THE COLLECTED WORKS OF
SAMUEL TAYLOR COLERIDGE · 4

THE FRIEND · II

General Editor: KATHLEEN COBURN
Associate Editor: BART WINER

THE COLLECTED WORKS

THE COLLECTED WORKS OF

Samuel Taylor Coleridge

The Friend

II

EDITED BY

Barbara E. Rooke

ROUTLEDGE & KEGAN PAUL

BOLLINGEN SERIES LXXV
PRINCETON UNIVERSITY PRESS

The Collected Works, sponsored by Bollingen Foundation,
is published in Great Britain
by Routledge & Kegan Paul Ltd
Broadway House, 68–74 Carter Lane, London EC4
and in the United States of America
by Princeton University Press, Princeton, New Jersey
The Collected Works constitutes
the seventy-fifth publication in Bollingen Series

The present work, number 4 of the Collected Works,
is in two volumes, this being 4: II

Designed by Richard Garnett
Printed in Great Britain by
Butler and Tanner Ltd, Frome and London

CONTENTS

LIST OF ILLUSTRATIONS

APPENDIX A

THE FRIEND

(1809–10, 1812)

[The following text is the original periodical *Friend* published at "weekly" intervals from 1 June 1809 to 15 March 1810. Only obvious typographical errors have been corrected. (Despite, or perhaps because of, Coleridge's assertion, below, that there "is one branch of learning, without which Learning itself cannot be railed at with common decency, namely, *Spelling*", his spelling idiosyncrasies have been retained.) Except for minor alterations of punctuation, all other changes made in the revised numbers issued in book form in 1812 are given in footnotes. The bracketed numbers within the text indicate the original periodical page numbers (the page numbers of the first twelve revised numbers differ slightly from those of the original); a word divided at the page break is considered part of the previous page. Editorial footnotes seek to elucidate passages found only in the periodical. Those footnotes to passages used again in 1818 are not repeated here: Appendix D, Collation Tables, and the index will help to locate them.]

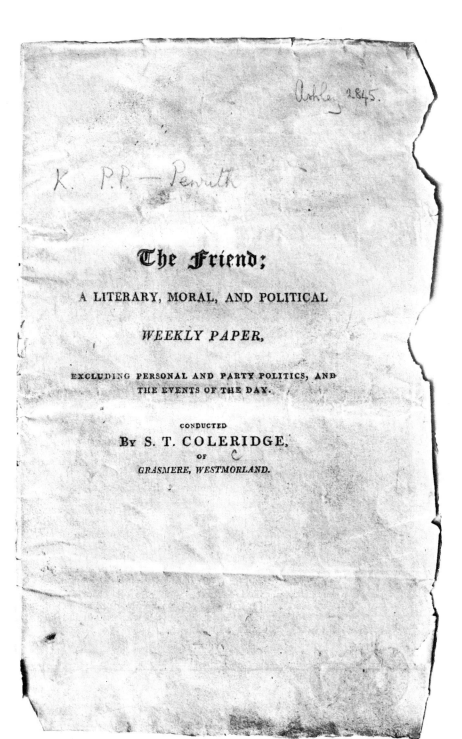

The Friend;

A LITERARY, MORAL, AND POLITICAL

WEEKLY PAPER,

EXCLUDING PERSONAL AND PARTY POLITICS, AND
THE EVENTS OF THE DAY.

CONDUCTED

By S. T. COLERIDGE,

OF

GRASMERE, WESTMORLAND.

1. *The Friend* (1809-10)
Title-page of the periodical, from a copy in the British Museum.

THE FRIEND

A LITERARY, MORAL, AND POLITICAL

WEEKLY PAPER,

EXCLUDING PERSONAL AND PARTY POLITICS,

AND THE EVENTS OF THE DAY

CONDUCTED

BY S. T. COLERIDGE,

OF

GRASMERE, WESTMORLAND[1]

---

[1] The 1812 title-page [p iii] reads: "THE FRIEND; A SERIES OF ESSAYS. BY S. T. COLE-RIDGE", followed by the motto "Accipe principium rursus, corpusque coactum | Desere: mutatâ melior procede figurâ. CLAUDIAN." The imprint is "London: Printed for Gale and Curtis, Paternoster-Row. 1812."

Facing the above title, now a half-title in 1812, is the notice [p iv]: "The first Twenty-eight Sheets of this Work were originally Published as the successive Numbers of a Weekly Paper; which was discontinued from the inconveniences and difficulties of the place, and the mode of Publication."

THE

FRIEND;

A

SERIES OF ESSAYS.

—

BY S. T. COLERIDGE.

R

"Accipe principium rursus, corpusque coactum
"Desere : mutatâ melior procede figurâ."

CLAUDIAN.

LONDON:
—
PRINTED FOR GALE AND CURTIS, PATERNOSTER-ROW.
—
1812.

2. *The Friend* (1812)
Title-page, from a copy in the British Museum.

THE FRIEND

No. 1. THURSDAY, June 1, 1809

Crede mihi, non est parvæ fiduciæ, polliceri opem decertantibus, consilium dubiis, lumen cæcis, spem dejectis, refrigerium fessis. Magna quidem hæc sunt, si fiant; parva, si promittantur. Verum ego non tam aliis legem ponam, quam legem vobis meæ propriæ mentis exponam: quam qui probaverit, teneat; cui non placuerit, abjiciat. Optarem, fateor, talis esse, qui prodesse possem quam plurimis.

PETRARCH: "De vita solitaria"

Believe me, it requires no little Confidence, to promise Help to the Struggling, Counsel to the Doubtful, Light to the Blind, Hope to the Despondent, Refreshment to the Weary. These are indeed great Things, if they be accomplished; trifles, if they exist but in a Promise. I however aim not so much to prescribe a Law for others, as to set forth the Law of my own Mind; which let the man, who shall have approved of it, abide by; and let him, to whom it shall appear not reasonable, reject it. It is my earnest wish, I confess, to employ my understanding and acquirements in that mode and direction, in which I may be enabled to benefit the largest number possible of my fellow-creatures.

IF it be usual with writers in general to find the first paragraph of their works that which has given them the most trouble with the least satisfaction,[1] THE FRIEND may be allowed to feel the difficulties and anxiety of a first introduction in a more than ordinary degree. He is embarassed by the very circumstances, that discriminate the plan and purposes of the present weekly paper from those of its periodical brethren, as well as from its more dignified literary relations, which come forth at once and in full growth from their parents. If it had been my[2] ambition to have copied[3] its whole scheme and fashion from the great founders of the race, THE TATLER AND SPECTATOR I should[4] indeed have exposed my[5] Essays to a greater hazard of unkind comparison. An imperfect imitation is often felt as a contrast. On the other hand, however, the very names and descriptions of the fictitious characters, which I[6] had proposed to assume in the course of my[7] work, would have put me[8] at once in possession of the stage; and my[9] first act have opened with a procession[10] of masks. Again,

[1] 1812 adds "the Author of".
[2] For "my" 1812 reads "his".
[3] For "to have copied" 1812 reads "to copy".
[4] For "I should" 1812 reads "he would".
[5] For "my" 1812 reads "his".
[6] For "I" 1812 reads "he".
[7] For "my" 1812 reads "his".
[8] For "me" 1812 reads "him".
[9] For "my" 1812 reads "his".
[10] For "procession" 1812 reads "succession".

if I were composing one work[1] on one given subject, the same acquaintance with its grounds and bearings, which had authorized me[2] to publish my[3] [3] opinions, would with its principles or fundamental facts have supplied me[4] with my[5] best and most appropriate commencement. More easy still would my task have been, had I planned "THE FRIEND" chiefly as a vehicle for a weekly descant on public characters and political parties. My perfect[6] freedom from all warping influences; the distance which permitted a distinct view of the game, yet secured me[7] from its passions; the LIBERTY OF THE PRESS; and its especial importance at the present period from—whatever event or topic might happen to form the great interest of the day; in short, the recipe[8] was ready to my hand, and it was framed so skilfully and has been practised with such constant effect, that it would have been affectation to have deviated from it. For originality for its own sake merely is idle at the best, and sometimes monstrous.[9] Excuse me therefore, gentle reader! if borrowing from my title a right of anticipation I avail myself of the privileges of a friend before I have earned them; and waiving the ceremony of a formal introduction, permit me to proceed at once to a subject,[10] trite indeed and familiar as the first lessons of childhood; which yet must be the foundation of my future Superstructure with all its ornaments, the hidden Root of the Tree, I am attempting to rear, with all its Branches and Boughs. But if from it[11] I have deduced my strongest moral motives for this[12] undertaking, it has at the same time been applied in suggesting the most formidable obstacle to my success—as far, I mean, as my Plan alone is concerned, and not the Talents necessary for its' Completion.[13]

Conclusions drawn from facts which subsist in perpetual flux, without definite place or fixed quantity, must always be liable to plausible objections, nay, often to unanswerable difficulties; and yet having their foundation in uncorrupted feeling are assented to by mankind at large, and in

---

[1] For "if . . . work" 1812 reads "if the Author had proposed to himself one unbroken work".

[2] For "me" 1812 reads "him".

[3] For "my" 1812 reads "his".

[4] For "me" 1812 reads "him".

[5] For "my" 1812 reads "his".

[6] For "My perfect" 1812 reads "Perfect".

[7] For "me" 1812 reads "the Looker-on".

[8] For "in short, the recipe" 1812 reads "this would have been my recipe! it".

[9] 1812 omits sentence.

[10] For "subject" 1812 reads "Principle".

[11] For "it" 1812 reads "this principle".

[12] For "this" 1812 reads "the present".

[13] In the specimen pages, this sentence and the last half of the preceding read: ". . . childhood, which yet, or rather my reflections on it, presented one of my strongest motives for this undertaking, and at the same time suggested the most formidable obstacle to its success. Thus too I shall be able more fully to state and explain the proposed difference of The Friend, in its plan and object, from my illustrious predecessors. As to the two other forms of publication which I have mentioned, this paper is sufficiently distinguished from the former, by its form and the generality of the title, and from the latter by the exclusion of personal politics and the events of the day already announced in the common title page of this and the future numbers": Forster MS 112 f 116.

all ages, as undoubted truths.[1] As our notions concerning them are almost equally obscure, so are our convictions almost equally vivid,[2] with those of our life and individuality. Regarded with awe, as guiding principles by the founders of law and religion, they are the favourite objects of attack with mock philosophers, and the demagogues in church, state, and literature; and the denial of them has in all times, though at various intervals, formed heresies and systems, which, after their day of wonder, are regularly exploded, and again as regularly [4] revived, when they have re-acquired novelty by courtesy of oblivion.

Among these universal persuasions we must place the sense of a self-contradicting principle in our nature, or a disharmony in the different impulses that constitute it—of[3] a something which essentially distinguishes man both from all other animals, that are known to exist, and from the idea of his own nature, or[4] conception of the original man. In health and youth we may indeed connect the glow and buoyance of our bodily sensations with the words of a theory, and imagine that we hold it with a firm belief. The pleasurable heat which the Blood or the Breathing generates, the sense of external reality which comes with the strong Grasp of the hand or the vigorous Tread of the foot, may indifferently become associated with the rich eloquence of a Shaftesbury, imposing on us man's possible perfections for his existing nature;[5] or with the cheerless and hardier impieties of a Hobbes, while cutting the gordian knot he denies the reality of either vice or virtue, and explains away the mind's self-reproach into a distempered ignorance, an epidemic affection of the human nerves and their habits of motion.[6] "Vain wisdom all, and false philosophy!"[7] I shall hereafter endeavour to prove, how distinct and different the sensation of positiveness is from the sense of certainty,[8] the turbulent heat of temporary fermentation from the mild warmth of essential life. Suffice it for the present to affirm, to declare it at least, as my own creed, that whatever humbles the heart and forces the mind inward, whether it be sickness, or grief, or remorse, or the deep yearnings of love (and there have been children of affliction, for whom all these have met and made up one complex suffering) in proportion as it acquaints us with "the thing, we are,"[9] renders us docile to the concurrent testimony of our fellow-men in all ages and in all nations. From PASCAL[10] in his closet, resting the arm, which

[1] 1812 adds: "Such are all those facts, the knowledge of which is not received from the senses, but must be acquired by reflection; and the existence of which we can prove to others, only as far as we can prevail on them to *go into themselves* and make their own minds the Object of their stedfast attention."

[2] The first statement of a recurring idea in *The Friend*; see above, I 106n, 179, and below, II 71–2.

[3] For "of" 1812 reads "the sense of".

[4] For "or" 1812 reads "from his

own".

[5] See Anthony Ashley Cooper, 3rd Earl of Shaftesbury *An Inquiry Concerning Virtue* bk I pt 3 sec 3: *Characteristicks* (1711) II 52–76.

[6] Hobbes *Leviathan* pt I ch 6, pt II ch 29.

[7] Milton *Paradise Lost* II 565.

[8] Another of C's distinctions: see *CN* II 3095 and *CL* III 48.

[9] Shakespeare *The Rape of Lucrece* line 149.

[10] Blaise Pascal (1623–62). C had read *Les Provinciales* (Cologne 1684);

supports his thoughtful brow, on a pile of demonstrations, to the poor pensive Indian, that seeks the missionary in the American wilderness, the humiliated self-examinant feels that there is Evil in our nature as well as Good, an EVIL and a GOOD for a just analogy to which he questions all other natures in vain. It is still the great definition of humanity, that we have a conscience, which no mechanic compost, no chemical combination, of mere appetence, [5] memory, and understanding, can solve; which is indeed an *Element* of our Being!—a conscience, unrelenting yet not absolute; which we may stupify but cannot delude; which we may suspend, but cannot annihilate; although we may perhaps find a treacherous counterfeit in the very quiet which we derive from its slumber, or its entrancement.

Of so mysterious a phænomenon we might expect a cause as mysterious. Accordingly, we find this (cause be it, or condition, or necessary accompaniment) involved and implied in the fact, which it alone can explain. For if our permanent Consciousness did not reveal to us our Free-agency, we should yet be obliged to deduce it, as a necessary Inference, from the fact of our Conscience: or rejecting both the one and the other, as mere illusions of internal Feeling, forfeit all power of thinking consistently with our Actions, or acting consistently with our Thought, for any single hour during our whole Lives. But I am proceeding farther than I had wished or intended. It will be long, ere I shall dare flatter myself, that I have won the confidence of my Reader sufficiently to require of him that effort of attention,[1] which the regular Establishment of this Truth would require.[2]

After the brief season of youthful hardihood, and the succeeding years of uneasy fluctuation, after long-continued and patient study of the most celebrated works, in the languages of ancient and modern Europe, in defence or denial of this prime Article of human Faith, which (save to the Trifler or the Worldling,) no frequency of discussion can superannuate, I at length satisfied my own mind by arguments, which placed me on firm land. This one conviction, determined, as in a mould, the form and feature of my whole system in Religion, in Morals, and even in Literature. These arguments were not suggested to me by Books, but forced on me by reflection on my own Being, and[3] Observation of the Ways of those about me, especially of little[4] Children. And as they had the power of fixing the same persuasion in some valuable minds, much interested, and not unversed in the controversy, and from the manner probably rather than the substance, appeared to them in some sort original—(for oldest Reasons will put on an impressive semblance of novelty, if they have indeed been drawn from the fountain-head of genuine self-research) [6] and since the arguments are neither abstruse, nor dependent on a long chain of Deduc-

---

his copy, with a ms note, is in VCL. See *CN* I 1647 and n. W. Schrickx has shown—"Coleridge and Friedrich Heinrich Jacobi" *Revue belge de philologie* XXXVI (1958) 818–19—that C's early quotation of Pascal's *Pensées* comes from Jacobi's *Hume* and *Über die*

Lehre des Spinoza; see above, I 154 and n 4, 155 and n 4.

[1] See above, I 16 and n 3.
[2] For "require" 1812 reads "demand".
[3] 1812 adds "by".
[4] 1812 omits "little".

tions, nor such as suppose previous habits of metaphysical disquisition; I shall deem it my Duty to state them with what skill I can, at a fitting opportunity, though rather as the Biographer of my own sentiments than a Legislator of the opinions of other men.

At present, however, I give it merely as an article of my own faith, closely connected with all my hopes of amelioration in man, and leading to the methods, by which alone I hold any fundamental or permanent amelioration practicable: that there is Evil distinct from Error and from Pain, an Evil in human nature which is not wholly grounded in the limitation of our understandings. And this too I believe to operate equally in subjects of Taste, as in the higher concerns of Morality. Were it my conviction, that our Follies, Vice, and Misery, have their entire origin in miscalculation from Ignorance, I should act irrationally in attempting other task than that of adding new lights to the science of moral Arithmetic, or new facility to its acquirement.[1] In other words, it would have been my worthy business to have set forth, if it were in my power, an improved system of Book-keeping for the Ledgers of calculating Self-love. If, on the contrary, I believed our nature fettered to all its' wretchedness of Head and Heart, by an absolute and innate necessity, at least by a necessity which no human power, no efforts of reason or eloquence could remove or lessen; (no, nor even prepare the way for such removal or diminution) I should then yield myself at once to the admonitions of one of my Correspondents[2] (unless indeed it should better suit my humour to do nothing than nothings, nihil quam nihili) and deem it even presumptuous to aim at other or higher object than that of *amusing*, during some ten minutes in every week, a small portion of the reading Public. Relaxed by these principles from all moral obligation, and ambitious of procuring Pastime and Self-oblivion for a Race, which could have nothing noble to remember, nothing desirable to anticipate, I might aspire even to the praise of the Critics and Dilettanti of the higher circles of Society; of some trusty Guide of blind Fashion; some pleasant Analyst of T ASTE, as it exists both in the Palate and the Soul; some living Guage and Mete-wand of past and present Genius. [7] But alas! my former studies would still have left a wrong Bias! If instead of perplexing my *common sense* with the Flights of Plato, and of stiffening over the meditations of the Imperial Stoic, I had been labouring to imbibe the gay spirit of a C ASTI, or had employed my erudition, for the benefit of the favoured Few, in elucidating the interesting Deformities of ancient Greece and India, what might I not have hoped from the Suffrage of those, who turn in weariness from the Paradise Lost, because compared with the prurient Heroes and grotesque Monsters of Italian Romance, or even with the narrative dialogues of the melodious Metastasio, that—"Adventurous Song,

> "Which justifies the ways of God to Man,"

has been found a poor Substitute for a Grimaldi, a most inapt medicine for

---

[1] For "acquirement" 1812 reads "acquirements".

[2] Probably Thomas Poole (see *CL* III 234); perhaps Daniel Stuart (see *CL* III 213).

an occasional propensity to yawn. For, as hath been decided, to fill up pleasantly the brief intervals of fashionable pleasures, and above all to charm away the dusky Gnome of Ennui, is the chief and appropriate Business of the Poet and—the *Novellist!* This duty unfulfilled, Apollo will have lavished his best gifts in vain; and Urania henceforth must be content to inspire Astronomers alone, and leave the Sons of Verse to more amusive Patronesses.

I must rely on my Readers' Indulgence for the pardon of this long and, I more than fear, prolix introductory explanation. I knew not by what means to avoid it without the hazard of becoming unintelligible in my succeeding Papers, dull where animation might justly be demanded, and worse than all, dull to no purpose. The Musician may tune his instrument in private, ere his audience have yet assembled: the Architect conceals the Foundation of his Building beneath the Superstructure. But an Author's Harp must be tuned in the hearing of those, who are to understand it's after harmonies; the foundation stones of his Edifice must lie open to common view, or his friends will hesitate to trust themselves beneath the roof. I foresee too, that some of my correspondents will quote my own opinions against me in confirmation of their former advice, and remind me that I have only in sterner language re-asserted the old adage,

> *Ille sinistrorsum, hic dextrorsum, unus utrique*
> *Error, sed variis illudit partibus omnes;*[1]

that the Will or Free Agency, by which I have endeavoured [8] to secure a retreat, must needs be deemed inefficient if error be universal; that to amuse, though only to amuse, our Visitors, is both Wisdom and Goodness, where it is presumption to attempt their amendment. And finally they will ask, by what right I affect to stand aloof from the crowd, even were it prudent; and with what prudence, did I even possess the right?[2]

This formidable Objection, (which however grounds itself on the false assumption, that I wage war with all amusement unconditionally, with all

[1] Horace *Satires* 2.3.50–1 (var). C seems to have been reading Burton's *Anatomy* (cf above, I 40–1 n 3, 249 n 1, and below, II 21 n 2, 30), for his quotation is given in the same words in Burton, where the lines are translated (3rd ed 1628) p 22 ("Democritus to the Reader"): "One reeles to this, another to that wall. | 'Tis the same Error that deludes them all."

[2] 1812 adds: "—'One of the later Schools of the Grecians (says Lord Bacon) is at a stand to think what should be in it that men should love Lies, where neither they make for pleasure, as with poets; nor for Advantage, as with the merchant; but for the Lie's sake. I cannot tell why, this same Truth is a naked and open day-light, that doth not shew the Masques and Mummeries and Triumphs of the present World half so stately and daintily, as Candle-lights. Truth may perhaps come to the Price of a Pearl, that sheweth best by day, but it will not rise to the price of a Diamond or Carbuncle, which sheweth best in varied lights. A mixture of Lies doth ever add pleasure. Doth any man doubt, that if there were taken from mens' minds vain opinions, flattering hopes, false valuations, imaginations *as one would*, and like the vinum Dæmonum (as a Father calleth poetry) but it would leave the minds of a number of men poor shrunken things, full of melancholy and Indisposition, and unpleasing to themselves?' "

delight from the blandishments of style, all interest from the excitement of Sympathy or Curiosity, when in truth I protest only against the habit of seeking in books for an idle and barren amusement) this objection of my friends brings to my recollection a fable or allegory, which I read during my Freshman's Term in Cambridge, in a modern Latin Poet: and if I mistake not, in one of the philosophical Poems of B. Stay, which are honoured with the prose commentary of the illustrious Boscovich.[1] After the lapse of so many years, indeed of nearly half my present Life, I retain no more of it than the bare outlines.

It was toward the close of that golden age (the tradition of which the self-dissatisfied Race of Men have every where preserved and cherished) when Conscience, or the effective Reason, acted in Man with the ease and uniformity of Instinct; when Labor was a sweet name for the activity of sane Minds in healthful Bodies, and all enjoyed in common the bounteous harvest produced, and gathered in, by common effort; when there existed in the Sexes, and in the Individuals of each Sex, just variety enough to permit and call forth the gentle restlessness and final union of chaste love and individual attachment, each seeking and finding the beloved *one* by the natural affinity of their Beings; when the dread Sovereign of the Universe was known only as the universal Parent, no Altar but the pure Heart, and Thanksgiving and grateful Love the sole Sacrifice—in this blest age of dignified Innocence one of their honored Elders, whose absence they were beginning to notice, entered with hurrying steps the place of their common assemblage at noon, and instantly attracted the general attention and wonder by the perturbation of his gestures, and by a strange Trouble both in his Eyes and over his whole Countenance. After a short but deep Silence, when the first Buz of varied Inquiry was becoming audible, [9] the old man moved toward a small eminence, and having ascended it, he thus addressed the hushed and listening Company.

"In the warmth of the approaching Mid-day as I was reposing in the vast cavern, out of which from its' northern Portal issues the River which [2] winds through our vale, a Voice powerful, yet not from its' loudness, suddenly hailed me. Guided by my Ear I looked toward the supposed place of the sound for some Form, from which it had proceeded. I beheld nothing but the glimmering walls of the cavern—again, as I was turning round, the same voice hailed me, and whithersoever I turned my face, thence did the voice seem to proceed. I stood still therefore, and in reverence awaited its' continuance. 'Sojourner of Earth! (these were its words) hasten to the meeting of thy Brethren, and the words which thou now hearest, the same do thou repeat unto them. On the thirtieth morning [3] from the morrow's sunrising, and during the space of thrice three Days and Nights, a thick cloud will cover the sky, and a heavy rain fall on the earth. Go ye therefore, ere the thirtieth sun ariseth, retreat to the Cavern of the River and there abide, till the Cloud [4] have passed away and the Rain be over and gone. For know ye of a certainty that whomever that Rain wetteth,

---

[1] See above, 1 9 and n 1. Ruggiero Giuseppe Boscovich (1711–87), Jesuit mathematician and physicist; like Stay, born in Dalmatia.

[2] For "which" 1812 reads "that".

[3] For "morning" 1812 reads "morn".

[4] For "Cloud" 1812 reads "Clouds".

on him, yea, on him and on his Children's Children will fall—the spirit of Madness.' Yes! Madness was the word of the voice: what this be, I know not! But at the sound of the word Trembling [1] and a Feeling, which I would not have had, came upon me,[2] and I remained even as ye beheld and now behold me."

The old man ended, and retired. Confused murmurs succeeded, and wonder, and doubt. Day followed day, and every day brought with it a diminution of the awe impressed. They could attach no image, no remembered sensations to the Threat. The ominous Morn arrived, the Prophet had retired to the appointed Cavern, and there remained alone during the space of the nine Days and Nights. On the tenth, he emerged from his place of Shelter, and sought his Friends and Brethren. But alas! how affrightful the change! Instead of the common Children of one great Family, working toward the same aim by Reason even as the Bees in their hives by Instinct, he looked and beheld, here a miserable wretch watching over a heap of hard and unnutritious [10] small substances, which he had dug out of the earth, at the cost of mangled limbs and exhausted faculties, and appearing to worship it with greater earnestness, than the Youths had been accustomed to gaze at their chosen Virgins in the first season of their choice. There he saw a former Companion speeding on and panting after a Butterfly, or a withered Leaf whirling onward in the breeze and another with pale and distorted countenance following close behind, and still stretching forth a dagger to stab his Precursor in the Back. In another place he observed a whole Troop of his fellow-men famished, and in fetters, yet led by one of their Brethren who had enslaved them, and pressing furiously onwards in the hope of famishing and enslaving another Troop moving in an opposite direction. For the first time, the Prophet missed his accustomed power of distinguishing between his Dreams, and his waking Perceptions. He stood gazing and motionless, when several of the Race gathered around him, and enquired of each other, Who is this fellow?[3] how strangely he looks! how wild!—a worthless Idler! exclaims one: assuredly, a very dangerous madman! cries a second. In short, from words they proceeded to violence: till harrassed, endangered, solitary in a world of forms like his own, without sympathy, without object of Love, he at length espied in some foss or furrow a quantity of the mad'ning water still unevaporated, and uttering the last words of Reason, "It is in vain to be sane in a World of Madmen," plunged and rolled himself in the liquid poison, and came out as mad and not more wretched than his neighbours and acquaintance.[4]

To such objections it would be amply sufficient, on my system of faith, to answer,[5] that though all men are in error, they are not all in the same

[1] For "Trembling" 1812 reads "Trembling came upon me,".

[2] 1812 deletes phrase.

[3] For "fellow" 1812 reads "Man".

[4] 1812 adds a new paragraph: "This tale or allegory seems to me to contain the objections to the practicability of my plan in all their strength. Either, says the Sceptic, you are the Blind offering to lead the Blind, or you are talking the language of Sight to those who do not possess the sense of Seeing."

[5] 1812 adds: "that we are not all blind, but all subject to distempers of 'the mental sight,' differing in kind and in degree;".

error, nor at the same time; and that each therefore may possibly heal the other (for the possibility of the cure is supposed in the free-agency) even as two or more physicians, all diseased in their general health yet under the immediate action of the disease on different days, may remove or alleviate the complaints of each other. But in respect to the *entertainingness* of moral writings, if in entertainment be included whatever delights the imagination or affects the generous passions, so far from rejecting such a mean of persuading the human soul, or of declaring it with Mr. Locke[1] a mere imposture, my very system compels me to defend not only the propriety but the [11] absolute necessity of adopting it, if we really intend to render our fellow-creatures better or wiser.

Previous to my ascent of Etna, as likewise of the Brocken in North Germany, I remember to have amused myself with examining the Album or Manuscript presented to Travellers at the first stage of the Mountain, in which on their return their Fore-runners had sometimes left their experience, and more often disclosed or betrayed their own characters. Something like this I have endeavoured to do relatively to my great predecessors in periodical Literature, from the Spectator to the Mirror,[2] or whatever later work of excellence[3] there may be. But the distinction between my proposed plan and all and each of theirs' I must defer to a future Essay. From all other works the FRIEND is sufficiently distinguished either by the very form and intervals of its Publication, or by its avowed exclusion of the Events of the Day, and of all personal Politics.

For a detail of the principal subjects, which I have proposed to myself to treat in the course of this work, I must refer to the Prospectus, printed at the end of this Sheet. But I own, I am anxious to explain myself more fully on the delicate subjects of Religion and Politics.[4] Of the former perhaps it may, for the present, be enough to say that I have confidence in myself that I shall neither directly or indirectly attack its Doctrines or Mysteries, much less attempt basely to undermine them by allusion, or tale, or anecdote. What more I might dare promise of myself, I reserve for another occasion. Of Politics[5] however I have many motives to declare my intentions more explicitly. It is my object to refer men to PRINCIPLES in all things; in Literature, in the Fine Arts, in Morals, in Legislation, in Religion. Whatever therefore of a political nature may be reduced to general Principles, necessarily indeed dependant on the circumstances of a Nation internal and external, yet not especially connected with this year or the preceding—this I do not exclude from my Scheme. Thinking it a sort of Duty to place my Readers in full possession both of my opinions and the only method in which I can permit myself to recommend them, and aware too of many calumnious accusations, as well as gross misapprehensions, of my political creed, I shall dedicate my second number entirely to the views, which a

---

[1] See *Essay Concerning Human Understanding* bk III ch 10 sec 34.

[2] An Edinburgh weekly modelled on the *Spectator*, written by members of a literary club. Of its 110 numbers, from 23 Jan 1779 to 27 May 1780, Henry Mackenzie (1745–1831) wrote forty-two.

[3] For "excellence" 1812 reads "merit".

[4] For "Religion and Politics" 1812 reads "RELIGION AND POLITICS".

[5] For "Of Politics" 1812 reads "Concerning POLITICS,".

British Subject in the present state of his Country ought to entertain of its actual and existing Constitution of Government.[1] If I can do no positive [12] good, I may perhaps aid in preventing others from doing harm. But all intentional allusions to particular persons, all support of, or hostility to, particular parties or factions, I now and for ever utterly disclaim. My Principles command this Abstinence, my Tranquillity requires it.

> TRANQUILLITY! thou better Name
> Than all the family of Fame!
> Thou ne'er wilt leave my riper age
> To low Intrigue, or factious Rage:
> For O! dear Child of thoughtful Truth,
> To thee I gave my early youth,
> And left the bark, and blest the steadfast shore,
> Ere yet the Tempest rose and scar'd me with its' Roar.
>
> Who late and lingering seeks thy shrine,
> On Him but seldom, Power divine,
> Thy Spirit rests! Satiety
> And Sloth, poor Counterfeits of Thee,
> Mock the tir'd Worldling. Idle Hope
> And dire Remembrance interlope,
> And vex the fev'rish Slumbers of the Mind:
> The Bubble floats before, the Spectre stalks behind!
>
> But me thy gentle Hand will lead,
> At morning, through th' accustom'd Mead;
> And in the sultry Summer's Heat
> Will build me up a mossy Seat;
> And when the Gust of Autumn crowds
> And breaks the busy moonlight Clouds,
> Thou best the Thought canst raise, the Heart attune,
> Light as the busy Clouds, calm as the gliding Moon.
>
> The feeling Heart, the searching Soul,
> To Thee I dedicate the whole!
> And while within myself I trace
> The Greatness of some future Race,
> Aloof with Hermit Eye I scan
> The present Works of present Man—
> A wild and dream-like trade of Blood and Guile
> Too foolish for a Tear, too wicked for a Smile![2]

---

[1] In No 2, C defers this "great Theme" to No 3, where it is also not carried out.

[2] *Ode to Tranquillity* (var; first published in the *M Post* 1801): *PW* (EHC) I 361–2. EHC's notes indicate the variants, but he is incorrect about "Slumbers" (line 15); the ms and *Friend* (1809 and 1812) all read "Slumbers". Copy R contains two interesting notes: C underlines the word "interlope" (line 14) and comments: "O Rhyme!

But I have transgressed from a Rule, which I had intended [13] to have established for myself, that of never troubling my Readers with my own Verses.

> *Ite hine, CAMÆNÆ! vos quoque, ite, suaves,*
> *Dulces Camœnœ! Nam (fatebimur verum)*
> *Dulces fuistis: et tamen meas chartas*
> *Revisitote; sed pudenter et raro.*
>
> VIRGIL: Catalect. VII[1]

I shall indeed very rarely and cautiously avail myself of this privilege. For long and early Habits of exerting my intellect in metrical composition have not so enslaved me, but that for some years I have felt and deeply felt, that the Poet's high Functions were not my proper assignment; that many may be worthy to listen to the strains of Apollo, neighbors of the sacred choir, and able to discriminate, and feel, and love its genuine harmonies; yet not therefore called to receive the Harp in their own hands, and join in the concert. I am content and gratified, that Spenser, Shakespere, Milton, have not been born in vain for me: and I feel it as a Blessing, that even among my Contemporaries I know one at least,[2] who has been deemed worthy of the Gift; who has received the Harp with Reverence, and struck it with the hand of Power.

Let me be permitted to conclude this prefatory Apology, or *Catalogue raisonnè* of my future work, by addressing myself more particularly to my learned and critical Readers. And that I may win the more on them, let me avail myself of the words of one, who was himself at once a great Critic and a great Genius:

Sic oportet ad librum, presertim miscellanei generis, legendum accedere lectorem, ut solet ad convivium conviva civilis. Convivator annititur omnibus satisfacere: et tamen si quid apponitur, quod hujus aut illius palato non respondeat, et hic et ille urbane dissimulant, et alia fercula probant, ne quid contristent convivatorem. Quis enim eum convivam ferat, qui tantum hoc animo veniat ad mensam, ut carpens quœ apponuntur nec vescatur ipse, nec alios vesci sinat! et tamen his quoque reperias inciviliores, qui palam, qui sine fine damnent ac lacerent opus, quod nunquam legerint. Ast hoc plusquam sycophanticum est damnare quod nescias.

ERASMUS

Rhyme! what hast thou not to answer for!"; he also marked the last couplet, commenting: "These two lines were composed during sleep.—S. T. Coleridge." See J. Wordsworth "Marginalia" 369.

[1] *Catalepton* 5.11–14 (var). Cf *CN* II 3200 and n. Tr H. R. Fairclough (LCL 1920): "Get ye hence, ye Muses! yea, away now even with you, ye sweet Muses! For the truth we must avow— ye have been sweet. And yet, come ye back to my pages, though with modesty and but seldom!"

[2] That is, Wordsworth. As early as 1800 C had felt the loss of his own poetic powers (*CL* I 623, II 831).

[14] PROSPECTUS[1]

OF

THE FRIEND,

A WEEKLY ESSAY, By S. T. COLERIDGE

(Extracted from a Letter to a Correspondent.)[2]

It is not unknown to you, that I have employed almost the whole of my Life in acquiring, or endeavouring to acquire, useful Knowledge by Study, Reflection, Observation, and by cultivating the Society of my Superiors in Intellect, both at Home and in foreign Countries. You know too, that at different Periods of my Life I have not only planned, but collected the Materials for, many Works on various and important Subjects: so many indeed, that the Number of my unrealized Schemes, and the Mass of my miscellaneous Fragments, have often furnished my Friends with a Subject of Raillery, and sometimes of Regret and Reproof. Waiving the Mention of all private and accidental Hindrances, I am inclined to believe, that this Want of Perseverance has been produced in the Main by an Over-activity of Thought, modified by a constitutional Indolence,[3] which made it more pleasant to me to continue acquiring, than to reduce what I had acquired to a regular Form. Add too, that almost daily throwing off my Notices or Reflections in desultory Fragments, I was still tempted onward by an increasing Sense of the Imperfection of my Knowledge, and by the Conviction, that, in Order fully to comprehend and develope any one Subject, it was necessary that I should make myself Master of some other, which again as regularly involved a third, and so on, with an ever-widening Horizon. Yet one Habit, formed during long[4] Absences from those, with

[1] There are three (slightly variant) versions of the Prospectus: the earlier two printed in Kendal, the third (in two sizes, some with a flyleaf) in London, dated 2 Feb 1809; see above, Introduction, I xxxix–xliv. In adding the Prospectus at the end of *Friend* No 1, C has made additional alterations in the London version. Some of the variant readings of these Prospectuses, as well as C's ms emendations in the Kendal copies sent to Poole and Stuart, are given in subsequent notes. The Poole Prospectus is in BM Add MS 35343 f 357; on f 358 is C's letter to Poole 4 Dec 1808 given in *CL* III 130–2. Three Prospectuses sent to Stuart are in BM Add MS 34046 ff 53 (first Kendal), 74–5 (second Kendal), 80–1 (second Kendal); f 53 is followed by the letter dated c 6 Dec 1808 in *CL* III 133–4; on f 75 (the flysheet of the Prospectus) is C's letter dated c 7 Feb 1809 in *CL* III 176; on f 81 (the

flysheet) the letter dated [8 Jan 1809] in *CL* III 162–5. The last corrected Prospectus was sent to Stuart with a "short advertisement for the News-papers", in SH's hand; see *CL* III 163 and n and below, I 20 n 2.

[2] "I wrote in the form of an Extract from a letter to a Correspondent . . . in some measure to cover over the indelicacy of speaking of myself to Strangers and to the Public . . .": *CL* III 151.

[3] Though friends chided, C is the most persistent of his accusers; see also below, II 36. For a list of some of C's "unrealized Schemes" see *CN* I and II Index 1: Coleridge: Projected Works.

[4] In the Kendal Prospectuses this read "Year-long"; C deleted the word "Year" in copies sent to Stuart. BM Add MS 34046 ff 53, 74. Jeffrey seems to have objected to "Year-long"; see C's letter to him 14 Dec 1808: *CL* III 150.

whom I could converse with full Sympathy, has been of Advantage to me —that of daily noting down, in my Memorandum or Common-place Books, both Incidents and Observations; whatever had occurred to me from without, and all the Flux and Reflux of my Mind within itself. The Number of these Notices, and their Tendency, miscellaneous as they were, to one common End (*"quid sumus et quid futuri gignimur,"*[1] *what we are and what we are born to become; and thus from the End of our Being to deduce its proper Objects*) first encouraged me to undertake the Weekly Essay, of which you will consider this Letter as the Prospectus.

Not only did the plan seem to accord better than any other with the Nature of my own Mind, both in its Strength and in its Weakness; but conscious that, in upholding some[2] Principles both of Taste and Philosophy, adopted by the great Men of Europe from the Middle of the fifteenth till toward the Close of the seventeenth Century, I must run Counter to many[3] Prejudices of many of my readers (*for old Faith is often modern Heresy*)[4] I perceived too in a periodical Essay the most likely Means of winning, instead of forcing my Way. [15] Supposing Truth on my Side, the Shock of the first Day might be so far lessened by Reflections of the succeeding Days, as to procure for my next Week's Essay a less hostile Reception, than it would have met with, had it been only the next Chapter of a present volume. I hoped to disarm the Mind of those Feelings, which preclude Conviction by Contempt, and, as it were, fling the Door in the Face of Reasoning by a *Presumption* of its Absurdity. A Motive too for honourable Ambition was supplied by the Fact, that every periodical Paper of the Kind now attempted, which had been conducted with Zeal and Ability, was not only well received at the Time, but has become permanently, and in the best Sense of the Word, popular. By honorable Ambition I mean the strong Desire to be useful, aided by the Wish to be generally acknowledged to have been so. As I feel myself actuated in no ordinary Degree by this Desire, so the Hope of realizing it appears less and less presumptuous to me, since I have received from Men of highest Rank and established Character in the Republic of Letters, not only strong Encouragements as to my own Fitness for the Undertaking, but likewise Promises of Support from their own Stores.[5]

---

[1] Persius *Satires* 3.67 (altered: C changed *victuri* to *futuri*, noted by the Bishop of Llandaff in his letter subscribing to *The Friend* 4 Dec 1808: DCL Folder C; see below, App F, II 473); quoted in the Introduction to Jeremy Taylor *Ductor dubitantium* (1660) xvi, where C may have seen it. C quotes the passage correctly in a letter to his brother George [10 Mar 1798]· *CL* I 397.

[2] The Kendal Prospectuses read "the"; C changed to "some" in those sent to Stuart. BM Add MS 34046 ff 74, 80.

[3] In one Stuart copy "many" was altered to "the". Ibid f 74.

[4] Cf Michael Drayton *Legend of T. Cromwell, Earl of Essex* line 909 (*B Poets* III 225): "What late was Truth, now turn'd to Heresy".

[5] In the Kendal Prospectuses the paragraph concluded: "I have even been authorized to mention their Names; but I dare not avail myself of the Permission, till the Nature of the Impression, made by my own Papers on the Readers of 'THE FRIEND,' shall have enabled me to conjecture, whether or no this, their Co-operation and Patronage, will tend to detract from their own well-earned Reputation

The *Object* of "THE FRIEND," briefly and generally expressed, is—to uphold those Truths and those Merits, which are founded in the nobler and permanent Parts of our Nature, against the Caprices of Fashion, and such Pleasures, as either depend on transitory and accidental Causes, or are pursued from less worthy Impulses. The chief *Subjects* of my own Essays will be:

The true and sole Ground of Morality, or Virtue, as distinguished from Prudence.

The Origin and Growth of moral Impulses,[1] as distinguished from external and immediate Motives.

The necessary Dependence of Taste on moral Impulses and Habits: and the Nature of Taste (relatively to Judgement in general and to Genius) defined, illustrated, and applied. Under this Head I comprize the Substance of the Lectures given, and intended to have been given, at the Royal Institution, on the distinguished English Poets, in illustration of the general Principles of Poetry;[2] together with Suggestions concerning the Affinity of the Fine Arts to each other, and the Principles common to them all: Architecture; Gardening; Dress; Music; Painting; Poetry.[3]

The opening out of new Objects of just Admiration in our own Language; and Information of the present State and past History of Swedish, Danish, German, and Italian Literature (to which, but as supplied by a Friend,[4] I may add the Spanish, Portuguese and French) as far as the same has not been already given to English Readers, or is not to be found in common French Authors.

Characters met with in real Life:—Anecdotes and Results of my own Life and Travels, &c. &c. as far as they are illustrative of general moral Laws, and have no immediate Bearing on personal or immediate Politics.

Education in its widest Sense, private, and national.

Sources of Consolation to the afflicted in Misfortune, or Disease, or Dejection of Mind,[5] from the Exertion and right Application of the Reason, the Imagination, and the moral Sense; and new Sources of Enjoyment opened out, or an

---

or at least from the Opinion of their Taste and Judgment." C deleted this from two copies sent to Stuart. BM Add MS 34046 ff 74, 80.

[1] Jeffrey objected to "moral Impulses"; see C's letter to him 14 Dec 1808: *CL* III 150.

[2] The lectures ("On the Principles of Poetry") began 15 Jan 1808; the date of the last lecture is uncertain, but was probably mid-June (see *CL* III 117 and n).

[3] The last six words were deleted from the London Prospectus, as they had been in Stuart's copies (BM Add MS 34046 ff 74v, 80v); "Dancing" had also been included in the earlier Prospectuses. Clarkson had written to C 7 Dec 1808: "I would strike out the Words 'Architecture, Gardening, Dress, Dancing, Music, Poetry, Painting'—The Sentence and Sentiment preceding does not need it—or, if all the

Words are not to be struck out, I would strike out Dress, Dancing, & Music, and add the others with &c &c at the End—My reason for the Alteration or Rejection is, that Quakers, to whom I might hand the Prospectus, might take fright—Such do not know the Liberality of your Views and wd be fearful, lest their Children should see these Essays, presuming that you might take the fashionable Side of the Question—": DCL Folder B. Here C omits only "Dancing". See C's letter to Pim Nevins c 31 Dec 1808: *CL* III 158–9.

[4] Probably Southey.

[5] In the Kendal Prospectuses this was "speculative Gloom"; in one Stuart Prospectus C altered this to "mental Gloom" (BM Add MS 34046 f 74v), in another, to "Distress of Mind" (f 80v).

Attempt (as an illustrious Friend once expressed the Thought to me) to add Sunshine to Daylight, by making the Happy more happy. In the words "Dejection of Mind" I refer particularly to [16] Doubt or Disbelief of the moral Government of the World, and the grounds and arguments for the religious Hopes of Human Nature.[1]

Such[2] are the chief Subjects, in the Developement of which I hope to realize, to a certain Extent, the great Object of my Essays. It will assuredly be my Endeavour, by as much Variety as is consistent with that Object, to procure *Entertainment* for my Readers, as well as *Instruction:* yet I feel myself compelled to hazard the Confession, that such of my Readers as make the *latter* the paramount Motive for their Encouragement of "THE FRIEND," will receive the largest Portion of the *former*. I have heard it said of a young Lady—if you are told before you see her, that she is handsome, you will think her ordinary; if that she is ordinary, you will think her handsome. I may perhaps apply this Remark to my own Essays —If Instruction and the Increase of honorable Motives and virtuous Impulses be chiefly expected, there will, I would fain hope, be felt no Deficiency of Amusement; but I must submit to be thought dull by those, who seek Amusement only. "THE FRIEND" will be distinguished from its celebrated Predecessors, the SPECTATOR, &c. as to its plan,[3] chiefly by the greater Length of the separate Essays, by their closer Connection with each other, and by the Predominance of one Object, and the common Bearing of all to one End.[4]

It would be superfluous to state, that I shall receive with Gratitude any Communications addressed to me: but it may be proper to say, that all Remarks and Criticisms in Praise or Dispraise of my Contemporaries (to which however nothing but a strong Sense of a moral Interest will ever lead me) will be written by myself only; both because I cannot have the same Certainty concerning the Motives of others, and because I deem it fit, that such Strictures should always be attended by the Name of their Author, and that one and the same Person should be solely responsible[5] for the Insertion as well as Composition of the same.[6]

[1] This sentence did not appear in the Kendal Prospectuses, and in the two Stuart copies mentioned in the above note C added in ms: "By the words, 'mental Gloom', I refer especially to Doubt or Disbelief of the moral Government of the world, and the Hopes connected with our religious Nature" (f 74ᵛ); "In 'Distress of Mind' I refer particularly to gloomy Doubt or Disbelief of the moral Government of the world and the Hopes given to Human Nature by Religion" (f 80ᵛ). Jeffrey had disliked "speculative Gloom"; C wrote him that the phrase was "almost as bad as picturesque Eye" and did not know how he "came to pass it". See C to Jeffrey 14 Dec

1808: *CL* III 149–50.

[2] 1812 omits this paragraph and the following two paragraphs.

[3] For this phrase the first Kendal Prospectus read "RAMBLER, WORLD, &c.".

[4] In the margin alongside this paragraph C wrote to Stuart: "I leave the insertion or omission of this § to *your* Judgment" (f 74ᵛ); "If you think this § might as well be omitted, omit it" (f 80ᵛ).

[5] The first Kendal Prospectus read "amenable".

[6] The first Kendal Prospectus concluded (before giving details of size and cost): "Let me conclude this Prospectus with a Quotation from Petrarch 'De

Each number will contain a stamped Sheet of large Octavo, like the present: and will be delivered, free of expence, by the Post, throughout the Kingdom, to Subscribers. The Price each Number one Shilling.[1] Orders for the FRIEND received by the Publisher, J. BROWN, PENRITH; by Messrs. LONGMAN, HURST, REES, and ORME, Paternoster Row; by CLEMENT, Bookseller, opposite ST. Clement's, Strand; LONDON. Orders likewise, and all Communications, to be addressed to S. T. COLERIDGE, Grasmere, KENDAL.

The mode of payment by Subscribers will be announced in a future Number: as soon as the arrangements have been completed.[2]

Vita Solitaria'", followed by the quotation used as the motto of No 1. C altered "Let me" to "I may not inaptly" on the Prospectuses sent to Poole and Stuart; it is also the reading of the revised Kendal version.

[1] The Kendal Prospectuses ended: "Each Number will contain a Sheet and a quarter, large Octavo, and will be regularly delivered, free of Expense, to Subscribers, living in Cities or Towns that have Communication with London by the Post. The Price, each Number one Shilling. Names of Subscribers, and Communications, to be addressed (Post paid) to Mr. COLERIDGE, Grasmere, Kendal. If a sufficient Number of Subscribers shall have been obtained, the Publication will commence on the first Saturday of January, 1809."

[2] At the foot of the Prospectus sent to Poole, C wrote: "Should there be so many scattered Subscribers that the large Number of separate Places should make up for the few ⟨Subscribers⟩ in each, THE FRIEND will then be stamped & sent by the Post, as newspapers—being printed on one Sheet, but on a Paper of larger size, and with 40 lines in each Page instead of 35, so that the quantity of matter will remain the same. But if the List of Subscribers shall have been furnished chiefly by the greater Cities and Towns, the Essays will then be forwarded by every Saturday's Mail from London in a Coach-parcel to some Friend or Bookseller in each place." BM Add MS 35343 f 357ᵛ. At the foot of the first Prospectus sent to Stuart C wrote a variant of this, beginning "If the large Number of separate Places should make up for the few Subscribers in each, THE FRIEND ..."; alongside which, Stuart noted: "not allow a weekly pub: without a Stamp". BM Add MS 34046 f 53ᵛ. At the foot of one Prospectus sent to Stuart, C added an advertisement (in SH's hand) to be inserted in newspapers: "On Saturday ——— will be published 'THE FRIEND' a weekly Essay, by S. T. Coleridge. The OBJECT of this work generally expressed, is—to uphold those Truths and those Merits which are founded in the nobler and permanent parts of our Nature against the Caprices of of Fashion, and such pleasures as either depend on transitory and accidental Causes, or are pursued from less worthy Impulses. A more detailed account of its purpose and chief objects Subjects will be found in the PROSPECTUS of 'THE FRIEND', which may be procured, gratis, from the Booksellers undermentioned. The events of the day, and all personal and immediate Politics will be excluded. Each Number will contain a Sheet of large octavo and will be delivered ——— ——— The names of those inclined to take in the work, and all communications, to be addressed (Post-paid) to MR COLERIDGE, Grasmere, Kendal: or ———". BM Add MS 34046 f 80ᵛ. C left it to Stuart "to fill up the Blanks". Ibid f 81; CL III 163.

THE FRIEND

No. 2. THURSDAY, JUNE 8, 1809

Whenever we improve, it is right to leave room for a further improvement. It is right to consider, to look about us, to examine the effect of what we have done. Then we can proceed with confidence, because we can proceed with intelligence. Whereas in hot reformations, in what men more zealous than considerate, call *making clear work*, the whole is generally so crude, so harsh, so indigested; mixed with so much imprudence and so much injustice; so contrary to the whole course of human nature and human institutions, that the very people who are most eager for it, are among the first to grow disgusted at what they have done. Then some part of the abdicated grievance is recalled from its exile in order to become a corrective of the correction. Then the abuse assumes all the credit and popularity of a Reform. The very Idea of purity and disinterestedness in Politics falls into disrepute, and is considered as a vision of hot and inexperienced men; and thus disorders become incurable, not by the virulence of their own quality, but by the unapt and violent nature of the remedies. "BURKE'S SPEECH" *on presenting to the House of Commons (on the 11th of February*, 1780.) A PLAN FOR THE BETTER SECURITY OF THE INDEPENDENCE OF PARLIAMENT.[1]

TO MY READERS

CONSCIOUS that I am about to deliver my sentiments on a subject of the utmost delicacy, to walk

> "*per ignes*
> "*Suppositos cineri doloso*"[2]

I have been tempted by my fears to preface them with a motto of unusual length,[3] from an Authority equally respected by both of the opposite[4] parties. I have selected[5] it from an Orator, whose eloquence has taken away for[6] Englishmen all cause of humiliation from[7] the names of Demosthenes and Cicero[8]: from a Statesman, who has left to our Language a bequest of Glory unrivalled and all our own, in the keen-eyed yet far-sighted genius, with which he has almost uniformly[9] made the most original

[1] Burke *Works* II (1792) 189–90. (See above, I 192 n 2.)

[2] Horace *Odes* 2.1.7–8; quoted in Burton (3rd ed 1628) 103. Tr C. E. Bennett *Horace. Odes and Epodes* (LCL 1924) 107: "over fires hidden beneath treacherous ashes". 1812 omits the quote and "to walk".

[3] For "been tempted . . . length," 1812 reads "selected the general motto to all my political lucubrations".

[4] 1812 omits "of the opposite".

[5] For "selected" 1812 reads "taken".

[6] For "has taken away for" 1812 reads "enables".

[7] For "all . . . from" 1812 reads "to repeat".

[8] 1812 adds "without humiliation".

[9] 1812 omits "almost uniformly".

and profound[1] general principles of political wisdom, and even the recondite laws of human passions, bear upon particular measures and[2] events. While of the Harangues of Pitt, Fox, and their elder compeers on the most important occurrences, we retain a few unsatisfactory fragments alone, the very Flies and Weeds of BURKE shine to us through the purest amber,[3] imperishably enshrined, and valuable from the precious material [18] of their embalmment. I have extracted the passage[4] from that BURKE whose latter exertions have rendered his works venerable, as oracular voices from the sepulchre of a Patriarch, to the Upholders of the Government and Society in their existing state and order; but from a Speech delivered by him while he was the most beloved, the proudest name with the more anxious Friends of Liberty; (I distinguish them in courtesy by the name of their own choice, not as implying any enmity to true Freedom in the characters of their opponents)[5] while he was the Darling of those, who believing mankind to have been improved are desirous to give to forms of government a similar progression.

From the same anxiety I have been led to introduce my opinions on this most hazardous subject by a preface of a somewhat personal character. And though the title of my address is general, yet, I own, I direct myself more particularly to those among my readers, who from various printed*

* 6 To cite one instance among many: while I was in Germany for the purpose of finishing my education, whither I was enabled to go by the munificence of my two honored Patrons,[7] whose names must not be profaned on such an occasion; and from which I returned before the proposed time, literally (I know not whether a Husband and Father ought to be ashamed of it) literally home-sick; one of the writers, concerned in the collection, inserted a note in the "Beauties of the Antijacobin," [8] which after having informed the Public that I had been dishonored at

---

1 For "most . . . profound" 1812 reads "profoundest".

2 1812 adds "passing".

3 C uses the metaphor often. He may have taken his image from Bacon; cf *Historia vitae et mortis* canon I explicatio: *Works* (1740) II 181.

4 Probably a "not" was accidentally omitted.

5 1812 omits the parenthetical phrase.

6 The footnote was misplaced in 1812; it appears there at foot of p 29, headed "*Note to line 16, page 18.*"

7 Josiah (1769–1843) and Thomas (1771–1805) Wedgwood.

8 *The Beauties of the Anti-Jacobin* (1799) 306n. In a note to the poem *New Morality* the editor of the *Beauties* did not accuse C of preaching Deism, but said that "To the disgrace of discipline, and a Christian University, this avowed Deist was not expelled" for the sin of "non-attendance at chapel". *The Poetry of the Anti-*

Jacobin appeared earlier the same year as the *Beauties*, but whereas the *Poetry* contained no prose and was expensive (2 vols 8º), the *Beauties* contained prose as well as poetry (with notes by the editor) and was cheaper: "to occupy a place on the tables, or in the pockets, of the middle class of society" (Advertisement p iv). Because the editor hoped that his volume would "not be displeasing to those Gentlemen who had the principal share in [the] composition" of the *Anti-Jacobin*, it seems unlikely that he was one of "those Gentlemen"— William Gifford, George Ellis, Canning, or J. Hookham Frere. L. Rice-Oxley *Poetry of the Anti-Jacobin* (Oxford 1924) 190 (basing his decision on annotated copies), attributes the lines on C to Frere and Canning, who were the main authors of the *New Morality*, with the help of Ellis and Gifford and, possibly, Pitt.

and unprinted calumnies have judged most [19] unfavourably of my political tenets; and to those, whose favour I have chanced to win in con-

Cambridge for preaching Deism (about the time, when I was deemed a perfect Bigot by the reigning *Philosophers* and their proselytes for my youthful ardor in defence of Christianity) concludes with these words: "Since this time he (*i.e.* S. T. Coleridge) has left his native Country, commenced Citizen of the World, *left his poor Children fatherless and his Wife destitute. Ex his disce* his friends—"[1] but I dare not desecrate their names. Suffice it to say, what may be said with severest truth, that it is absolutely impossible to select from the whole empire two men more exemplary in their domestic characters (both remarkably, and the one most awefully so) than the men, whose names were here printed at full length. Can it be wondered at, that some good men were not especially friendly to a Party, which encouraged and openly rewarded the Authors of such atrocious calumnies! ("Qualis es, nescio; sed per quales agis, scio et doleo")[2] Since this time, the envenomed weapon has been turned against themselves by one of their own agents.[3] And it behoves those to consider, who bring forward the *Gougers*[4] of slander to attack their real or imagined Enemies, that Savages are capricious in proportion as they are unprincipled: and when they have none else to attack, will turn round and assail their employers. For Attack is their vital Element: extract the venomous Sting, and the animal dies.

Again, will any man, who loves his Children and his Country, be slow to pardon me, if not in the spirit of vanity but of natural self-defence against yearly and monthly attacks on the very vitals of my character as an honest man and a loyal Subject, I prove the utter falsity of the charges by the only public means in my power, a citation from the last work published by me, in the close of the year 1798[5], and anterior to all the calumnies published to my dishonor. No one has charged me with seditious acts or conversation: if I have attempted [19] to do harm, by my works must it have been effected. By my works therefore must I be judged: (if indeed one obscure volume of juvenile poems, and one slight verse pamphlet of twenty pages, can without irony, be entitled *works*.)[6] The poem was written during the first alarm of Invasion, and left in the Press on my leaving my country for Germany. So few copies were printed, and of these so few sold, that to the great majority of my readers they will be any thing rather than a citation from a known publication—but my heart bears me witness, that I am aiming wholly at the moral confidence of my Readers in my principles, as a man, not at their praises of me, as a Poet; to which character, in its higher sense, I have already resigned all pretensions.

---

[1] *Beauties* 306n: " 'Ex uno disce' his associates Southey and Lambe".

[2] Source untraced. Tr: "I don't know what kind of person you are; but I know what kind of person you work through, and deplore it".

[3] Southey's copy of the 1812 *Friend* (later owned by SC) has a pencil note here suggesting *The Pursuits of Literature* ("A Satirical Poem in four Dialogues with Notes"), certainly an "envenomed weapon" directed against contemporary critics. There were sixteen editions between 1794 and 1812, each later one with additional notes carefully dated. The author,

T. J. Mathias (1754–1835), was a classicist and Italian scholar as well as a satirist. See above, I 210 n 3.

[4] Perhaps C's use of this American slang-word came from his reading of American travel-books—or from one of his American friends.

[5] *Fears in Solitude* was published (1798), with *France: an Ode* and *Frost at Midnight*, in a quarto pamphlet by J. Johnson in St Paul's Churchyard.

[6] *Poems on Various Subjects* (1796). The *Ode to the Departing Year* was also published in a quarto pamphlet in 1796.

sequence of a similar, though not equal, mistake. To both I affirm, that the
opinions and arguments, I am about to detail, have been the settled con-

————"Spare us yet awhile!
Father and God, O spare us yet awhile.
O let not English Women speed their flight
Fainting beneath the burthen of their Babes,
Of the sweet Infants, who but yesterday
Smiled at the bosom! Husbands, Brothers, all
Who ever gazed with fondness on the forms
Which grew up with you round the same fire-side,
And all who ever heard the Sabbath Bells
Without the Infidels' scorn; make yourselves strong,
Stand forth, be men, repel an impious race,
Impious and false, a light yet cruel race
That laugh away all virtue, mingling mirth
With deeds of murder! and still promising
Freedom, themselves too sensual to be free,
Poison Life's amities and cheat the heart
Of Faith and quiet Hope and all that soothes
And all that lifts the spirit! Stand ye forth,
Render them back upon th' insulted ocean
And let them float as idly on its waves
As the vile sea-weed, which the mountain blast
Sweeps from our Shores! And O! may we return
Not in a drunken triumph, but with awe,
Repentant of the wrongs, with which we stung
So fierce a race to Frenzy.
                    I have told,
O men of England! Brothers! I have told
Most bitter Truths but without bitterness.
Nor deem my zeal or factious or mistimed:
For never can true Courage dwell with them
Who playing tricks with Conscience dare not look
At their own vices. We have been too long
Dupes of a deep delusion. Some, belike,
Restless in enmity, have thought all change
Involv'd in change of constituted power,
As if a Government were but a Robe
On which our Vice and Wretchedness were sewn
Like fancy-points and fringes, with the Robe
Pull'd off at pleasure. . . . .
            . . . . others, meantime,
Dote with a mad Idolatry! and all
Who will not fall before their Images

[20]

And yield them worship, they are enemies
Even of their Country! *Such have I been deem'd.*
But O! dear Britain! O my Mother Isle!
Needs must thou be a name most dear and holy
To me a Son, a Brother, and a Friend,
A Husband, and a Parent, who revere
All Bonds of natural Love, and find them all
Within the circle of thy rocky shores!
O native Britain! O my Mother Isle!

victions of my mind for the last ten or twelve years, with some brief intervals of fluctuation, [20] and those only in lesser points, and known only to

> How should'st thou be aught else but dear and holy
> To me, who from thy seas and rocky shores,
> Thy quiet fields, thy streams and wooded Hills
> Have drunk in all my intellectual life,
> All sweet sensations, all ennobling thoughts,
> All adoration of the God in nature,
> All lovely and all honorable things,
> Whatever makes this mortal spirit feel
> The joy and greatness of its' future Being!
> There lives nor Form nor Feeling in my Soul
> Unborrowed from my Country. O divine
> And beauteous Island! thou hast been my sole
> And most magnificent Temple, in the which
> I walk with awe, and sing my stately songs
> Loving the God, who made me."
>
> *Fears of Solitude, a Poem* [1]

Most unaffected has been my wonder, from what causes a man who has published nothing with his name but a single forgotten volume of verses, thirteen
years ago, and a poem of two hundred lines a few years after, of which (to use
the words of a witty writer) I made the Public my Confidant and it kept the
secret,[2] should have excited such long and implacable malignity. And anony-
mously I have only contributed the foil of three or four small poems to the
volume of a superior mind,[3] and sent a few Essays to a Newspaper[4] in defence
of all that is dear, or abhorrence of what must be most detestable, to good men
and genuine Englishmen. With the exception of one solitary sonnet,[5] which in
what mood written, and by what accident published, personal delicacy forbids
me to explain, which was rejected indignantly from the second Edition of my
Poems, and re-inserted in the third in my absence and without my consent or
knowledge, I may safely defy my worst enemy to shew, in any of my few writings,
the least bias to Irreligion, Immorality, or Jacobinism: unless in the latter word,
be implied sentiments which have been avowed by men who without recantation,

---

[1] *Fears in Solitude* lines 129–66, 171–
197: *PW* (EHC) I 260–3 (where most of
the variants are noted).

[2] Cf his remark about his father, in
a letter to Poole Mar 1797: *CL* I 310.

[3] Wordsworth's; C's "foil of three
or four small poems" in the *Lyrical
Ballads* includes the *Rime of the
Ancient Mariner*.

[4] SC reprints sixty-two articles (and
part of one in a series by Poole) published in the *M Post* 1799–1802 (*EOT*
I 179–292, II 293–592).

[5] To Earl Stanhope (*PW*—EHC—I
89–90). See *CL* I 242, in which C is
"solicitous" to have it omitted from
his second edition, and *CL* III 27, in
which he says that it was inserted with-

out his consent in the first edition "by
the fool of a Publisher", "in direct contradiction, equally to my then, as to my
present principles", a sonnet written
"in ridicule and mockery . . . of French
Jacobin declamation". Cf his note in
the margin of SH's copy of *Poems*
(1803) 103, where he crossed out the
sonnet: "infamous Insertion! It was
written in ridicule of Jacobinical Bom-
bast put into the first Edition by a
blunder of Cottle's, rejected indignantly from the second & here maliciously reprinted in my Absence."
This copy is now in the Cornell University Library; see *The Cornell Wordsworth Collection* ed G. H. Healey
(Ithaca, N.Y. 1957) 264.

the Companions of my Fire-side. From both and from all my readers I solicit a gracious attention to the following explanations: first, on the congruity of this number[4] with the general Plan and Object of "The Friend;" and [21] secondly, on the charge of arrogance,[5] which may be adduced against the Author for the freedom, with which in this number[6] and in others that will follow on other subjects he presumes to dissent from men of established reputation, or even to doubt of the justice with which the public Laurel-crown, as symbolical of the *first* Class of Genius and Intellect, has been awarded to sundry writers since the Revolution, and permitted to wither around the brows of our elder Benefactors, from Hooker to Sir P. Sidney, and from Sir P. Sidney to Jeremy Taylor and Stillingfleet.[7]

First then, as to the consistency of the subject of the following Essay with the proposed Plan of my work, let something be allowed to honest personal motives, a justifiable solicitude to stand well with my Contemporaries in those points, in which I have remained unreproached by my own conscience. Des aliquid famæ.[8] A Reason of far greater importance is derived from the well-grounded Complaint of sober minds, concerning the mode by which political opinions of greatest hazard have been, of late years, so often propagated. This evil cannot be described in more just and lively language than in the words of Paley (p. 395 of the quarto edition of his Moral and Political Philosophy)[9] which, though by him applied to

direct or indirect, have been honored with the highest responsible offices of Government.[1]

This is the first time, that I have attempted to counteract the wanton calumnies of unknown and unprovoked persecutors. Living in deep retirement, I have become acquainted with the greater part only[2] years after they had been published and individually forgotten. But the general effect remained: and if my Readers knew the cruel hindrances, which they have opposed to me, in the bringing about the present undertaking, I have honorably erred in my notions of human nature, if I should not be more than forgiven: especially if the number of attacks on myself and on one still more and more deservedly dear to me,[3] should be more than equal to the number of the lines, in which I have, for the first time, been tempted to defend myself.

---

[1] C's note cannot be taken seriously. He fails to acknowledge *The Fall of Robespierre* (1794), *Conciones* (1795), and *The Watchman* (1796); and it would be easy to point out in them "a bias to Irreligion" (e.g. the "Essay on Fasts": *Watchman* No 2) and to "Jacobinism" (e.g. sentences in his first lecture, "Introductory Address", in *Conciones*, some of which he omitted when reprinting the speech in the 1818 *Friend*; see above, I 326–38 and nn). "If he was not a Jacobine, in the common acceptation of the name", RS wrote Danvers 15 Jun 1809, "I wonder who the Devil was": *S Letters* (Curry) I 511.

[2] 1812 transposes "only" before "become".

[3] Wordsworth.

[4] For "this number" 1812 reads "the following numbers".

[5] 1812 adds "or presumption".

[6] For "this number" 1812 reads "these numbers".

[7] See above, I 71 and n 1, 182 and n 3, 52 and n 1. Edward Stillingfleet (1635–99), bp of Worcester, whose *Origines sacrae* (1675) C annotated; see *C 17th C* 375–9.

[8] Source untraced. Tr: "Let something be allowed for rumour".

[9] *Principles of Moral and Political Philosophy* (1786) 395. Cf above, I 108 and n 3, 314–25 and nn.

Infidelity, hold equally of the turbulent errors of political Heresy. They are "served up in every shape, that is likely to allure, surprise, or beguile the imagination; in a fable, a tale, a novel, a poem; in interspersed and broken hints; remote and oblique surmises; in books of Travels, of Philosophy, of Natural History; in a word, in any form, rather than the right one, that of a professed and regular disquisition." Now in claiming for "THE FRIEND" a fair chance of unsuspected admission into the families of Christian Believers and quiet Subjects, I cannot but deem it incumbent on me to accompany my introduction with a full and fair statement of my own political system: not that any considerable portion of my Essays will be devoted to politics in any shape, for rarely shall I recur to them except as far as they may happen to be involved in some point of private morality; but that the Encouragers of this Work may possess grounds of assurance, that no tenets of a different tendency from these, I am preparing to state, will be met in it. I would fain hope, that even those persons [22] whose political opinions I may run counter to, will not be displeased at seeing the possible objections to their creed calmly set forth by one, who equally with themselves considers the love of true Liberty, as a part both of Religion and Morality, as a necessary condition of their general predominance, and ministring to the same blessed Purposes. The developement of my religious persuasions relatively to Religion in its great Essentials, will occupy a following number, in which (and throughout these Essays) my aim will be, seldom indeed to enter the Temple of Revelation (much less of positive Institution) but to lead my Readers to its' Threshhold, and to remove the prejudices with which the august edifice may have been contemplated from ill-chosen and unfriendly points of view.

But independently of this motive, I deem the subject of Politics, so treated as I intend to treat it, strictly congruous with my general Plan. For it was and is my prime object to refer men in all their actions, opinions, and even enjoyments to an appropriate Rule, and to aid them with all the means I possess, by the knowledge of the facts on which such Rule grounds itself. The rules of political prudence do indeed depend on local and temporary circumstances in a much greater degree than those of Morality or even those of Taste. Still however the circumstances being known, the deductions obey the same law, and must be referred to the same arbiter. In a late summary reperusal of our more celebrated periodical Essays, by the contemporaries of Addison and those of Johnson, it appeared to me that the objects of the Writers were, either to lead the reader from gross enjoyments and boisterous amusements, by gradually familiarizing them with more quiet and refined pleasures; or to make the habits of domestic life and public demeanour more consistent with decorum and good sense, by laughing away the lesser follies, and freaks of self-vexation; or to arm the yet virtuous mind with horror of the direr crimes and vices, by exemplifying their origin, progress and results, in affecting Tales and true or fictitious biography: or where (as in the Rambler)[1] it is intended to strike a yet deeper note, to support the cause of Religion and Morality by eloquent

---

[1] Johnson's *Rambler* was published twice weekly from Mar 1750 to Mar 1752; tax-free, it cost only twopence. It was corrected, collected in book form, and went through many editions during Johnson's lifetime.

declamation and dogmatic precept, such as may with propriety be addressed to those who require to be awakened rather than convinced, whose [23] conduct is incongruous with their own sober convictions; in short, to practical not speculative Heretics. Revered for ever be the names of these great and good men! Immortal be their Fame; and may Love and Honor and Docility of Heart in their readers, constitute its' essentials! Not without cruel injustice should I be accused or suspected of a wish to underrate their merits, because in journeying toward the same end I have chosen a different road. Not wantonly however have I ventured even on this variation. I have decided on it in consequence of all the Observations which I have made on my fellow-creatures, since I have been able to observe in calmness on the present age, and to compare its' phænomena with the best indications, we possess, of the character of the ages before us.

My time since earliest manhood has been pretty equally divided between deep retirement (with little other society than that of one family, and my Library) and the occupations and intercourse of (comparatively at least) public life both abroad[1] and in the British Metropolis. But in fact the deepest retirement, in which a well-educated Englishman of active feelings, and no misanthrope, can live at present, supposes few of the disadvantages and negations, which a similar place of residence would have involved, a century past. Independent of the essential knowledge to be derived from books, children, housemates, and neighbours, however few or humble; yet Newspapers,[2] their Advertisements,[3] Speeches in Parliament, Law-courts, and[4] Public Meetings, Reviews, Magazines, Obituaries, and (as affording occasional commentaries on all these)[5] that[6] diffusion of uniform[7] opinions,[8] of Behaviour and Appearance, of Fashions[9] in things external and internal, have combined to diminish, and often to render evanescent, the distinctions between the enlightened Inhabitants of the great city, and the scattered Hamlet. From all the facts however, that have occurred as subjects of reflection within the sphere of my experience, be they few or numerous, I have fully persuaded my own mind, that formerly MEN WERE WORSE THAN THEIR PRINCIPLES, but that at present THE PRINCIPLES ARE WORSE THAN THE MEN. For the former half of the proposition I might among a thousand other more serious and unpleasant proofs appeal even to the Spectators and Tatlers. It would not be easy perhaps to detect in [24] them any great corruption or debasement of the main foundations of Truth and Goodness; yet a man—I will not say of delicate mind and pure morals but—of common good manners, who means to read an essay, which he has opened upon at hazard in these

---

[1] C had been in Germany (1798–9) and in Malta and Italy (1804–6).

[2] A. Andrews *A History of British Journalism* (1859) II 39–40 gives the figures for newspapers in 1809: London 63, provinces 93, Scotland 24, Ireland 57.

[3] 1812 adds "their Reports of the".

[4] For "Law-courts, and" 1812 reads "in Law-courts, and in".

[5] 1812 adds "the frequency of Travelling, and the variety of character and object in the Travellers; and more than all".

[6] For "that" 1812 reads "the".

[7] 1812 deletes "uniform".

[8] 1812 adds "the uniformity".

[9] For "of Fashions" 1812 reads "and the *telegraphic* Spread and *beacon-like* Rapidity of Fashion".

Volumes, to a mixed company, will find it necessary to take a previous survey of its contents. If stronger illustration be required, I would refer to one of Shadwell's Comedies in connection with its Dedication to the Dutchess of Newcastle, encouraged, as he says, by the high delight with which her Grace had listened to the Author's private recitation of the Manuscript in her Closet.[1] A writer of the present Day, who should dare address such a composition to a virtuous Matron of high rank, would secure general infamy, and run no small risk of Bridewell and the Pillory. Why need I add the plays and poems of Dryden contrasted with his serious prefaces and declarations of his own religious and moral opinions? why the little success, except among the heroes and heroines of fashionable Life, of the two or three living Writers of prurient Love-odes (if I may be forgiven for thus profaning the word, Love)[2] and Novels at once terrific and libidinous.[3] These Gentlemen erred both in place and time, and have understood the temper of their age and country as ill as the precepts of that Bible, which, notwithstanding the atrocious Blasphemy[4] of one of them,[5] the great majority of their countrymen peruse with safety to their morals, if not improvement.

The truth of the latter half of the proposition in its' favourable part, is evidenced by the general anxiety on the subject of Education, the solicitous attention paid to several late works on its' general principles,[6] and the unexampled Sale of the very numerous large and small volumes published for the use of Parents and Instructors, and for the children given or intrusted to their Charge[7]. The first ten or twelve leaves of our old Almanac

[1] *The Humorists* (1671) is the only play of Thomas Shadwell dedicated to Margaret, Duchess of Newcastle. It is certainly outspoken, but there is no mention in the "Dedication" of Shadwell's reading the ms to her. In the dedication to William, Duke of Newcastle, of *The Virtuoso* (1676) Shadwell wrote that he had shown his grace "some part of this Comedy".

[2] Among the living writers C probably included Thomas Moore for his "wanton poems"; see a letter to Mary Robinson 27 Dec 1802: *CL* II 905.

[3] See above, I 29 and n 2; and see *Misc C* 355–82 (C's early reviews of novels).

[4] For "Blasphemy" 1812 reads "Blasphemies".

[5] Matthew Lewis *The Monk* (1796); see *Misc C* 374–5.

[6] C is thinking particularly of Bell's *The Madras School* (1808) and Joseph Lancaster's *Improvements in Education* (1803), and the controversy sparked by Mrs Trimmer and Joseph Fox over the priority of Bell's or Lancaster's system. C had borrowed sheets of Bell's book (*CL* III 86–7, 88–9) to prepare his lecture on education at the Royal Institution 3 May 1808; it lasted two and a quarter hours (*CL* III 98). C praised Bell and attacked Lancaster. Southey's *The Origin, Nature, and Object of the New System of Education* (1812), C maintained, was "a dilution of my Lecture at the R.I." (*CL* III 474), but he had borrowed a copy in 1813 while preparing his Bristol lecture on education in Nov of that year (*CL* III 455 and n).

[7] Maria Edgeworth (1767–1849) wrote several such volumes, including the *Parent's Assistant* (1796–1800). When he was in Germany C recommended her *Practical Education* (1798, written in collaboration with her father, Richard Lovell Edgeworth) to Mrs C as a guide for teaching young Hartley how to read (*CL* I 418); it had, he added, good things in it, "& some nonsense!" In his lecture on education (see note above), according to HCR, he "especially satirised the good books in Miss Edgeworth's style [*Moral Tales* (1801)]. 'I infinitely prefer the little

Books, and the copper-plates of old Ladies' Magazines and similar publications, will afford in the fashions and head-dresses of our Grandmothers, contrasted with the present simple ornaments of women in general, a less important but not less striking elucidation of my meaning. The wide diffusion of moral information, in no slight degree owing to the volumes of our popular Essayists, has undoubtedly been on the whole beneficent. But above all, the recent events, [25] (say rather, tremendous explosions) the thunder and earthquakes and deluge of the political world, have forced habits of greater thoughtfulness on the minds of men: particularly in our own Island, where the instruction has been acquired without the stupifying influences of terror or actual calamity. We have been compelled to acknowledge (what our Fathers would have perhaps called it want of liberality to assert) the close connection between private libertinism and national subversion. To those familiar with the state of morals and the ordinary subjects of after-dinner conversation, at least among the young men, in Oxford and Cambridge only twenty or twenty five years back, I might with pleasure point out, in support of my thesis, the present state of our two Universities, which has rather superseded, than been produced by, any additional vigilance or austerity of discipline.

The unwelcome remainder of the proposition, the "feet of iron and clay," [1] the unsteadiness, or falsehood or abasement of *the Principles*, which are taught and received by the existing generation, it is the chief purpose and general business of "THE FRIEND" to examine, to evince and, (as far as my own forces extend, increased by the contingents which, I flatter myself, will be occasionally furnished by abler patrons of the same Cause,) to remedy or alleviate. That my efforts will effect little, I am fully conscious; but by no means admit, that little is to be effected. The squire of low degree may announce the approach of puissant Knight; yea, the Giant may even condescend to lift up the feeble Dwarf and permit it to blow the Horn of Defiance on his Shoulders. [2]

PRINCIPLES therefore, their subordination, their connection, and their application, in all the divisions of our duties and of our pleasures—this is my Chapter of Contents. May I not hope for a candid interpretation of my motive, if I again recur to the possible apprehension, on the part of my readers, that THE FRIEND

"O'erlaid with Black, staid Wisdom's Hue" [3]

with eye fixed in abstruse research and brow of perpetual Wrinkle is to frown away the light-hearted Graces, and "unreproved Pleasures"; [4] or invite his Guests to a dinner of herbs in a Hermit's Cell? if I affirm, that my Plan does not in itself exclude either impassioned style or interesting Narrative, Tale, or Allegory, or Anecdote; and [26] that the defect will

books of "The Seven Champions of Christendom," "Jack the Giant Killer" . . . to your moral tales . . .' ". *Sh C* II 13. Mrs Barbauld's *Lessons for Children* (1779–1808) and *Hymns in Prose for Children* (1781) were also popular

and went through numerous editions.
1 Dan 2.33 (var).
2 See above, I 249 and n 1.
3 Milton *Il Penseroso* line 16.
4 Milton *L'Allegro* line 40.

originate in my Abilities not in my Wishes or Efforts, if I fail to bring forward,

> "due at my hour prepar'd
> For dinner savory fruits, of taste to please
> True appetite————————————
> In order, so contriv'd as not to mix
> Tastes, not well join'd, inelegant; but bring
> Taste after Taste upheld with kindliest Change."
>
> PAR. LOST. v[1]

I have said in my first Number, that my very system compels me to make every fair appeal to the Feelings, the Imagination, and even the Fancy. If these are to be withheld from the service of Truth, Virtue, and Happiness, to what purpose were they given? in whose service are they retained? I have indeed considered the disproportion of human Passions to their ordinary Objects among the strongest internal evidences of our future destination, and the attempt to restore them to their rightful Claimants, the most imperious Duty and the noblest Task of Genius. The verbal enunciation of this Master Truth could scarcely be new to me at any period of my Life since earliest Youth; but I well remember the particular time, when the words first became more than words to me, when they incorporated with a living conviction, and took their place among the realities of my Being. On some wide Common or open Heath, peopled with Ant-hills, during some one of the grey cloudy days of late Autumn, many of my Readers may have noticed the effect of a sudden and momentary flash of Sunshine on all the countless little animals within his view, aware too that the self-same influence was darted co-instantaneously over all their swarming cities as far as his eye could reach; may have observed, with what a kindly force the Gleam stirs and quickens them all! and will have experienced no unpleasurable shock of Feeling in seeing myriads of myriads of living and sentient Beings united at the same moment in one gay sensation, one joyous activity! But aweful indeed is the same appearance in a multitude of rational Beings, our fellow-men; in whom too the effect is produced not so much by the external occasion as from the active quality of their own thoughts. I had walked from Gottingen in the year 1799, to witness the arrival of the Queen of Prussia, on her visit to the Baron Von Hartzberg's Seat, five miles from the University. The spacious Outer Court of the Palace was [27] crowded with men and women, a sea of Heads, with a number of children rising out of it from their Father's shoulders. After a Buz of two hours' expectation, the avant-courier rode at full speed into the Court. At the trampling of the[2] Horses' Hoofs, and the loud cracks of his long whip,[3] the universal Shock and Thrill of Emotion—I have not language to convey it—expressed as it was in such manifold looks, gestures, and attitudes, yet[4] one and the same feeling in the eyes of all! Recovering from the first inevitable contagion of Sympathy, I involuntarily exclaimed, though in a language to myself alone intelligible, "O Man! ever nobler than thy circumstances! Spread but the mist of obscure feeling over any

---

[1] Milton *Paradise Lost* v 303–5, 334–336 (altered).
[2] For "the" 1812 reads "his".
[3] 1812 reverses the phrases.
[4] 1812 adds "with".

form, and even a woman, incapable of blessing or of injury to thee, shall be welcomed with an intensity of emotion adequate to the reception of the Redeemer of the World!"

It has ever been my opinion, that an excessive solicitude to avoid the use of our first personal pronoun more often has its' source in conscious selfishness than in true self-oblivion. A quiet observer of human Follies may often amuse or sadden his thoughts by detecting the perpetual feeling of purest Egotism through a long masquerade of *Tu-isms* and *Ille-isms*. Yet I can with strictest truth assure my Readers that with a pleasure combined with a sense of weariness I see the nigh approach of that point of my labours, in which I can convey my opinions and the workings of my heart without reminding the Reader obtrusively of myself. But the frequency, with which I have spoken in my own person, recalls my apprehensions to the second danger, which it was my hope to guard against; the probable charge of ARROGANCE,[1] both for daring to dissent from the opinions of great Authorities and, in my following numbers perhaps, from the general opinion concerning the true value of certain Authorities deemed great.[2]

As no man can rightfully be condemned without reference to some definite Law, by the knowledge of which he might have avoided the given fault, it is necessary so to define the constituent qualities and conditions of arrogance, that a reason may be assignable why we pronounce one man guilty and acquit another. For merely to *call* a person arrogant or most arrogant, can convict no one of the vice except perhaps the accuser. I was once present, when a young man who had left his Books and a Glass of Water to join a convivial party, each of whom had nearly [28] finished his second bottle, was pronounced very drunk by the whole party—"he looked so strange and pale!" The predominant Vice often betrays itself to an Observer, when it has deluded the Criminal's own consciousness, by his proneness on all occasions to suspect or accuse others of it. Now Arrogance,[3] like all other moral qualities, must be shewn by some act or conduct: and this too an act that implies, if not an immediate concurrence of the Will, yet some faulty constitution of the Moral Habits. For all criminality supposes its' essentials to have been within the power of the Agent. Either therefore the facts adduced do of themselves convey the whole proof of the charge, and the question rests on the truth or accuracy with which they have been stated; or they acquire their character from the circumstances. I have looked into a ponderous Review of the corpuscular philosophy by a Sicilian Jesuit, in which the acrimonious Father frequently expresses his doubt, whether he should pronounce Boyle and Newton more impious than *arrogant*,[4] or more arrogant[5] than impious. They had both attacked the reigning opinions on most important subjects, opinions sanctioned by the greatest names of antiquity, and by the general suffrage of their learned Contemporaries or immediate Predecessors. Locke was assailed with a full

---

[1] 1812 adds "or presumption".
[2] 1812 adds "The word, Presumption, I appropriate to the internal feeling, and Arrogance to the way and manner of outwardly expressing ourselves."

[3] 1812 adds "and Presumption,".
[4] For "*arrogant*" 1812 reads "*presumptuous*".
[5] For "arrogant" 1812 reads "presumptuous".

cry for his arrogance in declaring his sentiments concerning [1] the philosophical system at that time generally received by the Universities of Europe: and of late years Dr. Priestly bestowed the epithets of *arrogant* and *insolent* on Reid, Beattie, &c. for presuming to arraign certain opinions of Mr. Locke, himself repaid in kind by many of his own Countrymen for his theological Novelties. It will scarcely be affirmed, that these accusations were all of them just, or that any of them were fit or courteous. Must we therefore say, that in order to avow doubt or disbelief of a popular persuasion without arrogance, it is required that the dissentient should know himself to possess the genius, and foreknow that he should acquire the reputation of Locke, Newton, Boyle, or even of a Reid or a Beattie? But as this knowledge and prescience are impossible in the strict sense of the words, and could mean no more than a strong inward conviction, it is manifest that such a Rule, if it were universally established, would encourage the arrogant,[2] and condemn modest and humble minds alone to silence. And as this silence could not acquit the Individual's own mind of arrogance,[3] unless it were accompanied by conscious acquiescence, [29] Modesty itself must become an inert quality, which even in private society never displays its charms more unequivocally than in its' mode of reconciling itself with sincerity and intellectual courage.

We must seek then elsewhere for the true marks, by which arrogance [4] may be detected, and on which the charge may be grounded with little hazard of mistake or injustice. And as I confine my present observations to literary arrogance,[5] I deem such criteria neither difficult to determine or to apply. The first mark, as it appears to me, is a frequent bare *assertion* of opinions not generally received, without condescending to prefix or annex the facts and reasons on which such opinions were formed; especially if this absence of logical courtesy is supplied by contemptuous or abusive treatment of such as happen to doubt of or oppose the decisive *Ipse dixi.* But to assert, however nakedly, that a passage in a lewd Novel, which declares[6] the sacred Writings[7] more likely to pollute the young and innocent mind than a Romance notorious for its indecency,[8] argues equal impudence and ignorance in its' Author, at the time of writing and publishing it—*this* is not arrogance; although to a vast majority of the decent part of our Countrymen it would be superfluous as a Truism, if it were not sometimes an Author's duty to awake the Reader's indignation by the expression of his own, as well as to convey or revive knowledge.[9] A second species of this unamiable quality, which has been often distinguished

---

[1] For "arrogance . . . concerning" 1812 reads "presumption in having deserted".

[2] For "arrogant" 1812 reads "presumptuous".

[3] For "arrogance," 1812 reads "presumption".

[4] For "arrogance" 1812 reads "presumption or arrogance".

[5] For "literary arrogance" 1812 reads "literature".

[6] For "which declares" 1812 reads "describing".

[7] 1812 adds "as".

[8] 1812 adds "—to assert, I say, that *such* a passage".

[9] For "not sometimes . . . knowledge" 1812 reads "exclusively an Author's business to convey or revive knowledge, and not sometime his duty to awaken the indignation of his Reader by the expression of his own".

by the name of *Warburtonian* arrogance, betrays itself, not as in the former, by proud or petulant omission of proof or argument, but by the habit of ascribing weakness of intellect or want of taste and sensibility, or hardness of heart, or corruption of moral principle, to all who deny the truth of the doctrine, or the sufficiency of evidence, or the fairness of the reasoning adduced in its' support. This is indeed not essentially different from the first, but assumes a separate character from its' accompaniments: for though both the doctrine and its proofs may have been legitimately supplied by the understanding, yet the bitterness of personal crimination will resolve itself into naked assertion, and we are authorized by experience, and entitled on the principle of self-defence and by the law of fair Retaliation, in attributing it to a vicious temper arrogant from angry passions, or irritable from arrogance. This learned arrogance admits of many gradations, and is palliated or aggravated, accordingly as the Point in dispute [30] has been more or less controverted, as the reasoning bears a greater or smaller proportion to the virulence of the personal detraction, and as the Persons[1] or Parties, who are the Objects of it, are more or less respected, more or less worthy of respect*.

Lastly, it must be admitted as a just imputation of arrogance,[4] when an Individual obtrudes on the public eye with all the high pretensions of originality, opinions and observations, in regard to which he must plead wilful Ignorance in order to be acquited of dishonest Plagiarism. On the same seat must the writer be placed, who in a disquisition on any important subject proves, by his falsehoods of Omission or positive Error, that he has

* Had the Author of the Divine Legation of Moses more skilfully appropriated his coarse eloquence of Abuse, his customary assurances of the Ideotcy, both in head and heart, of all his opponents; if he had employed those vigorous arguments of his own vehement Humour in the defence of Truths, acknowleged and reverenced by learned men in general, or had confined them to the names of Chubb, Woolston, and other precursors of Mr. Thomas Payne, we should[2] perhaps still characterize his mode of controversy by its' rude violence; but not so often have heard his name used even by those who never read his writings, as a proverbial expression of learned Arrogance. But when a novel and doubtful Hypothesis of his own formation was the Citadel to be defended, and his mephetic hand-granados were thrown with the fury of lawless despotism at the fair reputations[3] of a Sykes and a Lardner, we not only confirm the verdict of his independent contemporaries, but cease to wonder, that arrogance should render men an object of contempt in many, and of aversion in all instances, when it was capable of hurrying a Christian Teacher of equal Talents and Learning into a slanderous vulgarity, which escapes our disgust only when we see the writer's own reputation the sole victim. But throughout his great work, and the pamphlets in which he supported it, he always seems to write, as if he had deemed it a duty of decorum to publish his fancies on the Mosaic Law as the Law itself was delivered "in thunders and lightnings" and had applied to his own Book instead of the sacred mount the menace—*There shall not a hand touch it but he shall surely be stoned or shot through.*

[1] For "Persons" 1812 reads "Person".

[2] For "should" 1812 reads "would".

[3] For "reputations" 1812 reads "reputation".

[4] For "arrogance," 1812 reads "presumption".

neglected to possess himself of the previous knowledge and needful information, which such acquirements as could alone authorize him to commence a public Instructor, and the Industry which that character makes his
indispensible duty, could not fail of procuring for him. If in addition to
this unfitness which every man possesses the means of ascertaining, his aim
should be to unsettle a general belief closely connected with public and
private quiet; and if his language and manner be avowedly calculated for
the illiterate (and perhaps licentious) part of his Countrymen; disgusting as
his *arrogance*[1] must appear, it is yet lost or evanescent in the close neighbourhood of his Guilt. That Hobbes translated Homer in English Verse
and published his Translation, furnishes no positive evidence of his Self-
conceit, though it implies a great lack of Self-knowledge [31] and of
acquaintance with the nature of Poetry. A strong wish often imposes itself
on the mind for an actual power: the mistake is favoured by the innocent
pleasure derived from the exercise of versification, perhaps by the approbation of Intimates; and the Candidate asks from more impartial Readers
that sentence, which Nature has not enabled him to anticipate. But when
the Philosopher of Malmesbury waged war with Wallis and the fundamental Truths of pure Geometry, every instance of his gross ignorance and
utter misconception of the very elements of the Science he proposed to
confute, furnished an unanswerable fact in proof of his gross *arrogance*.[2]
An illiterate mechanic who mistaking some disturbance of his nerves for a
miraculous call, proceeds alone to convert a tribe of Savages, whose
language he can have no natural means of acquiring, may have been misled
by impulses very different from those of high Self-opinion; but the illiterate
Perpetrator of "the Age of Reason," must have had his[3] very Conscience
stupified by the habitual intoxication of *his* arrogance,[4] and his common-
sense over-clouded by the vapours from his Heart.

As long therefore as I obtrude no unsupported assertions on my
Readers; and as long as I state my opinions and the evidence which induced or compelled me to adopt them, with calmness and that diffidence in
myself, which is by no means incompatible with a firm belief in the justness
of the opinions themselves; while I attack no man's private life from any
cause, and detract from no man's Honors in his public character, from the
truth of his doctrines, or the merits of his compositions, without detailing
all my reasons and resting the result solely on the arguments adduced;
while I moreover explain fully the motives of duty, which influenced me in
resolving to institute such investigation; while I confine all asperity of
censure, and all expressions of contempt, to gross violations of Truth,
Honor, and Decency, to the base Corrupter and the detected Slanderer;
while I write on no subject, which I have not studied with my best attention,
on no subject which my education and acquirements have incapacitated me
from properly understanding; and above all while I approve myself, alike
in praise and in blame, in close reasoning and in impassioned declama-

---

[1] For "*arrogance*" 1812 reads "presumption".

[2] For "gross *arrogance*" 1812 reads
"high presumption; and the confident
and insulting language of the attack

leaves the judicious reader in as little
doubt of his gross arrogance".

[3] For "his" 1812 reads "*his*".

[4] For "*his* arrogance" 1812 reads
"presumptuous arrogance".

tion, a steady F R I E N D to the two best and surest Friends of all men, T R U T H and H O N E S T Y; I will not fear an accusation of *Arrogance*[1] from the Good and the Wise, I shall pity it from the Weak, and despise it from the Wicked.[2]

[32] My inexperience of the Press, and the warmth of my feelings in addressing for the last time that portion of my countrymen who have given me their patronage, in my own name and personal character, have led me on to an extent that compels me to defer the investigation of the great Theme, announced in my first Essay and insinuated by the motto of the present, to the succeeding or third Number of T H E F R I E N D.[3] The necessity of collecting the lists of Subscribers (or by whatever other name I may call those who have honored this undertaking with their names and addresses for a trial of its' merits) from the different booksellers, and agents, and the propriety of forming some arrangement with regard to the mode of payment (which I propose to be at the close of each twentieth week) have made it advisable to defer the publication of the third number to Thursday, 22d. of June, (in London and places equi-distant from Penrith, on Saturday, the 24th.)

At the same time I take the opportunity of informing my known and unknown Patrons, that I am about to put to the Press a collection of the Poems written by me since the year 1795, several of which, of those at least of smaller size, have appeared in different Newspapers &c. in an incorrect state: and with this a collection of the Essays, chiefly on political subjects, from the year preceding the peace of Amiens, with a few of earlier date, to the return of our Troops from Spain. Of these Essays many were published in the Morning Post, during Lord Sidmouth's Administration and at the close of Mr. Pitt's first Ministry; the remainder, comprising all of later date, all that relate to our external affairs in America, the Mediterranean, and Egypt, are from MSS. The work will be printed in two Volumes on crown Octavo, wove paper, the price not exceeding 16 Shillings. The Poems and the Essays may be had separately.[4]

My principle Object in this publication, one volume of which will be preceded by a sketch of my Life, is to furnish undeniable proofs concerning falshoods and calumnies attached to my name, in the religious, and political, and literary opinions confidently attributed to me; and which from Indolence,[5] Indifference, and the affliction of ill-health I have permitted to pass unnoticed, although repeated or insinuated in many and various publications, year after year. But I would fain hope, if the hope can be entertained without self-delusion, that the effects of two thirds of my Life, dated from my earliest manhood, may not be wholly barren of instruction, in the facts and observations collected at home and abroad by my own experience, and the deductions from these and from the events known in common to all educated Englishmen.

---

[1] For *"Arrogance"* 1812 reads "either *Presumption* or *Arrogance*".

[2] No 2 of 1812 ends here, the following paragraphs having been deleted.

[3] Cf above, II 14.

[4] The first volume was finally realised in 1817, with the publication of *Sibylline Leaves*; the second volume, not until 1850, when SC published *Essays on His Own Times*.

[5] The second self-accusation of "indolence" in two numbers. This sketch of his life grew into the *Biographia Literaria* (1817).

As the assurance of a sale adequate to the expence of the Publication would relieve my mind from some anxiety, I have arranged that the Names of those disposed to take one or both of the volumes should be received by G. Ward, Bookseller and Stationer, Skinner Street; Clement, 201, Strand; London. By Messrs Constable and Co. Edinburgh, and by all the agents of the Friend: or may be transmitted to the Author, Grasmere, near Kendal.

THE FRIEND

No. 3. THURSDAY, AUGUST 10, 1809

ADVERTISEMENT[1]

THE Editor respectfully informs his Readers, that the Interruption of this Publication has been owing to disappointments in the receipt of, and an unexpected derangement in his plans of procuring, the Paper and Stamps; and to his resolve not to re-commence the Friend till he had placed himself out of the reach of all such accidents as might occasion the painful necessity of any future suspension or delay. Subscribers may be assured, that the greatest care will be taken henceforward, to prevent all irregularity in the forwarding of the Work to each, according to the directions which have been received; and it is hoped that any deficiency in this respect hitherto, will be attributed to the inexperience of the Editor, and the difficulty and awkwardness which are natural in a new undertaking, especially in so remote a part of the Kingdom. Those who have left their names and addresses at the Booksellers, without receiving the work by the Post in consequence, are solicited to repeat their orders, directed to J. Brown, Bookseller, Penrith: it being the object of the Stamp, to enable each Subscriber to receive the numbers at his own residence. The two first numbers are now reprinting.

ON THE COMMUNICATION OF TRUTH
AND THE RIGHTFUL LIBERTY OF THE PRESS
IN CONNECTION WITH IT

In eodem pectore nullum est honestorum turpiumque consortium: et cogitare optima simul et deterrima non magis est unius animi quam ejusdem hominis bonum esse ac malum. QUINTILIAN

There is no fellowship of Honor and Baseness in the same breast; and to combine the best and the worst designs is no more possible in one mind, than it is for the same man to be at the same instant virtuous and vicious.

[34] *Cognitio veritatis omnia falsa, si modo proferantur, etiam quæ prius inaudita erant, et dijudicare et subvertere idonea est.* AUGUSTINUS

A knowledge of the truth is equal to the task both of discerning and of confuting all false assertions and erroneous arguments, though never before met with, if only they may freely be brought forward.

AMONG the numerous artifices by which austere truths are to be softened down into palatable falsehoods, and Virtue and Vice, like the Atoms of Epicurus, to receive that insensible *clinamen* which is to

---

[1] 1812 deletes the "Advertisement"; see above, Introduction, I liv.

make them meet each other half way, I have[1] especial dislike to the expression PIOUS FRAUDS. Piety indeed shrinks from the very phrase, as an attempt to mix poison with the cup of Blessing: while the *expediency* of the measures which this phrase was framed to recommend or palliate, appears more and more suspicious, as the range of our experience widens, and our acquaintance with the records of History becomes more extensive and accurate. One of the most seductive arguments of Infidelity grounds itself on the numerous passages in the works of the Christian Fathers, asserting the lawfulness of Deceit for a good purpose. That the Fathers held almost without exception, "*Integrum omnino Doctoribus et cætûs Christiani Antistitibus esse, ut dolos versent, falsa veris intermisceant et imprimis religionis hostes fallant, dummodo veritatis commodis et utilitati inserviant,** " [2] is the unwilling confession of RIBOF: (*Program de Oeconomiâ Patrum*). St. Jerom, as is shewn by the citations of this learned Theologian, boldly attributes this *management* (*falsitatem dispensativam*) even to the Apostles themselves. But why [35] speak I of the advantage given to the opponents of Christianity? Alas! to this Doctrine chiefly, and to the practices derived from it, we must attribute the utter corruption of the Religion itself for so many ages, and even now over so large a portion of the civilized world. By a system of accommodating Truth to Falsehood, the Pastors of the Church gradually changed the life and light of the Gospel into the very superstitions which they were commissioned to disperse, and thus paganized Christianity, in order to *christen* Paganism. At this very hour Europe groans and bleeds in consequence.

So much in proof and exemplification of the probable *expediency* of pious deception, as suggested by its known and recorded consequences. An honest man, however, possesses a clearer light than that of History. He knows, that by sacrificing the law of his reason to the maxims of pretended Prudence, he purchases the sword with the loss of the arm which is to wield it. The duties which we owe to our own moral being, are the ground and condition of all other duties; and to set our nature at strife with itself for a good purpose, implies the same sort of prudence, as a priest

TRANSLATION

* "That wholly without breach of duty it is allowed to the Teachers and Heads of the Christian Church to employ artifices, to intermix falsehoods with truths, and especially to deceive the enemies of the faith, provided only they hereby serve the interests of Truth and the advantage of mankind."—I trust, I need not add, that the imputation of such principles of action to the first inspired Propagators of Christianity, is founded on the gross misconstruction of those passages in the writings of St. Paul, in which the necessity of employing different arguments to men of different capacities and prejudices, is supposed and acceded to. In other words, St. Paul strove to speak intelligibly, willingly sacrificed indifferent things to matters of importance, and acted courteously as a man in order to win attention as an Apostle. A Traveller prefers for daily use the coin of the nation through which he is passing, to bullion or the mintage of his own country: and is this to justify a succeeding Traveller in the use of counterfeit coin?

[1] 1812 adds "an".
[2] In 1812 the Latin was shifted to the footnote and the English placed in the body of the text and so needed no heading "TRANSLATION".

of Diana would have manifested, who should have proposed to dig up the celebrated charcoal foundations of the mighty Temple of Ephesus, in order to furnish fuel for the burnt-offerings on its' Altars. Truth, Virtue, and Happiness, may be distinguished from each other, but cannot be divided. They subsist by a mutual co-inherence, which gives a shadow of divinity even to our human nature. "Will ye speak deceitfully for God?" is a searching Question, which most affectingly represents the grief and impatience of an uncorrupted mind at perceiving a good cause defended by ill means: and assuredly if any temptation can provoke a well-regulated temper to intolerance, it is the shameless assertion, that Truth and Falsehood are indifferent in their own natures; that the former is as often injurious (and therefore criminal) as the latter, and the latter on many occasions as beneficial (and consequently meritorious) as the former.

These reflections were forced upon me by an accident during a short visit at a neighbouring house, as I was endeavouring to form some determinate principles of conduct in relation to my weekly labors—some rule which might guide my judgment in the choice of my subjects [36] and in my manner of treating them, and secure me from the disturbing forces of any ungentle moods of my own temper (and from such who dare promise himself a perpetual exemption?) as well as from the undue influence of passing events. I had fixed my eye, by chance, on the page of a bulky pamphlet[1] that lay open on the breakfast table, mechanically, as it were, imitating and at the same time preserving the mind's attention to its' own energies by a corresponding though idle stedfastness of the outward organ. In an interval or relaxation of the thought, as the mist gradually formed itself into letters and words, one of the sentences made its' way to me, and excited my curiosity by the boldness and strangeness of its' contents. I immediately recognized the work itself, which I had often heard discussed for evil and for good. I was therefore familiar with its general character, and extensive circulation, although partly from the seclusion in which I live, and my inability to purchase the luxuries of transitory literature on my own account, and partly too from the experience, that of all books I had derived the least improvement from those that were confined to the names and passions of my contemporaries: this was either the third or the fourth number which had come within my perusal. In this however I read not only a distinct avowal of the doctrine stated in my last paragraph, and which I had been accustomed to consider as an obsolete article in the creed of fanatical Antinomianism, but this avowal conveyed in the language of menace and intolerant contempt. I now look forward to the perusal of the whole series of the work, as made a point of duty to me by my knowledge of its' unusual influence on the public opinion; and in the mean time I feel it incumbent on me, as a joint measure of prudence and of honesty relatively to my own undertaking, to place immediately before my Readers, in the fullest and clearest light, the whole question of moral obligation respecting the communication of Truth, its' extent and conditions. I would

---

[1] The *Edinburgh Review*. De Quincey, in a letter to DW 16 Aug [1809], says that C was alluding to its review of William Belsham *History of Great Britain* (1805): *De Q to W* 244–5. See *Ed Rev* VI (Jul 1805) 421–8.

fain obviate all apprehensions either of my incaution or¹ insincere reserve,² by proving that the more strictly we adhere to the *Letter* of the moral law in this respect, the more compleatly shall we reconcile the law with prudence, and secure³ a purity in the principle without mischief from the practice. I would not, I could not dare, address my countrymen as a Friend, if I might not [37] justify the assumption of that sacred title by more than mere veracity, by open-heartedness. The meanest of men feels himself insulted by an unsuccessful attempt to deceive him; and hates and despises the man who had attempted it. What place then is left in the heart for Virtue to build on, if in any case we may dare practice on others what we should feel as a cruel and contemptuous Wrong in our own persons? Every parent possesses the opportunity of observing, how deeply children resent the injury of a delusion; and if men laugh at the falsehoods that were imposed on themselves during their childhood, it is because they are not good and wise enough to contemplate the Past in the Present, and so to produce by a virtuous and thoughtful sensibility that continuity in their self-consciousness, which Nature has made the law of their animal Life*. Alas!

* Ingratitude, sensuality, and hardness of heart, all flow from this source. Men are ungrateful to others only when they have ceased to look back on their former selves with joy and tenderness. They exist in fragments. Annihilated as to the Past, they are dead to the Future, or seek for the proofs of it every where, only not (where alone they can be found) in themselves. A contemporary poet has exprest and illustrated this sentiment with equal fineness of thought and tenderness of feeling:

> My heart leaps up when I behold
> A rain-bow in the sky!
> So was it, when my life began;
> So is it now I am a man;
> So let it be, when I grow old,
>   Or let me die.
> *The Child is Father of the Man,*
> *And I would wish my days to be*
> *Bound each to each by natural piety.*
>   WORDSWORTH

I am informed, that these very lines have been cited, as a specimen of despicable puerility. So much the worse for the citer. Not willingly in *his* presence would I behold the Sun setting behind our mountains, or listen to a tale of Distress or Virtue; I should be ashamed of the quiet tear on my own cheek. But let the Dead bury the Dead! The poet sang for the Living. Of what value indeed, to a sane mind, are the Likings or Dislikings of one man, grounded on the mere assertions of another? Opinions formed from opinions—what are they, but clouds sailing under clouds, which impress shadows upon shadows?

> Fungum pelle procul, jubeo! nam quid mihi Fungo?
> Conveniunt stomacho non minus ista suo.

I was always pleased with the motto placed under the figure of the Rosmary in old Herbals: Sus, apage! Haud tibi spiro.

¹ For "or" 1812 reads "on the one hand, or of any".
² For "reserve" 1812 reads "reserve on the other".
³ For "and secure" 1812 reads "thus securing".

the pernicious influence of this lax morality extends from the Nursery and the School to the Cabinet and Senate. It is a common weakness with men in power, who have used dissimulation successfully, to form a passion for the use of it, dupes to the love of duping! A pride is flattered by [38] these lies. He who fancies that he must be perpetually stooping down to the prejudices of his fellow-creatures, is perpetually reminding and re-assuring himself of his own vast superiority to them. But no real greatness can long co-exist with deceit. The whole faculties of man must be exerted in order to noble energies; and he who is not earnestly sincere, self-mutilated, self-paralysed, lives in but half his being.[1]

The latter part of the proposition, which has drawn me into this discussion, that I mean in which the morality of intentional falsehood is asserted, may safely be trusted to the reader's own moral sense. It will, however, be found in its proper nitch of Infamy, in some future number of THE FRIEND, among other enormities in taste, morals, and theology, with which our* literature continues to be outraged. The former sounds less offensively at the first hearing, only because it hides its' deformity in an equivocation, or double meaning of the word Truth. What may be rightly affirmed of Truth, used as synonimous with verbal accuracy, is transferred to it in its' higher sense of veracity. By *verbal* truth we mean no more than the correspondence of a given fact to given words. In *moral* truth, we moreover involve the intention of the speaker, that his words should correspond to his thoughts in the sense in which he expects them to be [39] understood by others: and in this latter import we are always supposed to use the word, whenever we speak of Truth absolutely, or as a possible subject of moral merit or demerit. It is verbally true, that in the sacred Scriptures

* Is it a groundless apprehension, that the Patrons and Admirers of such publications may receive the punishment of their indiscretion in the conduct of their Sons and Daughters? The suspicion of Methodism must be expected by every man of rank and fortune, who carries his examination respecting the Books which are to lie on his Breakfast-table, farther than to their freedom from gross verbal indecencies, and broad avowals of Atheism in *the Title-page*. For the existence of an intelligent first Cause may be ridiculed in the notes of one poem, or placed doubtfully as one of two or three possible hypotheses, in the very opening of another poem, and both be considered as works of safe promiscuous reading "virginibus puerisque:" and this too by many a Father of a family, who would hold himself highly culpable in permitting his Child to form habits of familiar acquaintance with a person of loose habits, and think it even criminal to receive into his house a private Tutor without a previous inquiry concerning his opinions and principles, as well as his manners and outward conduct. How little I am an enemy to free enquiry of the boldest kind, and where the Authors have differed the most widely from my own convictions and the general faith of mankind, provided only, the enquiry be conducted with that seriousness, which naturally accompanies the love of Truth, and is evidently intended for the perusal of those only, who may be presumed to be capable of weighing the arguments, I shall have abundant occasion of proving, in the course of this work. *Quin ipsa philosophia talibus e disputationibus non nisi beneficium recipit. Nam si vera proponit homo ingeniosus veritatisque amans, nova ad eam accessio fiet: sin falsa, refutatione eorum priores tanto magis stabilientur.* GALILÆI *Syst. Cosm.* p 42.

[1] 1812 transposes: "he who is not earnestly sincere, lives . . . self-paralysed".

it is written: "As is the good, so is the sinner, and he that sweareth as he that feareth an oath. A man hath no better thing under the sun, than to eat, and to drink, and to be merry. For there is one event unto all: the living know they shall die, but the dead know not any thing, neither have they any more a reward." But he who should repeat these words, with this assurance, to an ignorant man in the hour of his temptation, lingering at the door of the ale-house, or hesitating as to the testimony required of him in the Court of Justice, would, spite of this verbal truth, be a Liar, and the Murderer of his Brother's Conscience. Veracity therefore, not mere accuracy; to convey truth, not merely to say it; is the point of Duty in Dispute: and the only difficulty in the mind of an honest man arises from the doubt, whether more than *veracity* (i.e. the truth and nothing but the truth) is not demanded of him by the Law of Conscience, namely,[1] *Simplicity;* that is, the truth only, and the whole truth. If we can solve this difficulty, if we can determine the conditions under which the Law of universal Reason commands the communication of Truth independently of consequences altogether, we shall then be enabled to judge whether there is any such probability of *evil* consequences from such communication, as can justify the assertion of its' occasional criminality, as can perplex us in the conception, or disturb us in the performance, of our duty. (The existence of a rule of Right (*recta regula*) not derived from a calculation of consequences, and even independent of any experimental knowledge of its' practicability, but as an Idea co-essential with the Reason of Man, and its' necessary product, I have here intentionally *assumed,* in order that I may draw the attention of my Readers to this important question, of all questions indeed the most important, previous to the regular solution which I hope to undertake in my sixth or seventh Number.)[2]

The Conscience, or effective Reason, commands the design of conveying an *adequate* notion of the thing spoken of, when this is practicable; but at all events a *right* notion, or none at all. A School-master is under [40] the necessity of teaching a certain Rule in simple arithmetic empirically, (Do so and so, and the sum *will* always prove true) the necessary truth of the Rule (i.e. that the Rule having been adhered to, the sum *must* always prove true) requiring a knowledge of the higher mathematics for its demonstration. He, however, conveys a right notion, though he cannot convey the *adequate* one.

The moral law then permitting the one on the condition that the other is impracticable, and binding us to silence when neither is in our power, we must first enquire: What is necessary to constitute, and what may allowably accompany, a right though inadequate notion? And secondly, what are the circumstances, from which we may deduce the impracticability of conveying even a right notion, the presence or absence of which circumstances it therefore becomes our duty to ascertain? In answer to the first question, the Conscience demands: 1. That it should be the wish and design of the mind to convey the truth only; that if in addition to the negative loss implied in its' inadequateness, the notion communicated should *lead* to any positive error, the cause should lie in the fault or defect of the Recipient,

---

[1] For "namely," 1812 reads "whether it does not exact".

[2] For "in . . . Number.)" 1812 reads "hereafter."

not of the Communicator, whose paramount duty, whose inalienable right it is to preserve his own *Integrity*, the *integral* character of his own moral Being. Self-respect; the reverence which he owes to the presence of Humanity in the person of his Neighbour; the reverential upholding of the Faith of Man in Man; Gratitude for the particular act of Confidence; and religious awe for the divine [41] purposes in the gift of Language; are Duties too sacred and important to be sacrificed to the *Guesses* of an Individual, concerning the advantages to be gained by the breach of them. 2. It is further required, that the supposed error shall not be such as will pervert or materially vitiate the imperfect truth, in communicating which we had unwillingly, though not perhaps unwittingly, *occasioned* it. A Barbarian so instructed in the Power and Intelligence of the Infinite Being as to be left wholly ignorant of his moral attributes, would have acquired none but erroneous notions even of the former. At the very best, he would gain only a theory to satisfy his curiosity with; but more probably, would deduce the belief of a Moloch or a Baal. (For the Idea of an irresistible invisible Being naturally produces terror in the mind of uninstructed and unprotected man, and with terror there will be associated whatever had been accustomed to excite it, as Anger, Vengeance, &c.: as is proved by the Mythology of all barbarous nations.) This must be the case with all organized truths: the component parts derive their significance from the Idea of the whole. Bolingbroke removed Love, Justice, and Choice, from power and intelligence, and yet pretended to have left unimpaired the conviction of a Deity. He might as consistently have paralysed the optic nerve, and then excused himself by affirming, that he had, however, not touched the eye.

The third condition of a right though inadequate notion is, that the error occasioned be greatly outweighed by the importance of the truth communicated. The rustic would have little reason to thank the philosopher, who should give him true conceptions of the folly of believing in Ghosts,

---

* The best and most forcible sense of a word is often that, which is contained in its' Etymology. The Author of the Poems (*the Synagogue*) frequently affixed to Herbert's "Temple," gives the original purport of the word integrity, in the following lines (fourth stanza of the 8th poem.)

> Next to Sincerity, remember still,
> Thou must resolve upon *Integrity*.
> God will have *all* thou hast, thy mind, thy will,
> Thy thoughts, thy words, thy works.

And again, after some Verses on Constancy and Humility, the poem concludes with—

> He that desires to see
> The face of God, in his religion must
> Sincere, *entire*, constant, and humble be.

Having mentioned the name of *Herbert*, that model of a Man, a Gentleman, and a Clergyman, let me add, that the Quaintness of some of his Thoughts (not of his Diction, than which nothing can be more pure, manly, and unaffected,) has blinded modern readers to the great general merit of his Poems, which are for the most part exquisite in their kind.

Omens, Dreams, &c. at the price of[1] his faith in providence and in the continued existence of his fellow-creatures after their Death. The teeth of the old Serpent planted by the Cadmuses of French Literature, under Lewis XV. produced a plenteous crop of Philosophers and Truth-trumpeters of this kind, in the reign of his Successors. They taught many truths, historical, political, physiological, and ecclesiastical, and diffused their notions so widely, that the very Ladies and Hair-dressers of Paris became fluent *Encyclopædists:* and the sole price which their Scholars paid for these treasures of new information, was to believe Christianity an imposture, [42] the Scriptures a forgery, the worship (if not the belief) of God superstition, Hell a Fable, Heaven a Dream, our Life without Providence, and our Death without Hope. They became as Gods as soon as the fruit of this Upas Tree of Knowledge and Liberty had opened their eyes to perceive that they were no more than Beasts—somewhat more cunning perhaps, and abundantly more mischievous. What can be conceived more natural than the result,—that self-acknowledged Beasts should first act, and next suffer themselves to be treated as Beasts. We judge by comparison. To exclude the great is to magnify the little. The disbelief of essential Wisdom and Goodness, necessarily prepares the Imagination for the supremacy of Cunning with Malignity. Folly and Vice have their appropriate Religions, as well as Virtue and true Knowledge: and in some way or other Fools will dance round the golden Calf, and wicked men beat their timbrels and kettle-drums

> To Moloch, horrid king, besmeared with blood
> Of human sacrifice and parent's tears.

My feelings have led me on, and in my illustration I had almost lost from my view the subject to be illustrated. One condition yet remains: that the error foreseen shall not be of a kind to prevent or impede the after acquirement of that knowledge which will remove it. Observe, how graciously Nature instructs her human Children. She cannot give us the knowledge derived from sight without occasioning us at first to mistake Images of Reflection for Substances. But the very consequences of the delusion lead inevitably to its' detection; and out of the ashes of the error rises a new flower of knowledge. We not only see, but are enabled to discover by what means we see. So too we are under the necessity in given circumstances, of mistaking a square for a round object; but ere the mistake can have any practical consequences, it is not only removed, but in its' removal gives us the symbol of a new fact, that of distance. In a similar train of thought, though more fancifully, I might have elucidated the preceding Condition, and have referred our hurrying Enlighteners and revolutionary Amputators to the gentleness of Nature, in the Oak and the Beech, the dry foliage of which she pushes off only by the propulsion of the new buds, that supply its' place. [43] My friends! a cloathing even of withered Leaves is better than bareness.

Having thus determined the nature and conditions of a right notion, it remains to determine the circumstances which tend to render the communication of it impracticable, and obliges us of course, to abstain from the attempt—*obliges* us not to *convey* falsehood under the pretext of *saying*

[1] 1812 adds "abandoning".

truth. These circumstances, it is plain, must consist either in natural or moral impediments. The former, including the obvious gradations of constitutional insensibility and derangement, preclude all temptation to misconduct, as well as all probability of ill-consequences from accidental oversight, on the part of the communicator. Far otherwise is it with the impediments from moral causes. These demand all the attention and forecast of the genuine lovers of Truth in the matter, the manner, and the time of their communications, public and private; and these are the ordinary materials of the vain and the factious, determine them in the choice of their audiences and of their arguments, and to each argument give powers not its' own. They are distinguishable into two sources, the streams from which, however, must often become confluent, viz. hindrances from *Ignorance* (I here use the word in relation to the habits of reasoning as well as to the previous knowledge requisite for the due comprehension of the subject) and hindrances from predominant *passions.* Bold, warm, and earnest assertions, which gain credit partly from that natural generosity of the human heart which makes it an effort to doubt, and from[1] the habit formed by hourly acts of belief from infancy to age, and partly from the confidence which apparent Courage is wont to inspire, and from[2] the contagion of animal enthusiasm; arguments built on passing events and deriving an undue importance from the interest of the moment; startling particular facts; the display of defects without the accompanying excellencies, or of excellencies without their accompanying defects; the concealment of the general and ultimate result behind the scenery of local or immediate consequences; statement of conditional truths to those whose passions make them forget, that the conditions under which alone the statement is true, are not present, or even lead them to believe, that they are; chain[3] of questions, especially of such questions as those best authorized to propose are the slowest in [44] proposing; objections intelligible of themselves, the answers to which require the comprehension of a system;—all these a Demagogue might make use of, and in nothing deviate from the verbal truth. From all these the law of Conscience commands us to abstain, because such being the ignorance and such the passions of the supposed Auditors, we ought to deduce the impracticability of conveying not only adequate, but even right, notions of our own convictions, much less does it permit us to avail ourselves of the causes of this impracticability in order to procure nominal proselytes, each of whom will have a different, and all a false, conception of those notions that were to be conveyed for their truth's sake alone. Whatever is (or but for some defect in our moral character would have been) foreseen as preventing the conveyance of our thoughts, makes the attempt an act of self-contradiction: and whether the faulty cause exist in our choice of unfit words or our choice of unfit auditors, the result is the same and so is the guilt. We have voluntarily communicated falsehood.

Thus (without reference to *consequences,* if only one short digression be excepted) from the sole principle of Self-consistence or moral Integrity, we have evolved the clue of right Reason, which we are bound to follow in the

---

[1] 1812 deletes "from".   [3] For "chain" 1812 reads "chains".
[2] 1812 deletes "from".

communication of Truth. Now then we appeal to the judgment and experience of the Reader, whether he who most faithfully adheres to the letter of
the law of conscience, will not likewise act in strictest correspondence to
the maxims of prudence and sound policy. I am at least unable to recollect
a single instance, either in History or in my personal experience, of a preponderance of injurious consequences from the publication of any truth,
under the observance of the moral conditions above stated: much less can
I even imagine any case, in which Truth, as Truth, can be pernicious. But
if the assertor of the indifferency of Truth and Falsehood in their own
natures, attempt to justify his position by confining the word truth, in the
first instance, to the correspondence of given words to given facts, without
reference to the total impression left by such words; what is this more than
to assert, that *articulated sounds* are things of moral indifferency? and that
we may relate a fact accurately and nevertheless deceive grossly and
wickedly? Blifil related accurately Tom Jones's riotous joy during [45] his
Benefactor's illness, only omitting that this joy was occasioned by the
Physician's having pronounced him out of danger. Blifil was not the less
a Liar for being an accurate *matter-of-fact* Liar. *Tell-truths* in the service
of Falsehood we find every where, of various names and various occupations, from the elderly young women that discuss the Love-affairs of their
friends and acquaintance at the village Tea-tables, to the anonymous
calumniators of literary merit in Reviews, and the more daring Malignants,
who dole out Discontent, Innovation and Panic, in political Journals: and
a most pernicious Race of Liars they are! But whoever doubted it? Why
should our moral feelings be shocked, and the holiest words with all their
venerable associations be profaned, in order to bring forth a Truism? But
thus it is for the most part with the venders of startling paradoxes. In the
sense in which they are to gain for their Author the character of a bold
and original Thinker, they are false even to absurdity; and the sense in
which they are true and harmless, conveys so mere a Truism, that it even
borders on Nonsense. How often have we heard "THE RIGHTS OF
MAN—HURRA!——THE SOVEREIGNTY OF THE PEOPLE—HURRA!"
roared out by men who, if called upon in another place and before another
audience, to explain themselves, would give to the words a meaning, in
which the most monarchical of their political opponents would admit
them to be true, but which would contain nothing new, or strange, or
stimulant, nothing to flatter the pride or kindle the passions of the Populace. To leave a general confused impression of something great, and to
rely on the indolence of men's understandings and the activity of their
passions, for their resting in this impression, is the old artifice of public
Mountebanks, which, like stratagems in war, are never the less successful
for having succeeded a thousand times before.

But how will these Rules apply to the most important mode of communication? To that, in which one man may utter his thoughts to myriads
of men at the same time, and to myriads of myriads at various times and
through successions of generations? How do they apply to Authors, whose
foreknowledge assuredly does not inform them who, or how many, or of
what description their Readers will be? To[1] Books, which once published,

[1] For "To" 1812 reads "How do these Rules apply to".

are as likely to fall in the way of the Incompetent as of the Judicious, and will [46] be fortunate indeed if they are not many times looked at through the thick mists of ignorance, or amid the glare of prejudice and passion? —We answer in the first place, that this is not universally true. Relations of certain pretended miracles performed a few years ago, at Holywell, in consequence of Prayers to the Virgin Mary, on female servants, and these Relations moralized by the old Roman Catholic arguments without the old Protestant answers, have to my knowledge been sold by travelling Pedlars in villages and farm-houses, not only in a form which placed them within the reach of the narrowest means, but sold at a price less than their prime cost, and doubtless, to be thrown in occasionally as the *make-weight* of a bargain of Pins and Stay-tape. Shall I be told, that the publishers and reverend Authorizers of *these* base and vulgar delusions had exerted no *choice* as to the Purchasers and Readers? But waiving this, or rather having first pointed it out, as an important exception, we further reply: that if the Author have clearly and rightly established in his own mind the class of Readers, to which he means to address his communications; and if both in this choice, and in the particulars of the manner and matter of his work, he conscientiously observes all the conditions which Reason and Conscience have been shewn to dictate, in relation to those for whom the work was designed; he will, in most instances, have effected his design and realized the desired circumscription. The posthumous work of Spinoza (*Ethica ordine geometrico demonstrata*) may, indeed, accidentally fall into the hands of an incompetent reader. But (not to mention, that it is written in a dead language) it will be entirely harmless, because it must needs be utterly unintelligible. I venture to assert, that the whole first book, De Deo, might be read in a literal English Translation to any congregation in the kingdom, and that no Individual, who had not been habituated to the strictest and most laborious processes of Reasoning, would even suspect its' orthodoxy or piety, however heavily the few who listened would complain of its' Obscurity and want of Interest. This, it may be objected, is an extreme case. But it is not so for the present purpose. We are speaking of the probability of injurious consequences from the communication of Truth. This I have denied, if the right means have been adopted, and the necessary conditions adhered to, for its' *actual* communication. Now the Truths conveyed in a book are [47] either evident of themselves, or such as require a train of deductions in proof; and the latter will be either such as are authorized and generally received, or such as are in opposition to received and authorized opinions, or, lastly, truths presented for the appropriate test of examination, and still under trial (*adhuc sub lite*,)[1] of this latter class I affirm, that no instance can be brought of a preponderance of ill-consequences, or even of an equi-librium of advantage and injury, in which the understanding alone has been appealed to, by results fairly deduced from just premises, in terms strictly appropriate. Alas! legitimate reasoning is impossible without severe thinking, and thinking is neither an easy nor an amusing employment. The reader, who would follow a close reasoner to the summit and absolute principle of any one important subject, has chosen a Chamois-hunter for his Guide. Our Guide will, indeed,

[1] 1812 begins a new sentence with "Of".

take us the shortest way, will save us many a wearisome and perilous wandering, and warn us of many a mock road that had formerly led himself to the brink of chasms and precipices, or at best in an idle circle to the spot from whence he started; but he cannot carry us on his shoulders; we must strain our own sinews, as he has strained his; and make firm footing on the smooth rock for ourselves, by the blood of toil from our own feet. Examine the journals of our humane and zealous Missionaries in Hindostan. How often and how feelingly do they describe the difficulty of making the simplest chain of reasoning intelligible to the ordinary natives; the rapid exhaustion of their whole power of attention, and with what pain and distressful effort it is exerted, while it lasts. Yet it is among this class, that the hideous practices of self-torture chiefly, indeed almost exclusively, prevail. O if Folly were no easier than Wisdom, it being often so very much more grievous, how certainly might not these miserable men be converted to Christianity? But alas! to swing by hooks passed through the back, or to walk on shoes with nails of iron pointed upward on the soles, all this is so much less difficult, demands so very inferior an exertion of the Will than to *think*, and by thought to gain Knowledge and Tranquillity!

It is not true, that ignorant persons have no notion of the *advantages* of Truth and knowledge. They see, they acknowledge, those advantages in the conduct, the immunities, and the superior powers, of the Possessors. Were [48] these attainable by Pilgrimages the most toilsome, or Penances the most painful, we should assuredly have as many Pilgrims and as many Self-tormentors in the service of true Religion and Virtue, as now exist under the tyranny of Papal or Brahman Superstition. This Inefficacy[1] from the want of fit Objects, this[2] relative Weakness of legitimate Reason, and how narrow at all times its immediate sphere of action must be, is proved to us by the Impostures of all professions. What, I pray, is their fortress, the rock which is both their quarry and their foundation, from which and on which they are built? The desire of arriving at the end without the effort of thought and will which are the appointed means;[3] for though from the difference of the mode a difference of use is made requisite, yet the effort in conquering a bad passion, or in mastering a long series of linked truths, is *essentially* the same: in both we exert the same reason and the same will. Let us look backward three or four centuries. Then as now the great mass of mankind were governed by the three main wishes, the wish for vigor of body, including the absence of painful feelings: for wealth, or the power of procuring the external conditions of bodily enjoyment; these during life—and security from pain and continuance of happiness after death. Then, as now, men were desirous to attain them by some easier means than those of Temperance, Industry, and strict Justice. They gladly therefore applied to the Priest, who could ensure them happiness hereafter without the performance of their Duties here; to the Lawyer, who could make money a substitute for a right cause; to the Physician, whose medicines promised to take the sting out of the tail of their sensual

---

[1] 1812 transposes "of legitimate Reason" from below to here.

[2] 1812 adds "its' ".

[3] In 1812 the sentence ends here, the rest having been deleted.

Indulgences,[1] and let them fondle and play with Vice, as with a charmed Serpent; to the Alchemist, whose gold-tincture would enrich them without Toil or Economy; and to the Astrologer, from whom they could purchase foresight without Knowledge or Reflection. The established Professions were, without exception, no other than licenced modes of Witchcraft; the Wizards, who would now find their due reward in Bridewell, and their

(To be continued.)[2]

---

[1] For "Indulgences" 1812 reads "indulgencies".

[2] 1812 omits.

THE FRIEND

No. 4. THURSDAY, September 7, 1809

(Continued from page 48.)[1]

appropriate honors in the Pillory, sate then on episcopal thrones, candidates for Saintship, and already canonized in the belief of their deluded Contemporaries; while the one or two real Teachers and Discoverers of Truth were exposed to the hazard of Fire and Faggot, a Dungeon the best Shrine that was vouchsafed to a Roger Bacon and a Galileo! It is not so in our times. Heaven be praised, that in this respect at least we are, if not better, yet *better off* than our Forefathers. But to what, and to whom (under Providence) do we owe the Improvement? To any radical change in the moral affections of mankind in general? Perhaps, the great majority of men are now fully conscious, that they are born with the god-like faculty of Reason, and that it is the business of Life to develope and apply it? The Jacob's Ladder of Truth, let down from Heaven, with all its' numerous Rounds, is now the common High-way, on which we are content to toil upward to the Objects of our Desires? We are ashamed of expecting the end without the means? In order to answer these questions in the affirmative, I must have forgotten the Animal Magnetists, the proselytes of Brothers,[2] of Joanna Southcot, and some hundred thousand Fanatics less original in their creeds, but not a whit more rational in their expectations! I must forget the infamous Empirics, whose Advertisements pollute and disgrace all our Newspapers, and almost *paper* the walls of our Cities, and the vending of whose poisons and poisonous Drams (with shame and anguish be it spoken) supports a shop in every market-town! I must forget that other opprobrium of the Nation, that *Mother-vice*, the Lottery! I must forget, that a numerous class plead *Prudence* for keeping their fellow-men ignorant and incapable of intellectual enjoyments, and the *Revenue* for upholding such Temptations as men so ignorant will not withstand[3] —at every fiftieth door throughout the Kingdom, Temptations to the most [50] pernicious Vices, which fill the Land with mourning, and fit the labouring classes for Sedition and religious Fanaticism! Above all, I must forget the first years of the French Revolution, and the Millions throughout Europe who confidently expected the best and choicest Results of Knowledge and Virtue, namely, Liberty and universal Peace, from the votes of

---

[1] 1812 omits.
[2] 1812 adds "and".
[3] No 3 in 1812 ends here, no 4 beginning with the addition: "—yes! that even Senators and Officers of State hold forth the *Revenue* as a sufficient plea for upholding".

a tumultuous Assembly—that is, from the mechanical agitation of the air in a large Room at Paris—and this too in the most light, unthinking, sensual, and profligate of the European Nations, a Nation, the very phrases of whose language are so composed, that they can scarcely speak without lying!—No! Let us not deceive ourselves. Like the man, who used to pull off his Hat with great demonstration of Respect whenever he spoke of himself, we are fond of styling our own the *enlightened age:* though as Jortin, I think, has wittily remarked, the *golden* age would be more appropriate. But in spite of our great scientific Discoveries, for which Praise be given to whom the Praise is due, and in spite of that general indifference to all the Truths and all the Principles of Truth, which belonging to our permanent being, do not lie within the sphere of our senses, (which indifference makes Toleration so easy a Virtue with us, and constitutes nine-tenths of our pretended Illumination) it still remains the character of the mass of mankind to seek for the attainment of their necessary Ends by any means rather than the appointed ones, and for this cause only, that the latter implies[1] the exertion of the Reason and the Will. But of all things this demands the longest apprenticeship, even an apprenticeship from Infancy; which is generally neglected, because an excellence, that may and should belong to all men, is expected to come to every man of its' own accord.

To whom then do we owe our ameliorated condition? To the successive Few in every age (more indeed in one generation than in another, but relatively to the mass of Mankind always few) who by the intensity and permanence of their action have compensated for the limited sphere, within which it is at any one time intelligible; and whose good deeds Posterity reverence in their results, though the mode in which they[2] repair the inevitable Waste of Time, and the Style of their[3] Additions too generally furnish a sad proof, how little they[4] understand the Principles. I appeal to the Histories of the Jewish, the [51] Grecian, and the Roman Republics, to the Records of the Christian Church, to the History of Europe from the Treaty of Westphalia (1648). What do they contain but accounts of noble Structures raised by the Wisdom of the Few, and gradually undermined by the Ignorance and Profligacy of the Many. If therefore the Deficiency of good, which every way surround[5] us, originate in the general unfitness and aversion of Men to the process of Thought, that is, to continuous Reasoning, it must surely be absurd to apprehend a preponderance of evil from works which cannot act at all except as far as it can[6] call the reasoning faculties into full co-exertion with them.

Still, however, there are Truths so self-evident or so immediately and palpably deduced from those that are, or are acknowledged for such, that they are at once intelligible to all men, who possess the common advantages of the social state: although by sophistry, by evil habits, by the neglect, false persuasions, and impostures of an apostate Priesthood joined

---

[1] For "implies" 1812 reads "imply".
[2] For "they" 1812 reads "we".
[3] For "their" 1812 reads "our".
[4] For "they" 1812 reads "we".

[5] For "surround" 1812 reads "surrounds".
[6] For "it can" 1812 reads "they".

in one conspiracy with the violence of tyrannical Governors, the understandings of men may become so darkened and their Consciences so
lethargic,[1] there may arise a necessity of their republication, and that[2] too
with a voice of loud alarm, and impassioned Warning. Such were the
Doctrines proclaimed by the first Christians to the Pagan World; such
were the Lightnings flashed by Wickliff, Huss, Luther, Calvin, Zuinglius,
Latimer, &c. across the Papal darkness; and such in our own times the
agitating Truths, with which Thomas Clarkson, and his excellent Con-
federates, the Quakers, fought and conquered the legalized Banditti of
Men-stealers, the numerous and powerful Perpetrators and Advocates of
Rapine, Murder, and (of blacker guilt than either) Slavery. Truths of this
kind being indispensible to Man, considered as a moral being, are above
all expedience, all accidental consequences: for as sure as God is holy, and
Man immortal, there can be no evil so great as the Ignorance or Disregard
of them. It is the very madness of mock-prudence to oppose the removal
of a poisoned Dish on account of the pleasant sauces or nutritious viands
which would be lost with it: the dish contains destruction to that, for
which alone we ought to wish the palate to be gratified, or the body to
be nourished. The sole condition, therefore, imposed on us by the Law
of Conscience in these cases is, that we employ no [52] unworthy and
hetrogeneous means to realize the necessary end, that we entrust the event
wholly to the full and adequate promulgation of the Truth, and to those
generous affections which the constitution of our moral nature has linked
to the full perception of it. Yet Evil may, nay it will, be occasioned by it.[3]
Weak men may take offence, and wicked men avail themselves of it:
though we must not attribute to it[4] all the Evil, of which wicked men predetermined, like the Wolf in the fable, to create some occasion, may chuse
to make *it* the pretext. But that there ever was or ever can be a preponderance of Evil, I defy either the Historian to instance or the Philosopher to prove. *Avolent*[5]* *quantum volent paleæ levis fidei quocunque afflatu*
tentationum, eo purior massa frumenti in horrea domini reponetur, we are
entitled to say with Tertullian: and to exclaim with heroic Luther, *Aerger-*
niss[7] *hin, Aergerniss her! Noth bricht Eisen, und hat kein Aergerniss. Ich*
soll der schwachen Gewissen schonen so fern es ohne Gefahr meiner Seelen
geschehn mag. Wo nicht, so soll ich meiner Seelen rathen, es ärgere sich

---

* "Let it fly away, all that Chaff of light Faith that can fly[6] at any breath of
Temptation, the cleaner will the true Grain be stored up in the Granary of the
Lord." TERTULLIAN. "Scandal and offence! Talk not to me of Scandal and
Offence. Need breaks through Stone-walls, and recks not of Scandal. It is my
duty to spare weak Consciences as far as it may be done without hazard of my
Soul. Where not, I must take counsel for my Soul, though half or the whole
World should be scandalized thereby."

---

[1] 1812 adds "that".
[2] For "that" 1812 reads "this".
[3] 1812 omits "by it".
[4] For "it" 1812 reads "the Promulgation or to the truth promulgated".
[5] In 1812 the Latin was shifted to the
footnote and the English placed in the
body of the text.
[6] 1812 adds "off".
[7] In 1812 the English was placed in
the body of the text and the German in
the footnote.

daran die ganze oder halbe Welt. LUTHER felt and preached and wrote and acted, as beseemed a Luther to feel and utter and act. The truths, which had been outraged, he re-proclaimed in the spirit of outraged Truth, at the behest of his Conscience and in the service of the God of Truth. He did his duty, come good, come evil! and made no question, on which side the preponderance would be. In the one Scale there was Gold, and the Impress thereon the Image and Circumscription[1] of the Universal Sovereign. In all the wide and ever widthening[2] Commerce of mind with mind throughout the world, it is Treason to refuse it. Can this have a Counterweight? The other Scale indeed might have seemed full up to the very balance-yard; but of what worth and substance were its' contents? Were they *capable* of being counted or weighed against the former? The Conscience indeed is already violated when to moral good or evil we oppose things possessing no moral interest: and even if the Conscience [53] could waive this her preventive Veto, yet before we could consider the two-fold Results in the relations of Loss and Gain, it must be known whether their kind is the same or equivalent. They must first be valued and then they may be weighed or counted, if they are worth it. But in the particular case at present before us, the Loss is contingent, accidental;[3] the Gain essential and the Tree's own natural produce. The Gain is permanent, and spreads through all times and places; the Loss but temporary, and owing its' very being to Vice or Ignorance, vanishes at the approach of Know-ledge and moral Improvement. The Gain reaches all good men, belongs to all that love Light and desire an increase of Light; to all and of all times, who thank Heaven for the gracious Dawn, and expect the Noon-day; who welcome the first gleams of Spring, and sow their fields in confident Faith of the ripening Summer and the rewarding Harvest-tide! But the Loss is confined to the unenlightened and the prejudiced—say rather, to the weak and the prejudiced of one[4] generation. The prejudices of one age are con-demned even by the prejudiced of the succeeding ages: for endless are the modes of Folly, and the Fool joins with the Wise in passing sentence on all modes but his own. Who cried out with greater Horror against the Murderers of the Prophets, than those who likewise cried out, Crucify him! Crucify him!—The Truth-haters of every future generation will call the Truth-haters of the preceding ages by their true names: for even these the Stream of Time carries onward. In fine, Truth considered in itself and in the effects natural to it, may be conceived as a gentle Spring or Water-source, warm from the genial earth, and breathing up into the Snow-drift that is piled over and around its' outlet. It turns the obstacle into its' own form and character, and as it makes its' way increases its' stream. And should it be arrested in its' course by a chilling season, it suffers delay, not loss, and waits only for a change in the wind to awaken and again roll onwards.

---

[1] For "Circumscription" 1812 reads "Superscription".

[2] For "widthening" 1812 reads "widening".

[3] For "accidental" 1812 reads "and alien".

[4] For "one" 1812 reads "a single".

I semplici pastori
Sul Vesolo nevoso
Fatti curvi e canuti,
D' alto stupor son muti
Mirando al fonte ombroso
Il Po con pochi umori;
[54] *Poscia udendo gli onori*
Dell' urna angusta e stretta,
Che 'l Adda, che 'l Tesino
Soverchia in suo cammino
Che ampio al mar s' affretta,
Che si spuma, e si suona,
Che gli si da corona! *

CHIABRERA

Such are the good, that is, the natural Consequences of the promulgation to all of Truths which all are bound to know and to make known. The evils *occasioned* by it, with few and rare exceptions, have their origin in the attempts to suppress or pervert it; in the fury and violence of Imposture attacked or undermined in her strongholds, or in the extravagances of Ignorance and Credulity roused from their lethargy, and angry at the medicinal disturbance—awakening not yet broad awake, and thus blending the monsters of uneasy dreams with the real objects, on which the drowsy eye had alternately half-opened and closed, again half-opened and again closed. This *Re-action* of Deceit and Superstition, with all the trouble and tumult incident, I would compare to a Fire which bursts forth from some stifled and fermenting Mass on the first admission of Light and Air. It roars and blazes, and converts the already spoilt or damaged Stuff with all the straw and straw-like matter near it, first into flame and the next moment into ashes. The Fire dies away, the ashes are scattered on all the winds, and what began in Worthlessness ends in Nothingness. Such are the evil, that is, the casual consequences of the same promulgation.

It argues a narrow or corrupt nature to lose the general and lasting consequences of rare and virtuous Energy, in the brief accidents, which accompanied its' first movements—to set lightly by the emancipation of the Human [55] Reason from a legion of Devils, in our complaints and lamentations over the loss of a herd of swine! The Cranmers, Hampdens, and Sidneys; the Counsellors of our Elizabeth, and the Friends of our other great Deliverer the third William,—is it in vain, that *these* have been our Countrymen? Are we not the Heirs of their good deeds? And what are

---

* *Literal Translation.* "The simple Shepherds grown bent and hoary-headed on the snowy Vesolo, are mute with deep astonishment, gazing in the o'ershadowed fountain on the Po with his scanty waters; then hearing of the Honors of his confined and narrow Urn, how he receives as a Sovereign the ADDA and the TESINO in his course, how ample he hastens on to the Sea, how he foams, how mighty his Voice, and that to Him the Crown is assigned."

N.B. I give literal translations of my poetic as well as prose translations,[1] because the propriety of their introduction often depends on the exact sense and order of the words: which it is impossible always to retain in a metrical Version.

[1] For "translations" 1812 reads "Quotations".

noble Deeds but noble Truths realized? As Protestants, as Englishmen, as the Inheritors of so ample an estate of Might and Right, an estate so strongly fenced, so richly planted, by the sinewy arms and dauntless hearts of our Forefathers, we of all others have good cause to trust in the Truth, yea, to follow its' pillar of fire through the Darkness and the Desart, even though its Light should but suffice to make us certain of its' own presence. If there be elsewhere men jealous of the Light, who prophecy an excess of Evil over good from its' manifestation, we are entitled to ask them, on what experience they ground their Bodings? Our own Country bears no traces, our own history contains no records, to justify them. From the great æras of national illumination we date the commencement of our main national Advantages. The Tangle of Delusions, which stifled and distorted the growing Tree, have been torn away; the parasite Weeds, that fed on its' very roots, have been plucked up with a salutary violence. To us there remain only quiet duties, the constant care, the gradual improvement, the cautious unhazardous labors of the industrious though contented Gardener—to prune, to engraft, and one by one to remove from its' leaves and fresh shoots, the Slug and the Caterpillar. But far be it from us to undervalue with light and senseless detraction, the conscientious Hardihood of our Predecessors, or even to condemn in them that vehemence, to which the Blessings, it won for us, leave us now neither temptation or pretext. That the very terms, with which the Bigot or the Hireling would blacken the first Publishers of political and religious Truth, are, and deserve to be, hateful to us, we owe to the effects of its' publication. We ante-date the feelings in order to criminate the authors of our tranquillity, opulence, and security. But let us be aware. Effects will not, indeed, immediately disappear with their causes; but neither can they long continue without them. If by the *reception* of Truth in the spirit of Truth, we *became* what we [56] are; only by the *retention* of it in the same spirit, can we *remain* what we are. The narrow seas that form our boundaries, what were they in times of old? The convenient High-way for Danish and Norman Pirates. What are they now? Still but "a Span of Waters"—Yet

> *Even so* doth God protect us, if we be
> Virtuous and Wise. Winds blow and Waters roll,
> Strength to the Brave, and Power and Deity:
> Yet in themselves are nothing! One Decree
> Spake laws to *them*, and said that by the Soul
> Only the Nations shall be great and free.

Thus far then I have been conducting a cause between an Individual and his own mind. Proceeding on the conviction, that to Man is entrusted the nature, not the result of his actions, I have presupposed no calculations, I have presumed no foresight.—Introduce no contradiction into thy own consciousness. Acting or abstaining from action, delivering or withholding thy thoughts, whatsoever thou dost, do it *in singleness of heart*. In all things therefore let thy Means correspond to thy Purpose, and let thy Purpose be one with the Purport.—To this Principle I have referred the supposed Individual, and from this Principle solely I have deduced each particular of his Conduct. As far, therefore, as the Court of Conscience extends, (and in this Court alone I have been pleading hitherto) I have won the cause. It has been decided, that there is no just ground for apprehending Mischief from Truth communicated *conscientiously*, (i.e. with a strict observance of all the conditions required by the Conscience) that what is not so communicated, is Falsehood, and to the Falsehood, not to the Truth, must the consequences be attributed. Another and altogether different cause remains now to be pleaded; a different Cause, and in a different Court. The parties concerned are no longer the well-meaning Individual and his Conscience, but the Citizen and the State—the Citizen, who may be a fanatic as probably as a philosopher, and the State, which concerns itself with the Conscience only as far as it appears in the Action, or, still more accurately, in the fact; and which must determine the nature of the fact not only by a rule of Right formed from the modification of particular by general consequences, and thus reducing the freedom of each citizen [57] to the common measure in which it becomes compatible with the freedom of all; but likewise by the relation, which the Fact bears to its' own instinctive principle of Self-preservation. For every Depositary of the supreme Power must presume itself rightful: and as the source of law, not legally to be endangered. A form of government may indeed, in reality, be most pernicious to the governed, and the highest moral honor may await the patriot who risks his life in order by its' subversion to introduce a better and juster Constitution; but it would be absurd to blame the Law, by which his Life is declared forfeit. It were to expect, that by an involved contradiction, the Law should allow itself not to be Law, by allowing the State, of which it is a part, not to be a State. For as Hooker has well observed, the law of men's actions is one, if they be respected only as men; and another, when they are considered as parts of a body politic.

But though every Government subsisting in law (for pure lawless Despotism grounding itself wholly on terror precludes all consideration of Duty) though every government subsisting in Law must, and ought to, regard itself as the Life of the Body Politic, of which it is the Head, and consequently must punish every attempt against itself as an act of Assault or Murder, i.e. Sedition or Treason; yet still it ought so to secure the Life as not to prevent the conditions of its' growth, and of that Adaptation to Circumstances, without which its' very Life becomes insecure. In the application, therefore, of these principles to the public communication of Opinions by the most efficient means, the Press—we have to decide, whether consistently with them there should be any Liberty of the Press, and if this be answered in the affirmative, what shall be declared Abuses of that Liberty, and made punishable as such, and in what way the general Law shall be applied to each particular case.

First then, should there be any Liberty of the Press? We will not here mean, whether it should be permitted to print books at all; (for our Essay has little chance of being read in Turkey, and in any other part of Europe it cannot be supposed questionable) but whether by the appointment of a Censorship the Government should take upon itself the responsibility of each particular publication. In Governments purely monarchical (i.e. oligarchies under one head) the Balance of the Advantage [58] and disadvantage from this Monopoly of the Press will undoubtedly be affected by the general state of information; though after reading Milton's "Speech for the Liberty of unlicensed Printing,*" we shall probably be inclined to believe, that the best argument in favour of Licensing, &c. under *any* constitution is that, which supposing the Ruler to have a different Interest from that of his Country, and even from himself as a reasonable and moral Creature, grounds itself on the incompatibility of Knowledge with Folly, Oppression, and Degradation. What our prophetic Harrington said of religious, applies equally to literary Toleration. "If it be said that in France there is Liberty of Conscience in part, it is also plain that while the Hierarchy is standing, this Liberty is falling, and that if on the contrary, it comes to pull down the Hierarchy, it pulls down that Monarchy also: wherefore the Monarchy or Hierarchy will be beforehand with it, if they see their true Interest." On the other hand, there is no slight danger from general ignorance: and the only choice, which Providence has graciously left to a vicious Government, is either to fall *by* the People, if they are suffered to become enlightened, or *with* them, if they are kept enslaved and ignorant.

The nature of our Constitution, since the Revolution, the state of our literature, and the wide diffusion, if not of intellectual yet, of literary power, and the almost universal Interest in the productions of literature, have set the question at rest relatively to the British Press. However great the advantages of previous examination might be under other circumstances, in this Country it would be both impracticable and inefficient. I need only suggest in broken sentences—the prodigious number of Licensers that would be requisite—the variety of their attainments, and (inasmuch as the scheme must be made consistent with our religious freedom) the ludicrous variety of their principles and creeds, their number being so great, and each appointed Censor being himself a man of Letters, *quis custodiet ipsos custodes?*—If these numerous [59] Licensers hold their offices for Life, and independent of the Ministry *pro tempore*, a new, heterogeneous, and alarming Power is introduced, which can never be assimilated to the constitutional powers already existing:—if they are removeable at pleasure, that which is heretical and seditious in 1809, may become orthodox and loyal in 1810—and what man, whose attainments and moral respectability gave him even an endurable claim to this aweful Trust, would accept a situation at once so invidious and so precarious? And what institution can retain any useful influence in so free a nation, when its' abuses or inefficiences[2] have made it contemptible?—Lastly, and which of itself would suffice to justify the rejection of such a plan—unless all proportion between crime and punishment were abandoned, what penalties could the Law attach to the *assumption* of a Liberty, which it had denied, more severe than those which it now attaches to the *abuse* of the Liberty, which it grants? In all those instances at least, which it would be most the inclina-

---

* Il y a un voile qui doit toujour couvrir tout ce que l'on peut dire et tout ce qu'on peut croire D U D R O I T *des peuples* et de celui *des* princes, qui ne s'accordent jamais si bien ensemble que dans le silence.[1]   *Mem. du Card. de Retz*

How severe a satire where it can be justly applied! how false and calumnious if meant as a general maxim!

1 For "silence" 1812 reads "*silence*".   2 1812 omits "or inefficiences".

tion—perhaps the duty—of the State to prevent, namely, in seditious and incendiary publications (whether actually such, or only such as the existing Government chose so to denominate, makes no difference in the argument) the Publisher, who hazards the punishment now assigned to seditious publications, would assuredly hazard the penalties of unlicensed ones, especially as the very Practice of Licensing would naturally diminish the attention to the contents of the Works published, the chance of impunity therefore be so much greater, and the artifice of prefixing an unauthorized License so likely to escape Detection. It is a fact, that in many of the former German States in which Literature flourished, notwithstanding the establishment of Censors or Licensers, three fourths of the Books printed were unlicensed—even those, the contents of which were unobjectionable, and where the sole motive for evading the law must have been either the pride and delicacy of the Author, or the Indolence of the Bookseller—so difficult was the detection, so various the means of evasion, and worse than all, from the nature of the law and the affront it offers to the pride of human nature, such was the merit attached to the Breach of it—a merit commencing perhaps with Luther's Bible, and other prohibited works of similar great minds, published with no dissimilar purpose, and thence by many an intermediate [60] link of association finally connected with Books, of the very titles of which a good man would wish to remain ignorant. The interdictory Catalogues of the Roman Hierarchy always present to my fancy the muster-rolls of the two hostile armies of Michael and of Satan printed promiscuously, or extracted at hap-hazard, save only that the extracts from the former appear somewhat the more numerous. And yet even in Naples, and in Rome itself, whatever difficulty occurs in procuring any article catalogued in these formidable Folios must arise either from the scarcity of the work itself, or the absence of all interest in it: assuredly there is no difficulty in procuring from the most respectable Booksellers, the vilest provocatives to the basest crimes, though intermixed with gross lampoons on the Heads of the Church, the religious orders, and on religion itself. The Stranger is invited into an inner room, and the loathsome Wares presented to him with most significant Looks and Gestures, implying the hazard, and the necessity of secrecy. A respectable English Bookseller would deem himself insulted, if such works were even inquired after at his Shop.

We have therefore abundant reason to conclude, that the Law of England has done well and wisely in proceeding on the principle so clearly worded by Milton: that Books[1] should be as freely admitted into the world as any other Birth; and if it prove a monster, who denies but that it may justly be burnt and sunk into the sea. We have reason then, it appears,[2] to rest satisfied with our Laws, which no more prevent a book from coming into the world unlicensed, lest it should prove a Libel, than a Traveller from passing unquestioned through our Turnpike gates, because it is possible he may be a Highwayman. Innocence is presumed in both cases. The *publication* is a part of the offence, and its' necessary condition. Words are moral Acts, and words deliberately made public, the Law considers

---

[1] For "Books" 1812 reads "a Book".   [2] For "it appears" 1812 reads "I repeat".

in the same light as any other cognizable overt act. Here however a difficulty presents itself. Theft, Robbery, Murder, and the like, are easily defined: the degrees and circumstances likewise of these and similar actions are definite, and constitute specific offences, described and punishable each under its' own name. We have only to prove the fact and identify the offender. The Intention too, in so great a majority of cases, is clearly implied in the action, that the [61] Law can safely adopt it as its' universal maxim, that the proof of the malice is included in the proof of the fact, especially as the few occasional exceptions have their remedy provided in the prerogative of the supreme Magistrates.[1] But in the case of Libel, the degree *makes* the kind, the circumstances *constitute* the criminality; and both degrees and circumstances, like the ascending Shades of Color or the shooting Hues of a Dove's Neck, die away into each other, incapable of definition or outline. The eye of the understanding, indeed, sees the determinate difference in each individual case, but Language is most often inadequate to express what the eye perceives, much less can a general statute anticipate and pre-define it. Again: in other overt-acts a charge disproved leaves the Defendant either guilty of a different fault, or at best simply blameless. A man having killed a fellow-citizen is acquitted of Murder— the act was Manslaughter only, or it was justifiable Homicide. But when we reverse the iniquitous sentence passed on Algernon Sidney, during our perusal of his work on Government, at the moment we deny it to have been a traitrous Libel, our beating Hearts declare it to have been a benefaction to our Country, and under the circumstances of those times, the performance of an heroic Duty. From this cause therefore, as well as from a Libel's being a thing made up of degrees and circumstances (and these too discriminating offence from merit by such dim and ambulant boundaries) the Intention of the agent, wherever it can be independently or inclusively ascertained, must be allowed a great share in determining the character of the action, unless the Law is not only to be divorced from* moral Justice, but to wage open hostility against it.

Add too, that Laws in doubtful points are to be interpreted according to the design of the Legislator, where this can be certainly inferred. But the Laws of England, which owe their own present Supremacy and Absoluteness to the good sense and generous dispositions diffused by the Press, more, far more, than to any other single cause, must needs be presumed favourable to its' general influence, and even in the penalties attached to its' abuse [62] we must suppose it[2] actuated by the desire of preserving its' essential privileges. The Press is indifferently the passive Instrument of Evil† and of Good: yet the average result from Henry the 8th to the first

---

* According to the old adage: You are not hung for stealing a Horse, but that Horses may not be stolen. To what extent this is true, we shall have occasion to examine hereafter.

† There is some Good, however, even in its' Evil. "Good and Evil, we know in the field of this world, grow up together almost inseparably: and the knowledge of Good is so intervolved and interwoven with the knowledge of Evil, and

---

[1] For "Magistrates" 1812 reads "Magistrate".

[2] For "it" 1812 reads "the Legislature to have been".

Charles, was such a diffusion of religious Light as first redeemed and after-wards saved this Nation from the spiritual and moral death of Popery; and in the following period we owe to the Press[2] the gradual ascendancy of those wise political maxims, which casting philosophic truth in the moulds of national laws, customs, and existing orders of society, subverted the Tyranny without suspending the Government, and at length completed the mild and salutary Revolution, by the establishment of the House of Bruns-wick. To what must we attribute this vast over-balance of Good in the general effects of the Press, but to the over-balance of virtuous Intention in those who employed it[3]? The Law, therefore, will not refuse to manifest good Intention a certain weight even in cases of apparent error, lest it should discourage and scare away those, to whose [63] efforts we owe the comparative infrequency and weakness of Error on the whole. The Law may however, nay, it must demand, that the external Proofs of the Author's honest Intentions should be *supported* by the general style and matter of his work, by the circumstances and mode of its' publication, &c. A passage, which in a grave and regular disquisition would be blameless, might become highly libellous and justly punishable if it were applied to present measures or persons for immediate purposes, in a cheap and popular tract. I have seldom felt greater indignation than at finding in a large manufactory a

---

in so many cunning resemblances hardly to be discerned, that these confused seeds which were imposed on Psyche as an incessant labor to cull out and sort asunder, were not more intermixed.—As, therefore, the state of man now is, what wisdom can there be to chuse, what continence to forbear, without the knowledge of Evil? He that can apprehend and consider Vice with all her baits and seeming pleasures and yet abstain, and yet distinguish, and yet prefer that which is truly better, he is the true wayfaring Christian. I cannot praise a fugitive and cloistered virtue, that never sallies out and sees her Adversary—that which is but a youngling in the contemplation of Evil, and knows not the utmost that Vice promises to her followers, and rejects it, is but a *blank* Virtue, not a pure.— Since, therefore, the knowledge and survey of Vice is in this world so necessary to the constituting of human Virtue, and the scanning of Error to the confirma-tion of Truth, how can we more safely and with less danger, scout into the regions of Sin and Falsity, than by reading all manner of Tractates, and hearing all manner of reason?" *Milton's Speech for the Liberty of unlicensed Printing.* Again —but, indeed the whole Treatise is one Strain of moral wisdom and political prudence—"Why should we then affect a rigor contrary to the manner of God and of Nature, by abridging or scanting those means, which Books, freely per-mitted, are both to the trial of Virtue and the exercise of Truth? It would be better done to learn, that the Law must needs be frivolous, which goes to restrain things uncertainly and yet equally working to good and to evil. And were I the Chuser, a dram of well-doing should be preferred before many times as much the forcible hinderance of evil-doing. For God sure esteems the growth and completion of one virtuous person, more than the restraint of ten vicious."—Be it however observed, that nothing in these remarks countervenes the duty and necessity of choice and watchfulness on the part of Parents and Instructors. It is prettily said by one of the Fathers, that even in the Scriptures there are parts where the Elephant must swim, as well as others which the Lamb may ford.[1]

---

[1] See Gregory the Great *Epistola Missoria* ch 4: *Moralia* (Migne *PL* LXXV col 515).

[2] For "we . . . Press" 1812 reads "it is to the Press that we owe".

[3] For "it" 1812 reads "the Press".

sixpenny pamphlet, containing a selection of inflammatory paragraphs
from the prose-writings of Milton, without a hint given of the time, occasion, state of government, &c. under which they were written—not a hint,
that the Freedom, which we now enjoy, exceeds all that Milton dared hope
for, or deemed practicable; and that his political creed sternly excluded
the populace, and indeed the majority of the population, from all pretensions to political power. If the manifest bad intention would constitute
this publication a seditious Libel, a good intention equally manifest can
not justly be denied its' share of influence in producing a contrary verdict.

Here then is the difficulty. From the very nature of a Libel it is impossible so to define it, but that the most meritorious works will be found
included in the description. Not from any defect or undue severity in the
particular Statute, but from the very nature of the offence to be guarded
against, a work recommending Reform by the only rational mode of
recommendation, by the detection and exposure of corruption, abuse, or
incapacity, might, though it should breathe the best and most unadulterated
English feelings, be brought within the definition of Libel equally with the
vilest incendiary *Brochure*, that ever aimed at leading and misleading the
Multitude. Not a Paragraph in the Morning Post during the Peace of
Amiens, (or rather the experimental Truce so called) though to the immortal honour of the then Editor, it[1] was the chief *secondary* means of
producing that unexampled national unanimity, with which the war recommenced and has since been continued—not a Paragraph warning the
Nation, as need was and most imperious Duty commanded, of the perilous
designs and unsleeping ambition of our neighbour the mimic and Cari-
caturist of [64] Charlemagne* but was a punishable Libel. The Statute of

---

* *Charlemagne outré.* This phrase will call to mind the assumption of the iron
crown of Italy—the imperial coronation with the presence and authority of the
Holy Father—the imperial robe embroidered with bees in order to mark the
successor of Pepin—the late revocation of Charlemagne's grants to the Pope, &c.
The following extract will place the Usurper's[2] close imitation of Charlemagne in
a newer and more interesting light. I have translated it from a voluminous
German work, which, it is probable, few if any of my Readers will possess the
opportunity of consulting (Michael Ignaz Schmidt's History of the Germans: the
conclusion of the second chapter of the third Book, from Charles the Great to
Conrade the first.) But the passage itself contains so much matter for political
anticipation and well-grounded hope, as well as for amusing comparison, that I
feel no apprehension of my Readers' being disatisfied with the length of the
illustration. Let me, however, preface it with one remark. That Charlemagne,
for the greater part, created for himself the means of which he availed himself;
that his very education was his own work, and[3] unlike Peter the Great, he could
find no assistants out of his own realm; that he found in[4] the unconquerable
Courage and heroic Dispositions of the Nations he conquered,[5] a proof positive
of real superiority, indeed the sole positive proof of intellectual Power in a
Warrior: for how can we measure force but by the resistance to it? But all was
prepared for Buonaparte. Europe weakened in the very heart of all human
strength, namely, in moral and religious Principle, and at the same time accident-

---

1 For "it" 1812 reads "that News-   3 1812 adds "that".
paper".   4 1812 omits "he found in".
2 Bonaparte; see above, I 84.   5 1812 adds "supplied".

Libel is a vast Aviary, which incages the awakening Cock and the Geese whose alarm[1] preserved the Capitol, no less than the babbling Magpye and ominous Screech-owl.[2]

---

ally destitute of any one great or commanding mind: the French People, on the other hand, still restless from revolutionary Fanaticism; their civic Enthusiasm already passed into military Passion and the Ambition of Conquest; and alike by disgust, terror, and characteristic unfitness for Freedom, ripe for the reception of a Despotism. Add too, that the main obstacles to an unlimited System of Conquest and the pursuit of universal Monarchy had been cleared away for him by his Pioneers the Jacobins, viz. the influence of the great Land-holders, of the privileged and of the commercial Classes. Even the naval successes of Great Britain, by destroying the Trade, rendering useless the Colonies, and almost annihilating the Navy of France, were in some respects subservient to his designs by concentrating the Powers of the French Empire in its Armies, and supplying *them* out of the wrecks of all other Employments, save that of Agriculture. France had already approximated to the formidable state so prophetically described by Sir James Stuart, in his Political Economy, in which the Population should consist chiefly of Soldiers and Peasantry: at least the Interests of no other classes were regarded. The great merit of Buonaparte has been that of a skilful Steersman, who with his Boat in the most violent storm still keeps himself on the summit of the waves, which not he, but the winds, had raised. I will now proceed to my translation.

That Charles was an Hero, his Exploits bear evidence. The subjugation of the Lombards, protected as they were by the Alps, by Fortresses and fortified Towns, by numerous Armies, and by a great Name; of the Saxons, secured by their savage Resoluteness, by an untameable love of Freedom, by their desart Plains and enormous Forests, and by their own Poverty; the humbling of the Dukes of Bavaria, Aquitania, Bretagne, and Gascony;

(To be continued.)[3]

---

[1] For "alarm" 1812 reads "alarum".

[2] No 4 in 1812 continues (taking the opening of No 5) to "Ithuriel Spear, that", where it ends.

[3] 1812 omits.

THE FRIEND

No. 5. THURSDAY, September 14, 1809

(*Continued from page* 64.)[4]

And yet will we avoid this seeming injustice, we throw down all Fence and Bulwark of public Decency and public Opinion; political Calumny will soon join hands with private Slander; and every Principle, every Feeling,

---

[65] proud of their ancestry as well as of their ample domains; the almost entire extirpation of the Avars, so long the terror of Europe; are assuredly works, which demanded a courage and a firmness of mind, such as Charles only possessed.

How great his reputation was, and this too beyond the limits of Europe, is proved by the Embassies sent to him out of Persia, Palestine, Mauritania, and even from the Caliphs of Bagdad. If at the present day an Embassy from the Black or Caspian Sea comes to a Prince on the Baltic, it is not to be wondered at, since such are now the political relations of the four quarters of the World, that a blow which is given to any one of them is felt more or less by[1] the others. Whereas in the times of Charlemagne, the Inhabitants in one of the known parts of the World scarcely knew what was going on in the rest. Nothing but the extraordinary, all-piercing report of Charles's Exploits could bring this to pass. His greatness, which set the World in Astonishment, was likewise, without doubt, that which begot in the Pope and the Romans the first idea of the re-establishment of their Empire.

It is true, that a number of things united to make Charles a great Man—favourable circumstances of time, a nation already disciplined to warlike habits, a long life, and the consequent acquisition of experience, such as no one possessed in his whole Realm. Still, however, the principal means of his greatness Charles found in himself. His great mind was capable of extending its attention to the greatest multiplicity of affairs. In the middle of Saxony he thought on Italy and Spain, and at Rome he made provisions for Saxony, Bavaria, and Pannonia. He gave audience to the Ambassadors of the Greek Emperor and other Potentates, and himself audited the accounts of his own Farms, where every thing was entered even to the number of the Eggs. Busy as his mind was, his body was not less in one continued state of motion. Charles would see into every thing himself, and do every thing himself, as far as his powers extended: and even this it was too, which gave to his undertakings such a force and energy.[2]

But[3] with all this the government of Charles was the government of a Conqueror, that is splendid abroad and fearfully oppressive at home. What a grievance must it not have been for the People that Charles for forty years

---

1 1812 adds "all".

2 In 1812 the footnote in No 4 ends here.

3 In 1812 the footnote continuation begins in No 5 with this paragraph.

4 1812 omits.

that [66] binds the Citizen to his Country and the Spirit to its' Creator, will be undermined—not by reasoning, for from that there is no Danger; but—by the mere habit of hearing them reviled and scoffed at with im-

together dragged them now to the Elbe, then to the Ebro, after this to the Po, and from thence back again to the Elbe, and this not to check an invading Enemy, but to make conquests which little profited the French Nation! This must prove too much, at length, for a hired Soldier; how much more for Conscripts who did not live only to fight, but who were Fathers of Families, Citizens, and Proprietors? But above all, is it to be wondered at, that a Nation like the French, should suffer themselves to be used as Charles used them. But the People no longer possessed any considerable share of influence. All depended on the great Chieftains, who gave their willing [66] suffrage for endless Wars, by which *they* were always sure to win. They found the best opportunity, under such circumstances, to make themselves great and mighty at the expence of the Freemen resident within the circle of their baronial Courts; and when Conquests were made, it was far more for their advantage than that of the Monarchy. In the conquered Provinces there was a necessity for Dukes, Vassal Kings, and different high offices: all this fell to their share.

I would not say this if we did not possess incontrovertible original documents of those times, which prove clearly to us that Charles's government was an unhappy one for the People, and that this great Man, by his actions, laboured to the direct subversion of his first principles. It was his first pretext to establish a greater equality among the members of his vast community, and to make all free and equal Subjects under a common Sovereign. And from the necessity occasioned by continual War, the exact contrary took place. Nothing gives us a better notion of the interior state of the French Monarchy, than the third capitular of the year 811. (*compare with this the four or five quarto vols. of the present French Conscript Code*). All is full of complaint, the Bishops and Earls clamouring against the Freeholders, and these in their turn against the Bishops and Earls. And in truth the Freeholders had no small reason to be discontented and to resist, as far as they dared, even the Imperial Levies. A Dependant must be content to follow his Lord without further questioning: for he was paid for it. But a free Citizen, who lived wholly on his own property, might reasonably object to suffer himself to be dragged about in all quarters of the World, at the fancies of his Lord: especially as there was so much injustice intermixed. Those who gave up their properties entirely, or in part, of their own accord, were left undisturbed at home, while those, who refused to do this, were forced so often into service, that at length, becoming impoverished, they were compelled by want to give up, or dispose of their free tenures to the Bishops or Earls (*It would require no great ingenuity to discover parallels, or at least equivalent hardships to these, in the treatment of, and regulations concerning, the reluctant Conscripts. There is, I understand, an interesting article on this Subject in a late Number of the Edinburgh Review,*[1] *which I regret, that I have not had an opportunity of perusing.*)

It almost surpasses belief to what a height, at length, the aversion to War rose in the French Nation, from the multitude of the Campaigns and the grievances connected with them. The national vanity was now satiated by the frequency[2] of Victories: and the Plunder which fell to the lot of Individuals, made but a poor compensation for the Losses and Burthens sustained by their Families at home. Some, in order to become exempt from military service, sought for menial employ-

---

[1] See above, I 87 n 1. [2] For "frequency" 1812 reads "frequences".

punity. Were we to contemplate the Evils of a rank and unweeded Press only in its effect on the Manners of a People, and on the general tone of Thought and Conversation, the greater love we bore to Literature and to all the means and instruments [67] of human Improvement with the greater earnestness should we solicit the interference of Law: the more anxiously should we wish for some Ithuriel Spear, that might[1] remove from the ear of the Public, and expose in their own fiendish shape those Reptiles, which *inspiring venom and forging illusions as they list.*

> ——thence raise
> At least distemper'd discontented thoughts,
> Vain hopes, vain aims, inordinate desires.
> PARADISE LOST

The comparison of the English with the Anglo-American Newspapers, will best evince the difference between a lawless Press (lawless at least in practice and by connivance) and a Press at once protected and restrained by Law.[2]

How then shall we solve this Problem? Its Solution is to be found in that spirit which, like the universal menstruum sought for by the old Alchemists, can blend and harmonize the most discordant Elements—it is to be found in the spirit of a rational Freedom diffused and become national, in the consequent influence and controul of public opinion, and in its most precious organ, the Jury. It is to be found, wherever Juries are sufficiently enlightened to perceive the difference, and to comprehend the origin and necessity of the difference, between Libels and other criminal overt-acts, and are sufficiently independent to act upon the conviction, that in a charge of Libel the Degree, the Circumstances, and the Intention, constitute (not merely *modify*), the offence, give it its' Being, and determine its' legal name. The words "*maliciously* and advisedly," must here have a force of their own, and a proof of their own. They will consequently consider the written Law as a blank *power* provided for the punishment of the *Offender*, not as a *light* by which they are to determine and discriminate the *offence*. The Understanding and Conscience of the Jury are the Judges, *in toto:* the statute a blank *congé d'elire.* The Statute is the Clay and those

---

ments in the Establishments of the Bishops, Abbots, Abesses, and Earls. Others made over their free property to become tenants at will of such Lords as from their Age, or other circumstances, they thought would be called to no further military services. Others, even privately took away the life of their Mothers, Aunts, or other of their Relatives, in order that no family Residents might remain through whom their Names might be known, and themselves traced; others voluntarily made slaves of themselves, in order thus to render themselves incapable of the military rank.

[1] In 1812 No 5 begins with "might".

[2] The ms of *The Friend* continues with a cancelled sentence: "For the effect of the former we dare appeal to every well-educated Englishman, who has had the means of acquainting himself personally with the state of American Manners conversation before and since their Independence": Forster MS 112 f 21ᵛ.

the Potter's wheel. Shame fall on that Man, who shall labour to confound what reason and nature have put asunder, and who at once, as far as in him lies, would render the Press ineffectual and the Law odious; would lock up the main river, the Thames, of our intellectual commerce; would throw a bar across the stream, that [68] must render its' navigation dangerous or partial, using as his materials the very banks, that were intended to deepen its' channel and guard against its' innundations! Shame fall on him, and a participation in the infamy of those, who misled an English Jury to the murder of Algernon Sidney!

But though the virtuous intention of the Writer must be allowed a certain influence in facilitating his acquittal, the degree of his moral guilt is not the true index or mete-wand of his Condemnation. For Juries do not sit in a Court of Conscience, but of Law, they are not the Representatives of Religion, but the Guardians of external tranquillity. The leading Principle, the Pole Star, of the judgement in its' decision concerning the libellous nature of a published Writing, is its' more or less remote connection with after overt-acts, as the cause or occasion of the same. Thus the Publication of actual Facts may be and most often will be criminal and libellous, when directed against private Characters, not only because the charge will reach the minds of many who cannot be competent judges of the truth or falsehood of facts to which themselves were not witnesses, against a Man whom they do not know, or at best know imperfectly; but because such a Publication is of itself a very serious overt-act, by which the Author without authority and without trial, has inflicted punishment on a fellow subject, himself being Witness and Jury, Judge and Executioner. Of such Publications there can be no *legal* justification, though the wrong may be *palliated* by the circumstance that the injurious charges are not only true but wholly out of the reach of the Law. But in Libels on the Government there are two things to be balanced against each other, first the incomparably greater mischief of the overt acts, supposing them actually occasioned by the Libel—(as for instance the subversion of Government and Property, if the Principles taught by Thomas Paine had been realized, or if even an attempt had been made to realize them, by the many thousands of his Readers); and second, the very great improbability that such effects will be produced by such Writings. Government concerns all generally, and no one in particular. The facts are commonly as well known to the Readers, as to the Writer: and falsehood therefore easily detected. It is proved, likewise, by experience, that the frequency of open [69] political discussion, with all its blamable indiscretions, indisposes a Nation to overt acts of practical sedition or conspiracy. They talk ill, said Charles the fifth of his Belgian Provinces, but they suffer so much the better for it. His Successor thought differently: he determined to be Master of their Words and Opinions, as well as of their Actions, and in consequence lost one half of those Provinces, and retained the other half at an expence of strength and treasure greater than the original worth of the whole. An enlightened Jury, therefore, will require proofs of some more than ordinary malignity of intention, as furnished by the style, price, mode of circulation, and so forth; or of punishable indiscretion arising out of the state of the times, as of dearth for instance, or of whatever other calamity is likely to render the lower Classes turbulent and apt to be alienated from the Government of their Country. For the absence of a right disposition of mind must be considered both in Law and in Morals, as nearly equivalent to the presence of a wrong disposition. Under such circumstances the legal Paradox, that a Libel may be the more a Libel for being true, becomes strictly just, and as such ought to be acted upon. Concerning the right of punishing by Law the Authors of heretical or deistical Writings, I reserve my remarks for a future Number, in which I hope to state the grounds and limits of Toleration more accurately than they seem to me to have been hitherto traced.

I have thus endeavoured, with an anxiety which may perhaps have misled me into prolixity, to detail and ground the conditions under which the communication of Truth is commanded or forbidden to us as Individuals, by our Conscience; and those too, under which it is permissible by the Law which controls our Conduct as Members of the State. But is the Subject of sufficient importance to deserve so minute an examination? That[1] my Readers would look round the World, as it now is, and make to themselves a faithful Catalogue of its many Miseries! From what do these proceed, and on what do they depend for their continuance? Assuredly for the greater part on the actions of Men, and those again on the want of a vital Principle of virtuous action. We live by Faith. The essence of Virtue subsists in the Principle. And the Reality of this, as well as its Importance, is believed by all Men in Fact, few as there may be who, bring the [70] Truth forward into the light of distinct Consciousness. Yet all Men feel, and at times acknowledge to themselves, the true cause of their misery. There is no man so base, but that at some time or other, and in some way or other, he admits that he is not what he ought to be, though by a curious art of self-delusion, by an effort to keep at peace with himself as long and as much as possible, he will throw off the blame from the amenable part of his nature, his moral principle, to that which is independent of his will, namely, the degree of his intellectual faculties. Hence, for once that a man exclaims, how dishonest I am, on what base and unworthy motives I act, we may hear a hundred times, what a Fool I am! curse on my Folly?* and the like.

Yet even this implies an obscure sentiment, that with clearer conceptions in the understanding, the Principle of Action would become purer in the Will. Thanks to the image of our Maker not wholly obliterated from any human Soul, we dare not purchase an exemption from guilt by an excuse, which would place our amelioration out of our own power. Thus the very man, who will abuse himself for a fool but not for a Villain, would rather, spite of the usual professions to the contrary, be condemned as a Rogue by other men, than be acquitted as a Blockhead. But be this as it may, out

---

* We do not consider as exceptions the thousands that abuse themselves by rote in Lip-penitence, or the wild ravings of Fanaticism: for these Persons, at the very time they speak so vehemently of the wickedness and rottenness of their hearts, are then commonly the warmest in their own good opinion, covered round and comfortable in the *Wrap-rascal* of self-hypocrisy.

[1] For "That" 1812 reads "O that".

of himself, however, he sees plainly the true cause of our common complaints. Doubtless, there seem many physical causes of Distress, of Disease, of Poverty, and of Desolation—Tempests, Earthquakes, Volcanoes, wild or venomous Animals, barren soils, uncertain or tyrannous Climates, pestilential Swamps, and Death in the very Air we breathe. Yet when do we hear the general wretchedness of Mankind attributed to these? In Iceland, the Earth opened and sent forth three or more vast Rivers of Fire. The smoke and vapour from them dimmed the Light of Heaven through all Europe, for Months: even at Cadiz, the Sun and Moon, for several weeks, seemed turned to Blood. What was the amount of the injury to the human Race? Sixty men were destroyed, and of these the [71] greater part in consequence of their own imprudence. Natural Calamities that do indeed spread devastation wide (for instance the Marsh Fever), are, almost without exception, voices of Nature in her all-intelligible language—do this! or Cease to do that! By the mere absence of one Superstition, and of the Sloth engendered by it, the Plague would cease to exist throughout Asia and Africa. Pronounce meditatively the name of Jenner, and ask what might we not hope, what need we deem unattainable, if all the time, the effort, the skill, which we waste in making ourselves miserable through vice, and vicious through misery, were embodied and marshalled to a systematic War against the existing Evils of Nature? No, "*It is a wicked world!*" this is so generally the Solution, that this very Wickedness is assigned by selfish men, as their excuse for doing nothing to render it better, and for opposing those who would make the attempt. What have not Clarkson, Granville Sharp, Wilberforce, and the Society of the Friends, effected for the[1] English Nation, imperfectly as the intellectual and moral faculties of the People at large are developed at present? What may not be effected, if the recent discovery of the means of educating Nations (freed, however, from the vile sophistications and mutilations of ignorant Mountebanks), shall have been applied to its full extent? Would I frame to myself the most inspiriting[2] representation of future Bliss, which my mind is capable of comprehending, it would be embodied to me in the idea of BELL receiving, at some distant period, the appropriate reward of his earthly Labours, when thousands and ten thousands of glorified Spirits, whose reason and conscience had, through *his* efforts, been unfolded, shall sing the song of their own Redemption, and pouring forth Praises to God and to their Saviour, shall repeat *his* "new Name" in Heaven, give thanks for his earthly Virtues, as the chosen Instruments of Divine Mercy to them,[3] and not seldom, perhaps, turn their eyes toward *him*, as from the Sun to its image in the Fountain, with secondary gratitude and the permitted utterance of a human love! Were but a hundred men to combine a deep conviction that virtuous Habits may be formed by the very means by which knowledge is communicated, that men may be made better, not only in consequence, but *by* the mode and *in* the process, of instruction: were but an hundred men to combine [72] that clear conviction of this,

---

[1] 1812 adds "Honor, and, if we believe in a retributive Providence, for the continuance of the Prosperity of the".

[2] For "inspiriting" 1812 reads "inspirating"; see above, I 102 n 3.

[3] For "them" 1812 reads "themselves".

which I myself at this moment feel, even as I feel the certainty of my being, with the perseverance of a CLARKSON or a BELL, the promises of ancient prophecy would disclose themselves to our Faith, even as when a noble Castle hidden from us by an intervening mist, discovers itself by its reflection in the tranquil Lake, on the opposite shore of which we stand gazing. What an awful Duty, what a Nurse of all other, the fairest Virtues, does not hope[1] become! We are bad ourselves, because we despair of the goodness of others.

If then it be a Truth, attested alike by common feeling and common sense, that the greater part of human Misery depends directly on human Vices and the remainder indirectly, by what means can we act on Men so as to remove or preclude these Vices and purify their principle of moral election. The question is not by what means each man is to alter his own character—in order to this, all the means prescribed and all the aidances given by Religion, may be necessary for him. Vain, of themselves, may be

> ——the sayings of the wise
> In ancient and in modern books inroll'd
> . . . .
> Unless he feel within
> Some source of consolation from above,
> Secret refreshings, that repair his strength,
> And fainting spirits uphold.
>   SAMPSON AGONISTES

This is not the question. Virtue would not be Virtue, could it be *given* by one fellow-creature to another. To *make use* of all the means and appliances in our power to the actual attainment of Rectitude, is the abstract of the Duty which we owe to ourselves: to *supply* those means as far as we can, comprizes our Duty to others. The question then is, what are these means? Can they be any other than the communication of Knowledge, and the removal of those Evils and Impediments which prevent its' reception: it may not be in our power to combine both, but it is in the power of every man to contribute to the former, who is sufficiently informed to feel that it is his Duty. If it be said, that we should endeavour not so much to remove Ignorance, as to make the Ignorant religious, Religion herself, through her sacred [73] Oracles, answers for me, that all effective Faith presupposes Knowledge and individual Conviction. If the mere acquiescence in Truth, uncomprehended and unfathomed, were sufficient, few indeed would be the vicious and the miserable, in this Country at least, where speculative Infidelity is, Heaven be praised, confined to a small number. Like bodily Deformity, there is one instance here and another there; but three in one place are already an undue proportion. It is highly worthy of observation, that the inspired Writings received by Christians are distinguishable from all other Books pretending to Inspiration, from the Scriptures of the Bramins, and even from the Koran, in their strong and frequent recommendations of Truth. I do not here mean Veracity, which cannot but be enforced in every Code which

---

[1] For "hope" 1812 reads "HOPE".

appeals to the religious Principle of Man; but Knowledge. This is not only extolled as the Crown and Honor of a Man, but to seek after it is again and again commanded us as one of our most sacred Duties. Yea, the very perfection and final bliss of the glorified spirit is represented by the Apostle as a plain aspect, or intuitive beholding of Truth in its eternal and immutable Source. Not that Knowledge can of itself do all! The Light of Religion is not that of the Moon, light without heat; but neither is its warmth that of the Stove, warmth without light. Religion is the Sun, whose warmth indeed swells, and stirs, and actuates the Life of Nature, but who at the same time beholds all the growth of Life with a master-eye, makes all objects glorious on which he looks, and by that Glory visible to all others.

But though Knowledge be not the only, yet that it is an indispensible and most effectual Agent in the direction of our actions, one consideration will convince us. It is an undoubted Fact of human nature, that the sense of impossibility quenches all will. Sense of utter inaptitude does the same. The man shuns the beautiful Flame, which is eagerly grasped at by the Infant. The sense of a disproportion of certain after harm to present gratification, produces effects almost equally uniform: though almost perishing with thirst, we should dash to the earth a goblet of Wine in which we had seen a Poison infused, though the Poison were without taste or odour, or even added to the pleasures of both. Are not all our Vices equally inapt to the universal end of human [74] actions, the Satisfaction of the agent? Are not their pleasures equally disproportionate to the after harm? Yet many a Maiden, who will not grasp at the fire, will yet purchase a wreathe of Diamonds at the price of her health, her honor, nay (and she herself knows it at the moment of her choice), at the sacrifice of her Peace and Happiness. The Sot would reject the poisoned Cup, yet the trembling hand with which he raises his daily or hourly draught to his lips, has not left him ignorant that this too is altogether a Poison. I know, it will be objected, that the consequences foreseen are less immediate; that they are diffused over a larger space of time; and that the slave of Vice hopes well,[1] where no hope is. This, however, only removes the question one step further: for why should the distance or diffusion of known consequences produce so great a difference? Why are men the dupes of the present moment? Evidently because the conceptions are indistinct in the one case, and vivid in the other; because all confused conceptions render us restless; and because Restlessness can drive us to Vices that promise no enjoyment, no not even the cessation of that Restlessness. This is indeed the dread Punishment attached by Nature to habitual Vice, that its Impulses wax as its Motives wane. No object, not even the light of a solitary Taper in the far distance, tempts the benighted Mind from before; but its own restlessness dogs it from behind, as with the iron goad of Destiny. What then is or can be the preventive, the remedy, the counteraction, but the habituation of the Intellect to clear, distinct, and adequate conceptions concerning all things that are the possible objects of clear conception, and thus to remove our obscure notions and the vivid feelings which, when the objects

---

[1] 1812 omits "well,".

of these obscure notions are habitually present to the mind, become associated with them by a natural affinity, even as the element of thunder with the clouds[1]—to reserve these feelings[2] for those[3] objects, which their very sublimity renders indefinite, no less than their indefiniteness renders them sublime: Being, Form, Life, the Reason, the Law of Conscience, Freedom, Immortality, God! To connect with the objects of our senses the obscure notions and consequent vivid feelings, which are due only to our Ideas of immaterial and permanent Things, is profanation relatively to the heart, and superstition in the understanding. [75] It is in this sense, that the philosophic Apostle calls Covetousness Idolatry. Could we emancipate ourselves from the bedimming influences of Custom, and the transforming witchcraft of early associations, we should see as numerous Tribes of *Fetish-Worshippers* in the streets of London and Paris, as we hear of on the Coasts of Africa.

I am fully aware, that what I am writing and have written (in these latter paragraphs at least) will expose me to the Censure of some, as bewildering myself and Readers with Metaphysics; to the Ridicule of others as a School-boy declaimer on old and worn-out Truisms or exploded Fancies; and to the Objection of most as obscure. The last real or supposed defect requires and will receive a particular answer in a following Number, preparatory to the disquisition on the elements of our moral and intellectual faculties.[4] Of the two former, I shall take the present opportunity of declaring my sentiments: especially as I have already received a hint that my "idol, MILTON, has represented Metaphysics as the subjects which the bad Spirits in Hell delight in discussing." And truly, if I had exerted my subtlety and invention in persuading myself and others that we are but living machines, and that (as one of the late followers of Hobbes and Hartley has expressed the system) the Assassin and his Dagger are equally fit objects of moral esteem and abhorrence; or if with a Writer of wider influence and higher authority, I had reduced all Virtue to a selfish prudence eked out by Superstition (for assuredly, a creed which takes its central point in conscious selfishness, whatever be the forms or names that act on the selfish passion, a Ghost or a Constable, can have but a distant relationship

---

[1] For "to remove . . . clouds" 1812 reads "to reserve the deep feelings which belong*, as by a natural right to those obscure Ideas that are necessary to the moral perfection of the human being, notwithstanding, yea, even in consequence, of their obscurity", with the added footnote: "I have not expressed myself as clearly as I could wish. But the truth of the assertion, that deep feeling has a tendency to combine with obscure ideas in preference to distinct and clear notions, is proved in every Methodist meeting, and by the history of religious sects in general. The odium theologicum, or hatred excited by difference of faith, is even proverbial: and it is the common complaint of philosophers and philosophic Historians, that the passions of the Disputants are commonly violent in proportion to the subtlety and obscurity of the Questions in Dispute. Nor is this fact confined to professional Theologians: for whole nations have displayed the same agitations, and have sacrificed national policy to the more powerful Interest of a controverted Obscurity." Cf above, I 106 and n.

[2] 1812 adds "I repeat".

[3] 1812 omits "those".

[4] Cf below, II 152; the "disquisition" does not appear in *Friend* (1809–10).

to that Religion, which places its' Essence in our loving our Neighbour as ourselves, and God above all) I know not, by what arguments I could repel the sarcasm. But what are my Metaphysics, but the referring of the Mind to its' own Consciousness for Truths indispensible to its' own Happiness? To what purposes do I, or am I about, to employ them? To perplex our clearest notions and living moral instincts? To deaden the feelings of Will and free Power, to extinguish the Light of Love and of Conscience, to make myself and others Worth-less, Soul-less, God-less? No! To expose the Folly and the [76] Legerdemain of those who have thus abused the blessed machine of Language; to support all old and venerable Truths; and by them to support, to kindle, to project the Spirit; to make the Reason spread Light over our Feelings, to make our Feelings, with their vital warmth, actualize our Reason;—these are my objects, these are my subjects, and are these the Metaphysics which the bad Spirits in Hell delight in?

But how shall I avert the scorn of those Critics who laugh at the oldness of my Topics, Evil and Good, Necessity and Arbitrement, Immortality and the ultimate Aim. By what shall I regain their[1] favour? My Themes must be *new*, a French Constitution; a Balloon; a change of Ministry; a fresh Batch of Kings on the Continent, or of Peers in our happier Island; or who had the best of it of two parliamentary Gladiators, and whose Speech, on the subject of Europe bleeding at a thousand wounds, or our own Country struggling for herself and all human nature, was cheered by the greatest number of *Laughs, loud Laughs, and very loud Laughs:* (which, carefully marked by italics, form most conspicuous and strange parentheses in the Newspaper Reports). Or if I must be philosophical, the last chemical discoveries, provided I do not trouble my Reader with the Principle which gives them their highest Interest, and the character of intellectual grandeur to the Discoverer; or the last shower of stones, and that they were supposed, by certain Philosophers, to have been projected from some Volcano in the Moon, taking care, however, not to add any of their cramp[2] reasons for their[3] Opinion! Something new, however, it must be, quite new and quite out of themselves: for whatever is within them, whatever is deep within them, must be as old as the first dawn of human Reason. But to find no contradiction in the union of old and new, to contemplate the ANCIENT OF DAYS with feelings as fresh as if they then sprang forth at his own fiat, this characterizes the minds that feel the Riddle of the World, and may help to unravel it! To carry on the feelings of Childhood into the powers of Manhood, to combine the Child's sense of wonder and novelty with the Appearances which every day for perhaps forty years had rendered familiar,

> With Sun and Moon and Stars throughout the year,
> And Man and Woman——

[77] this is the character and privilege of Genius, and one of the marks which distinguish Genius from Talents. And so to represent familiar objects as to awaken the minds of others to a like freshness of sensation

---

1 For "their" 1812 reads "*their*".   cramp".
2 For "their cramp" 1812 reads "the   3 For "their" 1812 reads "this".

concerning them (that constant accompaniment of mental, no less than of bodily convalesence)—to the same modest questioning of a self-discovered and intelligent ignorance, which, like the deep and massy Foundations of a Roman Bridge, forms half of the whole Structure (*prudens interrogatio dimidium scientiæ*, says Lord Bacon)—this is the prime merit of Genius, and its' most unequivocal mode of manifestation. Who has not a thousand times, seen it snow upon water? Who has not seen it with a new feeling, since he has read Burns's comparison of sensual pleasure

> To snow that falls upon a river,
> A moment white—then gone for ever!

In Philosophy equally as in Poetry, Genius produces the strongest impressions of novelty, while it rescues the stalest and most admitted Truths from the Impotence caused by the very circumstance of their universal admission. Extremes meet—a proverb, by the bye, to collect and explain all the instances and exemplifications of which, would employ a Life. Truths, of all others the most awful and mysterious, yet being at the same time of universal interest, are too often considered as so true that they lose all the powers of Truth, and lie bed-ridden in the Dormitory of the Soul, side by side with the most despised and exploded Errors.

But as the Class of Critics whose contempt I have anticipated, commonly consider themselves as Men of the World, instead of hazarding additional sneers by appealing to the Authorities of *recluse* Philosophers (for such in spite of all History, the men who have distinguished themselves by profound thought, are generally deemed, from Plato and Aristotle to Tully, and from Bacon to Berkeley), I will refer them to the Darling of the polished Court of Augustus, to the Man, whose Works have been in all ages deemed the models of good sense, and are still the pocket-companion of those who pride themselves on uniting the Scholar with the Gentleman. This accomplished Man of the World has given us an account of the Subjects of Conversation between himself and the illustrious Statesmen who governed, and [78] the brightest Luminaries who then adorned the Empire of the civilized World:

> *Sermo oritur non de villis domibusve alienis*
> *Nec, male, nec ne lepus saltet. Sed quod magis ad nos*
> *Pertinet, et nescire malum est, agitamus: utrumne*
> *Divitiis homines, an sint virtute beati?*
> *Et quo sit natura boni? summumque quid eius?*
> HORAT. Serm. L. II. Sat. 6. v. 71*

Berkeley indeed asserts, and is supported in his Assertion by the great

LITERAL TRANSLATION

* The[1] Conversation arises not concerning the Country Seats or Families of Strangers, nor whether the dancing Hare performed well or ill. But we discuss what more nearly concerns us, and which it is an Evil not to know: whether Men are made happy by Riches or by Virtue? And in what consists the nature of Good and what is the ultimate or supreme Good? (*i.e. the Summum Bonum*).

[1] 1812 omits "The".

Statesmen, Lord Bacon and Sir Walter Raleigh, that without an habitual interest in these Subjects, a Man may be a dexterous Intriguer, but never can be a Statesman. Would to Heaven that the Verdict to be passed on my Labours depended on those who least needed them! The Water Lilly in the midst of Waters lifts up its' broad Leaves, and expands its' Petals at the first pattering of the Shower, and rejoices in the Rain with a quicker Sympathy, than the parched Shrub in the sandy Desert.

Chrisippus,[1] in one of his stoical Aphorisms (preserved by Cicero in his Dialogue de nat. deor. lib. 2. sect. 160.)[2] says: Nature has given to the Hog a *soul* instead of *salt*, in order to keep it from putrifying. This holds equally true of Man considered as an animal. Modern Physiologists have substituted the words vital power (*vis vitæ*)[3] for that of soul, and not without good reason: for from the effect we may fairly deduce the inherence of a power producing it, but are not entitled to *hypostasize*[4] this power (that is, to affirm it to be an individual substance) any more than the Steam in the Steam Engine, the power of Gravitation in the Watch, or the magnetic Influence in the Loadstone. If the Machine consist of Parts mutually dependant, as in the Time-piece or the Hog, we cannot dispart without destroying it: if otherwise, as in a mass of Loadstone and in the Polypus, the power is equally divisible with the substance. The most approved Definition of a living Substance is, that its' [79] vitality consists in the susceptibility of being acted upon by external stimulants joined to the necessity of re-action; and in the due balance of this action and re-action, the healthy state of Life consists. We must, however, further add the power of acquiring *Habits*, and Facilities by repetition. This being the generical idea of Life, is common to all living Beings; but taken exclusively, it designates the lowest Class, Plants and Plant Animals. An addition to the mechanism gives locomotion. A still costlier and more complex apparatus diversly organizes the impressions received from the external powers that fall promiscuously on the whole surface. The Light shines on the whole face, but it receives form and relation only in the Eyes. In *them* it is *organized.* To these *Organs* of sense we suppose (by analogy from our own experience) sensation attached, and these sensuous impressions acting on other parts of the Machine,[5] framed for other stimulants included in the Machine itself, namely, the Organs of Appetite; and these again work-

[1] In 1812 from here to the end of the following paragraph the passage is reduced to a footnote, which ends No 5. For the first part of the footnote, which C adds in 1812, see below, II 79 n 3.

[2] Chrysippus of Soli, in Cilicia (280–207 B.C.), quoted in Cicero *De natura deorum* 2.64 (§160). See *CN* I 1027 and n.

[3] Copy R has a comment at this point: "Imperfect and in part erroneous. *Life* can be defined only by Individuation & that which *manifests* its individuality is Life *to us,*—that, which existing, as a whole, contains in itself the principle of the specific form, by which it manifests itself as a whole.— Assimilation & the resistance of putrefaction, are effects, or involutes, not a definition of Life. Plants are Life dormant; Animals = Somnambulists; the mass of Mankind Day-dreamers; the Philosopher only awake." J. Wordsworth "Marginalia" 369.

[4] Cited in *OED* as the earliest use. A C coinage?

[5] Copy R alters to "other additaments to the Machine". J. Wordsworth 369.

ing on the instruments[1] of locomotion, and of[2] those by which the external substances corresponding to the sensuous impressions can be acted upon, (the Mouth, Teeth, Talons, &c.) constitute our whole idea of the perfect *Animal*. More than this Des Cartes denied to all other Animals but Man, and to Man himself as an animal: (for that this truly great Man considered Animals insensible, or rather *insensitive*, Machines, though commonly asserted, and that in Books of highest authority, is an error; and the charge was repelled with disdain by himself, in a Letter to Dr. Henry More, which, if I mistake not, is annexed to the small Edition of More's Ethics.)[3]

The strict analogy, however, between certain actions of sundry Animals and those of Mankind, forces upon us the belief, that they possess some share of a higher faculty: which, however closely united with Life in one person, can yet never be *educed* out of the mere idea of *vital power*. Indeed if we allow any force to the universal opinion, and almost instinct, concerning the difference between Plants and Animals, we must hold even sensation as a fresh power added to the Vis Vitæ, unless we would make an end of Philosophy, by comprizing all things in each thing, and thus denying that any one Power of the Universe can be affirmed to be itself and not another.[4] [80] However this may be, the Understanding or regulative faculty is manifestly distinct from Life and Sensation, its' *function* being to take up the *passive affections*[5] into distinct Thought of the Sense

[1] Copy R alters to "and these working back again toward the surface on the instruments". J. Wordsworth 369.

[2] For "of" 1812 reads "on".

[3] Henry More *Enchiridion ethicum* (1669) has an appended "Epistola H. Mori ad V. C." that is a close parallel of C's statement of the charge against Descartes; see esp pp 3–4. But the letter is by More, not to him. Tr: "Another example [of the second of Descartes' three errors] concerns living animals, which he takes to be soulless and insensitive Automata". More goes on to point out that Descartes said this in order to "secure untouched" the immortality of the human soul. Descartes' refutation is not found in this volume, but in his *Correspondance avec Arnaud et Morus* ed Geneviève Lewis (Paris 1953) 122 (letter dated 5 Feb 1649, sec 5), and see More's letter there pp 104–5 (11 Dec 1648), which also appears in More *A Collection of Several Philosophical Writings* (1712). C annotated More's *Theological Works* (1708); see *C 17th C* 316–21.

[4] Opposite this passage in Copy R, C wrote: "This as conveying the notion of Supervenience, as ab extra, instead of Evolution, ab intra, is erroneous: & the error of the Disciples of Hunter, as Abernethie—who are, however, the *best* of our English Physiologists. What follows is accurate, as *verbal* Definition." At the end of the footnote he wrote: "Be pleased to consult the Appendix, Note C. to the Lay-Sermon addressed to the Learned, published by Gale & Fennor [*SM* (1816) v–xxx, esp xi, in which the end of *The Friend* paragraph is reprinted and explained]—and I beseech you, do not be discouraged if either in this or in my Biographical Sketches you do not understand me at the first two or three Readings. Consider, how many years I have been toiling thro' mist and twilight; but I have not a fuller conviction of my own Life than I have of the Truth of my present convictions. They have taught me the difference in *kind* between the *sense* of certainty and the *sensation* of positiveness. '*I Am*', in *that I Am*': and St. Paul's Christ (as the Logos) the eternal *Yea* (Cor. 2. 1.) is the fontal Idea. See p. 88 [in 1809–10, pp 81–2n; below, II 79–82n]." J. Wordsworth 369. Cf 2 Cor 1.17–20.

[5] 1812 adds "of the Sense".

both[1] according to its' own essential forms.[*2] These Forms however, as they are first awakened by impressions from the Senses, so have they no Substance or Meaning unless in their application to Objects of the Senses; and if we would remove from them by careful Abstraction, all the influences and intermixtures of a yet far higher Faculty (Self consciousness for instance), it would be difficult, if at all possible, to distinguish its' Functions from those of Instinct, of which it would be no inapt Definition that it is a more or less limited Understanding without Self-consciousness, or spontaneous Origination.[3] Besides: the Understanding with all its axioms of

* Aristotle, the first systematic Anatomist of the Mind, constructed the first Numeration Table of these innate Forms or Faculties (N.B. not innate *Ideas* or *Notions*) under the name of Categories: which Table though both incomplete and erroneous, remains an unequivocal Proof of his Penetration and philosophical Genius. The best and most orderly arrangement of the original forms of the Understanding (the *Moulds* as it were both of our Notions and judgements concerning the Notices of the Senses) is that of Quantity, Quality, Relation, and Mode, each consisting of three Kinds. There is but one possible way of making an enumeration of them *interesting*, or even endurable to the general Reader: the history of the *origin* of certain useful Inventions in machinery, in the minds of the Inventors.

[1] For "Thought . . . both" 1812 reads "Thoughts and Judgements,".

[2] 1812 omits the footnote. In a letter to Poole 9 Oct 1809 C corrects the sentence as in the 1812 revision (above, II 76 n 5, 77 n 1), but continues the sentence: ". . . essential *forms*: formae formantes, in the language of Lord Bacon in contradistinction to the formae formatae." See *CL* III 235.

[3] For "or spontaneous Origination" 1812 reads "and without comprehension—that is, without the power of *concluding* the particular from the universal." Then follows the addition: "The few Readers, for whom this note is intended, will observe, that the word, understanding, may be used in two meanings, a wider and a narrower. In the first, it means the active power of the Soul, THOUGHT, as opposed to its' passive or merely recipient, property, the SENSE: (N.B. not the *Senses*, but that quality of the Soul which receive[s] impressions from the Senses, even as the Senses receive impressions from objects out of us,) so [Copy R begins a new sentence here] defined, it *includes* the Reason. In its' narrower meaning, the Understanding is used for the faculty, by which we form distinct *notions* of Things and *immediate*, positive judgements (ex. gr. Gold *is* a Body) in distinction from Reason or the faculty by which we form necessary conclusions, or *mediate* Judgements (ex. gr. Gold being a material Substance must be extended.) If the Reader will put up with scholastic Latinity, he may thus word the component faculties of the animal triplex: Vis sensitiva *per*cipit, Vis regulatrix *con*cipit, vis rationalis *comprehendit*: prima *imprimitur* per sensus; secunda impressiones multifarias in *notiones* individuas coadunat, pas [Copy R corrects to "has"] autem notiones *regulis* secundum analogiam subnectit, i.e. *experientiam* format; tertia et notiones individuas, et regulas experimentales, *Principiis* absolutis, seu *Legibus* necessariis subjungit et subjugat, et inde de rebus, quas *reales* esse experientia jam monstratum est, ipsa ultro demonstrans, quomodo sint *possibiles*, *scientiam* facit. Ratio, seu vis scientifica, est possibilitatis, vel essentiæ rerum, per leges earum constitutivas, intellectio." The Latin is almost certainly C's. Tr George Whalley: "The sensitive power *per*ceives, the regulative power *con*ceives, the rational power *understands:* the first *is impressed* through the senses; the second

sense, its Anticipations of Apperception, and its' Analogies of Experience,[1] has no appropriate Object, but the material World in Relation to our worldly Interests. The far-sighted Prudence of Man, and the more narrow, but at the same time far more certain and effectual, Cunning of the Fox, are both no other than a nobler Substitute *"for Salt, in order that the Hog may not putrify before its destined hour."* [2]

But[3] God created Man in his own Image: to be the Image of his own Eternity and Infinity[4] created he Man. He gave us Reason and with Reason Ideas of its own formation and underived from material Nature, self-consciousness, Principles, and above all, the Law of Conscience, which in the power of an holy and omnipotent Being *commands* us to attribute Reality—[5] among the numerous Ideas[6]

(To be continued.)[7]

---

unifies a variety of impressions into individual *notions,* but it organises [lit. binds under] these notions by analogy under *rules,* that is it gives form to *experience*; the third joins up and interrelates [lit. places under the yoke] both individual notions and experimental rules, under absolute *Principles* or necessary *Laws,* and so from things that are already shown by experience to be *real,* it makes *science,* moreover, showing how things are *possible.* Reason, or the scientific faculty, is the understanding of possibility, or the essence of things, through their constitutive laws."

1 For "Besides . . . Experience" 1812 reads "In its' narrower sense, I assert [Copy R corrects to: "*narrower* sense it is, that I assert"], that the Understanding, or *experiential* faculty thus distinguished from the Reason, or *sciential* power,".

2 Chrysippus; see above, II 75 and n 2.

3 1812 omits "But".

4 1812 omits "and Infinity".

5 For "He gave . . . Reality—" 1812

reads "Of Eternity and Self-existence what other Likeness is possible in a finite Being, but Immortality and moral Self-determination! In addition to Sensation, Perception, and practical Judgement (instinctive or acquirable) concerning the notices furnished by the organs of Perception, all which in *kind* at least, the Dog possesses in common with his Master; in *addition* to these, God gave us Reason, and with Reason he gave us reflective SELF-CONSCIOUSNESS; gave us PRINCIPLES, distinguished from the maxims and generalizations of outward Experience by their absolute and essential Universality and Necessity; and above all, by superadding to Reason the mysterious faculty of Free Will and consequent personal Amenability, he gave us CONSCIENCE—that Law of Conscience, which in the power, and as the indwelling WORD, of an holy and omnipotent Legislator *commands* us— from".

6 For "Ideas" 1812 reads "IDEAS".

7 1812 omits.

THE FRIEND

No. 6. THURSDAY, September 21, 1809

(Continued from page 80.)[1]

mathematical or[2] philosophical, which the Reason[3] by the necessity of its own excellence, creates for itself—to those, (and those only)[4] without which the Conscience[5] would be baseless and contradictory; namely,[6] to the Ideas of Soul, the[7] Free Will,[8] Immortality, and[9] God. To God as the Reality of the Conscience and the Source of all Obligation; to Free Will, as the power of the human being to maintain the Obedience, which God through the Conscience has commanded, against all the might of Nature; and to the immortality of the Soul as a State in which the weal and woe of man shall be proportioned to his moral Worth.*[10]

With this Faith all Nature,

—————————all the mighty World
Of Eye and Ear—————

* *Anima sapiens* (says Giordano Bruno, and let the sublime Piety of the Passage excuse some intermixture of Error, or rather let the words, as they well may, be interpreted in a safe sense) *Anima sapiens non timet mortem, immo interdum illam ultro appetit, illi ultro occurrit. Manet quippe substantiam omnem pro Duratione*

[1] 1812 omits.

[2] For "or" 1812 reads "and".

[3] In 1812 an asterisk is inserted here, with the following footnote: "The following paragraphs in this reprinted Copy I have transplanted from the Text to the Notes, in order that they may be read or passed over ad libitum. They are addressed to the Few among my Readers, who have directed their attention to psychological analysis: from the Rest I entreat that same toleration, which, if they are purchasers of new books, they must have been in the habit of giving to wide margins and empty spaces; which are called *Fat*, I believe, by the Printers, whether in consideration of the Good of the Trade in general and their own relief and profit in particular, or (*ex opposito*, as the Grammarians say) from the contrary effect on the Readers Information,

ut mons a non movenda [as mountain, so called because it does not move], I am unable to decide." Then follow the paragraphs beginning "Chrisippus".

[4] For "itself—to those . . . those only)" 1812 reads "itself, unconditionally *commands* us to attribute *Reality*, and actual *Existence*, to those Ideas, and to those only,".

[5] 1812 adds "itself".

[6] 1812 omits "namely".

[7] For "the" 1812 reads "of".

[8] 1812 adds "of".

[9] 1812 adds "of".

[10] In 1812 the text of No 5 ends here (with the concluding paragraph of what became a footnote), the footnote on Bruno deleted here and placed at the foot of p 88, with the heading "*Note to page* 80." No 6 in 1812 then begins: "With this Faith . . ."

presents itself to us, now as the Aggregate *Materials*[4] of Duty, and now as a Vision of the Most High revealing to us the mode, and time, and

---

Eternitas, pro Loco Immensitas, pro Actu Omniformitas. Non levem igitur ac futilem, atqui gravissimam perfectoque Homine dignissimam Contemplationis Partem persequimur ubi divinitatis, naturæque splendorem, fusionem, et communicationem, non in Cibo, Potu, et ignobiliore quâdam materiâ cum attonitorum seculo perquirimus; sed in augustâ Omnipotentis Regiâ, in immenso ætheris spacio, in infinitâ naturæ geminæ omnia fientis et omnia facientis potentiâ, unde tot astrorum, mundorum inquam et numinum, uni altissimo concinentium atque saltantium absque numero atque fine juxta propositos ubique fines atque ordines, contemplamur. Sic ex visibilium æterno, immenso et innumerabili effectu, sempiterna immensa illa Majestas atque bonitas intellecta conspicitur, proque suâ dignitate innumerabilium Deorum (mundorum dico) adsistentiâ concinentiâ, et gloriæ ipsius enarratione, immo ad oculos expressâ concione glorificatur. Cui Immenso mensum non quadrabit Domicilium atque Templum—ad cujus Majestatis plenitudinem agnoscendam atque percolendam, numerabilium ministorum nullus esset ordo. Eia igitur ad omniformis Dei omniformem Imaginem conjectemus oculos, vivum et magnum illius admiremar simulacrum!—Hinc miraculum magnum a Trismegisto appellabatar Homo, qui in Deum transeat quasi ipse sit Deus, qui conatur omnia fieri sicut Deus est omnia; ad objectum sine fine, ubique tamen finiendo, contendit, sicut infinitus est Deus, immensus ubique totus.

Translation. A wise Spirit does not fear death, nay, sometimes, (*as in cases of voluntary martyrdom*) seeks and goes forth to meet it, of its' own accord. For there awaits all actual Beings, for Duration an Eternity, for Place Immensity, for Action Omniformity. We pursue, therefore, a species of Contemplation not light or futile, but the weightiest and most worthy of an accomplished Man, while we examine and seek for, the splendor, the interfusion, and communication of the Divinity and of Nature, not in Meats or Drink, or any yet ignobler matter, with the Race of the Thunder-striken; (*i.e. minds stunned and stupified by superstitious fears.* BRUNO *here alludes, doubtless, to the gross absurdities of Transubstantiation*), but in the August palace of the Omnipotent, in the illimitable etherial space, in the infinite power, that creates all things, and is the abiding *Being* of all things. (*I have thought* [82] *myself allowed thus to render the less cautious expressions of the original, because the very same Latin words are to be found in the writings of Joannes Scotus Erigena,*[1] *who was doubtless a sincere Christian; and equivalent phrases occur in the mystic theology of one at least, if not more, of the early Greek Fathers.*[2] *It is most uncharitable to accuse a Writer of pantheism, for a few overcharged Sentences: especially as the Writer may have thought himself authorized by certain texts of St. John and St. Paul.*)[3]

---

[1] "Deus omnia sit, & omnia Deus sint", e.g., in Dedication [ii] of S. Maximus *Scholia in Gregorium theologum* printed with Joannes Scotus Erigena *De divisione naturae* (Oxford 1681). C's annotated copy of this volume is in the BM; for C's comment on the "Pantheism" of the above passage and others see *P Lects* (1949) 433–4. Cf *CN* I 1369, 1382 and nn.

[2] Cf an entry in *CN* III 3516: "Spinosism lurks in many of the definitions of the Schoolmen, but in some of

the Mystic Greek Fathers, & their Imitator Joannes Scotus Erigena, stands forth & shouts its presence—Of the former—36. Reg. [*Regulae theologicae* of Alanus Magnus] Mingarelli Fasciculus Anecdotorum, p. 171 et seq Ed. Rom. 1756. *Quotiescunque per pronomen demonstrativum de Deo fit sermo, cadit a demonstratione.*"

[3] See Col 1.17; Acts 17.28; 1 John 3.24, 4.13, 4.16.

[4] For "Aggregate *Materials*" 1812 reads "aggregated *Material*".

particular instance of applying [82] and realizing that universal Rule, pre-established in the Heart[1] of our Reason:[2] as

> The lovely shapes and sounds intelligible
> Of that Eternal Language, which our God
> Utters: Who from Eternity doth teach
> Himself in all, and all things in Himself![3]

There we may contemplate the Host of Stars, of Worlds and their guardian Deities (*i.e. presiding Angels*) numbers without number, each in its' appointed sphere, singing together, and dancing in adoration of the One Most High. Thus from the perpetual, immense, and innumerable goings on of the visible World, that sempiternal and absolutely infinite Majesty, is intellectually beheld, and is glorified according to his Glory, by the attendance, and choral symphonies, of innumerable gods, who utter forth the glory of their ineffable Creator in the expressive Language of Vision! To HIM illimitable, a limited Temple will not correspond—to the acknowledgement and due worship of the Plenitude of *his* Majesty there would be no proportion in any numerable Army of Ministrant Spirits. Let us then cast our Eyes upon the omniform Image of the Attributes of the all-creating Supreme, nor admit any representation of his Excellency but the living Universe, which he has created!—Thence was Man entitled by Trismegistus, "the great Miracle," inasmuch as he has been made capable of entering into Union with God, as if he were himself a divine nature; tries to *become* all things, even as in God all things *are;* and in limitless progression of limited States of Being, urges onward to the ultimate Aim, even as God is simultaneously infinite, and every where All!

I purpose hereafter, to give an account of the Life of Giordano Bruno, the Friend of Sir Philip Sidney, and who was burnt under pretence of Atheism, at Rome, in the year 1600; and of his Works, which are perhaps the scarcest Books ever printed. They are singularly interesting as portraits of a vigorous mind

---

[1] In 1812 there is an asterisk here, with the following footnote: "I earnestly entreat the Reader not to be dissatisfied either with himself or with the Author, if he should not at once understand the preceding paragraph; but rather to consider it as a mere annunciation of a magnificent Theme, the different parts of which are to be demonstrated and developed, explained, illustrated, and exemplified in the progress of the Work. I likewise entreat him to peruse with attention and with candour, the weighty Extract from the judicious HOOKER, prefaced as the Motto to the ninth Number of the Friend [below, II 122]. In works of Reasoning, as distinguished from narration of Events or statements of Facts; but more particularly in Works, the object of which is to make us better acquainted with our own nature, a Writer, whose meaning is every where comprehended as quickly as his sentences can be read, may indeed have produced an amusing Composition, nay, by awakening and re-enlivening our recollections, a useful one; but most assuredly he will not have *added* either to the stock of our Knowledge, or to the vigour of our Intellect. For how can we gather strength, but by exercise? How can a truth, new to us, be made our own without examination and self-questioning—any new truth, I mean, that relates to the properties of the mind, and its' various faculties and affections! But whatever demands effort, requires time. Ignorance seldom *vaults* into knowledge, but passes into it through an intermediate state of obscurity, even as Night into Day through Twilight."

[2] For "Reason . . . Himself!" 1812 reads "Reason!", omitting "as" and the lines of verse.

[3] *Frost at Midnight* lines 59–62 (var): *PW* (EHC) I 242.

If this be regarded as the dream of an Enthusiast, by such as

> deem themselves most free,
> When they within this gross and visible sphere,
> Chain down the winged soul, scoffing ascent,
> Proud in their meanness!————

by such as pronounce every man out of his *Senses* who has not lost his *Reason;* even such men[1] may find some weight in the historical Fact that from those chiefly,[2] who had[3] strengthened their Intellects and Feelings by the contemplation of universal Truths, and of[4] *Principles of Duty*, [83] the actions correspondent to which involve one half of their Consequences, and have Omnipotence, as the Pledge for the remainder—that chiefly from those have been derived to Mankind[5] the surest and most general *maxims of Prudence*, and with these that hardihood which completes the undertaking ere the contemptuous Calculator, who has left nothing omitted in his scheme of probabilities, except the might of the human mind, has finished his[6] proof of its impossibility. Though I have in this and the preceding Numbers quoted more frequently and copiously than I shall permit myself to do in future (yet I trust, such passages as will be original to a great majority of my Readers, either from the scarceness of the works, or[7] the Language in which they are written) I cannot deny myself the gratification of supporting this connection of practical Heroism with previous Habits of philosophic Thought, by a singularly appropriate passage from an Author whose Works can be called rare only from their being, I fear, rarely read, however commonly talked of. It is the instance of Xenophon as stated by Lord Bacon, who would himself furnish an equal instance, if there could be found an equal Commentator.

"It is of Xenophon the Philosopher, who went from Socrates's School into Asia, in the Expedition of Cyrus the younger, against King Artaxerxes. This Xenophon, at that time was very young, and never had seen the wars before; neither had any command in the army, but only followed the war as a Volunteer, for the Love and Conversation of Proxenus, his Friend. He was present when Falinus came in message from the great King to the Grecians, after that Cyrus was slain in the Field, and they, a handful of men, left to themselves in the midst of the King's territories,

struggling after truth, amid many prejudices, which from the state of the Roman Church, in which he was born, have a claim to much Indulgence. One of them (entitled Ember Week) is curious for its' lively accounts of the rude state of London, at that time, both as to the Streets and the manners of the Citizens. The most industrious Historians of Speculative Philosophy, have not been able to procure more than a few of his Works. Accidentally I have been more fortunate in this respect, than those who have written hitherto on the unhappy *Philosopher of Nola:* as out of eleven works, the titles of which are preserved to us, I have had an opportunity of perusing six. I was told, when in Germany, that there is a complete collection of them in the Royal Library at Copenhagen. If so, it is *unique.*

[1] For "such men" 1812 reads "these".

[2] For "those chiefly" 1812 reads "persons,".

[3] 1812 adds "previously".

[4] For "universal Truths, and of" 1812 reads "those".

[5] 1812 omits "to Mankind".

[6] 1812 adds "pretended".

[7] 1812 adds "from".

cut off from their Country by many navigable Rivers, and many hundred miles. The Message imported, that they should deliver up their arms and submit themselves to the King's mercy. To which message, before answer was made, divers of the Army conferred familiarly with Falinus, and amongst the rest Xenophon happened to say: Why, Falinus! we have now but these two things left, our Arms and our Virtue; and if we yield up our arms, how shall we make use of our Virtue? Whereto Falinus, smiling on him, said, 'If I be not deceived, Young Gentleman, you are an Athenian, and I believe, you study philosophy, and it is pretty that you say; but you are much abused, if you think your Virtue can withstand the King's Power.' Here was the Scorn: the Wonder followed—which was, that this young Scholar [84] or Philosopher, after all the Captains were murthered in parly, by treason, conducted those ten thousand foot, through the heart of all the Kings high Countries from Babylon to Grecia, in safety, in despight of all the King's Forces, to the Astonishment of the World, and the encouragement of the Grecians, in times succeeding, to make invasion upon the Kings of Persia; as was after purposed by Jason the Thessalian, attempted by Agesilaus the Spartan, and atchieved by Alexander the Macedonian, *all upon the ground of the act of that young Scholar.*"

Often have I reflected with awe on the great and disproportionate power, which an individual of no extraordinary talents or attainments may exert, by merely throwing off all restraint of Conscience. What then must not be the power, where an Individual, of consummate wickedness, can organize into the unity and rapidity of an individual will, all the natural and artificial forces of a populous and wicked nation? And could we bring within the field of imagination, the devastation effected in the moral world, by the violent removal of old customs, familiar sympathies, willing reverences, and habits of subordination almost naturalized into instinct,[1] the mild influences of reputation, and the other ordinary props and aidances of our infirm Virtue, or at least, if Virtue be too high a name, of our well-doing; and above all, if we could give form and body to all the effects produced on the Principles and Dispositions of Nations by the infectious feelings of Insecurity, and the soul-sickening sense of Unsteadiness in the whole Edifice of civil Society; the horrors of Battle, though the miseries of a whole War were brought together before our eyes in one disastrous Field, would present but a tame Tragedy in comparison.*

*[2] Nay, it would even present a sight of comfort and of elevation, if this Field of Carnage were the sign and result of a national Resolve, of a general Will so to die, that neither Deluge nor Fire should take away the name of Country[3] from their Graves, rather than to tread the same clods of Earth, no longer a Country, and themselves alive in nature but dead in infamy. What is Greece at this present moment? It is the Country[4] of the Heroes from Codrus to Philopæmen; and so it would be, though all the Sands of Africa should cover its Corn Fields and Olive Gardens, and not a Flower[5] left on Hybla[6] for a Bee to murmur in.

[1] For "instinct," 1812 reads "instinct; of".

[2] The footnote becomes text in 1812.

[3] For "Country" 1812 reads "COUN-TRY".

[4] For "Country" 1812 reads "COUN-TRY".

[5] 1812 adds "were".

[6] Copy R changes "Hybla" to "Hymettus".

If then the power with which Wickedness can invest the human being be thus tremendous, greatly does it behove us to enquire into its Source and Causes. So doing we shall quickly discover that it is not Vice, as Vice, which is thus mighty; but *systematic* Vice! Vice self-consistent and entire; Crime corresponding to Crime; Villainy entrenched and barricadoed by Villainy; this is the condition and main consistuent[1] of its power. The abandonment [85] of all *Principle* of Right enables the Soul to chuse and act upon a *Principle* of Wrong, and to subordinate to this one Principle all the various Vices of Human nature. For it is a mournful Truth, that as Devastation is incomparably an easier Work than Production, so all its means and instruments may be more easily arranged into a scheme and System. Even as in a Siege every Building and Garden which the faithful Governor must destroy as impeding the defensive means of the Garrison, or furnishing means of Offence to the Besieger, occasions a Wound in feelings which Virtue herself has fostered: and Virtue, because it is Virtue, loses perforce part of her energy in the reluctance, with which she proceeds to a business so repugnant to her wishes, as a choice of Evils. But to him[2] who has once said with his whole heart, Evil be thou my Good! has removed a world of Obstacles by the very decision, that he will have no Obstacles but those of force and brute matter. The road of Justice

"Curves round the corn-field and the hill of vines
Honouring the holy bounds of property!"

But the path of the Lightening is straight: and "straight the fearful Path

Of the cannon-ball. Direct it flies and rapid,
Shatt'ring that it *may* reach, and shatt'ring what it reaches."

Happily for Mankind, however, the obstacles which a consistent evil mind no longer finds in itself, it finds in its own unsuitableness to Human nature. A limit is fixed to its power: but within that limit, both as to the extent and duration of its influence, there is little hope of checking its career, if giant and united Vices are opposed only by mixed and scattered Virtues, and those too, probably, from the want of some combining Principle, which assigns to each its due Place and Rank, at civil War with themselves, or at best perplexing and counteracting each other. Thus even[3] in the present Hour of Peril we may[4] hear even good Men painting[5] the horrors and crimes of War, and softening or staggering the minds of their Brethren by details of individual wretchedness; thus under pretence of avoiding Blood, withdrawing the will from the defence of the very source of those blessings without which the blood would flow idly in our veins, and[6] lest a few should fall on the Bulwarks in glory, preparing us to give up the whole State to baseness, and the children of free Ancestors to become Slaves, and the Fathers of Slaves.

[1] In 1809–10, 1812, and 1818 "consistuent" (not in the *OED*), but changed to "constituent" by later editors.

[2] For "to him" 1812 reads "He".

[3] For "Thus even" 1812 reads "Even".

[4] For "we may" 1812 reads "do we not too often".

[5] For "painting" 1812 reads "declaiming on".

[6] For "veins, and" 1812 reads "veins! thus".

Machiavelli has well observed, "*Sono di tre generazioni Cervelli: l'uno intende per se; l' altro intende quanto da altri gli e mostro; il terzo non intende né per se stesso* [86] *ne per demostrazione d'altri.* There are Brains of three races. The one understands of itself; the other understands as much as is shewn it by others; the third neither understands of itself nor what is shewn it by others." I should have no hesitation in placing that Man in the third Class of Brains, for whom the History of the last twenty years has not supplied a copious comment on the preceding Text. The widest maxims of Prudence are like Arms without Hearts, disjoined from those Feelings which flow forth from Principle as from a fountain: and so little are even the genuine maxims of expedience likely to be perceived or acted upon by those who have been habituated to admit nothing higher than Expedience, that I dare hazard the assertion, that in the whole Chapter of Contents of European Ruin, every Article might be unanswerably deduced from the neglect of some maxim that had been repeatedly laid down, demonstrated, and enforced with a host of illustrations in some one or other of the Works of Machiavelli, Bacon, or Harrington. Indeed I can remember no one Event of importance which was not distinctly foretold, and this not by a lucky Prize drawn among a thousand Blanks out of the Lottery Wheel of Conjecture, but legitimately deduced as certain Consequences from established Premises. It would be a melancholy, but a very profitable employment, for some vigorous Mind, intimately acquainted with the recent History of Europe, to collect the weightiest Aphorisms of Machiavelli alone, and illustrating by appropriate Facts, the breach or observation of each to render less mysterious the[1] triumph of lawless Violence. The apt Motto to such a Work would be, "The Children of Darkness are wiser in their Generation than the Children of Light."

I see, however, one favourable symptom in the minds of men at present. The notion of our measureless superiority in Good Sense to our Ancestors, is somewhat less fashionable, than at the commencement of the French Revolution: we hear less of the jargon of *this enlightened Age*.[2] After having fatigued itself as Performer or Spectator of the giddy Figure-dance of political changes, Europe has seen the shallow Foundations of its self-complacent Faith give way; and we have now more reason to apprehend the stupor of Despondence, than the extravagances of idle Hope and unprincipled self-confidence. So grievously deceived by the showy mock theories of confident mock Thinkers, there seems a tendency in the public mind to shun all Thought, and to expect help from any quarter rather than from Seriousness and Reflection: As if some [87] invisible Power would think for us, when we gave up the pretence of thinking for ourselves. But in the first place, did those, who opposed the theories of Innovators, conduct their *untheoretic* Opposition with more Wisdom or to a happier Result? And secondly, are Societies now constructed on Principles so few and so simple, that we could, even if we wished it, act as it were by *Instinct*, like our distant Forefathers in the infancy of States? Doubtless, to act is nobler than to think; but as the old man doth not become a Child by means of his second Childishness, as little can a Nation exempt itself from the necessity of thinking, which has once learnt to think. Miserable is the

---

[1] 1812 adds "present".   [2] Cf above, I 61.

delusion of the present mad Realizer of mad Dreams, if he believe that he can transform the Nations of Europe into the unreasoning Hordes of a Babylonian or Tartar Empire, or even reduce the Age to the Simplicity so desirable for Tyrants of those Times, when the Sword and the Plough were the sole Implements of human Skill. Those are Epochs in the History of a People which having been, can never more recur. Extirpate all Civilization and all its Arts by the Sword, trample down all ancient Institutions, Rights, Distinctions, and Privileges, drag us backward to our old Barbarism, as Beasts to the Den of Cacus—deem you that thus you will re-create the unexamining and boisterous youth of the World, when the sole questions were—What is to be conquered? and who is the most famous Leader? Or shall I rather address myself to those, who think that as the Peace of Nations has been disturbed by the diffusion of Knowledge, falsely so called, and the excitement of Hopes that could not be gratified; that this Peace may be re-established by excluding the People from all Knowledge, all Thought, and all prospect of Amelioration? O never, never! Reflection, and stirrings of Mind, with all their Restlessness and all their Imperfections and Errors, are come into the World. The Powers that awaken and foster the Spirit of Curiosity and Investigation, are to be found in every Village; Books are in every Cottage. The Infant's cries are hushed with *picture-Books;* and the Child sheds his first bitter Tears over the Pages which will render it impossible for him, when a Man, to be treated or governed as a Child. The Cause of our disquietude must be the means of our Tranquillity: only by the Fire, which has burnt us, can we be enlightened to avoid a repetition of the Calamity.

In an Age in which artificial knowledge is received almost at the Birth, Intellect and Thought alone can be our Upholder and Judge. Let the importance of this [88] Truth procure pardon for its repetition. Only by means of Seriousness and Meditation and the free infliction of Censure in the spirit of Love, can the true Philanthropist of the present Time, curb in himself and his Contemporaries; only by these can he aid in preventing the Evils which threaten us, not from the terrors of an Enemy so much as from our fears of our own Thoughts, and our aversion to all the toils of Reflection—1 all must now be taught in sport—Science, Morality, yea, Religion itself. And yet few now sport from the actual impulse of a believing Fancy and in a happy Delusion. Of the most influencive Class, at least, of our literary Guides, (the anonymous Authors of our periodical Publications) the most part assume this Character from Cowardice or Malice, till having begun with studied ignorance and a premeditated levity, they at length realize the Lie, and end indeed in a pitiable destitution of all intellectual power.

To many I shall appear to speak insolently, because the PUBLIC (for that is the phrase which has succeeded to "THE TOWN," of the Wits of the reign of Charles the second)—the Public is at present accustomed to find itself appealed to as the infallible Judge, and each Reader complimented with excellencies, which if he really possessed, to what purpose is he a Reader, unless, perhaps, to remind himself of his own superiority? I confess that I think widely different. I have not a deeper Conviction on

1 For "Reflection—" 1812 reads "Reflection? For".

earth, than that the Principles both of Taste, Morals, and Religion, which are taught in the commonest Books of recent Composition, are false, injurious, and debasing. If my sentiments should be just, the consequences must be so important, that every well-educated Man, who professes them in sincerity, deserves a patient hearing. He may fairly appeal even to those whose persuasions are most opposed to his own, in the words of the Philosopher of Nola: "*Ad ist hæc quæso vos, qualiacunque primo videantur aspectu, adtendite, ut qui vobis forsan insanire videar, saltem quibus insaniam rationibus cognoscatis.*" What I feel deeply, freely will I utter. Truth is not Detraction: and assuredly we do not hate him, to whom we tell the Truth. But with whomsoever we play the Deceiver and Flatterer, him at the bottom we despise. We are indeed under a necessity to conceive a vileness in him, in order to diminish the sense of the Wrong we have committed, by the worthlessness of the object.

Through no excess of confidence in the strength of my talents, but with the deepest assurance of the Justice of my Cause, I bid defiance to all the Flatterers of the [89] Folly and foolish Self-opinion of the half-instructed Many; to all who fill the air with festal explosions and false fires sent up against the lightenings of Heaven, in order that the People may neither distinguish the warning Flash nor hear the threatening Thunder! Do we not stand alone in the World?

> Another year!—another deadly blow!
> Another mighty Empire overthrown!
> And we are left, or shall be left, alone;
> The last that dares to struggle with the Foe.
> 'Tis well! from this day forward we shall know
> That in ourselves our safety must be sought;
> That by our own right hands it must be wrought;
> That we must stand unprop'd or be laid low.
> O Dastard! whom such foretaste doth not cheer!
> We shall exult, if They, who rule the land,
> Be Men who hold its many blessings dear,
> Wise, upright, valiant; not a venal Band,
> Who are to judge of danger which they fear,
> And honour, which they do not understand.
>
> WORDSWORTH

P.S.[1] The next two or three Numbers of the FRIEND will have for their Subjects, Erroneous Principles of Political Philosophy, the Constitution of the British Government as it actually is, and the Principles of international Morality. The Author will then proceed to the Principles of morality, in confutation of the Systems of Hume and Paley,[2] and thence to the Principles of Taste, the insufficiency of the Faculty of Taste in itself to form right Judgements in the fine Arts, especially in Poetry,[3] and the necessary dependance of the Judgement on the moral Character. He will then pro-

---

[1] 1812 omits this entire "P.S.".

[2] Most of these subjects were eventually covered in *The Friend*; see Nos 7–11, 15, 22–4.

[3] See the essays "On the Principles of Genial Criticism Concerning the Fine Arts", which first appeared in *Felix Farley's Bristol Journal* in Aug and Sept 1814, and the "Fragment of an Essay on Taste. 1810", both reprinted in *BL* (1907) II 219–49.

ceed to examine, according to Principles, the Works of our most celebrated ancient and modern English Poets.

As I wish to commence the important Subject of—The *Principles* of political Justice with a separate Number of THE FRIEND,[1] and shall at the same time comply with the wishes communicated to me by one of my female Readers, who writes as the representative of many others: I shall conclude this Number with the following Fragment, or the third and fourth parts of a Tale consisting of six. The two last parts may be given hereafter, if the present should appear to have afforded pleasure, and to have answered the purpose of a relief and amusement to my Readers. The story,[2] as it is contained in the first and second parts, is as follows: Edward, a young farmer, meets at the house of Ellen, her bosom-friend, Mary, and commences an acquaintance, which ends in a mutual attachment. With her consent, and by the advice of their common friend, Ellen, he announces his hopes and intentions to Mary's Mother, a widow-woman bordering on her fortieth year, and from constant Health, the possession of a competent property, and from having had no other children but Mary and another Daughter (the Father died in their infancy) retaining, for the greater part, her personal attractions and comeliness of appearance; but a woman of low education and violent temper.

The answer which she at once returned to Edward's application, was remarkable—"Well, Edward! you are a handsome young fellow: and you shall have my Daughter." From *this* time all their Wooing passed under the Mother's Eyes: and in fine, she became herself enamoured of her future Son in law, and practised every art, both of endearment and of calumny, to transfer his affections from her daughter to herself. (The outlines of the Tale are positive Facts, and of no very distant date, though the author has purposely altered the names and the scene of action, as well as invented the characters [90] of the parties and the detail of the Incidents.) Edward, however, though perplexed by her strange detractions from her daughter's good qualities, yet in the innocence of his own heart still mistaking her encreasing fondness for motherly affection; she at length, overcome by her miserable passion, after much abuse of Mary's Temper and moral tendencies, exclaimed with violent emotion—O Edward! indeed, indeed, she is not fit for you—she has not a heart to love you as you deserve. It is I that love you! Marry me, Edward! and I will this very day settle all my property on you.—The Lover's eyes were now opened: and thus taken by surprize, whether from the effect of the horror which he felt, acting as it were hysterically on his nervous system, or that at the first moment he lost the sense of the guilt of the proposal in the feeling of its' strangeness and absurdity, he flung her from him and burst into a fit of Laughter. Irritated by this almost to frenzy, the Woman fell on her knees, and in a loud voice, that approached to a Scream, she prayed for a Curse both on him and on her own Child. Mary happened to be in the room directly

[1] See below, II 98.
[2] Cf *PW* (EHC) I 267–9, the reprinting (with changes) of this preface to *The Three Graves* as it appeared in

Sibylline Leaves. The two last parts of the poem were never written, and the first two parts (*PW*—EHC—I 269–75) were first published in *PW* (JDC).

above them, heard Edward's Laugh, and her Mother's blasphemous Prayer, and fainted away—He hearing the fall, ran upstairs, and taking her in his arms, carried her off to Ellen's Home; and after some fruitless attempts on her part, toward a reconciliation with her Mother, she was married to him.—And here the third part of the Tale begins.

I was not led to chuse this story from any partiality to tragic, much less, to monstrous events (though at the time that I composed the verses, somewhat more than twelve years ago,[1] I was less averse to such subjects than at present), but from finding in it a striking proof of the possible effect on the imagination, from an Idea violently and suddenly imprest on it. I had been reading Bryan Edwards's account of the effects of the *Oby* Witchcraft on the Negroes in the West Indies, and Hearne's deeply interesting Anecdotes of similar workings on the imagination of the Copper Indians: (those of my Readers, who have it in their power, will be well repaid for the trouble of referring to those Works, for the passages alluded to)[2] and I conceived the design of shewing, that instances of this kind are not peculiar to savage or barbarous tribes, and of illustrating the mode in which the mind is affected in these cases, and the progress and symptoms of the morbid action on the fancy from the beginning.

The Tale is supposed to be narrated by an old Sexton, in a country Church-yard to a Traveller, whose curiosity had been awakened by the appearance of three Graves, close by each other, to two only of which there were Grave-stones. On the first of these was the Name, and Dates, as usual: on the second no name, but only a Date, and the Words: The Mercy of God is infinite.

The language was intended to be *dramatic*, that is, suited to the narrator, and the metre to correspond to the homeliness of the Diction: and for this reason, I here present it not as the Fragment of a *Poem*, but of a Tale in the common ballad metre.[3]

THE THREE GRAVES,

A SEXTON'S TALE[4]

A FRAGMENT

T HE Grapes upon the vicar's wall
Were ripe as they could be;
And yellow leaves in sun and wind
Were falling from the tree.

[1] EHC in *PW* I 267n dates the composition 1798.

[2] See above, I 431n and n 7. See also *CN* II 2297 and n for these works in connexion with *The Three Graves*.

[3] In the preface to *Sibylline Leaves* C wrote that the poem was published "by the decisive recommendation of more than one of our most celebrated living Poets". It was "not presented as poetry" and was "in no way connected with the Author's judgment concerning poetic diction".

[4] In the ms of *The Friend*, cramped between the title and the text of the poem, is a note in C's hand, which has been crossed out: "N.B. Written by Sarah Stoddart for me, while the Book was yet an entire *Blank*. I have not *voluntarily* been guilty of any desacration of holy *Names*": Forster MS 112 f 33ᵛ. EHC (*PW* I 276n) reads ". . . Stoddart before her Brother was an entire Blank", but the writing is clear.

On the hedge-elms in the narrow lane
  Still swung the spikes of Corn:
Dear Lord! it seems but yesterday—
  Young Edward's marriage-morn.
Up thro' that wood behind the Church
  There leads from Edward's door
A mossy Track, all over-bough'd
  For half a mile or more.

[91]   And from their House-door by that Track
  The Bride and Bride-groom went:
Sweet Mary, tho' she was not gay,
  Seem'd cheerful and content.

But when they to the Church yard came,
  I've heard poor Mary say,
As soon as she stepp'd into the Sun,
  Her heart—it died away.

And when the Vicar join'd their hands,
  Her limbs did creep and freeze;
But when he pray'd, she thought she saw
  Her Mother on her knees.

And o'er the Church-path they return'd—
  I saw poor Mary's back
Just as she stepp'd beneath the boughs
  Into the mossy track.

Her feet upon the mossy track
  The Married Maiden set:
That moment—I have heard her say—
  She wish'd she could forget.

The Shade o'er-flush'd her limbs with heat—
  Then came a chill like Death:
And when the merry Bells rang out,
  They seem'd to stop her Breath.

Beneath the foulest Mother's curse
  No child could ever thrive:
A Mother is a Mother still;
  The holiest thing alive.

So five Months pass'd: the Mother still
  Would never heal the strife;
But Edward was a loving Man
  And Mary a fond wife.

"My Sister may not visit us,

The sheets were probably cut out of N 17, for the measurements and the watermark correspond, and some pages have been removed from it. The "holy Names" may refer to "ΣΑΡΑ" and "*Coleridge*", which are written on the top left and right corners of the notebook pages throughout. See *CN* II

General Notes. The prose introduction, however, was especially written for this number of *The Friend*. At the end of the poem in Copy R is C's note (J. Wordsworth "Marginalia" 369): "I regret that I wrote this in verse. You must read it purely as an *exercitatio psychologica*".

My Mother says her, nay:
O Edward! you are all to me,
I wish for your sake, I could be
    More lifesome and more gay.
I'm dull and sad! indeed, indeed
    I know, I have no reason!
Perhaps, I am not well in health,
    And 'tis a gloomy season."
'Twas a drizzly Time—no ice, no snow!
    And on the few fine days
She stirr'd not out lest she might meet
    Her Mother in the ways.
But Ellen, spite of miry ways
    And weather dank and dreary,
Trudg'd every day to Edward's house
    And made them all more cheary.
O! Ellen was a faithful Friend,
    More dear than any Sister!
As chearful too, as singing Lark;
And she ne'er left them till 'twas dark,
    And then they always miss'd her.

[92]

And now Ash-wednesday came—that day
    But few to Church repair:
For on that day you know, we read
    The Commination prayer.
Our late old Vicar, a kind Man,
    Once, Sir! he said to me,
He wish'd that service was clean out
    Of our good Liturgy.
The Mother walk'd into the Church—
    To Ellen's seat she went:
Tho' Ellen always kept her Church
    All Church-days during Lent.
And gentle Ellen welcom'd her
    With courteous looks and mild:
Thought she "what if her heart should melt
    And all be reconcil'd!"
The Day was scarcely like a Day—
    The Clouds were black outright:
And many a night with half a moon
    I've seen the Church more light.
The wind was wild; against the Glass
    The rain did beat and bicker;
The Church-tower singing over head—
    You could not hear the Vicar!
And then and there the Mother knelt
    And audibly she cried—
"O may a clinging curse consume
    This woman by my side!

O hear me, hear me, Lord in Heaven,
    Altho' thou take my life—
O curse this woman at whose house
    Young Edward woo'd his wife.
By night and day, in bed and bower,
    O let her cursed be!"
So having pray'd steady and slow,
    She rose up from her knee;
And left the Church, nor e'er again
    The Church-door entered she.
I saw poor Ellen kneeling still,
    So pale! I guess'd not why:
When she stood up, there plainly was
    A Trouble in her Eye.
And when the Prayers were done, we all
    Came round and ask'd her, why:
Giddy she seem'd and, sure, there was,
    A Trouble in her eye.
But ere she from the Church-door stepp'd,
    She smil'd and told us why:
"It was a wicked Woman's curse,
    Quoth she, and what care I?"
She smil'd and smil'd, and pass'd it off
    Ere from the door she stepp'd—
But all agree it would have been
    Much better, had she wept.

[93]　And if her heart was not at ease,
    This was her constant cry—:
"It was a wicked Woman's curse—
    God's good! and what care I?"
There was a Hurry in her Looks,
    Her struggles she redoubled:
"It was a wicked Woman's curse,
    And why should I be troubled?"
These tears will come! I dandled her,
    When 'twas the merest fairy!—
Good creature!—and she hid it all—
    She told it not to Mary.
But Mary heard the Tale—her arms
    Round Ellen's neck she threw:
"O Ellen, Ellen! She curs'd me,
    And now she has curs'd you!"
I saw young Edward by himself
    Stalk fast adown the lea:
He snatch'd a stick from every Fence,
    A Twig from every Tree.
He snapt them still with hand or knee,
    And then away they flew!
As if with his uneasy Limbs

He knew not what to do!
You see, good Sir! that single Hill?
This Farm lies underneath:
He heard it there—he heard it all,
    And only gnash'd his teeth.
Now Ellen was a darling Love
    In all his joys and cares;
And Ellen's name and Mary's name
Fast link'd they both together came,
    Whene'er he said his prayers.
And in the Moment of his Prayers
    He lov'd them both alike:
Yea, both sweet names with one sweet Joy
    Upon his heart did strike.
He reach'd his home, and by his looks
    They saw his inward strife;
And they clung round him with their arms,
    Both Ellen and his Wife.
And Mary could not check her tears,
    So on his breast she bow'd,
Then frenzy melted into grief
    And Edward wept aloud.
Dear Ellen did not weep at all,
    But closelier she did cling;
And turn'd her face, and look'd as if
    She saw some frightful Thing!

[94]   *THE THREE GRAVES,*

A SEXTON'S TALE

PART IV

To see a man tread over Graves
    I hold it no good mark:
'Tis wicked in the Sun and Moon,
    And bad luck in the dark.
You see that Grave? The Lord he gives,
    The Lord he takes away!
O Sir! the Child of my old Age
    Lies there, as cold as clay.
Except that Grave, you scarce see one
    That was not dug by me:
I'd rather dance upon them all
    Than tread upon these Three!
"Aye Sexton! 'tis a touching Tale—"
    You, Sir! are but a Lad:
This month I'm in my seventieth year
    And still it makes me sad.
And Mary's Sister told it me

For three good hours and more;
Tho' I had heard it in the main
From Edward's self before.
Well, it pass'd off—the gentle Ellen
Did well-nigh dote on Mary;
And she went oft'ner than before,
And Mary lov'd her more and more;
She manag'd all the Dairy.
To market She on Market Days,
To church on Sundays came:
All seem'd the same—all seem'd so, Sir!
But all was not the same.
Had Ellen lost her mirth? O no!
But she was seldom chearful;
And Edward look'd as if he thought
That Ellen's mirth was fearful.
When by herself she to herself
Must sing some merry rhyme—
She could not now be glad for hours
Yet silent all the time.
And when she sooth'd her friend, thro' all
Her soothing words 'twas plain
She had a sore grief of her own,
A Haunting in her brain.
And oft she said, "I'm not grown thin!"
And then her wrist she spann'd;
And once when Mary was downcast,
She took her by the hand,
And gaz'd upon her, and at first
She gently press'd her hand,

[95]

Then harder, till her Grasp at length
Did gripe like a convulsion:
"Alas!" said she—"we ne'er can be
Made happy by compulsion."
And once her both arms suddenly
Round Mary's neck she flung:
And her heart panted, and she felt
The words upon her tongue.
She felt them coming, but no power
Had she the words to smother;
And with a kind of shriek she cried,
"O Christ! you're like your Mother!—"
So gentle Ellen now no more
Could make this sad house cheary;
And Mary's melancholy ways
Drove Edward wild and weary.
Lingering he rais'd his latch at eve
Tho' tir'd in heart and limb:
He lov'd no other place, and yet

Home was no home to Him.[1]
One evening he took up a book
  And nothing in it read;
Then flung it down, and groaning cried,
  "O Heaven! that I were dead!"
Mary look'd up into his face,
  And nothing to him said;
She try'd to smile, and on his arm
  Mournfully lean'd her head!
And he burst into tears, and fell
  Upon his knees in prayers;
"Her heart is broke—O God! my Grief—
  It is too great to bear!"
'Twas such a foggy time as makes
  Old Sexton's Sir! like me,
Rest on their spades to cough; the Spring
  Was late uncommonly.
And then the hot days, all at once
  They came, one knew not how:
You look'd about for shade, when scarce
  A Leaf was on a Bough.
It happen'd then (—twas in the bower
  A furlong up the wood—
Perhaps you know the place, and yet
  I scarce know how you should).
No path leads thither: 'tis not nigh
  To any pasture plot;
But cluster'd near the chattering brook
  Some Hollies mark the spot.
Those Hollies, of themselves, a shape
  As of an arbour took;
A close round Arbour, and it stands
  Not three strides from the Brook.
Within this Arbour, which was still
  With scarlet berries hung,

[96]

Were these three Friends, one Sunday Morn,
  Just as the first bell rung—
'Tis sweet to hear a brook: 'tis sweet
  To hear the Sabbath Bell!
'Tis sweet to hear them both at once
  Deep in a woody Dell.
His Limbs along the moss, his head
  Upon a mossy heap,
With shut-up senses Edward lay:
That Brook, e'en on a working-day,
  Might chatter one to sleep.
And he had pass'd a restless night

[1] For a possible personal connexion with C's own domestic and love prob-lems cf *CL* IV 907, a letter to an un-known correspondent 8 Jan 1819.

And was not well in health!
The Women sate down by his side
And talk'd as 'twere by stealth.
"The Sun peeps thro' the close thick Leaves,
See, dearest Ellen! see—
'Tis *in* the Leaves! a little Sun,
No bigger than your ee.
A tiny Sun! and it has got
A perfect glory too:
Ten thousand threads and hairs of light
Make up a glory gay and bright
Round that small orb so blue."
And then they argued of those Rays
What colour they might be:
Says this, "they're mostly green!" says that,
"They're amber-like to me."
So they sat chatting, while bad thoughts
Were troubling Edward's rest;
But soon they heard his hard quick pants
And the thumping in his breast.
"A Mother too"! these self-same words
Did Edward mutter plain;
His face was drawn back on itself
With horror and huge pain.
Both groan'd at once, for both knew well
What thoughts were in his mind
When he wak'd up, and star'd like one
That hath been just struck blind.
He sate upright; and e're the Dream
Had had time to depart,
"O God, forgive me!" (he exclaim'd)
"I have torn out her heart!"
Then Ellen shriek'd, and forthwith burst
Into ungentle laughter;
And Mary shiver'd, where she sate
And never she smil'd after!

THE FRIEND

No. 7. THURSDAY, September 28, 1809

Dum POLITICI *sæpiuscule hominibus magis insidiantur quam consulunt, potius callidi quam sapientes;* THEORETICI *e contrario se rem divinam facere et sapientiæ culmen attingere credunt, quando humanam naturam, quæ nullibi est, multis modis laudare, et eam, quæ se verâ est, dictis lacessere norunt. Unde factum est, ut nunquam* Politicam *conceperint quæ possit ad usum revocari; sed quæ in Utopiä vel in illo poetarum aureo sæculo, ubi scilicet minime necesse erat, institui potuisset. At mihi plane persuadeo, Experientiam omnia civitatum genera, quæ concipi possunt ut homines concorditer vivant, et simul media, quibus multitudo dirigi, seu quibus intra certos limites contineri debeat, ostendisse: ita ut non credam, nos posse aliquid, quod ab experientâ sive praxi non abhorreat, cogitatione de hac re assequi, quod nondum expertum compertumque sit.*

Cum igitur animum ad Politicam *applicuerim, nihil quod novum vel inauditum est; sed tantum ea quæ cum praxi optime conveniunt, certâ et indubitatâ ratione demonstrare aut ex ipsâ humanæ naturæ conditione deducere, intendi. Et ut ea quæ ad hanc scientiam spectant, eâdem animi libertate, quâ res mathematicas solemus, inquirerem,* sedulo curavi humanas actiones non ridere, non lugere, neque detestari; sed intelligere. *Nec ad imperii securitatem refert quo animo homines inducantur ad res recte administrandum, modo res recte administrentur. Animi enim libertas, seu fortitudo, privata virtus est; at imperii virtus securitas.*

SPINOZA op. Post. p. 267

TRANSLATION

While the mere practical Statesman too often rather *plots* against mankind, than consults their interest, crafty not wise; the mere THEORISTS, on the other hand, imagine that they are employed in a glorious work, and believe themselves at the very summit of earthly Wisdom, when they are able, in set and varied language, to extol that Human Nature, which exists no where (except indeed in their own fancy) and to accuse and vilify our nature as it really is. Hence it has happened, that these men have never conceived a practicable scheme of civil policy, but at best such forms of government only, as might have been instituted in Utopia, or during the golden age of the Poets: that is to say, forms of Government excellently adapted for those who need no government at all. But I am fully persuaded, that experience has already brought to light all conceivable sorts of political Institutions under which human society can be maintained in concord, and likewise the chief means of directing the multitude, or retaining them within given boundaries: so that I can hardly believe, that on this subject the [98] deepest Research would arrive at any result not abhorrent from experience and practice, which has not been already tried and proved.

When, therefore, I applied myself to the study of political Economy, I proposed to myself nothing original or strange as the fruits of my reflections; but simply to demonstrate from plain and undoubted principles, or to deduce from the very condition and necessities of human nature, those plans and maxims which square the best with practice. And that in all things which relate to this province, I might conduct my investigations with the same freedom of intellect with which we proceed in questions of pure science, I sedulously disciplined my mind neither to laugh at, or bewail, or detest, the actions of men; but to understand them. For to the safety of the state it is not of necessary importance, what motives induce men to administer public Affairs rightly, provided only that public Affairs be rightly administered. For moral Strength, or freedom from the selfish Passions, is the Virtue of Individuals; but Security is the Virtue of a State.

ESSAY IV

ON THE PRINCIPLES OF POLITICAL PHILOSOPHY

ALL the different philosophical Systems of political Justice, all the Theories on the rightful Origin of Government, are reducible in the end to three Classes, correspondent to the three different points of view, in which the Human Being itself may be contemplated. The first denies all truth and distinct meaning to the words, RIGHT and DUTY, and affirming that the human mind consists of nothing but manifold modifications of passive sensation, considers Men as the highest sort of Animals indeed, but at the same time the most wretched; inasmuch as their defenceless nature forces them into Society, while such is the multiplicity of Wants engendered by the social state, that the Wishes of one are sure to be in contradiction with those of some other. The Assertors of this System consequently ascribe the Origin and continuance of Government to Fear, or the power of the Stronger, aided by the force of Custom. This is the System of Hobbes. Its Statement is its Confutation. It is, indeed, in the literal sense of the word *preposterous:* for Fear presupposes Conquest, and Conquest a previous union and agreement between the Conquerors. A vast Empire *may* perhaps be governed by Fear; at least the idea is not absolutely inconceivable, under circumstances [99] which prevent the consciousness of a common Strength. A million of men united by mutual Confidence and free intercourse of Thoughts, form one power, and this is as much a Real Thing as a Steam Engine; but a million of insulated Individuals is only an abstraction of the mind, and but one told so many times over without addition, as an Ideot would tell the Clock at noon—one, one, one, &c. But when, in the first Instances, the Descendants of one Family joined together to attack those of another Family, it is impossible that their Chief or Leader should have appeared to them stronger than all the rest together: they must therefore have *chosen* him, and this as for particular purposes, so doubtless under particular Conditions, expressed or understood. Such we know to be the case with the North American Tribes at present; such, we are informed by History, was the case with our own remote Ancestors. Therefore, even on the System of those who, in contempt of the oldest and most authentic records, consider the savage as the first and natural State of Man, Government must have *originated* in Choice and an Agreement. The apparent Exceptions in Africa and Asia are, if possible, still more subversive of this System: for they will be found to have originated in religious Imposture, and the first Chiefs to have secured a *willing* and enthusiastic Obedience to themselves, as Delegates of the Deity.

But the whole Theory is baseless. We are told by History, we learn from our Experience, we know from our own Hearts, that Fear of itself is utterly incapable of producing any regular, continuous and calculable effect, even on an Individual; and that the Fear, which *does* act systematically upon the mind, always presupposes a sense of Duty, as its Cause. The most cowardly of the European Nations, the Neapolitans and Sicilians, those among whom the fear of Death exercises the most tyrannous influence relatively to their own persons, are the very men who least fear to take away the Life of a Fellow-citizen by poison or assassination; while in Great Britain a Tyrant, who has abused the Power, which a vast property has given him, to oppress a whole Neighbourhood, can walk in safety unarmed, and unattended, amid a hundred men, each of whom feels his heart burn with rage and indignation at the sight of him. "It was this Man who broke my Father's heart—" or, "it is through [100] Him that my Children are clad in rags, and cry for the Food which I am no longer able to provide for them." And yet they dare not touch a hair of his head! Whence does this arise? Is it from a cowardice of *sensibility* that makes the injured man shudder at the thought of shedding blood? or from a cowardice of *selfishness* which makes him afraid of hazarding his own Life? Neither the one or the other! The Field of Talavera, as the most recent of an hundred equal proofs, has borne witness,

> That "bring a Briton fra his hill,
> . . . .
> Say, such is Royal George's will,
>   And there's the foe,
> He has nae thought but how to kill
>   Twa at a blow.
>
> Nae cauld, faint-hearted doubtings tease him;
> Death comes, wi' fearless eye he sees him;
> Wi' bloody hand a welcome gies him;
>   And when he fa's
> His latest draught o' breathin leaves him
>   In faint huzzas."

Whence then arises the difference of feeling in the former case? To what does the Oppressor owe his safety? To the spirit-quelling thought: the Laws of God and of my Country have made his Life sacred! I dare not touch a hair of his Head!—"'Tis Conscience that makes Cowards of us all" —but oh! it is Conscience too which makes Heroes of us all.

A truly great Man, (the best and greatest public character that I had ever the opportunity of making myself acquainted with) on assuming the command of a Man of War, found a mutinous Crew, more than one half of them uneducated Irishmen, and of the remainder no small portion had become Sailors by compromise of punishment. What terror could effect by severity and frequency of acts of discipline, had been already effected; and what *was* this effect? Something like that of a Polar Winter on a Flask of Brandy; the furious Spirit concentered itself with ten-fold strength at the heart; open violence was changed into secret plots and conspiracies; and the consequent orderliness of the Crew, as far as they were orderly, was but the brooding of a Tempest. The new Commander instantly commenced a System of Discipline as near as possible to that of ordinary Law—[101] as much as possible, he avoided, in his own person, the appearance of any will or arbitrary power to vary, or to remit, Punishment. The Rules to be observed, were affixed to a conspicuous part of the Ship, with the particular penalties for the breach of each particular rule; and care was taken that every Individual of the Ship should know and understand this Code. With a single exception in the case of mutinous behaviour, a space of twenty four hours was appointed between the first Charge and the second hearing of the Cause, at which time the accused Person was permitted and required to bring forward whatever he thought conducive to his Defence or Palliation. If, as was commonly the case (for the Officers well knew that the Commander would seriously resent in *them* all caprice of will, and by no means permit to others what he denied to himself) if no answer could be returned to the three questions—Did you not commit the act? Did you not know that it was in contempt of such a Rule, and in defiance of such a Punishment? And was it not wholly in your own power to have obeyed the one and avoided the other?—the Sentence was then passed with the greatest solemnity, and another but shorter space of time was again interposed between it and its actual execution. During this space the feelings of the Commander as a Man, were so well blended with his inflexibility as the organ of the Law; and how much he suffered previous to and during the execution of the Sentence, was so well known to the Crew, that it became a common saying with them, when a Sailor was about to be punished, "The Captain takes it more to heart than the Fellow himself." But whenever the Commander perceived any trait of pride in the Offender, or the germs of any noble Feeling, he lost no opportunity of saying—"It is not the pain that you are about to suffer which grieves me! you are none of you, I trust, such Cowards as to turn faint-hearted at the thought of *that!* but that, being a Man, and one who is to fight for his King and Country, you should have made it necessary to treat you as a vicious Beast, it is this that grieves me."

I have been assured, both by a Gentleman who was a Lieutenant on board that Ship at the time when the heroism of its Captain, aided by his characteristic calmness and foresight, greatly influenced the decision of the most glorious Battle recorded in the annals of our naval [102] Glory; and very recently by a grey-headed Sailor, who did not even know my Name, or could have suspected that I was previously acquainted with the circumstances—I have been assured, I say, that the success of this plan was such as astonished the oldest Officers, and convinced the most incredulous. Ruffians, who like the old Buccaneers, had been used to inflict torture on themselves for sport, or in order to harden themselves beforehand, were tamed and overpowered, how or why they themselves knew not. From the fiercest Spirits were heard the most earnest entreaties for the forgiveness of their Commander, not *before* the Punishment, for it was too well known that then they would have been to no purpose, but days after it, when the bodily pain was remembered but as a dream. An *invisible* Power it was, that quelled them, a Power, which was therefore irresistible, because it took away the very Will of resisting? It was the aweful power of L A W, acting on natures pre-configured to its influences. A Faculty was appealed to in the Offender's own being; a Faculty and a Presence, of which he had not been previously made aware—but it *answered* to the appeal! its real Existence therefore could not be doubted, or its reply rendered inaudible! and the very struggle of the wilder Passions to keep uppermost, counteracted its own purpose, by wasting in internal contest that Energy, which before had acted in its entireness on external resistance or provocation. Strength may be met with strength; the Power of inflicting pain may be baffled by the Pride of endurance; the eye of Rage may be answered by the stare of Defiance, or the downcast look of dark and revengeful Resolve; and with all this there is an outward and determined object to which the mind can attach its passions and purposes, and bury its own disquietudes in the full occupation of the Senses. But who dares struggle with an *invisible* Combatant? with an Enemy which exists and makes us know its existence—but *where* it is, we ask in vain?—No Space contains it—Time promises no control over it—it has no ear for my threats—it has no substance, that my hands can grasp, or my weapons find vulnerable—it commands and cannot be commanded—it acts and is insusceptible of my re-action—the more I strive to subdue it, the more am I compelled to think of it—and the more I think of it, the more do I find it to possess a reality out of myself, and not to be a phantom [103] of my own imagination; that all, but the most abandoned men, acknowledge its authority, and that the whole strength and majesty of my Country are pledged to support it; and yet that *for me* its power is the same with that of my own permanent Self, and that all the Choice, which is permitted to me, consists in having it for my Guardian Angel or my avenging Fiend! This is the Spirit of LAW! the Lute of Amphion, the Harp of Orpheus! This is the true necessity, which compels man into the social State, now and always, by a still-beginning, never-ceasing force of moral Cohesion.

Thus is Man to be governed, and thus only can he be *governed*. For from his Creation the objects of his Senses were to become his Subjects, and the Task allotted to him was to subdue the visible World within the sphere of action circumscribed by those Senses, as far as they could act in concert. What the Eye beholds the Hand strives to reach; what it reaches, it conquers and makes the instrument of further conquest. We can be subdued by that alone which is analogous in Kind to that by which we subdue, namely, by the invisible powers of our Nature, whose immediate presence is disclosed to our inner sense, and only as the Symbols and Language of which all shapes and modifications of matter become formidable to us.[1]

A Machine continues to move by the force which first set in it motion. If, therefore, the smallest number in any State, properly so called, hold together through the influence of any Fear that is antecedent to the sense of Duty, it is evident that the State itself could not have commenced through animal Fear. We hear, indeed, of conquests; but how does History represent these? Almost without exception as the substitution of one set of Governors for another: and so far is the Conqueror from relying on Fear alone to secure the obedience of the Conquered, that his first step is to demand an Oath of fealty from them, by which he would impose upon them the belief, that they become *Subjects:* for who would think of

[1] See above, I 172 n 1, for a cancelled passage in the ms of *The Friend.*

administering an Oath to a Gang of Slaves? But what can make the difference between Slave and Subject, if not the existence of an implied Contract in the one case, and not in the other? And to what purpose would a Contract serve if, however it might be *entered into* through Fear, it were deemed binding only in consequence of [104] Fear? To repeat my former illustration—where Fear alone is relied on, as in a Slave Ship, the chains that bind the poor Victims must be material chains: for these only can act upon feelings which have their source wholly in the material Organization. Hobbes has said, that Laws without the Sword are but bits of Parchment. How far this is true, every honest Man's heart will best tell him, if he will content himself with asking his own Heart, and not falsify the answer by his notions concerning the Hearts of other men. But were it true, still the fair answer would be—Well! but without the Laws the Sword is but a piece of Iron. The wretched Tyrant, who disgraces the present Age and Human Nature itself, has exhausted the whole magazine of animal Terror, in order to consolidate his truly satanic Government. But look at the new French Catechism, and in it read the misgivings of the Monster's Mind, as to the sufficiency of Terror alone! The System, which I have been confuting, is indeed so inconsistent with the Facts revealed to us by our own mind, and so utterly unsupported by any Facts of History, that I should be censurable in wasting my own time and my Reader's patience, by the exposure of its falsehood, but that the Arguments adduced have a value of themselves independent of their present application. Else it would have been an ample and satisfactory reply to an Assertor of this bestial Theory—Government is a thing which relates to Men, and what you say applies only to Beasts.

Before I proceed to the second of the three Systems, let me remove a possible misunderstanding that may have arisen from the use of the word Contract: as if I had asserted, that the whole Duty of Obedience to Governors is derived from, and dependent on, the *Fact* of an original Contract. I freely admit, that to make this the Cause and Origin of political Obligation, is not only a dangerous but an absurd Theory; for what could give moral force to the Contract? The same sense of Duty which binds us to keep it, must have pre-existed as impelling us to make it. For what man in his senses would regard the faithful observation of a contract entered into to plunder a Neighbour's House, but as a treble Crime? First the act, which is a crime of itself;—secondly, the entering into a Contract which it is a crime to observe, and yet a weakening of one of the main Pillars of human Confidence [105] *not* to observe, and thus voluntarily placing ourselves under the necessity of chusing between two evils;—and thirdly, the crime of chusing the greater of the two evils, by the unlawful observance of an unlawful Promise. But in my sense, the word Contract is merely synonimous with the sense of Duty acting in a specific direction and determining our moral relations, as members of a body politic. If I have referred to a supposed *origin* of Government, it has been in courtesy to a common notion: for I myself regard the supposition as no more than a means of simplifying to our Apprehension the ever-continuing causes of social union, even as the Conservation of the World may be represented as an act of continued Creation. For, what if an original Contract had *really* been entered into, and formally recorded? Still it could do no more than bind the contracting parties to act for the general good in the best manner, that the existing relations among themselves, (state of property, religion, &c.) on the one hand, and the external circumstances on the other (ambitious or barbarous Neighbours, &c.) required or permitted. In after times it could be appealed to only for the general principle, and no more, than the ideal Contract, could it affect a question of ways and means. As each particular Age brings with it its own exigencies, so must it rely on its own prudence for the specific measures by which they are to be encountered.

Nevertheless, it assuredly cannot be denied, that an original (in reality, rather an ever-originating) Contract is a very natural and significant mode of expressing the reciprocal duties of Subject and Sovereign, when we consider the utility of a real and formal State Contract, the Bill of Rights for instance, as a sort of *Est demonstratum* in politics; and the contempt lavished on this notion, though sufficiently compatible with the Tenets of a Hume, may well surprize us in the Writings of a Protestant Clergyman, who surely owed some respect to a mode of thinking which God himself had authorized by his own example, in the establishment of the Jewish Constitution. In this instance there was no necessity for *deducing* the will of God from the tendency of the laws to the general Happiness: his will was expressly declared. Nevertheless, it seemed good to the divine Wisdom, that there should be a covenant, an original contract, between himself as Sovereign, and the Hebrew Nation as Subjects. [106] This, I admit, was a *written* and formal Contract; but the Relations of Mankind, as members of a Body Spiritual, or religious Commonwealth, to the Saviour, as its' Head or Regent—is not this too styled a Covenant, though it would be absurd to ask for the material Instrument that contained it, or the time when it was signed or voted by the members of the Church collectively*?

With this explanation, the assertion of an original (still better, of a *perpetual*) Contract is rescued from all rational objection; and however speciously it may be urged, that History can scarcely produce a single example of a State dating its primary Establishment from a free and mutual Covenant, the answer is ready: if there be any difference between a Government and a band of Robbers, an act of consent must be supposed on the part of the People governed. Le plus Fort n'est jamais assez fort pour être *toujours* le maitre, s'il ne transforme sa force en droit et l'obeissance en devoir. Rousseau.—*Viribus* parantur provinciæ, *jure* retinentur. Igitur *breve* id gaudium, quippe Germani victi magis, quam domiti. Flor. iv. 12.

The second System corresponds to the second point of view under which the Human Being may be considered, namely, as an animal gifted with Understanding, or the faculty of suiting Measures to Circumstances. According to this Theory, every Institution of national origin needs no other Justification than a proof, that under the particular circumstances it

---

* It is perhaps to be regretted, that the words, old and new Testament, they having lost the sense intended by the Translators of the Bible, have not been changed into the old and new Covenant. We cannot too carefully keep in sight a notion, which appeared to the primitive Church the fittest and most scriptural mode of representing the sum of the Contents of the sacred Writings.

is EXPEDIENT. Having in my former Numbers expressed myself (so at least I am conscious I shall have appeared to do to many Persons) with comparative slight of the Understanding considered as the sole Guide of human Conduct, and even with something like contempt and reprobation of the maxims of Expedience, when represented as the only steady Light of the Conscience, and the absolute Foundation of all Morality; I shall perhaps seem guilty of an inconsistency, in declaring myself an Adherent of this second System, a zealous Advocate for deriving the origin [107] of all Government from human *Prudence*, and of deeming that to be just which Experience has proved to be expedient. From this charge of inconsistency* I shall best exculpate myself by the full statement of the third System, and by the exposition of its Grounds and Consequences.

* Distinct notions [1] do not suppose different *things.* When we make a threefold distinction in human nature, we are fully aware, that it is a distinction not a division, and that in every act of mind the *Man* unites the properties of Sense, Understanding, and Reason. Nevertheless, it is of great practical importance, that these distinctions should be made and understood, the ignorance or perversion of them being alike injurious; as the first French Constitution has most lamentably proved. It was fashion in the profligate times of Charles the second, to laugh at the Presbyterians, for distinguishing between the Person and the King; while in fact they were ridiculing the most venerable maxims of English Law.—The King never dies—The King can do no wrong, &c. and subverting the principles of genuine *Loyalty*, in order to prepare the minds of the People for Despotism.

Under the term SENSE, I comprize whatever is passive in our being, without any reference to the questions of Materialism or Immaterialism, all that Man is in common with animals, in *kind* at least—his sensations, and impressions whether of his outward senses, or the inner sense.[2] This in the language of the Schools, was called the vis receptiva, or *recipient* property of the soul, from the original constitution of which we perceive and imagine all things under the forms of Space and Time. By the Understanding,[3] I mean the faculty of thinking and forming *judgements* on the notices furnished by the Sense, according to certain rules existing in itself, which rules constitute its distinct nature. By the pure Reason,[4] I mean the power by which we become possessed of Principle, (the eternal Verities of Plato and Descartes) and of Ideas, (N.B. not images) as the ideas of a point, a line, a circle, in Mathematics; and of Justice, Holiness, Free-Will, &c. in Morals. Hence in works of pure Science the Definitions of necessity precede the Reasoning, in other works they more aptly form the Conclusion. I am not asking my Readers to admit the truth of these distinctions at present, but only to understand my words in the same sense in which I use them.

To many of my Readers it will, I trust, be some recommendation of these distinctions, that they are more than once expressed, and every where supposed, in the writings of St. Paul. I have no hesitation in undertaking to prove, that every Heresy which has disquieted the Christian Church, from Tritheism to Socinianism, has originated in and supported itself by, arguments rendered plausible only by the confusion of these faculties, and thus demanding for the Objects of one, a sort of evidence appropriated to those of another faculty.—

[1] For "notions" 1812 reads *"notions"*.   "UNDERSTANDING".
[2] 1812 adds "of Imagination".   [4] For "Reason" 1812 reads "REA-
[3] For "Understanding" 1812 reads   SON".

The third and last System then denies all rightful origin to Governments, except as far as they are derivable [108] from Principles contained in the REASON of Man, and judges all the relations of men in Society by the Laws of moral necessity, according to IDEAS (I here use the word in its highest and primitive sense, and as nearly synonimous with the modern word *ideal*) according to archetypal IDEAS co-essential with the Reason, and the consciousness of which is the sign and necessary product of its full developement. The following then is the fundamental Principle of this Theory: Nothing is to be deemed rightful in civil Society, or to be tolerated as such, but what is capable of being demonstrated out of the original Laws of the pure Reason. Of course, as there is but one System of Geometry, so according to this Theory there can be but one Constitution and one System of Legislation, and this consists in the freedom, which is the common Right of all Men, under the control of that moral necessity, which is the common Duty of all men. Whatever is not *every where* necessary, is *no where* right. On this assumption the whole Theory is built. To state it nakedly is to confute it satisfactorily. So at least it should seem! But in how winning and specious a manner this System may be represented even to minds of the loftiest order, if undisciplined, and unhumbled, by practical Experience, has been proved by the general impassioned admiration and momentous effects of Rousseau's *Du Contrat Social*, and the Writings of the French Economists, or as they more appropriately entitled themselves, *Physiocratic* Philosophers: and in how tempting and dangerous a manner it may be represented to the Populace, has been made too evident in our own Country, by the temporary effects of Paine's Rights of Man. Relatively, however, to this latter Work it should be observed, that it is not a *legitimate* Offspring of any one Theory, but a confusion of the immorality of the first System with the misapplied universal Principles of the last: and in this union, or rather lawless alternation, consists the essence of JACOBINISM, as far as Jacobinism is any thing but a term of abuse, or has any meaning of its own distinct from Democracy and Sedition.

A Constitution equally suited to China and America, or to Russia and Great Britain, must surely be equally unfit for both, and deserve as little respect in political, as a Quack's panacæa in medical, Practice. Yet there are [109] three weighty motives for a distinct exposition of this* Theory, and of the ground on which its' pretensions are bottomed: and I dare

---

These disquisitions have the misfortune of being in ill-report, as dry and unsatisfactory; but I hope, in the course of the work, to gain them a better character —and if elucidations of their practical importance from the most momentous events of History, can render them interesting, to give them that interest at least. Besides, there is surely some good in the knowledge of Truth, as Truth—(we were not made to live by Bread alone) and in the strengthening of the intellect. It is an excellent Remark of Scaliger's—"*Harum indagatio Subtilitatum, etsi non est utilis ad machinas farinarias conficiendas, exuit animum tamen inscitiæ rubigine acuitque ad alia.*" SCALIG. Exerc. 307. §§ 3. i.e. The investigation of these Subtleties, though it is of no use to the construction of machines to grind corn with, yet clears the mind from the rust of Ignorance, and sharpens it for other things.

* As "METAPHYSICS" are the science which determines what can, and what can not, be known of Being, and the Laws of Being, *a priori* (that is from those

affirm, that for the same reasons there are few subjects which in the present state of the World have a fairer claim to the attention of every serious Englishman, who is likely, directly or indirectly, as Partizan or as Opponent, to interest himself in schemes of Reform. The first motive is derived from the propensity of mankind to mistake the feelings of disappointment, disgust, and abhorrence occasioned by the unhappy effects or accompaniments of a particular System for an insight into the falsehood of its Principles which alone can secure its permanent rejection. For by a wise ordinance of Nature our feelings have no abiding-place in our memory, nay the more vivid they are in the moment of their existence the more dim and difficult to be remembered do they make the thoughts which accompanied them. Those of my Readers who at any time of their life have been in the habit of reading Novels may easily convince themselves of this Truth by comparing their recollections of those Stories which most excited their curiosity and even painfully affected their feelings, with their recollections of the calm and meditative pathos of Shakespere and Milton. Hence it is that human experience, like the Stern lights of a Ship at Sea, illumines only the path which we have passed over. The horror of the Peasants' War in Germany, and the direful effects of the Anabaptist Tenets, which were only nominally different from those of Jacobinism by the substitution of religious for philosophical jargon, struck all Europe for a time with affright. Yet little more than a Century was sufficient to obliterate all effective memory of those events: the same Principles budded forth anew and produced the same fruits from the imprisonment of Charles the first to the Restoration of his Son. In the succeeding Generations to the follies and vices of the European Courts, and to the oppressive privileges of the Nobility, were again transferred those feelings of disgust [110] and hatred, which for a brief while the Multitude had attached to the Crime[4] and Extravagances of political and religious Fanaticisms: and the same principles aided by circumstances and dressed out in the ostentatious garb of a fashionable Philosophy, once more rose triumphant, and effected the French Revolution. That Man has reflected little on Human Nature who does not perceive that the detestable maxims and correspondent crimes of the existing French Despotism, have already dimmed the recollections of the democratic phrenzy in the minds of men; by little and little, have drawn off to other objects the electric force of the feelings, which had massed and upheld those recollections; and that a favourable concurrence of Occasions is alone wanting to awaken the Thunder and precipitate the Lightening from the opposite quarter of the political Heaven. The true

---

necessities of the mind, or *forms*[1] of thinking, which, though first revealed to us by experience, must yet have pre-existed in order to make experience itself possible, even as the eye must exist previously[2] to any particular act of seeing, though by sight only can we know, that we have eyes)—so might the philosophy of Rousseau and his followers not inaptly be entitled, METAPOLITICS, and the Doctors of this School *Metapoliticians*.[3]

[1] For "*forms*" 1812 reads "forms".
[2] For "previously" 1812 reads "previous".

[3] For "*Metapoliticians*" 1812 reads "Metapoliticians".
[4] For "Crime" 1812 reads "Crimes".

origin of Human Events is so little susceptible of that kind of evidence which can compel our Belief even against our Will; and so many are the disturbing forces which modify the motion given by the first projection; and every Age has, or imagines it has its own circumstances which renders [1] past experience no longer applicable to the present case; that there will never be wanting answers, and explanations, and specious flatteries of hope. I well remember, that when the Examples of former Jacobins, Julius Cæsar, Cromwell, &c. were adduced in France and England at the commencement of the French Consulate, it was ridiculed as pedantry and Pedants ignorance, to fear a repetition of such Usurpation at the close of *the enlightened eighteenth Century.* Those who possess the *Moniteurs* of that date will find set proofs, that such results were little less than impossible, and that it was an insult to so philosophical an Age, and so enlightened a Nation, to dare direct the public eye towards them as Lights of admonition and warning.

It is a common foible with official Statesmen, and with those who deem themselves honoured by their acquaintance, to attribute great national Events to the influence of particular Persons, to the errors of one man and to the intrigues of another, to any possible spark of a particular occasion, rather than to the true cause, the predominant state of public Opinion. I have known Men who, with most significant nods, and the civil contempt of pitying half smiles, have declared the natural explanation of the French Revolution, to be the mere fancies of *Garretteers*, and then [111] with the solemnity of the Cabinet Minister,[2] have proceeded to explain the whole by —ANECDOTES. It is so stimulant to the pride of a vulgar mind, to be persuaded that it knows what few others know, and that it is the important depository of a sort of State Secret, by communicating which it confers an obligation on others! But I have likewise met with men of intelligence, who at the commencement of the Revolution were travelling on foot through the French Provinces, and they bear witness, that in the remotest Villages, every tongue was employed in echoing and enforcing the Doctrines of the Parisian Journalists, that the public Highways were crowded with Enthusiasts, some shouting the Watch-words of the Revolution, others disputing on the most abstract Principles of the universal Constitution, which they fully believed, that all the Nations of the Earth were shortly to adopt; the most ignorant among them confident of his fitness for the highest duties of a Legislator; and all prepared to shed their blood in the defence of the inalienable Sovereignty of the self-governed People. The more abstract the notions were, with the closer affinity did they combine with the most fervent feelings and[3] the immediate impulses to action. The Lord Chancellor Bacon lived in an Age of Court intrigues, and[4] familiarly acquainted with all the secrets of personal influence. He, if any Man, was qualified to take the guage and measurement of their comparative power, and he has told us, that there is one and but one infallible source of political prophesy, the knowledge of the predominant Opinions and the speculative Principles of men in general between the age of twenty and thirty. Sir Philip Sidney,

---

[1] For "renders" 1812 reads "render".
[2] For "the Cabinet Minister" 1812 reads "Cabinet Ministers".

[3] 1812 adds "all".
[4] 1812 adds "was".

the Favourite of Queen Elizabeth, the paramount Gentleman of Europe, the Nephew, and (as far as a good Man could be) the Confident[1] of the intriguing and dark-minded Earl of Leicester, was so deeply convinced that the Principles diffused through the majority of a Nation are the true Oracles from whence Statesmen are to learn wisdom, and that "when the People speak loudly it is from their being strongly possessed either by the Godhead or the Dæmon," that in the Revolution of the Netherlands he considered the universal adoption of one set of Principles, as a proof of the divine Presence. "If her Majesty," says he, "were the fountain; I would fear, considering what I daily find, that we should wax dry. But she is but a means which God useth." But if my Readers which[2] to see the Question of the efficacy of Principles and popular Opinions [112] for evil and for good proved and illustrated with an eloquence worthy of the Subject, I can refer him[3] with the hardiest anticipation of his[4] thanks, to the late Work "concerning the Relations of Great Britain, Spain, and Portugal," by my honoured Friend William Wordsworth* *quem quoties lego, non verba mihi videor audire, sed tonitrua!*

(*To be continued*)[5]

* I consider this reference to, and strong recommendation of the Work above-mentioned, not as a voluntary tribute of admiration, but as an act of mere justice both to myself and to the Readers of THE FRIEND. My own heart bears me witness, that I am actuated by the deepest sense of the truth of the Principles, which it has been and still more will be my endeavour to enforce, and of their paramount importance to the Well-being of Society at the present juncture: and that the duty of making the attempt, and the hope of not wholly failing in it, are, far more than the wish for the doubtful good of literary reputation or any yet meaner object, are my great and ruling Motives. Mr. Wordsworth I deem a fellow-labourer in the same vineyard, actuated by the same motives and teaching the same principles, but with far greater powers of mind, and an eloquence more adequate to the importance and majesty of the Cause. I am strengthened too by the knowledge, that I am not unauthorized by the sympathy of many wise and good men, and men acknowledged as such by the Public, in my admiration of his Pamphlet.—*Neque enim debet operibus ejus obesse, quod vivit. An si inter eos, quos nunquam vidimus, floruisset, non solum libros ejus, verum etiam imagines conquireremus, ejusdem nunc honor præsentis, et gratia quasi satietate languescit. At hoc pravum, malignumque est, non admirari hominem admiratione dignissimum, quia videre, complecti, nec laudare tantum, verum etiam amare contingit.* PLIN. Epist Lib. I.

It is hardly possible for a man of ingenuous mind to act under the fear that it shall be suspected by honest Men of the vileness of praising a Work to the Public, merely because he happens to be personally acquainted with the Author. That this is so commonly done in Reviews, furnishes only an additional proof of the morbid hardness produced in the moral sense by the habit of writing anonymous criticisms, especially under the further disguise of a pretended Board or Association of Critics, each man expressing himself to use the words of Andrew Marvel, as a *synodical individuum.* With regard however, to the probability of the Judgement being warped by partiality, I can only say that I judge of all

---

1 For "Confident" 1812 reads "Con-
fidante".
2 For "which" 1812 reads "wish".
3 For "him" 1812 reads "them".
4 For "his" 1812 reads "their".
5 1812 omits.

Works indifferently by certain fixed rules previously formed in my mind with all the power and vigilance of my Judgement; and that I should certainly of the two apply them with greater rigour to the production of a Friend than that of a Person indifferent to me. These Canons of criticism with the grounds on which each of them have been established, I shall lay before my Readers, preparatory to an analysis according to principles, of the merits and demerits of the ancient and modern English Poets.[1] But wherever I find in any Work all the conditions of excellence in its kind, it is not the accident of the Authors being my Contemporary or even my Friend, or the sneers of bad-hearted Men, that shall prevent me from speaking of it, as in my inmost convictions, I deem it deserves.

—————————————————————no, friend!
Though it be now the Fashion to commend,
As men of strong minds, those alone who can
Censure with judgement, no such piece of man
Makes up my spirit: where desert does live,
There will I plant my wonder, and there give
My best endeavours to build up his glory,
That truly merits!

Recommendatory Verses to one of the old Plays

[1] Cf above, II 87–8; a promise not fulfilled in *The Friend.*

THE FRIEND

(Continued from page 112.)

That erroneous political notions (they having become general and a part of the popular creed), have practical consequences, and these, of course, of a most fearful nature, is a Truth as certain as historic evidence can make it: and that when the feelings excited by these Calamities have passed away, and the interest in them has been displaced by more recent events, the same Errors are likely to be started afresh, pregnant with the same Calamities, is an evil rooted in Human Nature in the present state of general information, for which we have hitherto found no *adequate* remedy. (It may, perhaps, in the scheme of Providence, be proper and conducive to its ends, that no adequate remedy should exist: for the folly of men is the wisdom of God.) But if there be any means, if not of preventing yet of palliating the disease, and in the more favoured nations, of checking its progress at the first symptoms; and if these means are to be at all compatible with the civil and intellectual Freedom of Mankind, they are to be found only in an intelligible and thorough exposure of the error and through that discovery of the source, from which it derives its speciousness and powers of influence, on the human mind. This therefore is my first motive for undertaking the disquisition.

The second is, that though the French Code of revolutionary Principles, is now generally rejected as a *System*, yet every where in the speeches, and writings, of the English Reformers, nay, not seldom in those of their Opponents, I find certain maxims asserted or appealed to, which are not tenable, except as constituent parts of that System. Many of the most specious arguments in proof of the imperfection and injustice of the present Constitution of our Legislature will be found, on closer examination, to presuppose the truth of certain Principles, from which the Adducers of these arguments loudly profess their dissent. But in political changes no permanence [114] can be hoped for in the edifice, without consistency in the Foundation. The third motive is, that by detecting the true source of the influence of these Principles, we shall at the same time discover their natural place and object: and that in themselves they are not only Truths, but most important and sublime Truths, and that their falsehood and their danger consist altogether in their misapplication. Thus the dignity of Human Nature will be secured, and at the same time a lesson of Humility taught to each Individual, when we are made to see that the universal necessary Laws, and pure IDEAS of Reason, were given us, not for the[1] purpose of flattering our Pride and enabling us to become national Legis-

---

[1] 1812 omits "the".

lators, but that by an energy of continued self-conquest, we might establish
a free and yet absolute Government in our own Spirits.

ESSAY V

THE Intelligence, which produces or controls human actions and occurrences, is often represented by the Mystics under the name and notion
of the supreme Harmonist. I do not myself approve of these metaphors:
they seem to imply a restlessness to understand that which is not among
the appointed objects of our comprehension or discursive faculty.
But certainly there is one excellence in good music, to which, without
mysticism, we may find or make an analogy in the records of History.
I allude to that sense of *recognition*, which accompanies our sense of
novelty in the most original passages of a great Composer. If we listen
to a Symphony of CIMAROSA, the present strain still seems not only to
recal, but almost to *renew*, some past movement, another and yet the same!
Each present movement bringing back, as it were, and embodying the
Spirit of some melody that had gone before, anticipates and seems trying
to overtake something that is to come: and the Musician has reached the
summit of his art, when having thus modified the Present by the Past, he at
the same time weds the Past *in* the Present to some prepared and corres-
ponsive Future. The Auditor's thoughts and feelings move under the same
influence: retrospection blends with anticipation, and Hope and Memory (a
[115] female Janus) become one Power with a double Aspect. A similar
effect the Reader may produce for himself in the pages of History, if he will
be content to substitute an intellectual complacency for pleasurable sensation. The Events and Characters of one Age, like the Strains in Music,
recal those of another, and the variety by which each is individualized, not
only gives a charm and poignancy to the resemblance, but likewise renders
the whole more intelligible. Meantime, ample room is afforded for the
exercise both of the Judgement and the Fancy, in distinguishing cases of
real resemblance from those of intentional imitation, the analogies of
Nature revolving upon herself, from the masquerade Figures of Cunning
and Vanity.

It is not from identity of opinions, or from similarity of events and
outward actions, that a real resemblance in the radical character can be
deduced. On the contrary, Men of great and stirring Powers, who are
destined to mould the Age in which they are born, must first mould
themselves upon it. Mahomet born twelve Centuries later, and in the
heart of Europe, would not have been a false Prophet; nor would a false
Prophet of the present Generation have been a Mahomet in the sixth Century. I have myself, therefore, derived the deepest interest from the
comparison of Men, whose Characters at the first view appear widely dissimilar, who yet have produced similar effects on their different Ages, and
this by the exertion of powers which on examination will be found far more
alike, than the altered drapery and costume would have led us to suspect.
Of the Heirs of Fame few are more respected by me, though for very different qualities, than Erasmus and Luther: scarcely any one has a larger
share of my aversion than Voltaire; and even of the better-hearted Rousseau I was never more than a very lukewarm admirer. I should perhaps

too rudely affront the general opinion, if I avowed my whole Creed concerning the proportions of real Talent between the two Purifiers of revealed Religion, now neglected as obsolete, and the two modern Conspirators against its' authority, who are still the Alpha and Omega of Continental Genius. Yet when I abstract the questions of evil and good, and measure only the *effects* produced and the *mode* of producing them, I have repeatedly found the idea of Voltaire, Rousseau, and Robespierre, recal in a [116] similar cluster and connection that of Erasmus, Luther, and Munster.

Those who are familiar with the Works of Erasmus, and who know the influence of his Wit, as the Pioneer of the Reformation; and who likewise know, that by his Wit, added to the vast variety of knowledge communicated in his Works, he had won over by anticipation so large a part of the polite and lettered World to the Protestant Party, will be at no loss in discovering the intended counterpart in the Life and Writings of the veteran Frenchman. They will see, indeed, that the knowledge of the one was solid through its whole extent, and that of the other extensive at a cheap rate, by its superficiality; that the Wit of the one is always bottomed on sound sense, peoples and enriches the mind of the Reader with an endless variety of distinct images and living interest; and that his broadest laughter is every where translatable into grave and weighty truth: while the wit of the Frenchman, without imagery, without character, and without that pathos which gives the magic charm to genuine humour, consists, when it is most perfect in happy turns of phrase, but far too often in fantastic incidents, outrages of the pure imagination, and the poor low trick of combining the ridiculous with the venerable, where he, who does not laugh, abhors. Neither will they have forgotten, that the object of the one was to drive the Thieves and Mummers out of the Temple, while the other was propelling a worse Banditti, first to profane and pillage, and ultimately to raze it. Yet not the less will they perceive, that the *effects* remain parallel, the *circumstances* analagous, and the *instruments* the same. In each case the *effects* extended over Europe, were attested and augmented by the praise and patronage of thrones and dignities, and are not to be explained but by extraordinary industry and a life of Literature; in both instances the *circumstances* were supplied by an Age of Hopes and Promises—the Age of Erasmus restless from the first vernal influences of real knowledge, that of Voltaire from the hectic of imagined superiority: in the voluminous Works of both, the *instruments* employed are chiefly those of wit and amusive erudition, and alike in both the Errors and Evils (real or imputed) in Religion and Politics, are the objects of the Battery. And here we must stop. The two *Men* were *essentially* different. [117] Exchange mutually their dates and spheres of action, yet Voltaire, had he been ten-fold a Voltaire, could not have made up an Erasmus; and Erasmus must have emptied himself of half his greatness and all his goodness, to have become a Voltaire.

Shall we succeed better or worse with the next pair, in this our new Dance of Death, or rather of the Shadows which we have brought forth—two by two—from the historic Ark? In our first couple we have at least secured an honourable retreat, and though we failed as to the *Agents*, we have maintained a fair analogy in the *Actions* and the Objects. But the heroic

LUTHER, a Giant awaking in his strength! and the crazy ROUSSEAU, the Dreamer of love-sick Tales, and the Spinner of speculative Cobwebs; shy of light as the Mole, but as quick-eared too for every whisper of the public opinion; the Teacher of stoic *Pride* in his Principles, yet the Victim of morbid *Vanity* in his Feelings and Conduct! from what point of Likeness can we commence the Comparison between a Luther and a Rousseau? And truly had I been seeking for Characters that taken, as they really existed, closely resemble each other, and this too to our first apprehensions, and according to the common rules of biographical comparison, I could scarcely have made a more unlucky choice: unless I had desired that my Parallel of the German "Son of Thunder" and the Visionary of Geneva, should sit on the same bench with honest Fluellin's of Alexander the Great and Harry of Monmouth. Still, however, the same analogy would hold as in my former instance: the effects produced on their several Ages by Luther and Rousseau, were commensurate with each other, and were produced in both cases by (what their Contemporaries felt as) serious and vehement eloquence, and an elevated tone of moral feeling: and Luther, not less than Rousseau, was actuated by an almost superstitious hatred of Superstition, and a turbulent prejudice against Prejudices. In the relation too which their Writings severally bore to those of Erasmus and Voltaire, and the way in which the latter co-operated with them to the same general end, each finding its' own class of Admirers and Proselytes, the Parallel is complete. I cannot, however, rest here! Spite of the apparent incongruities, I am disposed to plead for a resemblance in the Men themselves, for that similarity in their *radical* natures, which I abandoned all pretence and desire of [118] shewing in the instances of Voltaire and Erasmus. But then my Readers must think of Luther not as he really was, but as he might have been, if he had been born in the Age and under the Circumstances of the Swiss Philosopher. For this purpose I must strip him of many advantages which he derived from his own Times, and must contemplate him in his natural weaknesses as well as in his original strength. Each referred all things to his own Ideal. The Ideal was indeed widely different in the one and in the other: and this was not the least of Luther's many advantages, or (to use a favourite phrase of his own) not one of his least favours of preventing Grace. Happily for him he had derived his standard from a common measure already received by the Good and Wise: I mean the inspired Writings, the study of which Erasmus had previously restored among the Learned. To know that[1] we are in sympathy with others, moderates our feelings as well as strengthens our convictions: and for the mind, which opposes itself to the faith of the multitude, it is more especially desirable, that there should exist an object out of itself, on which it may fix its attention, and thus balance its own energies.

Rousseau, on the contrary, in the inauspicious Spirit of his Age and Birth-place,* had slipped the Cable of his Faith, and steered by the

---

* Infidelity was so common in Geneva about that Time, that Voltaire in one of his Letters exults, that in this, Calvin's own City, some half dozen only of the most ignorant believed in Christianity under any form. This was, no doubt,

[1] For "that" 1812 reads "what".

Compass of unaided Reason, ignorant of the hidden Currents that were bearing him out of his Course, and too proud to consult the faithful Charts prized and held sacred by his Forefathers. But the strange influences of his bodily temperament on his understanding; his constitutional Melancholy pampered into a morbid excess by solitude; his wild Dreams of suspicion; his hypochondriacal Fancies of hosts of conspirators all leagued against him and his cause, and headed by some arch-enemy, to whose machinations he attributed every trifling mishap (all as much the creatures of his imagination, as if instead of Men he had conceived them to be infernal Spirits and Beings preternatural)—these, or at least the predisposition to them, existed in [119] the ground-work of his Nature: they were parts of Rousseau himself. And what corresponding in *kind* to these, not to speak of *degree*, can we detect in the Character of his supposed Parallel? This difficulty will suggest itself at the first thought, to those who derive all their knowledge of Luther from the meagre biography met with in "The Lives of eminent Reformers," or even from the ecclesiastical Histories of Mosheim or Milner: for a Life of Luther, in extent and style of execution proportioned to the grandeur and interest of the Subject, a Life of the *Man* Luther, as well as of Luther the *Theologian*, is still a desideratum in English Literature, though perhaps there is no Subject for which so many unused materials are extant, both printed and in manuscript.*

Whoever has sojourned in Eisenach, will assuredly have visited the †WARTEBURG, interesting by so many historical Associations, which stands on a high rock, about two miles to the south from the City Gate. To this Castle Luther was taken on his return from the imperial Diet, where Charles the fifth had pronounced the ban upon him, and limited his safe convoy to one and twenty days. On the last but one of these days, as he was on his way to Waltershausen (a town in the dutchy of Saxe Gotha, a few leagues to the south east of Eisenach) he was stopped in a hollow behind the Castle Altenstein, and carried to the Warteburg. The Elector of Saxony, who could not have refused to deliver up Luther, as one put in the ban by the Emperor and the Diet, had ordered John of Berleptsch, the Governor of the Warteburg, and Burckhardt von Hundt, the Governor of Altenstein, to take Luther to one or the other of these Castles, without acquainting him which; in order that he might be able, with safe conscience, to declare, that he did not know where Luther was. Accordingly they took

---

one of Voltaire's usual lies of exaggeration: it is not however to be denied, that here, and throughout Switzerland, he and the dark Master in whose service he employed himself, had ample grounds of triumph.

* The affectionate respect in which I hold the name of Dr. Jortin (one of the many illustrious Nurslings of the College to which I deem it no small honour to have belonged—Jesus, Cambridge) renders it painful to me to assert, that the above remark holds almost equally true of a Life of Erasmus. But every Scholar well read in the Writings of Erasmus and his illustrious Contemporaries, must have discovered, that Jortin had neither collected sufficient, nor the best, materials for his Work: and (perhaps from that very cause) he grew weary of his task, before he had made a full use of the scanty materials which he had collected.

† *Durch fluge durch Deutschland, die Niederlande und Frankreich: zweit. Theil,* *p.* 126.

him to the [120] Warteburg, under the name of the Chevalier (Ritter) George.

To this friendly Imprisonment the Reformation owes many of Luther's most important labours. In this Place he wrote his Works against auricular Confession, against Jacob Latronum, the tract on the abuse of Masses, that against clerical and monastic Vows, composed his Exposition of the 22, 27, and 68 Psalms, finished his Declaration of the Magnificat, began to write his Church Homilies, and translated the New Testament. Here too, and during this time, he is said to have hurled his inkstand at the Devil, the black spot from which yet remains on the stone wall of the room he studied in; which, surely, no one will have visited the Warteburg without having had pointed out to him by the good Catholic who is, or at least some few years ago was, the Warden of the Castle. He must have been either a very supercilious or a very incurious Traveller if he did not, for the gratification of his Guide at least, inform himself by means of his Penknife, that the said marvellous blot bids defiance to all the toils of the scrubbing Brush, and is to remain a sign for ever; and with this advantage over most of its kindred, that being capable of a double interpretation, it is equally flattering to the Protestant and the Papist, and is regarded by the wonder-loving Zealots of both Parties, with equal Faith.

Whether the great Man ever did throw his inkstand at his Satanic Majesty, whether he ever boasted of the Exploit, and himself declared the dark blotch on his Study Wall in the Warteburg, to be the result and relict of this Author-like hand-grenado (happily for mankind he used his inkstand at other times to better purpose, and with more effective hostility against the Arch-fiend), I leave to my Readers own Judgement; on condition, however, that he has previously perused Luther's Table Talk, and other Writings of the same stamp, of some of his most illustrious Contemporaries, which contain facts still more strange and whimsical, related by themselves and of themselves, and accompanied with solemn protestations of the Truth of their statements. Luther's Table Talk, which to a truly philosophic mind, will not be less interesting than Rousseau's Confessions, I have not myself the means of consulting at present, and cannot therefore say, whether this ink-pot Adventure is, or is [121] not, told or referred to in it; but many considerations incline me to give credit to the Story.

Luther's unremitting literary Labour and his sedentary mode of Life, during his confinement in the Warteburg, where he was treated with the greatest kindness, and enjoyed every liberty consistent with his own safety, had begun to undermine his former unusually strong health. He suffered many and most distressing effects of indigestion and a deranged state of the digestive Organs. Melanchthon, whom he had desired to consult the Physicians at Erfurth, sent him some de-obstruent medicines, and the advice to take regular and severe Exercise. At first he followed the advice, sate and laboured less, and spent whole days in the Chase; but, like the younger Pliny, he strove in vain to form a taste for this favourite Amusement of the "Gods of the Earth," as appears from a passage in his Letter to George Spalatin, which I translate for an additional reason: to prove to the Admirers of Rousseau (who perhaps will not be less affronted by this biographical Parallel, than the zealous Lutherans will be offended) that if my comparison should turn out groundless on the whole, the failure will not have arisen either from the want of sensibility in our great Reformer, or of angry aversion to those in high Places, whom he regarded as the Oppressors of their rightful equals. "I have been," he writes, "employed for two days in the sports of the field, and was willing myself to taste this bitter-sweet amusement of the great Heroes: we have caught two Hares, and one brace of poor little Partridges. An employment this which does not ill suit quiet leisurely folks: for even in the midst of the Ferrets and Dogs, I have had theological Fancies. But as much pleasure as the general appearance of the Scene and the mere looking-on occasioned me, even so much it pitied me to think of the mystery and emblem which lies beneath it. For what does this symbol signify, but that the Devil, through his god-less Huntsmen and Dogs, the Bishops and Theologians to wit, doth privily chase and catch the innocent poor little Beasts? Ah! the simple and credulous souls came thereby far too plain before my eyes. Thereto comes a yet more frightful mystery: as at my earnest entreaty we had saved alive one poor little Hare, and I had concealed it in the sleeve of my great Coat, and had strolled off a short distance [122] from it, the Dogs in the mean time found the poor Hare. Such too, is the fury of the Pope with Satan, that he destroys even the souls that had been saved, and troubles himself little about my pains and entreaties. Of such hunting then I have had enough." In another passage he tells his Correspondent, "you know it is hard to be a Prince, and not in some degree a Robber, and the greater a Prince the more a Robber." Of our Henry the eight he says, "I must answer the grim Lion that passes himself off for King of England. The ignorance in the Book is such as one naturally expects from a King; but the bitterness and impudent falsehood is quite leonine." And in his cir-cular letter to the Princes, on occasion of the Peasant's War, he uses a language so inflammatory, and holds forth a doctrine which borders so near on the holy right of Insurrection, that it may as well remain untrans-lated.

Had Luther been himself a Prince, he could not have desired better treatment than he received during his eight months stay in the Warteburg; and in consequence of a more luxurious diet than he had been accustomed to, he was plagued with temptations both from the "Flesh and the Devil." It is evident from his Letters* that he suffered under great irritability of his nervous System, the common effect of deranged Digestion in men of sedentary habits, who are at the same time intense thinkers: and this irritability added to, and revivifying the impressions made upon him in early life, and fostered by the theological Systems of his Manhood, is abundantly sufficient to explain all his Apparitions and all his nightly combats with evil Spirits. I see nothing improbable in the supposition,

* I can scarcely conceive a more delightful Volume than might be made from Luther's Letters, especially from those that were written from the Warteburg, if they were translated in the simple, sinewy, idiomatic, *hearty* mother-tongue of the original. A difficult task I admit—and scarcely possible for any man, however great his Talents in other respects, whose favourite reading has not lain among the English Writers from Edward the sixth to Charles the first.

that in one of those unconscious half sleeps, or rather those rapid alterna-
tions of the sleeping with the half waking state, which is *the true witching-
time,*

——————————————————"the season
Wherein the spirits hold their wont to walk"

the fruitful matrix of Ghosts—I see nothing improbable, that in some one
of those momentary Slumbers, into [123] which the suspension of all
Thought in the perplexity of intense thinking so often passes; Luther
should have had a full view of the Room in which he was sitting, of his
writing Table and all the Implements of Study, as they really existed, and
at the same time a brain-image of the Devil, vivid enough to have acquired
apparent *Outness*, and a distance regulated by the proportion of its distinctness to that of the objects really impressed on the outward senses.

I[1] will endeavour to make my meaning[2] more clear to those of my
Readers, who are fortunate enough to find it obscure in consequence of
their own good health and unshattered nerves. The Window of my
Library at Keswick is opposite to the Fire-place, and looks out on the very
large Garden that occupies the whole slope of the Hill on which the House
stands. Consequently, the rays of Light transmitted *through* the Glass,
(i.e. the Rays from the Garden, the opposite Mountains, the Bridge,
River, Lake, and Vale interjacent) and the rays reflected *from* it, (of
the Fire-place, &c.) enter the eye at the same moment. At the coming
on of Evening, it was my frequent amusement to watch the image or reflection of the Fire, that seemed burning in the bushes or between the trees in
different parts of the Garden or the Fields beyond it, according as there
was more or less Light; and which still arranged itself among the real
objects of Vision, with a distance and magnitude proportioned to its
greater or less faintness. For still as the darkness encreased, the Image of the
Fire lessened and grew nearer and more distinct; till the twilight had
deepened into perfect night, when all outward objects being excluded, the
window became a perfect Looking-glass: save only that my Books on the
side shelves of the Room were lettered, as it were, on their Backs with
Stars, more or fewer as the sky was more or less clouded (the rays of the
stars being at that time the only ones transmitted.) Now substitute the
Phantom from the[3] brain for the Images of *reflected* light (the Fire for
instance) and the Forms of the[4] room and its furniture for the *transmitted*
rays, and you have a fair resemblance of an Apparition, and a just conception of the manner in which it is seen together with real objects. As I
shall devote some future Numbers to the Subject of Dreams, Visions,
Ghosts, Witchcraft, &c. in which I shall first give, and then endeavour to
explain [124] the most interesting and best attested fact of each, which has
come within my knowledge, either from Books or from personal Testimony, I defer till then the explanation of the mode in which our Thoughts,

[1] In 1812 this long paragraph, with
its footnote, was transposed to the end
of the number, with the heading
"ILLUSTRATION OF THE PARAGRAPH,
P. 122 AND 123."

[2] 1812 adds "in p. 122–123" (i.e.
in the above paragraph, II 116–17).
[3] For "the" 1812 reads "Luther's".
[4] For "the" 1812 reads "his".

in states of morbid Slumber, become at times perfectly *dramatic* (for in certain sorts of dreams the dullest Wight becomes a Shakespeare) and by what Law the form of the Vision appears to talk to us its own thoughts in a voice as audible as the shape is visible; and this too oftentimes in connected trains, and sometimes even with a concentration of Power which may easily impose on the soundest judgements, uninstructed in the *Optics* and *Acoustics* of the inner sense, for Revelations and gifts of Prescience. I will only remark, in aid of the present case, that it would appear incredible to Persons not accustomed to these subtle notices of self observation, what small and remote resemblances, what mere *hints* of likeness from some real external object, (especially if the shape be aided by colour) will suffice to make a vivid thought consubstantiate with the real object, and derive from it an outward perceptibility.* Even when we are broad awake, if we are in [125] anxious expectation, how often will not the most confused sounds of nature be heard by us as articulate sounds? for instance, the babbling of a brook will appear, for a moment, the voice of a Friend, for whom we are waiting, calling out our own names, &c. A short meditation, therefore, on this Law of the imagination, that a Likeness in part tends to become a

* 1 A Lady once asked me if I believed in Ghosts and Apparitions, I answered with truth and simplicity: *No, Madam! I have seen far too many myself.* I have indeed a whole memorandum Book filled with records of these Phænomena, many of them interesting as facts and data for Psychology, and affording some valuable materials for a Theory of Perception and its dependence on the memory and Imagination. "In omnem actum Perceptionis imaginatio influit efficienter." WOLFE. But HE is no more, who would have realized this idea: who had already established the foundations and the law of the Theory; and for whom I had so often found a pleasure and a comfort, even during the wretched and restless nights of sickness, in watching and instantly recording these experiences of the world within us, of the "gemina natura, quæ fit et facit, et creat et creatur!" He is gone, my Friend! my munificent Co-patron, and not less the Benefactor of my Intellect!—He, who beyond all other men known to me, added a fine and ever-wakeful Sense of Beauty to the most patient Accuracy in experimental Philosophy and the profounder researches of metaphysical Science; he who united all the play and spring of Fancy with the subtlest Discrimination and an inexorable Judgement; and who controlled an almost painful exquisiteness of Taste by a Warmth of Heart, which in all the 2 relations of Life made allowances for faults as quick as the moral taste detected them; a Warmth of Heart, which was indeed noble and pre-eminent, for alas! the genial feelings of Health contributed no spark toward it! Of [125] these qualities I may speak, for they belonged to all mankind.—The higher virtues, that were blessings to his Friends, and the still higher that resided in and for his own Soul, are themes for the energies of Solitude, for the awfulness of Prayer!—virtues exercised in the barrenness and desolation of his animal being; while he thirsted with the full stream at his lips, and yet with unwearied goodness poured out to all around him, like the Master of a feast among his kindred in the day of his own gladness! Were it but for the remembrance of him alone and of his lot here below, the disbelief of a future state would sadden the earth around me, and blight the very grass in the Field.

1 In 1812 C's footnote becomes a final paragraph in the text, after "visit was repelled" (below, II 119), ending No 8.

2 For "all the" 1812 reads "the practical".

likeness of the whole, will make it not only conceivable but probable, that the Inkstand itself, and the dark-coloured Stone on the Wall, which Luther perhaps had never till then noticed, might have a considerable influence in the production of the Fiend, and of the hostile act with which his obtrusive visit was repelled.

If this Christian Hercules, this heroic Cleanser of the Augean Stable of Apostacy, had been born and educated in the present or the preceding Generation, he would, doubtless, have held himself for a Man of Genius and original Power. But with this faith alone he would scarcely have removed the Mountains which he did remove. The Darkness and Superstition of the Age, which required such a Reformer, had moulded his mind for the reception of ideas concerning himself, better suited to inspire the strength and enthusiasm necessary for the task of Reformation, ideas more in sympathy with the spirits whom he was to influence. He deemed himself gifted with supernatural influxes, an especial Servant of Heaven, a chosen Warrior, fighting as the General of a small but faithful troop, against an Army of evil Beings headed by the Prince of the Air. These were no metaphorical Beings in his Apprehension. He was a Poet indeed, as great a Poet as ever lived in any Age or Country; but his poetic images were so vivid, that they mastered the Poet's own mind! He was *possessed* with [126] them, as with substances distinct from himself: LUTHER did not *write*, he *acted* Poems. The Bible was a spiritual indeed, but not a *figurative* Armoury in his belief: it was the magazine of his warlike stores, and from thence he was to arm himself, and supply both Shield, and Sword, and Javelin, to the Elect. Methinks I see him sitting, the heroic Student, in his Chamber in the Warteburg, with his midnight Lamp before him, seen by the late Traveller in the distant Plain of *Bischofsroda*, as a Star on the Mountain! Below it lies the Hebrew Bible open, on which he gazes, his brow pressing on his palm, brooding over some obscure Text, which he desires to make plain to the simple Boor and to the humble Artizan, and to transfer its' whole force into their own natural and living Tongue. And he himself does not understand it! Thick Darkness lies on the original Text: he counts the Letters, he calls up the Roots of each separate Word, and questions them as the familiar Spirits of an Oracle. In vain thick Darkness continues to cover it! not a ray of meaning dawns through it. With sullen and angry Hope he reaches for the VULGATE, his old and sworn enemy, the treacherous confederate of the Roman Antichrist, which he so gladly, when he can, rebukes for idolatrous Falsehoods, which[1] had dared place

> "Within the sanctuary itself their shrines,
> Abominations!"————————

Now—O thought of humiliation—he must entreat its aid. See! there has the sly Spirit of Apostacy worked-in a phrase, which favours the doctrine of Purgatory, the intercession of Saints, or the efficacy of Prayers for the Dead. And what is worst of all, the interpretation is plausible. The original Hebrew might be forced into this meaning: and no other meaning seems to lie *in* it, none to hover *above* it in the heights of Allegory, none to lurk *beneath* it even in the depths of Cabala! This is the work of the Tempter!

---

[1] For "which" 1812 reads "that".

it is a cloud of Darkness conjured up between the Truth of the sacred Letters and the eyes of his Understanding, by the malice of the Evil One, and for a trial of his Faith! Must he then at length confess, must he subscribe the name of L U T H E R to an Exposition which consecrates a Weapon for the hand of the idolatrous Hierarchy? Never! never!

There still remains one auxiliary in reserve, the translation [127] of the Seventy. The Alexandrine Greeks, anterior to the Church itself, could intend no support to its corruptions—the Septuagent will have profaned the Altar of Truth with no incense for the Nostrils of the universal Bishop to snuff up. And here again his hopes are baffled! Exactly at this perplexed Passage had the Greek Translator given his Understanding a Holiday, and made his Pen supply its place. O honoured Luther! as easily mightest thou convert the whole City of Rome, with the Pope and the conclave of Cardinals inclusive, as strike a spark of Light from the Words, and *nothing-but-Words*, of the Alexandrine Version. Disappointed, despondent, enraged, ceasing to *think*, yet continuing his brain on the stretch, in solicitation of a Thought, and gradually giving himself up to angry Fancies, to recollections of past persecutions, to uneasy Fears and inward Defiances, and floating Images of the evil Being, their supposed personal Author, he sinks, without perceiving it, into a Trance of Slumber: during which his brain retains its' waking energies, excepting that what would have been mere *Thoughts* before, now (the action and counterweight of his outward senses and their impressions being withdrawn) shape and condense themselves into *Things*, into Realities! Repeatedly half-wakening, and his eyelids as often re-closing, the objects which really surround him form[1] the place and scenery of his Dream. All at once he sees the Arch-fiend coming forth on the Wall of the Room, from the very spot perhaps, on which his Eyes had been fixed vacantly during the perplexed moments of his former Meditation: the Ink-stand, which he had at the same time been using, becomes associated with it: and in that struggle of Rage, which in these distempered Dreams almost constantly precedes the helpless Terror by the pain of which we are finally awakened, he *imagines* that he hurls it at the Intruder, or not improbably in the first instant of awakening, while yet both his imagination and his eyes are possessed by the Dream, he *actually* hurls it! Some weeks after, perhaps, during which interval he had often mused on the incident, undetermined whether to deem it a Visitation of Satan to him in the body or out of the body, he discovers[2] the dark spot on his Wall, and receives it as a sign and pledge vouchsafed to him of the Event having actually taken place.

Such was Luther under the influences of the Age and [128] Country in and for which he was born. Conceive him a Citizen of Geneva, and a Contemporary of Voltaire; suppose the French Language his Mother-tongue, and the political and moral Philosophy of English Free-thinkers re-modelled by *Parisian Fort Esprits*, to have been the objects of his Study; —conceive this change of Circumstances, and Luther will no longer dream of Fiends or of Antichrist—but will he have no Dreams in their place? His melancholy will have changed its' Drapery; but will it find no new

---

[1] For "form" 1812 reads "from".   [2] 1812 adds "for the first time".

Costume wherewith to cloath itself? His impetuous temperament, his deep-working mind, his busy and vivid Imagination—would they not have been a *trouble* to him in a World, where nothing was to be altered, where nothing was to obey his Power, to cease to be that, which it had been, in order to realize his pre-conceptions of what ought to be? His Sensibility, which found Objects for itself, and shadows of human suffering in the harmless Brute, and even the Flowers which he trod upon—might it not naturally, in an unspiritualized Age, have wept and trembled, and dissolved over scenes of earthly Passion, and the struggles of Love with Duty? His Pity, that so easily passed into Rage, would it not have found in the inequalities of Mankind, in the oppressions of Governments, and the miseries of the governed, an entire instead of a divided Object? And might not a perfect Constitution, a Government of pure Reason, a renovation of the social Contract, have easily supplied the place of the reign of Christ in the new Jerusalem, of the restoration of the visible Church, and the Union of all Men by one Faith in one Charity? Henceforward, then, we will conceive his Reason employed in building up anew the Edifice of *earthly* Society, and his Imagination as pledging itself for the possible realization of the Structure. We will lose the great Reformer, who was born in an Age which needed him, in the Philosopher of Geneva, who was doomed to misapply his Energies to materials the properties of which he misunderstood, and happy only that he did not live to witness the direful effects of his System.

THE FRIEND

No. 9. THURSDAY, October 12, 1809

Albeit therefore, much of that we are to speak in this present Cause, may seem to a number perhaps tedious, perhaps obscure, dark and intricate, (for many talk of the Truth, which never sounded the depth from whence it springeth: and therefore, when they are led thereunto, they are soon weary, as men drawn from those beaten paths wherewith they have been inured;) yet this may not so far prevail, as to cut off that which the matter itself requireth, howsoever the nice humour of some be therewith pleased or no. They unto whom we shall seem tedious, are in no wise injured by us, because it is in their own hands to spare that labour which they are not willing to endure. And if any complain of obscurity, they must consider, that in these matters it cometh no otherwise to pass, than in sundry the works both of Art, and also of Nature, where that which hath greatest force in the very things we see, is, notwithstanding, itself oftentimes not seen. The stateliness of Houses, the goodliness of Trees, when we behold them, delighteth the eye: but that Foundation which beareth up the one, that Root which ministreth[1] unto the other nourishment and life, is in the bosom of the Earth concealed; and if there be occasion at any time to search into it, such labour is then more necessary than pleasant, both to them which undertake it and for the lookers on. In like manner, the use and benefit of good Laws, all that live under them, may enjoy with delight and comfort, albeit the grounds and first original causes from whence they have sprung, be unknown, as to the greatest part of men they are. But when they who withdraw their obedience, pretend that the Laws which they should obey are corrupt and vicious: for better examination of their quality, it behoveth the very Foundation and Root, the highest Well-Spring and Fountain of them to be discovered. Which because we are not oftentimes accustomed to do, when we do it, the pains we take are more needful a great deal than acceptable, and the Matters which we handle, seem by reason of newness, (till the mind grow better acquainted with them) dark, intricate, and unfamiliar. For as much help whereof, as may be in this case, I have endeavoured throughout the Body of this whole Discourse, that every former part might give strength to all that follow, and every latter bring some light to all before: so that if the judgements of men do but hold themselves in suspense, as touching these first more general Meditations, till in order they have perused the rest that ensue; what may seem dark at the first, will afterwards be found more plain, even as the latter particular decisions will appear, I doubt not, more strong when the other have been read before.—HOOKER'S ECCLESIAST. POLITY

---

[1] For "ministreth" 1812 reads "ministereth".

[130]   ESSAY VI

ON THE GROUNDS OF GOVERNMENT
AS LAID EXCLUSIVELY IN THE PURE REASON;
OR A STATEMENT AND CRITIQUE
OF THE THIRD SYSTEM OF POLITICAL PHILOSOPHY,
VIZ. THE THEORY OF ROUSSEAU AND THE FRENCH ECONOMISTS

M Y last was an Interlude. I now return to the theme announced in the
preceding Essay, to my promise of developing from its' embryo
Principles the Tree of French Liberty, of which the Declaration of the
Rights of Man, and the Constitution of 1791 were the Leaves, and the
succeeding and present State of France the Fruits. Let me not be blamed,
if for a brief while I have connected this System, though only in the
Imagination, though only as a *possible* case, with a name so deservedly
reverenced as that of Luther. It is some excuse, that to interweave with
the Reader's Recollections a certain Life and dramatic interest, during the
perusal of the abstract reasonings that are to follow, is the only means I
possess, of bribing his attention. We have most of us, at some period or
other of our Lives, been amused with Dialogues of the Dead. Who is
there, that wishing to form a probable opinion on the grounds of Hope and
Fear, for an injured People warring against mighty Armies, would not be
pleased with a spirited Fiction, which brought before him an old Numan-
tian discoursing on that subject in Elysium, with a newly-arrived Spirit from
the Streets of Saragossa or the Walls of Gerona?

But I have a better reason. I wished to give every fair advantage to the
Opinions, which I deemed it of importance to confute. It is bad policy to
represent a political System as having no charm but for Robbers and
Assassins, and no natural origin but in the brains of Fools or Madmen,
when Experience has proved, that the great danger of the System consists
in the peculiar fascination, it is calculated to exert on noble and imaginative Spirits; on all those, who in the amiable intoxication of youthful
Benevolence, are apt to mistake their own best Virtues and choicest
Powers for the average qualities and Attributes of the human Character.
The very Minds, which a good man would most wish to preserve or dis-
entangle from the Snare, are by these angry misrepresentations [131] rather
lured into it. Is it wonderful, that a Man should reject the arguments unheard, when his own Heart proves the falsehood of the Assumptions by
which they are prefaced? or that he should retaliate on the Aggressors
their own evil Thoughts? I am well aware, that the provocation was great,
the temptation almost inevitable; yet still I cannot repel the conviction
from my mind, that in part to this Error and in part to a certain inconsistency in his fundamental Principles, we are to attribute the small number of
Converts made by B URKE during his life time. Let me not be misunderstood. I do not mean, that this great Man supported different Principles at
different æras of his political Life. On the contrary, no Man was ever
more like himself! From his first published Speech on the American
Colonies to his last posthumous Tracts, we see the same Man, the same

Doctrines, the same uniform Wisdom of *practical* Councils, the same Reasoning and the same Prejudices against all abstract grounds, against all deduction of Practice from Theory. The inconsistency to which I allude, is of a different kind: it is the want of congruity in the Principles appealed to in different parts of the same Work, it is an apparent versatility of the Principle with the Occasion. If his Opponents are Theorists, *then* every thing is to be founded on PRUDENCE, on mere calculations of EXPEDIENCY: and every Man is represented as acting according to the state of his own immediate self interest. Are his Opponents Calculators? *Then* Calculation itself is represented as a sort of crime. God has given us FEELINGS, and we are to obey them! and the most absurd Prejudices become venerable, to which these FEELINGS have given Consecration. I have not forgotten, that Burke himself defended these half contradictions, on the pretext of balancing the too much on the one side by a too much on the other. But never can I believe, but that the straight line must needs be the nearest; and that where there is the most, and the most unalloyed Truth, there will be the greatest and most permanent power of persuasion. But the fact was, that Burke in his public Character found himself, as it were, in a Noah's Ark, with a very few Men and a great many Beasts! he felt how much his immediate Power was lessened by the very circumstance of his measureless Superiority to those about him: he acted, therefore, under a perpetual System of Compromise—a [132] Compromise of Greatness with Meanness; a Compromise of Comprehension with Narrowness; a Compromise of the Philosopher (who armed with the twofold knowledge of History and the Laws of Spirit, as with a Telescope, looked far around and into the far Distance) with the mere Men of Business, or with yet coarser Intellects, who handled a Truth, which they were required to receive, as they would handle an Ox, which they were desired to purchase. But why need I repeat what has been already said in so happy a manner by Goldsmith, of this great Man:

> "Who, born for the universe narrow'd his mind,
> And to party gave up what was meant for mankind.
> Tho' fraught with all learning, yet straining his throat,
> To persuade Tommy Townshend to give him a vote;
> Who too deep for his hearers, still went on refining,
> And thought of convincing, while they thought of dining."

And if in consequence it was his fate to "*cut blocks with a razor*," I may be permitted to add, that in respect of *Truth*, though not of *Genius*, the Weapon was injured by the misapplication.

THE FRIEND, however, acts and will continue to act under the belief, that the whole Truth is the best antidote to Falsehoods which are dangerous chiefly because they are half-truths: and that an erroneous System is best confuted, not by an abuse of Theory in general, nor by an absurd opposition of Theory to Practice, but by a detection of the Errors in the particular Theory. For the meanest of men has his Theory: and to think at all is to theorize. With these convictions I proceed immediately to the System of the Economists and to the Principles on which it is constructed, and from which it must derive all its strength.

The System commences with an undeniable Truth, and an important deduction therefrom equally undeniable. All voluntary Actions, say they, having for their Objects Good or Evil, are *moral* Actions. But all morality is grounded in the Reason. Every Man is born with the faculty of Reason: and whatever is without it, be the Shape what it may, is not a Man or PERSON, but a THING. Hence the sacred Principle, recognized by all Laws human and divine, the Principle indeed, which is the *ground-work* of all Law and Justice, that a Person can [133] never become a Thing, nor be treated as such without wrong. But the distinction between Person and Thing consists herein, that the latter may rightfully be used, altogether and merely, as a *Means*; but the former must always be included in the *End*, and form a part of the final Cause. We plant the Tree and we cut it down, we breed the Sheep and we kill it, wholly as *means* to our own *ends*. The Wood-cutter and the Hind are likewise employed as *Means*, but on an agreement of reciprocal advantage, which includes them as well as their Employer in the *end*. Again: as the faculty of Reason implies Free-agency, Morality (i.e. the dictate of Reason) gives to every rational Being the right of acting as a free agent, and of finally determining his conduct by his own Will, according to his own Conscience: and this right is inalienable except by guilt, which is an act of Self-forfeiture, and the Consequences therefore to be considered as the Criminal's own moral election. In respect of their Reason[1] all Men are equal. The measure of the Understanding and of all other Faculties of Man, is different in different Persons: but Reason is not susceptible of degree. For since it merely decides whether any given thought or action is or is not in contradiction with the rest, there can be no reason better, or more *reason*, than another.

REASON! best and holiest gift of Heaven and bond of union with the Giver. The high Title by which the Majesty of Man claims precedence above all other living Creatures! Mysterious Faculty, the Mother of Conscience, of Language, of Tears, and of Smiles![2] Calm and incorruptible Legislator of the Soul, without whom all its' other Powers would "meet in mere oppugnancy." Sole Principle of Permanence amid endless Change! in a World of discordant Appetites and imagined Self-interests the one only common Measure! which taken away,

> "Force should be right; or, rather right and wrong
> (Between whose endless jar justice resides)
> Should lose their names and so should justice too.
> Then every thing includes itself in power,
> Power into will, will into appetite;
> And appetite, an universal wolf,
> So doubly seconded with will and power,
> Must make perforce an universal prey!"

Thrice blessed faculty of Reason! all other Gifts, though [134] goodly and

[1] In 1812 an asterisk appears here, with the following footnote: "See this position fully explained, and the sophistry grounded on it detected and exposed, at the conclusion [pp 350-2; below, II 294-7] of the 21st No. of THE FRIEND."

[2] For a cancelled continuation in the ms see above, I 190 n 2.

of celestial origin, Health, Strength, Talents, all the powers and all the means of Enjoyment, seem dispensed by Chance or sullen Caprice—thou alone, more than even the Sunshine, more than the common Air, art given to all Men, and to every Man alike! To thee, who being one art the same in all, we owe the privilege, that of all we can become one, a living *whole!* that we have a COUNTRY! Who then shall dare prescribe a Law of moral Action for any rational Being, which does not flow immediately from that Reason, which is the Fountain of all Morality? Or how without breach of Conscience can we limit or coerce the Powers of a Free-Agent, except by a[1] coincidence with that Law in his own Mind, which is at once the Cause, the Condition, and the Measure of his Free-agency? Man must be *free;* or to what purpose was he made a Spirit of Reason, and not a Machine of Instinct? Man must *obey;* or wherefore has he a Conscience? The Powers, which create this difficulty, contain its solution likewise: for *their* Service is perfect Freedom. And whatever Law or System of Law compels any other service, disennobles our Nature, leagues itself with the Animal against the Godlike, kills in us the very Principle of joyous Well-doing, and fights against Humanity.

By the Application of these Principles to the social State there arises the following System, which as far as respects its' first grounds is developed the most fully by J. J. Rousseau in his Work *Du contrat social.* If then no Individual possesses the Right of prescribing any thing to another Individual, the rule of which is not contained in their common Reason, Society, which is but an aggregate of Individuals, can communicate this Right to no one. It cannot possibly make that rightful which the higher and inviolable Law of Human Nature declares contradictory and unjust. But concerning Right and Wrong the Reason of each and every Man is the competent Judge: for how else could he be an amenable Being, or the proper Subject of *any* Law? This Reason, therefore, in any one Man cannot even in the social state be rightfully subjugated to the Reason of any other. Neither an Individual, nor yet the whole Multitude which constitutes the State, can possess the Right of compelling him to do any thing, of which it cannot be demonstrated that his own Reason must join in prescribing [135] it. If therefore Society is to be under a *rightful* constitution of Government, and one that can impose on rational Beings a true and moral Obligation to obey it, it must be framed on such Principles that every Individual follows his own Reason while he obeys the Laws of the Constitution, and performs the Will of the State while he follows the Dictate[2] of his own Reason. This is expressly asserted by Rousseau, who states the problem of a perfect Constitution of Government in the following Words: *Trouver une forme d' Association—par laquelle chacun s'unissant à tous, n'obeisse pourtant qu' à lui même, et reste aussi libre qu' auparavant.* i.e. To find a form of Society according to which each one uniting with the whole shall yet obey himself only and remain as free as before. This right of the Individual to retain his whole natural Independence, even in the social State, is absolutely inalienable. He cannot possibly concede or compromise it: for this very Right is one of his most sacred Duties. He would sin against himself, and commit

---

[1] 1812 omits "a".   [2] For "Dictate" 1812 reads "Dictates".

high treason against the Reason which the Almighty Creator has given him, if he dared abandon its' exclusive right to govern his actions.

Laws obligatory on the Conscience, can only therefore proceed from that Reason which remains always one and the same, whether it speaks through this or that Person: like the voice of an external Ventriloquist, it is indifferent from whose lips it appears to come, if only it be audible. The Individuals indeed are subject to Errors and Passions, and each Man has his own defects. But when Men are assembled in Person or by real Representatives, the actions and re-actions of individual Self-love balance each other; errors are neutralized by opposite errors; and the Winds rushing from all quarters at once with equal force, produce for the time a deep Calm, during which the general Will arising from the general Reason displays itself. "It is fittest," says Burke himself, (see his Note on his Motion relative to the Speech from the Throne, Vol. II. Page 647. 4to Edit.) "It is fittest that sovereign Authority should be exercised where it is most likely to be attended with the most effectual correctives. These correctives are furnished by the nature and course of parliamentary proceedings, and by the infinitely diversified Characters who compose the two Houses. The fulness, the freedom, and publicity of discussion, [136] leave it easy to distinguish what are acts of power, and what the determinations of equity and reason. There Prejudice corrects Prejudice, and the different asperities of party zeal mitigate and neutralize each other."

This, however, as my Readers will have already detected, is no longer a demonstrable deduction from Reason. It is a mere *probability*, against which other probabilities may be weighed: as the lust of Authority, the contagious nature of Enthusiasm, and other of the acute or chronic diseases of deliberative Assemblies. But which of these results is the more probable, the correction or the contagion of Evil, must depend on Circumstances and grounds of Expediency: and thus we already find ourselves beyond the magic Circle of the pure Reason, and within the Sphere of the Understanding and the Prudence. Of this important fact Rousseau was by no means unaware in his Theory, though with gross inconsistency he takes no notice of it in his Application of the Theory to Practice. He admits the possibility, he is compelled by History to allow even the *probability*, that the most numerous popular Assemblies, nay even whole Nations, may at times be hurried away by the same Passions, and under the dominion of a common Error. This Will of all is *then* of no more value, than the Humours of any one Individual: and must therefore be sacredly distinguished from the pure Will which flows from universal Reason. To this point then I entreat the Reader's particular attention: for in this distinction, established by Rousseau himself, between the *Volonté de Tous* and the *Volonté generale* (i.e. between the collective Will, and a casual over-balance of Wills) the Falsehood or Nothingness of the whole System becomes manifest. For hence it follows, as an inevitable Consequence, that all which is said in the *Contrat social* of that sovereign Will, to which the right of universal Legislation appertains, applies to no one Human Being, to no Society or Assemblage of Human Beings, and least of all to the mixed Multitude that makes up the PEOPLE: but entirely and exclusively to REASON itself, which, it is true, dwells in every Man *potentially*, but actually and in perfect purity is found in no Man and in no Body of Men. This distinction the later Disciples of Rousseau chose completely to forget and, (a far more melancholy case!) the Constituent Legislators of France [137] forgot it likewise. With a wretched *parrotry* they wrote and harangued without ceasing of the *Volunté generale*—the *inalienable sovereignty* of the People: and by these high-sounding phrases led on the vain, ignorant, and intoxicated Populace to wild excesses and wilder expectations, which entailing on them the bitterness of disappointment, cleared the way for military Despotism, for the satanic Government of Horror under the Jacobins, and of Terror under the Corsican.

Luther lived long enough to see the consequences of the Doctrines into which indignant Pity and abstract ideas of Right had hurried *him*—to see, to retract, and to oppose them. If the same had been the lot of Rousseau, I doubt not, that his conduct would have been the same. In his whole System there is beyond controversy much that is true and well reasoned, if only its' application be not extended farther than the nature of the case permits. But then we shall find that little or nothing is won by it for the institutions of Society; and least of all for the constitution of Governments, the Theory of which it was his wish to ground on it. Apply his Principles to any case, in which the sacred and inviolable Laws of Morality are immediately interested, all becomes just and pertinent. No Power on Earth can oblige me to act against my Conscience. No Magistrate, no Monarch, no Legislature, can without Tyranny compel me to do any thing which the acknowledged Laws of God have forbidden me to do. So act that thou mayest be able without involving any contradiction to will that the Maxim of thy Conduct should be the Law of all intelligent Beings —is the one universal and sufficient Principle and Guide of Morality. And why? Because the *object* of Morality is not the outward act, but the internal Maxim of our Actions. And so far it is infallible. But with what shew of Reason can we pretend, from a Principle by which we are to determine the purity of our motives, to deduce the form and matter of a rightful Government, the main office of which is to regulate the outward Actions of particular Bodies of Men, according to their particular Circumstances? Can we hope better of Constitutions framed by ourselves, than of that which was given by Almighty Wisdom itself? The Laws of the Hebrew Commonwealth, which flowed from the pure Reason, remain and are immutable; but the Regulations dictated by Prudence, [138] though by the *Divine* Prudence, and though given in thunder from the Mount, have passed away; and while they lasted, were binding only for that one State whose particular Circumstances rendered them expedient.

Rousseau indeed asserts, that there is an inalienable sovereignty inherent in every human being possessed of Reason: and from this the Framers of the Constitution of 1791 deduce, that the People itself is its' own sole rightful Legislator, and at most dare only recede so far from its right as to delegate to chosen Deputies the Power of representing and declaring the general Will. But this is wholly without proof; for it has already been fully shewn, that according to the Principle out of which this consequence is attempted to be drawn, it is not the actual Man, but the abstract Reason alone, that is the sovereign and rightful Lawgiver. The confusion of two things so different is so gross an Error, that the Constituent Assembly could scarce proceed a step in their Declaration of Rights, without some glaring inconsistency. Children are excluded from all political Power—are they not human beings in whom the faculty of Reason resides? Yes? but in them the faculty is not yet adequately developed. But are not gross Ignorance, inveterate Superstition, and the habitual Tyranny of Passion and Sensuality, equal Preventives of the developement, equal impediments to the rightful exercise of the Reason, as Childhood and early Youth? Who would not rely on the judgement of a well-educated English Lad, bred in a virtuous and enlightened Family, in preference to that of a brutal Russian, who believes that he can scourge his wooden Idol into good humour, or attributes to himself the merit of perpetual Prayer, when he has fastened the Petitions, which his Priest has written for him, on the wings of a Windmill? Again: Women are likewise excluded—a full half, and that assuredly the most innocent the most amiable half, of the whole human Race, is excluded, and this too by a Constitution which boasts to have no other foundations but those of universal Reason! Is Reason then an affair of Sex? No! But Women are commonly in a state of *dependence*, and are not likely to exercise their Reason with freedom. Well! and does not this ground of exclusion apply with equal or greater force to the Poor, to the Infirm, to Men in embarrassed [139] Circumstances, to all in short whose maintenance, be it scanty or be it ample, depends on the Will of others? How far are we to go? Where must we stop? What Classes should we admit? Whom must we disfranchise? The objects, concerning whom we are to determine these Questions, are all Human Beings and differenced from each other by *degrees* only, and[1] these degrees too oftentimes changing. Yet the Principle on which the whole System rests is, that Reason is not susceptible of degree. Nothing therefore, which subsists wholly in degrees, the charges[2] of which do not obey any necessary Law, can be Subjects of pure Science, or determinable by mere Reason. For these things we must rely on our *Understandings*, enlightened by past experience and immediate Observation, and determining our choice by comparisons of Expediency.

It is therefore altogether a mistaken notion, that the Theory which would deduce the social Rights of Man and the sole rightful form of Government from principles of Reason, involves a necessary preference of the democratic, or even the representative, Constitutions. Accordingly, several of the French Economists, although Devotees of Rousseau and the physiocratic System, and assuredly not the least respectable of their Party either in Morals or in Intellect; and these too Men, who lived and wrote under the unlimited Monarchy of France, and who were therefore well acquainted with the evils connected with that System, did yet declare themselves for a pure Monarchy in preference to the Aristocratic, the popular, or the mixed form. These Men argued, that no other Laws being allowable but those which are demonstrably just, and founded in the simplest ideas of Reason, and of which every Man's Reason is the competent judge, it is indifferent whether one Man, or one or more Assemblies of men, give form and

---

[1] 1812 omits "and".   [2] For "charges" 1812 reads "changes".

publicity to them. For being matters of pure and simple Science, they require no experience in order to see their Truth, and among an enlightened People, by whom this System had been once solemnly adopted, no Sovereign would dare to make other Laws than those of Reason. They further contend, that if the People were not enlightened, a purely popular Government could not co-exist with this System of absolute Justice: and if it were adequately enlightened, the [140] influence of public Opinion would supply the place of formal Representation, while the *form* of the Government would be in harmony with the unity and simplicity of its' Principles. This they entitle *le Despotisme legal sous l'Empire de l'Évidence.* (The best statement of the Theory thus modified, may be found in *Mercier de la Riviere, l'ordre naturel et essentiel des sociétés politiques.*) From the proofs adduced in the preceding paragraph, to which many others might be added, I have no hesitation in affirming that this latter Party are the more consistent Reasoners.

It is worthy of remark, that the influence of these Writings contributed greatly, not indeed to raise the present Emperor, but certainly to reconcile a numerous class of Politicians to his unlimited Authority: and as far as his lawless Passion for War and Conquest allows him to govern according to any Principles, he favours those of the physiocratic Philosophers. His early education must have given him a predilection for a Theory conducted throughout with mathematical precision; its very simplicity promised the readiest and most commodious Machine for Despotism, for it moulds a Nation into as calculable a Power as an Army; while the stern and seeming greatness of the whole and its mock-elevation above human feelings, flattered his Pride, hardened his Conscience, and aided the efforts of Self-delusion. REASON is the sole Sovereign, the only rightful Legislator; but Reason to act on Man must be impersonated. The Providence which had so marvellously raised and supported him, had marked HIM out for the Representative of Reason, and had armed him with irresistible force, in order to realize its Laws. In Him therefore MIGHT becomes RIGHT, and HIS Cause and that of Destiny (or as the Wretch now chuses to word it, exchanging blind Nonsense for staring Blasphemy) HIS Cause and the Cause of God are one and the same. Excellent Postulate for a Choleric and self-willed Tyrant! What avails the impoverishment of a few thousand Merchants and Manufacturers? What even the general Wretchedness of millions of perishable men, for a short generation? Should these stand in the way of the chosen Conqueror, the Innovator, *Mundi*[1] *et Stupor Sæculorum,* or prevent "a constitution of Things, which erected on *intellectual* and [141] *perfect* foundations, groweth not old," but like the eternal Justice, of which it is the living Image,

———————————————————————"may despise
The strokes of Fate and see the World's last hour!"

For Justice, austere unrelenting Justice, is every where held up as the one Thing needful: and the only Duty of the Citizen, in fulfiling which he obeys all the Laws, is not to encroach on another's sphere of Action. The greatest

---

[1] For "Innovator, *Mundi*" 1812 reads "*Innovator Mundi*".

possible Happiness of a People is not, according to this System, the object of a Governor; but to preserve the Freedom of all by coercing within the requisite bounds the Freedom of each. Whatever a Government does more than this, comes of Evil: and its' best employment is the *repeal* of Laws and Regulations, not the Establishment of them. Each man is the best judge of his own Happiness, and to himself must it therefore be entrusted. Remove all the interferences of positive Statutes, all Monopoly, all Bounties, all Prohibitions, and all Encouragements of Importation and Exportation, of particular growth and particular manufactures; let the Revenues of the State be taken at once from the Produce of the Soil; and all things will then find their level, all irregularities will correct each other, and an indestructible Cycle of harmonious motions take place in the moral, equally as in the natural World. The business of the Governor is to watch incessantly, that the State shall remain composed of Individuals acting as Individuals, by which alone the Freedom of all can be secured. Its Duty is to take care, that itself remain the sole collective power, and that all the Citizens should enjoy the same Rights, and without distinction be subject to the same Duties.

Splendid Promises! Can any thing appear more equitable than the last Proposition, the equality of Rights and Duties? Can any thing be conceived more simple in the idea? But the execution—? let the four or five quarto Volumes of the Conscript Code be the Comment! But as briefly as possible I shall prove, that this System, as an exclusive Total, is under any form impracticable; and that if it were realized, and as far as it were realized, it would necessarily lead to general Barbarism and the most grinding Oppression; and that the final result of a general attempt to introduce it, must be a military Despotism inconsistent with the Peace and Safety of Mankind. [142] That Reason should be our Guide and Governor is an undeniable Truth, and all our notion of Right and Wrong is built thereon: for the whole moral Nature of Man originated and subsists in his Reason. From Reason alone can we derive the Principles which our Understandings are to apply, the Ideal to which by means of our Understandings we should endeavour to approximate. This however gives no proof, that Reason alone ought to govern and direct human beings, either as Individuals or as States. It ought not to do this, because it cannot. The Laws of Reason are unable to satisfy the first conditions of Human Society. We will admit, that the shortest Code of Law is the best, and that the Citizen finds himself most at ease where the Government least intermeddles with his affairs, and confines its efforts to the preservation of public tranquillity—we will suffer this to pass at present undisputed, though the examples of England, and before the late Events, of Holland and Switzerland, (surely the three happiest Nations of the World) to which perhaps we might add the major part of the former German free Towns, furnish stubborn facts in presumption of the contrary—yet still the proof is wanting, that the first and most general applications and exertions of the power of Man can be definitely regulated by Reason unaided by the positive and conventional Laws in the formation of which the Understanding must be our Guide, and which become just because they happen to be expedient.

The chief object, for which Men first formed themselves into a State was not the protection of their Lives but of their Property: For where the nature of the Soil and Climate precludes all Property but personal, and permits that only in its simplest forms, as in Greenland, men remain in the domestic State and form Neighbourhood[1] but not Governments. And in North America the Chiefs appear to exercise Government in those Tribes only which possess individual landed Property: among the rest the Chief is their General only, and Government is exercised only in Families by the Fathers of Families. But where individual landed Property exists, there must be inequality of Property: the nature of the Earth and the nature of the Mind unite to make the contrary impossible. But to suppose the Land the Property of the State and the Labour and the Produce to be equally divided among all the Members of the State, involves more than one contradiction: [143] for it could not subsist without gross injustice, except where the Reason of all and of each was absolute Master of the selfish passions, of Sloth, Envy, &c.; and yet the same State would preclude the greater part of the means, by which the Reason of man is developed. In whatever state of Society you would place it, from the most savage to the most refined, it would be found equally unjust and impossible; and were there a race of Men, a Country, and a Climate, that permitted such an order of things, the same Causes would render all Government superfluous. To Property, therefore, and to its inequalities, all human Laws directly or indirectly relate, which would not be equally Laws in the state of Nature. Now it is impossible to deduce the Right of Property from pure Reason. The utmost which Reason could give, would be a property in the *forms* of things, as far as the forms were produced by individual Power. In the *matter* it could give no Property. We regard Angels and glorified Spirits as Beings of pure Reason: and who ever thought of Property in Heaven? Even the simplest and most moral form of it, namely Marriage, (we know from the highest authority,) is excluded from the state of pure Reason. Rousseau himself expressly admits, that Property cannot be deduced from the Laws of Reason and Nature; and he ought therefore to have admitted at the same time, that his whole Theory was a thing of Air. In the most respectable point of view he could regard his System as analogous only to Geometry. (If indeed it be purely scientific, how could it be otherwise?) Geometry holds forth an *Ideal*, which can never be fully realized in Nature, even because it is Nature: because Bodies are more than Extension, and to pure extension of space only the mathematical Theorems wholly correspond. In the same manner the moral Laws of the intellectual World, as far as they are deducible from pure Intellect, are never perfectly applicable to our mixed and sensitive Nature, because Man is something besides Reason; because his Reason never acts by itself, but must cloath itself in the Substance of individual Understanding and specific Inclination, in order to become a Reality and an Object of Consciousness and Experience. It will be seen hereafter that together with this, the Key-stone of the Arch, the greater part and the most specious of the popular Arguments in favour of universal Suffrage fall in and are [144] crushed. I will mention one only at present. Major Cartwright, in his deduction of the Rights of the Subject

---

[1] For "Neighbourhood" 1812 reads "Neighbourhoods".

from Principles "not susceptible of proof, being self-evident—if one of which be violated all are shaken," affirms (Principle 98th, though the greater part indeed are moral Aphorisms, or blank Assertions, not scientific Principles) "that a Power which ought never to be used ought never to exist." Again he affirms that "Laws to bind all must be assented to by all, and consequently every Man even the poorest, has an equal Right to Suffrage:" and this for an additional reason, because "all without exception are capable of feeling Happiness or Misery, accordingly as they are well or ill governed." But are they not then capable of feeling Happiness or Misery, according as they do or do not possess the means of a comfortable Subsistence? and who is the Judge, what is a comfortable Subsistence, but the Man himself? Might not then on the same or equivalent Principles a Leveller construct a Right to equal Property? The Inhabitants of this Country without Property form, doubtless, a great majority: each of these has a Right to a Suffrage, and the richest Man to no more: and the object of this Suffrage is, that each Individual may secure himself a true efficient Representative of his Will. Here then is a legal power of abolishing or equalizing Property: and according to himself, *a Power which ought never to be used ought not to exist.*

Therefore, unless he carries his System to the whole length of common Labour and common Possession, a Right to universal Suffrage cannot exist; but if not to universal Suffrage, there can exist no *natural right* to Suffrage at all. In whatever way he would obviate this objection, he must admit *Expedience* founded on *Experience* and particular Circumstances, which will vary in every different Nation and in the same Nation at different times, as the Maxim of all Legislation and the Ground of all legislative Power. For his universal Principles, as far as they are Principles and universal, necessarily suppose uniform and perfect Subjects, which are to be found in the *Ideas* of pure Geometry and (I trust) in the *Realities* of Heaven, but never, never, in Creatures of Flesh and Blood.

THE FRIEND

No. 10. THURSDAY, October 19, 1809

"And it was no wonder if some good and innocent Men, especially such as He (LIGHTFOOT) who was generally more concerned about what was done in Judea many Centuries ago, than what was transacted in his own time in his own Country—it is no wonder if some such were for a while borne away to the approval of Opinions which they after more sedate Reflection disowned. Yet his Innocency from any self-interest or design, together with his Learning, secured him from the extravagancies of Demagogues, the People's Oracles."
LIGHTFOOT's *Works, Publisher's Preface to the Reader.*

ESSAY VII

ON THE ERRORS OF PARTY SPIRIT:
OR EXTREMES MEET

I HAVE never seen Major Cartwright, much less enjoy the honour of his acquaintance; but I know enough of his Character from the testimony of others and from his own Writings, to respect his Talents, and revere the purity of his Motives. I am fully persuaded, that there are few better Men, few more fervent or disinterested Adherents of their Country or the Laws of their Country, of whatsoever things are lovely, of whatsoever things are honourable! It would give me great pain, should I be supposed to have introduced disrespectfully a Name, which from my early youth I never heard mentioned without a feeling of affectionate Admiration. I have indeed quoted from this venerable Patriot, as from the most respectable English Advocate for the Theory, which derives the rights of Government, and the duties of Obedience to it, exclusively from principles of pure Reason. It was of consequence to my Cause, that I should not be thought to have been waging War against a Straw-Image of my own setting up, or even against a foreign Idol that had neither Worshippers nor Advocates in our own Country: and it was not less my object to keep my discussion aloof from those Passions, which more unpopular Names might have excited. I therefore introduced the name of Cartwright, as I had previously done that of Luther, in order [146] to give every fair advantage to a Theory, which I thought it of importance to confute; and as an instance, that though the System might be *made* tempting to the Vulgar, yet that, taken unmixed and entire, it was chiefly fascinating for lofty and imaginative Spirits, who mistook their own virtues and powers for the average character of Men in general.

Neither by fair statements nor by fair reasoning, should I ever give offence to Major Cartwright himself, nor to his judicious Friends. If I am in danger of offending them, it must arise from one or other of two Causes:

either that I have falsely represented his Principles, or his Motives and the tendency of his Writings. In the Book from which I quoted ("The Peoples Barrier against undue influence, &c.", the only one of Major Cartwrights which I possess) I am conscious that there are *six* foundations stated of constitutional Government. Therefore, it may be urged, the Author cannot be justly classed with those, who deduce our social Rights and correlative Duties exclusively from Principles of pure Reason, or unavoidable conclusions from such. My answer is ready. Of these six foundations three are but different words for one and the same, viz. the Law of Reason, the Law of God, and first Principles; and the three that remain cannot be taken as different, inasmuch as they are afterwards affirmed to be of no validity except as far as they are evidently deduced from the former; that is, from the PRINCIPLES implanted by GOD in the universal REASON of Man. These three latter foundations are, the *general* customs of the Realm, *particular* customs, and acts of Parliament. It might be supposed that the Author had not used his terms in the precise and single sense, in which they are defined in my former Essay: and that self-evident Principles may be meant to include the dictates of manifest Expedience, the Inducements[1] of the Understanding as well as the Prescripts of the pure Reason. But no! Major Cartwright has guarded against the possibility of this interpretation, and has expressed himself as decisively, and with as much warmth, against founding *Governments* on grounds of Expedience, as the Editor of the Friend has done against founding *Morality* on the same. Euclid himself could not have defined his words more sternly within the limit of pure Science; for instance, see the 1st. 2d. 3d. and 4th. primary Rules. [147] "A Principle is a manifest and simple proposition comprehending a certain Truth. Principles are the proof of every thing: but are not susceptible of external proof, being self-evident. If one Principle be violated, all are shaken. Against him, who denies Principles, all dispute is useless, and reason unintelligible, or disallowed, so far as he denies them. The Laws of Nature are immutable." Neither could Rousseau himself (or his Predecessors, the fifth Monarchy Men) have more nakedly or emphatically identified the foundations of Government in the concrete with those of religion and morality in the abstract: see Major Cartwright's Primary Rules from 31 to 39, and from 44 to 83. In these it is affirmed: that the legislative Rights of every Citizen are inherent in his nature; that being natural Rights they must be equal in all men; that a natural right is that right which a Citizen claims as being a *Man*, and that it hath no other foundation but his Personality or Reason; That Property can neither encrease or modify any legislative Right; that every one Man shall have one Vote however poor, and for any one Man, however rich, to have any more than one Vote, is against natural Justice, and an evil Measure; that it is better for a Nation to endure all Adversities, than to assent to one evil Measure; that to be free is to be governed by Laws, to which we have ourselves assented, either in Person or by a Representative, for whose election we have actually voted; that all not having a right of Suffrage are Slaves, and that a vast majority of the People of Great Britain are Slaves!

---

[1] For "Inducements" 1812 reads "Inductions".

To prove the total coincidence of Major Cartwright's Theory with that which I have stated (and I trust confuted) in the preceding Number, it only remains for me to prove, that the former, equally with the latter, confounds the sufficiency of the Conscience to make every Person a *moral* and amenable Being, with the sufficiency of Judgement and Experience requisite to the exercise of *political* Right. A single quotation will place this out of all doubt, which from its length I shall insert in a Note.*

[148] Great stress, indeed, is laid on the authority of our ancient Laws, both in this and the other Works of our patriotic Author; and whatever his System may be, it is impossible not to feel, that the Author himself possesses the heart of a genuine Englishman. But still his System can neither be changed nor modified by these appeals: for among the primary maxims, which form the ground-work of it, we are informed not only that Law in the abstract is the perfection of Reason; but that the Law of God and the Law of the Land are all one! What? The Statutes against Witches? Or those bloody Statutes against Papists, the abolition of which gave rise to the infamous Riots in 1780? Or (in the Author's own opinion) the Statutes of Disfranchisement and for making Parliaments septennial?—Nay! but (Principle 28) "an unjust Law is no Law:" and (P. 22.) against the Law of Reason neither prescription, statute, nor custom, may prevail; and if any

---

* "But the equality (observe Major Cartwright is here speaking of the *natural* right to universal Suffrage, and consequently of the universal right of eligibility, as well as of election, independent of Charter or of Property)—the equality and dignity of human nature in all men, whether rich or poor, is placed in the highest point of view by St. Paul, when he reprehends the Corinthian Believers for their litigations one with another, in the Courts of Law where Unbelievers presided; and as an argument of *the competency of all* [148] *Men* to judge for themselves, he alludes to that elevation in the Kingdom of Heaven which is promised to every man who shall be virtuous, or in the language of that time, a *Saint.* 'Do ye not know,' says he, 'that the Saints shall judge the world? And if the world shall be judged by you, are ye unworthy to judge the smallest matters? Know ye not that ye shall judge the Angels? How much more *things that pertain to this Life?*' If after such authorities, such manifestations of truth as these, any Christian through those prejudices which are the effects of long habits of injustice and oppression, and teach us to '*despise the poor*,' shall still think it right to exclude that part of the commonalty, consisting of '*Tradesmen, Artificers,* and Labourers,' or any of them from voting in elections of members to serve in parliament, I must sincerely lament such a persuasion as a misfortune both to himself and his Country. And if any man, (not having given himself the trouble to consider whether or not the Scripture be an authority, but who nevertheless is a friend to the rights of mankind) upon grounds of mere prudence, policy, or expediency, shall think it advisable to go against the whole current of our constitutional and law maxims, by which it is *self-evident* that every man, as being a MAN, created FREE, born to FREEDOM, and, without it, a THING, a SLAVE, a BEAST; and shall contend for drawing a line of exclusion at freeholders of forty *pounds* a year, or forty *shillings* a year, or *householders,* or *pot-boilers,* so that all who are below that line shall not have a vote in the election of a legislative Guardian,—which is taking from a citizen the power even of self-preservation,—such a man, I venture to say, is bolder than he who wrestled with the Angel; for he wrestles with God himself, who established *those principles in the eternal laws of nature, never to be violated* by any of his Creatures." P. 23 24.

such be brought against it, they be not prescriptions, statutes, nor customs, but things void: and (P. 29.) "What the Parliament doth shall be *holden for nought*, whensoever it shall enact that which is contrary to a *natural* Right!" We dare not suspect a grave Writer of such egregious trifling, as to mean no more by these assertions, than that what is wrong is not right; [149] and if more than this be meant, it must be that the Subject is not bound to obey any act of Parliament, which according to his conviction entrenches on a Principle of natural Right; which natural Rights are, as we have seen, not confined to the Man in his individual capacity, but are made to confer universal legislative privileges on every Subject of every State, and of the extent of which every man is competent to judge, who is competent to be the object of Law at all, i.e. every man who has not lost his Reason.

In the statement of his Principles therefore, I have not misrepresented Major Cartwright. Have I then endeavoured to connect public odium with his honoured name, by arraigning his Motives, or the Tendency of his Writings? The tendency of his Writings, in my inmost Conscience I believe to be perfectly harmless, and I dare cite them in confirmation of the opinions which it was the object of my 3d. and 4th. Numbers to establish, and as an additional proof, that no good Man communicating what he believes to be the Truth for the sake of Truth, and according to the rules of Conscience, will be found to have acted injuriously to the peace or interests of Society. The venerable State-Moralist (for this is his true character, and in this Title is conveyed the whole Error of his System) is incapable of aiding his arguments by the poignant condiment of personal slander, incapable of appealing to the envy of the Multitude by bitter declamation against the follies and oppressions of the higher Classes! He would shrink with horror from the thought of adding a false and unnatural influence to the cause of Truth and Justice, by details of present Calamity or immediate Suffering, fitted to excite the *fury* of the Multitude, or by promises of turning the current of the public Revenue into the channels* of individual Distress and Poverty, so as to bribe the Populace by selfish hopes! It does not belong to Men of his Character to delude the uninstructed into the belief, that their shortest way of obtaining the good things of this Life, is to commence busy Politicians, instead of remaining industrious Labourers. He knows, and acts on the Knowledge, that it is the [150] duty of the enlightened Philanthropist to plead *for* the poor and ignorant, not *to* them.

No!—From Works written and published under the control of austere Principles, and at the impulse of a lofty and generous enthusiasm, from Works rendered attractive only by the fervor of sincerity, and imposing only by the *Majesty of Plain Dealing*, no danger will be apprehended by a wise Man, no offence received by a good Man. I could almost venture to

---

* I had written a Note on this most interesting Subject, which insensibly grew under my pen to the length of a full Essay, and will form the next Number of THE FRIEND,[1] under the title of VULGAR ERRORS CONCERNING TAXES AND TAXATION.

[1] Actually, the one after the next, No 12.

warrant our Patriot's publications *innoxious,* from the single circumstance of their perfect freedom from *personal* themes in this AGE OF PERSONAL-ITY, this age of literary and political *Gossiping,* when the meanest Insects are worshipped with a sort of Egyptian Superstition, if only the brainless head be atoned for by the sting of *personal* malignity in the tail; when the most vapid Satires have become the objects of a keen public Interest purely from the number of contemporary characters *named* in the patch-work Notes (which possess, however, the comparative merit of being more poetical than the Text), and because, to increase the stimulus, the Author has sagaciously left his own *name* for whispers and conjectures!—In an Age, when even Sermons are published with a double Appendix stuffed with *names*—in a Generation so transformed from the characteristic reserve of Britons, that from the ephemeral Sheet of a London Newspaper to the everlasting Scotch Professorial Quarto, almost every Publication exhibits or flatters the epidemic Distemper; that the very "Last years Rebuses" in the Lady's Diary, are answered in a serious Elegy "*On my Father's Death,*" with the name and *habitat* of the elegiac Œdipus subscribed;—and "*other ingenious solutions were likewise given*" to the said *Rebuses*—not, as heretofore, by Crito, Philander, A B, X Y, &c. but—by fifty or sixty plain English Sirnames at full length, with their several places of Abode! In an Age, when a bashful *Philalethes* or *Philaleutheros*[1] is as rare on the title-pages and among the signatures of our Magazines, as a real name used to be in the days of our shy and notice-shunning Grandfathers! When (more exquisite than all) I see an EPIC POEM (Spirits of Maro and Mæonides, make ready to welcome your new Compeer!) advertized with the special recommendation, that the said EPIC POEM contains more than a hundred *names* of *living* Persons! No—if Works as abhorrent, as those of Major Cartwright, from all unworthy [151] provocatives to the vanity, the envy, and the selfish passions of mankind, could acquire a sufficient influence on the public mind to be mischievous, the plans proposed in his pamphlets would cease to be altogether visionary: though even then they could not ground their claims to actual adoption on self-evident Principles of pure Reason, but on the happy accident of the Virtue and Good Sense of that Public, for whose Suffrages they were presented. (Indeed with Major Cartwright's *Plans* I have no quarrel; but with the Principles, on which he grounds the obligations to adopt them.)

But I must not sacrifice Truth to my reverence for individual purity of Intention. The tendency of one good Man's Writings is altogether a different thing from the tendency of the System itself, when seasoned and served up for the unreasoning Multitude, as it has been by Men whose names I would not honour by writing them in the same sentence with Major Cartwright's. For this System has two sides, and holds out very different attractions to its Admirers that advance towards it from different points of the Compass. It possesses qualities, that can scarcely fail of winning over to its banners a numerous Host of shallow heads and restless tempers, Men who without Learning (or, as one of my Friends has forcibly expressed it, "*strong Book-mindedness*") live as Alms-folks on the

---

[1] For "Philaleutheros" 1812 reads "Phileleutheros".

opinions of their Contemporaries, and who, (well pleased to exchange the humility of regret for the self-complacent feelings of contempt) reconcile themselves to the *sans-culotterie* of their ignorance, by scoffing at the useless Fox-brush of Pedantry.* The attachment of this numerous Class is owing neither to the solidity and depth of *foundation* in this Theory, or to the strict *coherence* of its arguments; and still less to any genuine reverence for Humanity in the abstract. The physiocratic System promises to deduce all things and every [152] thing relative to Law and Government, with mathematical exactness and certainty, from a few individual and self-evident Principles. But who so dull, as not to be capable of apprehending a simple self-evident Principle, and of following a short demonstration? By this System (THE SYSTEM as its Admirers were wont to call it, even as they named the Writer who first applied it in systematic detail to the whole constitution and administration of civil Policy, (D Quesnoy, to wit) *le Docteur* or, THE TEACHER;) by this System the observation of Times, Places, relative Bearings, History, national Customs and Character, is rendered superfluous: all, in short, which according to the common notion makes the attainment of legislative Prudence a work of difficulty and long-continued effort, even for the acutest and most comprehensive minds. The cautious Balancing of comparative Advantages, the painful calculation of forces and counter-forces, the preparation of Circumstances, the lynx-eyed Watching for Opportunities, are all superseded; and by the magic Oracles of certain axioms and definitions it is revealed, how the World with all its concerns should be mechanized, and then let go on of itself. All the positive Institutions and Regulations, which the Prudence of our Ancestors had provided, are declared to be erroneous or interested Perversions of the natural Relations of Man; and the whole is delivered over to the faculty, which all Men possess equally, i.e. the *common* sense or universal Reason. "The science of Politics, it is said, is but the application of the common Sense, which every Man possesses, to a subject in which every Man is concerned." To be a Musician, an Orator, a Painter, a Poet, an Architect, or even to be a good Mechanist, presupposes *Genius;* to be an excellent Artizan or Mechanic, requires more than an average degree of *Talent;* but to be a Legislator requires nothing but *common Sense.* The commonest human intellect therefore suffices for a perfect insight into the whole Science of civil Polity, and qualifies the Possessor to sit in Judgement on the Constitution and Administration of his own Country, and of all other Nations. This must needs be agreeable Tidings to the great mass of Mankind. There is no Subject, which Men in general like better to

---

* "He (*Charles Brandon, Duke of Suffolk*) knowing that Learning hath no Enemy but Ignorance, did suspect always the want of it in those Men who derided the habit of it in others: like the Fox in the Fable, who being without a Tail, would persuade others to cut off theirs as a burthen. But he liked well the Philosopher's division of Men into three ranks—some who knew good and were willing to teach others; these he said were like Gods among Men—others who though they knew not much yet were willing to learn; these he said were like Men among Beasts—and some who knew not good and yet despised such as should teach them; these he esteemed as Beasts among Men." *Lloyd's State Worthies, p. 33.*

harangue on, than Politics: none, the deciding on which more flatters the sense of self-importance. For as to what Doctor Johnson calls [153] *plebeian envy*, I do not believe that the mass of men are justly chargeable with it in their political feelings; not only because envy is seldom excited except by definite and individual objects, but still more because it is a *painful* Passion, and not likely to co-exist with the high delight and self-complacency with which the harangues on States and Statesmen, Princes and Generals, are made and listened to in Ale-house Circles or promiscuous public meetings. A certain portion of this is not merely desirable, but necessary in a free Country. Heaven forbid! that the most ignorant of my Countrymen should be deprived of a Subject so well fitted to

> ————————"impart
> An hour's importance to the poor Man's heart!"

But a System which not only flatters the pride and vanity of men, but which in so plausible and intelligible a manner persuades them, not that *this* is wrong and that *that* ought to have been managed otherwise; or that Mr. X. is worth a hundred of Mr. Y., as a Minister or Parliament Man, &c. &c.; but that *all* is wrong and mistaken, nay, all most unjust and wicked, and that every man is *competent*, and in contempt of all rank and property, on the mere title of his *Personality*, possesses the *Right*, and is under the most solemn moral *obligation*, to give a helping hand toward overthrowing it: this confusion of political with religious claims, this transfer of the rights of Religion *disjoined* from the austere duties of Self-denial, with which religious rights exercised in their proper sphere cannot fail to be accompanied, and not only disjoined from Self-restraint, but *united* with the indulgence of those Passions (Self-will, love of Power, &c.) which it is the principal aim and hardest Task of Religion to correct and restrain—this, I say, is altogether different from the *Village Politics* of Yore, and may be pronounced alarming and of dangerous tendency by the boldest Advocates of Reform not less consistently, than by the most timid Eschewers of popular Disturbance.

Still, however, the System had its golden side for the noblest minds: and I should act the part of a Coward, if I disguised my Convictions, that the Errors of the Aristocratic Party were full as gross, and far less excusable. Instead of contenting themselves with opposing the real blessings of English Law to the splendid promises of [154] untried Theory, too large a part of those, who called themselves *Anti-Jacobins*, did all in their power to suspend those blessings; and thus furnished new arguments to the Advocates of Innovation, when they should have been answering the old ones. The most prudent, as well as the most honest mode of defending the existing arrangements, would have been, to have candidly admitted what could not with truth be denied, and then to have shewn that, though the things complained of were Evils, they were necessary Evils; or if they were *removable*, yet that the consequences of the *heroic* medicines recommended by the Revolutionists would be far more dreadful than the Disease. Now either the one or the other point, by the double aid of History, and a sound Philosophy, they *might* have established with a certainty little short of demonstration, and with such colours and illustrations as would have

taken strong hold of the very feelings which had attached to the democratic System all the good and valuable men of the Party. But instead of
this they precluded the possibility of being listened to even by the gentlest
and most ingenuous among the Friends of the French Revolution, denying
or attempting to palliate facts, that were equally notorious and unjusti-
fiable, and supplying the lack of Brain by an overflow of Gall. While they
lamented with tragic outcries the injured Monarch and the exiled Noble,
they displayed the most disgusting insensibility to the privations, sufferings,
and manifold oppressions, of the great mass of the continental Population,
and a blindness or callousness still more offensive to the crimes* and un-
utterable abominations of their oppressors. Not only was the Bastile
justified, but the Spanish Inquisition itself—and this in a pamphlet passionately extolled and industriously circulated by the adherents of the then
Ministry. Thus, and by their infatuated panegyrics on the former state of
France, they played into the hands of their worst and most dangerous
Antagonists. For these appeared to talk only the same language as the
Anti-jacobins themselves used, when they confounded the condition of the
English and French Peasantry, and quoted the authorities of Milton,
Sidney, and their immortal Compeers, as applicable [155] to present times
and the existing Government. For if the vilest calumnies of obsolete
Bigots were applied against these great Men by the one Party, with equal
plausibility might their authorities be adduced, and their arguments for
increasing the power of the People be re-applied to the existing Government,
by the other. If the most disgusting forms of Despotism were spoken of by
the one in the same respectful language as the executive Power of our own
Country, what wonder if the irritated Partizans of the other were able to
impose on the Populace the converse of the Proposition, and confounded
the executive branch of the English Sovereignty with the Despotisms of less
happy Lands? The first duty of a wise Advocate is to convince his Opponents, that he understands their Arguments and sympathizes with their
just Feelings. But instead of this, these pretended Constitutionalists recurred to the language of insult, and to measures of persecution. In order
to oppose Jacobinism they imitated it in its worst features; in personal
slander, in illegal violence, and even in the thirst for Blood. They justified
the corruptions of the State in the same spirit of Sophistry, by the same
vague arguments of general Reason, and the same disregard of ancient
Ordinances and established Opinions, with which the State itself had been
attacked by the Jacobins. The Wages of state-dependence were represented
as sacred as the Property won by Industry or derived from a long line of
Ancestors.

It was indeed evident to thinking men, that both parties were playing the
same game with different Counters. If the Jacobins ran wild with the
Rights of Man, and the abstract Sovereignty of the People, their Antagonists flew off as extravagantly from the sober good sense of our Forefathers
and idolized as pure an abstraction in the Rights of *Sovereigns*. Nor was

---

* I do not mean the Sovereigns, but the old Nobility of both Germany and
France. The extravagantly false and flattering picture, which BURKE gave of the
French Nobility and Hierarchy, has always appeared to me the greatest defect of
his, in so many respects invaluable Work.

this confined to Sovereigns. They defended the exemptions and privileges of all privileged Orders on the presumption of their inalienable *Right* to them, however inexpedient they might have been found, as universally and abstractly as if these privileges had been decreed by the supreme Wisdom instead of being the Offspring of Chance or Violence, or the inventions of human prudence. Thus while they deemed themselves defending, they were in reality blackening and degrading, the uninjurious and useful privileges of our English Nobility, which (thank Heaven!) rest on nobler and securer [156] grounds. Thus too the necessity of compensations for dethroned Princes was affirmed as familiarly, as if Kingdoms had been private Estates: and no more disapprobation was expressed at the transfer of five or ten millions of men from one Proprietor to another, than as many score head of Cattle. This most degrading and superannuated Superstition (or rather this Ghost of a defunct Absurdity raised by the Necromancy of the violent re-action which the Extreme of one System is so apt to occasion in the Adherents of its Opposite) was more than once allowed to regulate our measures in the conduct of a War, on which the Independence of the British Empire and the progressive Civilization of all Mankind depended. I could mention Possessions of paramount and indispensible Importance to first-rate national Interests, the nominal Sovereign of which had delivered up all his Sea-ports and Strong-holds to the French, and maintained a French Army in his Dominions—consequently, had by the law of Nations made his Territories French Dependencies—which Possessions were not to be touched, though the natural Inhabitants were eager to place themselves under our permanent protection—and why?—They were the *Property* of the King of——! All the grandeur and majesty of the Law of Nations, which taught our Ancestors to distinguish between a European Sovereign and the miserable Despots of oriental Barbarism, and to consider the former as the representative of the Nation which he governed, and as inextricably connected with its fortunes as *Sovereign*, were merged in the basest personality. Instead of the interest of mighty Nations, it seemed as if a mere Law-suit were carrying on between John Doe and Richard Roe—the happiness of millions was light in the balance, weighed against a theatric Compassion for one Individual and his Family, who (I speak from facts, that I myself know) if they feared the French more, hated us worse. Though the Restoration of good sense commenced during the Interval of the Peace of Amiens, yet it was not till the Spanish Insurrection that Englishmen of all Parties recurred *in toto* to the old English Principles, and spoke of their Hampdens, Sidneys, and Miltons, with the old enthusiasm. During the last War, an Acquaintance of mine (least of all Men a political Zealot) had *christened* a Vessel which he had just built—THE LIBERTY; and was seriously admonished by his aristocratic Friends to change it for some [157] other name. What? replied the Owner very innocently—should I call it THE FREEDOM? That (it was replied) would be far better, as people might then think only of Freedom of Trade; whereas LIBERTY has a *jacobinical* sound with it! Alas! (and this is an observation of Sir J. Denham and of Burke) is there then no medium between an Ague-fit and a Frenzy-fever?

I have said that to withstand the arguments of the lawless, the Anti-jacobins proposed to suspend the Law, and by the interposition of a particular Statute to eclipse the blessed light of the universal Sun, that Spies and Informers might tyrannize and escape in the ominous darkness. Oh! if these mistaken Men intoxicated with the alarm, and bewildered with the panic of Property, which they themselves were the chief Agents in exciting, had ever lived in a Country, where there was indeed a general disposition to change and Rebellion? Had they ever travelled through Sicily, or through France at the first coming on of the Revolution, or even alas! through too many of the Provinces of a Sister-Island, they could not but have shrunk from their own declarations concerning the state of Feeling and Opinion at that time predominant throughout Great Britain. There was a time (Heaven grant that that time may have passed by) when by crossing a narrow Strait they might have learnt the true symptoms of approaching Danger and have secured themselves from mistaking the Meetings and idle Rant of such Sedition, as shrunk appalled from the sight of a Constable, for the dire murmuring and strange consternation which precedes the storm or earthquake of national Discord. Not only in Coffee-houses and public Theatres, but even at the Tables of the wealthy, they would have heard the Advocates of existing Government defend their Cause in the language and with the tone of men, who are conscious that they are in a Minority. But in England, when the alarm was at the highest, there was not a City, no, not a Town in which a man suspected of holding democratic Principles could move abroad without receiving some unpleasant proof of the hatred, in which his supposed Opinions were held by the great majority of the People: and the only instances of popular Excess and indignation were on the side of the Government and the established Church. But why need I appeal to these invidious facts? Turn over the pages of History, and seek for a single instance of a Revolution [158] having been effected without the concurrence of either the Nobles, or the Ecclesiastics, or the monied Classes, in any Country in which the influences of Property had ever been predominant, and where the interests of the Proprietors were interlinked! Examine the Revolution of the Belgic Provinces under Philip the second; the civil Wars of France in the preceding generation, the History of the American Revolution, or the yet more recent Events in Sweden and in Spain; and it will be scarcely possible not to perceive, that in England, from 1791 to the Peace of Amiens, there were neither tendencies to Confederacy nor actual Confederacies, against which the existing Laws had not provided both sufficient safeguards and an ample punishment. But alas! the panic of Property had been struck in the first instance for Party purposes: and when it became general, its Propagators caught it themselves, and ended in believing their own Lie: even as our Bulls in Borrowdale sometimes run mad with the echo of their own bellowing. The consequences were most injurious. Our attention was concentred to a Monster which could not survive the convulsions in which it had been brought forth, even the enlightened Burke himself too often talking and reasoning as if a perpetual and organized Anarchy had been a possible thing! Thus while we were warring against French Doctrines, we took little heed whether the means, by which we attempted to overthrow them, were not likely to aid and augment the far more formidable evil of French Ambition. Like Children we ran away from the yelpings[1] of a Cur, and took shelter at the heels of a vicious War Horse. The conduct of the aristocratic Party was equally unwise in private life and to individuals, especially to the young and inexperienced, who were surely to be forgiven for having had their imagination dazzled, and their enthusiasm kindled, by a Novelty so specious, that even an old and tried Statesman had pronounced it "a stupendous monument of human Wisdom and human Happiness." This was indeed a gross Delusion, but assuredly for young men at least, a very venial one. To hope too boldly of Human Nature is a fault, which all good Men have an interest in forgiving. But instead of removing the Error in the only way, by which it could be, or even ought to have been removed, namely, having first sympathized with the warm benevolence and the [159] enthusiasm for Liberty, which was at the bottom of it; to have then shewn the young Enthusiasts, that Liberty was not the only Blessing of Society, and though desirable even for its own sake, yet that it was chiefly valuable as the means of calling forth and securing other advantages and excellencies, the activities of Industry, the security of Life and Property, the peaceful energies of Genius and manifold Talent, the developement of the moral Virtues, and the independence and dignity of the Nation itself in relation to foreign Powers: and that neither these nor Liberty itself could subsist in a Country so various in its Soils, so long inhabited and so fully peopled, as Great Britain, without difference of Ranks, and without Laws which recognized and protected the privileges of each. But instead of thus winning them back from the snare, they too often drove them into it by angry contumelies, which being in contradiction with each other, could only excite contempt for those that uttered them. To prove the folly of the Opinions, they were represented as the crude fancies of unfledged Wit and School-boy Statesmen; but when abhorrence was to be expressed, the self-same unfledged School-boys were invested with all the attributes of brooding Conspiracy and hoary-headed Treason. Nay, a sentence of absolute Reprobation was passed on them; and the speculative Error of Jacobinism was equalized to the mysterious Sin in Scripture, which in some inexplicable manner excludes not only Mercy but even Repentance. It became the Watch-word of the Party, "ONCE A JACOBIN ALWAYS A JACOBIN." And wherefore*? might the individual say, (who in his Youth or earliest Manhood had been enamoured of a System, which for *him* had combined the austere beauty of Science, at once with all the light and colours of Imagination, and with all the warmth of wide religious Charity, and who

---

* The Passage which follows is taken from an Essay of my own, published many years ago, in a morning Newspaper[2] (I hope the friendly Reader will forgive this little piece of vanity, which, however, I can assure him, respects my political Principles, not my literary Merits) which gave the first fair and philosophical statement and definition of Jacobinism and of Jacobin, as far as a Jacobin is not a mere word of abuse, or already expressed in Republican, Democrat, or Demagogue.

[1] For "yelpings" 1812 reads "yelping".

[2] "Once a Jacobin Always a Jaco-
bin" in the *M Post: EOT* II 542–52; see above, I 221 n 2.

overlooking its *ideal* Essence, had dreamt of actually building a Government on personal and natural Rights alone). And wherefore "Is Jacobinism an absurdity, and [160] have we no Understanding to detect it with? Is it productive of all misery and all horrors, and have we no natural Humanity to make us turn away with indignation and loathing from it? Uproar and confusion, insecurity of person and of property, the tyranny of Mobs or the domination of a soldiery; private houses changed to brothels, the ceremony of marriage but an initiation to harlotry, and marriage itself degraded to mere concubinage—these, the wiser Advocates of Aristocracy have said, and truly said, are the effects of Jacobinism! In private Life an insufferable licentiousness, and abroad an intolerable despotism! *'Once a Jacobin, always a Jacobin'*—O wherefore? Is it because the Creed which we have stated is dazzling at first sight to the young, the innocent, the disinterested, and to those, who judging of Men in general from their own uncorrupted hearts, judge erroneously, and expect unwisely? Is it, because it deceives the mind in its purest and most flexible period? Is it, because it is an Error, that every days experience aids to detect? An error against which all History is full of warning examples? Or is it because the experiment has been tried before our eyes and the error made palpable?

"From what source are we to derive this strange Phænomenon, that the Young and the Enthusiastic, who as our daily experience informs us, are deceived in their religious Antipathies, and grow wiser; in their Friendships, and grow wiser; in their modes of Pleasure, and grow wiser; should, if once deceived in a question of abstract Politics, cling to the Error for ever and ever? though in addition to the natural growth of judgement and information with increase of years, they live in the Age in which the tenets have been acted upon, and the consequences such that every good Man's heart sickens and his head turns giddy at the retrospect."

(To be continued.)[1]

The delay in the delivery of Nos. 8 and 9, has been occasioned, in the first instance, by the miscarriage of the stamps from London, and in the second, by an accidental mutilation of the Authors Manuscript in the printing office.[2]

---

[1] 1812 omits this line and the following paragraph.

[2] Rats in the printing-house ate the motto, and two fresh transcripts, entrusted to different carriers, failed to reach the printer; see above, Introduction, ɪ lvii.

THE FRIEND

No. 11. THURSDAY, OCTOBER 26, 1809

(Continued from page 160.)[1]

I was never myself, at any period of my life, a Convert to the System. From my earliest Manhood, it was an axiom in Politics with me, that in every Country where Property prevailed, Property must be the grand basis of the Government; and that that Government was the best, in which the Power or political Influence of the Individual was in proportion to his property, provided that the free circulation of Property was not impeded by any positive Laws or Customs, nor the tendency of Wealth to accumulate in abiding Masses unduly encouraged. I perceived, that if the People at large were neither ignorant nor immoral, there could be no motive for a sudden and violent change of Government; and if they were, there could be no hope but of a change for the worse. The Temple of Despotism, like that of the Mexican God, would be rebuilt with human skulls, and more firmly, though in a different architecture. Thanks to the excellent Education which I had received, my reason was too clear not to draw this "circle of Power" round me, and my spirit too honest to attempt to break through it. My feelings, however, and imagination did not remain unkindled in this general conflagration; and I confess I should be more inclined to be ashamed than proud of myself, if they had! I was a sharer in the general vortex, though my little World described the path of its Revolution in an orbit of its own. What I dared not expect from constitutions of Government and whole Nations, I hoped from Religion and a small Company of chosen Individuals, and formed a plan, as harmless as it was extravagant, of trying the experiment of human Perfectibility on the banks of the *Susquehannah;* where our little Society, in its second Generation, was to have combined the innocence of the patriarchal Age with the knowledge and genuine refinements of European culture: and where I had dreamt of beholding,[2] in the sober evening of my life,[3] the Cottages of Independence in the *undivided* Dale of Industry,

> "And oft, soothed sadly by some dirgeful wind,
> Muse on the sore ills I had left behind!"

[162] Strange fancies! and as vain as strange! yet to the intense interest and impassioned zeal, which called forth and strained every faculty of my intellect for the organization and defence of this Scheme, I owe much of whatever I at present possess, my clearest insight into the nature of

---

1 1812 omits *"from page* 160".   reads "dreamt that".
2 For "had . . . beholding," 1812   3 1812 adds "I should behold".

individual Man, and my most comprehensive views of his social relations, the true uses of Trade and Commerce, and how far the *Wealth*[1] of Nations promotes or impedes[2] their true *welfare* and inherent strength.[3] Nor were they less serviceable in securing myself, and perhaps some others, from the pitfalls of Sedition: and when we gradually alighted on the firm ground of common sense, from the gradually exhausted Balloon of youthful Enthusiasm, though the air-built Castles, which we had been pursuing, had vanished with all their pageantry of shifting forms and glowing colours, we were yet free from the stains and impurities which might have remained upon us, had we been travelling with the crowd of less imaginative malcontents, through the dark lanes and foul bye roads of ordinary Fanaticism.

But Oh! there were thousands as young and as innocent as myself who, not like me, sheltered in the tranquil nook or inland cove of a particular Fancy, were driven along with the general current! Many there were, young Men of loftiest minds, yea the prime stuff out of which manly Wisdom and practicable Greatness is to be formed, who had appropriated their hopes and the ardour of their souls to Mankind at large, to the wide expanse of national Interests, which then seemed fermenting in the French Republic as in the main Outlet and chief Crater of the volcanic Torrents, which,[4] like the Lavas of Vesuvius, were to subside into a soil of inexhaustible fertility on the circumjacent Lands, the old divisions and mouldering edifices of which they had covered or swept away—Enthusiasts of kindliest temperament, who to use the words of the Poet (having already borrowed the meaning and the metaphor) had approached

> —————————————"the shield
> Of human nature from the golden side,
> And would have fought even to the death to attest
> The quality of the metal which they saw."

My honoured Friend has permitted me to give a value and relief to the present Essay, by a quotation from one of [163] his unpublished Poems, the length of which I regret only from its forbidding me to trespass on his kindness by making it yet longer. I trust there are many of my Readers of the same Age with myself, who will throw themselves back into the state of thought and feeling, in which they were when France was reported to have solemnized her first sacrifice of error and prejudice on the bloodless altar of Freedom, by an Oath of Peace and Good-will to all Mankind——

> Oh! pleasant exercise of hope and joy!
> For mighty were the auxiliars, which then stood
> Upon our side, we who were strong in love!
> Bliss was it in that dawn to be alive,
> But to be young was very heaven! oh! times,

---

[1] 1812 adds "and relative *Power*".

[2] For "promotes or impedes" 1812 reads "promote or impede".

[3] For "strength" 1812 reads "*strength*".

[4] For "volcanic Torrents, which" 1812 reads "revolutionary Torrents; and who confidently believed, that these Torrents,".

In which the meagre stale forbidding ways
Of custom, law, and statute, took at once
The attraction of a country in Romance!
When Reason seem'd the most to assert her rights,
When most intent on making of herself
A prime Enchanter to assist the work,
Which then was going forward in her name!
Not favour'd spots alone, but the whole earth
The beauty wore of promise—that which sets
(To take an image which was felt no doubt
Among the bowers of paradise itself)
The budding rose above the rose full blown.
What temper at the prospect did not wake
To happiness unthought of? The inert
Were rous'd, and lively natures rapt away!
They who had fed their childhood upon dreams,
The play-fellows of fancy, who had made
All powers of swiftness, subtilty, and strength
Their ministers, used to stir in lordly wise
Among the grandest objects of the sense
And deal with whatsoever they found there
As if they had within some lurking right
To wield it;—they too, who of gentle mood
Had watch'd all gentle motions, and to these
Had fitted their own thoughts, schemers more mild
And in the region of their peaceful selves;——
Now was it that both found, the Meek and Lofty,
Did both find helpers to their heart's desire
And stuff at hand, plastic as they could wish!—
Were call'd upon to exercise their skill
Not in Utopia, subterraneous Fields,
Or some secreted Island, heaven knows where!
But in the very world, which is the world
Of all of us, the place where in the end
We find our happiness, or not at all!

WORDSWORTH

[164] The Peace of Amiens deserved the name of Peace, for it gave us unanimity at home, and reconciled Englishmen with each other. Yet it would be as wild a fancy as any of which we have treated, to expect that the violence of party Spirit is never more to return. Sooner or later the same causes, or their equivalents, will call forth the same opposition of opinion, and bring the same passions into play. Ample would be my recompence, could I foresee that this present Essay would be the means of preventing discord and unhappiness in a single Family; if its words of warning, aided by its tones of sympathy, should arm a single man of Genius against the fascinations of his own ideal World, a single Philanthropist against the enthusiasm of his own heart! Not less would be my satisfaction, dared I flatter myself that my lucubrations would not be altogether without effect on those who deem themselves Men of Judgement, faithful to the light of *Practice* and not to be led astray by the wandering fires of Theory! If I should aid in making these aware, that in recoiling with too incautious an abhorrence from the bugbears of innovation, they may sink all at once into

the slough of slavishness and corruption. Let such persons recollect, that the charms of hope and novelty furnish some palliation for the idolatry, to which *they* seduce the mind; but that the Apotheosis of familiar abuses and of the errors of selfishness, is the vilest of Superstitions. Let them recollect too, that nothing can be more incongruous than to combine the pusillanimity, which despairs of human improvement, with the arrogance, supercilious contempt, and boisterous anger, which have no pretensions to pardon except as the overflowings of ardent anticipation and enthusiastic faith! And finally, and above all, let it be remembered by both Parties, and indeed by Controversialists on all Subjects, that every speculative Error, which boasts a multitude of Advocates, has its *golden* as well as its dark side; that there is always some Truth connected with it, the exclusive attention to which has misled the understanding, some moral beauty which has given it charms for the heart. Let it be remembered, that no Assailant of an Error can reasonably hope to be listened to by its Advocates, who has not proved to them that he has seen the disputed Subject in the same point of view, and is capable of contemplating it with the same feelings as themselves (for why should we abandon a Cause at the persuasions of one, [165] who is ignorant of the reasons which have attached us to it?) Let it be remembered, that to write, however ably, merely to convince those who are already convinced, displays but the courage of a Boaster; and in any Subject to rail against the Evil before we have enquired for the Good, and to exasperate the Passions of those who think with us, by caricaturing the Opinions and blackening the Motives of our Antagonists, is to make the Understanding a Pandar of the Passions; and even though we should have defended the right cause, to gain for ourselves ultimately, from the Good and the Wise no other praise, than the supreme Judge awarded to the Friends of Job for their partial and uncharitable defence of his Justice: "My Wrath is kindled against you, for ye have not spoken of me *rightfully*."

TO CORRESPONDENTS

To R. L.

DEAR SIR,

WHEN I first undertook the present Publication for the sake and with the *avowed* object of referring Men in all things to PRINCIPLES or fundamental Truths, I was well aware of the obstacles which the plan itself would oppose to my success. For in order to the regular attainment of this object, all the driest and least attractive Essays must appear in the first fifteen or twenty Numbers, and thus subject me to the necessity of demanding effort or soliciting patience in that part of the Work, where it was most my interest to secure the confidence of my Readers by winning their favour. Though I dared warrant for the pleasantness of the Journey on the whole; though I might promise that the road would, for the far greater part of it, be found plain and easy, that it would pass through countries of various prospect and that at every stage there would be a change of company; it still remained a heavy disadvantage, that I had to start at the foot of a high and steep hill: and I foresaw, not without occasional feelings of despondency, that during the slow and laborious ascent it would require no common management to keep my Passengers in good humour with the Vehicle and its' Driver. As far as this inconvenience [166] could be palliated by sincerity and previous confession, I have no reason to accuse myself of neglect. In the Prospectus of THE FRIEND, which for this cause I re-printed and annexed to the first Number, I felt it my duty to inform such as might be inclined to patronize the Publication, that I must submit to be esteemed dull by those who sought chiefly for amusement: and this I hazarded as a *general* confession, though in my own mind I felt a chearful confidence that it would apply almost exclusively to the earlier Numbers. I could not therefore be surprized, however much I may have been depressed, by the frequency with which you hear The Friend complained of for its' abstruseness and obscurity; nor did the highly flattering expressions, with which you accompanied your communication, prevent me from feeling its' truth to the whole extent.

An Author's pen, like Children's legs, improves by exercise. That part of the blame which rests in[1] myself, I am exerting my best faculties to remove. A man long accustomed to silent and solitary meditation, in proportion as he encreases the power of thinking in long and connected trains, is apt to lose or lessen the talent of communicating his thoughts with grace and perspicuity. Doubless too, I have in some measure injured my style, in respect to its' facility and popularity, from having almost confined my reading, of late years, to the Works of the Ancients and those of the elder Writers in the modern languages. We insensibly imitate what we habitually admire; and an aversion to the epigrammatic unconnected periods of the fashionable *Anglo-gallican* Taste has too often made me willing to forget, that the stately march and difficult evolutions, which characterize the eloquence of Hooker, Bacon, Milton, and Jeremy Taylor, are, notwithstanding their intrinsic excellence, still less suited to a periodical Essay. This fault I am now endeavouring to correct; though I can never so far sacrifice my judgement to the desire of being immediately popular, as to cast my sentences in the French moulds, or affect a style which an ancient critic would have deemed purposedly invented for persons troubled with the asthma to read, and for those to comprehend who labour under the more pitiable asthma of a short-witted intellect. It cannot but be injurious to the human mind never to be called into effort and[2] the habit of receiving pleasure without any exertion [167] of thought, by the mere excitement of curiosity and sensibility, may be justly ranked among the worst effects of habitual novel reading. It is true that these short and unconnected sentences are easily and instantly understood: but it is equally true, that wanting all the cement of thought as well as of style, all the connections, and (if you will forgive so trivial a metaphor) all the *hooks-and-eyes* of the memory, they are as easily forgotten: or rather, it is scarcely possible that they should be remembered: Nor is it less true, that those who confine their reading to such books dwarf their own faculties, and finally reduce their Understandings to a deplorable imbecility: the

---

[1] For "in" 1812 reads "on".   [2] For "effort and" 1812 reads "effort:".

fact you mention, and which I shall hereafter make use of, is a fair instance and a striking illustration. Like idle morning Visitors, the brisk and breathless Periods hurry in and hurry off in quick and profitless succession; each indeed for the moments of its' stay prevents the pain of vacancy, while it indulges the love of sloth; but all together they leave the Mistress of the house (the soul I mean) flat and exhausted, incapable of attending to her own concerns, and unfitted for the conversation of more rational Guests.

I know you will not suspect me of fostering so idle a hope, as that of obtaining acquittal by recrimination; or think that I am attacking one fault, in order that its' opposite may escape notice in the noise and smoke of the battery. On the contrary, I shall do my best, and even make all allowable sacrifices, to render my manner more attractive and my matter more generally interesting. All the principles of my future Work, all the fundamental doctrines, in the establishment of which I must of necessity require the attention of my Reader to become my fellow-labourer; all the primary facts essential to the intelligibility of my principles, the existence of which facts I can prove to others only as far as I can prevail on them to retire *into themselves* and make their own minds the objects of their stedfast attention; these will, all together, not occupy more than six or seven of my future Essays, and between each of these I shall interpose one or more Numbers devoted to the rational *entertainment* of my various Readers; and, partly from the desire of gratifying particular requests, and partly as a specimen of the subjects which will henceforward have a due proportion of THE FRIEND allotted to them, I shall fill up the present Paper with a miscellany. I feel too deeply the importance [168] of the convictions, which first impelled me to the present undertaking, to leave unattempted any honourable means of recommending them to as wide a circle as possible; and though all the opinions which I shall bring forward in the course of the Work, on politics, morals, religion, literature, and the fine arts, will with all their applications, be strictly deducible from the principles established in these earlier Numbers; yet I doubt not, that being Truths and interesting Truths (and such, of course, I must be supposed to deem them) their intrinsic beauty will procure them introduction to the feelings of my Readers, even of those whose habits or avocations preclude the fatigue of close reasoning, and that[1] by the illustrations and the auxiliary and independent arguments appropriate to it, each[2] will of itself[3] become sufficiently intelligible and evident.

Hitherto, my dear Sir, I have been employed in laying the Foundations of my Work. But the proper merit of a foundation is its' massiveness and solidity. The conveniences and ornaments, the gilding and stucco work, the sunshine and sunny prospects, will come with the Superstructure. Yet I dare not flatter myself, that any endeavours of mine, compatible with the duty I owe to Truth and the hope of permanent utility, will render THE FRIEND agreeable to the majority of what is called the reading Public. I never expected it. How indeed could I, when I was to borrow so little from the influence of passing Events, and absolutely excluded from my plan all appeals to personal curiosity and personal interests. Yet even this

[1] 1812 adds "each Essay of itself,".   [3] 1812 omits "of itself".
[2] 1812 omits "each".

is not my greatest impediment. No real information can be conveyed, no important errors rectified, no widely injurious prejudices rooted up, without requiring some effort of thought on the part of the Reader. But the obstinate (and toward a contemporary Writer, the contemptuous) aversion to all intellectual effort is the mother evil of all which I had proposed to war against, the Queen Bee in the Hive of our errors and misfortunes, both private and national. The proof of the Fact, positively and comparatively, and the enumeration of its' various causes, will, as I have already hinted (P. 75)[1] form the preliminary Essay of the disquisition on the elements of our moral and intellectual faculties. To solicit the attention of those, on whom these debilitating causes have acted to their full extent, would be no less absurd than to recommend [169] exercise with the dumb bells, as the only mode of cure, to a patient paralytic in both arms. You, my dear Sir, well know, that my expectations were more modest as well as more rational. I hoped, that my Readers in general would be aware of the impracticability of suiting every Essay to every Taste in any[2] period of the work, and that they would not attribute wholly to the Author, but in part to the necessity of his plan, the austerity and absence of the lighter graces in the first fifteen or twenty Numbers. In my cheerful moods I sometimes flattered myself, that a few even among those, who foresaw that my lucubrations would at all times require more attention than from the nature of their own employments they could afford them, might yet find a pleasure in supporting The Friend during its' infancy, so as to give it a chance of attracting the notice of others, to whom its' style and subjects might be better adapted. But my main anchor was the Hope, that when circumstances gradually enabled me to adopt the ordinary means of making the Publication generally known, there might be found throughout the Kingdom a sufficient number of meditative minds, who, entertaining similar convictions with myself, and gratified by the prospect of seeing them reduced to form and system, would take a warm interest in the work from the very circumstance, that it wanted those allurements of transitory interest, which render particular patronage superfluous, and for the brief season of their Blow and Fragrance attract the eye of thousands, who would pass unregarded

—————————————————————————Flowers
Of sober tint, and Herbs of med'cinable powers.

I hoped, that a sufficient number of such Readers would gradually be obtained, as to secure for the Paper that small extent of circulation and immediate Sale, which would permit the Editor to carry it on to its' conclusion, and that they might so far interest themselves in recommending it to men of kindred judgements among their acquaintances, that the alterations in my list of Subscribers should not be exclusively of a discouraging nature. Hitherto, indeed, I have only to express gratitude and acknowledge constancy; but I do not attempt to disguise from myself that I owe this, in many instances, to a generous reluctance hastily to withdraw from an [170] Undertaking in its' first struggles, and before the Adventurer had had a fair opportunity of displaying the quality of his goods or the foundations of his credit.

[1] See above, II 72.   [2] For "any" 1812 reads "*any*".

*****—the one tantum vidi: the other I know by his works only and his public character.[1] To profess indifference to their praises would convict me either of insensibility or insincerity. Yet (and I am sure, that you will both understand, and sympathize with, the feeling) my delight was not unalloyed by a something like pain, as if I were henceforward less free to express my admiration of them with the same warmth and affection, which I have been accustomed to do, before I had even anticipated the honor of such a communication. You will therefore not judge me too harshly, if so confirmed and cheered, I have sometimes in the warmth of composition, and while I was reviewing the materials of the more important part of my intended Essays, if I have sometimes permitted my Hopes a bolder flight; and counted on a share of favour and protection from the soberly zealous among the professionally Learned,[2] when the Principles of The Friend shall have been brought into clear view, and Specimens have been given of the mode and the direction in which I purpose to apply and enforce them.

There are charges, the very suspicion of which is painful to an ingenuous mind in exact proportion as they are unfounded and inapplicable. I can bear with resignation a charge of enthusiasm. Even if accused of presumption, I will repay myself by deriving from the accusation an additional motive to increase watchfulness over myself, that I may remain entitled to plead, Not guilty! to it in the Court of my own conscience. But if my anxiety to obviate hasty judgements and misapprehensions is imputed to a less honorable[3] than the earnest wish to exert my best faculties as to the most beneficial purposes so in the way most likely to effectuate them, I can give but one answer, that however great my desires of *profit* may be, they cannot be greater than my ignorance of the world, if I have chosen a weekly paper planned, as the Friend is, written on such subjects and composed in such a style, as the most promising method of gratifying them.

S.T.C.

[171]   SONNETS[4]

Of mortal Parents is the Hero born
By whom the undaunted Tyrolese are led?
Or is it Tell's great Spirit from the dead
Returned to animate an age forlorn?
He comes like Phœbus through the gates of morn

---

[1] The "one I only saw" (cf Ovid *Tristia* 4.10.51: "Virgilium vidi tantum") is perhaps Walter Scott; there are several candidates for "the other" —among them, Walter Savage Landor and William Roscoe; see below, App E, II 457, 440, 454.

[2] For "a share of favour . . . Learned" the ms of *The Friend* (Forster MS 112 f 65ᵛ) originally read: "some support and protection from the established Clergy and from their Brethren who differ from them in [? notions/matters] of Church govern-ment, rather than points of Doctrine" —which, perhaps, indicates that, if this letter had a recipient, it was the Bishop of Llandaff. In ms the following paragraph began (ibid): "It is in the highest degree distressing to an ingenuous mind . . .".

[3] 1812 adds "motive".

[4] *Poems Dedicated to National Independence and Liberty* pt II Nos 9 (var) and 10: *WPW* III 129–30. The two sonnets were first published in *The Friend*.

When dreary darkness is discomfited:
Yet mark his simple state!—upon his head
A Heron's feather for a crest is worn.
O Liberty! they stagger at the shock,
The Murderers are aghast; they strive to flee
And half their Host is buried:—rock on rock
Descends:—beneath this godlike Warrior, see!
Hills, Torrents, Woods, embodied to bemock
The Tyrant, and confound his cruelty!　　　　W.W.

Advance—come forth from thy Tyrolean ground
Dear Liberty!—stern Nymph of soul untamed,
Sweet Nymph, oh! rightly of the mountains named!
Through the long chain of Alps, from mound to mound,
And o'er the eternal snows, like Echo, bound,
Like Echo when the Hunter-train at dawn
Have rouzed her from her sleep: and forest-lawn,
Cliffs, Woods, and Caves, her viewless steps resound
And babble of her pastime!—On! dread Power,
With such invisible motion speed thy flight,
Through hanging clouds, from craggy height to height,
Through the green vales and through the Herdsman's bower,
That all the Alps may gladden in thy might
Here, there, and in all places at one hour?　　　　W.W.

172]　　SPECIMENS OF RABBINICAL WISDOM,
SELECTED FROM THE MISHNA

1

The Lord helpeth both[1] man and beast

During his march to conquer the World, Alexander the Macedonian, came to a People in Africa who dwelt in a remote and secluded corner in peaceful huts, and knew neither War nor Conqueror. They led him to the hut of their Chief, who received him hospitably and placed before him golden Dates, golden Figs, and Bread of gold. Do you eat Gold in this Country! said Alexander. I take it for granted[2] that thou wert able to find eatable food in thine own Country. For what reason then art thou come among us? Your Gold has not tempted me hither, said Alexander, but I would willingly become acquainted with your Manners and Customs. So be it, rejoined the other. Sojourn among us as long as it pleaseth thee. At the close of this Conversation two Citizens entered as into their Court of Justice. The Plaintiff said, I bought of this Man a piece of Land, and as I was making a deep drain through it I found a Treasure. This is not mine, for I only bargained for the Land, and not for any treasure that might be concealed beneath it: and yet the former Owner of the Land will not receive it. The Defendant answered: I hope I have a Conscience as well as my Fellow-citizen. I sold him the Land with all it's contingent as well as existing advantages, and consequently the Treasure inclusively.

---

[1] 1812 omits "both".　　　　　　　[2] 1812 adds "(replied the Chief)".

The Chief, who was at the same time their supreme Judge, recapitulated their words, in order that the Parties might see whether or no he understood them aright. Then after some reflection said: Thou hast a Son, Friend, I believe? Yes! And thou (addressing the other) a Daughter? Yes!—Well then, let thy Son marry thy[1] Daughter, and bestow the Treasure on the young Couple for their marriage Portion.—Alexander seemed surprized and perplexed. Think you my sentence unjust? the Chief asked him—O no, replied Alexander, but it astonishes me. And how then, rejoined the Chief, would the Case have been decided in your Country?—To confess the truth, said Alexander, we should have taken both Parties [173] into Custody and have seized the Treasure for the King's use.—For the King's use, exclaimed the Chief, now in his turn astonished. Does the Sun shine on that Country?—O yes!—Does it rain there? Assuredly.—Wonderful! but are there tame Animals there that live on the grass and green herbs?—Very many, and of many kinds.—Aye, that must be the Cause, said the Chief, for the sake of those innocent Animals the All-gracious Being continues to let the Sun shine and the Rain drop down on your Country.

2

Whoso hath found a virtuous Wife, hath a greater treasure than costly Pearls

Such a Treasure had the celebrated Teacher R ABBI M EIR found. He sate, during the whole of one Sabbath day in the public School, and instructed the People. During his absence from his House, his two Sons died, both of them of uncommon beauty and enlightened in the Law. His Wife bore them to her Bed-chamber, laid them upon the marriage-bed, and spread a white covering over their Bodies. In the Evening Rabbi Meir came home. Where are my Sons, he asked, that I may give them my blessing? They are gone to the School, was the answer. I repeatedly looked round the School, he replied, and I did not see them there.—She reached to him a Goblet, he praised the Lord at the going out of the Sabbath, drank and again asked: where are my Sons, that they too may drink of the cup of blessing? They will not be far off, she said, and placed food before him that he might eat. He was in a gladsome and genial mood, and when he had said Grace after the meal, she thus addressed him. Rabbi, permit me[2] one question. Ask it then my Love, he replied. A few days ago a person entrusted some Jewels to my custody and now he demands them again, should I give them back to him? This is a question, said Rabbi Meir, which my Wife should not have thought it necessary to ask. What, wouldst thou hesitate or be reluctant to restore to every one his own?—O no, replied she,[3] but[4] I thought it best not to restore them without acquainting thee therewith. She then led him to their Chamber, and stepping to the Bed, took the white covering from the dead Bodies.—Ah, my Sons, my Sons, thus loudly lamented the Father, my Sons, the Light of mine Eyes and the Light of my [174] Understanding, I was your Father, but ye were

---

[1] For "thy" 1812 reads "*thy*".

[2] For "permit me" 1812 reads "with thy permission I would fain propose to thee".

[3] For "O . . . she," 1812 reads "No, she replied;".

[4] 1812 adds "yet".

my Teachers in the Law. The Mother turned away and wept bitterly. At length she took her Husband by the hand and said, Rabbi, didst thou not teach me that one[1] must not be reluctant to restore that which was entrusted to our keeping? See, the Lord gave, the Lord has taken away, and blessed be the name of the Lord! Blessed be the name of the Lord! echoed Rabbi Meir, and blessed be his name for thy sake too, for well is it written. Whoso hath found a virtuous Wife hath a greater Treasure than costly Pearls: She openeth her mouth with Wisdom, and in her tongue is the law of Kindness.

HYMN

Before Sun-rise, in the Vale of Chamouny[2]

HAST thou a charm to stay the morning Star
In his steep Course? So long he seems to pause
On thy bald aweful top, O sovran BLANC!
The Arve and Arveiron at thy base
Rave ceaselessly; but thou, dread aweful Form!
Risest from forth thy silent Sea of Pines
How silently! Around thee and above
Deep is the air and dark, transpicuous,[3] black,
An ebon Mass: methinks, thou piercest it,
As with a wedge! But when I look again,
It is thy own calm Home, thy crystal shrine,
Thy Habitation from eternity!
O dread and silent Mount! I gaz'd upon thee,
Till then,[4] still present to the bodily sense,
Didst vanish from my Thought: entranc'd in prayer
I worshipped THE INVISIBLE alone.
Yet[5] thou, meantime, wast working on my soul,

[1] For "one" 1812 reads "we".

[2] *PW* (EHC) I 376–80 (var). For this expansion of Sophie Christiane Friederika Brun's twenty-line *Chamouny beym Sonneraufgange: Gedichte* (1805) 1–2, see A. P. Rossiter in *TLS* (28 Sept 1951) 613. C's poem was first published in the *M Post* 11 Sept 1802 and reprinted in the *Poetical Register* for 1802. C's footnote on the next page (altered) follows the title in 1812.

[3] For "transpicuous" 1812 reads "substantial".

[4] For "then" 1812 reads "thou". See below, II 183, where C corrects and alters lines because "an imperfect Copy" had been sent to the printer. Some but not all of the corrections appear in 1812.

[5] For this and the following six lines 1812 substitutes:

Yet, like some sweet beguiling Melody
So sweet, we know not we are listening to it,
Thou, the meanwhile, wast blending with my Thought,
Yea, with my Life and Life's own secret Joy:
Till the dilating Soul, enrapt, transfus'd,
Into the mighty VISION passing, there
As in her natural form, swell'd vast to Heaven!

Awake, my Soul! not only passive praise
Thou owest! Not alone these swelling Tears,
Mute Thanks and secret extacy Awake,

Even like some sweet enchanting melody,
So sweet, we know not, we are list'ning to it.
But I awake, and with recover'd Will
And eager Thought self-conscious, utter now,
Not, as before, involuntary praise
And passive thanksgiving—Awake! Awake,
175]   Voice of sweet Song! Thou too,[1] my Heart, awake!
Green Vales and icy Cliffs, all join my Hymn.

Thou first and chief, unchanging silent Form![2]
O struggling with the Darkness, all the night,
And visited all night by troops of Stars,
Or when they climb the sky, or when they sink:
Companion of the Morning-star, at dawn,
Thyself Earth's rosy Star! and of the Dawn
Co-herald! Wake, O wake, and utter raise!

Who sank thy sunless Pillars deep in Earth?
Who fill'd thy Countenance with rosy light?
Who made thee Parent of perpetual Streams?
And you, ye five wild Torrents, fiercely glad!
Who call'd you forth from night and utter Death,
From dark and icy Caverns call'd you forth,
Down those precipitous, black, jagged Rocks
For ever shatter'd and the same for ever?
Who gave you your invulnerable Life,
Your Strength, your Speed, your Fury, and your Joy,
Unceasing Thunder and eternal Foam!
And who commanded (and the silence came)
Here let the Billows stiffen, and have Rest!

Ye Ice-falls! ye that from the Mountain's Brow
Adown enormous Ravines slope amain—
Torrents, methinks, that heard a mighty Voice,
And stopp'd at once amid their maddest Plunge!
Motionless Torrents! Silent Cataracts!
Who made you glorious, as the Gates of Heaven,
Beneath the keen full Moon? Who bade the Sun
Cloath you with Rainbows? Who with living* Flowers
Of loveliest Blue spread Garlands at your feet?

* Within a few paces of the Glaciers, the Gentiana major grows in immense
numbers. Besides the Rivers ARVE and Arveiron, which have their sources in
the foot of Mount Blanc, five conspicuous Torrents rush down its' sides.[3]

[1] For "Thou too" 1812 reads
"Awake".
[2] For "unchanging silent Form"
1812 reads "sole Sovran of the Vale".
See below, II 183, where C alters to
"stern Monarch of the Vale".
[3] In 1812 the footnote begins with
the second sentence, with the first sentence tacked on: ". . . its sides, and
within a few . . . in immense numbers
—with it's 'flowers of liveliest Blue.' "
Cf "loveliest Blue" and "living
Flowers" in the text of the poem. See
also *PW* (EHC) I 379n: "Its *blue* flower,

[176]   GOD! let the Torrents, like a shout of Nations,
          Answer! And let the Ice plains echo, GOD!
          God! sing, ye meadow streams! with gladsome voice!
          Ye Pine-groves, with your soft and soul-like Sounds!
          And they too have a Voice, you[1] Piles of Snow,
          And in their perilous Fall shall thunder GOD!

          Ye living Flowers, that skirt th' eternal Frost!
          Ye wild-goats sporting round the Eagle's nest!
          Ye Eagles, play-mates of the Mountain Storm!
          Ye Lightnings, the dread Arrows of the Clouds!
          Ye Signs and Wonders of the Element!
          Utter forth GOD, and fill the Hills with praise![2]

          Thou too, again, stupendous Mountain! thou—
          Who,[3] as once more I lift[4] my Head bow'd low,
          And to thy summit[5] upward from thy base
          Slow travel[6] with dim eyes suffus'd with tears,
          Solemnly seemest, like a vapours[7] Cloud,
          To rise before me—Rise, thou aweful Form![8]
          Rise, like a Cloud of Incense, from the Earth!
          Thou kingly Spirit thron'd among the Hills,
          Thou dread Ambassador from Earth to Heaven,
          Great Hierarch! tell thou the silent Sky,
          And tell the Stars, and tell yon rising Sun,
          EARTH with her thousand voices praises GOD!

                                      S. T. COLERIDGE

the colour of Hope: is it not a pretty emblem of Hope creeping onward even to the edge of the grave, to the very verge of utter desolation?"

[1] For "you" 1812 reads "yon"; corrected by C below, II 183.

[2] In 1812 the following stanza begins with the additional lines:

Thou too, hoar Mount! with thy sky-
     pointing Peaks,
Oft from whose feet the AVAL-
     ANCHE, unheard,
Shoots downward, glittering in the
     pure Serene,

Into the depth of Clouds that veil
     thy breast—
See below, II 183, for a slight change in the first line of this addition.

[3] For "Who," 1812 reads "That".

[4] For "lift" 1812 reads "raise".

[5] For "And . . . summit" 1812 reads "In adoration,".

[6] For "slow travel" 1812 reads "Slow-travelling".

[7] For "vapours" 1812 reads "vapoury".

[8] For "thou aweful Form!" 1812 reads "O ever rise,".

THE FRIEND

No. 12. THURSDAY, November 9, 1809

ON THE VULGAR ERRORS
RESPECTING TAXES AND TAXATION

IN a passage in the last Essay I referred to the second part of the "Rights of Man," in which Paine assures his Readers, that their Poverty is the consequence of Taxation; that Taxes are rendered necessary only by Wars and State-Corruption; that War and Corruption are entirely owing to Monarchy and Aristocracy; that by a Revolution and a brotherly alliance with the French Republic, our Land and Sea Forces, our Revenue Officers, and three-fourths of our Pensioners, Placemen, &c. &c., would be rendered superfluous; and that a small part of the Expences thus saved would suffice for the maintenance of the poor, the infirm, and the aged, throughout the kingdom. Would to Heaven! that the infamous mode of misleading and flattering the lower Classes were confined to the Writings of Thomas Paine. But how often do we hear, even from the mouths of our parliamentary Advocates for Popularity, the Taxes stated as so much money actually lost to the People; and a nation in Debt represented as the same both in Kind and Consequences, as an individual Tradesman on the brink of Bankruptcy. It is scarcely possible, that these Men should be themselves deceived; that they should be so ignorant of History as not to know that the freest Nations, being at the same time commercial, have been at all times the most heavily taxed; or so void of common sense as not to see that there is no analogy in the case of a Tradesman and his Creditors, to a Nation indebted to itself. Surely, a much fairer instance would be that of a Husband and Wife playing Cards at the same Table against each other, where what the one loses the other gains. Taxes may be indeed, and often are injurious to a Country, at no time, however, from their amount merely, but from the time or injudicious mode in which they are raised. A great Statesman, lately deceased, in one of his anti-ministerial harangues against some proposed [178] impost, said: the Nation has been already bled in every vein, and is faint with loss of blood. This Blood, however, was circulating in the mean time, through the whole Body of the State, and what was received into one chamber of the Heart, was instantly sent out again at the other Portal. Had he wanted a metaphor to convey the possible injuries of Taxation, he might have found one less opposite to the fact, in the known disease of aneurism, or relaxation of the coats of particular Vessels, by a disproportionate accumulation of Blood in them, which sometimes occurs, when the circulation has been suddenly and violently changed, and causes Helplessness, or even mortal stagnation, though the total quantity of Blood remains the same in the System at large.

But a fuller and fairer symbol of Taxation, both in its possible good and evil Effects, is to be found in the evaporation of Waters from the surface of the Planet. The Sun may draw up the moisture from the River, the Morass, and the Ocean, to be given back in genial Showers, to the Garden, the Pasture, and the Corn-field, but it may likewise force away the moisture from the fields of Tillage, to drop it on the stagnant Pool, the saturated Swamp, or the unprofitable Sand Waste. The Gardens in the South of Europe supply, perhaps, a not less apt illustration of a system of Finance judiciously conducted, where the Tanks or Reservoirs would represent the Capital of a Nation, and the hundred Rills hourly varying their channels and directions, under the Gardener's Spade, give a pleasing image of the dispersion of that capital through the whole Population, by the joint effect of Taxation and Trade. For Taxation itself is a part of Commerce, and the Government may be fairly considered as a great manufacturing House carrying on in different Places, by means of its Partners and Overseers, the Trades of the Shipbuilder, the Clothier, the Iron-founder, &c. &c.

There are so many real Evils, so many just causes of Complaint in the Constitution and Administration of Governments, our own not excepted, that it becomes the imperious Duty of every Well-wisher of his Country, to prevent, as much as in him lies, the feelings and efforts of his Compatriots from losing themselves on a wrong scent. Whether a System of Taxation is injurious or beneficial on the whole, is to be known, not by the amount of the sum taken from each Individual, but by that which remains [179] behind. A War will doubtless cause a stagnation of certain branches of Trade, and severe temporary distress in the Places where those branches are carried on: but are not the same effects produced in time of Peace by prohibitory edicts and commercial regulations of Foreign Powers, or by new Rivals with superior advantages in other Countries, or in different parts of the same? Bristol has, doubtless, been injured by the rapid Prosperity of Liverpool and its superior spirit of Enterprize; and the vast Machines of Lancashire have overwhelmed and rendered hopeless the domestic Industry of the Females in the Cottages and small Farm-houses of Westmorland and Cumberland. But if Peace has its stagnations as well as War, does not War create or re-enliven numerous branches of Industry as well as Peace? Is it not a fact, that not only our own military and naval Forces, but even a part of those of our Enemy are armed and cloathed by British Manufacturers? It cannot be doubted, that the whole of our immense military force is better and more expensively cloathed, and both these and our Sailors better fed, than the same Persons would be in their individual capacities: and this forms one of the real expences of War. Not, I say, that so much more money is raised, but that so much more of the means of comfortable existence are consumed, than would otherwise have been. But does not this, like all other Luxury, act as a stimulus on the producing Classes, and this in the most useful manner, and on the most important branches of production, on the Tiller, on the Grazier, the Clothier, and the maker of Arms? Had it been otherwise, is it possible that the receipts from the Property Tax should have increased instead of decreased, notwithstanding all the rage of our Enemy?

Surely, never from the beginning of the World was such a tribute of admiration paid by one Power to another, as Bonaparte within the last years has paid to the British Empire! With all the natural and artificial powers of almost the whole of continental Europe, with all the fences and obstacles of all public and private morality broken down before him, with a mighty Empire of fifty millions of Men, nearly two-thirds of whom speak the same Language, and are as it were fused together by the intensest nationality; with this mighty and swarming Empire organized in all its parts for War, and forming one huge Camp, and himself combining in his own person [180] the two-fold Power of Monarch and Commander in Chief; with all these advantages, with all these stupendous instruments and inexhaustible resources of Offence, this mighty Being finds himself imprisoned by the enemy whom he most hates and would fain despise, insulted by every wave that breaks upon his Shores, and condemned to behold his vast Flotillas as worthless and idle as the Sea-weed that rots around their keels! After years of haughty menace and expensive preparations for the Invasion of an Island, the trees and houses[1] of which are visible from the Roofs of his naval Store-houses, he is at length compelled to make open confession, that he possesses one mean only of ruining Great Britain. And what is it? The ruin of his own enslaved Subjects! To undermine the resources of one Enemy, he reduces the Continent of Europe to the wretched state in which it was before the wide diffusion of Trade and Commerce, deprives its' Inhabitants of comforts and advantages to which they and their Fathers had been, for more than a Century, habituated, and thus destroys, as far as his power extends, a principal source of Civilization, the origin of a *middle Class* throughout Christendom, and with it the true Balance of Society, the parent of international Law, the foster-nurse of general Humanity, and (to sum up all in one) the main Principle of Attraction and Repulsion, by which the Nations were rapidly though insensibly drawing together into one system, and by which alone they could combine the manifold Blessings of distinct character and national independence, with the needful stimulation and general influences of Intercommunity, and be virtually united without being crushed together by Conquest, in order to waste away under the Tabes and slow Putrefaction of a Universal Monarchy. This boasted Pacificator of the World, this *earthly Providence*,* as his Catholic Bishops blasphemously call him, professes to entertain no Hope of purchasing the destruction of Great [181] Britain at a less price than that of the Barbarism of all Europe! By the ordinary War of Government against Government, Fleets against Fleets, and Armies against Armies, he could effect nothing. His fleets might as well have been built at his own expence in *our* Dock-yards, as Tribute-offerings to the Masters of

---

* It has been well remarked, that there is something far more shocking in the Tyrant's pretensions to the gracious attributes of the Supreme Ruler, than in his most remorseless Cruelties. There is a sort of wild grandeur, not ungratifying to the imagination, in the answer of Timur Khan to one who remonstrated with him on the *inhumanity* of his devastations: Cur me Hominem putas, et non potius Iram Dei in terris agentem ob perniciem humani generis? Why do you deem me a *Man*, and not rather the incarnate Wrath of God acting on the earth for the ruin of Mankind?

[1] For "houses" 1812 reads "buildings".

the Ocean: and his Army of England lay encamped on his Coasts like Wolves baying the Moon!

Delightful to humane and contemplative minds was the Idea of countless individual efforts working together by a common instinct and to a common object, under the protection of an unwritten Code of Religion, Philosophy, and common Interest, which made Peace and Brotherhood co-exist with the most active Hostility. Not in the untamed Plains of Tartary, but in the very bosom of Civilization, and himself indebted to its' fostering care for his own education and for all the means of his elevation and power, did this genuine offspring of the old Serpent warm himself into the fiend-like resolve of waging War against Mankind and the quiet growth of the World's improvement, in an emphatic sense the enemy of the human Race. By these means only he deems Great Britain assailable (a strong presumption, that our prosperity is built on the common interests of mankind!—) this he acknowledges to be his only hope—and in this Hope he has been utterly baffled!

To what then do we owe our strength and our immunity? The sovereignty of Law; the incorruptness of its administration; the number and political importance of our religious Sects, which in an incalculable degree have added to the dignity of the Establishment; the purity, or at least the decorum of private Morals, and the independence, activity, and weight, of public Opinion? These and similar Advantages are doubtless the *materials* of the Fortress, but what has been the cement? What has bound them together? What has rendered Great Britain, from the Orkneys to the Rocks of Scilly, indeed and with more than metaphorical propriety a BODY POLITIC, our Roads, Rivers, and Canals being so truly the veins, arteries, and nerves, of the State, that every pulse in the Metropolis produces a correspondent pulsation in the remotest Village on its extreme Shores? What made the stoppage of the national Bank the conversation of a day without causing one irregular throb, or the stagnation of [182] the commercial Current in the minutest Vessel? I answer without hesitation, that the Cause and Mother Principle of this unexampled Confidence, of this *system* of Credit, which is as much stronger than mere positive Possessions, as the Soul of Man is than his Body, or as the force of a mighty Mass in free motion, than the pressure of its separate component parts would be in a state of rest—the main cause of this, I say, has been our NATIONAL DEBT. What its injurious effects on the Literature, the Morals, and religious Principles, have been, I shall hereafter develope with the same boldness. But as to our political Strength and circumstantial Prosperity, it is the National Debt which has wedded in indissoluble union all the interests of the State, the landed with the commercial, and the man of independent fortune with the stirring Tradesman and reposing Annuitant. It is the National Debt, which by the rapid nominal rise in the value of Things, has made it impossible for any considerable number of Men to retain their own former comforts without joining in the common Industry, and adding to the Stock of national Produce; which thus first necessitates a general activity, and then by the immediate and ample Credit, which is never wanting to him, who has any object on which his activity can employ itself, gives each Man the means not only of preserving but of encreasing and multiplying all his former enjoyments, and all the symbols of the rank in which he was born. It is this which has planted the naked Hills and enclosed the bleak Wastes, in the Lowlands of Scotland not less than in the wealthier Districts of South Britain: it is this, which leaving all the other causes of Patriotism and national Fervor undiminished and uninjured, has added to our public Duties the same feeling of Necessity, the same sense of immediate Self-interest, which in other Countries actuates the Members of a single Family in their conduct toward each other.

Somewhat more than a year ago, I happened to be on a visit with a Friend, in a small market town in the South West of England, when one of the Company turned the Conversation to the weight of Taxes and the consequent hardness of the times. I answered, that if the Taxes were a real weight, and that in proportion to their Amount, we must have been ruined long ago: for Mr. Hume, who had proceeded, as on a self-evident axiom, on the hypothesis, [183] that a debt of a Nation was the same as a debt of an individual, had declared our ruin arithmetically demonstrable, if the national debt increased beyond a certain sum. Since his time it has more than quintupled that sum, and yet——True, answered my Friend, but the Principle might be right though he might have been mistaken in the Time. But still, I rejoined, if the Principle were right, the *nearer* we came to that given point, and the greater and the more active the pernicious Cause became, the more manifest would its effects be. We might not be absolutely ruined, but our embarrassments would encrease in some proportion to their cause. Whereas instead of being poorer and poorer, we are richer and richer. Will any Man in his Senses contend, that the actual Labour and Produce of the Country has not only been decupled within half a century, but increased so prodigiously beyond that Decuple as to make six hundred millions a less weight to us than fifty millions were in the days of our Grandfathers? But if it really be so, to what can we attribute this stupendous progression of national Improvement, but to that system of credit and paper Currency, of which the national Debt is both the Reservoir and the Water-works? A constant Cause should have constant Effects: but if you deem that this is some anomaly, some strange exception to the general Rule, explain its mode of Operation, make it comprehensible, how a Cause acting on a whole Nation, can produce a regular and rapid encrease of Prosperity to a certain point, and then all at once pass from an Angel of Light into a Dæmon of Destruction? That an individual House may live more and more luxuriously upon borrowed Funds, and that when the suspicions of the Creditors are awakened, and their patience exhausted, the luxurious Spendthrift may all at once exchange his Palace for a Prison —this I can understand perfectly: for I understand, whence the luxuries could be produced for the Consumption of the individual House, and who the Creditors might be, and that it might be both their inclination and their interest to demand the debt, and to punish the insolvent Debtor. But who are a Nation's Creditors? The answer is, every Man to every Man. Whose possible interest could it be either to demand the Principal, or to refuse his share toward the means of paying the Interest? Not the Merchant's: for he would but provoke a crash of Bankruptcy, in which his own House would as necessarily be included, as a [184] single Card in a house of Cards! Not the Landholder's: for in the general Destruction of all Credit, how could he obtain payment for the Produce of his Estates? not to mention the improbability, that he would remain the undisturbed Possessor in so direful a Concussion—not to mention that on him must fall the whole weight of the public Necessities—not to mention, that from the Merchant's Credit depends the ever-encreasing value of his Land and the readiest means of improving it. Neither could it be the Labourer's Interest: for he must be either thrown out of employ, and lie like the Fish in the bed of a River from which the water has been diverted, or have the value of his labour reduced to nothing, by the inruption of eager Competitors. But least of all could it be the wish of the Lovers of Liberty, which must needs perish or be suspended, either by the horrors of anarchy, or by the absolute Power, with which the Government must be invested, in order to prevent them. In short, with the exception of Men desperate from guilt or debt, or mad with the blackest Ambition, there is no Class or Description of Men who can have the least Interest in producing or permitting a Bankruptcy. If then, neither Experience has acquainted us with any national impoverishment or embarrassment from the increase of national Debt, nor Theory renders such efforts comprehensible, (for the predictions of Hume went on the false assumption, that a part only of the Nation was interested in the preservation of the public Credit) on what authority are we to ground our apprehensions? Does History record a single Nation, in which relatively to Taxation there were no priviledged or exempted Classes, in which there were no compulsory prices of Labour, and in which the interest of all the different Classes and all the different Districts, were mutually dependent and vitally co-organized, as in Great Britain—has History, I say, recorded a single instance of such a Nation ruined or dissolved by the weight of Taxation? In France there was no public Credit, no communion of Interests: its unprincipled Government and the productive and taxable Classes were as two Individuals with separate Interests. Its Bankruptcy and the consequences of it are sufficiently comprehensible. Yet the *Cahiers*, or the instructions and complaints sent to the National Assembly, from the Towns and Provinces of France (an immense mass of Documents indeed, but without examination and patient perusal of [185] which, no Man is entitled to write a History of the French Revolution) these proved, beyond contradiction, that the amount of the Taxes was one only, and that a subordinate Cause of the revolutionary Movement. Indeed, if the amount of the Taxes could be disjoined from the mode of raising them, it might be fairly denied to have been a Cause at all. Holland was taxed as heavily and as equally as ourselves; but was it by Taxation that Holland was reduced to its present miseries?

The mode in which Taxes are supposed to act on the marketableness of our manufactures in foreign Marts, I shall examine in some future Number, when I shall endeavour to explain, in a more satisfactory way than has been hitherto done, to my apprehension at least, the real mode in which Taxes act, and how and why and to what extent they affect the Wealth, and what is of more consequence, the Well-being of a Nation. But in the present exigency, when the safety of the Nation depends, on the one hand, on the sense which the People at large have of the comparative excellencies of the Laws and Government, and on the firmness and wisdom of the Legislators and enlightened Classes in detecting, exposing, and removing its many particular Abuses and Corruptions on the other, right views on this Subject of Taxation are of such especial importance; and I have besides in my inmost nature such a loathing of factious Falsehoods and Mob-*sycophancy*, i.e. the flattering of the Multitude by *informing* against their Betters; that I cannot but revert to that point of the Subject from which I began, namely, that THE WEIGHT OF TAXES IS TO BE CALCULATED NOT BY WHAT IS PAID, BUT BY WHAT IS LEFT. What matters it to a Man, that he pays six times more Taxes than his Father did, if, notwithstanding, he with the same portion of exertion enjoys twice the Comforts which his Father did? Now this I solemnly affirm to be the case in general, throughout England, according to all the facts which I have collected during an examination of years, wherever I have travelled, and wherever I have been resident (I do not speak of Ireland, or the Lowlands of Scotland: and if I may trust to what I myself saw and heard there, I must even *except* the Highlands). In the Conversation which I have spoken of as taking place in the South West of England, by the Assistance of one or other of the Company, we went through every Family in [186] the town and neighbourhood, and my assertion was found completely accurate, though the Place had no one advantage over others and many disadvantages, that heavy one in particular, the non-residence and frequent change of its Rectors, the Living being always given to one of the Canons of Windsor, and resigned on the acceptance of better preferment. It was even asserted, and not only asserted but proved, by my Friend (who has from his earliest youth devoted a strong, original understanding, and a Heart warm and benevolent even to Enthusiasm, to the Service of the Poor and the labouring Class), that every sober Labourer, in that part of England at least, who should not marry till thirty, might, without any hardship or extreme self-denial, commence house-keeping at the age of thirty, with from a hundred to a hundred and twenty pounds belonging to him. I have no doubt, that on seeing this Essay, my Friend will communicate to me the proof in detail. But the price of Labour in the south-west of England is full one third less than in the greater number if not all of the Northern Counties. What then is wanting? Not the repeal of Taxes; but the encreased activity both of the Gentry and Clergy of the Land, in securing the *Instruction* of the lower Classes. A System of Education is wanting, such a system as that discovered, and to the blessing of thousands realized, by Dr. Bell, whom I never am or can be weary of praising, while my Heart retains any spark of regard for human nature or of reverence for human virtue!—A System, by which in the very act of receiving knowledge, the best virtues and most useful qualities of the moral Character are awakened, developed, and formed into habits. Were there a Bishop of Durham (no odds whether a temporal or a spiritual Lord) in every County or half County, and a Clergyman enlightened with the views, and animated with the spirit of Dr. Bell, in every Parish, we might bid defiance to the present weight of Taxes, and boldly challenge the whole World to shew a Peasantry as well fed and cloathed as the English, or with equal chance of improving their situation, and of securing an old Age of repose and Comfort to a Life of chearful Industry.

I will add one other Anecdote, as it demonstrates incontrovertibly the Error of the vulgar Opinion, that Taxes make things really dear, taking in the whole of a Man's expenditure. A Friend of mine, who has passed some [187] years in America, was questioned by an American Tradesman, in one of their Cities of the second Class, concerning the names and number of our Taxes and Rates. The answer seemed perfectly to astound him: and he exclaimed, "How is it possible that Men can live in such a Country? In *this* Land of Liberty we never see the face of a Tax-gatherer, nor hear of a Duty except in our Sea-ports." My Friend, who was perfect Master of the question, made semblance of turning off the Conversation to another Subject: and then, without any apparent reference to the former Topic, asked the American, for what sum he thought a Man could live in such and such a Style, with so many Servants, in a House of such dimensions and such a situation (still keeping in his mind the situation of a thriving and respectable Shop-keeper and Householder in different parts of England,) first supposing him to reside in Philadelphia or New York, and then in some Town of secondary importance. Having received a detailed answer to these questions, he proceeded to convince the American, that notwithstanding all our Taxes, a Man might live in the same Style, but with incomparably greater Comforts, on the same Income in London as in New York, and on a considerably less Income in Exeter or Bristol, than in any American provincial Town of the same relative importance. It would be insulting my Readers to discuss on how much less a Person may vegetate or brutalize in the back Settlements of the Republic, than he could live as a Man, as a rational and social Being, in an English Village; and it would be wasting time to inform him, that where Men are comparatively few, and unoccupied Land is in inexhaustible abundance, the Labourer and common Mechanic must needs receive (not only nominally but really) higher Wages than in a populous and fully occupied Country. But that the American Labourer is therefore happier, or even in possession of more Comforts and Conveniences of Life, than a sober or industrious English Labourer or Mechanic, remains to be proved. In conducting the comparison we must not however exclude the Operation of moral Causes, when these Causes are not accidental, but arise out of the nature of the Country and the constitution of the Government and Society. This being the case, take away from the American's Wages all the Taxes which his insolence, sloth, and attachment to spirituous [188] liquors impose on him, and judge of the remainder by his House, his Household Furniture, and Utensils— and if I have not been grievously deceived by those whose veracity and good sense I have found unquestionable in all other respects, the Cottage of an honest English Husbandman, in the Service of an enlightened and liberal Farmer, who is paid for his Labour at the price usual in Yorkshire or Northumberland, would, in the mind of a man in the same rank of life, who had seen a true account of the former,[1] excite no ideas favourable to emigration. This, however, I confess, is a balance of morals rather than of

---

[1] For "the former" 1812 reads "America".

circumstances: it proves, however, that where foresight and good morals exist, the TAXES do not stand in the way of an industrious Man's Comforts.

Dr. Price almost succeeded in persuading the English Nation (for it is a curious fact, that the fancy of its calamitous situation is a sort of necessary sauce without which our real prosperity would become insipid to us) Dr. Price, I say, alarmed the Country with pretended proofs that the Island was in a rapid state of depopulation, that England at the Revolution had been, Heaven knows how much! more populous; and that in Queen Elizabeth's time or about the Reformation (!!!) the number of Inhabitants in England might have been greater than even at the Revolution. My old mathematical Master, a Man of an uncommonly clear head, answered this blundering Book of the worthy Doctor's, and left not a stone unturned of the pompous Cenotaph in which the Effigy of the still living and bustling English Prosperity lay interred. And yet so much more suitable was the Doctor's Book to the purposes of Faction, and to the November mood of (what is called) the PUBLIC, that Mr. Wales's Pamphlet, though a Masterpiece of perspicacity as well as perspicuity, was scarcely heard of. This tendency to political Night-mares in our Countrymen reminds me of a Superstition, or rather nervous Disease, not uncommon in the Highlands of Scotland, in which Men, though broad awake, imagine they see themselves lying dead at a small distance from them. The act of Parliament for ascertaining the Population of the Empire has layed for ever this uneasy Ghost: and now, forsooth! we are on the brink of ruin from the excess of Population, and he who would prevent the Poor from rotting away in disease, misery, and wickedness, is an Enemy to his Country! A lately deceased Miser, of immense [189] Wealth, is reported to have been so delighted with this splendid Discovery, as to have offered a handsome Annuity to the Author, in part of payment, for this new and welcome piece of *Heart-armour*. This, however, we may deduce from the fact of our encreased Population, that if Cloathing and Food had *actually* become dearer in proportion to the means of procuring them, it would be as absurd to ascribe this effect to encreased Taxation, as to attribute the scantiness of Fare at a public Ordinary, to the Landlord's Bill, when twice the usual number of Guests had sat down to the same number of Dishes. But the fact is notoriously otherwise, and every man has the means of discovering it in his own House and in that of his Neighbours, provided that he makes the proper allowances for the disturbing forces of individual vice and imprudence. If this be the case, I put it to the Consciences of our literary Demagogues, whether a Lie, for the purposes of creating public disunion and dejection, is not as much a Lie, as one for the purpose of exciting discord among individuals. I entreat my Readers to recollect, that the present question does not concern the effects of Taxation on the public Independence and on the supposed balance of the three constitutional Powers (from which said balance, as well as from the balance of Trade, I own, I have never been able to elicit one ray of common sense.) That the nature of our Constitution has been greatly modified by the funding System, I do not deny: whether for good or for evil, on the whole, will form part of my Essay on the British Constitution as it actually exists.

There are many and great public Evils, all of which are to be lamented, some of which may be, and ought to be removed, and none of which can consistently with Wisdom or Honesty be kept concealed from the Public. As far as these originate in false PRINCIPLES, or in the contempt or neglect of right ones (and as such belonging to the Plan of THE FRIEND), I shall not hesitate to make known my opinions concerning them, with the same fearless simplicity with which I have endeavoured to expose the Errors of Discontent and the Artifices of Faction. But for the very reason that there are great Evils, the more does it behove us not to open out on a false scent. I will conclude this Essay with the examination of an article in a provincial Paper of a recent date, which is now lying before me; the accidental perusal of which [190] occasioned the whole of the preceding remarks. In order to guard against a possible mistake, I must premise, that I have not the most distant intention of defending the plan or conduct of our late Expeditions, and should be grossly calumniated if I were represented as an Advocate for carelessness or prodigality in the management of the public Purse. The public Money may or may not have been culpably wasted. I confine myself entirely to the general Falsehood of the Principle in the Article here cited; for I am convinced, that any hopes of Reform originating in such notions, must end in disappointment and public mockery.

'ONLY A FEW MILLIONS!

We have unfortunately of late been so much accustomed to read of millions being spent in one expedition, and millions being spent in another, that a comparative insignificance is attached to an immense sum of money, by calling it *only a few millions.* Perhaps some of our readers may have their judgment a little improved by making a few calculations, like those below, on the millions which it has been estimated will be lost to the nation by the late expedition to Holland; and then perhaps they will be led to reflect on the many millions which are annually expended in expeditions, which have almost invariably ended in absolute loss.

In the first place, with less money than it cost the nation to take Walcheren, &c. with the view of taking or destroying the French fleet at Antwerp, consisting of nine sail of the line, we could have completely built and equipped, ready for sea, a fleet of upwards of *one hundred sail of the line.*

Or, secondly, a new town could be built in every county of England, and each town consist of upwards of 1000 substantial houses for a less sum.

Or, thirdly, it would have been enough to give 100l. to 2000 poor families, in every county in England and Wales.

Or, fourthly, it would be more than sufficient to give a handsome marriage portion to 200,000 young women who probably, if they had even less than 50l. would not long remain unsolicited to enter the happy state.

Or, fifthly, a much less sum would enable the legislature to establish a life boat in every port in the United Kingdom, and provide for 10 or 12 men to be kept in constant attendance on each; and 100,000l. could be funded, the interest of which to be applied in premiums to those who should prove to be particularly active in saving lives from wrecks, &c. and to provide for the widows and children of those men who may accidentally lose their lives in the cause of humanity.

This interesting appropriation of 10 millions sterling, may lead our readers to think of the *great good* that can be done by *only a few millions*."

The Exposure of this Calculation will require but a few Sentences. These ten millions were expended, I presume, in Arms, Artillery, Ammunition, Cloathing, Provision, &c. &c. for about a hundred and twenty thousand British Subjects: and I presume that all these *Consumables* were produced by, and purchased from, other British Subjects. Now during the building of these new Towns, for a thousand Inhabitants each, in every County, or the distribution of the hundred pound Bank notes to the two thousand [191] poor Families, were the industrious Ship-builders, Clothiers, Charcoal-burners, Gunpowder-makers, Gunsmiths, Cutlers, Cannon-founders, Tailors, and Shoemakers, to be left unemployed and starving? or our brave Soldiers and Sailors to have remained without Food and Raiment? and where is the proof, that these ten millions, which (observe) all remain in the Kingdom, do not circulate as beneficially in the one way as they would in the other? Is it better to give money to the idle, or to give Houses to those who do not ask for them, or Towns to Counties which have already perhaps too many, or to afford opportunity to the industrious to earn their Bread, and to the enterprizing to better their Circumstances, and perhaps found new Families of independent Proprietors? The only mode, not absolutely absurd, of considering the Subject would be, not by the calculation of the *Money* expended, but of the Labour of which the money is a Symbol. But *then* the Question would be removed altogether from the Expedition: for assuredly, neither the Armies were raised, nor the Fleets built or manned for the sake of conquering the Isle of Walcheren, nor would a single Regiment have been disbanded, or a single Sloop paid off, though the Isle of Walcheren had never existed. The whole dispute, therefore, resolves itself to this one Question: whether our Soldiers and Sailors would not be better employed in making Canals, for instance, or cultivating Waste Lands, than in fighting or in learning to fight; and the Tradesman, &c. in making grey Coats instead of red or blue—and plough-shares, &c. instead of Arms. When I reflect on the state of China and the moral Character of the Chinese, I dare not positively affirm that it *would* be better. When the fifteen millions, which form our present Population, shall have attained to the same purity of Morals and of primitive christianity, and shall be capable of being governed by the same admirable Discipline, as the Society of the Friends, I doubt not that we should be all Quakers in this as in the other points of their moral Doctrine. But were this transfer of employment desirable, is it *practicable* at present, is it in our power? These Men *know*, that it is not. What then does all their Reasoning amount to? Nonsense!——

[192] SPECIMENS OF RABBINICAL WISDOM,

SELECTED FROM THE MISHNA[1]

3

He who taketh the side of Justice maketh the Land prosperous; he who withdraweth from the same is an accomplice in its destruction.

Rabbi Assi was sick, lay on his bed surrounded by his Disciples, and prepared himself for death. His Nephew came into him, and found him weeping. Wherefore weepest thou, Rabbi? he asked. Must not every look which thou castest back on thy past life, bring a thought of joy to thee? Hast thou not then sufficiently studied, not sufficiently taught the sacred Law? Lo! thy Disciples here are proofs of the contrary. Hast thou then, been backward in practising the works of Righteousness? Every

---

[1] See above, I 370 n 2. In place of this third selection of "Rabbinical Wisdom" 1812 prints the following:

EPIGRAMS

1.

What is an Epigram? A dwarfish Whole,
It's Body brevity, and wit it's Soul.

2.

An excellent Adage commands that we should
Relate of the Dead that alone which is good;
But of the great Lord, who here lies in lead,
We know nothing good but that he is dead.

3.

Here lies the Devil—ask no other name.
Well! but you mean Lord—Hush! we mean the same.

4.

An evil Spirits' on thee, friend! of late,
E'en from the day thou cam'st to thy estate:
Thy mirth all gone, thy kindness, thy discretion,
Th' Estate has prov'd to thee a most complete *Possession*.

For shame, old friend! would'st thou be truly blest,
Be thy wealth's Lord not Slave,
Possessor not *possess'd*!

5.

Did'st thou think less of thy dear Self,
Far more would others think of thee!
Sweet Anne! the knowledge of thy wealth
Reduces thee to poverty.
Boon Nature gave Wit, Beauty, Health,
On thee, as on her darling, pitching:
Could'st thou forget, thou'rt thus enrich'd,
That moment would'st thou become rich in;
And wert thou not so self-bewitch'd,
Sweet Anne! thou wert indeed bewitching!

6.

For a French House-dog's Collar.

When Thieves come, I bark; when Gallants, I am still;
So perform both my Master's and Mistress's will.

S. T. C.

See *PW* (EHC) II 963, 971, 964, 965, 966 (var). No 2 first appeared here; the other epigrams first appeared in the *M Post* in Sept and Oct 1802.

Man is satisfied that thou hast not. And thy Humility was the crown of all thy virtues! Never wouldst thou suffer thyself to be elected the Judge of the District, anxiously as the whole district wished it. It is even this, my Son, answered Rabbi Assi, which now troubles me. I had it in my power to exercise Right and Justice among the Children of Men, and out of mistaken Humility, I did not avail myself thereof. Whoso withdraweth himself from Justice is an accomplice in the ruin of the Land.

THE FRIEND

No. 13. THURSDAY, November 16, 1809

> It were a wantonness and would demand
> Severe reproof if we were men whose hearts
> Could hold vain dalliance with the misery
> Even of the dead; contented thence to draw
> A momentary pleasure, never mark'd
> By reason, barren of all future good.
> But we have known that there is often found
> In mournful thoughts, and always might be found
> A power to virtue friendly.—WORDSWORTH. MSS.

IT is gratifying to me to find from my correspondents, that the homeliness of the language and metre in the Fragment of "THE THREE GRAVES," has not prevented the philosophical interest of the Tale from being felt. In that rude Ballad, I attempted to exemplify the effect, which one painful idea vividly impressed on the mind, under unusual circumstances, might have in producing an alienation of the Understanding; and in the parts hitherto published, I have endeavoured to trace the progress to madness, step by step. But though the main incidents are facts, the detail of the circumstances is of my own invention: that is, not what I knew, but what I conceived likely to have been the case, or at least equivalent to it. In the present Number, I present an instance of the same causes acting upon the mind, to the production of conduct as wild as that of madness, but without any positive or permanent loss of the Reason or the Understanding; and this in a real occurrence, real in all its' parts and particulars. But in Truth this Tale overflows with a human interest, and needs no philosophical deduction to make it impressive. The account was published in the City in which the event took place, and in the same year I read it, when I was in Germany, and the impression made on my memory was so deep, that though I relate it in my own language, and with my own feelings, and in reliance on the fidelity of my recollection, I dare vouch for the accuracy of the narration in all important particulars.

The Imperial free Towns of Germany are, with only two or three exceptions, enviably distinguished by the [194] virtuous and primitive manners of the Citizens, and by the parental character of their several Governments. As exceptions, however, we must mention Aix la Chapelle, poisoned by French manners, and the concourse of Gamesters and Sharpers; and Nuremberg, whose industrious and honest Inhabitants deserve a better fate, than to have their lives and properties under the guardianship of a wolfish and merciless Oligarchy, proud from ignorance, and remaining ignorant through pride. It is from the small States of Germany, that our Writers on political Economy, might draw their most forcible instances of actually oppressive, and even mortal taxation, and gain the clearest insight into the causes and circumstances of the injury. One other remark, and I proceed to the Story. I well remember, that the event I am about to narrate, called forth, in several of the German periodical publications, the most passionate (and in more than one instance, blasphemous) declamations, concerning the incomprehensibility of the moral Government of the World, and the seeming injustice and cruelty of the dispensations of Providence. But, assuredly, every one of my Readers, however deeply he may sympathize with the poor Sufferers, will at once answer all such declamations by the simple reflection, that no one of these awful events could possibly have taken place under a wise Police and humane Government, and that men have no right to complain of Providence for evils which they themselves are competent to remedy by mere common sense, joined with mere common humanity.

MARIA ELEONORA SCHONING, was the Daughter of a Nuremberg Wire-drawer. She received her unhappy existence at the price of her Mother's Life, and at the age of seventeen she followed, as the sole Mourner, the bier of her remaining Parent. From her thirteenth year she had passed her Life at her Father's sick-bed, the gout having deprived him of the use of his limbs: and beheld the arch of Heaven only when she went to fetch food or medicines. The discharge of her filial duties occupied the whole of her time and all her thoughts. She was his only Nurse, and for the last two years they lived without a Servant. She prepared his scanty meal, she bathed his aching limbs, and though weak and delicate from constant confinement and the poison of melancholy thoughts, she [195] had acquired an unusual power in her arms, from the habit of lifting her old and suffering Father out of and into his bed of pain. Thus passed away her early youth in sorrow: she grew up in tears, a stranger to the amusements of Youth, and its more delightful schemes and imaginations. She was not, however, unhappy: she attributed, indeed, no merit to herself for her virtues, but for that reason were they the more her reward. *The peace, which passeth all understanding*, disclosed itself in all her Looks and Movements. It lay on her Countenance, like a steady unshadowed Moonlight: and her Voice, which was naturally at once sweet and subtle, came from her, like the fine flute-tones of a masterly performer, which still floating at some uncertain distance, seem to be created by the player, rather than to proceed from the instrument. If you had listened to it in one of those brief Sabbaths of the soul, when the activity and discursiveness of the Thoughts are suspended, and the mind quietly *eddies* round, instead of flowing onward (as at late evening in the Spring I have seen a Bat wheel in silent circles round and round a fruit-tree in full blossom, in the midst of which, as within a close Tent of the purest White, an unseen Nightingale was piping its' sweetest notes) in such a mood you might have half-fancied, half-felt, that her Voice had a separate Being of its' own—that it was a living Something, whose mode of existence was for the Ear only: so deep was her Resignation, so entirely had it become the unconscious Habit of her Nature, and in all, she did or said, so perfectly were both her movements and her utterance without effort and without the appearance of effort! Her dying Father's last words, addressed to the Clergyman who attended him, were his grateful testimony, that during his long and sore Trial, his good Maria had behaved to him like an Angel: that the most disagreeable offices and the least suited to her age and sex, had never drawn an unwilling look from her, and that whenever his eye had met her's, he had been sure to see in it either the tear of pity or the sudden smile expressive of her affection and wish to cheer him. God (said he) will reward the good Girl for all her long dutifulness to me! He departed during the inward Prayer, which followed these his last words. His wish will be fulfilled in Eternity; but for this World the Prayer of the dying Man was not heard!

[196] Maria sate and wept by the Grave, which now contained her Father, her Friend, the only bond by which she was linked to Life. But while yet the last sound of his death-bell was murmuring away in the air, she was obliged to return with two Revenue Officers, who demanded entrance into the house, in order to take possession of the papers of the deceased, and from them to discover whether he had always given in his income, and paid the yearly income-tax according to his Oath, and in proportion to his property.* After the few Documents had been looked through and collated with the Registers, the Officers found, or pretended to find, sufficient proofs, that the Deceased had not paid his Tax proportionably, which imposed on them the duty to put all the Effects under lock and seal. They therefore desired the Maiden to retire to an empty room, till the Ransom Office had decided on the Affair. Bred up in suffering, and habituated to immediate compliance, the affrighted and weeping Maiden obeyed. She hastened to the empty Garret, while the Revenue Officers placed the lock and seal upon the other doors, and finally took away the papers to the Ransom Office.

Not before evening did the poor faint Maria, exhausted with weeping, rouse herself with the intention of going to her bed: but she found the door of her Chamber sealed up and must pass the night on the floor of the Garret. The officers had had the humanity to place at the door the small portion of food that happened to be in the house. Thus passed several days, till the Officers returned with an order that MARIA ELEONORA SCHONING should leave the house without delay, the commission Court having confiscated the whole property to the City Treasury. The [197]

---

* This Tax called the Losung or Ransom, in Nuremberg, was at first a voluntary contribution: every one gave according to his liking or circumstances. But in the beginning of the 15th Century the heavy contributions levied for the service of the Empire, forced the Magistrates to determine the proportions and make the payment compulsory. At the time in which this Event took place, 1787, every Citizen must yearly take what was called his Ransom Oath (Losungseid) that the sum paid by him had been in the strict determinate proportion to his property. On the death of any citizen, the Ransom Office, or commissioners for this income or property tax, possess the right to examine his books and papers, and to compare his yearly payment as found in their Registers with the property he appears to have possessed during that time. If any disproportion appeared, if the yearly declarations of the Deceased should have been inaccurate in the least degree, his whole Effects are confiscated, and though he should have left Wife and Child, the state Treasury becomes his Heir.

Father before he was bed-ridden had never possessed any considerable property; but yet, by his industry, had been able not only to keep himself free from debt, but to lay up a small sum for the evil day. Three years of evil days, three whole years of sickness, had consumed the greatest part of this; yet still enough remained not only to defend his Daughter from immediate want, but likewise to maintain her till she could get into some Service or Employment, and have recovered her Spirits sufficiently to bear up against the hardships of Life. With this thought her dying Father had comforted himself, and this hope too proved vain!

A timid Girl, whose past life had been made up of sorrow and privation, she went indeed to solicit the commissioners in her own behalf; but these were, as is mostly the case on the Continent, Advocates—the most hateful Class, perhaps, of human society, hardened by the frequent sight of misery, and seldom superior in moral character to English Pettifoggers or Old Bailey Attornies. She went to them, indeed, but not a word could she say for herself. Her tears and inarticulate sounds—for these her Judges had no ears or eyes. Mute and confounded, like an unfledged Dove fallen out from its Mother's Nest, Maria betook herself to her home, and found the house door too, now shut upon her. Her whole wealth consisted in the clothes she wore. She had no Relations to whom she could apply, for those of her Mother had disclaimed all acquaintance with her, and her Father was a Nether Saxon by birth. She had no acquaintance, for all the Friends of old Schoning had forsaken him in the first year of his sickness. She had no Playfellow, for who was likely to have been the Companion of a Nurse in the room of a sick man? Surely, since the Creation never was a human Being more solitary and forsaken, than this innocent poor Creature, that now roamed about friendless in a populous City, to the whole of whose inhabitants her filial tenderness, her patient domestic goodness, and all her soft yet difficult virtues, might well have been the model.

> "But homeless near a thousand homes she stood,
> And near a thousand tables pin'd and wanted food!"

The night came, and Maria knew not where to find a shelter. She tottered to the Church-yard of the St. [198] James' Church in Nuremberg, where the Body of her Father rested. Upon the yet grassless grave she threw herself down; and could anguish have prevailed over youth, that night she had been in Heaven. The day came, and like a guilty thing, this guiltless, this good Being, stole away from the Crowd that began to pass through the Church-yard, and hastening through the Streets to the City Gate, she hid herself behind a garden hedge just beyond it, and there wept away the second day of her desolation. The Evening closed in: the pang of hunger made itself felt amid the dull aching of self-wearied anguish, and drove the Sufferer back again into the City. Yet what could she gain there? She had not the courage to beg, and the very thought of stealing never occurred to her innocent mind. Scarce conscious whither she was going, or why she went, she found herself once more by her Father's Grave, as the last relict of evening faded away in the horizon. I have sate for some minutes with my pen resting: I can scarce summon the courage to tell, what I scarce know, whether I ought to tell. Were I composing a Tale of Fiction, the

Reader might justly suspect the purity of my own heart, and most certainly would have abundant right to resent such an incident, as an outrage wantonly offered to his imagination. As I think of the circumstance, it seems more and more like a distempered dream: but alas! what is guilt so detestable other than a dream of madness, that worst madness, the madness of the heart? I cannot but believe, that the dark and restless passions must first have drawn the mind in upon themselves, and as with the confusion of imperfect sleep, have in some strange manner taken away the sense of reality, in order to render it possible for a human being to perpetrate what it is too certain that human beings have perpetrated. The Church-yards in most of the German Cities, and too often, I fear in those of our own Country, are not more injurious to health than to morality. Their former venerable character is no more. The religion of the place has followed its superstitions, and their darkness and loneliness tempt worse spirits to roam in them than those whose nightly wanderings appalled the believing hearts of our brave Forefathers! It was close by the new-made Grave of her Father, that the meek and spotless Daughter became the victim to brutal violence, which weeping and watching and cold and [199] hunger had rendered her utterly unable to resist. The Monster left her in a trance of stupefaction, and into her right hand, which she had clenched convulsively, he had forced a half-dollar.

It was one of the darkest nights of Autumn: in the deep and dead silence the only sounds audible were the slow blunt ticking of the Church Clock, and now and then the sinking down of bones in the nigh Charnel House. Maria, when she had in some degree recovered her senses, sate upon the Grave near which—not her innocence had been sacrificed, but that which, from the frequent admonitions and almost the dying words of her Father, she had been accustomed to consider as such. Guiltless, she felt the pangs of guilt, and still continued to grasp the Coin which the Monster had left in her hand, with an anguish as sore as if it had been indeed the wages of voluntary prostitution. Giddy and faint from want of food, her brain becoming feverish from sleeplessness, and this unexampled concurrence of calamities, this complication and entanglement of misery in misery! she imagined that she heard her Father's voice bidding her leave his sight. His last blessings had been conditional, for in his last hours he had told her, that the loss of her innocence would not let him rest quiet in his grave. His last blessings now sounded in her ears like curses, and she fled from the Church-yard as if a dæmon had been chasing her; and hurrying along the streets, through which it is probable her accursed Violator had walked with quiet and orderly step* to his place of rest and

* It must surely have been after hearing of or witnessing some similar event or scene of wretchedness, that the most eloquent of our Writers (I had almost said of our Poets) Jeremy Taylor, wrote the following paragraph, which, at least in Longinus's sense of the word, we may place among the most *sublime* passages in English Literature. "He that is no fool, but can consider wisely, if he be in love with this world we need not despair but that a witty man might reconcile him with tortures, and make him think charitably of the Rack, and be brought to admire the harmony that is made by a herd of evening Wolves when they miss their draught of blood in their midnight Revels. The groans of a man in a fit of

security, she was seized by the Watchmen of the night—a welcome prey, as they receive in Nuremberg half a Gulden from the police chest, for every Woman that they find in the Streets [200] after ten o'clock at night. It was midnight, and she was taken to the next Watch-house.

The sitting Magistrate, before whom she was carried the next morning, prefaced his first question with the most opprobious title that ever belonged to the most hardened Street-walkers, and which man born of woman should not address even those, were it but for his own sake. The frightful name awakened the poor Orphan from her dream of guilt, it brought back the consciousness of her innocence, but with it the sense likewise of her wrongs and of her helplessness. The cold hand of death seemed to grasp her, she fainted dead away at his feet, and was not without difficulty recovered. The Magistrate was so far softened, and only so far, as to dismiss her for the present; but with a menace of sending her to the House of Correction if she were brought before him a second time. The idea of her own innocence now became uppermost in her mind; but mingling with the thought of her utter forlornness, and the image of her angry Father, and doubtless still in a state of bewilderment, she formed the resolution of drowning herself in the river Pegnitz—in order (for this was the shape which her fancy had taken) to throw herself at her Father's feet, and to justify her innocence to him in the world of Spirits. She hoped, that her Father would speak for her to the Saviour, and that she should be forgiven. But as she was passing through the suburb, she was met by a Soldier's Wife, who during the life-time of her Father, had been occasionally employed in the house as a Chare-woman. This poor Woman was startled at the disordered apparel, and more disordered looks of her young Mistress, and questioned her with such an anxious and heart-felt tenderness, as at once brought back the poor Orphan to her natural feelings and the obligations of religion. As a frightened Child throws itself into the arms of its' Mother, and hiding its' head on her breast, half tells amid sobs what has happened to it, so did she [201] throw herself on the neck of the Woman who had uttered the first words of kindness to her since her Father's death, and, with loud weeping she related what she had endured and what she was about to have done, told her all her *affliction and her misery, the wormwood and the gall!* Her kind-hearted Friend mingled tears with tears,

---

the Stone are worse than all these; and the distractions of a troubled Conscience are worse than those groans: *and yet a careless merry sinner is worse than all that.* But if we could from one of the battlements of Heaven espy, how many men and women at this time lie fainting and dying for want of bread, how many young men are hewn down by the sword of War; how many poor Orphans are now weeping over the graves of their Father, by [200] whose life they were enabled to eat; if we could but hear how many Mariners and Passengers are at this present in a storm, and shriek out because their keel dashes against a Rock, or bulges under them; how many People there are that weep with want, and are mad with oppression, or are desperate by a too quick sense of a constant infelicity; in all reason we should be glad to be out of the noise and participation of so many evils. This is a place of sorrows and tears, of great evils and constant calamities: let us remove from hence, at least in affections and preparations of mind."

Holy Dying, Chap. 1. *Sect. 5.*

pressed the poor forsaken-one to her heart; comforted her with sentences out of the Hymn-book; and with the most affectionate entreaties conjured her to give up her horrid purpose, for that life was short, and heaven was for ever, and Christ a sure recompence.

Maria had been bred up in the fear of God: she now trembled at the thought of her former purpose, and followed her Friend Harlin, for that was the name of her Guardian Angel, to her home hard by. The moment she entered the door she sank down and lay at her full length, as if only to be motionless in a place of shelter had been the fulness of delight. As when a withered Leaf, that has been long whirled about by the gusts of Autumn, is blown into a Cave or hollow Tree, it stops suddenly, and all at once looks the very image of quiet. Such might this poor Orphan appear to the eye of a meditative imagination.

A place of shelter she had attained, and a Friend willing to comfort her, all that she could: but the noble-hearted Harlin was herself a daughter of calamity, one who from year to year must lie down in weariness and rise up to labour; for whom this World provides no other comfort but the Sleep which enables them to forget it; no other Physician but death, which takes them out of it! She was married to one of the City Guards, who, like Maria's Father, had been long sick and bed-ridden. Him, herself, and two little Children, she had to maintain by washing and *charing;* and sometime after Maria had been domesticated with them, Harlin told her that she herself had been once driven to a desperate thought by the cry of her hungry Children, during a want of employment, and that she had been on the point of killing one of the Little-ones, and of then surrendering herself into the hands of justice. In this manner, she had conceived, all would be well provided for; the surviving Child would [202] be admitted, as a matter of course, into the Orphan House, and her Husband into the Hospital; while she herself would have atoned for her act by a public execution, and, together with the Child that she had destroyed, would have passed into a state of bliss. All this she related to Maria, and these tragic ideas left but too deep and lasting impression on her mind. Weeks after, she herself renewed the conversation, by expressing to her Benefactress her inability to conceive how it was possible for one human being to take away the life of another, especially that of an innocent little Child. For that reason, replied Harlin, because it was so innocent and so good, I wished to put it out of this wicked world. Thinkest thou then, that I would have my head cut off for the sake of a wicked Child? Therefore it was little Nan, that I meant to have taken with me, who, as you see, is always so sweet and patient: little Frank has already his humours and naughty tricks, and suits better for this world. This was the answer. Maria brooded awhile over it in silence, then passionately snatched the Children up in her arms, as if she would protect them against their own Mother.

For one whole year the Orphan lived with the Soldier's Wife, and by their joint labours barely kept off absolute want. As a little Boy (almost a Child in size, though in his thirteenth year) once told me of himself, as he was

* I am ignorant, whether there be any classical authority for this word; but I know no other word that expresses occasional day-labour in the Houses of others.

guiding me up the Brocken, in the Hartz Forest, they had but "*little of that, of which a great deal tells but for little.*" But now came the second Winter, and with it came bad times, a season of trouble for this poor and meritorious household. The Wife now fell sick: too constant and too hard labour, too scanty and too innutritious food, had gradually wasted away her strength. Maria redoubled her efforts in order to provide bread and fuel for their washing which they took in; but the task was above her powers. Besides, she was so timid and so agitated at the sight of Strangers, that sometimes, with the best good-will, she was left without employment. One by one, every article of the least value which they possessed was sold off, except the Bed on which the Husband lay. He died just before the approach of Spring; but about the same time the Wife gave signs of convalescence. The Physician, though almost as poor as his Patients, had been kind to them: silver and gold had he none, but he occasionally brought a little Wine, and often assured [203] them that nothing was wanting to her perfect recovery, but better nourishment and a little wine every day. This, however, could not be regularly procured, and Harlin's spirits sank, and as her bodily pain left her she became more melancholy, silent, and self-involved. And now it was that Maria's mind was incessantly racked by the frightful apprehension, that her Friend might be again meditating the accomplishment of her former purpose. She had grown as passionately fond of the two Children as if she had borne them under her own heart; but the jeopardy in which she conceived her Friend's *salvation* to stand—*this* was her predominant thought. For all the hopes and fears, which under a happier lot would have been associated with the objects of the senses, were transferred, by Maria, to her notions and images of a future state.

In the beginning of March, one bitter cold evening, Maria started up and suddenly left the House. The last morsel of food had been divided betwixt the two Children for their breakfast, and for the last hour or more the little Boy had been crying for hunger, while his gentler Sister had been hiding her face in Maria's lap, and pressing her little body against her knees, in order by that mechanic pressure to dull the aching from emptiness. The tender-hearted and visionary Maiden had watched the Mother's eye, and had interpreted several of her sad and steady looks according to her preconceived apprehensions. She had conceived all at once the strange and enthusiastic thought, that she would in some way or other offer her own soul for the salvation of that of her Friends. The money which had been left in her hand, flashed upon the eye of her mind, as a single and connected image: and faint with hunger and shivering with cold, she sallied forth—in search of guilt! Awful are the dispensations of the Supreme, and in his severest judgements the hand of mercy is visible. It was a night so wild with wind and rain, or rather rain and snow mixed together, that a famished Wolf would have stayed in his Cave, and listened to a more fearful howl than his own. Forlorn Maria! thou wert kneeling in pious simplicity at the Grave of thy Father, and thou becamest the prey of a Monster! Innocent thou wert and without guilt didst thou remain. Now thou goest forth of thy own accord—but God will have pity on thee! Poor bewildered Innocent! in thy [204] spotless imagination dwelt no distinct conception of the evil which thou wentest forth to brave! To save the soul of thy Friend was the dream of thy feverish brain, and thou wert again apprehended as an Outcast of shameless sensuality, at the moment when thy too-spiritualized fancy was busied with the glorified forms of thy Friend and of her Little-ones interceding for thee at the Throne of the Redeemer! at this moment her perturbed fancy suddenly suggested to her a new Mean for the accomplishment of her purpose: and she replied to the Night-watch (who with a brutal laugh bade her expect on the morrow the unmanly punishment, which to the disgrace of human nature the laws of Protestant States (alas! even those of our own Country) inflict on female Vagrants) that she came to deliver herself up as an Infanticide. She was instantly taken before the Magistrate, through as wild and *pitiless a storm* as ever pelted on a houseless head! through as black and *"tyrannous a night"* as ever aided the workings of a heated brain! Here she confessed that she had been delivered of an Infant by the Soldier's Wife, Harlin, that she deprived it of life in the presence of Harlin, and according to a plan preconcerted with her, and that Harlin had buried it somewhere in the wood, but where she knew not. During this strange tale she appeared to listen with a mixture of fear and satisfaction, to the howling of the wind; and never sure could a confession of real guilt have been accompanied by a more dreadfully appropriate music! At the moment of her Apprehension she had formed the scheme of helping her Friend out of the World in a state of innocence. When the Soldier's Widow was confronted with the Orphan, and the latter had repeated her Confession to her face, Harlin answered in these words, "For God's sake, Maria! how have I deserved this of *thee?*" Then turning to the Magistrate, said, "I know nothing of this." This was the sole answer which she gave, and not another word could they extort from her. The instruments of torture were brought, and Harlin was warned, that if she did not confess of her own accord, the truth would be immediately forced from her. This menace convulsed Maria Schoning with affright: her intention had been to emancipate herself and her Friend from a life of unmixed suffering, without the crime of suicide in either, and with no guilt at all on the part of her Friend. The thought of her Friend's [205] being put to the torture had not occurred to her. Wildly and eagerly she pressed her Friend's hands, already bound in preparation for the torture—she pressed them in agony between her own, and said to her, "Anna! confess it! Anna, dear Anna! it will then be well with all of us! all, all of us! and Frank and little Nan will be put into the Orphan House!" Maria's scheme now passed, like a flash of Lightening, through the Widow's mind, she acceded to it at once, kissed Maria repeatedly, and then serenely turning her face to the judge, acknowledged that she had added to the guilt by so obstinate a denial, that all her Friend had said, had been true, save only that she had thrown the dead Infant into the River, and not buried it in the Wood.

They were both committed to prison, and as they both persevered in their common Confession, the process was soon made out and the condemnation followed the trial: and the sentence, by which they were both to be beheaded with the Sword, was ordered to be put in force on the next day but one. On the morning of the execution, the Delinquents were brought together, in order that they might be reconciled with each other, and join in common prayer for forgiveness of their common guilt. And now Maria's thoughts took another turn: the Idea that her Benefactress, that so very good a Woman, should be violently put out of Life, and this with an infamy on her name which would cling for ever to the little Orphans, overpowered her. Her own excessive desire to die scarcely prevented her from discovering the whole plan; and when Harlin was left alone with her, and she saw her Friend's calm and affectionate look, her fortitude was dissolved: she burst into loud and passionate weeping, and throwing herself into her Friend's arms, with convulsive sobs she entreated her forgiveness. Harlin pressed the poor agonized Girl to her arms: like a tender Mother, she kissed and fondled her wet cheeks, and in the most solemn and emphatic tones assured her, that there was nothing to forgive. On the contrary, she was her greatest Benefactress and the instrument of God's goodness to remove her at once from a miserable world and from the temptation of committing a heavy Crime. In vain! Her repeated promises, that she would answer before God for them both, could not pacify the tortured Conscience of Maria, till at length the presence of the Clergyman and the preparations for receiving the sacrament [206] occasioning the Widow to address her with—"See, Maria! this is the Body and Blood of Christ, which takes away all sin; let us partake together of this holy Repast with full trust in God and joyful hope of our approaching happiness." These words of comfort, uttered with cheering tones and accompanied with a look of inexpressible tenderness and serenity, brought back peace for a while to her troubled Spirit. They communicated together and on parting the magnanimous Woman once more embraced her young Friend: then stretching her hand toward Heaven said, "Be tranquil Maria! by tomorrow Morning we are *there*, and all our sorrows stay here behind us."

I hasten to the scene of the Execution: for I anticipate my Reader's feelings in the exhaustion of my own heart. Serene and with unaltered countenance the lofty minded Harlin heard the strokes of the death-bell, stood before the scaffold while the Staff was broken over her, and at length ascended the steps, all with a steadiness and tranquillity of manner which was not more distant from fear than from defiance and bravado. Altogether different was the state of poor Maria: with shattered nerves and an agonizing Conscience that incessantly accused her as the Murderess of her Friend, she did not walk but staggered towards the scaffold and stumbled up the steps. While Harlin, who went first, at every step turned her head round and still whispered to her, raising her eyes to heaven,— "but a few minutes, Maria! and we are there"! On the Scaffold she again bade her farewell, again repeating "Dear Maria! but one minute now, and we are together with God." But when she knelt down and her neck was bared for the stroke, the unhappy Girl lost all self-command and with a loud and piercing shriek she bade them hold and not murder the innocent. "She is innocent! I have born false Witness! I alone am the Murderess!" She rolled herself now at the feet of the Executioner, and now at those of the Clergymen, and conjured them to stop the execution: that the whole story had been invented by herself; that she had never brought forth, much less destroyed, an infant; that for her Friend's sake she made this discovery; that for herself she wished to die, and would die gladly, if they would take away her Friend, and promise to free her soul from the dreadful agony of having murdered her Friend by false witness. The Executioner asked Harlin, if there were any truth in what Maria Schoning had said. The Heroine answered with manifest reluctance: "most assuredly she [207] hath said the truth: I confessed myself guilty, because I wished to die and thought it best for both of us: and now that my hope is on the moment of its accomplishment, I cannot be supposed to declare myself innocent for the sake of saving my Life—but any wretchedness is to be endured rather, than that that poor Creature should be hurried out of the world in a state of despair."

The outcry of the attending Populace prevailed to suspend the Execution: a report was sent to the assembled Magistrates, and in the mean time one of the Priests reproached the Widow in bitter words for her former false confession. What? she replied sternly but without anger, "what would the truth have availed? Before I perceived my Friend's purpose, I did deny it: my assurance was pronounced an impudent lie: I was already bound for the torture, and so bound that the sinews of my hands started, and one of their Worships in the large white Peruke threatened that he would have me stretched till the Sun shone through me! and that then I should cry out, yes, when it was too late." The Priest was hard-hearted or superstitious enough to continue his reproofs, to which the noble Woman condescended no further answer. The other Clergyman, however, was both more rational and more humane. He succeeded in silencing his Colleague, and the former Half of the long Hour, which the Magistrates took in making speches on the *improbability* of the tale instead of re-examining the Culprits in person, he employed in gaining from the widow a connected account of all the circumstances, and in listening occasionally to Maria's passionate descriptions of all her Friend's goodness and magnanimity. For she had gained an influx of life and spirit from the assurance in her mind, both that she had now rescued Harlin from Death and was about to expiate the guilt of her purpose by her own execution. For the latter half of the time, the Clergyman remained in silence, lost in thought, and momently expecting the return of the Messenger. All which during the deep silence of this interval could be heard, was one exclamation of Harlin to her unhappy Friend—Oh! Maria! Maria! couldst thou but have kept up thy courage but for another minute, we should have been now in Heaven! The Messenger came back with an order from the Magistrates—to proceed with the Execution! With re-animated Countenance Harlin placed her neck on the block and her head was severed [208] from her body amid a general shriek from the Crowd. The Executioner fainted after the blow, and the under hangman was ordered to take his place. He was not wanted. Maria was already gone: her body was found as cold as if she had been dead for some hours. The Flower had been snapt in the storm, before the scythe of violence could come near it.

SONNET

*Suggested by the efforts of the Tyrolese,
contrasted with the present state of Germany*

Alas! what boots the long laborious quest
Of moral prudence sought through good and ill;
Or pain abstruse to elevate the will,
Or lead us on to that transcendent rest
Where every passion shall the sway attest
Of Reason seated on her sovereign hill;——
What is it but a vain and curious skill
If sapient Germany must lie deprest
Beneath the brutal sword?—Her haughty schools
Shall blush, and may not we with sorrow say,
A few strong instincts and a few plain rules,
Among the Herdsmen of the Alps, have wrought
More for mankind at this unhappy day
Than all the pride of intellect and thought?   W. W.[1]

In the HYMN in No. 11, the Reader will be pleased to make the following corrections and alterations, an imperfect Copy having been sent by mistake.[2]
Page 174, line 14, for *then* read *thou.*
    175,   3, read: *Thou first and chief, stern Monarch of the Vale!*
    176,   5, for *you* read *yon:*
and the beginning of the last paragraph, as follows:

And thou, hoar Mount! with thy sky-pointing Peaks,
Oft from whose feet the AVALANCHE unheard
Shoots downward, glittering in the pure Serene,
Into the depth of Clouds that veil thy Breast——
Thou too, again, stupendous Mountain! thou,
That, as once more I raise my head bow'd low
In Adoration, upward from thy Base
Slow-travelling with dim eyes suffus'd with tears,
Solemnly seemest, like a vapoury Cloud,
To rise before me—Rise, O ever rise,
Rise, like a Cloud of Incense, from the earth!
Thou kingly Spirit, &c. &c.

---

[1] *Poems Dedicated to National Independence and Liberty* pt II No 12 (var): *WPW* III 130. This sonnet was first published in *The Friend.*
[2] Although many of the changes listed here are made in No 11 of 1812, this section still appears in No 13 of 1812. See above, Introduction, I lxvi–lxviii, for a discussion of the correcting and the printing of the revised numbers.

THE FRIEND

No. 14. THURSDAY, November 23, 1809

'Tis true, IDOLOCLASTES SATYRANE
(So call him, for so mingling blame with praise
And smiles with anxious looks, his earliest friends,
Masking his birth-name, wont to character
His wild-wood fancy and impetuous zeal)
'Tis true, that passionate for ancient truths
And honoring with religious love the Great
Of elder times, he hated to excess,
With an unquiet and intolerant scorn,
The hollow Puppets of an hollow Age
Ever idolatrous, and changing ever
Its' worthless Idols!—Learning, Power, and Time,
(Too much of all!) thus wasting in vain war
Of fervid colloquy. Sickness, 'tis true,
Whole years of weary days, besieg'd him close
Even to the gates and outlets of his Life!
But it is true, no less, that strenuous, firm,
And with a natural gladness, he maintain'd
The Citadel unconquer'd, and in joy
Was strong to follow the delightful Muse.
For not a hidden path, that to the shades
Of the belov'd Parnassian forest leads,
Lurk'd undiscover'd by him; not a rill
There issues from the fount of Hippocrene,
But he had trac'd it upward to its' source
Thro' open glade, dark glen, and secret dell,
Knew the gay wild-flowers on its' banks, and cull'd
Its' med'cinable herbs. Yea, oft alone
Piercing the long-neglected holy cave,
The haunt obscure of old Philosophy,
He bade with lifted torch its' starry walls
Sparkle, as erst they sparkled to the flame
Of od'rous lamps tended by Saint and Sage.
O fram'd for calmer times and nobler hearts!
O studious Poet, eloquent for truth!
Philosopher, contemning wealth and death,
Yet docile, child-like, full of light and love!
Here, rather than on monumental stone,
This record of thy worth thy Friend inscribes
Thoughtful, with quiet tears upon his cheek.[1]*   S. T. C.

---

* Imitated, though in the movements rather than the thoughts, from the VIIth. of Gli Epitafi of *Chiabrera:*

Fu ver, che Ambrosio Salinero a torto
Si pose in pena d' odiose liti, &c.[2]

[1] *A Tombless Epitaph* (var): *PW* (EHC) I 413–14. See *PW* (EHC) I 413n and *CN* I 1729 and n.

[2] See Chiabrera *Opere* (2 vols Venice 1757) II 181 (*Gli Epitaffi*). See also above, I 65 and n 3.

[210] DURING my second Term at Cambridge I had, for my own amusement, commenced a Work on the plan of the well known
MISERIES OF HUMAN LIFE:[1] at least with the same Title, for by its Title
only, and the pleasure expressed by all who have spoken to me of it, am I
acquainted with that Publication. But at the same time I had meant to add,
as an Appendix, a Catalogue *raisonné* of the Sights, Incidents, and Employments, that leave us better men than they found us; or, to use my original
phrase, *of the Things that do a Man's Heart good.* If the seventeen or
eighteen years, which have elapsed since that period, would enable me
greatly to extend and diversify the former list, the latter, as more properly
the offspring of experience and reflection, would be augmented in a still
larger proportion. Among the addenda to this second Catalogue I should
rank foremost, a long winter evening devoted to the re-perusal of the
Letters of far distant, or deceased Friends. I suppose the Person so
employed to be one, whose time is seldom at his own disposal, and that
he finds himself alone in a quiet house, the other Inmates of which are
absent on some neighbourly visit. I have been led to this observation by
the numerous Letters (many of which had all the pleasure of novelty for
me, joined with the more tender charm of awakened recollection) from the
Friend,[2] with a slight sketch of whose character I have introduced the
present Number under the name, which he went by among his friends and
familiars, of SATYRANE, the Idoloclast, or breaker of Idols.

A few Seasons ago, I made the Tour of the northern Counties with him
and three other Companions. His extensive erudition, his energetic and
all too subtle intellect, the opulence of his imagination, and above all his
inexhaustible store of anecdotes, which always appeared to us the most
interesting when of himself, and his passionate love of mountain scenery,
which often gave an eloquence to his looks and made his very silence
intelligible, will for ever endear the remembrance of that Tour to the
Survivors. Various were our discussions, most often *with* him, but sometimes (when we had split our Party for a few hours) *concerning* him and
his opinions; not a few of which appeared, to some of us at least, sufficiently paradoxical, though there was nothing which he bore with less
patience than the hearing them thus characterized. Many and various
were our topics, often suggested by the objects and occurrences of the
moment, and often occasioned by the absence of other interest. O [211]
Satyrane! who would not have lost the sense of time and fatigue in thy
company? How often, after a walk of fifteen or twenty miles on rough
roads and through a dreary or uninteresting Country, have we seen our
proposed resting-place with a sort of pleasant surprize, all joining in the
same question, "who would have thought we had walked so far?" And

---

1 [James Beresford] *The Miseries of
Human Life; or the Groans of Samuel
Sensitive, and Timothy Testy. With a
Few Supplementary Sighs from Mrs.
Testy* . . . (1806). It contained miseries
of the "country", "sports", "reading
and writing", "travelling", etc. C's
plan for an Appendix was carried out

by others: see e.g. [Robert Heron] *The
Comforts of Human Life* . . . (1807) and
[John Britton] *The Pleasures of Human
Life* . . . or, "*the Miseries*", *Turned
Topsy Turvy* . . . (1807).
2 A self-disguise—"You will grin",
C wrote Southey, "at my *modest* ac-
count of Satyrane . . .": *CL* III 261.

then perhaps examined our Watches, as if half in doubt, or perhaps to contrast the length of time which had thus slipped away from us, with our own little sense of its' elapse. These discussions and the marked difference of our several Characters (though we were all old acquaintances, and with one exception, all of us fellow Cantabs) suggested to us the idea of a joint Work to be entitled, "TRAVELLING CONVERSATIONS." Since that time I have often renewed this idea in my mind, and pleased myself with the thought of realizing it. Independent of the delightful recollections, the lively portraiture and inward music, which would enliven my own fancy during the composition, it appeared to me to possess the merit of harmonizing an indefinite variety of matter by that unity of interest, which would arise from the Characters remaining the same throughout, while the Tour itself would supply the means of introducing the most different topics by the most natural connections. We had agreed to call each other by the names of our Walking-Sticks, each of which happened to be of a different Wood: Satyrane, however, excepted, who was well pleased to be called among us by his old College name, and not displeased with his learned Agnomen, when we used with mock solemnity to entreat a short reprieve for our prejudices from him, under the lofty title of "puissant and most redoubtable Idoloclastes." I flatter myself, that the Readers of THE FRIEND will consent to travel over the same road with the same fellow-Tourists. High indeed will be my gratification, if they should hereafter think of the *walk and talk* with the FRIEND's Satyrane, Holly, Larch, Hiccory, and Sycamore,[1] with a small portion of the delight with which they have accompanied THE SPECTATOR to *his* club, and made acquaintance with Will Honeycomb and the *inimitable* Sir Roger de Coverley. From any imitation indeed, I am precluded by the nature and object of my work: and for many reasons, the persons, whom I introduce, must be distinguished by their sentiments, their different kinds of information, and their different views of life and society, rather than by any prominent individuality of humour in [212] their personal Characters. What they were to myself, they will be to my Reader; glasses of different colours and various degrees of power, through which truth and error, happiness and misery, may be contemplated.

From his earliest youth Satyrane had derived his highest pleasures from the admiration of moral grandeur and intellectual energy; and during the whole of his short life he had a greater and more heart-felt delight in the superiority of other men to himself, than men in general derive from the belief of their own. His readiness to imagine a superiority where it did not exist, was indeed, for many years his predominant foible. His pain from the perception of inferiority in others, whom he had heard spoken of with any respect, was unfeigned and involuntary; and perplexed him, as a something which he did not comprehend. In the child-like simplicity of his nature he talked to all men, as if they were, at least, his equals in knowledge and talents; and his Familiars record many a whimsical anec-

[1] Cf *CN* i 774: "Travelling Conversations. The three Friends called by their Sticks—Larch, Hazel, & Lilack". C's fellow-tourists on the trip to Ger- many described in the following letters were John Chester and William and Dorothy Wordsworth.

dote, and many a ludicrous incident, connected with this Habit of his, of scattering the good seed on unreceiving soils. When he was at length compelled to see and acknowledge the true state of the morals and intellect of his contemporaries, his disappointment was severe, and his mind, always thoughtful, became pensive and almost gloomy: for to love and sympathize with mankind was a necessity of his nature. Hence, as if he sought a refuge from his own sensibility, he attached himself to the most abstruse researches, and seemed to derive his purest delight from subjects that exercised the strength and subtlety of his understanding without awakening the feelings of his heart.[1] When I first knew him, and for many years after, this was all otherwise. The sun never shone on a more joyous being! The Letters of earliest date, which I possess of his, were written to a common friend, and contain the accounts of his first travels. That I may introduce him to my Readers in his native and original character, I now place before them his first Letter, written on his arrival at Hamburg. From the remaining Series, written in the same or following year, I shall select and occasionally publish such letters as will give the liveliest idea of his opinions, and the different traits of his character at that period. I have only to premise, that Satyrane was incapable of ridiculing a foreigner merely for speaking English imperfectly; but the extravagant vanity that could prompt a man so speaking and pronouncing to pride himself on his excellence as [213] a Linguist, is as honest a subject of light satire, as an old Coquette, or as a Beau of threescore and ten exposing the infirmities of old age in a Reel on his Wedding-day.

LETTER I[2]

On Sunday Morning, September 16, 1798, the Hamburg Pacquet set sail from Yarmouth: and I, for the first time in my life, beheld my native land retiring from me. At the moment of its' disappearance—in all the Kirks, Churches, Chapels, and Meeting-houses, in which the greater number, I hope, of my Countrymen were at that time assembled, I will dare question whether there was one more ardent prayer offered up to Heaven, than that which I then preferred for my Country. Now then (said I to a Gentleman who was standing near me) we are out of our Country. Not yet, not yet! he replied, and pointed to the Sea; "This, too, is a Briton's Country." This bon mot gave a fillip to my spirits, I rose and looked round on my Fellow-passengers, who were all on the Deck. We were eighteen in number, videlicet, five Englishmen, an English Lady, a French Gentleman and his Servant, an Hanoverian and his Servant, a Prussian, a Swede, two Danes, and a Mulatto Boy, a German Tailor and his Wife (the smallest couple I ever beheld) and a Jew. We were all on the Deck; but in a short time I observed marks of dismay. The Lady retired to the Cabin in some confusion, and many of the Faces round me assumed a very doleful and frog-coloured appearance; and within an hour the number of those on Deck was lessened by one half. I was giddy, but not sick, and the giddiness soon went away, but left a feverishness and want of appetite which I

[1] Cf C's letter to Lady Beaumont 15 Apr 1810: *CL* III 287.

[2] "Satyrane's Letters", slightly revised, were reprinted in *BL* (1817) II 183–253, to fill out the second volume. For the original text of Letter I, to Mrs C 3 Oct 1798, see *CL* I 420–8; and cf *BL* (1817) II 183–204.

attributed, in great measure, to the *sæva Mephitis* of the Bilge-water; and it was certainly not decreased by the exportations from the Cabin. However, I was well enough to join the able-bodied Passengers, one of whom observed not inaptly, that Momus might have discovered an easier way to see a Man's Inside than by placing a Window in his breast. He needed only have taken a Salt-water trip in a pacquet-boat.

I am inclined to believe, that a Pacquet is far superior to a Stage-coach, as a means of making men open out to each other. In the latter the uniformity of posture disposes to dozing, and the definiteness of the period at which the Company will separate, makes each individual think more of those, *to* whom he is going, than of those *with* whom he is going. But at Sea more curiosity is [214] excited, if only on this account, that the pleasant or unpleasant qualities of your companions are of greater importance to you, from the uncertainty how long you may be obliged to house with them. Besides, if you are Countrymen, that now begins to form a distinction and a bond of Brotherhood; and if of different Countries, there are new incitements to conversation, more to ask and more to communicate. I found that I had interested the Danes in no common degree. I had crept into the Boat on the Deck and fallen asleep; but was awaked by one of them about three o'clock in the Afternoon, who told me that they had been seeking me in every hole and corner, and insisted that I should join their Party and drink with them. He talked English with such fluency, as left me wholly unable to account for the singular and even ludicrous incorrectness with which he spoke it. I went, and found some excellent Wines and a desert of Grapes with a Pine Apple. The Danes had christened me Docteur Teology, and dressed as I was all in black, with large shoes and black worsted stockings, I might certainly have passed very well for a Methodist Missionary. However I disclaimed my Title. What then may you be? A man of Fortune? No!—A Merchant? No! A Merchant's Traveller? No!—A Clerk? No!—Un Philosophe, perhaps? It was that time in my life, in which of all possible names and characters I had the greatest disgust to that of "un Philosophe."[1] But I was weary of being questioned, and rather than be Nothing, or at best only the abstract Idea of a Man, I submitted by a bow, even to the Aspersion implied in the word "un Philosophe."—The Dane then informed me, that all in the present Party were Philosophers likewise. Certes we were not of the Stoic School. For we drank and talked and sung, till we talked and sung all together; and then we rose and danced on the Deck a set of Dances, which in *one* sense of the word at least were very intelligibly and appropriately entitled *Reels*. The Passengers who lay in the Cabin below in all the agonies of Sea-sickness, must have found our Bacchanalian merriment

————————————————————————a tune
Harsh and of dissonant mood for their complaint.[2]

---

[1] Cf C's letter to his brother George c 10 Mar 1798 (*CL* I 395): "I deprecate the moral & intellectual habits of those men both in England & France, who have modestly assumed to themselves the exclusive title of Philo-sophers. . . . If I know my own opinions, they are utterly untainted with French metaphysics, French Ethics, & French Theology."

[2] Milton *Samson Agonistes* lines 661–2 (altered).

I thought so at the time; and (by way, I suppose, of supporting my newly
assumed philosophical Character) I thought too, how closely the greater
number of our Virtues are connected with the fear of Death, and how little
sympathy we bestow on Pain, where there is no Danger.

[215] The two Danes were Brothers. The one was a man with a clear
white complexion, white hair, and white eyebrows, looked silly, and nothing that he uttered gave the lie to his Looks. The other, whom, by way of
eminence I have called THE DANE, had likewise white hair, but was much
shorter than his Brother, with slender limbs, and a very thin face slightly
pock-fretten. This man convinced me of the justice of an old remark, that
many a faithful Portrait in our Novels and Farces has been rashly censured
for an outrageous Caricature, or perhaps Nonentity. I had retired to my
station in the Boat—he came and seated himself by my side, and appeared
not a little tipsy. He commenced the conversation in the most magnific
style, and as a sort of Pioneering to his own Vanity, he flattered me with
such grossness! The Parasites of the Old Comedy were modest in the
comparison. His language and accentuation were so exceedingly singular,
that I determined for once in my life to take notes of a Conversation.
Here it follows, somewhat abridged indeed, but in all other respects as
accurately as my memory permitted.

THE DANE. Vat Imagination! vat Language! vat vast Science! and vat
eyes! vat a milk-vite forehead!—O my heafen! vy, you're a Got!

ANSWER. You do me too much honour, Sir.

THE DANE. O me! if you should dink I is flattering you!—No, no, no!
I haf ten tousand a year—yes, ten tousand a year—yes, ten tousand pound
a year! Vell—and vat is dhat? a mere trifle! I 'ouldn't gif my sincere
heart for ten times dhe money.—Yes, you're a Got! I a mere man! But,
my dear Friend! dhink of me, as a man! Is, is—I mean to ask you now,
my dear Friend—is I not very eloquent? Is I not speak English very fine?

ANSW. Most admirably! Believe me, Sir! I have seldom heard even
a Native talk so fluently.

THE DANE. (*squeezing my hand with great vehemence*) My *dear* Friend!
vat an affection and fidelity we have for each odher! But tell me, do tell
me,—Is I not, now and den, speak some fault? Is I not in some wrong?

ANSW. Why, Sir! perhaps it might be observed by nice critics in the
English Language, that you occasionally use the word "Is" instead of
"am." In our best companies we generally say I am, and not I is or Ise.
Excuse me, Sir! it is a mere trifle.

THE DANE. O!—is, is, am, am, am. Yes, yes—I know, I know.

[216] ANSW. I am, thou art, he is, we are, ye are, they are.

THE DANE. Yes, yes—I know, I know—Am, am, am, is dhe Presens,
and Is is dhe Perfectum—yes, yes—and are is dhe Plusquam perfectum.

ANSW. And "Art," Sir! is——?

THE DANE. My dear Friend! it is dhe Plusquam perfectum, no, no—
dhat is a great lie. "Are" is the Plusquam perfectum—and "art" is dhe
Plusquamplue-perfectum—(*then swinging my hand to and fro and cocking
his little bright hazle eyes at me, that danced with vanity and wine*). You
see, my dear Friend! that I too have *some* Learning.

ANSW. Learning, Sir? Who dares suspect it? Who can listen to you for a minute, who can even look at you, without perceiving the extent of it?

THE DANE. My *dear* Friend!—(*then with a would-be-humble look, and in a tone of voice as if he was reasoning*) I could not talk so of Presens and Imperfectum, and Futurum and Plusquamplue perfectum, and all dhat, my dear Friend! widhout *some* Learning?

ANSW. Sir! a man like you cannot talk on any subject without discovering the depth of his information.

THE DANE. Dhe grammatic Greek, my Friend! Ha! ha! ha! (*laughing, and swinging my hand to and fro—then with a sudden transition to great solemnity*) Now I will tell you, my dear Friend! Dhere did happen about me vat dhe whole Historia of Denmark record no instance about no body else. Dhe Bishop did ask me all dhe questions about all dhe Religion in dhe Latin Grammar.

ANSW. The Grammar, Sir? The Language, I presume——

THE DANE (*a little offended*). Grammar is Language, and Language is Grammar—

ANSW. Ten thousand pardons!

THE DANE. Vell, and I was only fourteen years—

ANSW. Only fourteen years old?

THE DANE. No more. I vas fourteen years old—and he asked me all questions, Religion and Philosophy, and all in dhe Latin Language—and I answered him all every one, my dear Friend! all in dhe Latin Language.

ANSW. A Prodigy! an absolute Prodigy!

THE DANE. No, no, no! he was a Bishop, a great Superintendant.

ANSW. Yes! a Bishop.

THE DANE. A Bishop—not a mere Predicant, not a Prediger—

[217] ANSW. My dear Sir! we have misunderstood each other. I said that your answering in Latin at so early an age was a Prodigy, that is, a thing that is wonderful, that does not often happen.

THE DANE. Often! Dhere is not von instance recorded in dhe whole Historia of Denmark.

ANSW. And since then Sir——?

THE DANE. I was sent ofer to dhe Vest Indies—to our Island, and dhere I had no more to do vid Books. No! no! I put my genius another way—and I haf made ten tousand pound a year. Is not dhat *Genius*, my dear Friend!—But vat is money! I dhink dhe poorest man alive my equal. Yes, my dear Friend! my little Fortune is pleasant to my generous Heart, because I can do good—no man with so little a fortune ever did so much generosity—no person, no man person, no woman person ever denies it. But we are all Got's Children.

Here the Hanoverian interrupted us, and the other Dane, the Swede, and the Prussian, joined us, together with a young Englishman who spoke the German fluently, and interpreted to me many of the Prussian's Jokes. The Prussian was a travelling Merchant, turned of threescore, a hale man, tall, strong, and stout, full of stories, gesticulations, and buffoonery, with the soul as well as the look of a Mountebank, who while he is making you laugh, picks your pocket. Amid all his droll Looks and droll Gestures there remained one look untouched by laughter; and that one Look was the true face, the others were but its' mask. The Hanoverian was a pale, fat, bloated young man, whose Father had made a large Fortune in London, as an Army-contractor. He seemed to emulate the manners of young Englishmen of fortune. He was a good-natured Fellow, not without information or literature; but a most egregious Coxcomb. He had been in the habit of attending the House of Commons, and had once spoken, as he informed me, with great applause in a debating Society. For this he appeared to have qualified himself with laudable industry: for he was perfect in Walker's pronouncing Dictionary,[1] and with an accent, which forcibly reminded me of the Scotchman in Roderic Random, who professed to teach the English Pronunciation,[2] he was constantly *deferring* to my superior Judgment, whether or no I had pronounced this or that word with propriety or "the true delicacy." When he spoke, though it were only half a dozen sentences, he always rose; for which I could detect no other motive, than his partiality to that [218] elegant phrase so liberally introduced in the orations of our British Legislators, "While I am on my Legs." The Swede, whom for reasons that will soon appear, I shall distinguish by the name of "Nobility," was a strong-featured, scurvy-faced man, his complexion resembling in colour a red hot poker beginning to cool. He appeared miserably dependent on the Dane; but was however incomparably the best informed and most rational of the Party. Indeed his manners and conversation discovered him to be both a Man of the world and a Gentleman. The Jew was in the Hold; the French Gentleman was lying on the Deck so ill, that I could observe nothing concerning him except the affectionate attentions of his Servant to him. The poor Fellow was very sick himself, and every now and then ran to the side of the Vessel, still keeping his eye on his Master, but returned in a moment and seated himself again by him, now supporting his head, now wiping his forehead and talking to him all the while in the most soothing Tones. There had been a matrimonial squabble of a very ludicrous kind in the Cabin between the little German Tailor and his little Wife. He had secured two beds, one for himself, and one for her. This had struck the little Woman as a very cruel action; she insisted upon their having but one, and assured the Mate in the most piteous tones, that she was his lawful Wife. The Mate and the Cabin Boy decided in her favour, abused the little Man for his want of tenderness with much humour, and finally hoisted him into the same bed with his sea-sick Wife. This quarrel was interesting to me, as it procured me a bed, which I otherwise should not have had.

In the Evening at 7 o'Clock the Sea rolled higher, and the Dane by means of the greater agitation eliminated enough of what he had been swallowing to make room for a great deal more. His favourite potation was sugar and Brandy, i.e. a very little warm water with a large quantity of Brandy, Sugar, and Nutmeg. His servant boy, a black-eyed Mulatto, had a good-natured round face, exactly the colour of the skin of the kernel of the Walnut. The Dane and I were again seated, tete a tete in the Ship's Boat. The conversation, which was now indeed rather an oration, than a dialogue, became extravagant beyond all that I ever heard. He told me

---

[1] See above, I 469 and n 3.   *Roderick Random.* For C on the
[2] Tobias Smollett's *Adventures of*   humour in Smollett see *Misc C* 443.

that he had made a large fortune in the Island of Santa Cruz, and was now returning to Denmark to enjoy it. He expatiated on the Style in which he meant to live, and the great undertakings, [219] which he proposed to himself to commence, till the Brandy aiding his Vanity, and his Vanity and Garrulity aiding the Brandy, he talked like a madman—entreated me to accompany him to Denmark—there I should see his influence with the Government, and he would introduce me to the King, &c. &c. Thus he went on dreaming aloud, and then passing with a very lyrical transition to the subject of general Politics he declaimed, like a member of the Corresponding Society, *about* (not concerning) the Rights of Man, and assured me that notwithstanding his Fortune he thought the poorest man alive his Equal, "All are equal, my dear Friend! all are equal! Ve are all Got's Children. The poorest man haf the same Rights with me. Jack! Jack! some more sugar and Brandy. Dhere is dhat Fellow now! He is a Mulatto—but he is my equal.—That's right, Jack! (*taking the Sugar and Brandy*) Here you Sir! shake hands with dhis Gentleman! Shake hands with me, you dog! Dhere, dhere!—We are all equal my dear Friend!—Do I not speak like Socrates, and Plato, and Cato—they were all Philosophers, my dear Philosophe! all very great men!—and so was Homer and Virgil—but they were Poets, yes, yes! I know all about it!—But what can any body say more than this? we are all equal, all Got's Children. I haf ten tousand a year, but I am no more than the meanest man alive. I haf no pride; and yet, my dear Friend! I can say, Do! and it is done. Ha! ha! ha! my dear Friend! Now dhere is dhat Gentleman (*pointing to* "Nobility") he is a Swedish Baron—you shall see. Ho! (*calling to the Swede*) get me, will you, a bottle of Wine from the Cabin. SWEDE. Here, Jack! go and get your Master a bottle of Wine from the Cabin. *Dane.* No, no, no! do *you* go now—you go yourself—*you* go now! *Swede.* Pah!—*Dane.* Now go! Go, I pray you. AND THE SWEDE WENT!!

After this the Dane commenced an harangue on Religion, and mistaking me for "un Philosophe" in the continental sense of the word, he talked of Deity in a declamatory style very much resembling the devotional Rants of that rude Blunderer, Mr. Thomas Paine, in his Age of Reason,[1] and whispered in my ear, what damned *Hypocrism*[2] all Jesus Christ's Business was. I dare aver, that few men have less reason to charge themselves with indulging in *Persiflage* than myself. I should hate it if it were only that it is a Frenchman's vice, and feel a pride in avoiding it because our own language is too honest to have a word to express it by. But in this instance the temptation had [220] been too powerful, and I have placed it on the list of my offences. Pericles answered one of his dearest Friends who had solicited him on a case of life and death, to take an equivocal oath for his preservation: *Debeo amicis opitulari, sed usque ad Deos.**[3] Friendship herself must place her last and boldest step on this

* *Translation.* It behoves me to side with my Friends but only as far as the Gods.

[1] See above, I 32.

[2] A rare and obsolete form of "hypocrisy"; the *OED* cites Josuah

Sylvester's tr of Du Bartas.

[3] Aulus Gellius *Noctes Atticae* 1.3.20, where it is quoted in Greek.

side the altar. What Pericles would not do to save a Friend's life, you may be assured I would not hazard merely to mill the chocolate-pot of a drunken Fool's vanity till it frothed over. Assuming a serious Look, I professed myself a Believer, and sunk at once an hundred fathoms in his good graces. He retired to his Cabin, and I wrapped myself up in my great Coat, and looked at the Water. A beautiful white cloud of Foam at momently intervals coursed by the side of the Vessel with a roar, and little Stars of Flame danced and sparkled and went out in it: and every now and then light detachments of this white cloud-like foam darted off from the Vessel's side, each with its' own small constellation, over the sea, and scoured out of sight like a Tartar Troop over a Wilderness.

It was cold, the Cabin was at open War with my Olfactories, and I found reason to rejoice in my great Coat, a weighty high-caped, respectable Rug, the Collar of which turned over, and played the part of a Night-cap very passably. In looking up at two or three bright stars, which oscillated with the motion of the sails, I fell asleep, but was awakened at one o'clock, monday morning, by a shower of Rain. I found myself compelled to go down into the Cabin, where I slept very soundly, and awoke with a very good Appetite at Breakfast Time, my nostrils, the most placable of all the senses, reconciled to or indeed insensible of the Mephitis.

Monday September 17th, I had a long Conversation with the Swede, who spoke with the most poignant contempt of the Dane, whom he described as a Fool, purse-mad; but he confirmed the boasts of the Dane respecting the largeness of his Fortune, which he had acquired in the first instance as an Advocate, and afterwards as a Planter. From the Dane and from himself I collected that he was indeed a Swedish Nobleman, who had squandered a Fortune, that was never very large, and had made over his Property to the Dane, on whom he was now utterly dependent. He seemed to suffer very little pain from the [221] Dane's insolence. He was in high degree humane and attentive to the English Lady, who suffered most fearfully, and for whom he performed many little offices with a tenderness and delicacy which seemed to prove real goodness of Heart. Indeed, his general manners and conversation were not only pleasing, but even interesting; and I struggled to believe his insensibility respecting the Dane philosophical Fortitude. For though the Dane was now quite sober, his character oozed out of him at every pore. And after Dinner, when he was again flushed with wine, every quarter of an hour or perhaps oftener he would shout out to the Swede, "Ho! Nobility, go—do such a thing! Mr. Nobility!—tell the Gentlemen such a Story, and so forth," with an insolence which must have excited disgust and detestation, if his vulgar rants on the sacred rights of equality, joined to his wild havoc of general Grammar no less than of the English Language, had not rendered it so irresistibly laughable.

At four o'clock I observed a Wild Duck swimming on the waves, a single solitary wild duck. It is not easy to conceive, how interesting a Thing it looked in that round objectless Desert of Waters. I had associated such a feeling of immensity with the Ocean, that I felt exceedingly disappointed, when I was out of sight of all land, at the narrowness and *nearness,* as it were, of the circle of the Horizon. So little are images capable of satisfying the obscure feelings connected with words. In the evening the Sails were lowered, lest we should run foul of the Land, which can be seen only at a small distance. And at four o'clock, on Tuesday morning, I was awakened by the cry of Land! Land! It was an ugly Island Rock at a distance on our left, called Heiligeland,[1] well known to many Passengers from Yarmouth to Hamburg, who have been obliged by stormy weather to pass weeks and weeks in weary captivity on it, stripped of all their money by the exhorbitant demands of the Wretches who inhabit it. So at least the Sailors informed me.—About nine o'clock we saw the main land, which seemed scarcely able to hold its head above water, low, flat, and dreary, with light-houses and land-marks which seemed to give a character and language to the Dreariness. We entered the mouth of the Elbe, passing Neu-werk; though as yet the right bank only of the River was visible to us. On this I saw a Church, and thanked God for my safe Voyage, not without affectionate thoughts of those I had left in England. At eleven o'clock on the same morning we arrived at [222] Cuxhaven, the Ship dropped anchor, and the Boat was hoisted out, to carry the Hanoverian and a few others on shore. The Captain agreed to take us, who remained, to Hamburg for ten guineas, to which the Dane contributed so largely, that the other Passengers paid but half a guinea each. Accordingly we hauled anchor, and passed gently up the River. At Cuxhaven both sides of the River may be seen in clear weather; we could now see the right bank only. We passed a multitude of English Traders that had been waiting many weeks for a wind. In a short time both banks became visible, both flat and evidencing the labour of human hands by their extreme neatness. On the left Bank I saw a Church or two in the distance; on the right bank we passed by Steeple and Windmill and Cottage, and Windmill and single House, Windmill and Windmill, and neat single House, and Steeple. These were the objects and in the succession. The shores were very green and planted with Trees not inelegantly. Thirty five miles from Cuxhaven, the night came on us and as the Navigation of the Elbe is perilous, we dropped anchor.

Over what place, thought I, does the Moon hang to *your* eye, my dearest Friend? To me it hung over the left bank of the Elbe.[2] Close above the Moon was a huge Volume of deep black Cloud, while a very thin fillet crossed the middle of the orb, as narrow and thin and black as a ribbon of crape. The long trembling road of moonlight, which lay on the Water and reached to the stern of our Vessel, glimmered dimly and obscurely. We saw two or three lights from the right bank, probably from Bedrooms. I felt the striking contrast between the silence of this majestic Stream, whose banks are populous with men and women and children, and flocks and herds—between the silence by night of this peopled River, and the ceaseless noise, and uproar, and loud agitations of the desolate Solitude of the Ocean. The Passengers below had all retired to their Beds; and I felt the interest of this quiet scene the more deeply from the circumstance of having just quitted them. For the Prussian had during the whole of the evening displayed all his Talents to captivate the Dane, who had admitted

[1] The North Sea island, Heligoland.   [2] Cf C's letter to Mrs C 18 Sept 1798: *CL* I 415.

him into the train of his Dependents. The young Englishman continued to interpret the Prussian's Jokes to me. They were all without exception profane and abominable, but some sufficiently witty, and a few incidents, which he related in his own person, were valuable as illustrating the manners of the Countries in which they had taken place.

[223] Five o'clock on Wednesday morning we hauled the Anchor, but were soon obliged to drop it again in consequence of a thick fog, which our Captain feared would continue the whole day; but about nine it cleared off and we sailed slowly along, close by the shore of a very beautiful Island forty miles from Cuxhaven, the wind continuing slack. This Holme or Island is about a mile and a half in length, wedge-shaped, well wooded, with glades of the liveliest green, and rendered more interesting by the remarkably neat farm house on it. It seemed made for retirement without solitude—a place that would allure one's Friends while it precluded the impertinent calls of mere Visitors. The shores of the Elbe now became more beautiful, with rich meadows and trees running like a low wall along the River's edge; and peering over them, neat houses and (especially on the right bank) a profusion of steeple-spires, white, black, or red. An instinctive taste teaches men to build their churches in flat countries with spire-steeples, which as they cannot be referred to any other object, point as with silent finger to the sky and stars,[1] and sometimes when they reflect the brazen light of a rich though rainy sun-set, appear like a pyramid of flame burning heaven-ward. I remember once, and once only, to have seen a spire in a narrow valley of a mountainous country. The effect was not only mean but ludicrous, and reminded me against my will of an *extinguisher;* the close neighbourhood of the high mountain, at the foot of which it stood, had so completely dwarfed it, and deprived it of all connection with the sky or clouds. Forty six English miles from Cuxhaven, and sixteen from Hamburg, the Danish Village Veder[2] ornaments the left bank with its black steeple, and close by it the wild and pastoral Hamlet of Schulau. Hitherto both the right and left bank, green to the very brink and level with the River, resembled the shores of a park canal. The trees and houses were alike low, sometimes the low trees overtopping the yet lower houses, sometimes the low houses rising above the yet lower trees. But at Schulau the left bank rises at once forty or fifty feet, and stares on the River with its perpendicular fassade[3] of sand, thinly patched with tufts of green. The Elbe continued to present a more and more lively spectacle from the multitude of fishing boats and the flocks of sea gulls wheeling round them, the clamorous rivals and companions of the Fishermen; till we came to Blankaness,[4] a most interesting Village scattered amid scattered trees, over three hills [224] in three divisions. Each of the three hills stares upon the River, with faces of bare sand, with which the Boats with their bare poles, standing in files along the banks, made a sort of fantastic harmony. Between each fassade lies a green and woody dell, each deeper

---

[1] Cf WW *The Excursion* bk VI line 19: "And spires whose 'silent finger points to heaven' ". *WPW* v 187 (and 456, WW's note).

[2] The village of Vedder (or Veder).

[3] *CL* I 427 reads "Facing"; "fassade" (which is not in the *OED*) is both the German and the old French spelling of "façade".

[4] Blankenese.

than the other. In short it is a large Village made up of individual Cottages, each Cottage in the centre of its own little Wood or Orchard, and each with its own separate path: a Village with a labyrinth of paths, or rather a *neighbourhood* of Houses![1] It is inhabited by Fishermen and Boat-makers, the Blankanese Boats being in great request through the whole navigation of the Elbe. Here first we saw the Spires of Hamburg, and from hence as far as Altona the left bank of the Elbe is uncommonly pleasing, considered as the vicinity of an industrious and republican City—in that style of beauty, or rather prettiness, that might tempt the Citizen into the Country and yet gratify the taste which he had acquired in the Town. Summer Houses and Chinese show-work are every where scattered along the high and green banks; the boards of the farm-houses left unplaistered and gaily painted with green and yellow; and scarcely a tree not cut into shapes and made to remind the human being of his own power and intelligence instead of the wisdom of nature. Still, however, these are links of connection between Town and Country, and far better than the affectation of tastes and enjoyments for which mens' habits have disqualified them. Pass them by on Saturdays and Sundays with the Burgers of Hamburg smoking their Pipes, the Women and Children feasting in the Alcoves of Box and Yew, and it becomes a nature of its own. On Wednesday, four o'clock, we left the Vessel and passing with trouble through the huge masses of Shipping that seemed to choke the wide Elbe from Altona upward, we were at length landed at the Boom House,[2] Hamburg.

[1] Cf above, I 199–200 and 200 n 1.
[2] *CL* I 428 reads "boom [baum]-house". *Boomhaus* is Low German for "toll-house".

THE FRIEND

No. 15. THURSDAY, November 30, 1809

I have not intentionally either hidden or disguised the Truth, like an Advocate ashamed of his Client, or a bribed Accomptant who falsifies the quotient to make the Bankrupt's Ledgers square with the Creditor's Inventory. My conscience forbids the use of falsehood and the arts of concealment: and were it otherwise, yet I am persuaded, that a system which has produced and protected so great prosperity, cannot stand in need of them. If therefore Honesty and the Knowledge of the whole Truth be the things you aim at, you will find my principles suited to your ends: and as I like not the democratic forms, so am I not fond of any others above the rest. That a succession of wise and godly men may be secured to the nation in the highest power, is that to which I have directed your attention in this Essay, which if you will read, perhaps you may see the error of those principles which have led you into errors of practice. I wrote it purposely for the use of the multitude of well-meaning people, that are tempted in these times to usurp Authority and meddle with Government before they have any call from Duty or tolerable understanding of its' Principles. I never intended it for Learned Men versed in Politics; but for such as will be Practitioners before they have been Students.

BAXTER'S Holy Commonwealth, or Political Aphorisms

THE metaphysical (or as I have proposed to call them, *metapolitical*) reasonings hitherto discussed, belong to Government in the abstract. But there is a second class of Reasoners, who argue for a change in our government from former usage and from Statutes still in force or which have been repealed, (so these writers affirm) either through a corrupt influence, or to ward off temporary hazard or inconvenience. This Class, which is rendered illustrious by the names of many intelligent and virtuous Patriots, are Advocates for *reform* in the literal sense of the word. They wish to bring *back* the Government of Great Britain to a certain *form*, which they affirm it to have once possessed: and would melt the bullion anew in order to recast it in the original mould.

The answer to all arguments of this nature is obvious, and to my understanding appears decisive. These Reformers assume the character of Legislators or of Advisers of [226] the Legislature, not that of Law Judges or of appellants to Courts of Law. Sundry Statutes concerning the rights of electors and the mode of election still exist; so likewise do sundry statutes on other subjects (on Witchcraft for instance) which change of circumstances have rendered obsolete, or increased information shewn to be absurd. It is evident, therefore, that the expediency of the regulations prescribed by them and their suitableness to the existing circumstances of the Kingdom, must first be proved: and on this proof must be rested all rational claims for the enforcement of the Statutes that have not, no

197

less than for the re-enacting of those that have been, repealed. If the authority of the men, who first enacted the Laws in question, is to weigh with us, it must be on the presumption that they were wise men. But the wisdom of Legislation consists in the adaptation of Laws to Circumstances. If then it can be proved, that the circumstances, under which those laws were enacted, no longer exist; and that other circumstances altogether different, and in some instances opposite, have taken their place; we have the best grounds for supposing, that if the men were now alive, they would not pass the same Statutes. In other words, the spirit of the Statute interpreted by the intention of the Legislator would annul the Letter of it. It is not indeed impossible, that by a rare felicity of accident, the same law may apply to two sets of circumstances. But surely the *presumption* is, that regulations well adapted for the manners, the social distinctions, and the state of property, of opinion, and of external relations, of England in the reign of Alfred, or even in that of Edward the first, will not be well suited to Great Britain at the close of the reign of George the third. For instance: at the time when the greater part of the Cottagers and inferior Farmers were in a state of Villenage, when Sussex alone contained seven thousand and the Isle of Wight twelve hundred Families of Bondsmen, it was the Law of the Land that every *Freeman* should vote in the Assembly of the Nation personally or by his representative. An act of Parliament in the year 1660 confirmed what a concurrence of causes had previously effected:—every Englishman is now *born* free, the Laws of the Land are the Birth-right of every Native, and with the exception of a few honorary privileges all Classes obey the same Laws. Now, argues one of our political Writers, [227] it being made the Constitution of the Land by our Saxon Ancestors, that every Freeman should have a vote, and all Englishmen being now born free, *therefore*, by the Constitution of the Land, every Englishman has now a right to a vote. How shall we reply to this without breach of that Respect, to which the Reasoner at least, if not the Reasoning, is entitled? If it be the definition of a Pun, that it is the confusion of two different meanings under the same or some similar sound, we might almost characterize this argument as being grounded on a grave Pun. Our Ancestors established the right of voting in a particular Class of men forming at that time the middle rank of Society, and known to be all of them, or almost all, legal Proprietors—and these were then called the Freemen of England: *therefore* they established it in the lowest Classes of Society, in those who possess no Property, because these too are now called by the same name!! This is the same kind of Logic as that on the strength of which a Mameluke Bey extorted a large contribution from the Egyptian Jews: "it is my duty," said he, "to make men pay their just debts. *The Jews* borrowed a large Treasure from the Egyptians, which has not been repaid. But you are *the Jews*, and on you, therefore, I call for the repayment." Besides, if a law is to be interpreted by the known intention of its' makers, the Parliament in 1660, which declared all natives of England freemen, but neither altered nor meant thereby to alter the limitations of the right of election, did to all intents and purposes except that right from the common privileges of Englishmen, as Englishmen.

A moment's reflection may convince us, that every single Statute is made under the knowledge of all the other Laws, with which it is meant to co-exist, and by which its' action is to be modified and determined. In the legislative as in the religious Code, the text must not be taken without the context. Now, I think, we may safely leave it to the Reformers themselves to make choice between the civil and political privileges of Englishmen at present, considered as one Sum Total, and those of our Ancestors in any former period of our History, considered as another, on the old principle, *take one and leave the other; but whichever you take, take it all or none.* Laws seldom become obsolete as long as they are both useful and practicable; but should there be an exception, there [228] is no other way of reviving its' validity but by convincing the existing Legislature of its' undiminished practicability and expedience: which in all essential points is the same as the recommending of a new Law. And this leads me to the third Class of the Advocates of Reform, those, namely, who leaving ancient statutes to Lawyers and Historians, and universal Principles with the demonstrable deductions from them to the Schools of Logic, Mathematics, Theology, and Ethics, rest all their measures, which they wish to see adopted, wholly on their Expediency. Consequently, they must hold themselves prepared to give such proof, as the nature of comparative expediency admits, and to bring forward such evidence, as experience and the logic of probability can supply, that the plans which they recommend for adoption, are: first, practicable; secondly, suited to the existing circumstances; and lastly, necessary or at least requisite, and such as will enable the Government to accomplish more perfectly the ends for which it was instituted. These are the three indispensable Conditions of all prudent change, the Credentials, with which Wisdom never fails to furnish her public Envoys. Whoever brings forward a measure that combines this threefold excellence, whether in the Cabinet, the Senate, or by means of the Press, merits emphatically the title of a patriotic Statesman. Neither are they without a fair claim to respectful attention, as State-Counsellors, who fully aware of these conditions, and with a due sense of the difficulty of fulfilling them, employ their time and talents in making the attempt. An imperfect Plan is not necessarily a useless plan: and in a complex Enigma the greatest Ingenuity is not always shewn by him who first gives the compleat solution. The Dwarf sees farther than the Giant, when he has the Giant's shoulders to mount on.—It is, however, to Statesmen and State-Counsellors of this third Class, whom I would distinguish from the two former, i.e. from the METAPOLITICIANS and from the ANTIQUARIANS, by the name of PRACTICIANS, that I shall henceforward address myself, not as an Opponent, but as a Learner and Fellow-student: whenever I shall think it likely to gratify my readers that I should renew the Subject of Politics, by an examination of our Constitution, and of the expediency of a Change.

Thus, as perspicuously as I could, I have exposed the [229] erroneous Principles of political Philosophy, and pointed out the one only ground, on which the constitution of Governments can be either condemned or justified by wise men. By this sole test of general expedience, as determined by existing circumstances, I had intended to try both the present Government and the different plans which had been proposed for its' improvement, in detail; but as I find that after all possible compression, my Essay

on this subject could not be comprized in less than two Numbers, and it
being no part of my original plan, I shall inweave the *jet* of this most
important question in the miscellaneous Conversations of the Tourists
(See No. 14).¹ So not wholly dropping it, I may yet proceed without delay
to other Subjects, which I conceive more generally interesting, and which
are incomparably more agreeable to myself; namely, the Principles on
which we can alone deserve or procure happiness as individuals, and the
rules of right judgement concerning the Works of Nature and the Productions of human Genius.² To pourtray the *ideal* of a Moral Being, to
prove the close connection between moral worth and intellectual excellence
both in the production and appreciation of the works of genius, and to
apply this truth in detail to literature and the fine arts, was, and has always
remained, my strongest motive for the present undertaking. I would not,
however, willingly conclude this Essay, without something from which my
Readers individually may draw a practical advantage. If I interpret aright
the signs of the times, that branch of politics which relates to the necessity
and practicability of infusing new life into our Legislature, as the best
means of securing talent and wisdom in the Cabinet, will shortly occupy
the public attention with a paramount interest. I would gladly therefore
suggest the proper state of feeling and the right preparatory notions with
which this disquisition should be entered upon: and I do not know how
I can effect this more naturally, than by relating the facts and circumstances which influenced my own mind. I can scarcely be accused of
egotism as in the communications and conversations which I am about
to mention as having occurred to me during my residence abroad, I am
no otherwise the hero of the Tale, than as being the passive receiver or
auditor. But above all, let it not be forgotten, that in the following paragraphs I speak as a Christian Moralist, not as a Statesman.

[230] To examine any thing wisely, two conditions are requisite: first, a
distinct notion of the desirable ENDS, in the complete accomplishment of
which would consist the perfection of such a thing, or its' ideal excellence;
and, secondly, a calm and kindly mood of feeling, without which we shall
hardly fail either to overlook, or not to make due allowances for, the
circumstances which prevent these ends from being all perfectly realized
in the particular thing, which we are to examine. For instance, we must
have a general notion what a MAN can be and ought to be, before we can
even proceed to determine on the merits or demerits of any one Individual.
For the examination of our own Government, I prepared my mind, therefore, by the following short Catechism, on which I flatter myself the
remaining Contents of this Number will be found an amusing, if not an
instructive commentary.

In what do all States agree? A number of men—exert—powers—in
union. Wherein do they differ? 1st. In the quality and quantity of the
*powers. One State possesses Chemists, Mechanists, Mechanics of all kinds,
Men of Science; and the Arts of war and peace; and its' Citizens naturally
strong and of habitual courage: another State may possess none or a few only*

---

¹ Above, ii 186.
² C did not "proceed" in *The Friend*

with these principles and rules; see
above, ii 87 and n 3, 104.

of these, or the same more imperfectly. Or *of two States possessing the same in equal perfection the one is more numerous than the other, as France and Switzerland.* 2d. In the more or less perfect union of these powers. *Compare Mr. Leckie's valuable and authentic documents respecting the state of Sicily with No.* 12, *page* 181, 182, *of* THE FRIEND.[1] 3dly. In the greater or less activity of exertion. *Think of the ecclesiastical State and its' silent Metropolis and then of the County of Lancaster and the Towns of Manchester and Liverpool.* What is the condition of powers exerted in union by a number of men? A Government. What are the ends of Government? They are of two kinds, negative and positive. The negative ends of Government are the protection of Life, of personal Freedom, of Property, of Reputation, and of Religion, from foreign and from domestic attacks. The positive ends are, 1st. to make the means of subsistence more easy to each individual: 2d. that in addition to the necessaries of life he should derive from the union and division of labour a share of the comforts and conveniencies, which humanize and ennoble his nature; and at the same time the power of perfecting himself in his own branch of industry [231] by having those things which he needs, provided for him by others among his fellow-citizens; including the tools and raw or manufactured materials, necessary for his own Employment. *I knew a profound Mathematician in Sicily, who had devoted a full third of his life to the perfecting the discovery of the Longitude, and who had convinced not only himself but the principal Mathematicians of Messina and Palermo that he had succeeded; but neither throughout Sicily or Naples could he find a single Artist capable of constructing the instrument which he had invented.** 3dly. The hope of bettering his own condition and that of his children. *The civilized man gives up those stimulants of hope and fear which constitute the chief charm of the savage life: and yet his Maker has distinguished him from the Brute that perishes, by making Hope an instinct of his nature and an indispensible condition of his moral and intellectual progression. But a natural instinct constitutes a natural right, as far as its' gratification is compatible with the equal rights of others. Hence our Ancestors classed those who were bound to the soil* (addicti glebæ) *and incapable by law of altering their condition from that of their parents, as Bondsmen or Villains, however advantageously they might otherwise be situated. Reflect on the direful effects of Casts in Hindostan, and then transfer yourself in fancy to an English Cottage,*

---

* The good old Man, who is poor, old, and blind, universally esteemed for the innocence and austerity of his life not less than for his learning, and yet universally neglected except by persons almost as poor as himself, strongly reminded me of a German Epigram on Kepler, which may be thus translated:

> No mortal spirit yet had clomb so high
> As Kepler—yet his Country saw him die
> For very Want! the *Minds* alone he fed,
> And so the *Bodies* left him without bread.

The good old Man presented me with the book in which he has described and demonstrated his invention: and I should with great pleasure transmit it to any mathematician who would feel an interest in examining it and communicating his opinions on its merits.

[1] Above, II 162–3. Cf above, I 251 and n 2.

"Where o'er the cradled Infant bending
Hope has fixed her wishful gaze,"

and the fond Mother dreams of her Child's future fortunes—who knows but he may come home a rich Merchant, like such a one? or be a Bishop or a Judge? The prizes are indeed few and rare; but still they are possible: and the Hope is universal, and perhaps occasions more happiness than even its' fulfillment. (and lastly) the developement [232] of those faculties which are essential to his human nature by the knowledge of his moral and religious duties, and the increase of his intellectual powers in as great a degree as is compatible with the other ends of social union, and does not involve a contradiction. *The poorest Briton possesses much and important knowledge, which he would not have had, if Newton, Luther, Calvin, and their Compeers, had not existed; but it is evident that the means of Science and Learning could not exist, if all men had a right to be made profound Mathematicians or men of extensive Erudition. Still instruction is one of the ends of Government: for it is that only which makes the abandonment of the savage state an* ABSOLUTE DUTY: *and that Constitution is the best, under which the average sum of useful knowledge is the greatest, and the causes that awaken and encourage talent and genius, the most powerful and various.*

These were my preparatory notions. The influences under which I proceeded to re-examine our own Constitution, were the following, which I give, not exactly as they occurred, but in the order in which they will be illustrative of the different articles of the preceding paragraph. That we are better and happier than others is indeed no reason for our not becoming still better; especially as with States, as well as Individuals, not to be progressive is to be retrograde. Yet the comparison will usefully temper the desire of improvement with love and a sense of gratitude for what we already are.

I. A LETTER *received, at Malta, from an American Officer of high Rank, who has since received the thanks and rewards of the Congress for his Services in the Mediterranean*

SIR,   GRAND CAIRO, Dec. 13, 1804.

The same reason, which induced me to request Letters of introduction to his Britannic Majesty's Agents here, suggested the propriety of shewing an English jack at the main top-gallant mast head, on entering the port of Alexandria on the 26th ult. The signal was recognised; and Mr. B——— was immediately on board.

We found in port a Turkish Vice Admiral with a ship [233] of the line and six frigates; a part of which squadron is stationed there to preserve the tranquillity of the Country; with just as much influence as the same number of Pelicans would have on the same Station.

On entering and passing the streets of Alexandria I could not but notice the very marked satisfaction, which every expression and every countenance of all denominations of people, Turks and Frenchmen only excepted, manifested under an impression that we were the Avant-courier of an English Army. They had conceived this from observing the English Jack at our main, taking our flag perhaps for that of a saint, and because as is common enough every where, they were ready to believe what they wished. It would have been cruel to have undeceived them: consequently without positively assuming it, we passed in the character of Englishmen among the middle and lower orders of society, and as their Allies among those of better information. Wherever we entered or wherever halted, we were surrounded by the wretched Inhabitants; and stunned with their benedictions and prayers for blessings on us. "Will the English come? Are they coming? God grant the English may come! we have no commerce—we have no money—we have no bread! When will the English arrive?" My answer was uniformly, *Patience!* The same tone was heard at Rosetta as among the Alexandrians, indicative of the same dispositions; only it was not so loud, because the Inhabitants are less miserable, although without any traits of Happiness. On the fourth we left that Village for Cairo, and for our security as well as to facilitate our procurement of accommodations during our voyage, as well as our stay there, the Resident directed his Secretary, Capt. V——, to accompany us, and to give us lodgings in his house. We ascended the Nile leisurely, and calling at several Villages, it was plainly perceivable that the rational partiality, the strong and open expression of which proclaimed so loudly the feelings of the Egyptians of the Sea Coast, was general throughout the Country: and the prayers for the return of the English as earnest as universal.

On the morning of the sixth we went on shore at the village of Sabour. The Villagers expressed an enthusiastic gladness at seeing *red* and *blue* Uniforms and *round* Hats (the French, I believe, wear three-cornered ones.) Two days before, five hundred Albanian Deserters [234] from the Viceroy's army had pillaged and left this Village; at which they had lived at free quarters about four weeks.—The famishing Inhabitants were now distressed with apprehensions from another quarter. A Company of wild Arabs were encamped in sight. They dreaded their ravages and apprized us of danger from them. We were eighteen in the party, well armed; and a pretty brisk fire which we raised around the numerous flocks of Pigeons and other small fowl in the Environs, must have deterred them from mischief, if, as is most probable, they had meditated any against us. Scarcely, however, were we on board and under weigh, when we saw these mounted Marauders of the Desart fall furiously upon the herds of Camels, Buffaloes, and Cattle of the Village, and drove many of them off wholly unannoyed on the part of the unresisting Inhabitants, unless their *shrieks* could be deemed an annoyance. They afterwards attacked and robbed several unarmed boats, which were a few hours astern of us. The most insensible must surely have been moved by the situation of the Peasants of that Village. The while we were listening to their complaints, they kissed our hands and with prostrations to the ground, rendered more affecting by the inflamed state of the eyes almost universal amongst them, and which the new Traveller might venially imagine to have been the immediate effect of weeping and anguish, they all implored *English* succour. Their shrieks at the assault of the wild Arabs seemed to implore the same still more forcibly, while it testified what multiplied reasons they had to implore it. I confess, I felt an almost insurmountable impulse to bring our little party to their relief, and might perhaps have done a rash act, had it not been for the calm and just observation of Captain V——'s that "these were common occurrences, and that any relief, which we could afford, would not merely be only temporary, but would exasperate the Plunderers to still more atrocious outrages after our departure."

On the morning of the seventh we landed near a Village. At our approach the Villagers fled: signals of Friendship brought some of them to us. When they were told, that we were Englishmen, they flocked around us with demonstrations of joy, offered their services, and raised loud ejaculations for our establishment in the Country. Here we could not procure a pint of milk for our coffee. The Inhabitants had been plundered and chased from their [235] habitations by the Albanians and Desart Arabs, and it was but the preceeding day, they had returned to their naked Cottages.

Grand Cairo differs from the places already passed, only as the presence of the Tyrant stamps silence on the lips of misery with the seal of Terror. Wretchedness here assumes the form of Melancholy; but the few whispers that are hazarded, convey the same feelings and the same wishes. And wherein does this misery and consequent Spirit of Revolution consist? Not in any *form* of Government but in a formless Despotism, an Anarchy indeed! for it amounts literally to an annihilation of every thing that can merit the name of Government or justify the use of the word even in the laxest sense. Egypt is under the most frightful Despotism, yet has no Master! The Turkish Soldiery, restrained by no discipline, seize every thing by violence, not only all that their necessities dictate, but whatever their caprices suggest. The Mamelukes, who dispute with these the right of Domination, procure themselves subsistence by means as lawless though less insupportably oppressive. And the wild Arabs availing themselves of the occasion, plunder the defenceless wherever they find Plunder. To finish the whole, the talons of the Viceroy fix on every thing which can be changed into currency, in order to find the means of supporting an ungoverned, disorganized Banditti of foreign Troops, who receive the harvest of his oppression, desert and betray him. Of all this rapine, robbery, and extortion, the wretched Cultivators of the Soil are the perpetual Victims.—A spirit of Revolution is the natural consequence.

The reason the Inhabitants of this Country give for preferring the English to the French, whether true or false, is as natural as it is simple, and as influential as natural. "The English," say they, "pay for every thing—the French pay nothing, and take every thing." They do not like this kind of Deliverers.——

Well, thought I, after the perusal of this Letter, the Slave Trade (which had not then been abolished) is a dreadful crime, an *English* iniquity! and to sanction its' continuance under full conviction and parliamentary confession of its' injustice and inhumanity is, if possible, still blacker guilt. Would that our discontents were for a [236] while confined to our moral Wants! whatever may be the defects of our Constitution, we have at least an effective Government, and that too composed of Men who were born with us and are to die among us. We are at least preserved from the incursions of foreign enemies; the intercommunion of interests precludes

a civil War, and the Volunteer Spirit of the Nation equally with its laws,
give to the darkest lanes of our crowded Metropolis that quiet and security
which the remotest Villager at the cataracts of the Nile prays for in vain,
in his mud hovel!

> *Not yet enslaved nor wholly vile,*
> O Albion, O my Mother Isle!
> Thy Vallies fair, as Eden's bowers,
> Glitter green with sunny showers;
> Thy grassy uplands' gentle swells
> Echo to the bleat of flocks;
> (Those grassy hills, those glitt'ring dells
> Proudly ramparted with rocks)
> AND OCEAN MID HIS UPROAR WILD
> SPEAKS SAFETY TO HIS ISLAND-CHILD.
> Hence for many a fearless age
> Has social quiet lov'd thy shore;
> Nor ever sworded Warrior's rage
> Or sack'd thy towers or stain'd thy fields with gore.
>
> COLERIDGE'S POEMS

II. *Anecdote of* BUONAPARTE

Buonaparte, during his short stay at Malta, called out the Maltese Regiments raised by the Knights, amounting to fifteen hundred of the stoutest
young men of the Islands. As they were drawn up on the parade, he informed them, in a bombastic harangue, that he had restored them to
Liberty; but in proof that his attachment to them was not bounded by this
benefaction, he would now give them an opportunity of adding Glory to
Freedom—and concluding by asking who of them would march forward
to be his Fellow-soldier on the banks of the Nile, and contribute a flower
of Maltese heroism to the immortal wreaths of fame, with which he meant
to crown the Pyramids of Egypt! Not a man stirred: all gave a [237] silent
refusal. They were instantly surrounded by a Regiment of French Soldiers,
marched to the Marino, forced on board the Transports, and threatened
with death if any one of them attempted his escape, or should be discovered
in any part of the Islands of Malta or Goza. At Alexandria they were
always put in the front, both to save the French Soldiery and to prevent
their running away: and of the whole number fifty only survived to revisit
their native Country. From one of these Survivors I first learnt this fact,
which was afterwards confirmed to me by several of his remaining Comrades, as well as by the most respectable Inhabitants of Vilette.

This anecdote recalled to my mind an accidental conversation with an
old Countryman in a central district of Germany. I purposely omit names
because the day of retribution has come and gone by. I was looking at a
strong Fortress in the distance, which formed a highly interesting object in
a rich and varied landscape, and asked the old man, who had stopped to

gaze at me, it's name &c. adding—how beautiful it looks! It may be well enough to look at, answered he, but God keep all Christians from being taken thither! He then proceeded to gratify the curiosity, which he had thus excited, by informing me that the Baron —— had been taken out of his bed at midnight and carried to that Fortress—that he was not heard of for nearly two years, when a Soldier who had fled over the boundaries sent information to his family of the place and mode of his imprisonment. As I have no design to work on the feelings of my Readers, I pass over the shocking detail: had not the language and countenance of my informant precluded such a suspicion, I might have supposed that he had been repeating some tale of horror from a Romance of the dark ages. What was his crime? I asked—The report is, said the old Man, that in his capacity as Minister he had remonstrated with the —— concerning the extravagance of his Mistress, an outlandish Countess; and that she in revenge persuaded the Sovereign, that it was the Baron who had communicated to a Professor at Gottingen the particulars of the infamous sale of some thousand of his Subjects as Soldiers. On the same day I discovered in the Landlord of a small Public House one of the men who had been thus sold. He seemed highly delighted in entertaining an English Gentleman, and in once [238] more talking English after a lapse of so many years. He was far from regretting this incident in his life, but his account of the manner, in which they were forced away, accorded in so many particulars with Schiller's empassioned description of the same, or a similar scene, in his Tragedy of CABAL and LOVE, as to leave a perfect conviction on my mind, that the dramatic pathos of that description was not greater than its' historic fidelity.

As I was thus reflecting, I glanced my eye on the leading paragraphs of a London Newspaper, containing much angry declamation, and some bitter truths, respecting our military arrangements. It were in vain, thought I, to deny that the influence of parliamentary interest, which prevents the immense patronage of the Crown from becoming a despotic power, is not the most likely to secure the ablest Commanders or the fittest persons for the management of our foreign empire. However, thank Heaven! if we fight, we fight for our own King and Country: and grievances which may be publicly complained of, there is some chance of seeing remedied.

III. A celebrated Professor in a German University, shewed me a very pleasing Print entitled, "Toleration." A Catholic Priest, a Lutheran Divine, a Calvinist Minister, a Quaker, a Jew, and a Philosopher, were represented sitting round the same table over which a winged figure hovered in the attitude of protection. For this harmless Print, said my Friend, the Artist was imprisoned, and having attempted to make his escape, was sentenced to draw the Boats on the banks of the Danube with robbers and murderers: and there died in less than two months, from exhaustion and exposure. In your happy Country, Sir, this print would be considered as a pleasing scene from real life: for in every great Town throughout your empire you may meet with the original. Yes, I replied, as far as the *negative* ends of Government are concerned, we have no reason to complain. Our Government protects us from foreign enemies, and our Laws secure our lives, our personal freedom, our property, reputation, and religious rights, from domestic attacks. Our Taxes, indeed, are enormous—Oh! talk not of Taxes, said my Friend, till you have resided in a Country where the Boor disposes of his produce to Strangers for a foreign mart, not to bring back to his family the comforts and conveniences of foreign [239] manufactures, but to procure the coin which his Lord is to squander away in a distant land. Neither can I with patience hear it said, that your Laws act only to the *negative* ends of government. They have a manifold *positive* influence, and their incorrupt administration gives a colour to all your modes of thinking, and is one of the chief causes of your superior morality in private as well as public life.*

My limits compel me to strike out the different incidents, which I had written as a Commentary on the three former of the *positive* ends of Government. To the moral feelings of my Readers they might have been serviceable; but for their understandings they are superfluous. It is surely impossible to peruse them, and not admit that all three are realized under our Government to a degree unexampled in any other old and long peopled Country. The defects of our Constitution (in which word I include the Laws and Customs of the Land as well as it's scheme of Legislative and Executive power) must exist, therefore, in the fourth, namely, the production of the highest average of general information, of general moral and religious principles, and the excitements and opportunities which it affords, to paramount Genius and heroic power, in a sufficient number of its' Citizens. These are points in which it would be immorality to rest content with the presumption, however well founded, that we are better than others, if we are not what we ought to be ourselves, and not using the means of improvement. The first question then is, what is the FACT? The second: *supposing* a defect or deficiency in one or all of these points, and [240] that to a degree which may effect our power and prosperity if not our absolute safety, are the plans of Legislative Reform that have hitherto been proposed, fit or likely to remove such defect, and supply such deficiency? The third and last question is—Should there appear

---

* "The administration of Justice throughout the Continent is partial, venal, and infamous. I have, in conversation with many sensible men, met with something of content with their governments in all other respects than this; but upon the question of expecting justice to be really and fairly administered every one confessed there was no such thing to be looked for. The conduct of the Judges is profligate and atrocious. Upon almost every cause that comes before them, interest is openly made with the Judges; and woe betide the man who, with a cause to support had no means of conciliating favour either by the beauty of a handsome Wife or by other methods."—This quotation is confined in the original to France under the monarchy; I have extended the application, and adopted the words, as comprizing the result of my own experience: and I take this opportunity of declaring, that the most important parts of Mr. Leckie's Statement concerning Sicily I myself *know* to be accurate, and am authorized by what I myself saw there, to rely on the whole as a fair and unexaggerated representation.

reason to deny or doubt this, are there then any other means, and what are they?—Of these points hereafter and occasionally.

A French Gentleman in the reign of Lewis the 14th was comparing the French and English writers with all the boastfulness of national pre-possession. Sir! (replied an Englishman better versed in the principles of Freedom than the canons of criticism) there are but two Subjects worthy the human Intellect: POLITICS and RELIGION, our State here and our State hereafter: and on neither of these *dare* you write. Long may the envied Privilege be preserved to my Countrymen of writing and talking concerning both! Nevertheless, it behoves us all to consider, that to write or talk concerning any subject without having previously taken the pains to understand it, is a breach of Duty which we owe to ourselves, though it may be no offence against the Laws of the Land. The privilege of talking and even publishing Nonsense is necessary in a free state; but the more sparingly we make use of it, the better.

THE FRIEND

No. 16. THURSDAY, December 7, 1809

SATYRANE'S LETTERS

Letter II (To a Lady)[1]

RATZEBURG

Meine liebe Freundin,

See how natural the German comes from me, though I have not yet been six weeks in the Country!—almost as fluently as English from my neighbour the Amptschreiber (or Public Secretary) who as often as we meet, though it should be half a dozen times in the same day, never fails to greet me with—"* * *ddam your ploot unt Eyes, my dearest Englander! vhee goes it!*"—which is certainly a proof of great generosity on his part, these words being his whole stock of English. I had, however, a better reason than the desire of displaying my proficiency: for I wished to put you in good humour with a language, from the acquirement of which I have promised myself much edification and the means too of communicating a new pleasure to you and your Sister, during our winter Readings. And how can I do this better than by pointing out its' gallant attention to the Ladies? Our English affix, *ess*, is, I believe, confined either to words derived from the Latin, as *Actress, Directress*, &c. or from the French, as *Mistress, Duchess*, and the like. But the German, *in*, enables us to designate the Sex in every possible relation of life. Thus the Amptman's Lady is the Frau Amptman*in*—the Secretary's Wife (by the bye the handsomest Woman I have yet seen in Germany) is Die allerliebste Frau Amptschreiber*in*—the Colonel's Lady, Die Frau Obrist*in* or Colonel*lin*—and even the Parson's Wife, Die Frau Pastor*in*. But I am especially [242] pleased with their *Freundin*, which, unlike the *Amica* of the Romans, is seldom used but in its' best and purest sense. Now, I know, it will be said, that a Friend is already something more than a Friend, when a Man feels an anxiety to express to himself that this Friend is a female; but this I deny—in that sense at least in which the objection will be made. I would hazard the impeachment of heresy, rather than abandon my belief that there is a sex in our SOULS as well as in their perishable garments: and he who does not feel it, never truly loved a Sister—nay, is not capable even of loving a Wife as she deserves to be loved, if she indeed be worthy of that holy name.

Now I know, my gentle Friend, what you are murmuring to yourself— "This is so like him! running away after the first bubble, that chance has

---

[1] The "Lady" was Mrs C; actually this letter is a pastiche of letters to her and to Poole, to whom C had promised to write "alternately . . . twice every week" (*CL* I 415). Cf *CL* I 430– 440 for the original letters (to Poole 26 Oct 1798, to Mrs C 8 Nov 1798) and *BL* (1817) II 205–21 for later revisions of the letter published here.

blown off from the surface of his fancy; when one is anxious to learn where he is and what he has seen." Well then! that I am settled at Ratzeburg, with my motives and the particulars of my journey hither ——[1] will inform you. My first Letter to him,[2] with which doubtless he has edified your whole Fire-side, left me safely landed at Hamburg on the Elbe Stairs, at the Boom House. While standing on the Stairs, I was amused by the contents of the Passage Boat which crosses the River once or twice a day from Hamburg to Haarburg.[3] It was stowed close with all People of all Nations, in all sorts of Dresses; the Men all with pipes in their mouths, and these pipes of all shapes and fancies—straight and wreathed, simple and complex, long and short, cane, clay, porcelain, wood, tin, silver, and ivory; most of them with silver chains and silver bole-covers. Pipes and Boots are the first universal characteristic of the male Hamburgers that would strike the eye of a raw Traveller. But I forget my promise of journalizing as much as possible.—Therefore, *Septr. 19th. Afternoon.* My Companion,[4] who you recollect speaks the French Language with unusual propriety, had formed a kind of confidential acquaintance with the Emigrant, who appeared to be a man of sense, and whose manners were those of a perfect Gentleman. He seemed about fifty or rather more. Whatever is unpleasant in French manners from excess in the *Degree*, had been softened down by age or affliction, and all that is delightful in the *kind*, alacrity and delicacy in little attentions, &c. remained, and without bustle, gesticulation, [243] or disproportionate eagerness. His demeanour exhibited the minute philanthropy of a polished Frenchman, tempered by the sobriety of the English character disunited from its' reserve. There is something strangely attractive in the character of a *Gentleman* when you apply the word emphatically, and yet in that sense of the term which it is more easy to *feel* than to define. It neither includes the possession of high moral excellence nor, of necessity, even the ornamental graces of manner. I have now in my mind's eye a Person whose life would scarcely stand scrutiny even in the court of honour, much less in that of conscience; and his manners, if nicely observed, would of the two excite an idea of awkwardness rather than of elegance: and yet every one who conversed with him felt and acknowledged *the Gentleman*. The secret of the matter, I believe to be this—we feel the gentlemanly character present to us, whenever under all the circumstances of social intercourse, the trivial not less than the important, through the whole *detail* of his manners and deportment, and with the ease of a habit, a Person shews respect to others in *such a way*, as at the same time implies in his own feelings an habitual and assured anticipation of reciprocal respect from them to himself. This description will perhaps explain to you the ground of one of your own remarks, as I was englishing to you the interesting Dialogue concerning the causes of the corruption of eloquence.[5] "What perfect Gentlemen these old Romans must have been! I was impressed, I remember, with

[1] Poole.
[2] C's "first Letter" had been to his wife.
[3] Harburg, on the south bank of the Elbe.

[4] Wordsworth.
[5] Tacitus' *Dialogus de oratoribus* was once identified with Quintilian's lost dialogue, *De causis corruptae eloquentiae*; cf *BL* ch 3 (1907) I 40, 219.

the same feeling at the time I was reading a translation of Cicero's philosophical Dialogues and of his epistolary correspondence: while in Pliny's
Letters I seemed to have a different feeling—he gave me the notion of a
very *fine* Gentleman." [1]—You uttered the words as if you had felt that the
adjunct had injured the substance, and the encreased degree altered the
kind. Pliny was the Courtier of an absolute Monarch—Cicero an aristocratic Republican. For this reason the character of Gentleman, in the
sense to which I have confined it, is frequent in England, rare in France, and
found, where it is found, in age or the latest period of manhood; while
in Germany the character is almost unknown. But the proper *Antipode* of
a Gentleman is to be sought for among the Anglo-American Democrats.

I owe this digression, as an act of justice, to this [244] amiable Frenchman, and of humiliation for myself: for in a little controversy between us
on the subject of French Poetry, he made me feel my own ill behaviour
by the silent reproof of contrast, and when I afterwards apologized to him
for the warmth of my language, he answered me with a chearful expression
of surprize, and an immediate compliment, which a Gentleman might both
make with dignity and receive with pleasure. I was pleased, therefore, to
find it agreed on, that we should, if possible, take up our quarters in the
same House. My Friend went with him in search of an Hotel, and I to
deliver my Letters of recommendation.

I walked onward at a brisk pace, enlivened not so much by any thing I
actually saw, as by the confused sense that I was for the first time in my
life on the *Continent* of our Planet. I seemed to myself like a liberated Bird
that had been hatched in an aviary, who now after his first Soar of freedom
poises himself in the upper air. Very naturally I began to wonder at *all*
things, some for being so like and some for being so unlike the things in
England—Dutch Women with large umbrella hats shooting out half a
yard before them, with a prodigal plumpness of petticoat behind—the
Women of Hamburg with caps plated on the caul with silver or gold, or
both, bordered round with stiffened lace, which *stood out* before their eyes,
but not lower, so that the eyes sparkled through it—the Hanoverian
Women with the fore part of the head bare, then a stiff lace standing up
like a wall perpendicular on the cap, and the cap behind *tailed* with an
enormous quantity of ribbon which lies or tosses on the back:

> "Their visnomies seem'd like a goodly banner
> Spread in defiance of all enemies."
> S P E N S E R [2]

——The Ladies all in English dresses, all *rouged*, and all with bad teeth:
which you notice instantly from their striking contrast to the beautiful
mother-of-pearl whiteness and regularity of the teeth of the laughing, loud-
talking Country-women and Servant-girls, who with their clean white
stockings and with slippers without heel-quarters, tripped along the dirty
streets, as if they were secured by a charm from the dirt, and with a light-
ness which surprized me, who had always considered it as one [245] of the
annoyances of sleeping *in an Inn*, that I had to clatter up stairs in a pair of

---

[1] The above passage, which does not
appear in the letters to Mrs C and

Poole, is probably a later interpolation.
[2] *Amoretti* v lines 11–12 (altered).

them. The streets narrow; to my English nose sufficiently offensive, and explaining at first sight the universal use of Boots; without any appropriate path for the foot-passengers; the gable ends of the Houses all towards the street, some in the ordinary triangular form and *entire* as the botanists say, but the greater number notched and scolloped with more than Chinese grotesqueness—above all, I was struck with the profusion of windows, so large and so many, that the houses look all glass. Mr. Pitt's window Tax,[1] with its' pretty little *additionals* sprouting out from it like young toadlets on the back of a Surinam toad, would certainly improve the appearance of the Hamburg houses, which have a slight summer look, not *in keeping* with their size, incongruous with the climate, and precluding that feeling of retirement and self-content, which one wishes to associate with a house in a noisy city; but in truth a conflagration would be the previous requisite to the production of any architectural beauty in Hamburg: for verily it is a filthy Town. I moved on and crossed a multitude of ugly Bridges, with huge black deformities of water wheels close by them. The water intersects the City every where, and would have furnished to the genius of Italy the capabilities of all that is most beautiful and magnificent in architecture. It might have been the rival of Venice, and it is huddle and ugliness, stench and stagnation. The Jungfer Stieg[2] (i.e. young Ladies Walk) to which my Letters directed me, made an exception. It is a walk or promenade planted with treble rows of elm trees, which being yearly pruned and cropped, remain slim and dwarf-like. This walk occupies one side of a square piece of water, with many swans on it perfectly tame, and moving among the swans, shewy pleasure boats with ladies in them, rowed by their husbands or lovers. *

Some paragraphs have been here omitted—* * * *[3] thus embarrassed by sad and solemn politeness still more than by broken English, it sounded like the voice of an old friend when I heard the Emigrant's servant enquiring after me. He had come for the purpose of guiding me to our Hotel. Through streets and streets I pressed on as happy as a child and, I doubt not, with a childish expression of wonderment in my busy eyes, amused by the [246] wicker waggons with moveable benches across them, one behind the other, (these were the hackney coaches); amused by the sign-boards of the shops, on which all the articles sold within are painted, and that too very exactly, though in a grotesque confusion (a useful Substitute for language in this great mart of nations) amused with the incessant tinkling of the shop and house door bells, the bell hanging over each door and struck with a small iron rod at every entrance and exit;—and finally, amused by looking in at the windows, as I passed along; the ladies and gentlemen drinking coffee or playing cards, and the gentlemen all smoking. I wished myself a painter, that I might have sent you a sketch of one of the

---

[1] By 1766 the elder Pitt's government succeeded in raising the tax that had been levied on houses containing fifteen or more windows and lowering to seven the number of windows that made a house taxable. Householders began to brick up and plaster-and-lath their excess windows. C is probably thinking of the younger Pitt's window tax of 1797, which trebled his earlier (1792) graduated window tax.

[2] Jungfernstieg, in Hamburg.

[3] See *CL* I 432.

card parties. The long pipe of one gentleman rested on the table, its' bole half a yard from his mouth, fuming like a censer by the fish pool—the other gentleman, who was dealing the cards, and of course had both hands employed, held his pipe in his teeth, which hanging down between his knees, smoked beside his ancles. Hogarth[1] himself never drew a more ludicrous distortion both of attitude and physiognomy, than this effort occasioned: nor was there wanting beside it one of those beautiful female faces which the same Hogarth, in whom the Satyrist never extinguished that love of beauty which belonged to him as a Poet, so often and so gladly introduces as the central figure in a crowd of humourous deformities, which figure (such is the power of true genius!) neither acts, nor is *meant* to act as a contrast; but diffuses through all, and over each of the group, a spirit of reconciliation and human kindness; and even when the attention is no longer consciously directed to the cause of this feeling, still blends its' tenderness with our laughter: and thus prevents the instructive merriment at the whims of nature or the foibles or humours of our fellow-men from degenerating into the heart-poison of contempt or hatred.

Our Hotel DIE WILDE MAN, (the sign of which was no bad likeness of the Landlord, who had engrafted on a very grim face a restless grin, that was at every man's service, and which, indeed, like an Actor rehearsing to himself, he kept playing in *expectation* of an occasion for it)—neither our Hotel, I say, nor its Landlord were of the genteelest class; but it has one great advantage for a Stranger, by being in the market place, and the next neighbour of the huge Church of St. Nicholas: a church [247] with shops and houses built up against it, out of which *wens* and *warts* its' high massive steeple rises, *necklaced* near the top with a Round of large gilt balls. A better pole-star could scarcely be desired. Long shall I retain the impression made on my mind by the awful echo, so loud and long and tremulous, of the deep-toned clock within this church, which awoke me at two in the morning from a distressful dream,[2] occasioned, I believe, by the feather bed which is used here instead of bed clothes. I will rather carry my blanket about with me like a wild Indian, than submit to this abominable custom. Our Emigrant Acquaintance was, we found, an intimate friend of the celebrated Abbe de Lisle:[3] and from the large fortune which he possessed under the Monarchy, had rescued sufficient not only for independence, but for respectability. He had offended some of his Fellow-emigrants in London, whom he had obliged with considerable sums, by a refusal to make further advances, and in consequence of their intrigues had received an order to quit the kingdom. I thought it one proof of his innocence, that he attached no blame either to the alien act or to the Minister who had exerted it against him; and a still greater, that he spoke of London with rapture, and of his favourite Niece, who had married and settled in

---

[1] William Hogarth (1697–1764), to C one of England's five "unique" great men: see *C 17th C* 463, 657.

[2] Cf "I woke; it was the midnight hour, | The clock was echoing in the tower; | But though my slumber was gone by, | This dream it would not pass away—". *Christabel* lines 555-8: *PW* (EHC) I 232.

[3] Jean-Baptiste Isoard, called Delisle de Sales (1743–1816), author of over 100 volumes ranging from satiric poetry to *L'Histoire des hommes* (1781).

England, with all the fervor and all the pride of a fond parent. A Man sent by force out of a Country, obliged to sell out of the Stocks at a great loss, and exiled from those pleasures and that style of society which habit had rendered essential to his happiness, whose predominant feelings were yet all of a private nature, resentment for friendship outraged, and anguish for domestic affections interrupted—such a man, I think, I could dare warrant guiltless of *Espionage* in any service, most of all in that of the present French Directory. He spoke with extacy of Paris under the Monarchy: and yet the particular facts, which made up his description, left as deep a conviction on my mind, of French worthlessness, as his own tale had done of Emigrant ingratitude. Since my arrival in Germany I have not met a single Person, even among those who abhor the Revolution, that spoke with favor, or even charity, of the French Emigrants. Though the belief of their influence in the origination of this disastrous war (from the horrors of which North Germany deems itself only reprieved, not secured) may have some share in the general aversion with [248] which they are regarded; yet I am deeply persuaded that the far greater part is owing to their own profligacy, to their treachery and hard-heartedness to each other, and the domestic misery or corrupt principles which so many of them have carried into the families of their Protectors. My heart dilated with honest pride, as I recalled to mind the stern yet amiable characters of the English Patriots, who sought refuge on the Continent at the Restoration! O let not our civil war under the first Charles, be paralleled with the French Revolution! In the former the chalice overflowed from excess of Principle, in the latter from the fermentation of the dregs! The former was a civil war between the virtues and virtuous prejudices of the two parties, the latter between the vices. The Venetian Glass of the French Monarchy, shivered and flew asunder with the working of a double poison.

Septr. 20th. I was introduced to Mr. Klopstock, the brother of the Poet,[1] who again introduced me to Professor Ebeling,[2] an intelligent and lively man, though deaf: so deaf, indeed, that it was a painful effort to talk with him, as we were obliged to drop all our pearls into a huge ear-trumpet. From this courteous and kind-hearted man of letters (I hope the German Literati in general may resemble this first specimen) I heard a tolerable Italian Pun and an interesting Anecdote. When Buonaparte was in Italy, having been irritated by some instance of perfidy, he said, in a loud and vehement tone, in a public company—"'tis a true proverb, *Gli Italiani tutti Ladroni* (i.e. *the Italians all Plunderers*). A Lady had the courage to reply, "Non tutti; ma BUONA PARTE,'' (*not all, but a good part*, or *Buonaparte*). This, I confess, sounded to *my* ears, as one of the many good things that *might have been* said. The Anecdote is more valuable; for it instances the ways and means of French insinuation. HOCHE[3] had received much information concerning the face of the

[1] Victor Klopstock (1744–1811), "a sort of Merchant in the agency Line" as well as a newspaper proprietor (*CL* I 437). C called him Young Klopstock as a joke: he was younger than the poet, "altho' an old man"

(*CL* I 436).
[2] Christoph Daniel Ebeling (1741–1815); see *CN* I 337 and n.
[3] Louis-Lazare Hoche (1768–97), famous young general of the Revolution, the "Pacificator of the Vendée".

Country, from a Map of unusual fullness and accuracy, the Maker of which, he heard, resided at Dusseldorf. At the storming of Dusseldorf by the French army, HOCHE previously ordered, that the house and property of this Man should be preserved, and entrusted the performance of the order to an Officer on whose Troop he could rely. Finding afterwards that the Man had escaped before the storming commenced, Hoche exclaimed, "HE had no reason to flee! it is *for* such Men, not *against* them, that [249] the French Nation makes war and consents to shed the blood of its' Children." You remember Milton's Sonnet—

> "The great Emathian conqueror bid spare
> The house of Pindarus when temples and tower
> Went to the ground"——[1]

Now though the Dusseldorf Map-maker may stand in the same relation to the Theban Bard as the snail that marks its' path by lines of film on the wall it creeps over, to the Eagle that soars sun-ward and beats the tempest with its' wings; it does not therefore follow, that the Jacobin of France may not be as valiant a General and as good a Politician as the Madman of Macedon.[2]

From Professor Ebeling's Mr. Klopstock accompanied my Friend and me to his own house, where I saw a fine Bust of his Brother. There was a solemn and heavy greatness in his countenance which corresponded to my preconceptions of his style and genius.—I saw there, likewise, a very fine Portrait of Lessing,[3] whose Works are at present the chief object of my admiration. His eyes were uncommonly like mine, if any thing, rather larger and more prominent. But the lower part of his face and his nose—O what an exquisite expression of elegance and sensibility!—There appeared no depth, weight, or comprehensiveness, in the Forehead—The whole face seemed to say, that Lessing was a man of quick and voluptuous feelings; of an active but light fancy; acute; yet acute not in the observation of actual life, but in the arrangements and management of the Ideal World, i.e. in taste, and in metaphysics. I assure you, that I wrote these very words in my Memorandum Book with the portrait before my eyes, and when I knew nothing of Lessing but his name, and that he was a German Writer of eminence.[4]

We consumed two hours and more over a bad dinner, at the table d'Hote. "PATIENCE *at a German Ordinary, Smiling at Time.*"[5] The Germans are the worst cooks in Europe. There is placed for every two persons a bottle of common wine—Rhenish and Claret alternately; but in

[1] Sonnet VIII ("Captain or Colonel . . .") lines 10–12.

[2] Like Bonaparte, an earlier would-be world conqueror, Alexander the Great, was also a "madman" to C. For C's interest in Pindar see *CN* II esp 2881–2, 2886, 2911–12, 2986.

[3] C had planned to write a life of Lessing together with a study of German literature. See above, I 34 n 1.

[4] See *CN* I 337; and cf *CL* I 437. Cf also C's letter to Benjamin Flower 1

Apr 1796 (*CL* I 197): "The foremost infidel is Lessing. . . . His book is not yet translated, and is entitled, in German, 'Fragments of an Unknown Author.' It unites the wit of Voltaire with the subtlety of Hume, and the profound erudition of *our* Lardner. I had some thoughts of translating it . . .". See above, I 34 n 1.

[5] Cf Shakespeare *Twelfth Night* II iv 122–3 and *CN* I 339.

the houses of the opulent during the many and long intervals of the dinner, the Servants hand round glasses of richer wines. At the Lord of Culpin's they came in this order, Burgundy—Madeira—Port—Frontiniac—Pacchiaretti[1]—Old Hock—Mountain—Champagne—Hock again [250] — Bishop, and lastly, Punch. A tolerable quantum, methinks! The last dish at the Ordinary, viz. slices of roast pork (for all the larger dishes are brought in cut up and first handed round and then set on the table) with stewed prunes and other sweet fruits, and this followed by cheese and butter, with plates of Apples, reminded me of Shakespeare* and Shakespeare put it in my head to go to the French Comedy.[3] Bless me! why it is worse than our modern English Plays! The first Act informed me, that a Court Martial is to be held on a Count Vatron, who had drawn his sword on the Colonel, his Brother-in-law. The Officers plead in his behalf —in vain! His wife, the Colonel's Sister, pleads with most tempestuous agonies—in vain! She falls into hysterics and faints away, to the dropping of the inner Curtain! In the second act sentence of death is passed on the Count—his wife, as frantic and hysterical as before: more so (good industrious creature!) she could not be. The third and last act, the wife still frantic, very frantic indeed! the Soldiers just about to fire, the handkerchief actually dropped, when Reprieve! Reprieve! is heard from behind the scenes: and in comes Prince somebody, pardons the Count, and the wife is still frantic, only with Joy; That was all! O dear Lady! this is one of the cases, in which laughter is followed by melancholy: for such is the *kind* of Drama, which is now substituted every where for Shakespeare and Racine.[4] You well know, that I offer violence to my own feelings in joining these names; but however meanly I may think of the French serious Drama, even in it's most perfect specimens; and with whatever right I may complain of its perpetual falsification of the language, and of the connections and transitions of thought, which Nature has appropriated to states of passion: still, however, the French Tragedies are consistent works of art, and the Offspring of great intellectual power. Preserving a fitness in the parts, and a harmony in the whole, they form a nature of their own, though a false nature. Still they excite the minds of the Spectators to active thought, to a striving after ideal excellence. The Soul is not stupefied into mere sensations, by a worthless sympathy with our own

* "*Slender.* I bruised my shin with playing with sword and dagger for a dish of stewed prunes, and by my troth I cannot abide the smell of hot meat since." So again, *Evans.* "I will make an end of my dinner: there's Pippins and Cheese yet to come." [2]

[1] In *CL* I 439 it is "5. A Spanish Wine—I have forgot the name". See *CN* I 371, II 3040, entries perhaps to jog his memory.

[2] *Merry Wives of Windsor* I i 294–7 (var), I ii 12 (var).

[3] C saw a performance of *Le Comte de Waltron*, a French translation of a German comedy, *Der Graf von Walltron*, by Heinrich Ferdinand Möller:

see *CN* I 337 and n.

[4] Cf Wordsworth's statement in the Preface to *LB* (1800) I xix. The following discussion of drama does not appear in the original letters, but see *Sh C* II 284–5; C concluded his fifth lecture of 1813–14 with "some observations he penned after being present at the representation of a play in Germany".

ordinary sufferings, or an empty [251] curiosity for the Surprising, un-
dignified by the language or the situations which awe and delight the
imagination. What (I would ask of the Crowd, that press forward to
the pantomimic Tragedies and weeping Comedies of Kotzebue[1] and his
Imitators) what are you seeking? Is it Comedy? But in the comedy of
Shakespeare and Moliere[2] the more accurate my knowledge, and the more
profoundly I think, the greater is the satisfaction that mingles with my
laughter. For though the qualities which these Writers pourtray are ludicrous indeed, either from the kind or the excess, and exquisitely ludicrous,
yet are they the natural growth of the human mind and such as, with more
or less change in the drapery, I can apply to my own heart, or at least to
whole Classes of my fellow-creatures. How often are not the Moralist and
the Metaphysician obliged for the happiest illustrations of general truths
and the subordinate laws of human thought and action to quotations not
only from the tragic characters but equally from the Jaques, Falstaff, and
even from the Fools and Clowns of Shakespeare, or from the Miser,
Hypochondriast and Hypocrite of Moliere. Say not that I am recommending abstractions, for these Class-characteristics which constitute the in-
structiveness of a character, are so modified and particularized in each
Person of the Shakespearian Drama, that life itself does not excite more
distinctly that sense of individuality which belongs to real existence. Paradoxical as it may sound, one of the essential properties of Geometry is not
less essential to dramatic excellence, and (if I may mention his name without pedantry to a Lady) Aristotle has accordingly required of the Poet an
involution of the universal in the individual.[3] The chief differences are,
that in Geometry it is the universal truth which is uppermost in the consciousness, in Poetry the individual form in which it is cloathed. With the
Ancient and not less with the elder Dramatists of England and France,
both Comedy and Tragedy were considered as kinds of Poetry. They
neither sought in Comedy to make us laugh merely, much less to make
us laugh by wry faces, accidents of jargon, slang phrases for the day, or
the cloathing of common-place morals in metaphors drawn from the Shops
or mechanic occupations of their Characters. Nor did they condescend
in Tragedy to wheedle away the applause of the Spectators, by representing
before them fac-similes of their own mean selves in all their existing
meanness, or to work on [252] their sluggish sympathies by a pathos not a
whit more respectable than the maudlin tears of drunkenness. Their tragic
scenes were meant to affect us indeed, but within the bounds of pleasure,
and in union with the activity both of our Understanding and Imagination.
They wished to transport the mind to a sense of it's possible greatness, and
to implant the germs of that greatness during the temporary oblivion of

---

[1] August Friedrich Ferdinand von
Kotzebue (1761–1819). Cf *CL* I 378–9.
Kotzebue wrote almost 100 plays, but
another 200 were adaptations of his
plays by others or retouchings of his
own. Such plays as *The Stranger*,
Lovers' Vows, and *The Birthday* were
given season after season in London.

For C on "the German Beaumont and
Fletcher" see *Sh C* I 60.
  [2] C includes Molière in his brief list
of the "last of the Goths", i.e. those
whose Gothic blood had not been
adulterated with Celtic—praise from C.
See *C 17th C* 490.
  [3] *Poetics* 9.1–4 (esp 4) [1451[b] 7].

the worthless "thing, we are"[1] and of the peculiar state, in which each man *happens* to be; suspending our individual recollections and lulling them to sleep amid the music of nobler thoughts.

Hold! (methinks I hear the Spokesman of the crowd reply, and we will listen to him. I am the Plaintiff, and be He the Defendant.)

DEFENDANT. Hold! Are not our modern sentimental Plays filled with the best Christian morality?

PLAINTIFF. Yes! just as much of it, and just that part of it which you can exercise without a single christian virtue—without a single sacrifice that is really painful to you!—just as much as *flatters* you, sends you away pleased with your own hearts, and quite reconciled to your vices, which can never be thought very ill of, when they keep such good company, and walk hand in hand with so much compassion and generosity; Adulation so loathsome, that you would spit in the man's face who dared offer it to you in a private company, unless you interpreted it as insulting irony, you appropriate with infinite satisfaction, when you share the garbage with the whole stye, and gobble it out of a common trough. No Cæsar must pace your boards—no Antony, no royal Dane, no Orestes, no Andromache?

D. No: or as few of them as possible. What has a plain Citizen of London, or Hamburg, to do with your Kings and Queens, and your old school-boy Pagan Heroes? besides, every body knows the *stories:* and what curiosity can we feel——

P. What, Sir, not for the *manner?* not for the delightful language of the Poet? not for the situations, the action and reaction of the passions?

D. You are hasty, Sir, the only curiosity we feel is in the story, and how can we be anxious concerning the end of a Play, or be surprized by it, when we know how it will turn out.

P. Your pardon, for having interrupted you! we now [253] understand each other. You seek then, in a Tragedy, which wise men of old held for the highest effort of human genius, the same gratification, which you receive from a new Novel, the last German Romance, and other dainties of the same kind, which *can* be enjoyed but once. If you carry these feelings to the Sister Art of Painting, Michael Angelo's Sestine Chapel and the Scripture Gallery of Raphael, can expect no favour from you. *You know all about them beforehand;* and are, doubtless, more familiar with the subjects of those Paintings, than with the tragic Tales of the historic or heroic ages. There is a consistency, therefore, in your preference of Contemporary Writers: for the great Men of former times, those at least who were deemed great by our Ancestors, sought so little to gratify *this* kind of curiosity, that they seemed to have regarded the *Story* in a not much higher light, than the Painter regards his Canvass: as that *on*, not *by*, which they were to display their appropriate excellence. No work, resembling a Tale or Romance, can well shew less variety of invention in the incidents, or less anxiety in weaving them together, than the Don Quixote of CERVANTES.[2]

---

[1] See above, II 7 and n 9.

[2] For C on *Don Quixote* see also *TT* 11 Aug 1832. Lecture 6 of the 1813–14 ɩectures was to be "a philosophic analysis" of *Don Quixote (Sh C* II 257), and Lecture 8 of the 1818 lectures "Of the Life and *all* the Works of CERVANTES" (*Sh C* II 302–3).

Its' Admirers feel the disposition to go back and re-peruse some preceeding chapter, at least ten times for once that they find any eagerness to hurry forwards: or open the Book on those parts which they best recollect, even as we visit those friends oftenest whom we love most, and with whose characters and actions we are the most intimately acquainted. In the divine A R I O S T O (as his Countrymen call this, their darling Poet) I question whether there be a single *tale* of his own invention, or the elements of which were not familiar to the Readers of "old Romance."[1] I will pass by the ancient Greeks, who thought it even necessary to the Fable of a Tragedy, that its' substance should be previously known. That there had been at least fifty Tragedies with the same Title, would be one of the motives which determined Sophocles and Euripedes in the choice of Electra, as a Subject. But Milton——

D. Aye Milton, indeed! but do not Dr. Johnson and other great Men tell us, that nobody now reads Milton but as a task?[2]

P. So much the worse for them, of whom this can be truly said! But why then do you pretend to admire *Shakespeare?* The greater part, if not all, of his Dramas [254] were, as far as the names and the main incidents are concerned, already Stock Plays. All the *Stories*, at least, on which they are built, pre-existed in the Chronicles, Ballads, or Translations of contemporary or preceding English Writers. Why, I repeat, do you pretend to admire *Shakespeare?* is it, perhaps, that you only *pretend* to admire him? However, as once for all you have dismissed the well-known Events and Personages of History or the Epic Muse, what have you taken in their stead? Whom has *your* tragic Muse armed with her bowl and dagger? the sentimental Muse, I should have said, whom you have seated in the throne of Tragedy? What Heroes has *she* reared on her buskins?

D. O our good Friends and next-door-neighbours, honest Tradesmen, valiant Tars, high-spirited half-pay Officers, philanthropic Jews, virtuous Courtezans, tender-hearted Braziers, and sentimental Rat-catchers! (a little bluff or so, but all our very generous, tender-hearted characters are a little rude or misanthropic, and all our Misanthropes very tender-hearted.)

P. But I pray you, Friend, in what actions great or interesting, can such men be engaged?

D. They give away a great deal of money; find rich Dowries for young men and maidens who have all other good qualities; they brow-beat Lords, Baronets, and Justices of the Peace (for they are as bold as Hector), they rescue Stage Coaches at the instant they are falling down precipices; carry away Infants in the sight of opposing Armies; and some of our Performers act a muscular able-bodied man to such perfection, that our Dramatic Poets, who always have the Actors in their eye, seldom fail to make their favourite Male Character as strong as Sampson: and then they take such prodigious leaps!! And what is done on the Stage is more striking even than what is acted. I once remember such a deafening explosion, that I could not hear a word of the Play for half an act after it, and a little real gunpowder being set fire to at the same time, and smelt by all the Spectators, the naturalness of the scene was quite astonishing!

[1] For **C** on Ariosto see *TT* 12 Jul 1827; *Misc C* 148–9, 403.　　[2] See Johnson *Lives of the Poets* (1801) I 173.

P. But how can you connect with such Men and such Actions, that dependance of thousands on the fate of one, which gives so lofty an interest to the Personages of Shakespeare and the Greek Tragedians? How can you connect with them that sublimest of all feelings, the [255] power of Destiny and the controlling might of Heaven, which seems to elevate the Characters which sink beneath its' irresistible blow?

D. O mere fancies! We seek and find on the present Stage our own wants and passions, our own vexations, losses, and embarrassments.

P. It is your own poor pettifogging nature then, which you desire to? have represented before you? not human nature in its' heighth and vigour. But surely you might find the former with all its' joys and sorrows, more conveniently in your own houses and parishes.

D. True, but here comes a difference. Fortune is blind, but the Poet has his eyes open, and is besides as complaisant as Fortune is capricious. He makes every thing turn out exactly as we would wish it. He gratifies us by representing those as hateful or contemptible whom we hate and wish to despise.

P. (*aside*) That is, he gratifies your Envy by libelling your superiors.

D. He makes all those precise Moralists, who affect to be better than their Neighbours, turn out at last abject Hypocrites, Traitors, and hard-hearted Villains; and your Men of Spirit, who take their Girl and their Glass with equal freedom, prove the true Men of Honour, and (that no part of the Audience may remain unsatisfied) reform in the last scene, and leave no doubt on the minds of the Ladies, that they will make most faithful and excellent Husbands; though it does seem a pity, that they should be obliged to get rid of qualities which had made them so interesting! Besides, the Poor become rich all at once; and in the final matrimonial choice the opulent and high-born themselves confess, that VIRTUE IS THE ONLY TRUE NOBILITY,[1] AND THAT A LOVELY WOMAN IS A DOWRY OF HERSELF!![2]

P. Excellent! But you have forgotten those brilliant flashes of Loyalty, those patriotic praises of the King and old England, which, especially if conveyed in a Metaphor from the Ship or the Shop, so often solicit and so unfailingly receive the public plaudit! I give your prudence credit for the omission. For the whole System of your Drama is a moral and intellectual *Jacobinism* of the most dangerous kind, and those common-place rants of Loyalty are no better than hypocrisy in your Play-wrights, and your own sympathy with them a gross self-delusion. For [256] the whole secret of dramatic popularity with you, consists in the confusion and subversion of the natural order of things in their causes and effects, in the excitement of surprize, by representing the qualities of liberality, refined feeling, and a nice sense of honour (those things rather, which pass among you for such) in persons and in classes of life where experience teaches us least to expect them; and by rewarding with all the sympathies that are the dues of virtue, those criminals whom Law, Reason, and Religion, have excommunicated from our esteem!

And now good-Night! Truly! I might have written this last sheet

---

[1] Juvenal *Satires* 8.20.   [2] Cf Shakespeare *King Lear* I i 240.

without having gone to Germany,[1] but I fancied myself talking to you by your own fire-side, and can you think it a small pleasure to me to forget now and then, that I am not there. Besides, you and my other good Friends have made up your minds to me as I am, and from whatever place I write you will expect that part of my "Travels" will consist of the excursions in my own mind.

ADVERTISEMENT[2]

The Subscribers, who have not remitted their payment by other means, are respectfully requested, after the 20th Number, to order the money to be paid to Mr. George Ward, Bookseller, Skinner Street, Snow Hill. The Author takes the liberty of suggesting to his Readers, not resident in London, that it would be of very great advantage to him, especially under the heavy expences and many losses of an infant publication, if they could contrive, in the ordinary course of their Correspondence, to have the money paid by their friends in town, instead of remitting it by the post, which must needs subtract so large a part from the Sum Total of the Subscription.

---

[1] See above, II 216 n 4. The likelihood is that he wrote it years afterwards, for his 1808 lectures or for *The Friend* itself.

[2] See above, Introduction, I lxix–lxx.

TO THE EDITOR OF THE FRIEND

Sir,

I HOPE you will not ascribe to presumption, the liberty I take in address-ing you, on the subject of your Work. I feel deeply interested in the cause you have undertaken to support; and my object in writing this letter is to describe to you, in part from my own feelings, what I conceive to be the state of many minds, which may derive important advantage from your instructions.

I speak, Sir, of those who, though bred up under our unfavourable System of Education, have yet held at times some intercourse with Nature, and with those great minds whose works have been moulded by the Spirit of Nature: who, therefore, when they pass from the Seclusion and Con-straint of early Study, bring with them into the new scene of the world, much of the pure sensibility which is the spring of all that is greatly good in thought and action. To such the season of that entrance into the world is a season of fearful importance; not for the seduction of it's passions, but of it's opinions. Whatever be their intellectual powers, unless extraordin-ary circumstances in their lives have been so favourable to the growth of meditative genius, that their speculative opinions must spring out of their early feelings, their Minds are still at the mercy of fortune: they have no inward impulse steadily to propel them: and must trust to the chances of the world for a guide. And such is our present moral and intellectual State, that these chances are little else than variety of danger. There will be a thousand causes conspiring to complete the work of a false Education, and by enclosing the mind on every side from the influences of natural feeling, to degrade its inborn dignity, [258] and finally bring the heart itself under subjection to a corrupted understanding. I am anxious to describe to you what I have experienced or seen of the dispositions and feelings that will aid every other Cause of danger, and tend to lay the Mind open to the infection of all those falsehoods in opinion and sentiment, which constitute the degeneracy of the age.

Though it would not be difficult to prove, that the mind of the Country is much enervated since the days of her strength, and brought down from its moral dignity, it is not yet so forlorn of all good,—there is nothing in the face of the times so dark and saddening, and repulsive—as to shock the first feelings of a generous Spirit, and drive it at once to seek refuge in the elder ages of our greatness. There yet survives so much of the character bred up through long years of liberty, danger, and glory, that even what this age produces bears traces of those that are past, and it still yields enough of beautiful, and splendid, and bold, to captivate an ardent but untutored imagination. And in this real excellence is the beginning of danger: for it is the first spring of that excessive admiration of the age which at last brings down to its own level a mind born above it. If there existed only the general disposition of all who are formed with a high capacity for good, to be rather credulous of excellence than suspiciously and severely just, the error would not be carried far:—but there are, to a young Mind, in this Country and at this time, numerous powerful causes concurring to inflame this disposition, till the excess of the affection above the worth of its object, is beyond all computation. To trace these causes it will be necessary to follow the history of a pure and noble mind from the first moment of that critical passage from seclusion to the world, which changes all the circumstances of its intellectual existence, shews it for the first time the real scene of living men, and calls up the new feeling of numerous relations by which it is to be connected with them.

To the young adventurer in life, who enters upon his course with such a mind, every thing seems made for delusion. He comes with a spirit whose dearest feelings and highest thoughts have sprung up under the influences of Nature. He transfers to the realities of life the high wild fancies of visionary boyhood: he brings with him into the world the passions of solitary and untamed [259] imagination, and hopes which he has learned from dreams. Those dreams have been of the great and wonderful, and lovely, of all which in these has yet been disclosed to him: his thoughts have dwelt among the wonders of Nature, and among the loftiest spirits of Men —Heroes, and Sages, and Saints;—those whose deeds, and thoughts, and hopes, were high above ordinary Mortality, have been the familiar Companions of his soul. To love and to admire has been the joy of his existence. Love and admiration are the pleasures he will demand of the world. For these he has searched eagerly into the ages that are gone: but with more ardent and peremptory expectation he requires them of that in which his own lot is cast:—for to look on life with hopes of happiness is a necessity of his nature, and to him there is no happiness but such as is surrounded with excellence.

See first how this spirit will affect his judgment of moral character, in those with whom chance may connect him in the common relations of life. It is of those with whom he is to live, that his Soul first demands this food of her desires. From their conversation, their looks, their actions, their lives, she asks for excellence. To ask from all and too ask in vain, would be too dismal to hear: it would disturb him too deeply with doubt and perplexity, and fear. In this hope, and in the revolting of his thoughts from the possibility of disappointment, there is a preparation for self-delusion: there is an unconscious determination that his soul shall be satisfied; an obstinate will to find good everywhere. And thus his first study of mankind is a continued effort to read in them the expression of his own feelings. He catches at every uncertain shew and shadowy resemblance of what he seeks; and unsuspicious in innocence, he is first won with those appearances of good which are in fact only false pretensions. But this error is not carried far: for there is a sort of instinct of rectitude, which like the pressure of a talisman given to baffle the illusions of enchantment, warns a pure mind against hypocrisy.—There is another delusion more difficult to resist and more slowly dissipated. It is when he finds, as he often will, some of the real features of excellence in the purity of their native form. For then his rapid imagination will gather round them all the kindred features that are wanting to perfect beauty; and make for him, where he could not find, the moral creature of his [260] expectation:—peopling, even from this human world, his little circle of affection, with forms as fair as his heart desired for its love.

But when, from the eminence of life which he has reached, he lifts up his eyes, and sends out his spirit to range over the great scene that is opening before him and around him,—the whole prospect of civilized life—so wide and so magnificent:—when he begins to contemplate, in their various stations of power or splendour, the leaders of mankind—those men on whose wisdom are hung the fortunes of nations—those whose genius and valour wield the heroism of a people;—or those, in no inferior "pride of place," whose sway is over the Mind of Society,—Chiefs in the realm of Imagination.—Interpreters of the Secrets of Nature,—Rulers of Human Opinion—what wonder, when he looks on all this living scene, that his heart should burn with strong affection, that he should feel that his own happiness will be for ever interwoven with the interests of mankind?—Here then the sanguine hope with which he looks on life, will again be blended with his passionate desire of excellence; and he will still be impelled to single out some, on whom his imagination and his hopes may repose. To whatever department of human thought or action his mind is turned with interest, either by the sway of public passion or by its own impulse—among Statesmen, and Warriors, and Philosophers, and Poets, he will distinguish some favoured names on which he may satisfy his admiration. And there, just as in the little circle of his own acquaintance, seizing eagerly on every merit they possess, he will supply more from his own credulous hope, completing real with imagined excellence, till living men, with all their imperfections, become to him the representatives of his perfect ideal creation:—Till, multiplying his objects of reverence, as he enlarges his prospect of life, he will have surrounded himself with idols of his own hands, and his imagination will seem to discern a glory in the Countenance of the Age, which is but the reflection of its own effulgence.

He will possess, therefore, in the creative power of generous hope, a preparation for illusory and exaggerated admiration of the age in which he lives:—and this pre-disposition will meet with many favouring circumstances, when he has grown up under a System of Education like ours, which (as perhaps all Education must that is placed [261] in the hands of a distinct and embodied Class, who therefore bring to it the peculiar and hereditary prejudices of their Order) has controuled his imagination to a reverence of former times, with an unjust contempt of his own.—For no sooner does he break loose from this Controul, and begin to feel, as he contemplates the world for himself, how much there is surrounding him on all sides, that gratifies his noblest desires, than there springs up in him an indignant sense of injustice, both to the age and to his own mind: and he is impelled warmly and eagerly to give loose to the feelings that have been held in bondage, to seek out and to delight in finding excellence that will vindicate the insulted world, while it justifies too, his resentment of his own undue subjection, and exalts the value of his new-found liberty.

Add to this, that secluded as he has been from knowledge, and, in the imprisoning circle of one System of ideas, cut off from his share in the thoughts and feelings that are stirring among men, he finds himself, at the first steps of his liberty, in a new intellectual world. Passions and powers which he knew not of, start up in his Soul. The human Mind, which he had seen but under one aspect, now presents to him a thousand unknown and beautiful forms. He sees it, in its varying powers, glancing over Nature with restless curiosity, and with impetuous energy, striving for ever against the barriers which she has placed around it; sees it with divine power creating from dark materials living beauty, and fixing all its high and transported fancies in imperishable forms.—In the world of Knowledge, and Science, and Art, and Genius, he treads as a stranger:—in the confusion of new sensations, bewildered in delights, all seems beautiful; all seems admirable. And therefore he engages eagerly in the pursuit of false or insufficient Philosophy; he is won by the allurements of licentious Art; he follows with wonder the irregular transports of undisciplined Imagination.—Nor, where the objects of his admiration are worthy, is he yet skilful to distinguish between the acquisitions which the age has made for itself, and that large proportion of its wealth which it has only inherited: but in his delight of discovery and growing knowledge, all that is new to his own mind seems to him new-born to the world.—To himself every fresh idea appears instruction; every new exertion, acquisition of [262] power: he seems just called to the consciousness of himself, and to his true place in the intellectual world; and gratitude and reverence towards those to whom he owes this recovery of his dignity, tends much to subject him to the dominion of minds that were not formed by Nature to be the leaders of opinion.

All the tumult and glow of thought and imagination, which seizes on a mind of power in such a scene, tends irresistibly to bind it by stronger attachment of love and admiration to its own age. And there is one among the new emotions which belong to its entrance on the world—one—almost the noblest of all—in which this exaltation of the Age is essentially mingled. The faith in the perpetual progression of human nature towards perfection, gives birth to such lofty dreams, as secure to it the devout assent of Imagination; and it will be yet more grateful to a heart just opening to hope, flushed with the consciousness of new strength, and exulting in the prospect of destined achievements. There is, therefore, almost a Compulsion on generous and enthusiastic Spirits, as they trust that the future shall transcend the present, to believe that the present transcends the past. It is only on an undue love and admiration of their own Age, that they can build their confidence in the amelioration of the human race. Nor is this faith,—which, in some shape, will always be the creed of virtue,—without apparent reason, even in the erroneous form in which the young adopt it. For there is a perpetual acquisition of knowledge and art,—an unceasing progress in many of the modes of exertion of the human mind,—a perpetual unfolding of virtues with the changing manners of society:—and it is not for a young mind to compare what is gained with what has passed away; to discern, that amidst the incessant intellectual activity of the race, the intellectual power of individual minds may be falling off;—and that amidst accumulating knowledge lofty Science may disappear:—and still less, to judge, in the more complicated moral character of a people, what is progression, and what is decline.

Into a mind possessed with this persuasion of the perpetual progress of man, there may even imperceptibly steal both from the belief itself, and from many of the views on which it rests—something like a distrust of the wisdom of great men of former ages, and with the reverence—which [263] no delusion will ever overpower in a pure mind—for their greatness, a fancied discernment of imperfection;—of incomplete excellence, which wanted for its accomplishment the advantages of later improvements: there will be a surprise, that so much should have been possible in times so ill prepared: and even the study of their works may be sometimes rather the curious research of a speculative Enquirer, than the devout contemplation of an Enthusiast; the watchful and obedient heart of a disciple listening to the inspiration of his Master.

Here then is the power of delusion that will gather round the first steps of a youthful spirit, and throw enchantment over the world in which it is to dwell.—Hope realizing its own dreams:—Ignorance dazzled and ravished with sudden sunshine:—Power awakened and rejoicing in its own consciousness:—Enthusiasm kindling among multiplying images of greatness and beauty; and enamoured, above all, of one splendid error:—and, springing from all these, such a rapture of life and hope, and joy, that the soul, in the power of its happiness, transmutes things essentially repugnant to it, into the excellence of its own nature:—these are the spells that cheat the eye of the Mind with illusion. It is under these influences that a young man of ardent spirit gives all his love, and reverence, and zeal, to productions of Art, to theories of Science, to Opinions, to Systems of feeling, and to Characters distinguished in the World, that are far beneath his own original dignity.

Now as this delusion springs not from his worse but his better nature, it seems as if there could be no warning to him from within of his danger: for even the impassioned joy which he draws at times from the works of Nature, and from those of her Mightier Sons, and which would startle him from a dream of unworthy passion, serves only to fix the infatuation:—for those deep emotions, proving to him that his heart is uncorrupted, justify to him *all* its workings, and his mind confiding and delighting in itself, yields to the guidance of its own blind impulses of pleasure. His chance, therefore, of security, is the chance that the greater number of objects occurring to attract his honourable passions, may be worthy of them. But we have seen that the whole power of circumstances is collected to gather round him such objects and influences as will bend his high passions to unworthy enjoyment. He [264] engages in it with a heart and understanding unspoiled: but they cannot long be misapplied with impunity. They are drawn gradually into closer sympathy with the falsehoods they have adopted, till, his very nature seeming to change under the Corruption, there disappears from it the capacity of those higher perceptions and pleasures to which he was born: and he is cast off from the communion of exalted minds, to live and to perish with the age to which he has surrendered himself.

If minds under these circumstances of danger are preserved from decay and overthrow, it can seldom, I think, be to themselves that they owe their deliverance. It must be to a fortunate chance which places them under the influence of some more enlightened mind, from which they may first gain suspicion and afterwards wisdom. There is a Philosophy, which, leading them by the light of their best emotions to the principles which should give life to thought and law to genius, will discover to them in clear and perfect evidence, the falsehood of the Errors that have misled them; and restore them to themselves. And this Philosophy they will be willing to hear and wise to understand: but they must be led into its mysteries by some guiding hand; for they want the impulse or the power to penetrate of themselves the recesses.

If a superior Mind should assume the protection of others just beginning to move among the dangers I have described, it would probably be found, that delusions springing from their own virtuous activity, were not the only difficulties to be encountered. Even after suspicion is awakened, the subjection to falsehood may be prolonged and deepened by many weaknesses both of the intellectual and moral nature; weaknesses that will sometimes shake the authority of acknowledged Truth.—There may be intellectual indolence; an indisposition in the mind to the effort of combining the ideas it actually possesses, and bringing into distinct form the knowledge, which in its elements is already its own:—there may be, where the heart resists the sway of opinion, misgivings and modest self-mistrust, in him who sees, that if he trusts his heart, he must slight the judgment of all around him:—there may be a too habitual yielding to authority, consisting, more than in indolence or diffidence, in a conscious helplessness, an incapacity of the mind to maintain itself in its own place against the weight of general opinion;—and [265] there may be too indiscriminate, too undisciplined a sympathy with others, which by the mere infection of feeling will subdue the reason.—There must be a weakness in dejection to him who thinks, with sadness, if his faith be pure, how gross is the error of the multitude, and that multitude how vast:—A reluctance to embrace a creed that excludes so many whom he loves, so many whom his youth has revered:—a difficulty to his understanding to believe that those whom he knows to be, in much that is good and honourable, his superiors, can be beneath him in this which is the most important of all:—a sympathy pleading importunately at his heart to descend to the fellowship of his brothers, and to take their wisdom and faith for his own.—How often, when under the impulses of those solemn hours, in which he has felt with clearer insight and deeper faith his sacred truths, he labours to win to his own belief those whom he loves, will he be checked by their indifference or their laughter! and will he not bear back to his meditations a painful and disheartening sorrow,—a gloomy discontent in that faith which takes in but a portion of those whom he wishes to include in all his blessings? Will he not be enfeebled by a distraction of inconsistent desires, when he feels so strongly that the faith which fills his heart, the circles within which he would embrace all he loves—would repose all his wishes and hopes, and enjoyments, is yet incommensurate with his affections?

Even when the Mind, strong in reason and just feeling united, and relying on its strength, has attached itself to Truth, how much is there in the course and accidents of life that is for ever silently at work for its degradation. There are pleasures deemed harmless, that lay asleep the recollections of innocence:—there are pursuits held honourable, or imposed by duty, that oppress the moral spirit:—above all there is that perpetual connexion with ordinary minds in the common intercourse of society;—that restless activity of frivolous conversation, where men of all characters and all pursuits mixing together, nothing may be talked of that is not of common interest to all—nothing, therefore, but those obvious thoughts and feelings that float over the surface of things:—and all which is drawn from the depth of Nature, all which impassioned feeling has made original in thought, would be misplaced and obtrusive. The talent that is allowed to shew itself [266] is that which can repay admiration by furnishing entertainment:—and the display to which it is invited is that which flatters the vulgar pride of society, by abasing what is too high in excellence for its sympathy. A dangerous seduction to talents—which would make language—that was given to exalt the soul by the fervid expression of its pure emotions—the instrument of its degradation. And even when there is, as the instance I have supposed, too much uprightness to choose so dishonourable a triumph, there is a necessity of manners, by which every one must be controled who mixes much in society, not to offend those with whom he converses by his superiority; and whatever be the native spirit of a mind, it is evident that this perpetual adaptation of itself to others—this watchfulness against its own rising feelings, this studied sympathy with mediocrity—must pollute and impoverish the sources of its strength.

From much of its own weakness, and from all the errors of its misleading activities, may generous youth be rescued by the interposition of an enlightened mind: and in some degree it may be guarded by instruction against the injuries to which it is exposed in the world. *His* lot is happy who owes this protection to friendship: who has found in a friend the watchful guardian of his mind. He will not be deluded, having that light to guide: he will not slumber, with that voice to inspire; he will not be desponding or dejected, with that bosom to lean on.—But how many must there be whom Heaven has left unprovided, except in their own strength; who must maintain themselves, unassisted and solitary, against their own infirmities and the opposition of the world! For such there may be yet a protector. If a Teacher should stand up in their generation conspicuous above the multitude in superior power, and yet more in the assertion and proclamation of disregarded Truth—to Him—to his cheering or summoning voice all hearts would turn, whose deep sensibility has been oppressed by the indifference, or misled by the seduction of the times. Of one such Teacher who has been given to our own age, you have described the power when you said, that in his annunciation of truths he seemed to speak in thunders. I believe that mighty voice has not been poured out in vain: that there are hearts that have received into their inmost depths all its varying tones: and that even now, there are many to [267] whom the name of

Wordsworth calls up the recollection of their weakness, and the conscious-ness of their strength.

To give to the reason and eloquence of one Man, this complete control over the minds of others, it is necessary, I think, that he should be born in their own times. For thus whatever false opinion of pre-eminence is attached to the Age, becomes at once a title of reverence to him: and when with distinguished powers he sets himself apart from the Age, and above it as the Teacher of high but ill-understood truths, he will appear at once to a generous imagination, in the dignity of one whose superior mind outsteps the rapid progress of society, and will derive from illusion itself the power to disperse illusions. It is probable too, that he who labours under the errors I have described, might feel the power of Truth in a writer of another age, yet fail in applying the full force of his principles to his own times: but when he receives them from a living Teacher, there is no room for doubt or misapplication. It is the errors of his own generation that are denounced; and whatever authority he may acknowledge in the instructions of his Master, strikes, with inevitable force, at his veneration for the opinions and characters of his own times.—And finally, there will be gathered round a living Teacher, who speaks to the deeper soul, many feelings of human love, that will place the infirmities of the heart peculiarly under his controul; at the same time that they blend with and animate the attachment to his cause. So that there will flow from him something of the peculiar influence of a friend: while his doctrines will be embraced and asserted, and vindicated, with the ardent zeal of a disciple, such as can scarcely be carried back to distant times, or connected with voices that speak only from the grave.

I have done what I proposed. I have related to you as much as I have had opportunities of knowing of the difficulties from within and from without, which may oppose the natural developement of true feeling and right opinion, in a mind formed with some capacity for good: and the resources which such a mind may derive from an enlightened contemporary writer.—If what I have said be just, it is certain that this influence will be felt more particularly in a work, adapted by its mode of publication, to address the feelings of the time, and to bring to its readers repeated ad-monition and repeated consolation.

[268] I have perhaps presumed too far in trespassing on your attention, and in giving way to my own thoughts: but I was unwilling to leave any thing unsaid which might induce you to consider with favour the request I was anxious to make, in the name of all whose state of mind I have described, that you would at times regard us more particularly in your instructions. I cannot judge to what degree it may be in your power to give the Truth you teach a controul over understandings that have matured their strength in error; but in our Class I am sure you will have docile learners.

M<small>ATHETES</small>

The Friend might rest satisfied that his exertions thus far have not been wholly unprofitable, if no other proof had been given of their influence, than that of having called forth the foregoing Letter, with which he has been so much interested, that he could not deny himself the pleasure of communicating it to his Readers.—In answer to his Correspondent, it need scarcely here be repeated, that one of the main purposes of his work is to weigh, honestly and thoughtfully, the moral worth and intellectual power of the Age in which we live; to ascertain our gain and our loss; to determine what we are in ourselves positively, and what we are compared with our Ancestors; and thus, and by every other means within his power, to discover what may be hoped for future times, what and how lamentable are the evils to be feared, and how far there is cause for fear. If this attempt should not be made wholly in vain, my ingenuous Correspondent, and all who are in a state of mind resembling that of which he gives so lively a picture, will be enabled more readily and surely to distinguish false from legitimate objects of admiration: and thus may the personal errors which he would guard against, be more effectually prevented or removed, by the developement of general truth for a general purpose, than by instructions specifically adapted to himself or to the Class of which he is the able Representative. There is a life and spirit in knowledge which we extract from truths scattered for the benefit of all, and which the mind, by its own activity, has appropriated to itself—a life and a spirit, which is seldom found in knowledge communicated by formal and direct precepts, even [269] when they are exalted and endeared by reverence and love for the Teacher.

Nevertheless, though I trust that the assistance which my Correspondent has done me the honour to request, will in course of time flow naturally from my labours, in a manner that will best serve him, I cannot resist the inclination to connect, at present, with his Letter a few remarks of direct application to the subject of it—*remarks*, I say, for to such I shall confine myself, independent of the main point out of which his complaint and request both proceed, I mean the assumed inferiority of the present Age in moral dignity and intellectual power, to those which have preceded it. For if the fact were true, that we had even surpassed our Ancestors in the best of what is good, the main part of the dangers and impediments which my Correspondent has feelingly pourtrayed, could not cease to exist for minds like his, nor indeed would they be much diminished; as they arise out of the Constitution of things, from the nature of Youth, from the laws that govern the growth of the Faculties, and from the necessary condition of the great body of Mankind. Let us throw ourselves back to the age of Elizabeth, and call up to mind the Heroes, the Warriors, the Statesmen, the Poets, the Divines, and the Moral Philosophers, with which the reign of the Virgin Queen was illustrated. Or if we be more strongly attracted by the moral purity and greatness, and that sanctity of civil and religious duty, with which the Tyranny of Charles the first was struggled against, let us cast our eyes, in the hurry of admiration, round that circle of glorious Patriots—but do not let us be persuaded, that each of these, in his course of discipline, was uniformly helped forward by those with whom he associated, or by those whose care it was to direct him. Then as now existed objects, to which the wisest attached undue importance; then as now judgment was misled by factions and parties—time wasted in controversies fruitless, except as far as they quickened the faculties; then as now Minds were venerated or idolized, which owed their influence to the weakness of their Contemporaries rather than to their own power. Then, though great

Actions were wrought, and great works in literature and science produced, yet the general taste was capricious, fantastical, or grovelling: and in this point as in all others, was Youth subject to delusion, frequent in proportion [270] to the liveliness of the sensibility, and strong as the strength of the imagination. Every Age hath abounded in instances of Parents, Kindred, and Friends, who, by indirect influence of example, or by positive injunction and exhortation have diverted or discouraged the Youth, who, in the simplicity and purity of Nature, had determined to follow his intellectual genius through good and through evil, and had devoted himself to knowledge, to the practice of Virtue and the preservation of integrity, in slight of temporal rewards. Above all, have not the common duties and cares of common life, at all times exposed Men to injury, from causes whose action is the more fatal from being silent and unremitting, and which, wherever it was not jealously watched and steadily opposed, must have pressed upon and consumed the diviner spirit.

There are two errors, into which we easily slip when thinking of past times. One lies in forgetting, in the excellence of what remains, the large overbalance of worthlessness that has been swept away. Ranging over the wide tracts of Antiquity, the situation of the Mind may be likened to that of a Traveller* in some unpeopled part of America, who is attracted to the burial place of one of the primitive Inhabitants. It is conspicuous upon an eminence, "a mount upon a mount!" He digs into it, and finds that it contains the bones of a Man of mighty stature: and he is tempted to give way to a belief, that as there were Giants in those days, so that all Men were Giants. But a second and wiser thought may suggest to him, that this Tomb would never have forced itself upon his notice, if it had not contained a Body that was distinguished from others, that of a Man who had been selected as a Chieftain or Ruler for the very reason that he surpassed the rest of his Tribe in stature, and who now lies thus conspicuously inhumed upon the mountain-top, while the bones of his Followers are laid unobstrusively together in their burrows upon the Plain below. The second habitual error is, that in this comparison of Ages we divide time merely into past and present, and place these in the balance to be weighed against each other, not considering that the present is in our estimation not more than a period of thirty years, or half a century at [271] most, and that the past is a mighty accumulation of many such periods, perhaps the whole of recorded time, or at least the whole of that portion of it in which our own Country has been distinguished. We may illustrate this by the familiar use of the words Ancient and Modern, when applied to Poetry—what can be more inconsiderate or unjust than to compare a few existing Writers with the whole succession of their Progenitors? The delusion, from the moment that our thoughts are directed to it, seems too gross to deserve mention; yet Men will talk for hours upon Poetry, balancing against each other the words Ancient and Modern, and be unconscious that they have fallen into it.

These observations are not made as implying a dissent from the belief of my Correspondent, that the moral spirit and intellectual powers of this Country are declining; but to guard against *unqualified* admiration, even

* Vide Ashe's Travels in America.

in cases where admiration has been rightly fixed, and to prevent that depression, which must necessarily follow, where the notion of the peculiar unfavourableness of the present times to dignity of mind, has been carried too far. For in proportion as we imagine obstacles to exist out of ourselves to retard our progress, will, in fact, our progress be retarded.——Deeming then, that in all ages an ardent mind will be baffled and led astray in the manner under contemplation, though in various degrees, I shall at present content myself with a few practical and desultory comments upon some of those general causes, to which my Correspondent justly attributes the errors in opinion, and the lowering or deadening of sentiment, to which ingenuous and aspiring Youth is exposed. And first, for the heart-cheering belief in the perpetual progress of the Species towards a point of unattainable perfection. If the present Age do indeed transcend the past in what is most beneficial and honorable, he that perceives this, being in no error, has no cause for complaint; but if it be not so, a Youth of genius might, it should seem, be preserved from any wrong influence of this faith, by an insight into a simple truth, namely, that it is not necessary, in order to satisfy the desires of our Nature, or to reconcile us to the economy of Providence, that there should be at all times a continuous advance in what is of highest worth. In fact it is not, as a Writer of the present day has admirably observed, in the power of fiction, to pourtray in words, or of the imagination [272] to conceive in spirit, Actions or Characters of more exalted virtue, than those which thousands of years ago have existed upon earth, as we know from the records of authentic history. Such is the inherent dignity of human nature, that there belong to it sublimities of virtue which all men may attain, and which no man can transcend: And, though this be not true in an equal degree, of intellectual power, yet in the persons of Plato, Demosthenes, and Homer,—and in those of Shakespeare, Milton, and Lord Bacon,—were enshrined as much of the divinity of intellect as the inhabitants of this planet can hope will ever take up its abode among them. But the question is not of the power or worth of individual Minds, but of the general moral or intellectual merits of an Age—or a People, or of the human Race. Be it so—let us allow and believe that there is a progress in the Species towards unattainable perfection, or whether this be so or not, that it is a necessity of a good and greatly-gifted Nature to believe it—surely it does not follow, that this progress should be constant in those virtues, and intellectual qualities, and in those departments of knowledge, which in themselves absolutely considered are of most value—things independent and in their degree indispensible. The progress of the Species neither is nor can be like that of a Roman road in a right line. It may be more justly compared to that of a River, which both in its smaller reaches and larger turnings, is frequently forced back towards its fountains, by objects which cannot otherwise be eluded or overcome; yet with an accompanying impulse that will ensure its advancement hereafter, it is either gaining strength every hour, or conquering in secret some difficulty, by a labour that contributes as effectually to further it in its course, as when it moves forward uninterrupted in a line, direct as that of the Roman road with which we began the comparison.

(To be continued.)

THE FRIEND

No. 18. THURSDAY, DECEMBER 21, 1809

I PRESENT my readers, in this Number, with four original Sonnets from Mr. Wordsworth, on the same subject as his three former, in Numbers 11 and 13;[1] and as its' conclusion. To make the *set* complete (if I may use so trivial a phrase) I have prefixed his Sonnet on Switzerland from his "Poems," having always thought it one of the noblest Sonnets in our Language, and the happiest comment on the line of Milton—"The *mountain* Nymph, sweet Liberty,"[2] which would be no inapt motto for the whole collection.

SONNETS

Thought of a Briton on the Subjugation of SWITZERLAND[3]

Two Voices are there; one is of the Sea,
One of the Mountains; each a mighty Voice:
In both from age to age thou didst rejoice,
They were thy chosen Music, Liberty!
There came a Tyrant, and with holy glee
Thou fought'st against Him; but hast vainly striven!
Thou from thine Alpine Holds at length art driven,
Where not a torrent murmurs heard by thee.
Of one deep bliss thine ear hath been bereft:
Then cleave, O cleave to that which still is left!
For, high-soul'd Maid! what sorrow would it be,
That mountain Floods should thunder as before,
And Ocean bellow from his rocky shore,
And neither awful Voice be heard by thee!

Feelings of the TYROLESE[4]

The Land we from our Fathers had in trust
And to our Children will transmit, or die:
This is our maxim, this our piety;
And God and Nature say, that it is just.

---

[1] See above, II 153-4, 183.
[2] *L'Allegro* line 36.
[3] *Poems Dedicated to National Independence and Liberty* pt I No 12: *WPW*

III 115.
[4] Ibid pt II Nos 11, 13, 14: *WPW* III 130 (var), 131 (var).

That which we *would* perform in arms—we *must!*
We read the dictate in the Infant's eye,
In the Wife's smile, and in the placid sky,
And at our feet, amid the silent dust
Of them that were before us.—Sing aloud
Old Songs, the precious music of the heart!
Give, Herds and Flocks! your voices to the wind!
While we go forth, a self-devoted crowd,
With weapons in the fearless hand, to assert
Our virtue, and to vindicate mankind!

[274] And is it among rude untutor'd vales,
There, and there only, that the heart is true?
And rising to repel or to subdue,
Is it by rocks and woods that man prevails?
Ah no!—though Nature's dread protection fails,
There is a bulwark in the *soul*.—This knew
Iberian Burghers, when the sword they drew
In Zaragoza, naked to the gales
Of fiercely-breathing War. The truth was felt
By Palafox, and many a brave Compeer,
Like him, of noble birth and noble mind:
By Ladies, meek-eyed Women without fear,
And Wanderers[1] of the Street, to whom is dealt
The bread which without industry they find.

O'er the wide earth, on mountain and on plain
Dwells in the affections and the soul of man
A Godhead, like the universal PAN*
But more exalted, with a brighter train.
And shall his bounty be dispensed in vain,
Shower'd equally on city and on Field,
And neither hope nor steadfast promise yield
In these usurping times of fear and pain?
Such doom awaits us!—Nay, forbid it Heaven!
We know the arduous strife, the eternal laws
To which the triumph of all good is given,
High sacrifice and labour without pause
Even to the death:—else wherefore should the eye
Of man converse with immortality?

*————————"universal Pan
Knit with the graces and the hours in dance
Led on the eternal spring."—————— MILTON[2]

[1] In a list of "Errata" at the end of No 19 C notes that "Wanderers" should be read as "Beggars", a reading not found when the poem was first col-lected, *Poems* (1815); nor does de Selin-court give it as a variant in *WPW*.
[2] *Paradise Lost* IV 266-8.

On the report of the submission of the TYROLESE[1]
It was a *moral* end for which they fought;
Else how, when mighty Thrones were put to shame,
Could They, poor Shepherds, have preserv'd an aim,
A Resolution or enlivening thought?
Nor hath that moral good been vainly sought;
For in their magnanimity and fame
Powers have they left—an impulse—and a claim
Which neither can be overturn'd nor bought.
Sleep, Warriors, sleep! among your hills repose!
We know that Ye beneath the stern controul
Of awful prudence keep the unvanquished soul.
And when impatient of her guilt and woes
Europe breaks forth, then Shepherds, shall ye rise
For perfect triumph o'er your enemies.   W.W.

[275] I am indebted to an accomplished Correspondent for the following elegant Copy of Verses,[2] imitated from a French Poem addressed to Madame Buonaparte, when she was Madam Beauharnois. I do not remember to have read a more pleasing combination of beautiful Images and intelligible Allegory with a play of words. Those Hyper-critics, who will discover that two different meanings are confounded under one word, namely, Age and the sensation of Time, &c.[3] will have caught a Fire-fly, as it was flitting to and fro in a Grove at twilight, to transfix it with a pin, and pore over it in broad day.

Destined with restless foot to roam,
    Old TIME, a venerable sage,
Reaches a river's brink, and—"come,"
    He cries—"have pity on my age.
What! on these banks forgotten I,
    Who mark each moment with my glass?
Hear, Damsels, hear my suppliant cry,
    And courteously help TIME to pass."

[1] *Poems Dedicated to National Independence and Liberty* pt II No 15 (entitled *On the Final Submission of the Tyrolese*): *WPW* III 131–2.

[2] The Rev Francis Wrangham (1769–1842), whom C had known at Cambridge. A *Friend* subscriber, he wrote to C 27 Nov 1809: ". . . The verses on the other page (a translation *done* by myself about a fortnight ago from some French lines ascribed to Mme. Buonaparte while Mme. Beauharnois) I send you as a proof that *I* have not ceased to jingle rhymes. To the severer strains of poetry, you know, I was always a stranger. These light things occupy my mind, now & then, during a solitary

ride. The allegory, I think, is elegant, the managing of it (in the *original*, at least) pretty—and the *verité renfermée*, according to some Commentators, but too generally true." DCL Folder B. The poem was reprinted (with the French original by the Vicomte Alexandre Joseph Pierre de Ségur, *Le Voyage de l'amour et du tems*) under the title *The Ferry* in Wrangham *Sermons, Practical and Occasional; Dissertations, Translations* (3 vols 1816) III 306–9.

[3] In the list of "Errata" at the end of No 19 "two different . . . Time, &c." is corrected to "the words 'Time' and 'pass' are each used in three different senses".

Disporting on the farther shore,
    Full many a gentle Nymph look'd on;
And fain to speed his passage o'er,
    Bade Love, their boatman, fetch the crone:
But one, of all the group most staid,
    Still warn'd her venturous mates—"Alas!
How oft has shipwreck whelm'd the Maid,
    Whose pity would help TIME to pass!"

Lightly his boat across the stream
    LOVE guides, his hoary freight receives,
And fluttering 'mid the sunny gleam,
    His canvas to the breezes gives:
And plying light his little oars—
    In treble now and now in bass,
"See, girls," th' enraptur'd Urchin roars,
"How gaily LOVE makes TIME to pass."

But soon—'tis LOVE'S proverbial crime—
    Exhausted, he his oars let fall;
And soon those oars are snatch'd by TIME,
    And—heard ye not the rallier's call?—
"What! tired so soon of thy sweet toil,
    Poor Child! thou sleepest!—I, alas!
In graver strain repeat the while
    My Song—'Tis TIME makes LOVE to pass!"

                                            F.W.

276]   *SATYRANE'S LETTERS*

LETTER III[1]

                                            RATZEBURG
No little Fish thrown back again into the Water, no Fly unimprisoned from a child's hand, could more buoyantly enjoy it's element, than I this clean and peaceful house, with this lovely view of the town, groves, and lake of Ratzeburg, from the window at which I am writing. My spirits certainly, and my health I fancied, were beginning to sink under the noise, dirt, and unwholesome air, of our Hamburg Hotel. I left it on Sunday, Sept. 23d. with a Letter of introduction from the Poet Klopstock, to the Amptman of Ratzeburg.[2] The Amptman received me with kindness, and introduced me to the worthy Pastor, who agreed to board and lodge me for any length of time not less than a month. The Vehicle, in which I took my place, was considerably larger than an English Stage Coach, to which it bore much the same proportion and rude resemblance, that an Elephant's ear does to the human. Its top was composed of naked boards of different colours, and seeming to have been parts of different wainscots.

[1] Cf *CL* I 445–9, 460–1, 453–8, 441–5 (Satyrane's Letter III is a pastiche of four letters) and *BL* (1817) II 232–53 for   later revisions.
[2] "Amtman Braunes": *CL* I 448.

Instead of windows there were leathern curtains with a little eye of glass in each: they perfectly answered the purpose of keeping out the prospect and letting in the cold. I could observe little, therefore, but the inns and farm houses at which we stopped. They were all alike, except in size: one great room, like a barn, with a hay-loft over it, the straw and hay dangling in tufts through the boards which formed the ceiling of the room, and the floor of the loft. From this room, which is paved like a street, sometimes one, sometimes two smaller ones, are enclosed at one end. These are commonly floored. In the large room the Cattle, Pigs, Poultry, Men, Women, and Children, live in amicable community: yet there was an appearance of cleanliness and rustic comfort. One of these houses I measured. It was an hundred feet in length. The apartments were taken off from one corner. Between these and the stalls there was a small inter-space, and here the breadth was forty eight feet, but thirty two where the stalls were; of course, the stalls were on each side eight feet in depth. The faces of the Cows, &c. [277] were turned towards the room; indeed they were in it, so that they had at least the comfort of seeing each others faces. Stall-feeding is universal in this part of Germany, a practice concerning which the Agriculturalist and the Poet are likely to entertain opposite opinions—or at least, to have very different feelings. The wood work of these buildings on the outside is left unplaistered, as in old houses among us, and being painted red and green, it cuts and tesselates the buildings very gaily. From within three Miles of Hamburg almost to Molln, which is thirty miles from it, the Country, as far as I could see it, was a dead flat, only varied by woods. At Molln it became more beautiful. I observed a small Lake nearly surrounded with groves,[1] and a Palace in view belonging to the King of Great Britain and inhabited by the Inspector of the Forests. We were nearly the same time in travelling the thirty five miles from Hamburg to Ratzeburg, as we had been in going from London to Yarmouth, one hundred and twenty six miles.

The Lake of Ratzeburg runs from south to north, about nine miles in length, and varying in breadth from three miles to half a mile. About a mile from the southernmost point it is divided into two, of course very unequal, parts by an Island, which being connected by a Bridge and a narrow slip of land with the one shore, and by another Bridge of immense length with the other shore, forms a complete Isthmus. On this Island the town of Ratzeburg is built. The Pastor's house or Vicarage, together with the Amptman's, Amptschrieber's, and the Church, stands near the summit of a hill, which slopes down to the slips[2] of land and the little Bridge, from which, through a superb military gate, you step into the Island-Town of Ratzeburg; This again is itself a little hill, by ascending and descending which, you arrive at the long Bridge, and so to the other shore. The water to the south of the town is called the little Lake, which however almost engrosses the beauties of the whole: The shores being just often enough green and bare to give the proper effect to the magnificent groves which occupy the greater part of their circumference. From the turnings, wind-ings, and indentations of the shore, the views vary almost every ten steps,

[1] Möllner See.   No 19 "slips" is corrected to "Slip".
[2] In the list of "Errata" at the end of

and the whole has a sort of majestic beauty, a feminine grandeur. At the north of the great Lake, and peeping over it, I see the seven Church towers [278] of Lubec,[1] at the distance of twelve or thirteen miles, yet as distinctly as if they were not three. The only defect in the view is, that Ratzeburg is built entirely of red bricks, and all the houses roofed with red tiles. To the eye, therefore, it presents a clump of brick-dust red. Yet this evening, Octr 10th. twenty minutes past five, I saw the town perfectly beautiful, and the whole softened down into *complete keeping*, if I may borrow a term from the Painters. The sky over Ratzeburg and all the east, was a pure evening blue, while over the west it was covered with light sandy clouds. Hence a deep red light spread over the whole prospect, in undisturbed harmony with the red town, the brown-red woods, and the yellow-red reeds on the skirts of the Lake. Two or three boats, with single persons paddling them, floated up and down in the rich light, which not only was itself in harmony with all, but brought all into harmony.

I should have told you that I went back to Hamburg on Thursday (Sept. 27th.) to take leave of my Friend, who travels southward,[2] and returned hither on the Monday following. From Empfelde, a village half way from Ratzeburg, I walked to Hamburg through deep sandy roads and a dreary flat: the soil every where white, hungry, and excessively pulverized; but the approach to the City is pleasing. Light cool Country Houses, which you can look through and see the Gardens behind them, with arbours and trellis work, and thick vegetable walls, and trees in cloisters and piazzas, each house with neat rails before it, and green seats within the rails. Every object, whether the growth of Nature or the work of Man, was neat and artificial. It pleased me far better, than if the houses and gardens, and pleasure fields, had been in a nobler taste: for this nobler taste would have been mere apery. The busy, anxious, money-loving, Merchant of Hamburg could only have *adopted*, he could not have *enjoyed*, the simplicity of Nature. The mind begins to love nature by imitating human conveniences in Nature; but this is a step in intellect, though a low one—and were it not so, yet all around me spoke of innocent enjoyment and sensitive comforts, and I entered with unscrupulous sympathy into the enjoyments and comforts even of the busy, anxious, money-loving Merchants of Hamburg. In this charitable and *catholic* mood I reached the vast ramparts of the City. These are huge green cushions, one [279] rising above the other, with trees growing in the inter-spaces, pledges and symbols of a long peace. Of my return I have nothing worth communicating, except that I took extra post, which answers to posting in England. These North-German Post Chaises are uncovered wicker carts. An English dust-cart is a piece of finery, a chef d'oeuvre of mechanism, compared with them: and the horses! a Savage might use their ribs instead of his fingers for a numeration table. Wherever we stopped, the Postillion fed his cattle with the brown rye bread of which he eat himself, all breakfasting together, only the Horses had no gin to their water, and the Postillion no water to his gin.

---

[1] The towers of the Domkirche, Marienkirche, and Holsten-Tor in Lübeck.

[2] Wordsworth went (among other places) to Goslar, at the foot of the Harz Mts, where he stayed several months.

Now and henceforward for subjects of more interest to you, and to the objects in search of which I left you; namely, the Literati and Literature of Germany. Believe me, I walked with an impression of awe on my spirits, as B——[1] and myself accompanied Mr. Klopstock to the House of his Brother, the Poet, which stands about a quarter of a mile from the City Gate. It is one of a row of little common-place Summer-houses, (for so they looked) with four or five rows of young meagre elm trees before the windows, beyond which is a Green, and then a dead flat intersected with several roads. Whatever beauty (thought I) may be before the Poet's eyes at present, it must certainly be purely of his own creation. We waited a few minutes in a neat little parlour, ornamented with the figures of two of the Muses and with Prints, the subjects of which were from Klopstock's Odes.[2] The Poet entered. I was much disappointed in his countenance, and recognized in it no likeness to the Bust. There was no comprehension in the forehead, no weight over the eye-brows, no expression of peculiarity, moral or intellectual on the eyes, no massiveness in the general countenance. He is if any thing rather below the middle size. He wore very large half-boots which his legs filled, so fearfully were they swoln. However, though neither B—— nor myself could discover any indications of sublimity or enthusiasm in his phisiognomy, we were both equally impressed with his liveliness, and his kind and ready courtesy. He talked in French with my Friend, and with difficulty spoke a few sentences to me in English. His enunciation was not in the least affected by the entire want of his upper teeth. The conversation began on his part by the expression of his rapture at the [280] surrender of the detachment of French Troops under General Humbert.[3] Their proceedings in Ireland with regard to the Committee, which they had appointed, with the rest of their organizing System, seemed to have given the Poet great Entertainment. He then declared his sanguine belief in Nelson's victory,[4] and anticipated its' confirmation with a keen and triumphant pleasure. His words, tones, looks, implied the most vehement Anti-Gallicanism. The subject changed to Literature, and I enquired in Latin concerning the History of German Poetry and the elder German Poets.[5] To my great astonishment he confessed, that he knew very little on the subject. He had indeed occasionally read one or two of their elder Writers, but not so as to enable him to speak of their merits. Professor Ebeling, he said, would probably give me every information of this kind: the subject had not particularly excited his curiosity. He then talked of Milton and Glover,[6] and thought Glover's blank verse superior to Milton's.

---

[1] That is, Wordsworth.

[2] Friedrich Gottlieb Klopstock (1724–1803). The *Oden* (1771) bk II includes one entitled "Die beyden Musen" (pp 150–3).

[3] In the middle of a rebellion in Ireland Gen J.-R.-M. Humbert (1755–1823) led a French expeditionary force that landed in Aug 1798 and, after initial success, surrendered 9 Sept to Cornwallis.

[4] At Aboukir Bay 1 Aug 1798.

[5] "He answered in French, & Wordsworth interpreted it to me": *CL* I 442.

[6] Richard Glover (1712 85), author of the blank-verse epic *Leonidas* (1737; enlarged 1770), which was translated into French prose (1738) and German (1766).

B—— and myself expressed our surprize: and my Friend gave his definition and notion of harmonious verse, that it consisted (the English iambic blank verse above all) in the apt arrangement of pauses and cadences, and the sweep of whole paragraphs,

> —————"with many a winding bout
> Of linked sweetness long drawn out," [1]

and not in the even flow, much less in the prominence or antithetic vigour, of single lines which were indeed injurious to the total effect, except where they were introduced for some specific purpose. Klopstock assented, and said that he meant to confine Glover's superiority to single lines. He told us that he had read Milton, in a prose translation, when he was fourteen.*[2] I understood him thus myself, and B—— interpreted Klopstock's French as I had already construed it. He appeared to know very little of Milton— or indeed of our Poets in general. He spoke with great indignation of the English prose translation of his Messiah.[3] All the Translations had been bad, very bad—but the English was *no* translation—there were pages on pages, not in the Original:—and half the Original was not to be found in the Translation. B—— [281] told him that I intended to translate a few of his Odes as specimens of German Lyrics[4]—he then said to me in English, "I wish you would render into English some select Passages of the Messiah, and *revenge* me of your Countryman!" It was the liveliest thing which he produced in the whole conversation. He told us, that his first Ode was fifty years older than his last. I looked at him with much emotion —I considered him as the venerable Father of German Poetry; as a good Man; as a Christian; seventy four years old; with legs enormously swoln; yet active, lively, chearful, and kind, and communicative. My eyes felt as if a tear were swelling into them. In the Portrait of Lessing there was a Toupee Periwig which enormously injured the effect of his Phisiognomy— Klopstock wore the same, powdered and frizzled. By the bye, old Men ought never to wear powder—the contrast between a large snow-white wig and the colour of an old man's skin is disgusting, and wrinkles in such a neighbourhood appear only channels for dirt. It is an honour to Poets

---

* This was accidentally confirmed to me by an old German Gentleman at Helmstadt, who had been Klopstock's school and bedfellow. Among other boyish anecdotes he related, that the young Poet set a particular value on a translation of the Paradise Lost, and always slept with it under his pillow.

---

[1] Milton *L'Allegro* lines 139–40.
　[2] A French prose translation of Milton's poetical works appeared in 1753, a French prose translation of *Paradise Lost, Le Paradis perdu,* in 1729 (many editions). A German translation of *Paradise Lost* appeared as early as 1682, and there were several later ones.
　[3] *Der Messias* (1749) appeared in an English translation, begun by Mary and completed by Joseph Collyer, *The Messiah. Attempted from the German of Mr. Klopstock* (1763), which went

through four editions by 1769. C wrote a "malicious Motto" on Klopstock's *Messias*:
Tale tuum carmen nobis, divine Poeta,
Quale *Sopor*!
Letter to William Sotheby 13 Jul 1802: *CL* ii 811. The motto—from Virgil *Eclogues* 5.45–6—may be tr: "Of such a nature is thy song to us, divine Poet, as *Sleep*!"
　[4] If C translated any of Klopstock's odes, no translations are extant.

and Great Men,[1] that you think of them as parts of Nature; and any thing of trick and fashion wounds you in them, as much as when you see venerable Yews clipped into miserable peacocks.—The Author of the Messiah should have worn his own grey hair.—His Powder and Periwig were to the Eye, what MR. Virgil would be to the ear.

Klopstock dwelt much on the superior power which the German Language possessed, of concentrating meaning. He said, he had often translated parts of Homer and Virgil, line by line, and a German line proved always sufficient for a Greek or Latin one. In English you cannot do this. I answered, that in English we could commonly render one Greek heroic line in a line and a half of our common heroic metre, and I conjectured that this line and a half would be found to contain no more syllables, than one German or Greek hexameter. He did not understand* me: and I who

---

* [2] Klopstock's observation was partly true and partly erroneous. In the literal sense of his words, and if we confine the comparison to the average of space required for the expression of the same thought in the two languages, it is erroneous. I have translated some German hexameters into English hexameters, and find, that on the average three lines English will express four lines German. The reason is evident: our language abounds in monosyllables [282] and dissyllables. The German not less than the Greek, is a polysyllabic Language. But in another point of view the remark was not without foundation. For the German possessing the same unlimited privilege of forming compounds, both with prepositions and with epithets as the Greek, it can express the richest single Greek word in a single German one, and is thus freed from the necessity of weak or ungraceful paraphrases. I will content myself with one example at present, viz. the use of the prefixed particles *ver, zer, ent,* and *weg*, thus reissen to rend, verreissen to rend away, zerreissen to rend to pieces, *entreissen* to rend off or out of a thing, in the active sense: or schmelzen to melt—ver, zer, ent, schmelzen—and in like manner through all the verbs neuter and active.[3] If you consider only how much we should feel the loss of the prefix *be*, as in bedrop̄t, besprinkle, besot, especially in our poetical Language, and then think that this same mode of composition is carried through all their simple and compound prepositions, and many of their adverbs; and that with most of these the Germans have the same privilege as we have, of dividing them from the verb and placing them at the end of the sentence; you will have no difficulty in comprehending the reality and the cause, of this superior power in the German of condensing meaning, in which it's great Poet exulted. It is impossible to read half a dozen pages of Wieland[4] without perceiving that in this respect the German has no rival but the Greek, and yet I seem to feel that concentration or condensation is not the happiest mode of expressing this excellence, which seems to consist not so much in the less time required for conveying an impression, as in the unity and simultaneousness with which the impression is conveyed. It tends to make their language more picturesque: it *depictures* images

---

[1] In the list of "Errata" at the end of No 19 C inserts the words "in general".

[2] Cf a ms deletion at the beginning of this note: "I have since made myself acquainted with Voss's incomparable Translation of Homer, and with the first Edition of it; and I find that". Forster MS 112 f 72ᵛ. Johann Heinrich Voss's translations of the *Odyssey*

(1781) and the *Iliad* (1793) C called "truly marvellous"; see his letter to J. H. Frere 16 Jul 1816: *CL* IV 655.

[3] See *CN* II 3160: "O for the power to persuade all the writers of G.B. to adopt the ver, zer, and ab of the German—why not verboil, zerboil? . . ."

[4] See below, II 245 and n 1.

wished to hear his opinions, not to correct them, was glad that he did not.

[282] We now took our leave. At the beginning of the French Revolution Klopstock wrote Odes of congratulation. He received some honorary presents from the French Republic (a golden Crown I believe) and, like our Priestly, was invited to a seat in the Legislature, which he declined. But when French Liberty metamorphosed herself into a Fury, he sent back these presents with a Palinodia, declaring his abhorrence of their proceedings: and since then he has been perhaps more than enough an Anti-Gallican. I mean, that in his just contempt and detestation of the crimes and follies of the Revolutionists he suffers himself to forget, that the Revolution itself is a process of the Divine Providence; and that as the folly of Men is the wisdom of God, so are their iniquities instruments of his goodness. From Klopstock's House we walked to the Ramparts, discoursing together on the Poet and his conversation, till our attention was diverted to the beauty and singularity of the sunset and it's effects on the objects round us. There were Woods in the distance. A rich sandy light (nay, of a much deeper colour than [283] sandy) lay over these woods that blackened in the blaze. Over that part of the woods, which lay immediately under the intenser light, a brassy mist floated. The Trees on the Ramparts, and the People moving to and fro between them, were cut or divided into equal segments of deep shade and brassy light. Had the Trees, and the bodies of the Men and Women, been divided into equal segments by a rule or pair of Compasses, the portions could not have been more regular. All else was obscure. It was a fairy scene! and to encrease its romantic character, among the moving objects thus divided into alternate shade and brightness, was a beautiful Child dressed with the elegant simplicity of an English child, riding on a stately Goat, the saddle, bridle, and other accoutrements of which were in a high degree costly and splendid. Before I quit the subject of Hamburg, let me say, that I remained a day or two longer than I otherwise should have done, in order to be present at the feast of St. Michael, the Patron Saint of Hamburg, expecting to see the civic pomp of this commercial Republic. I was however disappointed. There were no processions, two or three sermons were preached to two or three old Women in two or three Churches, and St. Michael and his patronage wished elsewhere by the higher classes, all places of entertainment, Theatre, &c. being shut up on this day. In Hamburg, there seems to be no religion at all: in Lubec it is confined to the Women. The Men seem determined to be divorced from their wives in the other world, if they cannot in this. You will not easily

---

better. We have obtained this power in part by our compound verbs derived from the Latin: and the sense of it's great effect no doubt induced our Milton both to the use and the abuse of Latin derivatives. But still these prefixed particles conveying no separate or separable meaning to the mere English Reader, cannot possibly act on the mind with the force or liveliness of an original and homogeneous language, such as the German is: and besides are confined to certain words.[1]

[1] Cf *CL* I 450–1, letters to WW on German hexameters, which seem to be a continuing discussion of this conversation on German prosody (at which, of course, WW was also present).

conceive a more singular sight, than is presented by the vast aisle of the principal Church at Lubec[1] seen from the Organ-loft: for being filled with female Servants and Persons in the same class of life, and all their caps having gold and silver cauls, it appears like a rich pavement of gold and silver.

I will conclude this Letter with the mere transcription of notes, which my Friend B—— took of his conversations with Klopstock, during the interviews that took place after my departure.[2] On these I shall make but one remark at present, and that will appear a presumptuous one; namely, that Klopstock's remarks on the venerable Sage of Koenigsburg are to my own knowledge injurious and mistaken; and so far is it from being true, that his system is now given up, that throughout the Universities of Germany there is not a single Professor, who is not either a [284] Kantean, or a disciple of Fichte whose system is built on the Kantean, and presupposes it's truth; or lastly who, though an antagonist of Kant as to his theoretical work, has not embraced wholly or in part his moral system, and adopts part of his nomenclature. "Klopstock having wished to see the Calvary of Cumberland,[3] and asked what was thought of it in England, I went to Remnant's (the English Bookseller)[4] where I procured the Analytical Review, in which is contained the review of Cumberland's Calvary.[5] I remembered to have read there some specimens of a blank verse translation of the Messiah. I had mentioned this to Klopstock, and he had a great desire to see them. I walked over to his house and put the book into his hands. On adverting to his own Poem, he told me he began the Messiah when he was seventeen: he devoted three entire years to the plan without composing a single line. He was greatly at a loss in what manner to execute his work. There were no successful specimens of versification in the German language before this time. The first three cantos he wrote in a species of measured or numerous prose. This, though done with much labour and some success, was far from satisfying him. He had composed hexameters both Latin and Greek as a school exercise, and there had been also in the German language attempts in that style of versification. These were only of very moderate merit.—One day he was struck with the idea of what could be done in this way—he kept his room a whole day, even went without his dinner, and found that in the evening he had written twenty-three hexameters, versifying a part of what he had before written in prose.

[1] The Marienkirche.

[2] C had gone to Ratzeburg. What follows within quotation marks is presumably a report from Wordsworth, who dined with the poet at his brother's country-place and "sustained an animated conversation with [him] during the whole afternoon": *DWJ* (26 Sept 1798) i 25. See also *CL* i 444.

[3] Richard Cumberland (1732–1811), playwright and poet, satirised as Sir Fretful Plagiary in Sheridan's *Critic*. Cumberland's *Calvary; or the Death of Christ* (1792), one of his contemporaries claimed, combined the excellences of Shakespeare and Milton—"of which", says Sir Leslie Stephen in the *DNB*, "he has certainly made pretty free use".

[4] The bookseller Joseph Johnson had given C an order for £30 on William Remnant. See *CL* i 417 and n.

[5] *Analytical Review* xiii (Jun 1792) 121–38; the reviewer, "R. R.", calls Klopstock second to Milton as an epic poet and translates parts of *Messias* bks ii and iv (pp 130 8).

From that time, pleased with his efforts, he composed no more in prose. To-day he informed me that he had finished his plan before he read Milton. He was enchanted to see an Author who before him had trod the same path. This is a contradiction of what he said before.[1] He did not wish to speak of his poem to any one till it was finished: but some of his Friends who had seen what he had finished, tormented him till he had consented to publish a few books in a journal. He was then I believe very young, about twenty-five. The rest was printed at different periods, four books at a time. The reception given to the first specimens was highly flattering. He was nearly thirty years in finishing the whole Poem, but of these thirty years not more than two were employed in the composition [285]. He only composed in favourable moments; besides he had other occupations. He values himself upon the plan of his Odes, and accuses the modern lyrical Writers of gross deficiency in this respect. I laid the same accusation against Horace: he would not hear of it—but waived the discussion. He called Rousseau's Ode to Fortune[2] a moral Dissertation, in Stanzas. I spoke of Dryden's St. Cecilia; but he did not seem familiar with our Writers. He wished to know the distinctions between our dramatic and epic blank verse. He recommended me to read his Herman[3] before I read either the Messiah or the Odes. He flattered himself that some time or other his dramatic poems would be known in England. He had not heard of Cowper. He thought that Voss in his translation of the Iliad[4] had done violence to the idiom of the Germans, and had sacrificed it to the Greek, not remembering sufficiently that each language has it's particular spirit and genius. He said Lessing was the first of their dramatic Writers. I complained of Nathan[5] as tedious. He said there was not enough of action in it; but that Lessing was the most chaste of their Writers. He spoke favourably of Goethe; but said that his 'Sorrows of Werter' was his best work, better than any of his Dramas: he preferred the first written[6] to the rest of Goethe's Dramas. Schiller's 'Robbers' he found so extravagant, that he could not read it. I spoke of the scene of the setting sun.[7] He did not know it. He said Schiller could not live. He thought Don Carlos the best of his Dramas; but said that the plot was inextricable—It was evident, he knew little of Schiller's Works: indeed he said, he could not read them. Burgher[8] he said was a true Poet, and would live; that Schiller, on the contrary, must soon be forgotten; that he gave himself up to the imitation of Shakespeare, who often was extravagant, but that Schiller was ten thousand times more so. He spoke very slightingly of Kotzebue, as an immoral Author in the first place, and next as deficient in power. At Vienna, said he, they are

---

[1] See above, ii 240.

[2] Jean-Baptiste Rousseau (1671–1741); see his *Odes* bk ii no 6: *Œuvres complètes* (Paris 1797) i 107–13.

[3] *Hermanns Schlacht* (1769).

[4] Voss (1751–1826); see above, ii 241 n 2.

[5] Lessing's *Nathan der Weise* (1779).

[6] *Götz von Berlichingen* (1773).

[7] That is, iii ii.

[8] Gottfried August Bürger (1747–1794), author of the famous ballad *Lenore* (1772). Two weeks earlier C had written that "Bürger of all the German Poets pleases me the most": *CL* i 438. For C's and WW's controversy over Bürger's merits as a poet see *CL* i 565–6, a letter to William Taylor, one of several translators of *Lenore* (*CN* i 1132n).

transported with him; but we do not reckon the people of Vienna either the wisest or the wittiest People of Germany. He said Wieland was a charming Author and a sovereign Master of his own language:[1] that in this respect Goethe could not be compared to him, or indeed could any body else. He said that his fault was to be fertile to exuberance. I told him the Oberon had just [286] been translated into English. He asked me, if I was not delighted with the Poem. I answered, that I thought the Story began to flag about the seventh or eighth book; and observed that it was unworthy of a man of genius to make the interest of a long poem turn entirely upon animal gratification. He seemed at first disposed to excuse this by saying, that there are different subjects for poetry, and that Poets are not willing to be restricted in their choice. I answered, that I thought the *passion* of Love as well suited to the purposes of Poetry as any other passion; but that it was a cheap way of pleasing to fix the attention of the Reader through a long poem on the mere *appetite*. Well! but, said he, you see, that such Poems please every body. I answered, that it was the province of a great Poet to raise People up to his own level, not to descend to their's. He agreed, and confessed, that on no account whatsoever would he have written a work like the Oberon. He spoke in raptures of Wieland's style, and pointed out the passage where Retzia is delivered of her Child,[2] as exquisitely beautiful. I said that I did not perceive any very striking passages; but that I made allowance for the imperfections of a Translation. Of the thefts of Wieland he said, they were so exquisitely managed, that the greatest writers might be proud to steal as he did. He considered the books and fables of old Romance Writers in the light of the ancient mythology, as a sort of common property, from which a man was free to take whatever he could make a good use of. An Englishman had presented him with the Odes of Collins, which he had read with pleasure. He knew little or nothing of Gray except his Essay in the Church-yard. He complained of the Fool in Lear. I observed, that he seemed to give a terrible wildness to the distress; but still he complained. He asked whether it was not allowed, that Pope had written rhyme poetry with more skill than any of our Writers.—I said, I preferred Dryden, because his couplets had greater variety in their movement. He thought my reason a good one; but asked whether the rhyme of Pope were not more exact. This question I understood as applying to the final terminations,[3] and observed to him that I believed it was the case; but that I thought it was easy to excuse some inaccuracy in the final sounds, if the general sweep of the verse was superior. I told him that we were not so exact with regard to the final[4] endings of lines [287] as the French. He did not seem to know that we made no distinction between masculine and feminine (i.e. single or double,) rhymes: at least he put inquiries to me on this subject. He seemed to think, that no

---

[1] Christoph Martin Wieland (1733–1813). His *Oberon* was published in 1780, and William Sotheby's translation in 1798. C (c 20 Nov 1797) wrote that he was translating *Oberon* (*CL* I 357); for what became of this translation see Werner W. Beyer *The En-*chanted Forest* (New York 1963) 37–65.

[2] *Oberon* can VIII sts 69–80.

[3] In the list of "Errata" at the end of No 19 "as . . . terminations" is corrected to "literally".

[4] In the "Errata" the word "final" is omitted.

language could ever be so far formed as that it might not be enriched by idioms borrowed from another tongue. I said this was a very dangerous practice; and added that I thought Milton had often injured both his prose and verse by taking this liberty too frequently. I recommended to him the prose works of Dryden as models of pure and native English. I was treading upon tender ground, as I have reason to suppose that he has himself liberally indulged in the practice.

"The same day I dined at Mr. Klopstocks, where I had the pleasure of a third interview with the Poet. We talked principally about indifferent things. I asked him what he thought of Kant. He said that his reputation was much on the decline in Germany. That for his own part he was not surprized to find it so, as the Works of Kant were to him utterly incomprehensible—that he had often been pestered by the Kanteans; but was rarely in the practice of arguing with them. His custom was to produce the book, open it and point to a passage, and beg they would explain it.[1] This they ordinarily attempted to do by substituting their own ideas. I do not want, I say, an explanation of your own ideas, but of the passage which is before us. In this way I generally bring the dispute to an immediate conclusion. He spoke of Wolfe as the first Metaphysician they had in Germany.[2] Wolfe had followers; but they could hardly be called a sect, and luckily till the appearance of Kant, about fifteen years ago, Germany had not been pestered by any sect of Philosophers whatsoever; but that each man had separately pursued his enquiries uncontrolled by the dogmas of a Master. Kant had appeared ambitious to be the founder of a Sect, that he had succeeded: but that the Germans were now coming to their senses again. That Nicolai[3] and Engel[4] had in different ways contributed to disenchant the Nation; but above all the incomprehensibility of the Philosopher and his philosophy. He seem[ed] pleased to hear, that as yet Kant's doctrines had not met with many Admirers in England—did not doubt but that we had too much wisdom to be duped by a Writer who set at defiance the common sense and common understandings of Men. [288] We talked of Tragedy. He seemed to rate highly the power of exciting tears—I said that nothing was more easy than to deluge an audience, that it was done every day by the meanest Writers."

I must remind you, my Friend, first, that these Notes, &c. are not intended as specimens of Klopstock's intellectual power or even "*colloquial*

---

[1] The "book" was probably Kant's *Kritik der reinen Vernunft* (Riga 1781, revised 1787).

[2] Christian von Wolff, whom Kant criticised for giving a wrong direction to all investigations into the nature and origin of our knowledge; see *Kritik der reinen Vernunft* i pt 1 §8. See also above, i 146 and n 2.

[3] Among the others whom this well-known critic, Christoph Friedrich Nicolai (1733–1811), attacked were Goethe, Schiller, Herder, Wieland, and

Fichte. In his copy of Nicolai's *Über meine gelehrte Bildung* . . . (Berlin and Stettin 1799), now in the BM, C has written some devastating comments on this "Gooseander arching its neck in imitation of the Swans": "Hoot! Hoot! Pretty Poll! Pretty Poll!" . . . "Old Nic. the Berlin book-scribling Book-shopster & Book-monger" . . . "impertinent Blockhead!"

[4] Johann Jakob Engel (1741–1802); see above, i 370 n 2.

prowess," to judge of which by an accidental conversation, and this with Strangers, and those too Foreigners, would be not only unreasonable, but calumnious. Secondly, I attribute little other interest to the remarks than what is derived from the celebrity of the Person who made them. Lastly, if you ask me, whether I have read the Messiah, and what I think of it? I answer—as yet the first four books only: and as to my opinion (the reasons of which hereafter) you may guess it from what I could not help muttering to myself, when the good Pastor this morning told me, that Klopstock was the German Milton—"a very *German* Milton indeed"!!!—Heaven preserve you, and

SATYRANE

TO CORRESPONDENTS

I thank the "*Friend's friend and a Cantab*"[1] for his inspiriting Letter, and assure him, that it was not without it's intended effect, of giving me encouragement. That this was not needless, he would feel as well as know, if I could convey to him the anxious thoughts and gloomy anticipations, with which I write any single paragraph, that demands the least effort of attention, or requires the Reader to enter into himself and question his own mind as to the truth of that which I am pressing on his notice. But both He and my very kind Malton Correspondent,[2] and all of similar dispositions, may rest assured, that with every imaginable endeavour to make THE FRIEND, *collectively*, as *entertaining* as is compatable with the main Object of the Work, I shall never so far forget the duty, I owe to them and to my own heart, as not to remember that *mere* amusement is *not* that main Object. I have taken upon myself (see No. 11.)[3] all the blame that I could acknowledge without adulation to my readers and hypocritical mock-humility. But the principal source of the obscurity imputed must be sought for in the want of *interest* concerning the truths themselves. (REVEL. III. 17.)[4] My sole Hope (I dare not say expectation) is, that if I am enabled to proceed with the work through an equal number of Essays with those already published, it will gradually find for itself it's appropriate Public.

S. T. COLERIDGE

---

[1] For this anonymous letter of encouragement, see below, App F, II 500 1.

[2] William Wray, a Malton attorney; for his letter, see below, App F, II 501–2; see also above, Introduction, I lxi n 5.

[3] The letter to R.L., above, II 149–53.

[4] "Because thou sayest, I am rich, and increased with goods, and have need of nothing; and knowest not that thou art wretched, and miserable, and poor, and blind, and naked". Perhaps C means Rev 3.16: ". . . because thou art lukewarm, and neither cold nor hot, I will spue thee out of my mouth".

THE FRIEND

No. 19. THURSDAY, December 28, 1809

EPITAPHS

TRANSLATED FROM CHIABRERA

I

There never breath'd a man who when his life
Was closing might not of that life relate
Toils long and hard.—The Warrior will report
Of wounds, and bright swords flashing in the field,
And blast of trumpets. He, who hath been doomed
To bow his forehead in the courts of kings,
Will tell of fraud and never-ceasing hate,
Envy, and heart-inquietude derived
From intricate cabals of treacherous friends.
I, who on ship-board lived from earliest youth,
Could represent the countenance horrible
Of the vex'd waters, and the indignant rage
Of Auster and Bootes. Forty years
Over the well-steer'd Gallies did I rule;
From huge Pelorus to the Atlantic pillars
Rises no mountain to mine eyes unknown;
And the broad gulphs I travers'd—oft—and oft.
Of every cloud which in the heavens might stir
I knew the force; and hence the rough sea's pride
Avail'd not to my Vessel's overthrow.

What noble pomp and frequent have not I
On regal decks beheld! yet in the end
I learn that one poor moment can suffice
To equalize the lofty and the low.
We sail the sea of life—a *calm* One finds
And One a *tempest*—and, the voyage o'er,
Death is the quiet haven of us all.
If more of my condition ye would know,
Savona was my birth-place, and I sprang
Of noble Parents: sixty years and three
Lived I—then yielded to a slow disease.[1]

[1] See *Epitaphs Translated from Chia-* *Opere* (1757) II 191–2 (*Epitaffi* xxv).
brera IV: *WPW* IV 250 (var); Chiabrera

II

Destined to war from very infancy
Was I, Roberto Dati, and I took
In Malta the white symbol of the Cross.
Nor in life's vigorous season did I shun
Hazard or toil; among the Sands was seen
Of Lybia, and, not seldom, on the Banks
Of wide Hungarian Danube, 't was my lot
To hear the sanguinary trumpet sounded.
So liv'd I, and repined not at such fate;
This only grieves me, for it seems a wrong,
That stripp'd of arms I to my end am brought
On the soft down of my paternal home.
Yet haply Arno shall be spared all cause
To blush for me. Thou loiter not nor halt
In thy appointed way, and bear in mind
How fleeting and how frail is human life.[1]

[291]

Ma pianger non si dee, come per tempo
Dal Mondo uscito. Voi, Mortali, errate,
Per vero dir, nel conto della vita—
Sol numerate gli anni, e non guardate
All' opre gloriose di Virtute.*

CHIABRERA[2]

"*Does* Fortune favour Fools? Or how do you explain the origin of the Proverb, which, differently worded, is to be found in all the languages of Europe?"

This Proverb admits of various explanations according to the mood of mind, in which it is used. It may arise from pity, and the soothing persuasion that Providence is eminently watchful over the helpless, and extends an especial care to those who are not capable of caring for themselves. So used, it breathes the same feeling as "God tempers the wind to the shorn Lamb"—or, the more sportive adage, that "the Fairies take care of Children and tipsy Folk." The persuasion itself, in addition to the general religious feeling of Mankind, and the scarcely less general love of the marvellous, may be accounted for from our tendency to exaggerate all effects, that seem disproportionate to their visible cause, and all circumstances that are in any way strongly contrasted with our notions of the Persons under them. Secondly, it arises from the safety and success which an ignorance of danger and difficulty sometimes actually assists in

* *Literal Translation.* But we ought not to lament, as if he had departed early from the World: It is you, Mortals, in truth, that err in your calculation of Life: you count the years only, and do not look to the glorious works of Virtue.

[1] See *Epitaphs* VI: *WPW* IV 251;   [2] Chiabrera II 181 (*Epitaffi* VI).
Chiabrera II 189 (*Epitaffi* XIX).

procuring; inasmuch as it precludes the despondence, which might have kept the more foresighted from undertaking the enterprize, the depression which would retard its' progress, and those overwhelming influences of terror in cases where the vivid perception of the danger constitutes the greater part of the danger itself. Thus men are said to have swooned and even died at the sight of a narrow Bridge, over which they had rode, the night before, in perfect safety; or at tracing their footmarks along the edge of a Precipice which the darkness had concealed from them. A more obscure cause, yet not wholly to be omitted, is afforded by the [292] undoubted fact, that the exertion of the reasoning faculties tends to extinguish or bedim those mysterious instincts of skill, which, though for the most part latent, we nevertheless possess in common with other animals.

Or the Proverb may be used *invidiously:* and Folly in the vocabulary of Envy or Baseness may signify courage and magnanimity. Hardihood and Fool-hardiness are indeed as different as green and yellow, yet will appear the same to the jaundiced eye. Courage multiplies the chances of success by sometimes *making* opportunities, and always availing itself of them: and in this sense Fortune may be said to *favour Fools* by those, who however prudent in their own opinion are deficient in valour and enterprize. Again: an eminently good and wise Man, for whom the praises of the judicious have procured a high reputation even with the world at large, proposes to himself certain objects, and adapting the right means to the right end attains them: but his objects not being what the world calls Fortune, neither money nor artificial rank, his admitted inferiors in moral and intellectual worth, but more prosperous in their worldly concerns, are said to have been favoured by Fortune and he slighted: although the fools did the same in their line as the wise man in his: they adapted the appropriate means to the desired end and so succeeded. In this sense the Proverb is current by a misuse, or a catachresis at least, of both the words, Fortune and Fools.

> How seldom Friend! a good great man inherits
> Honour or wealth with all his worth and pains!
> It sounds, like stories from the land of spirits,
> If any man obtain that which he merits,
> Or any merit that which he obtains.
>
> REPLY
>
> For shame, dear Friend! renounce this canting strain!
> What would'st thou have a good great man obtain?
> Place? Titles? Salary? a gilded Chain?
> Or Throne of Corses which his sword hath slain?
> Greatness and goodness are not *means* but *ends!*
> Hath he not always treasures, always friends,
> The good great Man? Three treasures, LOVE, and LIGHT,
> And CALM THOUGHTS regular as infant's breath:
> And three firm friends, more sure than day and night,
> HIMSELF, his MAKER, and the Angel DEATH.
>
> S.T.C.

[293] But, lastly, there is, doubtless, a true meaning attached to Fortune, distinct both from Prudence and from Courage; and distinct too from that absence of depressing or bewildering Passions, which (as, according to my favourite Proverb, "extremes meet,") the Fool not seldom obtains in as great perfection by his ignorance, as the wise Man by the highest energies of thought and self-discipline. L U C K has a real existence in human affairs from the infinite number of powers, that are in action at the same time, and from the co-existence of things contingent and accidental (such as to *us* are at least accidental) with the regular appearances and general laws of Nature. A familiar instance will make these words intelligible. The moon waxes and wanes according to a necessary law.—The clouds likewise, and all the manifold appearances connected with them, are governed by certain laws no less than the phases of the moon. But the laws which determine the latter, are known and calculable: while those of the former are hidden from us. At all events, the number and variety of their effects baffle our powers of calculation: and that the sky is clear or obscured at any particular time, we speak of, in common language, as a matter of *accident*. Well! at the time of the full moon, but when the sky is completely covered with black clouds, I am walking on in the dark, aware of no particular danger: a sudden gust of wind rends the cloud for a moment, and the moon emerging discloses to me a chasm or precipice, to the very brink of which I had advanced my foot. This is what is meant by *Luck*, and according to the more or less serious mood or habit of our mind we exclaim, how lucky! or, how providential! The co-presence of numberless Phænomena, and the co-existence of those, which from the complexity or subtlety of their determining causes are called *contingencies*, with any regular or necessary Phænomenon (as the clouds with the moon for instance) occasions *coincidences*, which, when they are attended by any advantage or injury, and are at the same time incapable of being calculated or foreseen by human prudence, form good or ill *Luck*. On a hot sunshiny afternoon came on a sudden storm and spoilt the Farmer's hay: and this is called ill Luck. We will suppose the same event to take place, when meteorology shall have been perfected into a Science, and provided itself with unerring instruments; but which the Farmer had neglected to examine. This is no longer ill Luck, [294] but Imprudence. Now apply this to our proverb. Unforeseen Coincidences may have greatly helped a Man, yet if they have done for him only what possibly from his own abilities he might have effected for himself, his good Luck will excite less attention and the instances be less remembered. That clever men should attain their objects seems natural, and we neglect the circumstances that perhaps produced that success of themselves without the intervention of Skill or Foresight; but we dwell on the fact and remember it, as something strange, when the same happens to a weak or ignorant man. So too, though the latter should fail in his undertakings from concurrences that might have happened to the wisest man, yet his failure being no more than might have been expected and accounted for from his folly, it lays no hold on our attention, but fleets away among the other undistinguished waves in which the stream of ordinary life murmurs by us, and is forgotten. Had it been as true as it was notoriously false, that those all-embracing Discoveries, which have shed a

dawn of *Science* on the *Art* of Chemistry, and give no obscure promise of some one great constitutive Law, in the light of which dwell dominion and the power of Prophecy; if these discoveries, instead of having been as they really were, preconcerted by meditation, and evolved out of his own intellect, had occurred by a set of lucky *accidents* to the illustrious Father and Founder of philosophic Alchemy; if they had presented themselves to Professor D A V Y exclusively in consequence of his *luck* in possessing a particular Galvanic Battery, if this Battery, as far as D A V Y was concerned, had itself been an *accident*, and not desired and obtained by him for the purpose of ensuring the testimony of experience to his Principles, and in order to bind down material Nature under the inquisition of Reason, and force from her, as by torture, unequivocal answers to *prepared* and *preconceived* questions—yet still they would not have been talked of or described, as instances of *Luck*, but as the natural results of his skill and knowledge. But should an accident have disclosed similar Discoveries to a Mechanic at Birmingham or Sheffield, and if the Man should grow rich in consequence, and partly by the envy of his Neighbours, and partly with good reason, be considered by them as a man *below par* in the general powers of his understanding; then, "O what a lucky Fellow!—Well, Fortune *does* favour Fools— [295] that's for certain!—It is always so!"— And forthwith the Exclaimer relates half a dozen similar instances. Thus accumulating the one sort of facts and never collecting the other, we do, as Poets in their diction, and Quacks of all denominations do in their reasoning, put a part for the whole, and at once soothe our envy and gratify our love of the marvellous, by the sweeping Proverb, "FORTUNE FAVOURS FOOLS."

The philosophic Ruler, who secured the favours of Fortune by seeking Wisdom and knowledge in preference to them, has pathetically observed— "The heart knoweth its own bitterness; and there is a joy in which the stranger intermedleth not." A simple Question founded on a trite Proverb, with a discursive answer to it, would scarcely suggest to an indifferent Person, any other notion than that of a mind at ease, amusing itself with it's own activity. Once before (I believe about this time last year) I had taken up the old memorandum Book, from which I have now transcribed the introductory Paragraphs, and they had then attracted my notice by the name of the extraordinary Man mentioned in the last illustration. Exasperated by the base and cowardly attempt, that had been made, to detract from the honours due to his astonishing genius, I had slightly altered the concluding sentences, substituting the more recent for his earlier Discoveries; and without the most distant intention of publishing what I then wrote, I had expressed my own convictions for the gratification of my own feelings, and finished by tranquilly paraphrasing into a chemical Allegory, the homeric adventure of Menelaus with Proteus. Oh! with what different feelings, with what a sharp and sudden emotion did I re-peruse the same question yester-morning, having by accident opened the book at the page, upon which it was written. I was moved; for the particular satisfaction expressed at my answer by him, who proposed the question to me, had been the occasion of my noting down the substance of it.[1] I was moved:

[1] See above, I 533, Sir A. Ball putting the question to C.

because to this conversation, I was indebted for the friendship and confidence, with which he afterwards honoured me; and because it recalled the memory of one of the most delightful mornings I ever passed; when, as we were riding together, the same person related to me the principal events of his own Life, and introduced them by adverting to this conversation. It recalled too [296] the deep impression left on my mind by that narrative, the impression, that I had never known any analogous instance, in which a man so successful, had been so little indebted to Fortune, or lucky accidents, or so exclusively both the Architect and Builder of his own success. The sum of his History may be comprised in this one sentence: Hæc, sub numine, nobismet fecimus, sapientia duce, fortuna permittente. (i.e. These things, under God, we have done for ourselves, through the guidance of wisdom, and with the permission of Fortune.) Luck *gave* him nothing: in her most generous moods, she only worked with him as with a Friend, not for him as for a Fondling; but more often she simply stood neuter and suffered him to work for himself. Ah! how could I be otherwise than deeply affected, by whatever reminded me of that daily and familiar intercourse with him, which made the fifteen months from May 1804, to October 1805, in many respects, the most memorable and instructive period of my life?—for there was still lying on my table the Paper which, the day before, had conveyed to me the unexpected and most awful tidings of this Man's death! his Death in the fulness of all his powers, in the rich autumn of ripe, yet undecaying Manhood! I once knew a Lady, who after the loss of a lovely Child, continued for several days in a state of seeming indifference, the weather, at the same time, as if in unison with her, being calm, though gloomy: till one morning a burst of sunshine breaking in upon her, and suddenly lighting up the room where she was sitting, she dissolved at once into tears, and wept passionately. In no very dissimilar manner, did the sudden gleam of recollection at the sight of this memorandum act on myself. I had been stunned by the intelligence, as by an outward blow, till this trifling incident startled and disentranced me: (the sudden pang shivered through my whole frame:) and if I repressed the outward shews of sorrow, it was by force that I repressed them, and because it is not by tears that I ought to mourn for the loss of Sir Alexander Ball.

He was a Man above his Age: but for that very reason the Age has the more need to have the master features of his character pourtrayed and preserved. This I feel it my duty to attempt,[1] and this alone: for having received neither instructions nor permission from the Family of the Deceased, I cannot think myself allowed to enter into the [297] particulars of his private History, strikingly as many of them would illustrate the elements and composition of his mind. For he was indeed a living confutation of the assertion attributed to the Prince of Conde, that no Man appeared great to his Valet de Chambre—a saying which, I suspect, owes it's currency less to it's truth, than to the envy of mankind and the misapplication of the word great to actions unconnected with Reason and Free will. It will be sufficient[2] for my purpose to observe, that the purity

---

[1] See above, 1 534 n 1, for a cancelled ms passage.

[2] See above, 1 535 n 2, for a cancelled ms passage.

and strict propriety of his conduct, which precluded rather than silenced calumny, the evenness of his Temper and his attentive and affectionate Manners, in private life, greatly aided and encreased his public utility: and, if it should please Providence, that a portion of his spirit should descend with his Mantle, the virtues of SIR ALEXANDER BALL, as a Master, a Husband, and a Parent, will form a no less remarkable epoch in the History of Maltese Morality, than his wisdom, as a Governor, has made in that of their outward circumstances. That the private and personal qualities of a first Magistrate should have political effects, will appear strange to no reflecting Englishman, who has attended to the workings of mens' minds during the first ferment of revolutionary principles, and must therefore have witnessed the influence of the King's domestic character in counteracting them. But in Malta there were circumstances which rendered such an example peculiarly requisite and beneficent. The very existence, for so many generations, of an Order of Lay Cælibates in that Island, who abandoned even the outward semblances of an adherence to their vow of chastity, must have had pernicious effects on the morals of the inhabitants. But when it is considered too that the Knights of Malta had been for the last fifty years or more a set of useless Idlers, generally illiterate,* for they thought literature no part of a Soldier's excellence and yet effeminate, for they were Soldiers in name only; that they were, moreover, all of them *aliens*, who looked upon themselves not merely as of a superior rank to the native Nobles, but as beings of a different [298] race, (I had almost said, *species*), from the Maltese collectively; and finally that these Men possessed exclusively the government of the Island; it may be safely concluded that they were little better than a perpetual Influenza, relaxing and diseasing the hearts of all the families within their sphere of influence. Hence the Peasantry, who fortunately were below their reach, notwithstanding the more than childish ignorance in which they were kept by their Priests, yet compared with the middle and higher classes, were both in mind and body, as ordinary men compared with dwarfs. Every respectable family had some one Knight for their Patron, as a matter of course; and to him the honour of a Sister or a Daughter was sacrificed, equally as a matter of course. But why should I thus disguise the truth? Alas! in nine instances out of ten, this Patron was the common Paramour of every Female in the Family. Were I composing a State-memorial, I should abstain from all allusion to *moral* good or evil, as not having now first to learn, that with Diplomatists, and with practical Statesmen of every denomination, it would preclude all attention to it's other contents, and with no result but that of securing for it's Author's name the *official* private mark of exclusion or dismission, as a weak or suspicious Person. But among those for whom I am now writing, there are I trust many, who will think it not the

* The personal effects of every Knight were, after his death, appropriated to the Order, and his Books, if he had any, devolved to the public Library. This Library therefore, which has been accumulating from the time of their first settlement in the Island, is a fair criterion of the nature and degree of their literary Studies, as an average. Even in respect to works of military science it is contemptible—as the sole public Library of so numerous and opulent an Order, *most* contemptible—and in all other departments of Literature it is below contempt.

feeblest reason for rejoicing in our possession of Malta, and not the least worthy motive for wishing it's retention, that one source of human misery and corruption has been dried up. Such persons will hear the name of Sir Alexander Ball with additional reverence, as of one who has made the protection of Great Britain a double blessing to the Maltese, and broken, *"the bonds of iniquity"* as well as unlocked the fetters of political oppression.[1]

When we are praising the Departed by our own fire-sides, we dwell most fondly on those qualities which had won our personal affection, and which sharpen our individual regrets. But when impelled by a loftier and more meditative Sorrow, we would raise a public monument to their memory, we praise them appropriately when we relate their actions faithfully: and thus preserving their example for the imitation of the Living, alleviate the Loss, while we demonstrate it's magnitude. My funeral Eulogy of Sir Alexander Ball, must therefore be a narrative of his Life; and this Friend of Mankind will be defrauded of [299] honour in proportion as that narrative is deficient and fragmentary. It shall, however, be as complete as my information enables, and as prudence and a proper respect for the feelings of the Living permit me to render it. His Fame (I adopt the words of one of our elder Writers) is so great throughout the World that he stands in no need of an encomium: and yet his worth is much greater than his Fame. It is impossible not to speak great things of him, and yet it will be very difficult to speak what he deserves. But custom requires that something should be said: it is a duty and a debt which we owe to ourselves and to mankind, not less than to his memory: and I hope his great Soul, if it hath any knowledge of what is done here below, will not be offended at the smallness even of my Offering.

After my next number, which will contain the conclusion of No. 17, (for I must not disappoint the expectations raised by the masterly* comments on the Letter of Mathetes) I shall proceed with these sketches of the Life and Character of the late Admiral Sir Alexander Ball, under three heads; first, as a naval officer; secondly, as entrusted with the Government of Malta; and lastly, of his opinions and principles, as learnt from his own conversation.[3] Ah! how little, when among the subjects of THE FRIEND I promised "Characters met with in real Life," did I anticipate the sad Event, which compels me to weave on a Cypress branch, those sprays of Laurel, which I had destined for his Bust not his Monument! He lived as we should all live; and, I doubt not, left the world as we should all wish to leave it. Such is the power of dispensing blessings, which Providence has attached to the truly great and good, that they cannot even die without advantage to their fellow-creatures: for Death consecrates their Example; and the wisdom, which might have been slighted at the Council Table,

* Of course I here imply, that these comments were themselves a communication to THE FRIEND. The Writer was present at the receipt of Mathetes' Letter, and much interested by it's contents: His remarks on which were so judicious and conceived in so manly and original a style of thinking, that I requested him to reduce them into form and permit them to be annexed to the Letter.[2]

[1] See above, I 537 n 2, for a cancelled ms passage.

[2] Cf above, I 377 n 2.

[3] The life of Ball continues in Nos 21, 22, 26, and 27.

becomes oracular from the Shrine. Those rare excellencies, which make our grief poignant, make it likewise profitable; and the Tears, which wise men shed for the departure of the Wise, are [300] among those that are preserved in Heaven. It is the fervent aspiration of my spirit, that I may so perform the task which private gratitude, and public duty impose on me, that "as God hath cut this tree of Paradise down, from it's seat of Earth, the dead Trunk may yet support a part of the declining Temple, or at least serve to kindle the Fire on the Altar." BP. JER. TAYLOR.

CHRISTMAS WITHIN DOORS,

IN THE NORTH OF GERMANY

EXTRACTED FROM SATYRANE'S LETTERS

RATZEBURG

There is a Christmas custom here which pleased and interested me.—The Children make little presents to their Parents, and to each other; and the Parents to the Children. For three or four months before Christmas the Girls are all busy, and the Boys save up their pocket-money, to make or purchase these presents. What the Present is to be is cautiously kept secret, and the Girls have a world of contrivances to conceal it—such as working when they are out on visits and the others are not with them; getting up in the morning before day-light, &c. Then on the evening before Christmas day one of the Parlours is lighted up by the Children, into which the Parents must not go: a great yew bough is fastened on the Table at a little distance from the wall, a multitude of little Tapers are fastened in the bough, but not so as to burn it till they are nearly burnt out, and coloured paper, &c. hangs and flutters from the twigs.—Under this Bough the Children lay out in great order the presents they mean for their Parents, still concealing in their pockets what they intend for each other. Then the Parents are introduced—and each presents his little Gift—and then bring out the rest one by one from their pockets, and present them with kisses and embraces.—Where I witnessed this scene, there were eight or nine Children, and the eldest Daughter and the Mother wept aloud for joy and tenderness; and the tears ran down the face of the Father, and he clasped all his Children so tight to his breast—it seemed as if he did it to stifle the sob that was rising within him.—I was very much affected.—The Shadow of the [301] Bough and its appendages on the wall, and arching over on the Ceiling, made a pretty Picture—and then the raptures of the *very* little Ones, when at last the twigs and their needles began to take fire and *snap*— O it was a delight for them!—On the next day, in the great Parlour, the Parents lay out on the table the Presents for the Children: a scene of more sober joy succeeds, as on this day, after an old custom, the Mother says privately to each of her Daughters, and the Father to his Sons, that which he has observed most praise-worthy and that which was most faulty in their conduct.—Formerly, and still in all the smaller Towns and Villages throughout North Germany, these Presents were sent by all the Parents to some one Fellow who in high Buskins, a white Robe, a Mask, and an enormous flax Wig, personates Knecht Rupert, i.e. the Servant Rupert. On Christmas Night he goes round to every House and says, that Jesus Christ, his Master, sent him thither—the Parents and elder Children receive him with great pomp of reverence, while the little ones are most terribly frightened—He then enquires for the Children, and according to the character which he hears from the Parent, he gives them the intended Present, as if they came out of Heaven from Jesus Christ.—Or, if they should have been bad Children, he gives the Parents a Rod, and in the name of his Master, recommends them to use it frequently.—About seven or eight years old the Children are let into the secret, and it is curious how faithfully they keep it!

CHRISTMAS OUT OF DOORS

The whole Lake of Ratzeburg is one mass of thick transparent ice—a spotless Mirror of nine miles in extent! The lowness of the Hills, which rise from the shores of the Lake, preclude the awful sublimity of Alpine scenery, yet compensate for the want of it by beauties, of which this very lowness is a necessary condition. Yester-morning I saw the lesser Lake completely hidden by Mist; but the moment the Sun peeped over the Hill, the mist broke in the middle, and in a few seconds stood divided, leaving a broad road all across the Lake; and between these two Walls of mist the sunlight *burnt* upon the ice, forming a [302] road of golden fire, intolerably bright! and the mist-walls themselves partook of the blaze in a multitude of shining colours. This is our second Frost. About a month ago, before the Thaw came on, there was a storm of wind; during the whole night, such were the thunders and howlings of the breaking ice, that they have left a conviction on my mind, that there are Sounds more sublime than any Sight *can* be, more absolutely suspending the power of comparison, and more utterly absorbing the mind's self-consciousness in it's total attention to the object working upon it. Part of the ice which the vehemence of the wind had shattered, was driven shore-ward and froze anew. On the evening of the next day, at sun-set, the shattered ice thus frozen, appeared of a deep blue, and in shape like an agitated sea; beyond this, the water, that ran up between the great Islands of ice which had preserved their masses entire and smooth, shone of a yellow green; but all these scattered Ice-islands, themselves, were of an intensely bright blood colour —they seemed blood and light in union! On some of the largest of these Islands, the Fishermen stood pulling out their immense Nets through the holes made in the ice for this purpose, and the Men, their Net-Poles, and their huge Nets, were a part of the glory; say rather, it appeared as if the rich crimson light had shaped itself into these forms, figures, and attitudes, to make a glorious vision in mockery of earthly things.

The lower Lake is now all alive with Scaters, and with Ladies driven onward by them in their ice cars. Mercury, surely, was the first maker of Scates, and the wings at his feet are symbols of the invention. In scating there are three pleasing circumstances: the infinitely subtle particles of Ice, which the Scate cuts up, and which creep and run before the Scate like a low mist, and in sun-rise or sun-set become coloured; second, the shadow of the Scater in the water seen through the transparent Ice; and third, the melancholy undulating sound from the Scate, not without variety; and when very many are scating together, the sounds and the noises give an impulse to the icy Trees, and the woods all round the Lake *tinkle!*

Here I stop, having in truth transcribed the preceding in great measure, in order to present the lovers of Poetry with a descriptive passage, extracted, with the Author's [303] permission, from an unpublished Poem on the growth and revolutions of an individual mind, by WORDSWORTH.

> ——————an Orphic Tale indeed,
> A Tale divine of high and passionate thoughts
> To their own music chaunted!   S.T.C.

GROWTH OF GENIUS FROM THE INFLUENCES OF NATURAL OBJECTS, ON THE IMAGINATION IN BOYHOOD, AND EARLY YOUTH

Wisdom and Spirit of the Universe!
Thou Soul, that art the Eternity of Thought!
And giv'st to forms and images a breath
And everlasting motion! not in vain,
By day or star-light, thus from my first dawn
Of Childhood didst Thou intertwine for me
The passions that build up our human Soul,
Nor with the mean and vulgar works of Man
But with high objects, with enduring things,
With Life and Nature: purifying thus
The elements of feeling and of thought,
And sanctifying by such discipline
Both pain and fear, until we recognize
A grandeur in the beatings of the heart.
　　　Nor was this fellowship vouchsaf'd to me
With stinted kindness. In November days
When vapours rolling down the vallies made
A lonely scene more lonesome; among woods
At noon, and mid the calm of summer nights,
When by the margin of the trembling Lake,
Beneath the gloomy hills I homeward went
In solitude, such intercourse was mine;
'Twas mine among the fields both day and night
And by the waters all the summer long.
　　　And in the frosty season when the sun
Was set, and, visible for many a mile
The cottage windows through the twilight blazed,
I heeded not the summons:—happy time
It was indeed for all of us, to me
It was a time of rapture! clear and loud
The village clock toll'd six, I wheel'd about,

[304]   Proud and exulting, like an untir'd horse
          That car'd not for its home.—All shod with steel
          We hiss'd along the polish'd ice, in games
          Confederate, imitative of the Chace
          And woodland pleasures, the resounding horn,
          The Pack loud bellowing, and the hunted hare.
          So through the darkness and the cold we flew,
          And not a voice was idle: with the din
          Meanwhile the precipices rang aloud,
          The leafless trees and every icy crag
          Tinkled like iron, while the distant hills
          Into the tumult sent an alien sound
          Of melancholy not unnoticed, while the stars
          Eastward, were sparkling clear, and in the west
          The orange sky of evening died away.
               Not seldom from the uproar I retired
          Into a silent bay or sportively
          Glanc'd sideway, leaving the tumultuous throng
          To cut across the image of a Star
          That gleam'd upon the ice: and oftentimes
          When we had given our bodies to the wind,
          And all the shadowy banks on either side
          Came sweeping through the darkness spinning still
          The rapid line of motion, then at once
          Have I reclining back upon my heels
          Stopp'd short, yet still the solitary Cliffs
          Wheel'd by me even as if the earth had roll'd
          With visible motion her diurnal round!
          Behind me did they stretch in solemn train
          Feebler and feebler, and I stood and watch'd
          Till all was tranquil as a summer sea.

Errata

No. 18. p. 274, l. 13, for Wanderers, read Beggars.
          p. 275, l. 6 and 7, read "that the words 'Time' and 'pass' are each
               used in three different senses"—instead of "that two—Time
               &c."
          p. 277, l. 3,[1] for *slips*, read Slip.
          p. 281, l. 20, after great men—insert *in general*.
          p. 286, l. 39, 40, substitute "literally" for "as applying to the final
               terminations," and omit the word "*final*" in the last line.

[1] An error for line "31"; see above, II 237 n 2.

THE FRIEND

THE remarks, which were called forth by the letter of Mathetes, given in the 17th Number, concluded with a comparison of the progress of the human race to that of a river. We will now resume the subject, carrying on the same illustration.[1] It suffices to content the mind, though there may be an apparent stagnation, or a retrograde movement in the Species, that something is doing which is necessary to be done, and the effects of which, will in due time appear;—that something is unremittingly gaining, either in secret preparation or in open and triumphant progress. But in fact here, as every where, we are deceived by creations which the mind is compelled to make for itself: we speak of the Species not as an aggregate, but as endued with the form and separate life of an Individual. But human kind, what is it else than myriads of rational beings in various degrees obedient to their Reason; some torpid, some aspiring; some in eager chace to the right hand, some to the left; these wasting down their moral nature, and these feeding it for immortality? A whole generation may appear even to sleep, or may be exasperated with rage—they that compose it, tearing each other to pieces with more than brutal fury. It is enough for complacency and hope, that scattered and solitary minds are always labouring somewhere in the service of truth and virtue; and that by the sleep of the multitude, the energy of the multitude may be prepared; and that by the fury of the people, the chains of the people may be broken. Happy moment was it for England when her Chaucer, who has rightly been called the morning star of her literature, appeared above the horizon—when her Wickliff, like the Sun, "shot orient beams" through the night of Romish superstition!—Yet may the darkness and the desolating hurricane which immediately followed in the wars of York and Lancaster, be deemed in their turn a blessing, with which the Land has been visited.

[306] May I return to the thought of progress, of accumulation, of increasing light, or of any other image by which it may please us to represent the improvement of the Species? The hundred years that followed the Usurpation of Henry the fourth, were a hurling-back of the mind of the Country, a delapidation, an extinction; yet institutions, laws, customs, and habits, were then broken down, which would not have been so readily, nor perhaps so thoroughly destroyed by the gradual influence of increasing knowledge; and under the oppression of which, if they had continued to exist, the virtue and intellectual Prowess of the succeeding Century could not have appeared at all, much less could they have displayed themselves with that eager haste, and with those beneficent triumphs which will to the end of time be looked back upon with admiration and gratitude.

[1] See above, II 232. In Copy R, Wordsworth "Marginalia" 369. C again notes "Wordsworth's": J.

If the foregoing obvious distinctions be once clearly perceived, and steadily kept in view,—I do not see why a belief in the progress of human Nature towards perfection, should dispose a youthful mind, however enthusiastic, to an undue admiration of his own Age, and thus tend to degrade that mind.

But let me strike at once at the root of the evil complained of in my Correspondent's Letter.—Protection from any fatal effect of seductions, and hindrances which opinion may throw in the way of pure and high-minded Youth, can only be obtained with certainty at the same price by which every thing great and good is obtained, namely, steady dependence upon voluntary and self-originating effort, and upon the practice of self-examination, sincerely aimed at and rigorously enforced. But how is this to be expected from Youth? Is it not to demand the fruit when the blossom is barely put forth, and is hourly at the mercy of frosts and winds? To expect from Youth these virtues and habits, in that degree of excellence to which in mature years they *may* be carried, would indeed be preposterous. Yet has youth many helps and aptitudes, for the discharge of these difficult duties, which are withdrawn for the most part from the more advanced stages of Life. For Youth has its own wealth and independence; it is rich in health of Body and animal Spirits, in its sensibility to the impressions of the natural universe, in the conscious growth of knowledge, in lively sympathy and familiar communion with the generous actions recorded [307] in History, and with the high passions of Poetry; and, above all, Youth is rich in the possession of Time, and the accompanying consciousness of Freedom and Power. The Young Man feels that he stands at a distance from the Season when his harvest is to be reaped,—that he has leisure and may look around—may defer both the choice and the execution of his purposes. If he makes an attempt and shall fail, new hopes immediately rush in, and new promises. Hence, in the happy confidence of his feelings, and in the elasticity of his spirit, neither worldly ambition, nor the love of praise, nor dread of censure, nor the necessity of worldly maintenance, nor any of those causes which tempt or compel the mind habitually to look out of itself for support; neither these, nor the passions of envy, fear, hatred, despondency, and the rankling of disappointed hopes (all which in after life, give birth to, and regulate the efforts of Men, and determine their opinions), have power to preside over the choice of the Young, if the disposition be not naturally bad, or the circumstances have not been in an uncommon degree unfavourable.

In contemplation, then, of this disinterested and free condition of the youthful mind, I deem it in many points peculiarly capable of searching into itself, and of profiting by a few simple questions—such as these that follow. Am I chiefly gratified by the exertion of my power from the pure pleasure of intellectual activity, and from the knowledge thereby acquired? In other words, to what degree do I value my faculties and my attainments for their own sakes? or are they chiefly prized by me on account of the distinction which they confer, or the superiority which they give me over others? Am I aware that immediate influence and a general acknowledgment of merit, are no necessary adjuncts of a successful adherence to study and meditation, in those departments of knowledge which are of most value to mankind? that a recompence of honours and emoluments is far less to be expected—in fact, that there is little natural connection between them? Have I perceived this truth? and, perceiving it, does the countenance of philosophy continue to appear as bright and beautiful in my eyes? —has no haze bedimmed it? has no cloud passed over and hidden from me that look which was before so encouraging? Knowing that it is my duty, and feeling that it is my inclination, to mingle as a social Being with my fellow Men; prepared also to submit cheerfully to [308] the necessity that will probably exist of relinquishing, for the purpose of gaining a livelihood, the greatest portion of my time to employments where I shall have little or no choice how or when I am to act; have I, at this moment, when I stand as it were upon the threshold of the busy world, a clear intuition of that pre-eminence in which virtue and truth (involving in this latter word the sanctities of religion) sit enthroned above all dominations and dignities which, in various degrees of exaltation, rule over the desires of Men?— Do I feel that, if their solemn Mandates shall be forgotten, or disregarded, or denied the obedience due to them when opposed to others, I shall not only have lived for no good purpose, but that I shall have sacrificed my birth-right as a Rational being; and that every other acquisition will be a bane and a disgrace to me? This is not spoken with reference to such sacrifices as present themselves to the Youthful imagination in the shape of crimes, acts by which the conscience is violated; such a thought, I know, would be recoiled from at once, not without indignation; but I write in the spirit of the ancient fable of Prodicus, representing the choice of Hercules.— Here is the WORLD, a female figure approaching at the head of a train of willing or giddy followers:—her air and deportment are at once careless, remiss, self-satisfied, and haughty:—and there is INTELLECTUAL PROWESS, with a pale cheek and serene brow, leading in chains Truth, her beautiful and modest Captive. The One makes her salutation with a discourse of ease, pleasure, freedom, and domestic tranquillity; or, if she invite to labour, it is labour in the busy and beaten track, with assurance of the complacent regards of Parents, Friends, and of those with whom we associate. The promise also may be upon her lip of the huzzas of the multitude, of the smile of Kings, and the munificent rewards of senates. The Other does not venture to hold forth any of these allurements; she does not conceal from him whom she addresses the impediments, the disappointments, the ignorance and prejudice which her follower will have to encounter, if devoted when duty calls, to active life; and if to contemplative, she lays nakedly before him, a scheme of solitary and unremitting labour, a life of entire neglect perhaps, or assuredly a life exposed to scorn, insult, persecution, and hatred; but cheered by encouragement from a grateful few, by applauding conscience, and by a prophetic anticipation, perhaps, of fame—a late, though lasting [309] consequence. Of these two, each in this manner soliciting you to become her adherent, you doubt not which to prefer,—but oh! the thought of moment is not preference, but the *degree* of preference; the passionate and pure choice, the inward sense of absolute and unchangeable devotion.

I spoke of a few simple questions—the question involved in this deliberation *is* simple; but at the same time it is high and awful: and I would

gladly know whether an answer can be returned satisfactory to the mind.—
We will for a moment suppose that it can not; that there is a startling and
a hesitation.—Are we then to despond? to retire from all contest? and to
reconcile ourselves at once to cares without generous hope, and to efforts
in which there is no more Moral life than that which is found in the business and labours of the unfavoured and unaspiring many? No—but, if the
enquiry have not been on just grounds satisfactorily answered, we may
refer confidently our Youth to that Nature of which he deems himself an
enthusiastic follower, and one who wishes to continue no less faithful and
enthusiastic.—We would tell him that there are paths which he has not
trodden; recesses which he has not penetrated, that there is a beauty
which he has not seen, a pathos which he has not felt—a sublimity to
which he hath not been raised. If he have trembled, because there has
occasionally taken place in him a lapse, of which he is conscious; if he
foresee open or secret attacks, which he has had intimations that he will
neither be strong enough to resist, nor watchful enough to elude, let him not
hastily ascribe this weakness, this deficiency, and the painful apprehensions accompanying them, in any degree to the virtues or noble qualities
with which Youth by Nature is furnished; but let him first be assured,
before he looks about for the means of attaining the insight, the discriminating powers, and the confirmed wisdom of Manhood, that his soul has
more to demand of the appropriate excellences of Youth, than Youth has
yet supplied to it;—that the evil under which he labours is not a super-
abundance of the instincts and the animating spirit of that age, but a falling
short, or a failure.—But what can he gain from this admonition? he cannot
recal past time; he cannot begin his journey afresh; he cannot untwist the
links by which, in no undelightful harmony, images and sentiments are
wedded in [310] his mind. Granted that the sacred light of Childhood is
and must be for him no more than a remembrance. He may, notwithstanding, be remanded to Nature; and with trust-worthy hopes; founded
less upon his sentient than upon his intellectual Being—to Nature, not as
leading on insensibly to the society of Reason; but to Reason and Will,
as leading back to the wisdom of Nature. A re-union, in this order accomplished, will bring reformation and timely support; and the two powers of
Reason and Nature, thus reciprocally teacher and taught, may advance
together in a track to which there is no limit.

We have been discoursing (by implication at least) of Infancy, Childhood, Boyhood, and Youth, of pleasures lying upon the unfolding Intellect plenteously as morning dew-drops—of knowledge inhaled insensibly like a fragrance—of dispositions stealing into the Spirit like music
from unknown quarters—of images uncalled for and rising up like ex-
halations—of hopes plucked like beautiful wild flowers from the ruined
tombs that border the high-ways of antiquity, to make a garland for a
living forehead;—in a word, we have been treating of Nature as a Teacher
of Truth through joy and through gladness, and as a Creatress of the faculties by a process of smoothness and delight. We have made no mention of
fear, shame, sorrow, nor of ungovernable and vexing thoughts; because,
although these have been and have done mighty service, they are overlooked in that stage of life when youth is passing into manhood—

overlooked, or forgotten. We now apply for succour which we need, to a faculty that works after a different course: that faculty is Reason: she gives much spontaneously, but she seeks for more; she works by thought, through feeling; yet in thoughts she begins and ends.

A familiar incident may elucidate this contrast in the operations of Nature, may render plain the manner in which a process of intellectual improvements, the reverse of that which Nature pursues is by Reason introduced: There never perhaps existed a School-boy who, having when he retired to rest, carelessly blown out his candle, and having chanced to notice as he lay upon his bed in the ensuing darkness, the sullen light which had survived the extinguished flame, did not, at some time or other, watch that light as if his mind were bound to it by a spell. It fades and revives— gathers to a [311] point—seems as if it would go out in a moment—again recovers it's strength, nay becomes brighter than before: it continues to shine with an endurance, which in its apparent weakness is a mystery— it protracts its existence so long, clinging to the power which supports it, that the Observer, who had laid down in his bed so easy-minded, becomes sad and melancholy: his sympathies are touched—it is to him an intimation and an image of departing human life,—the thought comes nearer to him—it is the life of a venerated Parent, of a beloved Brother or Sister, or of an aged Domestic; who are gone to the grave, or whose destiny it soon may be thus to linger, thus to hang upon the last point of mortal existence, thus finally to depart and be seen no more—This is Nature teaching seriously and sweetly through the affections—melting the heart, and, through that instinct of tenderness, developing the understanding.— In this instance the object of solicitude is the bodily life of another. Let us accompany this same Boy to that period between Youth and Manhood, when a solicitude may be awakened for the moral life of himself.—Are there any powers by which, beginning with a sense of inward decay that affects not however the natural life, he could call up to mind the same image and hang over it with an equal interest as a visible type of his own perishing Spirit?—Oh! surely, if the being of the individual be under his own care—if it be his first care—if duty begin from the point of accountableness to our Conscience, and, through that, to God and human Nature; —if without such primary sense of duty, all secondary care of Teacher, of Friend, or Parent, must be baseless and fruitless; if, lastly, the motions of the Soul transcend in worth those of the animal functions, nay give to them their sole value; then truly are there such powers: and the image of the dying taper may be recalled and contemplated, though with no sadness in the nerves, no disposition to tears, no unconquerable sighs, yet with a melancholy in the soul, a sinking inward into ourselves from thought to thought, a steady remonstrance, and a high resolve.—Let then the Youth go back, as occasion will permit, to Nature and to Solitude, thus admonished by Reason, and relying upon this newly-acquired support. A world of fresh sensations will gradually open upon him as his mind puts off its infirmities, and as instead of being propelled restlessly towards others in admiration, or too hasty love, he makes it his [312] prime business to understand himself. New sensations, I affirm, will be opened out—pure, and sanctioned by that reason which is their original Author; and precious feelings of disinterested, that is self-disregarding joy and love may be regenerated and restored:—and, in this sense, he may be said to measure back the track of life he has trod.

In such disposition of mind let the Youth return to the visible Universe; and to conversation with ancient Books; and to those, if such there be, which in the present day breathe the ancient spirit: and let him feed upon that beauty which unfolds itself, *not* to his eye as it sees carelessly the things which cannot possibly go unseen, and are remembered or not as accident shall decide, but to the thinking mind; which searches, discovers, and treasures up,—infusing by meditation into the objects with which it converses an intellectual life; whereby they remain planted in the memory, now, and for ever. Hitherto the Youth, I suppose, has been content for the most part, to look at his own mind, after the manner in which he ranges along the Stars in the firmament with naked unaided sight: let him now apply the telescope of Art—to call the invisible Stars out of their hiding places; and let him endeavour to look through the system of his being, with the organ of Reason; summoned to penetrate, as far as it has power, in discovery of the impelling forces and the governing laws.

These expectations are not immoderate: they demand nothing more than the perception of a few plain truths; namely, that knowledge efficacious for the production of virtue, is the ultimate end of all effort, the sole dispenser of complacency and repose. A perception also is implied of the inherent superiority of Contemplation to Action. The FRIEND does not in this contradict his own words, where he has said heretofore, that "doubtless it is nobler to Act than to Think." In those words, it was his purpose to censure that barren contemplation, which rests satisfied with itself in cases where the thoughts are of such quality that they may be, and ought to be, embodied in Action. But he speaks now of the general superiority of thought to action;—as preceding and governing all action that moves to salutary purposes: and, secondly, as leading to elevation, the absolute possession of the individual mind, and to a consistency or harmony of the Being within itself, which no outward agency can reach to disturb or to [313] impair:—and lastly as producing works of pure science; or of the combined faculties of imagination, feeling, and reason;—works which, both from their independence in their origin upon accident, their nature, their duration, and the wide spread of their influence, are entitled rightly to take place of the noblest and most beneficent deeds of Heroes, Statesmen, Legislators, or Warriors.

Yet, beginning from the perception of this established superiority, we do not suppose that the Youth, whom we wish to guide and encourage, is to be insensible to those influences of Wealth, or Rank, or Station, by which the bulk of Mankind are swayed. Our eyes have not been fixed upon virtue which lies apart from human Nature, or transcends it. In fact there is no such Virtue. We neither suppose nor wish him to undervalue or slight these distinctions as modes of power, things that may enable him to be more useful to his contemporaries; nor as gratifications that may confer dignity upon his living person; and, through him, upon those who love him; nor as they may connect his name, through a Family to be founded by his success, in a closer chain of gratitude with some portion of posterity, who shall speak of him, as among their Ancestry, with a more tender interest than the mere general bond of patriotism or humanity would supply. We suppose no indifference to, much less a contempt of, these rewards; but let them have their due place; let it be ascertained, when the Soul is searched into, that they are only an auxiliary motive to exertion, never the principal or originating force. If this be too much to expect from a Youth who, I take for granted, possesses no ordinary endowments, and whom circumstances with respect to the more dangerous passions have favoured, then, indeed, must the noble Spirit of the Country be wasted away: then would our Institutions be deplorable; and the Education prevalent among us utterly vile and debasing.

But my Correspondent, who drew forth these thoughts, has said rightly, that the character of the age may not without injustice be thus branded: he will not deny that, without speaking of other Countries, there is in these Islands, in the departments of Natural philosophy, of mechanic ingenuity, in the general activities of the country, and in the particular excellence of individual Minds, in high stations civil or military, enough to excite admiration and love in the sober-minded, and more than enough [314] to intoxicate the Youthful and inexperienced.—I will compare, then, an aspiring Youth, leaving the Schools in which he has been disciplined, and preparing to bear a part in the concerns of the World, I will compare him in this season of eager admiration, to a newly-invested Knight appearing with his blank unsignalized Shield, upon some day of solemn tournament, at the Court, of the Fairy-Queen, as that Sovereignity was conceived to exist by the moral and imaginative genius of our divine Spenser. He does not himself immediately enter the lists as a combatant, but he looks round him with a beating heart; dazzled by the gorgeous pageantry, the banners, the impresses, the Ladies of overcoming beauty, the Persons of the Knights —now first seen by him, the fame of whose actions is carried by the Traveller, like merchandize, through the World; and resounded upon the harp of the Minstrel.—But I am not at liberty to make this comparison. If a Youth were to begin his career in such an Assemblage, with such examples to guide and to animate, it will be pleaded, there would be no cause for apprehension: he could not falter, he could not be misled. But ours, is notwithstanding its manifold excellences, a degenerate Age: and recreant Knights are among us, far outnumbering the true. A false Gloriana in these days imposes worthless services, which they who perform them, in their blindness, know not to be such; and which are recompenced by rewards as worthless—yet eagerly grasped at, as if they were the immortal guerdon of Virtue.

I have in this declaration insensibly overstepped the limits which I had determined not to pass:—let me be forgiven; for it is hope which hath carried me forward. In such a mixed assemblage as our age presents, with its genuine merit and its large overbalance of alloy, I may boldly ask into what errors, either with respect to Person or Thing, could a young Man fall, who had sincerely entered upon the course of moral discipline which has been recommended, and to which the condition of youth, it has been proved, is favourable? His opinions could no where deceive him beyond the point to which, after a season, he would find that it was salutary for him to have been deceived. For, as that Man cannot set a right value upon health who has never known sickness, nor feel the blessing of ease who has been through his life a stranger to pain, so can there be no confirmed and passionate love of [315] truth for him who has not experienced the hollowness of error.—Range against each other as Advocates, oppose as Combatants, two several Intellects, each strenuously asserting doctrines which he sincerely believes; but the one contending for the worth and beauty of that garment which the other has outgrown and cast away. Mark the superiority, the ease, the dignity, on the side of the more advanced Mind, how he overlooks his subject, commands it from centre to circumference, and hath the same thorough knowledge of the tenets which his Adversary, with impetuous zeal, but in confusion also, and thrown off his guard at every turn of the argument, is labouring to maintain! If it be a question of the fine Arts (Poetry for instance) the riper mind not only sees that his opponent is deceived; but, what is of far more importance, sees *how* he is deceived. The imagination stands before him with all its imperfections laid open; as duped by shews, enslaved by words, corrupted by mistaken delicacy and false refinement,—as not having even attended with care to the reports of the senses, and therefore deficient grossly in the rudiments of her own power. He has noted how, as a supposed necessary condition, the Understanding sleeps in order that the Fancy may dream. Studied in the history of Society, and versed in the secret laws of thought, he can pass regularly through all the gradations, can pierce infallibly all the windings, which false taste through ages has pursued—from the very time when first, through inexperience, heedlessness, or affectation, she took her departure from the side of Truth, her original parent.—Can a disputant thus accoutred be withstood?—to whom, further, every movement in the thoughts of his Antagonist is revealed by the light of his own experience; who, therefore, sympathises with weakness gently, and wins his way by forebearance; and hath, when needful, an irresistible power of onset,—arising from gratitude to the truth which he vindicates, not merely as a positive good for Mankind, but as his own especial rescue and redemption.

I might here conclude: but my Correspondent towards the close of his letter, has written so feelingly upon the advantages to be derived, in his estimation, from a living Instructor, that I must not leave this part of the Subject without a word of direct notice. The Friend cited, some time ago, a passage from the prose works of Milton, [316] eloquently describing the manner in which good and evil grow up together in the field of the World almost inseparably; and insisting, consequently, upon the knowledge and survey of vice as necessary to the constituting of human virtue, and the scanning of Error to the confirmation of Truth. If this be so, and I have been reasoning to the same effect in the preceding paragraph, the fact, and the thoughts which it may suggest, will, if rightly applied, tend to moderate an anxiety for the guidance of a more experienced or superior Mind. The advantage, where it is possessed, is far from being an absolute good: nay, such a preceptor, ever at hand, might prove an oppression not to be thrown off, and a fatal hindrance. Grant that in the general tenor of his intercourse with his Pupil he is forbearing and circumspect, inasmuch as he is rich in that knowledge (above all other necessary for a teacher) which cannot exist without a liveliness of memory, preserving for him an unbroken image of the winding, excursive, and often retrograde course, along which his own intellect has passed. Grant that, furnished with these distinct remembrances, he wishes that the mind of his pupil should be free to luxuriate in the enjoyments, loves, and admirations appropriate to its age; that he is not in haste to kill what he knows will in due time die of itself; or be transmuted, and put on a nobler form and higher faculties otherwise unattainable. In a word, that the Teacher is governed habitually by the wisdom of Patience waiting with pleasure. Yet perceiving how much the outward help of Art can facilitate the progress of Nature, he may be betrayed into many unnecessary or pernicious mistakes where he deems his interference warranted by substantial experience. And in spite of all his caution, remarks may drop insensibly from him which shall wither in the mind of his pupil a generous sympathy, destroy a sentiment of approbation or dislike, not merely innocent but salutary; and for the inexperienced Disciple how many pleasures may be thus cut off, what joy, what admiration, and what love! while in their stead are introduced into the ingenuous mind misgivings, a mistrust of its own evidence, dispositions to affect to feel where there can be no real feeling, indecisive judgements, a superstructure of opinions that has no base to support it, and words uttered by rote with the impertinence of a Parrot or a Mocking-bird, yet which may not be listened to with the same indifference, as [317] they cannot be heard without some feeling of moral disapprobation.

These results, I contend, whatever may be the benefit to be derived from such an enlightened Teacher, are in their degree inevitable. And by this process, humility and docile dispositions may exist towards the Master, endued as he is with the power which personal presence confers; but at the same time they will be liable to over-step their due bounds, and to degenerate into passiveness and prostration of mind. This towards him! while, with respect to other living Men, nay even to the mighty Spirits of past times, there may be associated with such weakness a want of modesty and humility. Insensibly may steal in presumption and a habit of sitting in judgement in cases where on sentiment ought to have existed but diffidence or veneration. Such virtues are the sacred attributes of Youth; its appropriate calling is not to distinguish in the fear of being deceived or degraded, not to analyze with scrupulous minuteness, but to accumulate in genial confidence; its instinct, its safety, its benefit, its glory, is to love, to admire, to feel, and to labour. Nature has irrevocably decreed, that our prime dependance in all stages of life after Infancy and Childhood have been passed through (nor do I know that this latter ought to be excepted) must be upon our own minds; and that the way to knowledge shall be long, difficult, winding, and often times returning upon itself.

What has been said is a mere sketch; and that only of a part of the interesting Country into which we have been led: but my Correspondent will be able to enter the paths that have been pointed out. Should he do this and advance steadily for a while, he needs not fear any deviations from the truth which will be finally injurious to him. He will not long have his admiration fixed upon unworthy objects; he will neither be clogged nor drawn aside by the love of friends or kindred, betraying his understanding through his affections; he will neither be bowed down by conventional arrangements of manners producing too often a lifeless decency: nor will the rock of his Spirit wear away in the endless beating of the waves of the World: neither will that portion of his own time, which he must surrender to labours by which his livelihood is to be earned or his social duties performed, be unprofitable to himself indirectly, while it is directly useful to others: for that [318] time has been primarily surrendered through an act of obedience to a moral law established by himself, and therefore he moves then also along the orbit of perfect liberty.

Let it be remembered, that the advice requested does not relate to the government of the more dangerous passions, or to the fundamental principles of right and wrong as acknowledged by the universal Conscience of Mankind. I may therefore assure my Youthful Correspondent, if he will endeavour to look into himself in the manner which I have exhorted him to do, that in him the wish will be realized, to him in due time the prayer granted, which was uttered by that living Teacher of whom he speaks with gratitude as of a Benefactor, when, in his character of philosophical Poet, having thought of Morality as implying in its essence voluntary obedience, and producing the effect of order, he transfers in the transport of imagination, the law of moral to physical natures, and, having contemplated, through the medium of that order, all modes of existence as subservient to one spirit, concludes his address to the power of Duty in the following words:

> To humbler functions, awful Power!
> I call thee; I myself commend
> Unto thy guidance from this hour;
> Oh, let my weakness have an end!
> Give unto me, made lowly wise,
> The spirit of self-sacrifice;
> *The confidence of reason give;*
> *And in the light of truth thy Bondman let me live!*

M. M.[1]

[319]   EPITAPH

FROM THE ITALIAN OF CHIABRERA[2]

> NOT without heavy grief of heart did He,
> On whom the duty fell, (for at that time
> The Father sojourned in a distant Land)
> Deposit in the hollow of this Tomb
> A Brother's Child, most tenderly beloved!
> FRANCESCO was the name the Youth had borne
> POTZZOBONNELLI his illustrious House;
> And when beneath this stone the Corse was laid
> The eyes of all Savona stream'd with tears.

[1] See above, I 405 n 2.
[2] See *Epitaphs Translated from Chiabrera* VIII: *WPW* IV 252–3; Chiabrera *Opere* II 182–3 (*Epitaffi* IX on Francesco Pozzobonello).

Alas! the twentieth April of his life
Had scarcely flowered: and, at this early time,
By genuine virtue he inspired a hope
That greatly cheared his country; to his kin
He promis'd comfort; and the flattering thoughts
His Friends had in their fondness entertained,
He suffer'd not to languish or decay.
Now is there not good reason to break forth
Into a passionate lament?—O Soul!
Short while a Pilgrim in our nether world,
Do thou enjoy the calm empyreal air,
And round this earthly tomb let roses rise,
An everlasting spring! in memory
Of that delightful fragrance which was once
From thy mild manners quietly exhaled.

[320]   EPITAPH

                FROM THE ITALIAN OF CHIABRERA[1]

PAUSE, courteous Spirit!—Balbi supplicates
That Thou, with no reluctant voice, for him
Here laid in mortal darkness, wouldst prefer
A prayer to the Redeemer of the world.
This to the dead by sacred right belongs,
All else is nothing.—Did occasion suit
To tell his worth, the marble of this tomb
Would ill suffice: for Plato's love sublime
And all the wisdom of the Stagyrite
Enriched and beautified his studious mind;
With Archimedes also he conversed
As with a chosen Friend; nor did he leave
Those laureat wreathes ungathered which the Nymphs
Twine on the top of Pindus.—Finally,
Himself above each lower thought uplifting,
His ears he clos'd to listen to the Song
Which Sion's Kings did consecrate of old,
And fixed his Pindus upon Lebanon.
A blessed Man! who of protracted days
Made not, as thousands do, a vulgar sleep,
But truly did he live his life. Urbino
Take pride in him.—O Passenger farwell!

---

[1] See *Epitaphs* IX: *WPW* IV 253 (var); Chiabrera II 192–3 (*Epitaffi* XXVII on Bernardino Baldi). In the ms of *The Friend* the correct "Baldi" was altered to "Balbi".

THE FRIEND

THURSDAY, January 11, 1810

The Friend regards the following as a supernumerary Essay, and has there-fore dated but not numbered it. As nearly one half relates to the circum-stances of the Publication, he leaves it wholly to the Discretion of those who receive it, to pay the usual price or not—for the names of those, who may have given orders for the discontinuance of the work, after the 20th number, have not yet been received, with very few exceptions.[1]

IRUS

IRUS, the forlorn Irus, whose nourishment consisted in bread and water, whose cloathing of one tattered mantle, and whose bed of an arm-full of straw, this same Irus, by a rapid transition of fortune, became the most prosperous mortal under the sun. It pleased the Gods to snatch him at once out of the dust, and to place him by the side of Princes. He beheld himself in the possession of incalculable treasures. His palace excelled even the temple of the Gods in the pomp of it's ornaments; his least sumptuous cloathing was of purple and gold, and his table might well have been named the compendium of Luxury, the summary of all that the voluptuous ingenuity of men had invented for the gratification of the palate. A numerous train of admiring Dependents followed him at every step; those to whom he vouchsafed a gracious look, were esteemed already in the high road of fortune, and the favoured individual who was permitted to kiss his hand, appeared to be the object of common envy. The name of Irus sounding in his ears an unwelcome memento and perpetual reproach of his former poverty, he for this reason named himself Ceraunius, or the Lightening-flasher, and the whole people celebrated this splendid change of title by public rejoicings. The Poet, who a few years ago had [322] personified poverty itself under his former name of Irus, now made a discovery which had till that moment remained a profound secret, but was now received by all with implicit faith and warmest approbation. Jupiter, forsooth, had become enamoured of the Mother of Ceraunius, and assumed the form of a mortal in order to enjoy her love. Hence-forward, they erected altars to him, they swore by his name, and the Priests discovered in the entrails of the sacrificial victim, that THE GREAT CERAUNIUS, this worthy son of Jupiter, was the sole Pillar of the Western World. Toxaris, his former neighbour, a man whom good fortune, un-wearied industry, and rational frugality, had placed among the richest

[1] See above, Introduction, I lxix-lxx.

271

citizens, became the first victim of the pride of this new demi-god. In the time of his poverty *Irus* had repined at his luck and prosperity, and irritable from distress and envy, had conceived that Toxaris had looked contemptuously at him; and now was the time that *Ceraunius* would make him feel the power of him, whose father grasped the Thunder-bolt. Three Advocates, newly admitted into the recently established Order of the Cygnet, gave evidence, that Toxaris had denied the Gods, committed peculations on the sacred Treasury, and encreased his treasures by acts of sacrilege. He was hurried off to Prison and sentenced to an ignominious death, and his wealth confiscated to the use of Ceraunius, the earthly Representative of the Deities. Ceraunius now found nothing wanting to his felicity but a Bride worthy of his rank and blooming honours. The most illustrious of the Land were Candidates for his alliance. Euphorbia, the daughter of the noble Saxones, was honoured with his final choice. To nobility of birth nature had added for Euphorbia a rich dowry of beauty, a nobleness both of look and stature. The flowing ringlets of her hair, her lofty forehead, her brilliant eyes, her stately figure, her majestic gait, had enchanted the haughty Ceraunius: and all the Bards told what the inspiring Muses had revealed to them, that Venus more than once had pined with jealousy at the sight of her superior charms. The day of the espousal arrived, and the illustrious Son of Jove was proceeding in pomp to the Temple, when the anguish-stricken wife of Toxaris, with his innocent children, suddenly threw themselves at his feet, and with loud lamentations entreated him to spare the Life of her husband. Enraged by this interruption, [323] Ceraunius spurned her from him with his feet and—Irus awaked, and found himself lying on the same straw on which he had lain down, and with his old tattered mantle spread over him. With his returning Reason, Conscience too returned. He praised the Gods and resigned himself to his lot. Ceraunius indeed had vanished, but the innocent Toxaris was still alive, and Irus poor yet guiltless.

Can my Reader recollect no character now on Earth, who sometime or other will awake from his Dream of Life, poor as Irus, with all the guilt and impiety of Ceraunius?

> *Ante quod est in me, postque* ————————
> *Omnis habet geminas hinc atque hinc Janua frontes,*
> *Equibus* Hæc *Populum spectat,* illa *Larem:*
> *Utque sedens primi vester prope limina tecti*
> *Janitor, egressus introitusque videt,*
> *Sic Ego* ————
>
> Ovid: Fastor: Lib. 1* [1]

---

* *Interpretation.* What is before in me, and behind—Every House-door has two Fronts, the one of which looks to the People in the Road or Street, the other to the family at Home: and as the Porter sitting near the threshold within the Porch, beholds the goings-out and comings-in, (or the exits and the entrances) thus now do I—.

[1] *Fasti* 1.114, 135–9 (var).

TO MY SUBSCRIBERS;
AND TO THE READERS OF THE FRIEND IN GENERAL[1]

I have always looked forward to the present Number of THE FRIEND, as its first proper starting-post;[2] for the twenty Numbers preceding I regarded as a preparatory heat, in order to determine whether or no I should be admitted, as a Candidate, on that longer course, on which alone the speed and strength of the Racer can be fairly proved. But dropping the metaphor, and with it all desire to give dignity to a Subject, which ought to rest wholly on it's propriety and necessity, as I am speaking of the *Publication* rather than of the work, so let me speak as the Publisher rather than as the Author. By the exertions of my private acquaintances, aided by the small degree of public interest which attached to my character from my juvenile poems, and still more perhaps from the [324] favourable reception of my Lectures at the Royal Institution,[3] a sufficient number of Names were procured to permit me to make the *experiment*, which it would not only have been imprudent, but absolutely out of my power to have tried at my own risk: which risk however I have found far less guarded against, than from my estrangement from business, and the habits of business, I had been able to anticipate. Intreating the patience of the Reader solely on the ground of his doing by others as he would himself be done by, I will endeavour to make myself fully intelligible; and explain first the nature of the risk, and next my reasons for calling my work an *Experiment*. It is indeed a matter of blank necessity, that I should do so, if THE FRIEND is to proceed at all with his weekly efforts in the present or any similar form.

I was not so ignorant of mankind as to expect that my Essays would be found interesting in the hurry and struggle of active Life. All the passions, which are there at work, it was my object to preclude: and I distinctly foresaw, that by rejecting all appeals to personal passions, and party spirit, and all interest grounded wholly on the cravings of curiosity, and the love of novelty for it's own sake, I at the same time precluded three-fourths of the ordinary readers of periodical publications, whether Reviews, Magazines, or Newspapers. I might however find dispersedly what I could not hope to meet with collectively. I thought it not improbable, that there might be individuals scattered throughout the kingdom, to whom the very absence of such stimilants would prove a recommendation to the work, and that when the existence of such a work was generally known, a sufficient number of persons able and willing to patronize it might gradually be collected—sufficient, I mean, first to render it *possible* for the Author so to employ his time and powers, and secondly, to repay the expences of the publication. On this account, and on this only, the Friend was printed on stamped paper, that it might thus go free by the General Post to all parts of the Kingdom, even where there was no communication with London by means of the Booksellers, or a very infrequent one. Could

---

[1] See above, Introduction, I lxix–lxx.
[2] When revising the material for the 1818 *Friend* C did in fact use part of this number (pp 327–30; below, II 276–8)

for an early essay, Essay II of vol I. See also below, App C, II 386 (ff 91–2ᵛ), for a passage deleted from the ms.
[3] See above, II 18 n 2.

this have been done uniformly, it would have been neither a Loss or a Gain to the Author as the Proprietor of the work, as the price of the stamp was no more than the deduction of 30 per cent. made by the Booksellers from the sale-price of every publication that passes through [325] their hands. But as I had to advance the money both for the Paper* and for the Stamps, for at least the first four and twenty numbers, and as the arrival of them from London cannot be calculated upon within less than six weeks, as I have learnt by sad† experience, I ought to have made it a condition that a notice of six weeks must be given of the intention to discontinue the work—a notice less by half the time than what is required by all the Publishers of Newspapers, even in London, where the Stamps can be procured daily, and no necessity exists of a large stock of stamped paper on hand. But this I neglected from unwise delicacy, an habitual turning away from all thoughts relating to money, and from a self-flattering persuasion, that those who after the perusal of my prospectus had determined on giving the work a trial, would be sensible of the difficulties it had to struggle with, and whether satisfied or not with it's style of execution, yet for the earnest wish of THE FRIEND, not only to please them but to please them in such a way as might leave them permanently better pleased with themselves, would be disposed rather to lessen than increase them. If therefore THE FRIEND is permitted to proceed, it must be understood, that for the next twenty numbers a notice of six weeks will be expected from those who wish to discontinue the publication. At the same time I must intreat those who may have sent orders for its discontinuance, with their payment of the Subscription for the numbers preceding, not to be surprized or offended by the receipt of the present number: for neither I nor the Printer have, or possibly can have received their order.

From the same unacquaintedness with business and delusory hopes, I had suggested to the Subscribers, that by desiring their acquaintance in London—not by an especial Letter, but in the course of their other correspondence, to pay in the £1 at Mr. G. WARD'S instead of inclosing the note in a letter, they would without any loss to themselves very considerably lessen my expences.¹ The Blame be upon myself! But I certainly had not anticipated, [326] that this suggestion would have occasioned such a number of letters (and those not post-paid) desiring my friend to call on persons, each residing in some different part of the eight square miles occupied by the metropolis and it's suburbs: for this so far from diminishing any expence, must be double to that of receiving the £1 note by the post—which letter would detract ten per cent from the whole sum payed. I am not surprized, that my respected Friend has declined so troublesome a commission: greatly as so unexpected a circumstance has embarrassed

---

* The paper, of which I am sorry to hear so many, I fear, just complaints, costs me 52s. 6d. a ream, exclusive of the carriage from London to Penrith—the stamp three-pence halfpenny for each sheet—add the expences of the printing, &c.

† According to the *professions* of the persons concerned, goods delivered to the Waggon-office, in London, ought to arrive at Penrith on the 10th day; but the truth is, as I have stated it.

¹ See the "Advertisement" at the end of No 16 (above, II 221).

me.[1] I can only at present request those who have not paid their Subscriptions, to pay it to the Post-master of the place, at or near which they reside, with instructions to forward it to the Post-master at Kendal: when the receipt which they receive from the Post-master, will be a receipt for the Friend.

One other observation, and I quit for ever a subject which cannot be so tiresome to the Reader, as it is painful and hateful to the Writer. This is, that I must request again, and more earnestly, that all Letters whatsoever, addressed either to Mr. Brown, at Penrith, or to myself at Grasmere, should be post-paid: indeed, by the united consequences of folly and malignity, I have no other resource left, during the publication of the Friend, than to return all not post-paid, unopened; and no Letters will find me, that are not addressed either to Mr. Brown, if they contain orders, or to myself if they contain communications or suggestions. My private friends will be informed of this regulation, and will see, that living as I do, five miles from the place where the Letters are left, and nineteen miles from the Post-office at Kendal, and receiving my letters too by different hands, and neighbourly good offices, it is altogether out of my power to draw any intelligible line of distinction; and that considering the painful accidents that may take place in consequence of this regulation, no motive short of blank compulsion would have led me to adopt it. Among other things of the kind, a person signing himself "Carlyol" has addressed a threatening and abusive letter to me from Dover. I shall not tell him, that such an act was ungentlemanly, unmanly, and unchristian, for this would be to him the same "learned non*sence* and unintelligible Jar*gin*," for which he abuses me; but some other points I may venture to press on his attention. First, that it was a lack of common honesty [327] in him to write a letter with a fictitious signature, and not pay the postage: secondly, that it was injudicious to address the letter to me, as the Editor of the Courier is alone responsible for the appearance of the passages which have offended him, and the other admirers of Buonaparte, in that paper:[2] thirdly, that there is one branch of learning, without which Learning itself cannot be railed at with common decency, namely, *Spelling*: and lastly, that unintelligibility is a very equivocal charge. It certainly may arise from the author, especially if he should chance to be deficient in that branch of Erudition, last-mentioned; but it may likewise, and often does, arise from the Reader, and this from more than one cause. He may have an ideotic understanding, and what is far more common, as well as incomparably more lamentable,—he may have an *ideotic heart!* To this last cause must we attribute the commission of such crimes, as provoke the vengeance of the Law, by men who cannot but have heard from the Pulpit truths and warnings, which, though evident to their *understandings*, were, unhappily

[1] See C's letter to Ward c early Jan 1810: *CL* iii 267–70.

[2] See "Letters on the Spaniards" i *Courier* (7 Dec 1809): *EOT* ii 593, where C thanks the editor for printing an extract from *The Friend*. SC is mistaken (in her note to this passage, *EOT* iii 1024–5) in dating the appearance of this extract 25 Nov 1811; it was 25 Nov 1809. Two other passages on Napoleon, from *The Friend*, were published in the *Courier* 12 Sept and 13 Nov 1809 (information from D. V. Erdman).

for them, religious non*sence* and unintelligible Jar*gin* to their bad *hearts*. And I feel it my duty to press on my Correspondent's reflection, the undoubted fact, that a man may be quite fool enough to be a rogue, and yet not *appear* fool enough to save him from the legal consequences of his roguery.

A few words will explain my reason for having called the present undertaking an experiment. From periodical Literature the general Reader deems himself entitled to expect amusement, and some degree of information, and if the Writer can convey any instruction at the same time and without demanding any additional thought (as the Irishman, in the hackneyed jest, is said to have passed off a light Guinea between two good Halfpence) this supererogatory merit will not perhaps be taken amiss. Now amusement in and for itself may be afforded by the gratification either of the Curiosity or of the Passions. I use the former word as distinguished from the love of knowledge, and the latter in distinction from those emotions which arise in well-ordered minds, from the perception of Truth or Falsehood, Virtue or Vice, and which are always preceded by Thought, and linked with it. Again, all information sought for without any wish of becoming wiser or better thereby, I class among the gratifications of mere Curiosity, whether it be sought for in a light Novel [328] or a grave History: we may therefore omit the word information, as included either in amusement or instruction. Now my experiment regarded not the two elements themselves, which serious Readers at least persuade themselves, they pursue, but a change of the usual *order*, in which periodical Writers have in general attempted to convey them. Having myself experienced that no delight either in kind or degree, was equal to that which accompanies the distinct perception of a fundamental Truth, relative to our moral Being; having, long after the completion of what is ordinarily called a learned Education, discovered a new World of intellectual profit opening on me—not from any new opinions, but lying, as it were, at the roots of those which I had been taught in Childhood in my Catechism and Spelling-book; there arose a soothing hope in my mind that a lesser Public might be found, composed of Persons susceptible of the same Delight, and desirous of attaining it by the same process, rendered as much easier to them, than it had been to me, as the united efforts of my understanding and imagination were able to render it. In short, I wished to convey not instruction merely, but fundamental instruction; not so much to shew my Reader this or that Fact, as to kindle his own Torch for him, and leave it to himself to chuse the particular Objects, which he might wish to examine by it's light. THE FRIEND did not indeed exclude from his Plan occasional interludes, and vacations of innocent entertainment and promiscuous information, but still in the main to propose to himself the communication of such delight, as rewards the march of Truth, rather than to collect the flowers which diversify it's track, and present them apart from the homely yet foodful or medicinable herbs, among which they had grown. To refer men's opinions to their absolute Principles, and thence their Feelings to the appropriate Objects, and in their due degrees; and finally, to apply the Principles thus ascertained, first to subjects of Taste or the fine Arts; then to the schemes of private and national Education; and last of all, to the particular Duties, Joys, and Afflictions of private Life—these were to be the Objects and the Contents of his Work. Themes like these not even the genius of a Plato or a Bacon could render intelligible, without demanding from the Reader, THOUGHT sometimes, and ATTENTION generally. By THOUGHT I here mean the voluntary production [329] in our own minds of those states of consciousness, to which, as to his fundamental facts, the Writer has referred us: while ATTENTION has for it's object the order and connection of Thoughts and Images, each of which is in itself already and familiarly known. Thus the elements of Geometry require Attention only; but the analysis of our primary Faculties, and the investigation of all the absolute grounds of Religion and Morals, are impossible without energies of Thought in addition to the effort of Attention. THE FRIEND never attempted to disguise from his Readers that both Attention and Thought were Efforts, and the latter a most difficult and laborious Effort; (see Nos. 3. and 4. P. 46. 51.)[1] nor from himself, that to require it often or for any continuance of time was incompatible with the nature of a periodical Publication, even were it less incongruous than it unfortunately is with the present habits and pursuits of Englishmen. Accordingly after a careful re-perusal of the preceding Numbers, I can discover but four passages which supposed in the Reader any energy of thought and voluntary abstraction, and of these four two should have been (and in the re-printed Numbers will be) placed in the Notes, to be read or passed over ad libitum.[2] But Attention, I confess, two thirds of the Work hitherto have required. On whatever subject the mind feels a lively interest, attention, though always an effort, becomes a delightful effort, and I should be quite at ease could I secure for the whole Work as much of it, as a Card Party of earnest Whist-Players often expend in a single Evening, or a Lady in the making up of a fashionable Dress. But where no interest previously exists, attention (as every School-master knows) can be procured only by Terror: which is the true reason, why the majority of mankind learn nothing systematically, except as School-boys or Apprentices. Here then was the *experiment:* whether throughout the Kingdom the Author could procure four or five Hundred Readers, who were desirous to derive pleasure from the consciousness of being instructed or ameliorated, and who felt a sufficient *interest* as to the foundations of their own Opinions in Literature, Politics, Morals, and Religion, to afford that degree of Attention, without which, however men may deceive themselves, no actual progress ever was or ever can be made in that knowledge, which supplies at once strength and nourishment.

[330] During the composition of this last Paragraph I have been aware that I shall appear to have been talking arrogantly and with an unwarrantable assumption of superiority, but a moment's reflection will enable my Reader to acquit me of this charge, as far as it is, or ought to be a charge. He will recollect, that I have been giving the History of my own mind, and that if it had been my duty to believe, that the main obstacle to the success

---

of my undertaking existed not in the minds of others, but in my own insufficiency and inferiority, I ought not to have undertaken it at all. To a sincere and sensible mind, it cannot but be disgusting to find an Author writing on Subjects, to the investigation of which he professes to have devoted the greater portion of his Life, and yet appealing to all his Readers promiscuously, as his full and competent judges, and thus soliciting their favour by a mock modesty, which either convicts him of gross hypocrisy or the most absurd presumption. For what can be conceived at once more absurd and presumptuous, than for a man to write and publish Books for the instruction of those who are wiser than himself, more learned, and more judicious! Humility like all other virtues, must exist in Harmony with Truth. My heart bears me witness, that I would gladly give up all the pleasures which I can ever derive from literary Reputation, could I receive instead of them a deep conviction, that THE FRIEND has failed in pleasing no one, whose own superiority had not rendered the Essays tiresome because superfluous. And why should that be deemed a mark of self-sufficiency in an Author, which would be thought only common sense in a Musician or a Painter, namely, the supposition that he understands and can practice those arts, to which he has devoted his best faculties during life, in consequence of a particular predilection for them, better than the mass of mankind, who have given their time and thoughts to other pursuits? There is one species of presumption among Authors which is truly hateful, and which betrays itself when Writers who in their Prefaces have prostrated themselves before the superiority of their Readers, as supreme Judges, will yet in their works pass judgements on Plato, Milton, Shakespeare, Spenser, and their Compeers, in blank assertions and a peremptory ipse-dixi, and with a grossness of censure, which a sensible School-master would not apply to the exercises of the youths in [331] his upper forms. I *need* no outward remembrances of my own inferiority, but I possess them on almost every shelf of my Library; and the very book, which I am now using as my writing-desk (Lord Bacon's Novum Organon)[1] inspires an awe and heart-felt humility, which I would not exchange for all the delight which Napoleon can enjoy at the moment that his crowned Courtiers hail him Emperor of Emperors and Lord Paramount of the West!

As the week, which is to decide on the continuance of THE FRIEND, coincides with the commencement of the New Year, the present address has not inappropriately taken its character from the *two-faced* God, to whom the first month is indebted for its name: it being in part retrospective and in part prospective. Among the various reasons, which Ovid in the passage from which I have taken my motto, has made Janus himself assign for his *bi-front* appearance, he has omitted the most obvious intention of the Emblem, that of instructing his Worshippers to commence the new Year with a religious as well as prudential review of their own conduct and its consequences, during the past year: and thus to look onward to the year before them with wiser plans, and with strengthened or amended resolutions. I will apply this to my own conduct as far as it concerns the present Publication, and having already sufficiently informed the Reader

---

[1] C was using the first volume of the folio edition in 4 vols, *Works* (1740); see above, I 10 n 3, 482-3 and nn.

of the general idea, which I had proposed to myself, I will now with the same simplicity communicate my own calm judgement on the manner in which that idea has been so far realized, and the outline filled up. My first Number bears the marks of the effort and anxiety with which it was written, and is composed less happily than I could wish. It assuredly had not the cheerful and winning aspect, which a door-keeper presenting the bill of Fare ought to possess. Its' object, however was so far answered, as it announced distinctly the fundamental position or grand *postulate* on which the whole Superstructure, with all its supporting beams and pillars, was to rest. I call it a Postulate, not only because I deferred the Proofs but because, strictly speaking, it was not susceptible of any proof from without. The sole possible question was—Is it, or is it not, a Fact? and for the answer every human Being must be referred to his own Consciousness. This Postulate is the fact of *Free-agency;* thence of a moral *responsibility*; and thence the existence of *Evil;* of Evil essentially such, not by accident of outward circumstances, not derived from it's [332] physical consequences, or from any cause, out of itself. *Omnia exeunt in mysterium,*[1] says a Schoolman: i.e. *There is nothing, the absolute ground of which is not a Mystery.* The contrary were indeed a contradiction in terms: for how can that, which is to explain all things, be susceptible of an explanation? It would be to suppose the same thing first and second at the same time. Had I rested here, I should merely have placed my Creed in direct opposition to that of the Necessitarians, who assume (for observe *both* Parties begin in an *Assumption*, and cannot do otherwise) that motives act on the Will, as bodies act on bodies; and that whether mind and matter are essentially the same or essentially different, they are both alike under one and the same Law of compulsory Causation. But this was far from exhausting my intention. I meant at the same time to oppose the Disciples of SHAFTESBURY, and those who have been well called the pious Deists of the last Century,[2] who substituted one Faith for another, in order to distinguish them from the Infidels of the present age, who *persuade* themselves, (for the thing itself is not possible) that they reject all Faith. I declared my dissent from these too, because they imposed upon themselves an *Idea* for a Reality: a most sublime Idea indeed, and so necessary to human Nature, that without it no Virtue is conceivable, but still an Idea! In contradiction to their splendid but delusory Tenets, I professed a deep conviction that Man was a *fallen* Creature, not by accidents of bodily constitution, or any other cause, which *human* Wisdom in a course of ages might be supposed capable of removing; but diseased in his *Will*, in that Will which is the true and only strict synonime of the word, I, or the intelligent Self. Thus at each of these two opposite Roads (the Philosophy of Hobbes and that of Shaftesbury, so *call* them, not that Hobbes or Shaftesbury were the original Authors of the opinions) I had placed a directing

---

[1] Source untraced. This passage (including the following paragraph to ". . . ameliorating both ourselves and others") was used with a few changes in *AR* (1825) 135–9 (Preliminary Aphorisms on Spiritual Religion).

[2] Such writers as Anthony Collins (see above, I 426 n 3), Thomas Woolston (1670–1733), Thomas Chubb (1679–1747), John Toland (1670–1722), and Matthew Tindal (c 1653–1733).

Post, informing my Fellow-travellers, that on neither of these Roads could they see the Truths to which I was to direct their attention. But the place of starting was at the meeting of *four* Roads, and one only was the right road. I proceeded therefore to preclude the opinion of those likewise, who indeed agreed with me as to the moral Responsibility of Man in opposition to Hobbes and the Anti-Moralists, and that He was a fallen Creature, essentially diseased, in opposition to Shaftesbury and the Misinterpreters of Plato; but who differ from me [333] in exaggerating the diseased *weakness* of the Will into an absolute privation of all Freedom, thereby making moral responsibility, not a mystery *above* comprehension, but a direct contradiction, of which we do distinctly comprehend the absurdity. Among the many dreadful consequences of this Doctrine (which, as Extremes meet[1] yet preserve their separate identity, is the same notion, intellectually considered, as that of Hobbes, but embraced under the influence of very different feelings) among the consequences of this Doctrine, is that direful one of swallowing up all the Attributes of the supreme Being in the one Attribute of infinite Power, and thence deducing that Things are good and wise because they were created, and not created through Wisdom and Goodness. Thence too the awful Attribute of *Justice* is explained away into a mere right of absolute *Property;* the sacred distinction between Things and Persons is erased; and the selection of Persons for Virtue and Vice in this Life, and for eternal Happiness or Misery in the next, is represented as the result of a mere *Will,* acting in the blindness and solitude of it's own Infinity. The Title of a Work written by the great and pious Boyle is "Of the Awe, which the human Mind owes to the supreme Reason." [2] This, in the language of these gloomy Doctors, must be translated into— "the horror, which a Being capable of eternal Pleasure or Pain, is compelled to feel from the idea of an infinite Power, about to inflict the latter on an immense majority of human Souls, without any power on their part either to prevent it or the actions which are (not indeed it's causes but) it's assigned *signals,* and preceding links of the same iron chain!"

Against these Tenets I maintained, that a Will conceived separate from Intelligence is a Non-entity, and a mere Phantasm of Abstraction; and that a Will not *free* is an absolute contradiction. It might be an Instinct, an Impulse, a plastic Power, and, if accompanied with consciousness, a desire; but a Will it *could* not be; and this *every* Human Being *knows* with equal *clearness,* though different minds may *reflect* on it with different degrees of *distinctness;* for who would not smile at the notion of a Rose *willing* to put forth it's Buds and expand them into Flowers? That such a phrase would be deemed a *poetic* Licence proves the difference in the things: for all metaphors are grounded on an apparent likeness of things essentially different. I concluded therefore, and on this Conclusion rested the whole [334] rationality of the Work which I had undertaken, that the human Will, though diseased, is yet free, and being at the same time an Intelligence, must be capable of being acted upon by different forms of Intelligence; that the opposite assertion contradicts the whole Tenor of the

---

[1] See above, i 110 and n 5.
[2] Robert Boyle *Of the High Veneration Man's Intellect Owes to God; Peculiarly for His Wisdom and Power* (1685).

Gospel, which informs us, not simply that Christ brought Immortality into the World, but LIGHT and Immortality; and by a mystery awfully significant, attributes in the divine Economy the *origination* and *peculiar* office of Redemption to the WORD, or *intelligential* Wisdom, which from all Eternity is with God and is God. I utterly disclaimed the idea, that any *human* Intelligence, with whatever power it might manifest itself, was *alone* adequate to the office of restoring health to the Will: but at the same time I held it impious and absurd to hold, that the Creator would have *given* us the faculty of Reason, or that the Redeemer would in so many varied forms of Argument and Persuasion have *appealed* to it, if it had been either totally useless or wholly impotent, and I saw that these Truths were only to be reconciled by the position, that the imperfect human understanding could be exerted effectually only in *subordination* to, and a dependent *alliance* with, the means and aidances supplied by the all-perfect and supreme Reason; but that under these conditions it was not only an admissible, but a necessary, instrument of ameliorating both ourselves and others.[1] The final deduction was easy. If Man be a free Agent, his Good and Evil must not be judged of according to the nature of his *outward* Actions, or the mere *legality* of his Conduct; but by the final Motive and Intention of the Mind. Now the final Motive of an intelligent Will is a *Principle*: and consequently to refer the opinions of Men to Principles (that is, to absolute and necessary instead of secondary and contingent, grounds) is the best and only secure way of referring the Feelings of Men to their proper objects. In the union of both consists the Perfection of the human Character.

The same subject was illustrated in my second Essay, and reasons assigned from the peculiar circumstances of the Age, and the present state of the Minds of Men, for giving *this* particular direction to the serious Studies of Men, instead of the more easy and attractive mode of Instruction adapted by my Illustrious Predecessors in periodical Literature. At the same time being conscious, how many Authorities of recent, but for that reason more influencive, reputation, I must of necessity contravene in the support and application of my Principles, both in Criticism and Philosophy, I thought it requisite to state the true nature of PRESUMPTION and ARROGANCE, and thus, if it were possible, preclude the charge in cases where I had not committed the Offence. (In this Essay I had made a confusion between Arrogance and Presumption,[2] which is corrected in the re-printed Copies.) The object of the four next Numbers was to demonstrate the *innoxiousness* of Truth, if only the conditions were preserved which the Reason and Conscience dictated; to shew at large *what* those conditions were which ought to regulate the conduct of the Individual, in the communication of Truth; and by what Principles the civil Law ought to be governed [335] in the Punishment of Libels. Throughout the whole of these Numbers, and more especially in the two latter, I again and again recalled the attention of the Reader, to the paramount importance of PRINCIPLES, alike for their moral and their intellectual, for their private and their national Consequences; the importance, I say, of Prin-

[1] See above, I 96.

[2] See above, II 32-6 and nn, and Introduction, I lxxxix.

ciples of Reason, as distinct from, and paramount to, the maxims of Prudence, even for Prudence sake! Some of my Readers will probably have seen this subject supported by other and additional arguments in my seventh Letter, "on the Grounds of Hope for a People warring against Armies," published during the last month, in the Courier.[1] In the mean time I was aware, that in *thus* grounding my opinions in Literature, Morals, and Religion, I should frequently use the same or similar Language as had been applied by Rousseau, the French physiocratic Philosophers, and their Followers in England, to the nature and rightful origin of civil Government. The remainder of my Work therefore, hitherto has been devoted to the purpose of averting this mistake, as far as I have not been compelled by the general Taste of my Readers to interrupt the systematic progress of the Plan by Essays of a lighter kind, or which at least required a less effort of Attention. In Truth, since my twelfth Number I have not had courage to renew any Subject which *did* require Attention. The way to be admired is to tell the Reader what he knew before, but cloathed in a statelier phraseology, and embodied in apt and lively illustrations. To attempt to make a Man wiser is of necessity to remind him of his ignorance: and in the majority of instances, the pain actually felt is so much greater than the pleasure anticipated, that it is natural that men should attempt to shelter themselves from it by contempt or neglect. For a living Writer is yet sub judice: and if we cannot follow his conceptions or enter into his feelings, it is more consoling to our Pride, as well as more agreeable to our indolence, to consider him as lost beneath, than as soaring out of our sight above us. Itaque id agitur, ut ignorantia etiam ab ignominiâ liberetur.[2] Happy is that Man, who can truly say, with Giordano Bruno, and whose circumstances at the same time permit him to *act* on the sublime feeling—

> "Procedat nudus, quem non ornant Nubilæ,
> Sol! Non conveniunt Quadrupedum Phaleræ
> Humano Dorso! *Porro Veri species*
> *Quæsita, inventa, et patefacta, me efferat!*
> *Etsi nullus intelligat,*
> *Si cum Naturâ sapio et sub numine,*
> *Id vere plusquam satis est.*" [3]

Should the number of Subscribers remaining on my List be sufficient barely to pay the expences of the Publication, I shall assuredly proceed in the present form, at least till I have concluded all the Subjects which have

[1] "Letters on the Spaniards" VII *Courier* (22 Dec 1809): *EOT* II 652–61.

[2] Source untraced. Tr: "So it comes about that even ignorance is absolved of disgrace".

[3] The poem is to be found in the Cambridge University Library copy of the rare 1591 edition of Bruno's *De monade*, just before the numbered pages and following the index. Tr George Whalley (*P Lects*—1949—325):

"Wings are not for mortals. Let the sun | Go naked, unadorned by any cloud. | Vision of truth! quested, found, revealed, | Take me—though none may follow where I go. | If I am wise with Nature by God's bounty | That is enough indeed, more than enough." For a text (which varies from copy to copy) and tr see *P Lects* (1949) 325 (Lect 11), 451–2; and cf *CN* I 929 and n.

been left imperfect in the preceding Essays. And this, as far as I can at present calculate, will extend the present Volume to the twenty-eighth or perhaps thirtieth Number. The first place will be given to "Fragments and sketches of the Life of the late Admiral Sir Alexander Ball." I shall next finish the important [336] Subject left incomplete at the 9th No. and demonstrate that Despotism and Barbarism are the natural result of a national attempt to realize anti-feudalism, or the System of philosophical Jacobinism. This position will be illustrated and exemplified at each step by the present state of France, and the Essay will conclude with a detailed analysis of the Character of BUONAPARTE (*promised* by the Author so many years ago in the Morning Post, as a Companion to the Character of Mr. Pitt, which I have been requested, by Men of the highest reputation in the philosophical and literary World, to re-publish in a more permanent form.)[1] In the third place, I shall conduct the subject of Taxation to a conclusion, my Essay on which has been grossly misunderstood. These misconceptions and misrepresentations I shall use my best efforts to remove; and then develope the influences of Taxation and a national Debt, on the *Foreign Trade* of Great Britain: and lastly (the only mournful part of the Tale) on the Principles and intellectual Habits of the Country. And the Volume, whether it be destined to stand alone or as the first of a Series, will conclude with a philosophical examination of the British Constitution in all it's branches separately and collectively.[2] To the next or 21st Number, I shall annex a Note of explanation, requested by many intelligent Readers, concerning my use of the Words Reason and Understanding, as far as is requisite for the full comprehension of the political Essays from the 7th to the 11th Nos.[3] But as I am not likely to receive back my List of Subscribers from London within less than ten days, and must till then remain ignorant of the Names of those who may have given orders for the discontinuance of the Friend, I am obliged to suspend the Publication for one Week. I cannot conclude this Address without expressions of gratitude to those who have written me Letters of encouragement and respect; but at the same time entreat, that in their friendly efforts to serve the Work by procuring new names for it, they will apply to such only as, they have cause to believe, will be actually pleased with a work of this kind. Such only can be of real advantage to THE FRIEND: and even if it were otherwise, He ought not to wish it. Yet I have no reason to feel shame in adding, that without efforts of this kind, appropriately directed, and by those who have felt themselves interested, and in some instances perhaps instructed by his Writings, THE FRIEND has little chance of extending his periodical labours beyond the first Volume. An author's success ought

---

[1] See *EOT* II 319–29 (*M Post* 19 Mar 1800) and SC's note II 329, and *CL* I 623. Southey wrote to C: "There is scarcely anything you could do which would excite so much notice [for *The Friend*] as if you were *now* to write the character of Bonaparte, announced in former times for 'To-morrow,' and to-morrow and to-morrow . . .": *S Life* (CS) III 264. Neither the character of Bonaparte nor the system of philosophical Jacobinism appears in the final numbers.

[2] The conclusion of the essay on taxation and the examination of the Constitution are two more unfulfilled promises.

[3] See below, II 294–7.

always to depend on feelings inspired exclusively by his Writings, and on the sense of their having been useful to the Person who recommends them. On this supposition, and on this only, such recommendation becomes a Duty.

*** *The numbers wanting will be sent to such Subscribers, who have informed the Printer what numbers they have not received, in the course of the next fortnight: and either complete Sets or particular Numbers may after that time be procured from Messrs. Longman and Co. London, by the usual orders to the Country Booksellers.*

THE FRIEND

No. 21, THURSDAY, JANUARY 25, 1810

A PREFATORY OBSERVATION ON MODERN BIOGRAPHY

The History of Times representeth the magnitude of Actions and the *public* faces or deportment of Persons, and passeth over in silence the smaller passages and motions of Men and Matters. But such being the workmanship of God, that he doth hang the greatest weight upon the smallest wires, maxima e minimis suspendens: it comes therefore to pass, that Histories do rather set forth the pomp of business than the true and inward resorts thereof. But Lives, if they be well written, *propounding to themselves a Person to represent* in whom actions both greater and smaller, public and private, have a commixture, must of necessity contain a more true, native, and lively representation.—LORD BACON.

MANKIND in general are so little in the habit of looking steadily at their own meaning, or of weighing the words by which they express it, that the Writer, who is careful to do both, will sometimes mislead his Readers through the very excellence which qualifies him to be their Instructor: and this with no other fault on his part, than the modest mistake of supposing in those, to whom he addresses himself, an intellect as watchful as his own. The inattentive Reader adopts as unconditionally true, or perhaps rails at his Author for having stated as such, what upon examination would be found to have been duly limited, and would so have been understood, if opaque spots and false refractions were as rare in the mental as in the bodily eye. The motto, for instance, to this Paper has more than once served as an excuse and authority for huge volumes of biographical minutiæ, which render the real character almost invisible, like clouds of dust on a Portrait, or the counterfeit frankincense which smoke-blacks the favorite idol of a catholic Village. Yet Lord Bacon, by the words which I have marked in italics, evidently confines the Biographer to such facts as are either susceptible of some useful general inference, or tend to illustrate those qualities which distinguished the Subject of them from ordinary men; while the passage in general was meant to guard the Historian against considering, as trifles, all that might appear so to those, who recognize no greatness in the mind, and can conceive no dignity in any incident, which does not act on their [338] senses by it's external accompaniments, or on their curiosity by it's immediate consequences. Things apparently insignificant are recommended to our Notice, not for their own sakes, but for their bearings or influences on things of importance: in other words, when they are insignificant in appearance only.

An inquisitiveness into the minutest circumstances and casual sayings of eminent contemporaries, is indeed quite natural; but so are all our follies, and the more natural they are, the more caution should we exert in guarding against them. To scribble Trifles even on the perishable glass of an Inn window, is the mark of an Idler; but to engrave them on the Marble Monument, sacred to the memory of the departed Great, is something worse than Idleness. The spirit of genuine Biography is in nothing more conspicuous, than in the firmness with which it withstands the cravings of worthless curiosity, as distinguished from the thirst after useful knowledge. For, in the first place, such anecdotes as derive their whole and sole interest from the great name of the Person, concerning whom they are related, and neither illustrate his general character nor his particular Actions,—would scarcely have been noticed or remembered except by men of weak minds: it is not unlikely therefore, that they were misapprehended at the time, and it is most probable that they have been related as incorrectly, as they were noticed injudiciously. Nor are the consequences of such garulous Biography merely negative. For as insignificant stories can derive no real respectability from the eminence of the Person who happens to be the subject of them, but rather an additional deformity of disproportion, they are apt to have their insipidity seasoned by the same bad passions, that accompany the habit of gossiping in general; and the misapprehensions of weak men meeting with the misinterpretations of malignant men, have not seldom formed the ground work of the most grievous calumnies. In the second place, these trifles are subversive of the great end of Biography, which is to fix the attention and to interest the feelings of men, on those qualities and actions which have made a particular Life worthy of being recorded. It is no doubt, the duty of an honest Biographer, to pourtray the prominent imperfections as well as excellencies of his Hero; but I am at a loss to conceive, how this can be deemed an excuse for heaping together a multitude of particulars, which can prove nothing of any man that might not have been safely taken [339] for granted of all men. In the present age (emphatically the age of personality!) there are more than ordinary motives for withholding all encouragement from this mania of busying ourselves with the names of others, which is still more alarming as a symptom, than it is troublesome as a disease. The Reader must be still less acquainted with contemporary Literature than myself—a case not likely to occur—if he needs *me* to inform him, that there are men, who trading in the silliest anecdotes, in unprovoked abuse and senseless eulogy, think themselves nevertheless employed both worthily and honourably, if only all this be done "*in good set terms,*" and from the Press, and of *public* Characters: a class which has encreased so rapidly of late, that it becomes difficult to discover what Characters are to be considered as private. Alas! if these wretched misusers of language and the means of giving wings to thought, and of multiplying the presence of an individual mind, had ever known, how great a thing the possession of any one simple Truth is, and how mean a thing a mere Fact is, except as seen in the light of some comprehensive Truth; if they had but once experienced the unborrowed complacency, the inward independence, the home-bred strength, with which every clear conception of the Reason is accompanied, they would shrink from their own Pages as at the remembrance of a crime. For a crime it is (and the Man, who hesitates in pronouncing it such, must be ignorant of what mankind owe to Books, what he himself owes to them in spite of his ignorance) thus to introduce the spirit of vulgar scandal, and personal inquietude into the Closet and the Library, environing with evil passions the very Sanctuaries, to which we should flee for refuge from them! For to what do these Publications appeal, whether they present themselves as Biography or as anonymous Criticism, but to the same feelings which the Scandal-bearers and Time-killers of ordinary life seek to gratify in themselves and their Listeners? And both the Authors and Admirers of such Publications, in what respect are they less Truants and Deserters from their own Hearts, and from their appointed Task of understanding and amending them, than the most garrulous female Chronicler, of the goings-on of yesterday in the Families of her Neighbours and Towns-folk?—As to myself, and my own present attempt to record the Life and Character of the late Admiral Sir Alexander Ball,[1] I have already stated, that I consider myself as debarred from all circumstances, not appertaining to his [340] conduct or character as a public Functionary, that involve the names of the Living for good or for evil. Whatever facts and incidents I relate of a private nature, must for the most part concern Sir Alexander Ball exclusively, and as an insulated Individual. But I needed not this restraint. It will be enough for me, still as I write, to recollect the Form and Character of Sir Alexander Ball himself, to represent to my own feelings the inward contempt, with which he would have abstracted his mind from worthless anecdotes[2] and petty personalities; a contempt rising into indignation, if ever an illustrious Name were used as the thread to string them upon. If this recollection be my Socratic Dæmon to warn and to check me, I shall on the other hand derive encouragement from the remembrance of the tender patience, the sweet gentleness, with which he was wont to tolerate the tediousness of well-meaning Men; and the inexhaustible attention, the unfeigned interest, with which he would listen for hours where the conversation appealed to Reason, and like the Bee made Honey while it murmured.

SKETCHES AND FRAGMENTS
OF THE LIFE AND CHARACTER
OF THE LATE ADMIRAL SIR ALEXANDER BALL

Si partem tacuisse velim, quodcumque relinquam,
Majus erit. Veteres actus, primamque juventam
Prosequar? Ad sese mentem præsentia ducunt.
Narrem justitiam? Resplendet gloria Martis.
Armati referam vires? Plus egit inermis.
CLAUDIAN DE LAUD. STIL.

There is something (says Harrington in the Preliminaries to his Oceana) first in the making of a Commonwealth, then in the governing of it, and last of all in the leading of it's armies, which though there be great Divines, great Lawyers, great Men in all Professions, seems to be peculiar only to the genius of a Gentleman. For so it is in the universal series of History, that if any man has founded a Commonwealth, he was first a Gentleman.

---

[1] See above, II 253, 255 and nn.   [2] Cf above, II 18.

Such also, he adds, as have got any fame as civil Governors, have been Gentlemen, or persons of known Descents. Sir Alexander Ball was a Gentleman by Birth; a younger Brother of an old and respectable Family in Gloucestershire. He went into the Navy at an early age from his own choice, and as he himself told me, in consequence of the deep impression and vivid images which were left on his mind by the perusal of Robinson [341] Crusoe. It is not my intention to detail the steps of his promotion, or the Services in which he was engaged as a Subaltern. I recollect many particulars indeed, but not the dates, with such distinctness as would enable me to state them (as it would be necessary to do if I stated them at all) in the order of time. These dates might perhaps have been procured from the Metropolis: but incidents that are neither characteristic nor instructive, even such as would be expected with reason in a regular Life, are no part of my plan; while those which are both interesting and illustrative I have been precluded from mentioning, some from motives which have been already explained, and others from still higher considerations; especially in the present state of the Country, and in a Work which, from it's form and price, cannot be secure of being circulated exclusively among Men of Reflection, or even in the educated classes of Society.[1] The most important result may be comprised in the reflection with which he himself once concluded a long and affecting narration, that no Body of Men can for any length of time be safely treated otherwise than as rational Beings; and that, therefore, the education of the lower classes was of the utmost consequence to the permanent security of the Empire, even for the sake of our Navy. The dangers apprehended from the education of the lower Classes, arose entirely from it's not being universal, and from the unusualness in the lowest classes of *those* accomplishments, which He, like Doctor Bell, regarded as one of the *means* of Education, and not as Education itself.* If, he observed, the lower Classes in general possessed but one Eye or one Arm, the few who were so fortunate as to possess two, would naturally become vain and restless, and consider themselves as entitled to a higher situation. He illustrated this by the faults attributed to learned Women, and that the same objections were formerly made to educating Women at all; namely, that their Knowledge made them vain, affected, and neglectful of their proper duties. Now that all Women of Condition are well-educated, we hear no more of these apprehensions, or observe any instances to justify them. Yet if a Lady understood the Greek one [342] tenth part as well as the whole circle of her acquaintances understood the French Language, it would not surprize us to find her less pleasing from the consciousness of her superiority in the possession of an unusual Advantage. Sir Alexander Ball quoted the speech of an old Admiral, one of whose two great wishes was to have a Ship's Crew composed altogether of serious Scotchmen. He spoke with great reprobation of the vulgar

---

* Which consists in *educing*, or to adopt Dr. Bell's own expression, *eliciting* the faculties of the Human Mind, and at the same time subordinating them to the Reason and Conscience; varying the means of this common end according to the sphere and particular mode, in which the Individual is likely to act and become useful.

[1] Cf above, I 53–4.

notion, the worse Man, the better Sailor. Courage, he said, was the natural product of familiarity with Danger, which thoughtlessness would oftentimes turn into Fool-hardiness; and that he had always found the most usefully brave Sailors the gravest and most rational of his crew. The best Sailor he ever had, first attracted his notice by the anxiety which he expressed concerning the means of remitting some money which he had received in the West Indies, to his Sister in England; and this Man without any tinge of Methodism, was never heard to swear an Oath, and was remarkable for the firmness with which he devoted a part of every Sunday to the reading of his Bible. I record this with satisfaction as a testimony of great weight, and in all respects unexceptionable; for Sir Alexander Ball's opinions throughout Life remained unwarped by zealotry, and were those of a mind seeking after Truth, in calmness and complete self-possession. He was much pleased with an unsuspicious testimony furnished by Dampier (Vol. 2. Part 2. Page 89,) "I have particularly observed," writes this famous old Navigator, "there and in other places, that such as had been well-bred, were generally most careful to improve their time, and would be very industrious and frugal where there was any probability of considerable gain; but on the contrary, such as had been bred up in ignorance and hard labour, when they came to have plenty would extravagantly squander away their time and money in drinking and *making a bluster.*" Indeed it is a melancholy proof, how strangely power warps the minds of ordinary men, that there can be a doubt on this subject among persons who have been themselves educated. It tempts a suspicion, that unknown to themselves they find a comfort in the thought, that their inferiors are something less than Men, or have an uneasy half-consciousness that, if they were otherwise, they would themselves have no claim to be their superiors. For a sober Education naturally inspires self-respect, but he, who respects himself, will respect others; and he who respects both himself and others, must of necessity be a brave [343] Man. The great importance of this Subject, and the increasing interest which good men of all denominations feel in the bringing about of a national Education, must be my excuse for having entered so minutely into Sir Alexander Ball's opinions on this head, in which, however, I am the more excuseable, being on that part of his Life which I am obliged to leave almost a blank.[1]

During his Lieutenancy, and after he had perfected himself in the knowledge and duties of a practical Sailor, he was compelled by the state of his health to remain in England for a considerable length of time. Of this he industriously availed himself to the acquirement of substantial knowledge from books; and during his whole life afterwards, he considered those as his happiest hours, which, without any neglect of official or professional duty, he could devote to reading. He preferred, indeed he almost confined himself to History, political Œconomy, Voyages and Travels, Natural History, and latterly Agricultural Works: in short, to such Books as contain specific Facts, or practical Principles capable of specific application. His active Life, and the particular objects of immediate utility, some one of which he had always in his view, precluded a taste for works of pure Speculation and abstract Science, though he highly honoured those

[1] See above, I 541 n 2, for a cancelled ms passage.

who were eminent in these respects, and considered them as the benefactors of Mankind, no less than those who afterwards discovered the mode of applying their Principles, or who realized them in Practice. Works of Amusement, as Novels, Plays, &c. did not appear even to amuse him: and the only poetical Composition, of which I have ever heard him speak, was a Manuscript Poem written by one of my Friends, which I read to his Lady in his presence.[1] To my surprize, he afterwards spoke of this with warm interest; but it was evident to me, that it was not so much the poetic merit of the Composition that had interested him, as the Truth and psychological insight with which it represented the practicability of reforming the most hardened minds, and the various accidents which may awaken the most brutalized Person to a recognition of his nobler Being. I will add one remark of his on knowledge acquired from Books, which appears to me both just and valuable. The prejudice against such knowledge, he said, and the custom of opposing it to that which is learnt by practice, originated in those times when books were almost confined to Theology, and to logical and metaphysical Subtleties; but that at present there is scarcely any [344] practical knowledge, which is not to be found in books: The press is the means by which intelligent Men now converse with each other, and persons of all classes and all pursuits convey, each the contribution of his individual experience. It was therefore, he said, as absurd to hold book-knowledge at present in contempt, as it would be for a man to avail himself only of his own eyes and ears, and to aim at nothing which could not be performed exclusively by his own arms. The use and necessity of personal experience consisted in the power of chusing and applying what had been read, and of discriminating by the light of analogy, the practicable from the impracticable, and probability from mere plausibility. Without a judgement matured and steadied by actual experience, a man would read to little or perhaps to bad purpose; but yet that experience, which in exclusion of all other knowledge has been derived from one Man's life, is in the present day scarcely worthy of the name—at least for those who are to act in the higher and wider spheres of duty. An ignorant General, he said, inspired him with terror; for if he were too proud to take advice he would ruin himself by his own blunders; and if he were not, by adopting the worst that was offered. A great Genius may indeed form an exception; but we do not lay down rules in expectation of wonders. A similar remark I remember to have heard from a gallant Officer, who to eminence in professional Science and the gallantry of a tried Soldier, adds all the accomplishments of a sound Scholar, and the powers of a man of Genius.

One incident, which happened at this period of Sir Alexander's life, is so illustrative of his character, and furnishes so strong a presumption, that the thoughtful humanity by which he was distinguished, was not wholly the growth of his latter years, that, though it may appear to some trifling in itself, I will insert it in this place, with the occasion on which it was communicated to me. In a large party at the grand Master's Palace, I had observed a naval Officer of distinguished merit listening to Sir Alexander Ball, whenever he joined in the conversation, with so marked a pleasure,

[1] WW's *Peter Bell*; see above, I 543n and n 1.

that it seemed as if his very voice independent of what he said, had been delightful to him: and once as he fixed his eyes on Sir Alexander Ball, I could not but notice the mixed expression of awe and affection, which gave a more than common interest to so manly a countenance. During his stay in the Island this Officer honoured me not unfrequently with his visits; [345] and at the conclusion of my last conversation with him, in which I had dwelt on the wisdom of the Governor's* conduct in a recent and difficult emergency, he told me that he considered himself as indebted to the same excellent Person for that which was dearer to him than his life. Sir Alexander Ball, said he, has (I dare say) forgotten the circumstance; but when he was Lieutenant Ball, he was the Officer whom I accompanied in my first *boat*-expedition, being then a Midshipman and only in my fourteenth year. As we were rowing up to the Vessel which we were to attack, amid a discharge of musquetry, I was overpowered by fear, my knees trembled under me, and I seemed on the point of fainting away. Lieutenant Ball who saw the condition I was in, placed himself close beside me, and still keeping his countenance directed toward the enemy, took hold of my hand, and pressing it in the most friendly manner, said in a low voice "Courage, my dear Boy! don't be afraid of yourself! you will recover in a minute or so—I was just the same, when I first went out in this way." Sir, added the officer to me, it was as if an Angel had put a new Soul into me. With the feeling, that I was not yet dishonoured, the whole burthen of agony was removed; and from that moment I was as fearless and forward as the oldest of the boats crew, and on our return the Lieutenant spoke highly of me to our Captain. I am scarcely less convinced of my own being, than that I should have been what I tremble to think of, if, instead of his humane encouragement, he had at that moment scoffed, threatened, or reviled me. And this was the more kind in him because, as I afterwards understood, his own conduct in his first trial, had evinced to all appearances the greatest fearlessness, and that he said this therefore only to give me heart, and restore me to my own good opinion.—This anecdote, I trust, will have some weight with those who may have lent an ear to any of those vague calumnies from which no naval Commander can secure his good name, who knowing the paramount necessity of regularity and strict [346] discipline in a Ship of war, adopts an appropriate plan for the attainment of these objects, and remains constant and immutable in the execution. To an Athenian, who, in praising a public Functionary had said, that every one either applauded him or left him without censure, a Philosopher replied—"How seldom then must he have done his Duty!"

Of Sir Alexander Ball's character, as Captain Ball, of his measures as a

---

* Such Sir Alexander Ball was in reality, and such was his general appellation in the Mediterranean: I adopt this Title therefore, to avoid the ungraceful repetition of his own name on the one hand, and on the other the confusion of ideas, which might arise from the use of his real Title, viz. "His Majesty's civil Commissioner for the Island of Malta and it's Dependencies; and Minister Plenipotentiary to the Order of St. John." This is not the place to expose the timid and unsteady policy which continued the latter Title, or the petty jealousies which interfered to prevent Sir Alexander Ball from having the Title of Governor, from one of the very causes which rendered him fittest for the Office.

Disciplinarian, and of the wise and dignified principle on which he grounded those measures, I have already spoken in a former part of this Work, and must content myself therefore with referring the Reader to the 7th No. of THE FRIEND, page 100, entreating him to re-peruse that passage as belonging to this place, and as a part of the present narration.[1] Ah! little did I expect at the time I wrote that account, that the motives of delicacy, which then impelled me to withhold the Name, would so soon be exchanged for the higher duty which now justifies me in adding it! At the thought of such events the language of a tender superstition is the voice of Nature itself, and those facts alone presenting themselves to our memory which had left an impression on our hearts, we assent to, and adopt the Poet's pathetic complaint:

> ————"O Sir! the good die first,
> And those whose hearts are dry as summer dust,
> Burn to the socket."————

That the humane plan described in the Pages now referred to, that a system in pursuance of which the Captain of a Man of war uniformly regarded his Sentences not as dependent on his own Will, or to be affected by the state of his feelings at the moment, but as the pre-established, determinations of known Laws, and himself as the Voice of the law in pronouncing the sentence, and it's Delegate in enforcing the execution, could not but furnish occasional food to the spirit of Detraction, must be evident to every reflecting mind. It is indeed little less than impossible, that he who in order to be effectively humane, determines to be inflexibly just, and who is inexorable to his own feelings when they would interrupt the course of justice; who looks at each particular act by the light of all its' consequences, and as the representative of ultimate good or evil, should not sometimes be charged with Tyranny by weak minds: and it is too certain that the calumny will be willingly believed and eagerly propagated by all those, who would shun the presence of an eye keen in the detection of imposture, incapacity, and misconduct, [347] and of a resolution as steady in their exposure. We soon hate the Man whose qualities we dread, and thus have a double interest, an interest of passion as well as of policy, in decrying and defaming him. But good men will rest satisfied with the promise made to them by the divine Comforter, that BY HER CHILDREN SHALL WISDOM BE JUSTIFIED.

At the close of the American War, Captain Ball was entrusted with the protection and convoying of an immense mercantile Fleet to America, and by his great prudence and unexampled attention to the interests of all and each, endeared his name to the American Merchants, and laid the foundation of that high respect and predilection which both the Americans and their Government ever afterwards entertained for him. My recollection does not enable me to attempt any accuracy in the date or circumstances, or to add the particulars of his services in the West Indies, and on the Coast of America, I now therefore merely allude to the fact with a prospective reference to opinions and circumstances, which I shall have to mention hereafter. Shortly after the general Peace was established, Captain Ball, who was now a married man, passed some time with his Lady in

[1] See above, II 99–101, written a month before the death of Ball.

France, and, if I mistake not, at Nantz. At the same time, and in the same Town, among the other English Visitors Lord (then Captain) Nelson, happened to be one. In consequence of some punctilio, as to whose business it was to pay the compliment of the first call, they never met, and this trifling affair occasioned a coldness between the two naval Commanders, or in truth a mutual prejudice against each other. Some years after, both their Ships being together close off Minorca and near Port Mahon, a violent Storm nearly disabled Lord Nelson's Vessel, and in addition to the fury of the wind, it was night-time and the thickest darkness. Captain Ball however brought his Vessel at length to Nelson's assistance, took his Ship in tow, and used his best endeavours to bring her and his own Vessel into Port Mahon. The difficulties and the dangers encreased. Nelson considered the case of his own Ship as desperate, and that unless she was immediately left to her own fate, both Vessels would inevitably be lost. He, therefore, with the generosity natural to him, repeatedly requested Captain Ball to let him loose; and on Captain Ball's refusal, he became impetuous, and enforced his demand with passionate threats. Captain Ball then himself took the speaking Trumpet, which the fury of the [348] wind and waves rendered necessary, and with great solemnity and without the least disturbance of temper, called out in reply: "I feel confident that I can bring you in safe; I therefore must not, and by the help of Almighty God! I will not leave you." What he promised he performed; and after they were safely anchored, Nelson came on board of Ball's Ship, and embracing him with all the ardour of acknowledgement, exclaimed—a Friend in need is a Friend indeed! At this time and on this occasion commenced that firm and perfect friendship between these two great Men, which was interrupted only by the death of the former. The pleasing task of dwelling on this mutual attachment I defer to that part of the present sketch which will relate to Sir Alexander Ball's opinions of men and things. It will be sufficient for the present to say, that the two Men, whom Lord Nelson especially honoured, were Sir Thomas Troubridge and Sir Alexander Ball; and once, when they were both present, on some allusion made to the loss of his Arm, he replied: "Who shall dare tell me, that I want an Arm, when I have three right arms—this (putting forward his own) and Ball and Troubridge."

In the Plan of the Battle of the Nile it was Lord Nelson's design, that Captains Troubridge and Ball should have led up the attack. The former was stranded: and the latter by accident of the wind, could not bring his Ship into the line of battle till some time after the engagement had become general. With his characteristic forecast and activity of (what may not improperly be called) practical imagination, he had made arrangements to meet every probable contingency. All the shrouds and sails of the Ship, not absolutely necessary for it's immediate management, were thoroughly wetted and so rolled up, that they were as hard and as little inflamable as so many solid cylinders of wood; every Sailor had his appropriate place and function, and a certain number were appointed as the firemen, whose sole duty it was to be on the watch if any part of the Vessel should take fire: and to these men exclusively the charge of extinguishing it was committed. It was already dark when he brought his Ship into action, and laid her alongside the l'Orient. One particular only I shall add to the known account of the memorable engagement between these Ships, and this I received from Sir Alexander Ball himself. He had previously made a combustible preparation, but which, from the nature of the engagement to be expected, he had purposed [349] to reserve for the last emergency. But just at the time when from several symptoms he had every reason to believe, that the Enemy would soon strike to him, one of the Lieutenants, without his knowledge, threw in the combustible matter: and this it was that occasioned the tremendous explosion of that Vessel, which with the deep silence and interruption of the Engagement which succeeded to it, has been justly deemed the sublimest war incident recorded in History. Yet the incident which followed, and which has not, I believe, been publicly made known, is scarcely less impressive, though it's sublimity is of a different character. At the renewal of the battle Captain Ball, though his Ship was then on fire in three different parts, laid her along side a French eighty-four: and a second longer obstinate contest began. The firing on the part of the French Ship having at length for some time slackened, and then altogether ceased, and yet no sign given of surrender, the senior Lieutenant came to Captain Ball and informed him: that the *hearts* of his Men were as good as ever, but that they were so completely exhausted, that they were scarcely capable of lifting an arm. He asked therefore, whether, as the Enemy had now ceased firing, the Men might be permitted to lie down by their Guns for a short time. After some reflection, Sir Alexander acceded to the proposal, taking of course the proper precautions to rouze them again at the moment he thought requisite. Accordingly, with the exception of himself, his Officers, and the appointed Watch, the Ship's Crew lay down, each in the place to which he was stationed, and slept for twenty minutes. They were then rouzed; and started up, as Sir Alexander expressed it, more like men out of an Ambush than from sleep, so co-instantaneously did they all obey the summons! They recommenced their fire, and in a few minutes the Enemy surrendered: and it was soon after discovered, that during that interval, and almost immediately after the French Ship had first ceased firing, the Crew had sunk down by their Guns, and there slept, almost by the side, as it were, of their sleeping Enemy.

Whatever other incidents, I propose to mention relating to Sir Alexander Ball as a naval Commander, will either appear among the proofs and illustrations with which I shall accompany the analysis of his Character; or will be better related under the head of MALTA, as appertaining to the conquest of that Island, and forming a part of those services which secured for himself the devout and filial [350] attachment of the Maltese. The conduct of Sir Alexander Ball in relation to Malta, will be the subject, therefore, of the next Number.[1]

NOTE in explanation of the assertion in No. 9, that all men possess REASON in the same degree.[2]

Every Man must feel, that though he may not be exerting different faculties, he is exerting his faculties in a different way, when in one instance he

---

[1] See below, II 298.   [2] See above, II 125 and n 1.

begins with some one self-evident truth, (that the radii of a circle, for instance, are all equal), and in consequence of this being true, sees at once, without any actual experience, that some other thing must be true likewise, and that this being true, some *third* thing must be equally true, and so on till he comes, we will say, to the properties of the Lever, considered as the spoke of a circle; which is capable of having all it's marvellous powers demonstrated even to a Savage who had never seen a Lever, and without supposing any other previous knowledge in his mind, but this one, that there is a conceivable figure, all possible lines from the middle to the circumference of which are of the same length: or when, in the second instance, he brings together the facts of experience, each of which has it's own separate value, neither encreased nor diminished by the truth of any other fact which may have preceded it; and making these several facts bear upon some particular project, and finding some in favour of it, and some against it, determines for or against the project, according as one or the other class of facts preponderate: as, for instance, whether it would be better to plant a particular spot of ground with Larch, or with Scotch Fir, or with Oak in preference to either. Surely every Man will acknowledge, that his mind was very differently employed in the first case from what it was in the second; and all men have agreed to call the results of the first class the truths of *science*, such as not only are true, but which it is impossible to conceive otherwise: while the results of the second class are called *facts*, or things of *experience*: and as to these latter we must often content ourselves with the greater *probability*, that they are so, or so, rather than otherwise—nay, even when we have no doubt that they are so in the particular case, we never presume to assert that they must continue so always, and under all circumstances. On the contrary, our conclusions depend altogether on contingent *circumstances*. Now when the mind is employed, as in the case first-mentioned, I call it *Reason*, or more definitely, [351] the pure Reason; but, in the second case, the *Understanding* or *Prudence*.

This Reason applied to the *motives* of our conduct, and combined with the sense of our moral responsibility, is called the *Conscience:* and as the Reason consists wholly in a man's power of seeing, whether any two ideas, which happen to be in his mind, are, or are not in contradiction with each other, it follows of necessity, not only that all men have Reason, but that every man has it in the same degree. For Reason does not consist in the Ideas, or in their clearness, but simply, when they *are* in the mind, in seeing whether they contradict each other or no.

And again as in the determinations of Conscience, the only knowledge required is that of my own *intention*—whether in doing such a thing, instead of leaving it undone, I did what I should think right if any other Person had done it; it follows that in the mere question of guilt or innocence, all men have not only Reason equally, but likewise all the materials on which the Reason, considered as *Conscience*, is to work. But when we pass out of ourselves, and speak, not exclusively of the *agent as meaning* well or ill, but of the action in it's consequences, then of course experience is required, judgment in making use of it, and all those other qualities of the mind which are so differently dispensed to different persons, both by (nature and education) and though *the reason itself* is the same in all men, yet the means of exercising it, and the materials (i.e. the facts and ideas) on which it is exercised, being possessed in very different degrees by different persons, the *practical Result* is, of course, equally different—and the whole ground work of Rousseau's Philosophy ends in a mere Nothingism. —Even in that branch of Knowledge, in which the *ideas*, on the congruity of which with each other, the Reason is to decide, are all possessed alike by all men, namely, in Geometry, (for all men in their senses possess all the component images, viz. *simple* curves and straight lines) yet the power of *attention* required for the perception of linked Truths, even of *such* Truths, is so very different in A and in B that Sir Isaac Newton professed that it was in this power only that he was superior to ordinary men. In short, the sophism is as gross as if I should say—The *Souls* of all men have the *faculty* of Sight in an *equal* degree—forgetting to add, that this faculty cannot be exercised without *eyes*, and that some men are blind and others short-sighted, &c.—and should then take advantage of this omission to conclude against the use or necessity of [352] spectacles, microscopes, &c.—or chusing the sharpest-sighted men for our Guides.

Having exposed the gross sophism, I must warn against an opposite error—namely, that if Reason, as distinguished from Prudence, consists merely in knowing that Black cannot be White—or when a man has a clear conception of an inclosed figure, and another equally clear conception of a straight line, his Reason teaches him that these two conceptions are incompatible in the same object, i.e. that two straight lines *cannot* include a space——the said Reason must be a very *insignificant* faculty. But a moment's steady self-reflection will shew us, that in the simple determination "Black is not White"—or, "that two straight Lines cannot include a space"—all the powers are implied, that distinguish Man from Animals— first, the power of *reflection*—2d. of *comparison*—3d. and therefore of *suspension* of the mind—4th ergo of a controlling Will, and the power of acting from *Notions*, instead of mere Images exciting appetites, from *Motives*, not mere dark *instincts*.—Was it an insignificant thing to weigh the Planets, and determine all their courses, and prophecy every possible relation of the Heavens a thousand years hence? Yet all this mighty Pile of Science is nothing but a *linking* together of the truths of the same kind as, *the whole is greater than it's part:*—or, if A and B = C, then A = B— or 3 + 4 − 7, therefore 7 | 5 = 12, and so forth. X is to be found either in A or B or C or D: It is not found in A, B, or C,—therefore it is to be found in D.—What can be simpler? Apply this to an animal—a Dog misses his master where four roads meet—he has come up one, smells to two of the others, and then with his head aloft darts forward to the third road without any examination.—If this was done by a conclusion, the Dog would have *Reason*—how comes he then never to shew it in his *ordinary* habits? Why does this story excite either wonder or incredulity? —If the Story be a fact, and not a fiction, I should say—the Breeze brought his Master's scent down the 4th Road, to the Dog's nose, and that *therefore* he did not put it down to the Road, as in the two former instances. So aweful and almost miraculous does the simple act of concluding, that *take* 3 from 4, *there remains one,* appear to us when attributed to the most sagacious of all animals.

This is the whole that is necessary to be understood in order to find no difficulty in comprehending the reasoning of Nos. 7, 8, 9, and 10, of *The Friend.*

THE FRIEND

No. 22, THURSDAY, JANUARY 31,[1] 1810

⁑ *Orders for discontinuance received henceforward, cannot be complied with till the sixth Number from the receipt of the Letter: and all such orders, whether containing money or not, will, it is requested, be addressed directly to Mr. Brown, Printer, Penrith. Those Subscribers who have not remitted the sum for the first twenty Numbers, are solicited to pay the same either to Mr. G. Ward, Bookseller, Skinner-Street, or to the Post-master of the town at or near which they reside; to be repaid by the Post-master at Kendal, or inclosed in a letter (post paid) to Mr. Coleridge, Grasmere, Kendal; or (if containing orders) to Mr. Brown, Penrith. A more regular and uniform plan of Receipt will be formed and made known six weeks before the next payment.*[2]

ARMATI REFERAM VIRES? PLUS EGIT INERMIS.

CLAUDIAN

MY preceding Number, in strict correspondence with its' Title, presented merely *Sketches* and *Fragments* of the Life and Character of Sir ALEXANDER BALL. The chief causes that withheld me from attempting a regular Biography, were the consciousness of a constitutional inability in myself to retain Names and Dates, joined with a diffidence in the accuracy of my recollection respecting facts and events, which, at the time I heard them narrated, had not particularly interested me; or (to speak more correctly) which had faded in my memory in consequence of the vivid impression left by other facts, that appeared to me more illustrative of the Narrator's character, or bearing a closer reference to scenes and circumstances, in which I had been myself personally present. I resembled a Man who having dug up in separate pieces the greater and more important part of a Mammoth Skeleton, yet through ignorance of all its' anatomy, and having besides forgotten or confused the arrangement, in which the fragments were originally presented to him, becomes incapable of representing [354] a just and coherent figure of the whole animal. Where these causes did not act, prudential reasons, and motives of personal delicacy, supplied their place. My Readers therefore will kindly consider what I have hitherto related, in the light of a mere introduction to that part of my subject, of which I am more compleatly master; and which besides, if not more important in itself, yet possesses in a greater degree that species of interest, that connection with general Principles, by which

---

[1] An error for "February 1".   lxix–lxx, and below, App E, ii 407–9.
[2] See above, Introduction, i lxiii,

(as far as the public taste will permit) I would wish that every Number of THE FRIEND should be more or less marked. I proceed therefore to the conduct and character of Sir Alexander Ball, as the Conqueror, Governor, and Legislator of Malta.

> *Insula parva situ sed rebus maxima gestis,*
> *Africæ et Europæ ac Asiæ contermina, Pauli*
> *Hospes, et alborum procerum gratissima nutrix*.*
> VINCENZO LITTARA[1]

For the perfect comprehension of Sir Alexander Ball's views and objects, and in order justly to estimate the nature and extent of his services, as a Man and as a Statesman, relatively both to Malta and to Great Britain, it will be useful to prefix a few remarks on the original grounds of the present war; in what sense Malta is to be considered as the cause of it; and lastly, in what the real importance of the Island consists. I shall do this the more gladly, first, because there are many erroneous opinions on this point, still current, and which, if they are suffered to remain unconfuted, may act to the prejudice of our national interests; secondly, because the facts and arguments, by which they are to be confuted, apply closely to the present assertions and general temper of a clamourous and, it is to be feared, encreasing party among us, and will, I hope, throw some additional light on those Principles, by which alone the War can be prosecuted with effect, or a Peace concluded with safety and honor; and lastly, because the considerations I am about to submit to the Reader, were written by me during my residence at Malta—were written at the instance of Sir Alexander Ball, and after many conversations with him on the subject, and when written, [355] were read and approved of by him, and must therefore be deemed as a part of his own opinions, and as such not merely preparatory to, but a natural part of, the plan which I first proposed to myself. Little prospective wisdom can that man obtain, who hurrying onward with the current, or rather torrent, of Events, feels no interest in their importance, except as far as his curiosity is excited by their novelty; and to whom all reflection and retrospect are wearisome. If ever there were a time when the formation of just *public* Principles becomes a duty of *private* Morality; when the principles of *Morality in general* ought to be made bear on our public suffrages, and to effect every great national determination; when, in short, his COUNTRY should have a place by every Englishman's Fire-side; and when the feelings and truths, which give dignity to the Fire-side and tranquillity to the Death-bed, ought to be present and influencive in the Cabinet and the Senate—that time is now

---

* An Island small in size but great by illustrious exploits, the joint neighbour of Africa, Europe, and Asia, the hospitable entertainer of St. Paul, and the delightful nurse of the Nobles of the white Cross.

[1] Quoted (var: *mater* for *nutrix*) on the title-page of Charles Wilkinson *Epitome of the History of Malta and Gozo* (1804). C copied the lines into a notebook, where they are followed by the geographical measurements of Malta, given by Wilkinson p 80; see *CN* II 2459, 2460 and nn.

with us. Never can Englishmen too often be warned, that where Ambition admits no boundary but that of its' own power, and all the *Vices* are allied and systematized against us; there can be no hope of successful resistance, but in an equal union of all the *Virtues* of the human character: and that this is not possible without a clear insight into those Principles, which measure and reconcile their different claims of different virtues, and allot to each its' time, its' place, its' function, and its' degree. If the present Empire of France be rightly considered as one bad great Man wielding the strength and weaponry of millions, in all just proportion the Kingdom, that is to resist him, and which must perish if it does not resist him adequately, ought to be (as Milton with his accustomed grandeur hath expressed it) "but as one vast Personage, one mighty growth and stature of an honest Man, as big and compact in virtue as in body." [1] Scarcely can that be too often enforced, the practice of which is both necessary and inexhaustible: and the principle of Evil fights his battles cheap, if he may still use the same Sword, and good Men not employ the same Buckler.

In a rich commercial State, a War seldom fails to become unpopular by length of continuance. The last War, which *towards its' close*, had become just and necessary, perhaps beyond any former example, had yet causes of unpopularity peculiar to itself. Exhaustion is the natural [356] consequence of excessive stimulation, in the feelings of Nations equally, as in those of Individuals. Wearied out by overwhelming Novelties; stunned, as it were, by a series of strange explosions; sick too of hope long delayed; and uncertain as to the real object and motive of the War, from the rapid change and general failure of its' ostensible objects and motives; the public mind, for many months preceding the signing of the Preliminaries, had lost all its' tone and elasticity. The consciousness of mutual errors and mutual disappointments, disposed the great majority of all Parties to a spirit of diffidence and toleration, which, amiable as it may be in Individuals, yet in a Nation, and above all in an opulent and luxurious Nation, is always too nearly akin to apathy and selfish indulgence. An unmanly impatience for Peace became only not universal. After as long a resistance as the nature of our Constitution and national Character permitted or even endured, the Government applied at length the only remedy adequate to the greatness of the Evil, a remedy which the magnitude of the Evil justified, and which nothing but an Evil of that magnitude could justify. At a high price they purchased for us the *name* of Peace, at a time when the views of France became daily more and more incompatible with our vital interests. Considering the Peace as a mere Truce of experiment, wise and temperate Men regarded with complacency the Treaty of Amiens, for the very reasons that would have ensured the condemnation of any other Treaty under any other circumstances. Its' palpable deficiencies were its' antidote: or rather they formed its' very essence, and declared at first sight, what alone it was or was meant to be. Any attempt at that time and in this Treaty, to have secured Italy, Holland and the German Empire, would have been in the literal sense of the word, *preposterous*. The Nation

[1] Milton *Of Reformation . . . in England*: *Works* (1738) I 14 (var).

would have withdrawn all faith in the pacific intentions of the Ministers, if the negociation had been broken off on a plea of this kind: for it had taken for granted the extreme desirableness, nay the necessity of a Peace, and, this once admitted, there would, no doubt, have been an absurdity in continuing the War for objects, which the War furnished no means of realizing. If the First Consul had entered into stipulations with us respecting the Continent, they would have been observed only as long as his interest from other causes might have dictated; [357] they would have been signed with as much sincerity and observed with as much good faith, as the article actually inserted in the Treaty of Amiens, respecting the integrity of the Turkish Empire. This article indeed was wisely insisted on by us, because it affected both our national honour, and the interests of our Indian empire immediately; and still more, perhaps, because this of all others was the most likely to furnish an early proof of the First Consul's real dispositions. But deeply interested in the fate of the Continent, as we are thought to be, it would nevertheless have been most idle to have abandoned a Peace, supposing it at all desirable, on the ground that the French Government had refused that, which would have been of no value had it been granted.

Indeed there results one serious disadvantage from insisting on the rights and interests of Austria, the Empire, Switzerland, &c. in a Treaty between England and France: and, as it should seem, no advantage to counterbalance it. For so, any attack on those rights instantly pledges our character and national dignity to commence a War, however inexpedient it might happen to be, and however hopeless: while if a War were expedient, any Attack on these Countries by France furnishes a justifiable cause of war in its' essential nature, and independently of all positive Treaty. Seen in this light, the Defects of the Treaty of Amiens will become it's real Merits. If the Government of France made Peace in the spirit of Peace, then a friendly Intercourse and the humanizing Influences of Commerce and reciprocal Hospitality, would gradually bring about in both Countries the dispositions necessary for the calm discussion and sincere conclusion of a genuine, efficient, and comprehensive Treaty. If the contrary proved the fact, the Treaty of Amiens contained in itself the principles of it's own Dissolution. It was what it ought to be. If the First Consul had both meant and dealt fairly by us, the Treaty would have *led* to a true Settlement; but he acting, as all prudent men expected that he would act, it supplied just reasons for the commencement of war—and at it's decease left us, as a legacy, Blessings that assuredly far outweighed our Losses by the Peace. It left us popular Enthusiasm, national Unanimity, and simplicity of Object: and removed one inconvenience, which cleaved to the last War, by attaching to the right objects, and enlisting under their proper Banners, the scorn and hatred of Slavery, the [358] passion for Freedom, all the high Thoughts and high Feelings that connect us with the honored names of past Ages, and inspire sentiments and language, to which our Hampdens, Sidneys, and Russels, might listen without jealousy.

The late Peace then was negociated by the Government, ratified by the Legislature, and received by the Nation, as an Experiment: as the only means of exhibiting such proof, as would be satisfactory to the People in

their then Temper, whether Buonaparte devoting his Ambition and Activity to the re-establishment of Trade, colonial tranquillity, and social
morals, in France, would abstain from *insulting*, *alarming*, and *endangering*,
the British Empire. And these thanks at least were due to the First Consul,
that he did not long delay the Proof. With more than papal Insolence he
issued Edicts of Anathema against us, and excommunicated us from all
interference in the Affairs of the Continent. He *insulted* us still more
indecently by pertinacious demands respecting our constitutional Laws and
Rights of Hospitality; by the official publication of Sebastiani's Report;
and by a direct personal outrage offered in the presence of all the foreign
Ministers to the King, in the person of his Ambassador. He both insulted
and alarmed us by a display of the most perfidious Ambition in the subversion of the Independence of Switzerland, in the avowal of designs
against Egypt, Syria, and the Greek Islands, and in the mission of military
Spies to Great Britain itself. And by forcibly maintaining a French Army
in Holland, he at once insulted, alarmed, and endangered us. What can
render a War just (presupposing it's expedience) if Insult, repeated Alarm,
and Danger, do not? And how can it be expedient for a rich, united, and
powerful Island-Empire to remain in nominal Peace and unresenting
Passiveness with an insolent neighbour, who has proved, that to wage
against it an unmitigated war of Insult, Alarm, and Endangerment is both
his Temper and his System?

Many attempts were made by Mr. Fox to explain away the force of the
greater number of the Facts here ennumerated; but the great fact, for
which alone they have either force or meaning, the great ultimate fact, that
Great Britain had been insulted, alarmed, and endangered by France, Mr.
Fox himself expressly admitted. But the Opposers of the present War
concentre the strength of their cause in the following brief Argument.
Supposing, say [359] they, the grievances set forth in our Manifesto to be
as notorious as they are asserted to be, yet more notorious they cannot be
than that other fact, which utterly annuls them as reasons for a War—
the fact, that Ministers themselves regard them only as the pompous
Garnish of the Dish. It stands on record, that Buonaparte might have
purchased our Silence for ever, respecting these Insults and Injuries, by a
mere acquiescence on his Part in our Retention of Malta. The whole
Treaty of Amiens is little more than a perplexed Bond of Compromise
respecting Malta. On Malta we rested the peace: for Malta we renewed
the War. So say the Opposers of the present War. As it's Advocates, we
do not deny the fact as stated by them: but we hope to atchieve all, and
more than all the purposes of such denial, by an Explanation of the Fact.
The difficulty then resolves itself into two questions: first, in what sense
of the words can we be said to go to War for Malta alone? Secondly,
wherein does the importance of Malta consist? The answer to the second
will be involved in the biography: while the attempt to settle the first
Question, so at the same time elucidate the LAW OF NATIONS and it's
identity with the law of Conscience, will occupy the remainder of the
present Number.

I. *In what sense can we be affirmed to have renewed the War
for Malta alone?*

If we had known or could reasonably have believed, that the Views of
France were and would continue to be friendly or negative toward Great
Britain, neither the Subversion of the independence of Switzerland, nor the
maintenance of a French Army in Holland, would have furnished any
prudent ground for War. For the only way by which we could have
injured France, namely, the destruction of her commerce and navy, would
increase her means of continental conquests, by concentring all the resources and energies of the French Empire in her military powers: while
the losses and miseries which the French People would suffer in consequence, and their magnitude, compared with any advantages that might
accrue to them from the extension of the *name* France, were facts which,
we knew by experience, would weigh as nothing with the existing Government. Its' attacks on the independence of its' continental neighbours,
becomes motives for the commencement of hostility to *us*, only as far as
[360] they give *proofs* of a hostile intention toward ourselves, and facilitate
the realizing of such intention. If any events had taken place, increasing
the *means* of injuring this Country, even though these events furnished no
moral ground of complaint against France (such, for instance, might be
the great extension of her population and revenue, from freedom and a
wise government) much more, if they were the fruits of iniquitous ambition,
and therefore in themselves involved the *probability* of an hostile intention
to us—then, I say, every after occurrence becomes important, and both a
just and expedient ground of war, in proportion, not to the importance of
the thing in itself, but to the quantity of evident *proof* afforded by it of an
hostile design in the Government, by whose power our interests are endangered. If by demanding the immediate evacuation of Malta, when he
had himself done away the security of its' actual independence (on *his*
promise of preserving which *our* pacific promises rested as on their sole
foundation) and this too, after he had openly avowed such designs on
Egypt, as not only in the opinion of *our* Ministers, but in his own opinion,
made it of the greatest importance to this Country, that Malta should not
be under French Influence; if by this conduct the First Consul exhibited a
decisive *proof* of his intention to violate our rights and to undermine our
national interests; then all his preceding actions on the Continent became
proofs likewise of the same intention; and any *one** of these aggressions

* An hundred Cases might be imagined, which would place this assertion in it's
true light. Suppose, for instance, a country according to the laws of which a
Parent might not disinherit a Son without having first convicted him of some one
of sundry crimes enumerated in a specific Statute. Caius, by a series of vicious
actions, has so nearly convinced his Father of his utter worthlessness, that the
Father resolves on the next provocation to use the very first opportunity of legally
disinheriting this Son. The provocation occurs, and in itself furnishes this opportunity: and Caius is disinherited, though, for an action much less glaring and intolerable, than most of his preceding delinquencies had been. The Advocates of
Caius complain, that he should be thus punished for a comparative trifle, so many
worse misdemeanors having been passed over. The Father replies: this, his last
action, is not the *cause* of the disinheritance; but the *means* of disinheriting him. I

involves the meaning of the whole. Which of them is to *determine* as to war, must be decided by other and prudential considerations. Had the First [361] Consul acquiesced in our detention of Malta, he would thereby have furnished such proof of pacific intentions, as would have led to further hopes, as would have lessened our alarm from his former acts of ambition, and relatively to us have altered in some degree their nature.

It should never be forgotten, that a Parliament or national Council is essentially different from a Court of Justice, alike in its' objects and its' duties. In the latter, the Juror lays aside his private knowledge and his private connections, and judges exclusively according to the evidence adduced in the Court: in the former, the Senator acts upon his own internal convictions, and oftentimes upon private information which it would be imprudent or criminal to disclose. Though his ostensible Reason ought to be a true and just one, it is by no means necessary, that it should be his sole or even his chief reason. In a Court of Justice the Juror attends to the character and general intentions of the accused party, exclusively as adding to the probability of his having or not having committed the one particular action then in question. The Senator, on the contrary, when he is to determine on the conduct of a foreign Power, attends to particular actions chiefly in proof of character and existing intentions. Now there were many and very powerful Reasons why, though appealing to the former actions of Buonaparte as confirmations of his hostile spirit and alarming Ambition, we should nevertheless make MALTA the direct Object and final Determinant of the War. Had we gone to war avowedly for the Independence of Holland and Switzerland, we should have furnished Buonaparte with a *colourable pretext* for annexing both countries immediately to the French Empire, which,* if he should do (as if his power continues, he most assuredly will sooner or later) by a mere act of violence, and undisguised tyranny, there will follow a *moral* weakening of his power in the minds of men, which may prove of *incalculable* advantage to the independence and well-being of Europe; but which, unfortunately, for this very reason, that it is not to be *calculated*, is too often disregarded by ordinary Statesmen. At all events, it would have been made the plea for banishing, plundering, and perhaps murdering numbers of virtuous [362] and patriotic Individuals, as being the Partizans of *"the Enemy of the Continent."* Add to this, that we should have appeared to have rushed into a War for objects, which by war we could not hope to realize; we should have exacerbated the misfortunes of the Countries of which we had elected ourselves the Champions; and the War would have appeared a

---

punished him *by* it rather than *for* it. In truth, it was not for any of his *actions*, that I have thus punished him, but for his *vices;* that is, not so much for the injuries which I have suffered, as for the *dispositions* which these actions *evinced;* for the insolent and alarming *intentions*, of which they are *proofs*. Now of this habitual temper, of these dangerous purposes, his last action is as true and compleat a manifestation, as any or all of his preceding offences; and it therefore may and must be taken, as their common *representative*.

* The Reader will bear in mind, that this disquisition was written, as it now appears, in the year 1804, (with the exception of the latter paragraphs, which I have therefore included in crotchets.)

mere War of Revenge and Reprisal, a circumstance always to be avoided where it is possible. The ablest and best men in the Batavian Republic, those who felt the insults of France most acutely, and were suffering from her oppressions the most severely, entreated our Government, through their Minister, that it would not make the state of Holland the great ostensible Reason of the War. The Swiss Patriots too believed, that we could do nothing to assist them at that time, and attributed to our forbearance the comparatively timid use, which France has made hitherto of her absolute power over that country. Besides Austria, whom the changes on the Continent much more nearly concerned than England, having refused all co-operation with us, there is reason to fear that an opinion (destructive of the one great blessing purchased by the Peace, our national unanimity) would have taken root in the popular mind, that these Changes were mere pretexts. Neither should we forget, that the last war had left a dislike in our countrymen to continental interference, and a not unplausible persuasion, that where a nation has not sufficient sensibility to its' wrongs to commence a war against the aggressor, unbribed and ungoaded by Great Britain, a war begun by the government of such a nation, at the instance of our Government, has little chance of other than a disastrous result, considering the character and revolutionary resources of the Enemy. Whatever may be the strength or weakness of this argument, it is however certain, that there was a strong predilection in the British People for a Cause indisputably and peculiarly British. And this feeling is not altogether ungrounded. In practical politics and the great expenditures of national power, we must not pretend to be too far-sighted: otherwise even a transient Peace would be impossible among the European Nations. To future and distant Evils we may always oppose the various unforeseen Events that are ripening in the womb of the Future. Lastly, it is chiefly to immediate and unequivocal attacks on our own Interests and [363] Honor, that we attach the notion of RIGHT with a full and efficient feeling. Now, though we may be first stimulated to action by probabilities and prospects of Advantage, and though there is a perverse restlessness in human nature, which renders almost all wars popular at their commencement, yet a nation always needs a sense of positive RIGHT to *steady* its' spirit. There is always needed some one reason, short, simple, and independent of complicated calculation, in order to give a sort of muscular strength to the public mind, when the power that results from enthusiasm, animal spirits, and the charm of novelty, has evaporated.

There is no feeling more honorable to our nature, and few that strike deeper root when our nature is happily circumstanced, than the jealousy concerning a positive Right independent of an immediate Interest. To surrender, in our national character, the merest Trifle, that is strictly our Right, the merest Rock on which the waves will scarcely permit the Sea-fowl to lay its' Eggs, at the demand of an insolent and powerful Rival, on a shop-keeper's calculation of Loss and Gain, is in its' final, and assuredly not very distant consequences, a Loss of every thing—of national Spirit, of national Independence, and with these of the very wealth, for which the low calculation was made. This feeling in individuals, indeed and in private life, is to be sacrificed to Religion. Say rather, that by Religion it is transmuted into a higher Virtue, growing on an higher and engrafted Branch, yet nourished from the same root; that it remains in its' essence the same Spirit, but

> Made pure by Thought, and naturaliz'd in Heaven;

and he who cannot perceive the moral differences of national and individual duties, comprehends neither the one or the other, and is not a whit the better Christian for being a bad Patriot. Considered nationally, it is as if the Captain of a Man of War should strike and surrender his colours under the pretence, that it would be folly to risk the lives of so many good Christian Sailors for the sake of a *few yards of coarse Canvas!* of such reasoners we take an indignant leave in the words of an obscure Poet,

> Fear never wanted arguments: you do
> Reason yourselves into a careful bondage,
> Circumspect only to your Misery.
> [364]   I could urge Freedom, Charters, Country, Laws,
> Gods, and Religion, and such precious names—
> Nay, what you value higher, *Wealth!* But that
> You sue for bondage, yielding to demands
> As impious as they're insolent, and have
> Only this sluggish name—TO PERISH FULL!
>
> CARTWRIGHT

And here we find it necessary to animadvert on a principle asserted by Lord Minto (*in his Speech, June 6th,* 1803, *and afterwards published at full length*) that France had an undoubted Right to insist on our abandonment of Malta, a Right not given, but likewise not abrogated, by the Treaty of Amiens. Surely in this effort of candour his Lordship must have forgotten the circumstances on which he exerted it. The case is simply thus: the British Government was convinced, and the French Government admitted the Justice of the Conviction, that it was of the utmost importance to our interests, that Malta should remain uninfluenced by France. The French Government binds itself down by a solemn Treaty, that it will use its' best endeavours in conjunction with us, to secure this independence. This promise was no act of liberality, no generous free-gift on the part of France. No! we purchased it at a high price. We disbanded our forces, we dismissed our Sailors, and we gave up the best part of the fruits of our naval victories. Can it therefore with a shadow of plausibility be affirmed, that the Right to insist on our evacuation of the Island, was unaltered by the Treaty of Amiens, when this demand is strictly tantamount to our surrender of all the advantages which we had bought of France at so high a price? tantamount to a direct breach on her part, not merely of a solemn Treaty, but of an absolute Bargain? It was not only the perfidy of unprincipled Ambition—the demand was the fraudulent trick of a Sharper. For what did France? She sold us the Independence of Malta: then exerted her power and annihilated the very possibility of that independence, and lastly, demanded of us that we should leave it bound hand and foot for her to seize without trouble, whenever her ambitious Projects led her to regard such seizure as expedient. We bound ourselves to surrender it to the Knights of Malta—not surely to Joseph, Robert, or Nicolas, but to a known order, cloathed with certain powers, and capable of exerting them in consequence of certain Revenues. We found no such order. The men indeed and the name [365] we found: and even so, if we had purchased Sardinia of its' Sovereign for so many millions of money, which through our national credit, and from the equivalence of our national Paper to Gold and Silver, he had agreed to receive in Bank Notes, and he had received them—doubtless, he would have the Bank Notes, even though immediately after our payment of them, we had for this very purpose forced the Bank Company to break. But would he have received the Debt due to him? It is nothing more or less than a practical *Pun*, as wicked though not quite so ludicrous, as the (in all senses) *execrable* Pun of Earl Goodwin, who requesting *Basium* (i.e. a kiss) from the Archbishop, thereupon seized on the Archbishop's Manor of Baseham.

A Treaty is a Writ of mutual Promise between two independent States, and the Law of Promise is the same to Nations as to Individuals. It is to be sacredly performed by each party in that sense in which it knew and permitted the other party to understand it, at the time of the contract. Any thing short of this is criminal deceit in Individuals, and in Governments impious perfidy. After the conduct of France in the affair of the Guarantees, and of the Revenues of the Order, we had the same right to preserve the Island independent of France by a British Garrison, as a lawful Creditor has to the Household goods of a fugitive and dishonest Debtor.

One other assertion of his Lordship's, in the same speech, bears so immediately on the plan of THE FRIEND, as far as it proposed to investigate the *principle* of international, no less than of private morality, that I feel myself in some degree under an obligation to notice it. A Treaty (says his Lordship) ought to be strictly observed by a nation in its' literal sense, even though the utter ruin of that nation should be the certain and foreknown consequence of the observance. Previous to any remarks of my own on this high flight of diplomatic virtue, we will hear what Harrington has said on this subject. "A man may devote himself to Death or Destruction to save a nation; but no nation will devote itself to Death or Destruction to save mankind. Machiavel is decried for saying, 'that no consideration is to be had of what is just or unjust, of what is merciful or cruel, of what is honourable or ignominious, in case it be to save a state or to preserve liberty:' which as to the manner of expression may perhaps [366] be crudely spoken. But to imagine, that a Nation will devote itself to Death or Destruction any more after Faith given, or an Engagement thereto tending, than if there had been no Engagement made or Faith given, were not Piety but Folly."—Crudely spoken indeed! and not less crudely thought, nor is the matter much mended by the commentator. Yet every Man, who is at all acquainted with the world and its' past History, knows that the *fact* itself is truly stated: and what is more important in the present argument, he cannot find in his heart a full, deep, and downright verdict, that it *should* be otherwise. The consequences of this perplexity in the moral feelings, are not seldom extensively injurious. For men hearing the duties, which would be binding on two individuals living under the same Laws, insisted on as equally obligatory on two independent states, in extreme cases, where they see clearly the impracticability of realizing such a notion; and having at the same time a dim half-consciousness, that two States can never be placed exactly on the same ground as two Individuals; relieve themselves from their perplexity by cutting what they cannot untie, and assert, that *national policy* cannot in all cases be subordinated to the Laws of Morality: in other words, that a Government may act with injustice, and yet remain blameless. This assertion was hazarded (I record it with unfeigned regret) by a Minister of State, on the affair of Copenhagen. Tremendous assertion! that would render every complaint, which we make, of the abominations of the French Tyrant, hypocrisy, or mere incendiary declamation for the simple-headed multitude! But, thank heaven! it is as unnecessary and unfounded, as it is tremendous. For what is a Treaty? a voluntary contract between two *Nations.* So we will state it in the first instance. Now it is an impossible case, that any nation can be supposed by any other to have intended its' own absolute Destruction in a Treaty, which its' interests alone could have prompted it to make. The very thought is self-contradictory. Not only Athens (we will say) could not have intended this to have been understood in any specific promise made to Sparta; but Sparta could never have imagined, that Athens had so intended it. And Athens itself must have known, that had she even affirmed the contrary, Sparta could not have believed—nay, would have been under a moral *obligation* not to have [367] believed her.—Were it possible to suppose such a case—for instance, such a Treaty made by a single besieged Town, under an independent government, as that of Numantia—it becomes no longer a state, but the act of a certain number of Individuals voluntarily sacrificing themselves, each to preserve his separate honor. For the state was already destroyed by the circumstances, which alone could make such an engagement conceivable.—But we have said, *Nations.*—Applied to England and France, relatively to treaties, this is but a form of speaking. The treaty is really made by some half dozen, or perhaps half a hundred individuals, possessing the *Government* of these countries. Now it is a universally admitted part of the Law of Nations, that an Engagement entered into by a Minister, with a foreign power, when it was known to this Power, that the Minister in so doing had exceeded and contravened his Instructions, is altogether nugatory. And is it to be supposed for a moment, that a whole nation, consisting of perhaps twenty millions of human souls, could ever have invested a few Individuals, whom, altogether for the promotion of its' welfare it had intrusted with its' Government, with the right of signing away its' existence?

SPECIMENS OF RABBINICAL WISDOM

SELECTED FROM THE MISHNA[1]

4

Conversation of a Philosopher with a Rabbi

Your God in his Book calls himself a jealous God who can endure no other God beside him, and on all occasions makes manifest his abhorrence of idolatry. How comes it then that he threatens and seems to

---

[1] See above, I 370 and n 2.

hate the worshippers of false Gods more than the false Gods themselves?
—A certain King, replied the Rabbi, had a disobedient Son. Among other
worthless tricks of various kinds, he had the baseness to give his Dogs his
Father's name and titles. Should the King shew his Anger on the Prince
or the Dogs?—Well turned, rejoined the Philosopher: but if your God
destroyed the objects of idolatry he would take away the temptation to
it.—Yea, retorted the Rabbi, if the Fools worshipped such things only as
were of no further use than that to which their Folly applied them, if the
Idol were always as worthless as the [368] Idolatry is contemptible. But
they worship the Sun, the Moon, the Host of Heaven, the Rivers, the Sea,
Fire, Air—and what not? Would you that the Creator, for the sake of
these Fools, should ruin his own Works and disturb the Laws appointed
to Nature by his own Wisdom? If a Man steals grain and sows it, should
the seed not shoot up out of the Earth because it was stolen? O no! the
wise Creator lets nature run her own course, for her course is his own
appointment. And what if the Children of Folly abuse it to evil? The
day of reckoning is not far off, and Men will then learn, that human
Actions re-appear in their consequences by as certain a Law as the green
Blade rises up out of the buried corn seed.

To the doctrine of retribution after Death, the Philosopher made the
following objection. When the soul is disunited from the body, to which
will belong the guilt of the offences committed during Life? Certainly not
to the body, for this, when the soul takes its departure, lies like a clod of
earth, and without the soul would never have been capable of offending:
and as little would the soul have defiled itself with sin but for it's union
with the flesh. Which of the two then is the proper object of the divine
Justice? God's Wisdom only, answered the Rabbi, fully comprehends the
ways of his justice. Yet the Mortal may without offence, if with humility,
strive to render the same intelligible to himself and his fellows. A Householder had in his fruit-garden two Servants, the one lame and the other
blind. Yonder, said the lame Man to the blind, on those Trees I see most
delicious fruit hang, take me on thy shoulders and we will pluck thereof.
This they did and thus robbed their Benefactor, who had maintained them,
as unprofitable servants, out of his mere goodness and compassion. The
Master discovered the theft, and called the two Ingrates to account. Each
threw off the blame from himself, the one urging in his defence his incapability of seeing the Fruit, and the other the want of power to get at
it. What did the Master of the House do? He placed the lame Man upon
the blind, and punished them in the same posture in which they had committed the Offence. So will the Judge of the world do with the soul and
body of Man.

THE FRIEND

No. 23, THURSDAY, FEBRUARY 8, 1810

ONLY a few privileged Individuals are authorized to pass into the Theatre without stopping at the Door-keeper's box; but every man of decent appearance may put down the Play-price there, and thenceforward has as good a right as the Managers themselves not only to see and hear, as far as his place in the House, and his own ears and eyes permit him, but likewise to express audibly his approbation or disapprobation of what may be going forward on the Stage. If his feelings happen to be in unison with those of the Audience in general, he may without breach of decorum persevere in his notices of applause or dislike, till the wish of the House is complied with. If he finds himself unsupported, he rests contented with having once exerted his common right, and on that occasion at least gives no further interruption to the amusement of those, who feel differently from him. So it is, or so it should be, in Literature. A few extraordinary minds may be allowed to pass a mere *opinion:* though in point of fact, those who alone are entitled to this privilege, are ever the last to avail themselves of it. Add too, that even the mere opinions of such men may in general be regarded either as promissory Notes, or as receipts referring to a former payment. But every man's *opinion* has a right to pass into the common Auditory, if his *reason* for the opinion is paid down at the same time: for arguments are the sole current coin of intellect. The degree of influence to which the opinion is entitled, should be proportioned to the weight and value of the Reasons for it: and whether these are shillings or pounds sterling, the man, who has given them, remains blameless, provided he contents himself with the place to which they have entitled him, and does not attempt by strength of lungs to counter-balance its' disadvantages, or expect to exert as immediate an influence in the back seats of the upper Gallery, as if he had paid in gold and been seated in the Stage box.

[370] But unfortunately (and here commence the points of difference between the theatric and the literary Public) in the great Theatre of Literature there are no authorized Door-keepers: for our anonymous Critics are self-elected. I shall not fear the charge of calumny if I add, that they have lost all credit with wise men, by unfair dealing: such as their refusal to receive an honest man's money, (that is, his argument) because they anticipate and dislike his opinion, while others of suspicious character and the most unseemly appearance, are suffered to pass without payment, or by virtue of *orders* which they have themselves distributed to known Partizans. Sometimes the honest man's intellectual coin is refused under pretence, that it is light or counterfeit, without any proof given either by

the money scales, or by sounding the coin in dispute together with one of known goodness. We may carry the metaphor still farther. It is by no means a rare case, that the money is returned because it had a different sound from that of a counterfeit, the brassy blotches on which seemed to blush for the impudence of the silver wash in which they were inisled, and rendered the mock coin a lively emblem of a lie self-detected. Still oftener does the rejection take place by a mere act of insolence, and the blank assertion, that the Candidate's money is light or bad, is justified by a second assertion, that he is a Fool or Knave for offering it.

The second point of difference explains the preceding, and accounts both for the want of established Door-keepers in the Auditory of Literature, and for the practices of those, who under the name of Reviewers volunteer this office. There is no royal Mintage for Arguments, no ready means, by which all men alike, who possess common sense, may determine their value and intrinsic worth at the first sight or sound. Certain forms of natural Logic indeed there are, the inobservance of which is decisive against an argument; but the strictest adherence to them is no proof of it's actual (though an indispensible condition of its' possible) validity: In the Arguer's own conscience there is no doubt, a certain value, and an infallible criterion of it, which applies to all Arguments equally: and this is the sincere conviction of the mind itself. But for those, to whom it is offered, these are only *conjectural* marks; yet such as will seldom mislead any man of plain sense, who is both honest and [371] observant. These characteristics THE FRIEND attempted to comprize in the concluding paragraph of his second Number, and has described them more at large in the Essay, which follows, "On the communication of Truth." If the honest warmth, which results from the strength of the particular conviction, be tempered by the modesty which belongs to the sense of general fallibility; if the emotions, which accompany all vivid perceptions, are preserved distinct from the expression of personal passions, and from appeals to them in the heart of others; if the Reasoner asks no respect for the opinion, as *his* opinion, but only in proportion as it is acknowledged by that Reason, which is common to all men; and, lastly, if he supports an opinion on no subject which he has not previously examined, and furnishes proof both that he possesses the means of enquiry by his education or the nature of his pursuits, and that he has endeavoured to avail himself of those means; then, and with these conditions, every human Being is authorized to make public the *grounds* of any opinion which he holds, and of course the opinion itself, as the object of them, consequently, it is the duty of all men, not always indeed to attend to him, but, if they do, to attend to him with respect, and with a sincere as well as apparent toleration. I should offend against my own Laws, if I disclosed at present the nature of my convictions concerning the degree, in which this virtue of Toleration is possessed and practised by the majority of my Contemporaries and Countrymen, but if the contrary Temper is felt and shewn in instances where all the conditions have been observed, which have been stated at full in the second and three following Numbers of this work, and the chief of which I have just now recapitulated; I have no hesitation in declaring that whatever the opinion may be, and however opposite to the Hearer's or Reader's previous persuasions, one or other or all of the following defects must be taken for granted. Either the intolerant Person is not master of the grounds on which his own Faith is built, which therefore neither is or can be his own *Faith*, though it may very easily be his *Liking* his imagined *Interest*, and his *Habit* of thought: and he is angry, not at the opposition to Truth, but at the interruption of his own indolence and intellectual slumber, or possibly at the apprehension, that his temporal advantages are threatened, or at least the ease of mind, in which he had been accustomed to enjoy [372] them. Or, secondly, he has no love of Truth for its' own sake; no reverence for the divine command to seek earnestly after it, which command, if it had not been so often and solemnly given by Revelation, is yet involved and expressed in the gift of Reason, and in the dependence of all our virtues on its' developement; and no moral and religious awe for freedom of thought, though accompanied both by sincerity and humility; nor for the right of free communication which is ordained by God, together with that freedom, if it be true that God has ordained us to live in Society, and has made the progressive improvement of all and each of us depend on the reciprocal aids, which directly or indirectly each supplies to all, and all to each. But if his alarm and his consequent intolerance, are occasioned by his eternal rather than temporal interests, and if as is most commonly the case, he does not deceive himself on this point, gloomy indeed, and erroneous beyond idolatry, must have been his notions of the Supreme Being! For surely the poor Heathen who represents to himself the divine attributes of Wisdom, Justice, and Mercy, under multiplied and forbidden Symbols in the powers of Nature or the Souls of Extraordinary Men, practises a Superstition which (though at once the cause and effect of blindness and sensuality) is less incompatible with inward piety and true religious feeling, than the Creed of that Man, who in the spirit of his practice though not in direct words, loses sight of all these attributes, and substitutes "servile and thrall-like fear instead of the adoptive and chearful boldness, which our new alliance with God requires of us as Christians." * Such fear-ridden and thence angry Believers, or rather *Acquiescents*, would do well to re-peruse the Book of Job, and observe the sentence passed by the All-just on the Friends of the Sufferer, who had hoped, like venal advocates, to *purchase* the favour of Deity by uttering Truths, of which in their own hearts they had neither conviction nor comprehension. [373] THE TRUTH FROM THE LIPS DID NOT ATONE FOR THE LIE IN THE HEART, while the rashness of agony in the scarching and bewildered Complainant, was forgiven in consideration of his sincerity and integrity in not disguising the true dictates of his Reason and Conscience, but avowing his incapability of solving a problem

---

* *Milton's Reformation in England.* "For in every deed, the superstitious Man by his good will is an Atheist; but being scared from thence by the pangs of conscience, shuffles up to himself such a God and such a Worship, as is most accordant to his Fear: which Fear of his as also his Hope, being fixed only upon the Flesh, renders likewise the whole faculty of his Apprehension carnal, and *all the inward acts of Worship issuing from the native strength of the Soul, run out lavishly to the upper Şkin, and there harden into a crust of Formality.* Hence men came to scan the Scriptures by the *Letter*, and in the covenant of our Redemption magnified the external signs more than the quickening power of the *Spirit*."

by his Reason, which before the Christian Dispensation the Almighty was pleased to solve only by declaring it to be beyond the limits of human Reason. Having insensibly passed into a higher and more serious style than I had first intended, I will venture to appeal to these Self-obscurants, whose Faith dwells in the Land of the Shadow of Darkness, these Papists without a Pope, and Protestants who protest only against all protesting; and will appeal to them in words which yet more immediately concern them as Christians, in the hope that they will lend a fearless ear to the learned Apostle, when he both assures and labours to persuade them, that they *were called in Christ to all perfectness in spiritual knowledge and full assurance of understanding in the mystery of God.* There can be no End without means: and God furnishes no means that exempt us from the task and duty of joining our own best endeavours. The original Stock, or wild olive tree, of our natural powers, was not given us to be burnt or blighted, but to be *grafted on.* We are not only not forbidden to examine and propose our doubts, so it be done with humility and proceed from a real desire to know the Truth; but we are repeatedly commanded so to do: and with a most unchristian spirit must that Man have read the preceding passages, if he can interpret any one sentence as having for its' object to excuse a too numerous class, who, to use the words of St. Augustine, *quærunt non ut fidem sed ut infidelitatem inveniant:* i.e. such as examine not to find reasons for Faith, but pretexts for Infidelity.

I have so often suffered from having ventured to avow my doubts concerning the Truth of certain opinions, which had been sanctified in the minds of my Hearers, by the Authority of some reigning great name, even though in addition to my own reasons, I had all the greatest Names from the Reformation to the Revolution on my side, that I could not summon courage, without some previous pioneering, to declare publicly, that the Principles of Morality taught in the present Work will be in direct opposition to the System of the late Dr. Paley. [374] This confession I should have deferred to a future time, but that my present Subject (viz. the grounds of international Morality) compels me to advert to a fundamental point in Paley's System of moral and political Philosophy, that Chapter, I mean, which treats of GENERAL CONSEQUENCES, as the chief and best criterion of the Right or Wrong of particular Actions. Now this Doctrine I conceive to be neither tenable in Reason nor Safe in Practice: and the following are the grounds of my Opinion:

First; this criterion is purely *ideal,* and so far possesses no advantages over the former more rigid systems of Morality: while it labours under defects, with which those are not justly chargeable. It is *ideal:* for it depends on, and must vary with, the notions of the Individual, who in determining the nature of an action is to make the calculation of it's general consequences: and, as in all other calculation, the result depends on that faculty of the Soul in the decrees of which men most vary from each other, and which is itself most affected by accidental advantages or disadvantages of Education, natural Talent, and acquired Knowledge—the faculty, I mean, of Foresight and systematic Comprehension. But surely Morality, which is of equal importance to all men, ought to be grounded, if possible, in that part of our Nature which in all Men may and ought to be the same: in the Conscience and the common sense. Secondly; this criterion confounds Morality with Law; and when the Author adds, that in all probability the divine Justice will be regulated in the final Judgement by a similar rule, he draws away the attention from the *Will*, that is from the inward motives and impulses which constitute the Essence of *Morality*, to the outward Act: and thus changes the Virtue commanded by the Gospel into the mere Legality, which was to be enlivened by it. One of the most persuasive, if not one of the strongest, arguments for a future state, rests on the belief, that although by the necessity of things our outward and temporal welfare must be regulated by our outward actions, which alone can be the objects and guides of human Law, there must yet needs come a juster and more appropriate sentence hereafter, in which our *intentions* will be considered, and our Happiness and Misery made to accord with the grounds of our Actions. Our Fellow-creatures can only judge what we *are* by what we *do;* but in the eye of our Maker what we *do* is of no worth, [375] except as it flows from what we *are*. Though the Fig-tree should produce no visible Fruit, yet if the living Sap is in it, and if it has struggled to put forth Buds and Blossoms which have been prevented from maturing by inevitable contingencies of tempests or untimely frosts, the virtuous Sap will be accounted as Fruit: and the curse of Barrenness will light on many a Tree, from the Boughs of which hundreds have been satisfied, because the omniscient Judge knows, that the Fruits were threaded to the Boughs artificially by the outward working of base Fear and selfish Hopes, and were neither nourished by the love of God or of man, nor grew out of the graces engrafted on the Stock by Religion. This is not, indeed, all that is meant in the Apostles use of the word Faith, as the sole principle of Justification, but it is included in his meaning and forms an essential part of it: and I can conceive no thing more groundless, than the alarm, that this Doctrine may be prejudicial to outward utility and active well-doing. To suppose that a Man should cease to be *beneficent* by becoming *benevolent*, seems to me scarcely less absurd, than to fear that a fire may prevent heat, or that a perennial fountain may prove the occasion of Drought. Just and generous Actions may proceed from bad Motives, and both may, and often do, originate in *parts* and as it were *fragments*, of our Nature. A lascivious Man may sacrifice half his Estate to rescue his Friend from Prison, for he is constitutionally sympathetic, and the better part of his Nature happened to be uppermost: the same Man shall afterwards exert the same disregard of money in an attempt to seduce that Friend's Wife or Daughter. But Faith is a *total* act of the soul: it is the *whole* state of the mind, or it is not at all! and in this consists its' power, as well as its' exclusive worth.

This Subject is of such immense importance to the Welfare of all men, and the understanding of it to the present tranquility of many thousands at this time and in this Country, that should there be but one only of all my Readers, who should receive conviction or an additional light from what is here written, I dare hope that a great majority of the rest would in consideration of that solitary effect think these Paragraphs neither wholly uninteresting or altogether without value. For this cause I will endeavour so to explain this Principle, that it may be intelligible to the simplest capacity. The Apostle tells those, who [376] would substitute Obedience for Faith (addressing the Man as Obedience personified) "*Know that thou bearest not the Root, but the ROOT thee*"—a sentence which, methinks, should have rendered all disputes concerning Faith and good Works impossible among those, who profess to take the Scriptures for their Guide. It would appear incredible, if the fact were not notorious, that two Sects should ground and justify their opposition to each other, the one on the words of the Apostle, that we are justified by Faith, i.e. the inward and absolute ground of our Actions; and the other on the declaration of Christ, that he will judge us according to our Actions. As if an Action could be either good or bad disjoined from its' Principle! as if it could be, in the christian and only proper sense of the word an *Action* at all, and not rather a mechanic series of lucky or unlucky motions! Yet it may be well worth the while to shew the beauty and harmony of these twin Truths, or rather of this one great truth considered in its' two principal bearings. God will judge each man before all Men: consequently he will judge us relatively to man. But man knows not the heart of man; scarcely does any one know his own. There must therefore be outward and visible signs, by which men may be able to judge of the inward state: and thereby justify the ways of God to their own spirits, in the Reward or Punishment of themselves and their Fellow-men. Now good Works are these Signs, and as such become necessary. In short there are two Parties, God and the human Race: and both are to be satisfied! first, *God*, who seeth the Root and knoweth the Heart: therefore there must be Faith, or the entire and absolute Principle. Then *Man*, who can judge only by the Fruits: therefore that Faith must bear Fruits of Righteousness, that Principle must *manifest* itself by Actions. But that which God sees, *that* alone justifies: what Man sees, does *in this life* shew, that the justifying Principle may be the root of the thing seen; but in the final Judgement the acceptance of these actions will shew that this Principle actually *was* the Root. In this world a good Life is a *presumption* of a good Man: his virtuous actions are the only possible, though still ambiguous, manifestations of his virtue: but the absence of a good Life is not only a presumption, but a proof of the contrary, as long as it continues. Good Works may exist *without* saving Principles, and therefore *cannot* contain in themselves [377] the Principle of Salvation; but saving Principles never did, never can, exist without good Works. On a subject of such infinite importance, I have feared prolixity less than obscurity. Men often talk against Faith, and make strange monsters in their imagination of those, who profess to abide by the words of the Apostle interpreted literally: and yet in their ordinary feelings they themselves judge and act by a similar Principle. For what is Love without kind offices, wherever they are possible? (and they are always possible, if not by actions commonly so called, yet by kind Words, by kind Looks; and, where even these are out of our power, by kind Thoughts and fervent Prayers!) yet what noble mind would not be offended, if he were supposed to value the serviceable offices equally with the Love that produced them; or if he were thought to value the Love for the sake of the Services, and not the Services for the sake of the Love?

I return to the question of general consequences, considered as the criterion of moral actions. The admirer of Paley's System is required to suspend for a short time the objection, which, I doubt not, he has already made, that general consequences are stated by Paley as the Criterion of the Action, not of the Agent. I will endeavour to satisfy him on this point, when I have completed my present chain of argument. It has been shewn, that this criterion is no less *ideal* than that of any former System: that is, it is no less incapable of receiving any external, experimental proof, compulsory on the understandings of all men, such as the criteria exhibited in Chemistry. Yet, unlike the elder Systems of Morality, it remains in the World of the Senses, without deriving any evidence therefrom: the Agent's mind is compelled to go out of itself in order to bring back *conjectures*, the probability of which will vary with the shrewdness of the Individual. But this criterion is not only ideal: it is likewise imaginary. If we believe in a scheme of Providence, all Actions alike work for good: there is not the least ground for supposing, that the crimes of Nero were less instrumental in bringing about our present advantages, than the virtues of the Antonines. Lastly; the criterion is either nugatory or false. It is demonstrated, that the only *real* consequences cannot be meant. The Individual is to *imagine*, what the general consequences *would* be all [378] other things remaining the same, if all men were to act as he is about to act. I scarcely need remind the Reader, what a source of self delusion and sophistry is here opened to a mind in a state of temptation. Will it not say to itself, I know that all men *will not* act so: and the immediate good consequences, which I shall obtain, are *real*, while the bad consequences are imaginary and improbable? When the foundations of Morality have once been laid in outward consequences, it will be in vain to recall to the mind, what the consequences would be, were all men to reason in the same way: for the very excuse of this mind to itself is, that neither its' action nor its' reasoning is likely to have any consequences at all, its' immediate object excepted. But suppose the mind in its' sanest state. How can it possibly form a notion of the nature of an action considered as indefinitely multiplied, unless it has previously a distinct notion of the nature of the single action itself, which is the multiplicand? If I conceive a Crown multiplied a hundred fold, the single Crown enables me to understand what a hundred Crowns are; but how can the notion hundred teach me, what a Crown is? For the Crown substitute X. Y. or abracadabra, and my imagination may multiply it to infinity, and I remain as much at a loss as before. But if there be any means of ascertaining the Action in and for itself, what further do we want? Would we give light to the Sun, or look at our own fingers through a Telescope? The nature of every action is determined by all its' circumstances: alter the circumstances and a similar set of *motions* may be repeated, but they are no longer the same or similar Action. What would a Surgeon say, if he were advised not to cut off a limb, because if all men were to do the same, the consequences would be dreadful? Would not his answer be—"Whoever does the same under the same circumstances, and with the same motives, will do right; but if the circumstances and motives are different, what have I to do with it?" I confess myself unable to divine any possible use, or even meaning, in this doctrine of general consequences, unless it be, that in all our actions we are bound to consider the effect of our example, and to guard as much as possible against the hazard of their being misunderstood. I will not slaughter a Lamb, or drown a litter of Kittens in the presence of my child of four years old, because the child cannot understand my action, but [379] will understand that his Father has inflicted pain, and taken away life from beings, that had never offended him. All this is true, and no man in his senses ever thought otherwise. But methinks it is strange to state that, as a criterion of morality, which is no more than an accessary aggravation of an action bad in its' own nature, or a ground of caution as to the mode and time, in which we are to do or suspend what is in itself good or innocent.

The duty of setting a good Example is no doubt a most important Duty; but the example is good or bad, necessary or unnecessary, according as the Action may be, which has a chance of being imitated. I once knew a small, but (in outward circumstances at least) respectable Congregation, four-fifths of whom professed that they went to Church *entirely* for the example's sake; in other words to cheat each other and act a common Lie! These *rational* Christians had not considered, that example may encrease the good or evil of an action, but can never constitute either. If it was a *foolish thing* to kneel, when they were not inwardly praying, or to sit and listen to a discourse of which they believed little and cared nothing, they were setting a foolish *example*. Persons in their *respectable* circumstances do not think it necessary to clean shoes, that by their example they may encourage the shoe-black in continuing *his* occupation: and Christianity does not think so meanly of herself, as to fear that the poor and afflicted will be a whit the less pious, though they should see reason to believe that those, who possessed the good things of the present life, were determined to leave all the blessings of the future for their more humble inferiors. If I have spoken with bitterness, let it be recollected that my subject is Hypocrisy.

It is likewise fit, that in all our actions we should have considered, how far they are likely to be misunderstood, and from superficial resemblances to be confounded with, and so appear to authorize, actions of a very different character. But if this caution be intended for a moral rule, the misunderstanding must be such as might be made by persons who are neither very weak nor very wicked. The apparent resemblances between the good action we were about to do, and the bad one which might possibly be done in mistaken imitation of it, must be obvious: or that which makes them essentially different, must be subtle or recondite. For what is there which a wicked man blinded [380] by his passions may not, and which a madman will not misunderstand? It is ridiculous to frame rules of Morality with a view to those, who are fit objects only for the Physician or the Magistrate. The question may be thus illustrated. At Florence there is an unfinished bust of Brutus, by Michael Angelo, under which a Cardinal wrote the following distich:

> Dum Bruti effigiem sculptor de marmore finxit,
> In mentem sceleris venit, et abstinuit.

As the Sculptor was forming the Effigy of Brutus, in marble, he recollected his act of guilt and refrained.

An English Nobleman, indignant at this distich, wrote immediately under
it the following:
Brutum effinxisset sculptor, sed mente recursat
Multa viri virtus; sistit et obstupuit.

*The Sculptor would have framed a Brutus, but the vast and manifold virtue of the
Man flashed upon his thought: he stopped and remained in astonished admiration.*

Now which is the nobler and more moral Sentiment, the Italian Cardinal's, or the English Nobleman's? The Cardinal would appeal to the
doctrine of general consequences, and pronounce the death of Cæsar a
murder, and Brutus an Assassin. For, (he would say) if one man may be
allowed to kill another, because he thinks him a Tyrant, religious or
political phrenzy may stamp the name of Tyrant on the best of Kings:
regicide will be justified under the pretence of tyrannicide, and Brutus be
quoted as authority for the Clements and Ravilliacs. From Kings it may
pass to Generals and Statesmen, and from these to any Man, whom an
enemy or enthusiast may pronounce unfit to live. Thus we may have a
Cobler of Messina in every City, and Bravos in our Streets, as common
as in those of Naples, with the names of Harmodius, Aristogeiton,[1] and
Brutus, on their Stilettos. The Englishman would commence his answer
by commenting on the words "because he *thinks* him a Tyrant." No! he
would reply, not because the Patriot *thinks* him a Tyrant; but because he
knows him to be so, and knows likewise, that the vilest of his slaves cannot
deny the fact, that he has by [381] violence raised himself above the Laws
of his Country; because he knows, that all good and wise men equally
with himself abhor the fact! If there be no such state, as that of being
broad awake, or no means of distinguishing it when it exists; if because
men sometimes dream that they are awake, it must follow that no man,
when awake, can be sure that he is not dreaming; if because an Hypo-
chondriac is positive, that his legs are cylinders of glass, all other men are
to learn modesty, and cease to be so positive, that their legs are legs; what
possible advantage can *your* criterion of GENERAL CONSEQUENCES possess over any other rule of direction? If no man can be sure, that what
he *thinks* a Robber with a pistol at his Breast demanding his purse, may
not be a good Friend enquiring after his health; or that a Tyrant (the son
of a cobler perhaps, who at the head of a regiment of perjured Traitors,
has driven the representatives of his Country out of the Senate at the
point of the bayonet, subverted the Constitution, which had trusted, enriched, and honored him, trampled on the Laws which before God and
Man he had sworn to obey, and finally raised himself above all Law) may
not, in spite of his own and his Neighbours' knowledge of the contrary,
be a lawful King, who has received his power, however despotic it may be,
from the Kings his Ancestors, who exercises no other power, than what
had been submitted to for centuries and been acknowledged as the Law
of the Country; on what ground can you possibly expect less fallibility,
or a result more to be relied upon, in the same man's calculation of your
general consequences? Would *he*, at least, find any difficulty in converting
your criterion into an authority for his act? What should prevent a man,
whose perceptions and judgements are so strangely distorted, from arguing,

---

[1] See above, I 321 and n 1.

that nothing is more devoutly to be wished for, as a general consequence, than that every Man, who by violence places himself above the Laws of his Country, should in all Ages and Nations be considered by Mankind, as placed by his own act out of the protection of Law, and be treated by them as any other noxious wild beast would be? Do you think it necessary to try Adders by a Jury? Do you hesitate to shoot a mad Dog, because it is not in your power to have him first tried and condemned at the Old Bailey? On the other hand, what consequence can be conceived more detestable, than one which would set a bounty on the most [382] enormous crime in human nature, and establish it as a law of Religion and Morality, that the accomplishment of the most atrocious guilt, invests the Perpetrator with impunity, and renders his person for ever sacred and inviolable? For madmen and enthusiasts what avail your moral criterions? But as to your Neapolitan Bravos, if the act of Brutus when *"in pity to the general wrong of Rome, He slew his best Lover for the good of Rome,"* authorized by the Laws of his Country, in manifest opposition to all selfish interests, in the face of the Senate, and instantly presenting himself and his cause first to that Senate, and then to the assembled Commons, by them to stand acquitted or condemned—if such an act as this, with all its' vast out-jutting circumstances of distinction, can be confounded by any mind not frantic with the crime of a cowardly skulking Assassin, who hires out his dagger for a few crowns to gratify a hatred not his own, or even with the deed of that Man, who makes a compromise between his revenge and his cowardice, and stabs in the dark the enemy whom he dared not meet in the open field, or summon before the laws of his Country—*what* actions can be so different, that they may not be equally confounded? The ambushed Soldier must not fire his musquet, lest *his* example should be quoted by the Villain, who to make sure of his booty, discharges his piece at the un-suspicious Passenger, from behind a hedge.—The Physician must not administer a solution of arsenic to the leprous, lest *his* example should be quoted by professional poisoners. If no distinction, full and satisfactory to the conscience and common sense of mankind be afforded by the detestation and horror excited in all men, (even in the meanest and most vicious, if they are not wholly monsters) by the act of the Assassin, con-trasted with the fervent admiration felt by the good and wise in all ages, when they mention the name of Brutus; contrasted with the fact that the honor or disrespect, with which that name was spoken of, became an historic criterion of a noble or a base Age; and if it is in vain, that our own hearts answer to the question of the Poet

> "Is there among the adamantine spheres
> Wheeling unshaken through the boundless void,
> Aught that with half such majesty can fill
> The human bosom, as when Brutus rose
> [383]   Refulgent from the stroke of Cæsar's fate
> Amid the croud of Patriots; and his arm
> Aloft extending, like eternal Jove,
> When guilt brings down the thunder, call'd aloud
> On Tully's name, and shook his crimson sword,
> And bade the Father of his Country, Hail!

> For lo the Tyrant prostrate on the dust
> And Rome again is free!"—

If I say, all this be fallacious and insufficient, can we have any firmer reliance on a cold ideal calculation of imaginary GENERAL CONSEQUENCES, which, if they were general, could not be *consequences* at all: for they would be effects of the frenzy or frenzied wickedness, which alone could confound actions so utterly dissimilar? No! (would the ennobled Descendant of our Russells or Sidneys conclude) No! Calumnious Bigot, never yet did a human being become an assassin from his own or the general admiration, of the Hero, Brutus; but I dare not warrant, that villains might not be encouraged in their trade of secret murder, by finding their own guilt attributed to the Roman Patriot, and might not conclude, that if Brutus be no better than an Assassin, an Assassin can be no worse than Brutus. I request, that the preceding may not be interpreted as my own settled judgement on the moral nature of Tyrannicide. I think with Machiavel and with Spinosa, for many and weighty reasons assigned by those Philosophers, that it is difficult to conceive a case, in which a good man would attempt Tyrannicide, because it is difficult to conceive one, in which a wise man would recommend it. In a small State, included within the walls of a single City, and where the tyranny is maintained by foreign Guards, it may be otherwise; but in a Nation or Empire it is perhaps inconceivable, that the circumstances which made a Tyranny possible, should not likewise render the removal of the Tyrant useless. The patriot's sword may cut off the Hydra's head; but he possesses no brand to staunch the active corruption of the body, which is sure to re-produce a Successor.

I must now in a few words answer the objection to the former part of my argument (for to that part only the objection applies,) namely that the doctrine of general consequences was stated as the criterion of the Action, not of the Agent. I might answer, that the Author himself had in [384] some measure justified me in not noticing this distinction by holding forth the probability, that the supreme judge will proceed by the same rule. The Agent may then safely be included in the Action, if both here and hereafter the Action only and its' general consequences will be attended to. But my main ground of justification is, that the distinction itself is merely logical, not real and vital. The character of the agent is determined by his view of the action: and that System of Morality is alone true and suited to human nature, which unites the intention and the motive, the warmth and the light, in one and the same act of mind. This alone is worthy to be called a moral Principle. Such a Principle may be extracted, though not without difficulty and danger, from the ore of the stoic Philosophy; but it is to be found unalloyed and entire in the christian System, and is there called FAITH.

A single Paragraph will enable me to apply the result to the question of international Morality and at the same time will establish the true nature and obligation of the Law of Nations, which was a necessary part of my plan, and which I knew no more interesting or shorter method of introducing and accomplishing, than in connection with the subject of Biography, which I shall re-commence in the next number.[1]

[1] The law of nations is the subject of No 24; the biography of Ball recom-   mences in No 26.

THE FRIEND

No. 24, THURSDAY, FEBRUARY 15, 1809[1]

ON THE LAW OF NATIONS

IT were absurd to suppose, that Individuals should be under a law of moral obligation, and yet that a million of the same individuals, acting collectively or through representatives, should be exempt from all law: for Morality is no accident of human nature, but its' essential characteristic. A being absolutely without morality is either a beast or a fiend, according as we conceive this want of conscience to be natural or self-produced; or (to come nearer to the common notion, though with the sacrifice of austere accuracy) according as the being is conceived without the law, or in unceasing and irretrievable rebellion to it. Yet were it possible to conceive a man wholly immoral, it would remain impossible to conceive him without a moral obligation to be otherwise: and none, but a madman, will imagine that the essential qualities of any thing can be altered by its' becoming part of an aggregate; that a grain of corn, for instance, shall cease to contain flour, as soon as it is part of a peck or bushel. It is therefore grounded in the nature of the thing, and not by a mere fiction of the mind, that wise men, who have written on the Law of Nations, have always considered the several States of the civilized world, as so many Individuals, and equally with the latter under a moral obligation to exercise their free agency within such bounds, as render it compatible with the existence of free agency in others. We may represent to ourselves this original free agency, as a right of commonage, the formation of separate States as an enclosure of this Common, the Allotments awarded severally to the co-proprietors as constituting national Rights, and the Law of Nations as the common Register Office of their title deeds. But in all Morality, though the principle, which is the abiding *spirit* of the Law, remains perpetual and unaltered, even as that supreme Reason in whom and from whom it has its' being, yet the *Letter* of the Law, that is, the application of it to particular instances and the mode of realizing it in actual practice, must be modified by the existing circumstances. *What* we should desire to do, the conscience alone will inform us; but *how* and *when* we are to [386] make the attempt, and to what extent it is in our power to accomplish it, are questions for the judgement, and require an acquaintance with facts and their bearings on each other. Thence the improve-

---

[1] A misprint corrected to "1810" while the issue was being printed: one of the BM copies (C 126 b 8) has the right date; all other copies I have seen have the wrong date. The same BM copy does not make the correction cited in the note below, II 331 n 1.

ment of our judgement, and the increase of our knowledge, on all subjects included within our sphere of action, are not merely advantages recommended by prudence, but absolute duties imposed on us by conscience.

As the circumstances then, under which men act as Statesmen, are different from those under which they act as Individuals, a proportionate difference must be expected in the practical rules by which their public conduct is to be determined. Let me not be misunderstood: I speak of a difference in the practical rules not in the moral law itself which these rules point out the means of administering in particular cases, and under given circumstances. The spirit continues one and the same, though it may vary its' form according to the element into which it is transported. This difference with its' grounds and consequences it is the province of the philosophical Jus-publicist to discover and display: and exactly in this point (I speak with unfeigned diffidence) it appears to me that the Writers* on the Law of Nations, whose works I have had the opportunity of studying, have been least successful. In what does the Law of Nations differ from the Laws enacted by a particular State for its' own Subjects? The solution is evident. The law of nations considered apart from the common Principle of all Morality is not fixed or positive in itself, nor supplied with any regular means of being enforced. Like those duties in private Life which, for the same reasons, Moralists have entitled imperfect duties (though the most atrocious guilt may be involved in the omission or violation of them), the law of nations appeals only to the conscience and prudence of the Parties concerned. Wherein then does it differ from the moral laws which the Reason, considered as Conscience, dictates for the conduct of Individuals? This is a more difficult question; but my answer would be determined by, and grounded on, the obvious differences [387] of the circumstances in the two cases. Remember, then, that we are now reasoning, not as Sophists or System-mongers, but as Men anxious to discover what is right in order that we may practice it, or at least give our suffrage and the influence of our opinion in recommending its' practice. We must therefore confine the question to those cases, in which honest Men and real Patriots can suppose any controversy to exist between real patriotism and common honesty. The objects of the Patriot are, that his countrymen should, as far as circumstances permit, enjoy what the Creator designed for the enjoyment of Animals endowed with reason, and of course develope those faculties which were given them to be developed. He would do his best that every one of his Countrymen should possess whatever all men may and should possess, and that a sufficient number should be enabled and encouraged to acquire those excellencies which, though not

---

* Grotius, Bykenshoek, Puffendorf, Wolfe, and Vattel; to whose Works I must add, as comprizing whatever is most valuable in the preceding Authors, with many important improvements and additions, Robinson's Reports of the Causes of the Court of Admiralty under Sir W. Scott: to whom international Law is under no less obligation than the Law of commercial proceedings was to the late Lord Mansfield. As I have never even seen Sir W. Scott, nor either by myself or my connections enjoy the honour of the remotest acquaintance with him, I trust that even by those who may think my opinions erroneous, I shall at least not be suspected of intentional flattery.

necessary or possible *for* all men, are yet *to* all men useful and honourable. He knows, that Patriotism itself is a necessary link in the golden chain of our affections and virtues, and turns away with indignant scorn from the false Philosophy or mistaken Religion, which would persuade him that Cosmopolitism is nobler than Nationality, and the human Race a sublimer object of love than a People; that Plato, Luther, Newton, and their Equals, formed themselves neither in the Market nor the Senate, but in the World and for all Men of all Ages. True! But where and among whom are these giant exceptions produced? In the wide Empires of Asia, where millions of human Beings acknowledge no other bond but that of a common Slavery, and are distinguished on the Map but by a name which themselves perhaps never heard, or hearing abhor? No! In a circle defined by human affections, the first firm sod within which becomes sacred beneath the quickened step of the returning Citizen—here, where the powers and interests of men spread without confusion through a common sphere, like the vibrations propagated in the air by a single voice, distinct yet coherent, and all uniting to express one thought and the same feeling! here where even the common Soldier dares force a passage for his Comrades by gathering up the Bayonets of the Enemy into his own breast: because his Country "*expected every Man to do his duty!*" and this, not after he has been hardened by habit but, as probably, in his first battle; not reckless or hopeless, but braving death from a keener sensibility to those blessings, which [388] make life dear, to those qualities which render himself worthy to enjoy them! Here, where the royal crown is loved and worshipped as a glory around the sainted head of FREEDOM! Where the Rustic at his plough whistles with equal enthusiasm, "*God save the King*" and "*Britons never shall be Slaves;*" or, perhaps, leaves one Thistle unweeded in his Garden, because it is the symbol of his dear native Land!* *Here*, from within *this* circle defined, as light by shade, or rather as light within light by its' intensity, only within these magic circles rise up the awful Spirits, whose words are Oracles for Mankind, whose love embraces all Countries, and whose voice sounds through all Ages! Here and here only may we confidently expect these mighty minds to be reared and ripened, whose names are naturalized in foreign lands, the sure Fellow-travellers of Civilization! and yet render their own Country dearer and more proudly dear to their own Countrymen. This is indeed Cosmopolitism, at once the Nursling and the Nurse of patriotic affection! This, and this alone, is genuine Philanthropy, which like the Olive Tree, sacred to concord and to

* I cannot here refuse myself the pleasure of recording a speech of the Poet Burns, related to me by the Lady to whom it was addressed. Having been asked by her, why in his more serious Poems he had not changed the two or three Scotch words which seemed only to disturb the purity of the style! the Poet with great sweetness, and his usual happiness in reply, answered, why in truth it would have been better, but—

> The rough bur-thistle spreading wide
> Amang the bearded bear,
> I turn'd the weeder-clips aside
> An' spar'd the symbol dear.

An Author may be allowed to quote from his own Poems, when he does it with as much modesty and felicity, as Burns did in this instance.

wisdom, fattens not exhausts the soil, from which it sprang, and in which it remains rooted. It is feebleness only, which cannot be generous without injustice, or just without ceasing to be generous. Is the morning Star less brilliant, or does a ray less fall on the golden fruitage of the earth, because the Moons of Saturn too feed their lamps from the same Sun? Even Germany, though curst with a base and hateful brood of Nobles and Princelings, cowardly and ravenous Jackals to the very Flocks entrusted to them as to Shepherds, who hunt for the Tyger and whine and wag their tails for his bloody offal—even Germany, whose ever-changing boundaries superannuate the last year's Map, and are altered as easily as the hurdles of a temporary sheep-fold, is still remembered with filial love and a Patriot's pride, when the thoughtful German hears the names of Luther and Leibnitz. "Ah! why, he sighs, [389] why for herself in vain should my Country have produced such a host of immortal minds!" Yea, even the poor enslaved, degraded, and barbarized Greek, can still point to the Harbour of Tenedos, and say—"there lay *our* Fleet when we were besieging Troy." Reflect a moment on the past History of *this* wonderful People! what were they while they remained free and independent? when Greece resembled a collection of Mirrors set in a single frame, each having its' own focus of patriotism, yet all capable, as at Marathon and Platea, of converging to one point and of consuming a common Foe? What were they then? The Fountains of light and civilization, of truth and of beauty, to all Mankind! they were the thinking Head, the beating Heart, of the whole World! they lost their independence, and with their independence their patriotism: and became the Cosmopolites of Antiquity. It has been truly observed (by the Author of the work for which PALM was murdered) that after the first acts of severity the Romans treated the Greeks not only more mildly than their other Slaves and Dependants, they behaved to them even affectionately and munificiently. The victor Nation felt reverentially the presence of the visible and invisible Deities that gave sanctity to every Grove, every Fountain, and every Forum. "Think (writes Pliny to one of his Friends) that you are sent into the Province of Achaia, that true and genuine Greece, where civilization, letters, even corn, are believed to have been discovered; that you are sent to administer the affairs of free States, that is, to men eminently free, who have retained their natural right by valour, by services, by friendship, lastly by treaty and by religion. Revere the Gods their founders, the sacred influences represented in those Gods, revere their ancient glory and this very old age which in Man is venerable, in Cities sacred. Cherish in thyself a reverence of Antiquity, a reverence for their great Exploits, a reverence even for their Fables. Detract nothing from the proud pretensions of any State; keep before thine eyes that this is the Land which sent us our institutions, which gave us our laws, not after it was subjugated, but in compliance with *our* petition.* " And what came out of these Men, who were *eminently free* without Patriotism, because without national Independence? (which eminent Freedom, however, Pliny himself, in the very next sentence, styles the shadow and residuum of Liberty) While they were intense Patriots, they were the benefactors of all Mankind, legislators [390] for

* Plin. Epist. Lib. VIII.

the very Nation that afterwards subdued and enslaved them. When, therefore, they became pure Cosmopolites, and no partial affections interrupted their Philanthropy, and when yet they retained their Country, their Language, and their Arts, what noble Works, what mighty Discoveries, may we not expect from them? If the applause of a little City (a first rate Town of a country not much larger than Yorkshire) and the encouragement of a Pericles, produced a Phidias, a Sophocles, and a constellation of other Stars scarcely inferior in glory, what will not the applause of the World effect, and the boundless munificence of the World's imperial Masters? Alas! no Sophocles appeared, no Phidias was born! individual genius fled with national Independence, and the best products were cold and laborious copies of what their Fathers had thought and invented in grandeur and majesty. At length nothing remained, but dastardly and cunning Slaves who avenged their own ruin and degradation by assisting to degrade and ruin their Conquerors; and the golden Harp of their divine Language remained only as the frame on which Priests and Monks spun their dirty cobwebs of Sophistry and Superstition!

If then in order to be Men we must be Patriots, and Patriotism cannot exist without national Independence, we need no new or particular Code of Morals to justify us in placing and preserving our Country in that relative situation, which is most favourable to its' independence. But the true Patriot is aware, that this Object is not to be accomplished by a system of general Conquest, such as was pursued by Philip of Macedon and his Son, nor yet by the political annihilation of the one State, which happens to be its' most formidable Rival: the unwise measure recommended by Cato, and carried into effect by the Romans, in the instance of Carthage. Not by the latter: for Rivalry between two Nations conduces to the Independence of both, calls forth or fosters all the virtues, by which national Security is maintained. Still less by the former: for the victor Nation itself must at length, by the very extension of its' own Conquests, sink into a mere Province; nay, it will most probably become the most abject portion of the Empire, and the most cruelly oppressed, both because it will be more feared and suspected by the common Tyrant, and because it will be the sink and centre of his luxury and corruption. Even in cases of actual injury and just alarm, the Patriot sets bounds to the reprisal of national vengeance, and contents [391] himself with such securities as are compatible with the welfare, though not with the ambitious projects of the Nation, whose aggressions had given the provocation: for as Patriotism inspires no super-human faculties, neither can it dictate any conduct which would require such. He is too conscious of his own ignorance of the future, to dare extend his calculations into remote periods; nor, because he is a Statesman, arrogates to himself the cares of Providence and the government of the World. How does he know, but that the very Independence and consequent Virtues of the Nation, which in the anger of cowardice he would fain reduce to absolute insignificance, and rob even of its' ancient Name, may in some future emergence be the destined Guardians of his own Country; and that the power, which now alarms, may hereafter protect and preserve it. The experience of History authorizes not only the possibility, but even the probability, of such an event. An American Commander, who has deserved and received the highest honours which his grateful Country, through her assembled Representatives, could bestow upon him, once said to me with a sigh: In an evil hour for my Country did the French and Spaniards abandon Louisiana to the United States; we were not sufficiently a Country before; and should we ever be mad enough to drive the English from Canada and her other North American Provinces, we shall soon cease to be a Country at all. Without local attachment, without national honor, we shall resemble a swarm of Insects that settle on the fruits of the Earth to corrupt and consume them, rather than Men who love and cleave to the Land of their Forefathers. After a shapeless anarchy, and a series of civil wars, we shall at last be formed into many countries; unless the Vices engendered in the process should demand a further punishment, and we should previously fall beneath the despotism of some military Adventurer, like a Lion, consumed by an inward disease, prostrate and helpless, beneath the beak and talons of a Vulture, or yet meaner bird of Prey.

The same sanity of mind will the true Patriot display, in all that regards the internal prosperity of his Country. He will reverence not only whatever tends to make the component Individuals more happy, and more worthy of happiness; but likewise whatever tends to bind them more closely together, as a People; that as a multitude of parts and functions make up one human body, so the whole multitude of his Countrymen may, by the visible and invisible influences of religion, language, laws, customs, [392] and the reciprocal dependence and re-action of trade and agriculture, be organized into one body politic. But much as he desires to see *all* become A WHOLE, he places limits even to this wish, and abhors that System of Policy, which would blend men into a State by the dissolution of all those virtues, which make them happy and estimable as Individuals. Sir James Stuart (Polit. Econ. Vol. 1. P.88.) after stating the case of the Vine-Dresser, who is Proprietor of a bit of Land, on which grain (enough, and no more) is raised for himself and family—and who provides for their other wants of cloathing, salt, &c. by his extra labour, as a Vine-dresser, observes—"From this example we discover the difference between Agriculture exercised *as a trade*, and *as a direct means of subsisting*. We have the two species in the Vine-dresser: he labours the vine-yard as a trade, and his spot of ground for subsistence. We may farther conclude, that as to the last part he is only useful to himself: but as to the first he is useful to the society and becomes a member of it: consequently were it not for his trade, the State would lose nothing, although the Vine-dresser and his Land were both swallowed up by an earthquake."

Now this contains the sublime philosophy of the sect of Economists. They worship a kind of non-entity under the different words, the state, the whole, the society, &c. and to this Idol they make bloodier sacrifices than ever the Mexicans did to Tescalipoca. *All*, that is, each and every sentient being in a given tract, are made diseased and vicious, in order that *each* may become useful to *all*, or the State, or the Society,—that is, to the *word, all*, the word state, or the word society! The absurdity may be easily perceived by omitting the words relating to this idol—as for instance—in a former paragraph of the same (in most respects) excellent work: "If it therefore happens that an additional number produced do more than feed themselves, then I perceive no advantage gained from their production." What? no advantage gained by, for instance, ten thousand happy, intelligent, and immortal Beings having been produced?—O yes! but no advantage "to this Society."—What is this Society? this "whole?" this "State?" is it any thing else but a word of convenience to express at once the whole number of confederated individuals living in a certain district? Let the sum total of each man's happiness, be supposed = 1000: and suppose ten thousand men produced, who neither made swords or poison, or found corn or clothes for those [393] who did—but who procured by their labour food and raiment for themselves, and for their children— would not that Society be richer by 10,000,000 parts of Happiness? And think you it possible, that ten thousand happy human beings can exist together without encreasing each other's happiness? or that it will not overflow into countless channels, and* diffuse itself through the rest of the Society.

The poor Vine-dresser rises from sweet sleep, worships his Maker, goes with his wife and children into his little plot—returns to his hut at noon, and eats the produce of the similar labour of a former day. Is he useful? No! not yet.—Suppose then, that during the remaining hours of the day he endeavoured to provide for his moral and intellectual appetites, by physical experiments and philosophical research, by acquiring knowledge for himself, and communicating it to his wife and children. Would he be useful then? "*He* useful! The State would lose nothing, although the Vine-dresser, and his Land were both swallowed up by an earthquake!" Well then, instead of devoting the latter half of each day to his closet, his laboratory, or to neighbourly conversation, suppose he goes to the vine-yard, and from the ground which would maintain in health, virtue, and wisdom, twenty of his fellow-creatures, helps to raise a quantity of liquor that will disease the bodies, and debauch the souls of an hundred—Is he useful *now*?—O yes!—a very useful Man, and a most excellent Citizen!!

In what then *does* the Law between State and State differ from that between Man and Man? For hitherto we seem to have discovered no variation. According to THE FRIEND's best understanding, it differs in this one point: that the influence of *example* in any extraordinary case, as the possible occasion of an action apparently like though in reality very different, is of considerable importance in the moral calculations of an Individual; but of little, if any, in those of a Nation. The reasons are evident. In the first place, in cases, concerning which there can be any dispute between an honest Man and a true Patriot, the circumstances, which at

---

* Well, and in the spirit of genuine Philosophy, does the Poet describe such beings as Men

"Who being innocent do for that cause
Bestir them in good deeds"———
WORDSWORTH

Providence, by the ceaseless activity which it has implanted in our nature, has sufficiently guarded against an innocence without virtue.

once authorize and [394] discriminate the measure, are so marked and peculiar and notorious, that it is incapable of being drawn into a precedent by any other State under dissimilar circumstances; except perhaps as a mere pretext for an action, which had been predetermined without reference to this authority, and which would have taken place, though it had never existed. But if so strange a thing *should* happen, as a second coincidence of the same circumstances, or of circumstances sufficiently similar to render the prior measure a fair precedent; then, if the one action was justifiable, so will the other be; and without any reference to the former, which in this case may be useful, as a light, but cannot be requisite, as an authority. Secondly, in extraordinary cases it is ridiculous to suppose, that the conduct of States will be determined by example. We know that they neither will, nor in the nature of things can be determined by any other consideration, but that of the imperious circumstances, which render a particular measure advisable. But lastly, and more important than all, Individuals are and must be under positive Laws: and so very great is the advantage, which results from the regularity of legal decisions, and their consequent capability of being foreknown and relied upon, that equity itself must sometimes be sacrificed to it. For the very letter of a positive law is part of its' spirit. But States neither are, nor can be, under positive Laws. The only fixed part of the Law of Nations is the spirit: the Letter of the Law consists wholly in the circumstances, to which the Spirit of the Law is applied. It is mere puerile declamation to rail against a Country, as having imitated the very measures for which it had most blamed its' ambitious Enemy, if that Enemy have previously changed all the relative circumstances which *had* existed for *him*, and therefore rendered *his* conduct iniquitous; but which, having been removed, however iniquitously, cannot without absurdity be supposed any longer to control the measures of an innocent Nation, necessitated to struggle for its' own safety, especially when the measures in question were adopted for the very purpose of *restoring* those circumstances. There are times, when it would be wise to regard Patriotism as a light that is in danger of being blown out, rather than as a fire which needs to be fanned, by the winds of party spirit. There are times, when party spirit, without any unwonted excess, may yet become faction; and though in general not less useful than natural in a free Government, may under particular emergencies [395] prove fatal to Freedom itself. I trust, I am writing to those who think with me, that to have blackened a Ministry, however strong or rational our dislike may be of the Persons who compose it, is a poor excuse and a miserable compensation for the crime of unnecessarily blackening the character of our Country. Under this conviction I request my Reader to cast his eye back on my last argument, and then to favour me with his patient attention while I attempt at once to explain its' purport and to shew its' cogency.

Let us transport ourselves in fancy to the Age and Country of the Patriarchs or, if the Reader prefers it, to some small Colony uninfluenced by the Mother Country, which has not organized itself into a State, or agreed to acknowledge any one particular Governor. We will suppose this Colony to consist of from twenty to thirty Households, or separate Establishments, differing greatly from each other in the number of retainers and in extent of possessions. Each Household, however, possesses its' own domain, the least not less than the greatest, in full right: and its' Master is an independent Sovereign within his own boundaries. This mutual understanding and tacit agreement, we may well suppose to have been the gradual result of many feuds, which had produced misery to all, and real advantage to none: and that the same sober and reflecting Persons, dispersed through the different establishments, who had brought about this state of things, had likewise coincided in the propriety of some other prudent and humane regulations, which from the authority of these wise men on points, in which they were unanimous, and from the evident good sense of the rules themselves, were acknowledged throughout the whole Colony, though they were never voted into a formal Law, though the determination of the cases, to which these rules were applicable, had been entrusted to no one recognized judge, or their enforcement of, delegated to any particular Magistrate. The chief of these virtual Laws, we may safely conclude, would be: that as no man ought to interfere in the affairs of another against his will, so if any Master of a household, instead of employing himself in the improvement of his own fields and flocks, or in the better regulation of his own Establishment, should be foolish and wicked enough to employ his children and servants in breaking down the fences and taking possession of the lands and property of a Fellow-colonist, or in turning the head of the Family out of his House, and forcing those that remained to acknowledge [396] himself as their Governor instead, and to obey whomever he might please to appoint as his deputy, then that it became the duty and interest of the other Colonists to join against the Aggressor, and to do all in their power to prevent him from accomplishing his bad purposes, or to compel him to make restitution and compensation. The mightier the aggressor, and the weaker the injured party, the more cogent would the motive become for restraining the one and protecting the other. For it was plain, that he, who was suffered to overpower, one by one, the weaker Proprietors, and render the members of their establishment subservient to his will, must soon become an over-match for those who were formerly his equals: and the mightiest would differ from the meanest only by being the last victim. This allegoric fable faithfully pourtrays the Law of Nations and the balance of power among the European States. Let us now give the sequel, as the historian of this imaginary Colony, and relate, that in the second or third generation the Proprietors too generally disregarded the good old opinion, that what injured any could be of real advantage to none; and treated those, who still professed it, as fit only to instruct Children in their Catechism. By the Avarice of some, the Cowardice of others, and by the Corruption and want of Foresight in the greater part, the former state of things had been completely changed, and the tacit compact set at nought, the general acknowledgement of which had been so instrumental in producing this State and in preserving it, as long as it lasted. The stronger had preyed on the weaker, whose wrongs, however, did not remain long unavenged: for the same selfishness and blindness to the future, which had induced the wealthy to trample on the rights of the poorer proprietors, prevented them from assisting each other effectually, when they were themselves attacked, one after the other, by the most powerful of all: and from a concurrence of circumstances attacked so successfully, that of the whole Colony few remained, that were not, directly or indirectly, the Creatures and Dependents of this one over-grown Establishment. Say rather, of its' new Master, an adventurer whom Chance and Poverty had brought thither, and who in better times would have been employed in the swine-yard, or the slaughter-house, from his ignorance and stupid aversion to all the Arts that tended to improve either the land or those that were to be maintained by its' produce. He was however eminent for other qualities, which were still better suited to promote his power among those degenerate [397] colonists: for he feared neither God nor his own Conscience. The most solemn oaths could not bind him; the most deplorable calamities could not awaken his pity; and when others were asleep, he was either brooding over some scheme of robbery and murder, or with a part of his Banditti actually employed in laying waste his neighbour's fences, or in undermining the walls of their houses. His natural cunning, undistracted by any honest avocations, and meeting with no obstacle either in his head or heart, and above all having been quickened and strengthened by constant practice and favoured by the times with all conceivable opportunities, ripened at last into a surprizing *Genius* for oppression and tyranny: and, as we must distinguish him by some name, we will call him MISETES. The only Estate, which remained able to bid defiance to this common Enemy, was that of PAMPHILUS, superior to Misetes in wealth, and his equal in strength; though not in the power of doing mischief, and still less in the wish. Their characters were indeed perfectly contrasted: for it may be truly said, that throughout the whole Colony there was not a single Establishment, which did not owe some of its' best buildings, the encreased produce of its' fields, its' improved implements of industry, and the general more decent appearance of its' Members, to the information given and the encouragements afforded by Pamphilus and those of his household. Whoever raised more than they wanted for their own establishment, were sure to find a ready purchaser in Pamphilus, and oftentimes for articles which they had themselves been before accustomed to regard as worthless, or even as nuisances: and they received in return things necessary or agreeable, and always in one respect at least useful, that they roused the Purchasers to industry and its' accompanying virtues. In this intercommunion all were benefited: for the wealth of Pamphilus was increased by the increasing Industry of his Fellow-colonists, and their Industry needed the support and encouraging Influences of Pamphilus's Capital. To this good man and his estimable Household Misetes bore the most implacable Hatred, had publicly sworn that he would root him out; the only sort of Oath which he was not likely to break by any want of will or effort on his own part. But fortunately for Pamphilus, his main property consisted of one compact Estate divided from Misetes and the rest of the Colony by a wide and dangerous river, with the exception of one small plantation which belonged to an independent Proprietor [398] whom we will name LATHRODACNUS: a man of no influence in the Colony, but much respected by Pamphilus. They were indeed relations by blood originally and afterwards by intermarriages; and it was to the power and protection of Pamphilus that Lathrodacnus owed his independence and prosperity, amid the general distress and slavery of the other Proprietors. Not less fortunately did it happen, that the means of passing the River were possessed exclusively by Pamphilus and his above mentioned Kinsman; and not only the Boats themselves, but all the means of constructing and navigating them. As the very existence of Lathrodacnus, as an independent Colonist, had no solid ground, but in the strength and prosperity of Pamphilus; and as the interests of the one in no respect interfered with those of the other; Pamphilus for a considerable time remained without any anxiety, and looked on the river-craft of Lathrodacnus with as little alarm, as on those of his own Establishment. It did not disquiet him, that Lathrodacnus had remained neutral in the quarrel: and though many advantages, which in peaceful times would have belonged to Pamphilus, were now transferred to his Neighbour, and had more than doubled the extent and profit of his concern, Pamphilus, instead of repining at this, was glad that some good at least to some one came out of the general evil. Great then was his surprize, when he discovered, that without any conceivable reason Lathrodacnus had employed himself in building and collecting a very unusual number of such Boats, as were of no use to him in his traffic, but designed exclusively as ferry-boats: and what was still stranger and more alarming, that he chose to keep these in a bay on the other side of the river, opposite to the one small Plantation, along side of Pamphilus' Estate, from which plantation Lathrodacnus derived the materials for building them. Willing to believe this conduct a transient whim of his Neighbour's, occasioned partly by his vanity, and partly by envy (to which latter passion the want of a liberal education and the not sufficiently comprehending the grounds of his own prosperity, had rendered him subject) Pamphilus contented himself for a while with urgent yet friendly remonstrances. The only answer, which Lathrodacnus vouchsafed to return, was: that by the Law of the Colony, which Pamphilus had made so many professions of revering, every Proprietor was an independent Sovereign within his own boundaries; that the Boats were his own, and the opposite shore, to which they were [399] fastened, part of a field which belonged to him; and, in short, the[1] Pamphilus had no right to interfere with the management of his Property, which, trifling as it might be compared with that of Pamphilus, was no less sacred by the Law of the Colony. To this uncourteous rebuff Pamphilus replied with a fervent wish, that Lathrodacnus could with more propriety have appealed to a law, as still subsisting, which, he well knew, had been effectually annulled by the unexampled tyranny and success of Misetes, together with the circumstances which had given occasion to the law, and made it wise and practicable. He further urged, that this law was not made for the benefit of any one Man, but for the common safety and advantage of all: that it was absurd to suppose that either he (Pamphilus) or that Lathrodacnus himself, or any other Proprietor, ever did or could acknowledge this law in the sense, that it was to survive the very circumstances which made it just and proper, much less could they have even tacitly assented to it, if

[1] For "the" 1812 reads "that"—the only textual change that seems to have been made since No 12. See above, II 321 n 1.

they had ever understood it as authorizing one Neighbour to endanger the absolute ruin of another, who had perhaps fifty times the property to lose, and perhaps ten times the number of souls to answer for, and yet forbidding the injured person to take any steps in his own defence: and, lastly, that this Law gave no right without imposing a corresponding duty, and therefore if Lathrodacnus insisted on the *rights* given him by the law, he ought at the same time to perform the *duties* which it required, and join heart and hand with Pamphilus in his endeavours to defend his independence, to restore the former state of the Colony, and with this to re-enforce the old Law, in opposition to Misetes, who had enslaved the one and set at nought the other. So ardently was Pamphilus attached to the Law, that excepting his own safety and independence, there was no price which he would not pay, no sacrifice which he would not make for its' restoration. His reverence for the very memory of the law was such, that the mere appearance of transgressing it would be a heavy affliction to him. In the hope therefore of gaining from the avarice of Lathrodacnus that consent, which he could not obtain from his justice or neighbourly kindness, he offered to give him in full right a Plantation ten times the value of all his boats, and yet, whenever the Colony should once more be settled, to restore the Boats: if he would only permit Pamphilus to secure them during the present state of things, on his side of the River, retaining whatever he really wanted for the passage of his own Household. To all these persuasions and entreaties Lathrodacnus turned a deaf ear; and Pamphilus remained agitated and undetermined, till at length he received certain intelligence, that Lathrodacnus had called a Council of the chief members of his Establishment, in consequence of the threats of Misetes, that he would treat him as the Friend and Ally of Pamphilus, if he did not declare himself his Enemy. Partly for the sake of a large Meadow belonging to him on the other side of the River, which it was not easy to secure from the Tyrant, but still more from envy and the irritable temper of a proud inferior, Lathrodacnus, and with him the majority of his advisers (though to the great discontent of the few wise heads among them) settled it finally, that if he should be again pressed on this point by Misetes, he would [400] join him and commence hostilities against his old Neighbour and Kinsman. It is indeed but too probable, that he had long brooded over this scheme, for to what other end could he have strained his income and over-worked his servants, in building and fitting up such a number of passage-boats? As soon as this information was received by Pamphilus, and this from a quarter which it was impossible for him to discredit, he obeyed the dictates of self-preservation, took possession of the passage-boats by force, and brought them over to his own grounds; but without any further injury to Lathrodacnus, and still urging him to accept a compensation and continue in that amity which was so manifestly their common interest. Instantly, a great outcry was raised against Pamphilus, who was charged in the bitterest terms with having first abused Misetes, and then imitated him in his worst acts of violence. In the calmness of a good conscience Pamphilus contented himself with the following reply: "Even so, if I were out on a shooting Party with a Quaker for my companion, and saw coming on towards us an old Footpad and Murderer, who had made known his intention of killing me wherever he might meet me; and if my companion the Quaker would neither give me up his Gun, nor even discharge it as (we will suppose) I had just before unfortunately discharged my own; if he would neither promise to assist me nor even promise to make the least resistance to the Robber's attempt to disarm himself; you might call me a Robber for wresting this Gun from my companion, though for no other purpose, but that I might at least do for by myself, what he *ought* to have done, but *would* not do either for, or with me!" Even so, and as plausibly, you might exclaim: "O the Hypocrite Pamphilus, who has not been deafened with his complaint against Robbers and Footpads? and lo! he himself has turned Foot-pad and commenced by robbing his peaceful and unsuspecting Companion of his double-barrelled Gun!" It is the business of THE FRIEND to lay down Principles not to make the applications of them to particular, much less, to recent cases. If any such there be, to which these Principles are fairly applicable, the Reader is no less master of the facts than the Writer of the present Essay. If not, the Principles remain: and the Friend has finished the Task, which the Plan of his Work imposed on him, of proving the identity of international Law and the Law of Morality in *spirit*, and the reasons of their difference in *practice*, in those extreme cases in which alone they have been allowed to differ.

THE FRIEND

No. 25, THURSDAY, February 22, 1810

EPITAPHS

TRANSLATED FROM CHIABRERA[1]

PERHAPS some needful service of the State
Drew TITUS from the depth of studious bowers,
And doomed him to contend in faithless courts,
Where gold determines between right and wrong.
Yet did at length his loyalty of heart
And his pure native genius lead him back
To wait upon the bright and gracious Muses
Whom he had early lov'd. And not in vain
Such course he held! Bologna's learned schools
Were gladdened by the Sage's voice, and hung
With fondness on those sweet Nestrian strains.
There did he live content; and all his thoughts
Were blithe as vernal flowers.—O human life,
That never art secure from dolorous change!
Behold a high injunction suddenly
To Arno's side conducts him, and he charm'd
A Tuscan audience: but full soon was call'd
To the perpetual silence of the grave.
Mourn, Italy, the loss of him who stood
A Champion steadfast and invincible,
To quell the rage of literary War!

2[2]

O Thou who movest onward with a mind
Intent upon thy way, pause though in haste!
'Twill be no fruitless moment. I was born
Within Savona's walls of gentle blood,
On Tiber's banks my youth was dedicate
To sacred studies; and the Roman Shepherd
Gave to my charge Urbino's numerous Flock.

[1] See *Epitaphs Translated from Chiabrera* II: *WPW* IV 248–9 (var); Chiabrera *Opere* II 185–6 (*Epitaffi* XIV). In Copy R, C notes "Wordsworth's": J. Wordsworth "Marginalia" 369. DW, in a letter to Lady Beaumont 28 Feb 1810, corrects "Nestrian" to "Nestorian" in line 11 above. See *WL (M)* I 357–8.

[2] See *Epitaphs* III: *WPW* IV 249 (var); Chiabrera II 182 (*Epitaffi* VIII).

[402]
                Much did I watch, much laboured; nor had power
                To escape from many and strange indignities;
                Was smitten by the great ones of the World
                But did not fall, for virtue braves all shocks,
                Upon herself resting immoveably.
                Me did a kindlier fortune then invite
                To serve the glorious Henry, King of France,
                And in his hands I saw a high reward
                Stretch'd out for my acceptance—but Death came.—
                Now, Reader, learn from this my fate—how false
                How treacherous to her promise is the World,
                And trust in God—to whose eternal doom
                Must bend the sceptred Potentates of Earth.

IN this, and some preceding Numbers, has been given a selection of Epitaphs from the Italian Poet CHIABRERA; in one instance imitated, and in the others carefully translated. The perusal of the original collection afforded me so much pleasure that I was induced to think upon the nature of that species of composition with more care than I had previously bestowed upon the Subject: the result of my reflections may perhaps be interesting to the Readers of THE FRIEND. An attempt will be made to unfold the Laws of Taste and Criticism systematically, as soon as certain topics, which have already been entered upon, shall be concluded: in the mean while, I wish to avail myself of the present occasion to tempt the more practised Reader into a short prelusive exercise of powers which he will hereafter be called upon to put forth in good earnest; and, in respect to those Persons who are unfamiliar with such speculations, my labour, in the present Essay, may be likened to that of a Teacher of Geology, who, to awaken the curiosity of his Pupils, and to induce them to prepare for the study of the inner constitution of the Planet, lectures with a few specimens of fossils and minerals in his hand, arranged in their several classes, and the beauty of which he points out to their attention.

"To define an Epitaph," says Dr. Johnson,[1] "is useless; every one knows that it is an inscription on a Tomb. An Epitaph, therefore, implies no particular character of writing, but may be composed in verse or prose. It is indeed commonly panegyrical; because we are seldom distinguished with a Stone but by our Friends; but it [403] has no rule to restrain or mollify it, except this, that it ought not to be longer than common beholders may have leisure or patience to peruse." From this introduction the Critic immediately proceeds to a review of the metrical Epitaphs of Pope. This summary opinion is delivered with such laxity that, even on that account, the passage would not have deserved to be quoted, if it had not been forced upon the notice of our Countrymen, by the place which it occupies in the book entitled, "The Lives of the most eminent English Poets," by the same Writer. I now solicit the Reader's attention to a more

[1] See *Lives of the Poets* (1801) III 199 (var) (the essay, "A Dissertation on the Epitaphs Written by Pope", that Johnson appended to his "Life" of Pope).

comprehensive view of the subject; and shall endeavour to treat it with more precision.[1]

It needs scarcely be said, that an Epitaph presupposes a Monument upon which it is to be engraven. Almost all Nations have wished that certain external signs should point out the places where their Dead are interred. Among savage Tribes unacquainted with Letters, this has mostly been done either by rude stones placed near the Graves, or by Mounds of earth raised over them. This custom proceeded obviously from a twofold desire; first, to guard the remains of the deceased from irreverent approach or from savage violation; and, secondly, to preserve their memory. Never any, says Cambden,[2] neglected burial but some savage Nations; as the Bactrians which cast their dead to the dogs; some varlet Philosophers, as Diogenes, who desired to be devoured of fishes; some dissolute Courtiers, as Mecænas, who was wont to say, Non tumulum curo; se pelit natura relictos.

> I'm careless of a Grave:—Nature her dead will save.

As soon as Nations had learned the use of letters, Epitaphs were inscribed upon these Monuments; in order that their intention might be more surely and adequately fulfilled. I have derived Monuments and Epitaphs from two sources of feeling: but these do in fact resolve themselves into one. The invention of Epitaphs, Weever, in his discourse of funeral Monuments, says rightly,[3] "proceeded from the presage or fore-feeling of Immortality, implanted in all men naturally, and is referred to the Scholars of Linus the Theban Poet, who flourished about the year of the World two thousand seven hundred; who first bewailed this Linus their Master, when he was slain, in doleful verses then called of him Œlina, afterwards Epitaphia, [404] for that they were first sung at burials, after engraved upon the Sepulchres."

And, verily, without the consciousness of a principle of Immortality in the human soul, Man could never have had awakened in him the desire to live in the remembrance of his fellows; mere love, or the yearning of Kind

[1] WW wrote this "Essay on Epitaphs", the introductory paragraph of which (II 334) is probably C's. See W. J. B. Owen "The Text of Wordsworth's Essay upon Epitaphs" *N & Q* CCI (1956) 214–15. According to DW, WW "did not intend it to be published now; but Coleridge was in such bad spirits that when the time came he was utterly unprovided, and besides had been put out of his regular course by waiting for books to consult respecting Duty; so my brother's essay, being ready, was sent off". DW to Lady Beaumont 28 Feb 1810: *WL (M)* I 358–9. WW wrote "two more essays on the same subject, which will appear when there is need". Ibid I 359. These essays, which C planned to use in a revived *Friend* (see above, Introduction, I lxxvi–lxxvii), were first printed from ms by A. B. Grosart *The Prose Works of William Wordsworth* (1876) II 41–75. In the second essay WW says that translating the Chiabrera epitaphs led him to write the essay.

[2] See William Camden *Remaines concerning Britaine* (1636) 360 (var), which does not contain the translation of Maecenas's words. However, the passage comes from John Weever *Antient Funeral Monuments, of Great Britain . . .* (1767) xxiv (var), where the translation *is* given.

[3] Weever p ix.

towards Kind, could not have produced it. The Dog or Horse perishes in the field, or in the stall, by the side of his Companions, and is incapable of anticipating the sorrow with which his surrounding Associates shall bemoan his death, or pine for his loss; he cannot pre-conceive this regret, he can form no thought of it; and therefore cannot possibly have a desire to leave such regret or remembrance behind him. Add to the principle of love, which exists in the inferior animals, the faculty of reason which exists in Man alone; will the conjunction of these account for the desire? Doubtless it is a necessary consequence of this conjunction, yet not I think as a direct result, but only to be come at through an intermediate thought, viz. that of an intimation or assurance within us, that some part of our nature is imperishable. At least the precedence in order of birth, of one feeling to the other is unquestionable. If we look back upon the days of childhood, we shall find that the time is not in remembrance when, with respect to our own individual Being, the mind was without this assurance; whereas, the wish to be remembered by our Friends or Kindred after Death, or even in Absence, is, as we shall discover, a sensation that does not form itself till the *social* feelings have been developed, and the Reason has connected itself with a wide range of objects. Forlorn, and cut off from communication with the best part of his nature, must that Man be, who should derive the sense of immortality, as it exists in the mind of a child, from the same unthinking gaiety or liveliness of animal Spirits with which the Lamb in the meadow, or any other irrational Creature, is endowed; who should ascribe it, in short, to blank ignorance in the Child; to an inability arising from the imperfect state of his faculties to come, in any point of his being, into contact with a notion of Death; or to an unreflecting acquiescence in what has been instilled in to him! Has such an unfolder of the mysteries of Nature, though he may have forgotten his former self, ever noticed the early, obstinate, and unappeaseable inquisitiveness of Children upon the subject of origination? This single [405][1] fact proves outwardly the monstrousness of those suppositions: for, if we had no direct external testimony that the minds of very young Children meditate feelingly upon Death and Immortality, these enquiries, which we all know they are perpetually making concerning the *whence*, do necessarily include correspondent habits of interrogation concerning the *whither*. Origin and tendency are notions inseparably co-relative. Never did a Child stand by the side of a running Stream, pondering within himself what power was the feeder of the perpetual current, from what neverwearied sources the body of water was supplied, but he must have been inevitably propelled to follow this question by another: "towards what abyss is it in progress? what receptacle can contain the mighty influx?" and the spirit of the answer must have been, though the word might be Sea or Ocean, accompanied perhaps with an image gathered from a Map, or from the real object in Nature—these might have been the *letter*, but the *spirit* of the answer must have been *as* inevitably, a receptacle without bounds or dimensions, nothing less than infinity. We may, then, be justified in asserting that the sense of Immortality, if not co-existent and twin

[1] In the BM copy of the 1812 edition, pp 405–6 were bound out of place, following p 410.

birth with Reason, is among the earliest of its' Offspring: and we may further assert, that from these conjoined, and under their countenance, the human affections are gradually formed and opened out. This is not the place to enter into the recesses of these investigations; but the subject requires me here to make a plain avowal that, for my own part, it is to me inconceivable, that the sympathies of love towards each other, which grow with our growth, could ever attain any new strength, or even preserve the old, after we had received from the outward senses the impression of Death, and were in the habit of having that impression daily renewed and it's accompanying feeling brought home to ourselves, and to those we love; if the same were not counteracted by those communications with our internal Being, which are anterior to all these experiences, and with which revelation coincides, and has through that coincidence alone (for otherwise it could not possess it) a power to affect us. I confess, with me the conviction is absolute, that, if the impression and sense of Death were not thus counterbalanced, such a hollowness would prevade the whole system of things, such a want of correspondence and consistency, a disproportion [406] so astounding betwixt means and ends, that there could be no repose, no joy. Were we to grow up unfostered by this genial warmth, a frost would chill the spirit, so penetrating and powerful, that there could be no motions of the life of love; and infinitely less could we have any wish to be remembered after we had passed away from a world in which each man had moved about like a shadow.

Simonides, it is related, upon landing in a strange Country, found the Corse of an unknown person, lying by the Sea side; he buried it, and was honoured throughout Greece for the piety of that Act.[1] Another ancient Philosopher, chancing to fix his eyes upon a dead Body, regarded the same with slight, if not with contempt; saying, "see the Shell of the flown Bird." But it is not to be supposed that the moral and tender hearted Simonides was incapable of the lofty movements of thought, to which that other Sage gave way at the moment while his soul was intent only upon the indestructible being; or, on the other hand, that he, in whose sight a lifeless human Body was of no more value than the worthless Shell from which the living fowl had departed, would not, in a different mood of mind, have been affected by those earthly considerations which had incited the philosophic Poet to the performance of that pious duty with respect to the latter,[2] we may be assured that, if he had been destitute of the capability of communing with the more exalted thoughts that appertain to human Nature, he would have cared no more for the Corse of the Stranger than for the dead body of a Seal or Porpoise which might have been cast up by the Waves. We respect the corporeal frame of Man, not merely because it is the habitation of a rational, but of an immortal Soul. Each of these Sages was in sympathy with the best feelings of our Nature; feelings which, though they seem opposite to each other, have another and a finer connection than that of contrast.—It is a connection formed through the

---

[1] Simonides of Cos (c 556–469 B.C.), Greek lyric poet. The saying "Poetry is vocal painting, as painting is silent poetry" is attributed to him.

[2] DW, in the letter to Lady Beaumont cited above, corrects to "... pious duty. And with regard to this latter". *WL* (*M*) I 357–8.

subtle progress by which, both in the natural and the moral world, qualities pass insensibly into their contraries, and things revolve upon each other. As, in sailing upon the orb of this Planet, a voyage, towards the regions where the sun sets, conducts gradually to the quarter where we have been accustomed to behold it come forth at its' rising; and, in like manner, a voyage towards the east, the birth-place in our [407] imagination of the morning, leads finally to the quarter where the Sun is last seen when he departs from our eyes; so, the contemplative soul, travelling in the direction of mortality, advances to the Country of everlasting Life; and, in like manner, may she continue to explore those chearful tracts, till she is brought back, for her advantage and benefit, to the land of transitory things—of sorrow and of tears.

On a midway point, therefore, which commands the thoughts and feelings of the two Sages whom we have represented in contrast, does the Author of that species of composition, the Laws of which it is our present purpose to explain, take his stand. Accordingly, recurring to the twofold desire which has been deduced from the higher feeling, namely,[1] the consciousness of immortality, it may be said, that a sepulchral Monument is a tribute to a Man as a human Being; and that an Epitaph, (in the ordinary meaning attached to the word) includes this general feeling and something more; and is a record to preserve the memory of the dead, as a tribute due to his individual worth, for a satisfaction to the sorrowing hearts of the Survivors, and for the common benefit of the living: which record is to be accomplished, not in a general manner, but in *close connection with the bodily remains of the deceased:* and these, it may be added, among the modern Nations of Europe are deposited within, or contiguous to their places of worship. In ancient times, as is well known, it was the custom to bury the dead beyond the Walls of Towns and Cities; and among the Greeks and Romans they were frequently interred by the way-sides.

I could here pause with pleasure, and invite the Reader to indulge with me in contemplation of the advantages which must have attended such a practice. I could ruminate upon the beauty which the Monuments, thus placed, must have borrowed from the surrounding images of Nature—from the trees, the wild flowers, from a stream running perhaps within sight or hearing, from the beaten road stretching it's weary length hard by. Many tender similitudes must these objects have presented to the mind of the Traveller, leaning upon one of the Tombs, or reposing in the coolness of it's shade, whether he had halted from weariness or in compliance to the invitation, "Pause Traveller!" so often found upon the Monuments. And to it's Epitaph also must have been supplied strong [408] appeals to visible appearances or immediate impressions, lively and affecting analogies of Life as a Journey—Death as a Sleep overcoming the tired Wayfarer—of Misfortune as a Storm that falls suddenly upon him—of Beauty as a Flower that passeth away, or of innocent pleasure as one that may be gathered—of Virtue that standeth firm as a Rock against the beating Waves; —of Hope "undermined insensibly like the Poplar by the side of the

---

[1] DW corrects to ". . . twofold desire, namely, to guard the remains of the deceased, and to preserve their memory, which has been deduced from the higher feeling". *WL (M)* i 358.

River that has fed it," [1] or blasted in a moment like a Pine-tree by the stroke of lightening upon the Mountain top—of admonitions and heart-stirring remembrances, like a refreshing Breeze that comes without warning, or the taste of the waters of an unexpected Fountain. These, and similar suggestions must have given, formerly, to the language of the senseless stone a voice enforced and endeared by the benignity of that Nature with which it was in unison.—We in modern times have lost much of these advantages: and they are but in a small degree counterbalanced to the Inhabitants of large Towns and Cities, by the custom of depositing the Dead within, or contiguous to, their places of worship; however splendid or imposing may be the appearances of those Edifices, or however interesting or salutary the recollections associated with them. Even were it not true that Tombs lose their monitory virtue when thus obtruded upon the notice of Men occupied with the cares of the World, and too often sullied and defiled by those cares, yet still, when Death is in our thoughts, nothing can make amends for the want of the soothing influences of Nature, and for the absence of those types of renovation and decay, which the fields and woods offer to the notice of the serious and contemplative mind. To feel the force of this sentiment, let a man only compare in imagination the unsightly manner in which our Monuments are crowded together in the busy, noisy, unclean, and almost grassless Church-yard of a large Town, with the still seclusion of a Turkish Cemetery, in some remote place, and yet further sanctified by the Grove of Cypress in which it is embosomed. Thoughts in the same temper as these, have already been expressed with true sensibility by an ingenious [2] Poet of the present day. The subject of his Poem is "All Saint's Church, Derby:" he has been deploring the forbidden and unseemly appearance of its' burial-ground, and uttering a wish, that in past times the practices had been adopted of interring the Inhabitants of large Towns in the Country.—

[409]
    "Then in some rural, calm, sequestered spot,
    Where healing Nature her benignant look
    Ne'er changes, save at that lorn season, when,
    With tresses drooping o'er her sable stole,
    She yearly mourns the mortal doom of man,
    Her noblest work, (so Israel's virgins erst,
    With annual moan upon the mountains wept
    Their fairest gone) there in that rural scene,
    So placid, so congenial to the wish
    The Christian feels, of peaceful rest within
    The silent grave, I would have stray'd:

. . . .
    —wandered forth, where the cold dew of heaven
    Lay on the humbler graves around, what time
    The pale moon gazed upon the turfy mounds,
    Pensive, as though like me, in lonely muse,
    'Twere brooding on the Dead inhum'd beneath.
    There, while with him, the holy Man of Uz,
    O'er human destiny I sympathiz'd,

---

[1] Source not traced.
[2] DW, in the letter to Lady Beaumont cited above, corrects to "ingenuous". *WL (M)* 1 358.

Counting the long, long periods prophecy
Decrees to roll, ere the great day arrives
Of resurrection, oft the blue-eyed Spring
Had met me with her blossoms, as the Dove
Of old, return'd with olive leaf, to cheer
The Patriarch mourning o'er a world destroy'd:
And I would bless her visit; for to me
'Tis sweet to trace the consonance that links
As one, the works of Nature and the word
Of God."——

JOHN EDWARDS[1]

A Village Church-yard, lying as it does in the lap of Nature, may indeed be most favourably contrasted with that of a Town of crowded Population; and Sepulture therein combines many of the best tendencies which belong to the mode practised by the Ancients, with others peculiar to itself. The sensations of pious chearfulness, which attend the celebration of the Sabbath-day in rural places, are profitably chastised by the sight of the Graves of Kindred and Friends, gathered together in that general Home towards which the thoughtful yet happy Spectators themselves are journeying. Hence a Parish Church, in the stillness of the Country, is a visible centre of a community of the living and the dead; a point to which are habitually referred the nearest concerns of both.

[410] As, then, both in Cities and in Villages, the Dead are deposited in close connection with our places of worship, with us the composition of an Epitaph naturally turns still more than among the Nations of Antiquity, upon the most serious and solemn affections of the human mind; upon departed Worth—upon personal or social Sorrow and Admiration—upon Religion individual and social—upon Time, and upon Eternity. Accordingly it suffices, in ordinary cases, to secure a composition of this kind from censure, that it contains nothing that shall shock or be inconsistent with this spirit. But to entitle an Epitaph to praise more than this is necessary. It ought to contain some Thought or Feeling belonging to the mortal or immortal part of our Nature touchingly expressed; and if that be done, however general or even trite the sentiment may be, every man of pure mind will read the words with pleasure and gratitude. A Husband bewails a wife; a Parent breathes a sigh of disappointed Hope over a lost Child; a Son utters a sentiment of filial reverence for a departed Father or Mother; a Friend perhaps inscribes an encomium recording the companionable qualities, or the solid virtues, of the Tenant of the Grave, whose departure has left a sadness upon his memory. This, and a pious admonition to the Living, and a humble expression of Christian confidence in Immortality, is the language of a thousand Church yards; and it does not often happen that any thing, in a greater degree discriminate or appropriate to the Dead or to the Living, is to be found in them. This want of discrimination has

---

[1] John Edwards *All-Saints' Church, Derby* (1805) 40–1 (9 lines omitted). WW's copy of the work is in DCL. Edwards was a friend of C and the poet James Montgomery; he was a *Friend* subscriber and sent C a few poems for the periodical; see below, App E, II 426.

been ascribed by the Critic above quoted, to two causes; first, the scantiness of the Objects of human praise; and, secondly, to the want of variety in the Characters of Men; or to use his own words, "to the fact, that the greater part of Mankind have no Character at all." [1] This is language which may be holden without blame among the generalities of common conversation; but does not become a Critic and a Moralist speaking seriously upon a serious Subject. The objects of admiration in Human Nature are not scanty but abundant; and every Man has a Character of his own, to the eye that has skill to perceive it. The real cause of the acknowledged want of discrimination in sepulchral memorials is this: That to analyse the Characters of others, especially of those whom we love, is not a common or natural employment of Men, at any time. We are not anxious [411] unerringly to understand the constitution of the Minds of those who have soothed, who have cheered, who have supported us; with whom we have been long and daily pleased or delighted. The affections are their own justification. The Light of Love in our Hearts is a satisfactory evidence that there is a flame of worth in the minds of our friends or kindred, whence that Light has proceeded. We shrink from the thought of placing their merits and defects to be weighed against each other in the nice balance of pure intellect; nor do we find much temptation to detect the shades by which a good quality or virtue is discriminated in them from an excellence known by the same general name as it exists in the mind of another; and least of all do we incline to these refinements when under the pressure of Sorrow, Admiration, or Regret, or when actuated by any of those feelings which incite men to prolong the memory of their Friends and Kindred, by records placed in the bosom of the all-uniting and equalizing Receptacle of the Dead.

The first requisite, then, in an Epitaph is, that it should speak, in a tone which shall sink into the heart, the general language of humanity as connected with the subject of Death—the source from which an Epitaph proceeds, of death and of life. To be born and to die are the two points in which all men feel themselves to be in absolute coincidence. This general language may be uttered so strikingly as to entitle an Epitaph to high praise; yet it cannot lay claim to the highest unless other excellencies be superadded. Passing through all intermediate steps, we will attempt to determine at once what these excellencies are, and wherein consists the perfection of this species of composition. It will be found to lie in a due proportion of the common or universal feeling of humanity to sensations excited by a distinct and clear conception, conveyed to the Reader's mind, of the Individual, whose death is deplored and whose memory is to be preserved; at least of his character as, after death, it appeared to those who loved him and lament his loss. The general sympathy ought to be quickened, provoked, and diversified, by particular thoughts, actions, images,—circumstances of age, occupation, manner of life, prosperity which the Deceased had known, or adversity to which he had been subject; and these ought to be bound together and solemnized into one harmony by the general sympathy. The two powers [412] should temper, restrain, and

<hr>

[1] See Johnson *Lives of the Poets* (1801) III 209.

exalt each other. The Reader ought to know who and what the Man was
whom he is called upon to think of with interest. A distinct conception
should be given (implicitly where it can, rather than explicitly) of the
Individual lamented. But the Writer of an Epitaph is not an Anatomist
who dissects the internal frame of the mind; he is not even a Painter who
executes a portrait at leisure and in entire tranquillity: his delineation, we
must remember, is performed by the side of the Grave; and, what is more,
the grave of one whom he loves and admires. What purity and brightness
is that virtue cloathed in, the image of which must no longer bless our living
eyes! The character of a deceased Friend or beloved Kinsman is not seen,
no—nor ought to be seen, other than as a Tree through a tender haze or a
luminous mist, that spiritualizes and beautifies it; that takes away indeed,
but only to the end that the parts which are not abstracted may appear
more dignified and lovely, may impress and affect the more. Shall we say
then that this is not truth, not a faithful image; and that accordingly the
purposes of commemoration cannot be answered?—It *is* truth, and of the
highest order! for, though doubtless things are not apparent which did
exist, yet, the object being looked at through this medium, parts and proportions are brought into distinct view which before had been only
imperfectly or unconsciously seen: it is truth hallowed by love—the joint
offspring of the worth of the Dead and the affections of the Living! This
may easily be brought to the test. Let one, whose eyes have been sharpened
by personal hostility to discover what was amiss in the character of a good
man, hear the tidings of his death, and what a change is wrought in a
moment!—Enmity melts away; and, as it disappears, unsightliness, disproportion, and deformity, vanish; and, through the influence of com-
miseration, a harmony of love and beauty succeeds. Bring such a Man to
the Tomb-stone on which shall be inscribed an Epitaph on his Adversary,
composed in the spirit which we have recommended. Would he turn from
it as from an idle tale? Ah! no—the thoughtful look, the sigh, and perhaps
the involuntary tear, would testify that it had a sane, a generous, and good
meaning; and that on the Writer's mind had remained an impression
which was a true abstract of the character of the deceased; that his gifts and
graces were remembered in the simplicity in [413] which they ought to be
remembered. The composition and quality of the mind of a virtuous man,
contemplated by the side of the Grave where his body is mouldering,
ought to appear and be felt as something midway between what he was on
Earth walking about with his living frailties, and what he may be presumed to be as a Spirit in Heaven.

It suffices, therefore, that the Trunk and the main Branches of the Worth
of the Deceased be boldly and unaffectedly represented. Any further detail,
minutely and scrupulously pursued, especially if this be done with laborious
and antithetic discriminations, must inevitably frustrate it's own purpose;
forcing the passing Spectator to this conclusion,—either that the Dead did
not possess the merits ascribed to him, or that they who have raised a
monument to his memory and must therefore be supposed to have been
closely connected with him, were incapable of perceiving those merits;
or at least during the act of composition had lost sight of them; for, the
Understanding having been so busy in it's petty occupation, how could the

heart of the Mourner be other than cold? and in either of these cases, whether the fault be on the part of the buried Person or the Survivors, the Memorial is unaffecting and profitless.

Much better is it to fall short in discrimination than to pursue it too far, or to labour it unfeelingly. For in no place are we so much disposed to dwell upon those points, of nature and condition, wherein all Men resemble each other, as in the Temple where the universal Father is worshipped, or by the side of the Grave which gathers all Human Beings to itself, and "equalizes the lofty and the low." [1] We suffer and we weep with the same heart; we love and are anxious for one another in one spirit; our hopes look to the same quarter; and the virtues by which we are all to be furthered and supported, as patience, meekness, good-will, temperance, and temperate desires, are in an equal degree the concern of us all. Let an Epitaph then, contain at least these acknowledgments to our common nature; nor let the sense of their importance be sacrificed to a balance of opposite qualities or minute distinctions in individual character; which if they do not, (as will for the most part be the case) when examined, resolve themselves into a trick of words, will, even when they are true and just, for the most part be grievously out of place; for, as it is probable that few only have [414] explored these intricacies of human nature, so can the tracing of them be interesting only to a few. But an Epitaph is not a proud Writing shut up for the studious; it is exposed to all, to the wise and the most ignorant; it is condescending, perspicuous, and lovingly solicits regard; it's story and admonitions are brief, that the thoughtless, the busy and indolent, may not be deterred, nor the impatient tired; the stooping Old Man cons the engraven record like a second horn-book;—the Child is proud that he can read it—and the Stranger is introduced by it's mediation to the company of a Friend: it is concerning all, and for all:—in the Churchyard it is open to the day; the sun looks down upon the stone, and the rains of Heaven beat against it.

Yet, though the Writer who would excite sympathy is bound in this case more than in any other, to give proof that he himself has been moved, it is to be remembered, that to raise a Monument is a sober and a reflective act; that the inscription which it bears is intended to be permanent and for universal perusal; and that, for this reason, the thoughts and feelings expressed should be permanent also—liberated from that weakness and anguish of sorrow which is in nature transitory, and which with instinctive decency retires from notice. The passions should be subdued, the emotions controlled; strong indeed, but nothing ungovernable or wholly involuntary. Seemliness requires this, and truth requires it also: for how can the Narrator otherwise be trusted? Moreover, a Grave is a tranquillizing object; resignation, in course of time, springs up from it as naturally as the wild flowers, besprinkling the turf with which it may be covered, or gathering round the monument by which it is defended. The very form and substance of the monument which has received the inscription, and the appearance of the letters, testifying with what a slow and laborious hand they must have been engraven, might seem to reproach the

[1] Source not traced.

Author who had given way upon this occasion to transports of mind, or to quick turns of conflicting passion; though the same might constitute the life and beauty of a funeral Oration or elegiac Poem.

These sensations and judgements, acted upon perhaps unconsciously, have been one of the main causes why Epitaphs so often personate the Deceased, and represent him as speaking from his own Tomb-stone. The departed [415] Mortal is introduced telling you himself that his pains are gone; that a state of rest is come; and he conjures you to weep for him no longer. He admonishes with the voice of one experienced in the vanity of those affections which are confined to earthly objects, and gives a verdict like a superior Being, performing the office of a Judge, who has no temptations to mislead him, and whose decision cannot but be dispassionate. Thus is Death disarmed of its' sting, and affliction unsubstantialized. By this tender fiction the Survivors bind themselves to a sedater sorrow, and employ the intervention of the imagination in order that the reason may speak her own language earlier than she would otherwise have been enabled to do. This shadowy interposition also harmoniously unites the two worlds of the Living and the Dead by their appropriate affections. And I may observe, that here we have an additional proof of the propriety with which sepulchral inscriptions were referred to the consciousness of Immortality as their primal source.

I do not speak with a wish to recommend that an Epitaph should be cast in this mould preferably to the still more common one, in which what is said comes from the Survivors directly; but rather to point out how natural those feelings are which have induced men, in all states and ranks of Society, so frequently to adopt this mode. And this I have done chiefly in order that the laws, which ought to govern the composition of the other, may be better understood. This latter mode, namely, that in which the Survivors speak in their own Persons, seems to me upon the whole greatly preferable: as it admits a wider range of notices; and, above all, because, excluding the fiction which is the ground-work of the other, it rests upon a more solid basis.

Enough has been said to convey our notion of a perfect Epitaph; but it must be observed that one is meant which will best answer the *general* ends of that species of composition. According to the course pointed out, the worth of private life, through all varieties of situation and character, will be most honourably and profitably preserved in memory. Nor would the model recommended less suit public Men, in all instances save those persons who by the greatness of their services in the employments of Peace or War, or by the surpassing excellence of their works in Art, Literature, or Science, have made [416] themselves not only universally known, but have filled the heart of their Country with everlasting gratitude. Yet I must here pause to correct myself. In describing the general tenor of thought which Epitaphs ought to hold, I have omitted to say, that, if it be the *actions* of a Man, or even some *one* conspicuous or beneficial act of local or general utility which has distinguished him and excited a desire that he should be remembered, then, of course, ought the attention to be directed chiefly to those actions or that act; and such sentiments dwelt upon as naturally arise out of them or it. Having made this necessary distinction I proceed.—
The mighty Benefactors of mankind, as they are not only known by the

immediate Survivors, but will continue to be known familiarly to latest Posterity, do not stand in need of biographic sketches, in such a place; nor of delineations of character to individualize them. This is already done by their actions, in the Memories of Men. Their naked names, and a grand comprehensive sentiment of civic Gratitude, patriotic Love, or human Admiration; or the utterance of some elementary Principle most essential in the constitution of true Virtue; or an intuition, communicated in adequate words, of the sublimity of intellectual power;—these are the only tribute which can here be paid—the only offering that upon such an Altar would not be unworthy!

> What needs my Shakespeare for his honoured bones
> The labour of an age in piled stones,
> Or that his hallowed reliques should be hid
> Under a star-y-pointing pyramid?
> Dear Son of Memory, great Heir of Fame,
> What need'st thou such weak witness of thy name?
> Thou in our wonder and astonishment
> Hast built thyself a live-long Monument.
> And so sepulchred, in such pomp dost lie,
> That Kings for such a Tomb would wish to die.[1]

---

[1] Milton *On Shakespear. 1630* lines 1–8, 15–16.

THE FRIEND

No. 26, THURSDAY, March 1, 1810

SKETCHES AND FRAGMENTS
OF THE LIFE AND CHARACTER
OF THE LATE ADMIRAL SIR ALEXANDER BALL

(Continued from Number 22.)

An accessibility to the sentiments of others on Subjects of importance often accompanies feeble minds, yet is not the less a true and constituent part of practical greatness, when it exists wholly free from that passiveness to impression which renders counsel itself injurious to certain characters, and from that weakness of heart which in the literal sense of the word is always *craving* advice. Exempt from all such imperfections, say rather in perfect harmony with the excellencies that preclude them, this openness to the influxes of good sense and information, from whatever quarter they might come, equally characterized both Lord Nelson and Sir Alexander Ball, though each displayed it in the way best suited to his natural temper. The former with easy hand collected, as it passed by him, whatever could add to his own stores, appropriated what he could assimilate, and levied subsidies of knowledge from all the accidents of social life, and familiar intercourse. Even at the jovial board, and in the height of unrestrained merriment, a casual suggestion, that flashed a new light on his mind, changed the boon companion into the Hero and the Man of Genius; and with the most graceful transition he would make his company as serious as himself. When the taper of his genius seemed extinguished, it was still surrounded by an inflammable atmosphere of it's own, and rekindled at the first approach of light, and not seldom at a distance which made it seem to flame up self-revived. In Sir Alexander Ball, the same excellence was more an affair of system: and he would listen, even to weak men, with a patience, which in so careful an economist of time, always demanded [418] my admiration, and not seldom excited my wonder. It was one of his maxims, that a man may suggest what he cannot give: adding, that a wild or silly plan had more than once, from the vivid sense, and distinct perception of its folly, occasioned him to see what ought to be done in a new light, or with a clearer insight. There is, indeed, a hopeless sterility, a mere negation of sense and thought, which suggesting neither difference nor contrast, cannot even furnish hints for recollection. But on the other hand, there are minds so whimsically constituted, that they may sometimes be profitably interpreted by contraries, a process of which the great Tycho Brache is said to have availed himself in the case of the Fool, who used to sit and mutter at his Feet while he was studying. A mind of this sort we may compare to a Magnetic Needle, the poles of which had been suddenly reversed by a flash of lightening, or other more obscure accident of Nature. It may be safely concluded, that to those whose judgement or information he respected, Sir Alexander Ball did not content himself with giving access and attention. No! he seldom failed of consulting them whenever the subject permitted any disclosure; and where secrecy was necessary, he well knew how to acquire their opinions without exciting even a conjecture concerning his immediate object.

Yet, with all this readiness of attention, and with all this zeal in collecting the sentiments of the well-informed, never was a man more completely uninfluenced by authority than Sir Alexander Ball, never one who sought less to tranquilize his own doubts by the mere suffrage and coincidence of others. The ablest suggestions had no conclusive weight with him, till he had abstracted the opinion from its author, till he had reduced it into a part of his own mind. The thoughts of others were always acceptable, as affording him at least a chance of adding to his materials for reflection; but they never directed his judgement, much less superseded it. He even made a point of guarding against additional confidence in the suggestions of his own mind, from finding that a person of talents had formed the same conviction: unless the person, at the same time, furnished some new argument, or had arrived at the same conclusion by a different road. On the latter circumstance he set an especial value, and, I may almost say, courted the company and conversation [419] of those, whose pursuits had least resembled his own, if they were men of clear and comprehensive faculties. During the period of our intimacy, scarcely a week passed, in which he did not desire me to think on some particular subject, and to give him the result in writing. Most frequently by the time I had fulfilled his request, he would have written down his own thoughts, and then, with the true simplicity of a great mind, as free from ostentation, as it was above Jealousy, he would collate the two papers in my presence, and never expressed more pleasure than in the few instances, in which I had happened to light on all the arguments and points of view which had occurred to himself, with some additional reasons which had escaped him. A single new argument delighted him more than the most perfect coincidence, unless, as before stated, the train of thought had been very different from his own, and yet just and logical. He had one quality of mind, which I have heard attributed to the late Mr. Fox, that of deriving a keen pleasure from clear and powerful reasoning for its own sake, a quality in the intellect which is nearly connected with veracity and a love of justice in the moral character.*

* It may not be amiss to add, that the pleasure from the perception of Truth was so well poised and regulated by the equal or greater delight in Utility, that his love of real accuracy was accompanied with a proportionate dislike of that hollow appearance of it, which may be produced by turns of phrase, words placed in balanced antithesis, and those epigrammatic points that pass for subtle and luminous distinctions with ordinary Readers, but are most commonly translatable into mere truisms or trivialities, if indeed they contain any meaning at all. Having observed in some casual conversation, that though there were doubtless *masses* of matter unorganized, I saw no ground for asserting a mass of unorganized *matter;*

Valuing in others merits which he himself possessed, Sir Alexander Ball felt no jealous apprehension of great talent. Unlike those vulgar Functionaries, whose Place is too big for them, a truth which they attempt to disguise from themselves, and yet feel, he was under no necessity of arming himself against the Natural Superiority of Genius by factitious contempt and an industrious association of extravagance and impracticability, with every deviation from the ordinary routine; as the Geographers in the middle ages used to designate on their meagre Maps, the greater part of the World, as Desarts or Wildernesses, inhabited [420] by Griffins and Chimæras. Competent to weigh each system or project by its own arguments, he did not need these preventive charms and cautionary amulets against delusion. He endeavoured to make talent instrumental to his purposes in whatever shape it appeared, and with whatever imperfections it might be accompanied; but wherever talent was blended with moral worth, he sought it out, loved, and cherished it. If it had pleased Providence to preserve his life, and to place him on the same course on which Nelson ran his race of Glory, there are two points in which Sir Alexander Ball would most closely have resembled his illustrious Friend. The first is, that in his enterprizes and engagements he would have thought nothing done, till all had been done that was possible:

"Nil actum reputans, si quid supresset agendum."

The second, that he would have called forth all the talent and virtue that existed within his sphere of influence, and created a band of Heroes, a gradation of officers, strong in head and strong in heart, worthy to have been his Companions and his Successors in Fame and public Usefulness.

Never was greater discernment shewn in the selection of a fit agent, than when Sir Alexander Ball was stationed off the Coast of Malta to intercept the supplies destined for the French Garrison, and to watch the movements of the French Commanders, and those of the Inhabitants who had been so basely betrayed into their power. Encouraged by the well-timed promises of the English Captain, the Maltese rose through all their Casals (or Country Towns) and themselves commenced the work of their emancipation, by storming the Citadel at Civita Vecchia, the ancient Metropolis of Malta, and the central height of the Island. Without discipline, without a military Leader, and almost without arms, these brave peasants succeeded, and destroyed the French Garrison by throwing them over the battlements into the trench of the Citadel. In the course of this blockade, and of the tedious siege of Vallette, Sir Alexander Ball displayed all that strength of character, that variety and versatility of talent, and that sagacity, derived in part from habitual circumspection, but which, when the occasion demanded it, appeared intuitive and like an instinct; at the union of which, in the same Man, one of our oldest naval Commanders once told me, [421] "he could never exhaust his wonder." The Citizens of Vallette were fond of relating their astonishment, and that of the French, at Captain Ball's Ship

Sir A. B. paused, and then said to me, with that frankness of manner which made his very rebukes gratifying, "The distinction is just, and, now I understand you, abundantly obvious; but hardly worth the trouble of your inventing a puzzle of words to make it appear otherwise." I trust the rebuke was not lost on me.

wintering at anchor out of the reach of the Guns, in a depth of fathom unexampled, on the assured impracticability of which the Garrison had rested their main hope of regular supplies. Nor can I forget, or remember without some portion of my original feeling, the solemn enthusiasm with which a venerable old man, belonging to one of the distant Casals, shewed me the Sea Coombe, where their Father BALL, (for so they commonly called him) first landed; and afterwards pointed out the very place, on which he first stepped on their Island, while the countenances of his Townsmen, who accompanied him, gave lively proofs, that the old man's enthusiasm was the representative of the common feeling. There is no reason to suppose, that Sir Alexander Ball was at any time chargeable with that weakness so frequent in Englishmen, and so injurious to our interests abroad, of despising the Inhabitants of other Countries, of losing all their good qualities in their vices, of making no allowance for those vices, from their religious or political impediments, and still more of mistaking for vices, a mere difference of manners and customs. But if ever he had any of this erroneous feeling, he completely freed himself from it, by living among the Maltese during their arduous trials, as long as the French continued masters of the Capital. He witnessed their virtues, and learnt to understand in what various shapes and even disguises the valuable parts of human Nature may exist. In many Individuals, whose littleness and meanness in the common intercourse of life would have stamped them at once as contemptible and worthless, with ordinary Englishmen, he had found such virtues of disinterested patriotism, fortitude, and self-denial, as would have done honour to an ancient Roman.

There exists in England, a *gentlemanly* character, a *gentlemanly* feeling, very different even from that, which is the most like it, the character of a well-born Spaniard, and unexampled in the rest of Europe. This feeling probably *originated* in the fortunate circumstance, that the Titles of our English Nobility follow the law of their Property, and are inherited by the eldest Sons only. From this source, under the influences of our Constitution, and of our astonishing Trade, it has diffused itself in [422] different modifications through the whole Country. The uniformity of our Dress among all classes above that of the day labourer, while it has authorized all classes to assume the appearance of Gentlemen, has at the same time inspired the wish to conform their manners, and still more their ordinary actions in social intercourse, to their notions of a Gentleman, the most commonly received attribute of which, is a certain generosity in trifles. On the other hand, the encroachments of the lower classes on the higher, occasioned, and favoured by this resemblance in exteriors, and the absence of any cognizable marks of distinction, have rendered each class more reserved and jealous in their general communion, and far more than our Climate, or natural Temper, have caused that haughtiness and reserve in our outward demeanor, which is so generally complained of among Foreigners. Far be it from me to depreciate the value of this gentlemanly feeling: I respect it under all its forms and varieties, from the House of Commons, to the Gentlemen in the one shilling Gallery. It is always the ornament of Virtue, and oftentimes a support; but it is a wretched substitute for it. Its *worth*, as a moral good, is by no means in proportion to its' *value*, as a social advantage. These observations are not irrelevant: for to the want of reflection, that this diffusion of gentlemanly feeling among us, is not the growth of our moral excellence, but the effect of various accidental advantages peculiar to England; to our not considering that it is unreasonable and uncharitable to expect the same consequences, where the same causes have not existed to produce them; and, lastly, to our proneness to regard the absence of this character (which, as I have before said, does, for the greater part, and, in the common apprehension, consist in a certain frankness and generosity in the detail of action) as decisive against the sum total of personal or national worth; we must, I am convinced, attribute a large portion of that conduct, which in many instances has left the Inhabitants of Countries conquered or appropriated by Great Britain, doubtful whether the various solid advantages which they derived from our protection and just government, were not bought dearly by the wounds inflicted on their feelings and prejudices, by the contemptuous and insolent demeanour of the English, as individuals. The Reader who bears this remark in mind, will meet, in the [423] course of this narration, more than one passage that will serve as its' comment and illustration.

It was, I know, a general opinion among the English in the Mediterranean, that Sir Alexander Ball thought too well of the Maltese, and did not share in the enthusiasm of Britons, concerning their own superiority. To the former part of the charge, I shall only reply at present, that a more venial, and almost desirable fault, can scarcely be attributed to a Governor, than that of a strong attachment to the People whom he was sent to govern. The latter part of the charge is false, if we are to understand by it, that he did not think his Countrymen superior on the whole to the other Nations of Europe: but it is true, as far as relates to his belief, that the English think themselves still better than they are: that they dwelt on, and exaggerated their National Virtues, and weighed them by the opposite *vices* of Foreigners, instead of the virtues, which those Foreigners possessed, and they themselves wanted. Above all, as Statesmen, we must consider qualities by their practical uses. Thus—he entertained, no doubt, that the English were superior to all others in the kind, and the degree of their courage, which is marked by far greater enthusiasm, than the courage of the Germans and northern Nations, and by a far greater steadiness and self-subsistence, than that of the French. It is more closely connected with the character of the Individual. The courage of an English army is the sum total of the courage which the individual Soldiers bring with them to it, rather than of that which they derive from it. When I was at Naples, a Russian and an English Regiment were drawn up together in the same square: "See," said a Neapolitan to me, who had mistaken me for one of his Countrymen, "there is but one face in that whole Regiment, while in *that*" (*pointing to the English*) "every Soldier has a face of his own.") On the other hand, there are qualities scarcely less requisite to the completion of the military character, in which the English are inferior to the Continental Nations; as for instance, both in the power and the disposition to endure privations; in the friendly temper necessary, when troops of different Nations are to act in concert; in their obedience to the regulations of their commanding Officers, respecting the treatment of the Inhabitants of the countries through which they are marching, as well as in many other points, not immediately connected [423] with their conduct in the field; but, above all, in sobriety and temperance during the siege of Vallette, especially during the sore distress to which the Besiegers were for sometime exposed from the failure of provision, Sir Alexander Ball had an ample opportunity of observing and weighing the separate merits and demerits of the Natives, and of the English Troops: and surely since the publication of Sir John Moore's campaign, there can be no just offence taken, though I should say, that before the walls of Vallette, as well as in the plains of Gallicia an indignant Commander might, with too great propriety, have addressed the English Soldiery in the words of an old Dramatist—

> Will you still owe your virtues to your bellies?
> And only then think nobly when y' are full?
> Doth Fodder keep you honest? Are you bad
> When out of Flesh? And think you't an excuse
> Of vile and ignominious actions, that
> Y' are lean and out of liking?
>   CARTWRIGHT'S LOVE'S CONVERT

From the first insurrectionary movement to the final departure of the French from the Island, though the civil and military powers and the whole of the Island, save Vallette, were in the hands of the Peasantry, not a single act of excess can be charged against the Maltese, if we except the razing of one House at Civita Vecchia belonging to a notorious and abandoned Traitor, the Creature and Hireling of the French. In no instance did they injure, insult, or plunder, any one of the native Nobility, or employ even the appearance of force toward them, except in the collection of the Lead and Iron from their Houses and Gardens, in order to supply themselves with bullets: and this very appearance was assumed from the generous wish to shelter the Nobles from the resentment of the French, should the patriotic efforts of the Peasantry prove unsuccessful. At the dire command of famine the Maltese Troops did indeed once force their way to the Ovens, in which the Bread for the British Soldiery was baked, and were clamorous that an equal division should be made. I mention this unpleasant circumstance, because it brought into proof the firmness of Sir Alexander Ball's character, his presence of mind, and generous disregard of danger and personal responsibility, where the slavery or emancipation, [425] the misery or the happiness, of an innocent and patriotic People were involved; and because his conduct in this exigency evinced, that his general habits of circumspection and deliberation were the results of wisdom and complete self-possession, and not the easy virtues of a spirit constitutionally timorous and hesitating. He was sitting at Table with the principal British Officers, when a certain General addressed him in strong and violent terms concerning this outrage of the Maltese, reminding him of the necessity of exerting his commanding influence in the present case, or the consequences must be taken. "What," replied Sir Alexander Ball, "would you have us do? would you have us threaten death to Men dying with Famine? Can you suppose that the hazard of being shot will weigh with whole Regiments acting under a common necessity? Does not the extremity of hunger take away all difference between Men and Animals? and is it not as absurd to appeal to the prudence of a body of men starving, as to a herd of famished Wolves? No, General, I will not degrade myself or outrage humanity by menacing Famine with Massacre! More effectual means must be taken." With these words he rose and left the room, and having first consulted with Sir Thomas Troubridge, he determined at his own risk on a step, which the extreme necessity warranted, and which the conduct of the Neapolitan Court amply justified. For this Court, though terrorstricken by the French, was still actuated by hatred to the English, and a jealousy of their power in the Mediterranean: and this in so strange and senseless a manner, that we must join the extremes of imbecility and treachery in the same Cabinet, in order to find it comprehensible.* Though the very existence of Naples and Sicily, as a Nation, depended wholly and exclusively on British support; [426] though the Royal Family owed their personal safety to the British Fleet; though not only their Dominions and their Rank, but the Liberty and even the Lives of Ferdinand and his Family, were interwoven with our success; yet with an infatuation scarcely credible, the most affecting representations of the distress of the Besiegers, and of the utter insecurity of Sicily if the French remained possessors of Malta, were treated with neglect; and the urgent remonstrances for the permission of importing corn from Messina, were answered only by sanguinary Edicts precluding all supply. Sir Alexander Ball sent for his senior Lieutenant, and gave him orders to proceed immediately to the Port of Messina, and there to seize and bring with him to Malta the Ships laden with corn, of the number of which Sir Alexander had received accurate information. These orders were executed without delay, to the great delight and profit of the Ship Owners and Proprietors; the necessity of raising the Siege was removed; and the Author of the measure waited in calmness for the consequences that might result to himself personally. But not a complaint, not a murmur, proceeded from the Court of Naples. The sole result was, that the Governor of Malta became an especial object of its' hatred, its' fear, and its' respect.

The whole of this tedious Siege, from its' commencement to the signing of the Capitulation, called forth into constant activity the rarest and most difficult virtues of a commanding mind; virtues of no shew or splendour in the vulgar apprehension, yet more infallible characteristics of true greatness than the most unequivocal displays of enterprize and active daring.

* It cannot be doubted, that the Sovereign himself was kept in a state of delusion. Both his understanding and his moral principles are far better than could reasonably be expected from the infamous mode of his Education: if indeed the systematic preclusion of all knowledge, and the unrestrained indulgence of his passions, adopted by the Spanish Court for the purposes of preserving him dependent, can be called by the name of Education. Of the other influencing Persons in the Neapolitan Government, Mr. Leckie has given us a true and lively account. It will be greatly to the advantage of the present narration, if the Reader should have previously perused Mr. Leckie's Pamphlet on the state of Sicily: the facts which I shall have occasion to mention hereafter will reciprocally confirm and be confirmed by the documents furnished in that most interesting Work; in which I see but one blemish of importance, namely, that the Author appears too frequently to consider justice and true policy as capable of being contradistinguished.

Scarcely a day passed, in which Sir Alexander Ball's patience, forbearance, and inflexible constancy, were not put to the severest trial. He had not only to remove the misunderstandings that arose between the Maltese and their Allies, to settle the differences among the Maltese themselves, and to organize their efforts: he was likewise engaged in the more difficult and unthankful task of counteracting the weariness, discontent, and despondency, of his own Countrymen—a task, however, which he accomplished by management and address, and an alternation of real firmness with apparent yielding. During many months he remained the only Englishman, who did not think the Siege hopeless, and the Object worthless. He often spoke of the time in [427] which he resided at the country seat of the Grand Master at St. Antonio, four miles from Vallette, as perhaps the most trying period of his Life. For some weeks Captain Vivian was his sole English Companion, of whom, as his partner in anxiety, he always expressed himself with affectionate esteem. Sir Alexander Ball's presence was absolutely necessary to the Maltese, who, accustomed to be governed by him, became incapable of acting in concert without his immediate influence. In the out-burst of popular emotion, the impulse, which produces an insurrection, is for a brief while its' sufficient pilot: the attraction constitutes the cohesion, and the common provocation supplying an immediate object, not only unites, but directs, the multitude. But this first impulse had passed away, and Sir Alexander Ball was the one Individual who possessed the general confidence. On him they relied with implicit faith: and even after they had long enjoyed the blessings of British government and protection, it was still remarkable with what child-like helplessness they were in the habit of applying to him, even in their private concerns. It seemed as if they thought him made on purpose to think for them all. Yet his situation at St. Antonio was one of great peril: and he attributed his preservation to the dejection, which had now begun to prey on the spirits of the French Garrison, and which rendered them unenterprizing and almost passive, aided by the dread which the nature of the Country inspired. For subdivided as it was into small Fields, scarcely larger than a Cottage Garden, and each of these little squares of land inclosed with a substantial stone wall, and from the necessity of being perfectly level, rising in tiers above each other, the whole of the inhabited part of the Island was an effective Fortification for all the purposes of annoyance and defensive Warfare. Sir Alexander Ball exerted himself successfully in procuring information respecting the state and temper of the Garrison, and by the assistance of the Clergy and the almost universal fidelity of the Maltese, contrived, that the Spies in the pay of the French should be in truth his own most confidential Agents. He had already given splendid proofs that he could out-fight them; but here, and in his after diplomatic intercourse previous to the recommencement of the War, he likewise out-witted them. He once told me with a smile, as we were conversing on the practice of laying wagers, that he was sometimes inclined [428] to think that the final perseverance in the Siege was not a little indebted to several valuable bets of his own, he well knowing at the time, and from information which himself alone possessed, that he should certainly lose them. Yet this artifice had a considerable effect in suspending the impatience of the Officers, and in supplying topics for dispute and conversation. At length, however, the two French Frigates, the sailing of which had been the subject of these Wagers, left the great Harbour on the 24th of August, 1800, with a part of the Garrison, and one of them soon became a prize to the English. Sir Alexander Ball related to me the circumstances which occasioned the escape of the other; but I do not recollect them with sufficient accuracy to dare repeat them in this place. On the 15th of September following, the Capitulation was signed, and after a blockade of two years the English obtained possession of Vallette, and remained masters of the whole Island and its' Dependencies.

Anxious not to give offence, but more anxious to communicate the truth, it is not without pain that I proceed to give my sentiments on this capitulation, by which Malta was delivered up to his Britannic Majesty and his Allies, without the least mention made of the Maltese. With a warmth honourable both to his head and his heart, Sir Alexander Ball pleaded, as not less a point of sound policy than of plain justice, that the Maltese, by some Representative, should be made a Party in the capitulation, and a joint Subscriber in the signature. They had never been the Slaves or the Property of the Knights of St. John, but Freemen and the true landed Proprietors of the Country, the civil and military government of which, under certain restrictions, had been vested in that Order; yet checked by the rights and influences of the Clergy and the native Nobility, and by the Customs and ancient Laws of the Island. This trust the Knights had with the blackest treason and the most profligate perjury, betrayed and abandoned. The right of Government of course reverted to the landed Proprietors and the Clergy. Animated by a just sense of this right, the Maltese had risen of their own accord, had contended for it in defiance of death and danger, had fought bravely, and endured patiently. Without undervaluing the military assistance afterwards furnished by Great Britain (though how scanty this was before the arrival of General Pigot is well known) it remained [429] undeniable, that the Maltese had taken the greatest share both in the fatigues and in the privations consequent on the Siege; and that had not the greatest virtues and the most exemplary fidelity been uniformly displayed by them, the English Troops, (they not being more numerous than they had been for the greater part of the two years) could not possibly have remained before the Fortifications of Vallette, defended as that City was by a French Garrison, that greatly outnumbered the British Besiegers. Still less could there have been the least hope of ultimate success; as if any part of the Maltese Peasantry had been friendly to the French or even indifferent, if they had not all indeed been most zealous and persevering in their hostility towards them; it would have been impracticable so to blockade that Island as to have precluded the arrival of supplies. If the Siege had proved unsuccessful, the Maltese were well aware that they should be exposed to all the horrors which revenge and wounded pride could dictate to an unprincipled, rapacious, and sanguinary Soldiery; and now that success has crowned their efforts, is this to be their reward, that their own Allies are to bargain for them with the French as for a herd of Slaves, whom the French had before purchased from a former Proprietor? If it be urged, that there is no established Government in Malta, is it not equally true, that through the whole population of the Island there is not a single Dissentient? and thus that the chief inconvenience, which an established authority is to obviate, is virtually removed by the admitted fact of their unanimity? And have they not a Bishop, and a dignified Clergy, their Judges and municipal Magistrates, who were at all times sharers in the power of the Government, and now, supported by the unanimous suffrage of the Inhabitants, have a rightful claim to be considered as it's Representatives? Will it not be oftener said than answered, that the main difference between French and English injustice rests in this point alone, that the French siezed on the Maltese without any previous pretences of Friendship, while the English procured possession of the Island by means of their friendly promises, and by the co-operation of the Natives afforded in confident reliance on these promises? The impolicy of refusing the signature on the part of the Maltese was equally evident: since such refusal could answer no one purpose but that of alienating their affections by a wanton insult to their feelings. [430] For the Maltese were not only ready but desirous and eager to place themselves at the same time under British protection, to take the oaths of loyalty as Subjects of the British Crown, and to acknowledge their Island to belong to it. These representations, however, were over-ruled: and I dare affirm, from my own experience in the Mediterranean, that our conduct in this instance, added to the impression which had been made at Corsica, Minorca, and elsewhere, and was often referred to by Men of reflection in Sicily, who have more than once said to me: "A connection with Great Britain, with the consequent extension and security of our Commerce, are indeed great blessings: but who can rely on their permanence? or that we shall not be made to pay bitterly for our zeal as Partizans of England, whenever it shall suit it's plans to deliver us back to our old Oppressors."

(To be continued.)

TO CORRESPONDENTS

A valued Correspondent[1] objects to the latter part of No. 24. "It might seem," he observes, "that THE FRIEND was afraid of his Opinion, by the attempt to disguise it in an Allegory; at least the application should have been openly avowed." The following considerations will, I trust, remove this objection.

It was once said to me, when the Copenhagen affair was in dispute, "You do not see the enormity, because it is an affair between State and State: conceive a similar case between Man and Man, and you would both see and abhor it." Now, I was neither defending or attacking the measure itself, for my arguments were confined to the *grounds*, which had been taken both in the arraigning of that measure, and in its' defence, because I thought both equally untenable. I was not enough master of facts to form a decisive opinion on the enterprize, even for my own mind; but I had no hesitation in affirming, that the *principles*, on which it was *defended* in

---

[1] Unidentified; possibly Poole.

the legislature, appeared to me fitter objects of indignant reprobation, than the act itself. This having been premised, I answer to the assertion above stated, by asserting the direct contrary: [431] namely, that were a similar case conceived between Man and Man, the severest arraigners of the measure, would, *on their grounds* find nothing to blame in it. How was I to prove this assertion? Clearly, by imagining some case between individuals living in the same relations toward each other, in which the several states of Europe exist, or existed. My Allegory, therefore, so far from being a disguise, was a necessary part of the main argument, *a case in point*, to prove the identity of the Law of Nations with the Law of Conscience. We have only to conceive Individuals in the same relations as States, in order to learn that the rules emanating from international Law, differ from those of private honesty, solely through the difference of the circumstances.

But why did not THE FRIEND avow the *application* of the principle to the seizure of the Danish Fleet? Because I did not possess sufficient evidence to prove to others, or even to decide for myself, that my Principle *was* applicable to this particular act. In the case of Pamphilus and Lathrodacnus, the prudence and necessity of the measure was certain; and, this taken for granted, I shewed it's perfect rightfulness. In the affair of Copenhagen I had no doubt of our *right* to do as we did, *supposing* the necessity, or at least the extreme prudence, of the measure; *taking for granted*, that there existed a motive adequate to the action, and that the action was an adequate means of realizing the motive.

But this I was not authorized to take for granted in the real, as I had been in the imaginary, Case. I see many reasons for the affirmative, and many for the negative. For the former, the certainty of an hostile design on the part of the Danes, the alarming state of Ireland, that vulnerable heel of the British Achilles! and the immense difference between military and naval superiority. Our naval power collectively may ride in defiance of the whole world; but it is widely scattered, and a combined operation from the Baltic, Holland, Brest, and Lisbon, might easily bring together a Fleet double to that which we could bring against it at the instant, or for the short time that might be necessary to convey 30 or 40,000 Men to Ireland. On the other hand, it is equally clear that Buonaparte needs Sailors rather than Ships; and that we took the Ships and left him the Danish Sailors. It appears from the papers lately published, that the French Fleet at Antwerp is in [432] fact manned, in part, by those very Sailors. But I repeat, that THE FRIEND had no concern with the Expedition itself; but only with the grounds or principles on which it had been attacked or defended. Those who attacked it denied the right altogether, however imperious the motive might be: and I appear to myself to have shewn, in opposition to such Reasoners, that no such right existed, or is deducible either from international Law or the Law of private morality. Those again, who defended it, conceded that it was a violation of right; but affirmed, that such violation was justified by the urgency of the motive. It was asserted (as I have before noticed, in the introduction to the subject p. 366)[1] that *national policy*

---

[1] See above, II 308.

cannot in all cases be subordinated to the Laws of Morality; in other words, that a Government may act with injustice, and yet remain blameless. To prove this assertion as groundless and unnecessary as it is tremendous, formed the chief object of the whole disquisition. I trust then, that my Correspondent will rest satisfied, that it is not only the profession and pretext of THE FRIEND, but his constant plan and actual intention, to establish PRINCIPLES; that he refers to particular facts for no other purpose, than that of giving illustration and interest to those Principles; and that to invent Principles with a view to particular cases, whether with the motive of attacking or arraigning a transitory Cabinet, is a baseness which will scarcely be attributed to THE FRIEND by any one who understands the Work, even though the suspicion should not have been precluded by a knowledge of the Author. S.T.C.

THE FRIEND

No. 27, THURSDAY, MARCH 15, 1810

SKETCHES AND FRAGMENTS
OF THE LIFE AND CHARACTER
OF THE LATE ADMIRAL SIR ALEXANDER BALL

(Continued.)

CAPTAIN BALL's services in Malta were honoured with his Sovereign's approbation, transmitted in a letter from the Secretary Dundas, and with a Baronetcy. A thousand pounds* were at the same time directed to be paid him from the Maltese Treasury. The best and most appropriate addition to the applause of his King and his Country, Sir Alexander Ball found in the feelings and faithful affection of the Maltese. The enthusiasm manifested in reverential gestures and shouts of triumph whenever their Friend and Deliverer appeared in public, was the utterance of a deep feeling, and in no wise the mere ebullition of animal sensibility: which is not indeed a part of the Maltese character. The truth of this observation will not be doubted by any person, who has witnessed the religious Processions [434] in honour of the favourite Saints, both at Vallette and at Messina or Palermo, and who must have been struck with the contrast between the apparent apathy, or at least the perfect sobriety, of the Maltese, and the fanatical agitations of the Sicilian Populace. Among the latter each Man's soul seems hardly containable in his body, like a prisoner, whose Jail is on fire, flying madly from one barred outlet to another; while the former might suggest the suspicion, that their bodies were on the point of

---

* I scarce know whether it be worth mentioning, that this Sum remained undemanded till the Spring of the year 1805: at which time the Writer of these Sketches, during an examination of the Treasury Accounts, observed the circumstance and noticed it to the Governor, who had suffered it to escape altogether from his memory, for the latter years at least. The value attached to the Present by the Receiver, must have depended on his construction of its purpose and meaning: for, in a pecuniary point of view, the sum was not a moiety of what Sir Alexander had expended from his private fortune during the blockade. His immediate appointment to the Government of the Island, so earnestly prayed for by the Maltese, would doubtless have furnished a less questionable proof that his services were as highly estimated by the Ministry as they were graciously accepted by his Sovereign. But this was withheld as long as it remained possible to doubt, whether great talents, joined to local experience, and the confidence and affection of the Inhabitants, might not be dispensed with in the Person entrusted with that Government.

sinking into the same slumber with their understandings. But their political Deliverance was a thing that came home to their hearts, and intertwined with their most empassioned recollections, personal and patriotic. To Sir Alexander Ball exclusively (with what justice it is not for me to decide) the Maltese themselves attributed their emancipation: on him too they rested their hopes of the future. Whenever he appeared in Vallette, the Passengers on each side, through the whole length of the street stopped, and remained uncovered till he had passed: the very clamours of the Market Place were hushed at his entrance, and then exchanged for shouts of joy and welcome. Even after the lapse of years he never appeared in any one of their Casals,* which did not lie in the direct road between Vallette and St. Antonio, his Summer Residence, but the Women and Children, with such of the Men who were not at labour in their fields, fell into ranks, and followed, or preceded him, singing the Maltese Song which had been made in his honour, and which was scarcely less familiar to the Inhabitants of Malta and Goza, than God save the King to Britons. *When he went to the Gate through the City, the young Men refrained talking; and the Aged arose and stood up. When the ear heard, then it blessed him; and when the eye saw him, it gave witness to him: because he delivered the Poor that cried, and the Fatherless, and those that had none to help them. The blessing of them that were ready to perish came upon him; and he caused the Widow's heart to sing for joy.*

[435] These feelings were afterwards amply justified by his administration of the Government; and the very excesses of their gratitude on their first deliverance, proved in the end, only to be acknowledgements antedated. For some time after the departure of the French, the distress was so general and so severe, that a large proportion of the lower classes became Mendicants, and one of the greatest thoroughfares of Vallette still retains the name of the "*Nix Mangiare Stairs*," from the crowd who used there to assail the ears of the Passengers with cries of "nix mangiare," or "nothing to eat," the former word *nix*, being the low German pronunciation of *nichts*, nothing. By what means it was introduced into Malta, I know not; but it became the common vehicle both of solicitation and refusal, the Maltese thinking it an English word, and the English supposing it to be Maltese. I often felt it as a pleasing remembrancer of the evil day gone by, when a tribe of little children, quite naked, as is the custom of that climate, and each with a pair of gold ear-rings in his ears, and all fat and beautifully proportioned, would suddenly leave their play, and, looking round to see that their Parents were not in sight, change their shouts of merriment for "*nix mangiare!*" awkwardly imitating the plaintive tones of mendicancy; while the white teeth in their little swarthy faces gave a splendor to the happy and confessing laugh, with which they received the good-humoured rebuke or refusal, and ran back to their former sport.

* It was the Governor's custom to visit every Casal throughout the Island once, if not twice, in the course of each Summer; and during my residence there, I had the honour of being his constant, and most often, his only Companion in these rides; to which I owe some of the happiest and most instructive hours of my life. In the poorest House of the most distant Casal two rude paintings were sure to be found: A Picture of the Virgin and Child; and a Portrait of Sir Alexander Ball.

In the interim between the capitulation of the French Garrison and Sir Alexander Ball's appointment as his Majesty's civil Commissioner for Malta, his zeal for the Maltese was neither suspended nor unproductive of important benefits. He was enabled to remove many prejudices and misunderstandings; and to persons of no inconsiderable influence gave juster notions of the true importance of the Island to Great Britain. He displayed the magnitude of the Trade of the Mediterranean in it's existing state; shewed the immense extent to which it might be carried, and the hollowness of the opinion, that this Trade was attached to the south of France by any natural or indissoluble bond of connection. I have some reason likewise for believing, that his wise and patriotic representations prevented Malta from being made the seat and pretext for a numerous civil establishment, in hapless imitation of Corsica, [436] Ceylon, and the Cape of Good Hope. It was at least generally rumoured, that it had been in the contemplation of the Ministry to appoint Sir Ralph Abercrombie as Governor, with a salary of £10,000 a year, and to reside in England, while one of his Countrymen was to be the Lieutenant Governor at £5,000 a year; to which were to be added a long et cetera of other Offices and Places of proportional emolument. This threatened appendix to the State Calendar may have existed only in the imaginations of the Reporters, yet inspired some uneasy apprehensions in the minds of many well-wishers to the Maltese, who knew that—for a foreign Settlement at least, and one too possessing in all the ranks and functions of Society, an ample Population of it's own— such a stately and wide-branching Tree of Patronage, though delightful to the Individuals who are to pluck it's golden Apples, sheds, like the Manchineel, unwholesome and corrosive dews on the multitude who are to rest beneath it's shade. It need not however be doubted, that Sir Alexander Ball would exert himself to preclude any such intention, by stating and evincing the extreme impolicy and injustice of the plan, as well as it's utter inutility, in the case of Malta. With the exception of the Governor, and of the Public Secretary, both of whom undoubtedly should be natives of Great Britain, and appointed by the British Government, there was no civil Office that could be of the remotest advantage to the Island which was not already filled by the Natives, and the functions of which none could perform so well as they. The number of Inhabitants (he would state) was prodigious compared with the extent of the Island, though from the fear of the Moors one fourth of it's surface remained unpeopled and uncultivated. To deprive therefore the middle and lower Classes of such Places, as they had been accustomed to hold, would be cruel: while the Places held by the Nobility, were, for the greater part, such as none but Natives could perform the duties of. By any innovation we should affront the higher classes and alienate the affections of all, not only without any imaginable advantage but with the certainty of great loss. Were Englishmen to be employed, the salaries must be encreased four-fold, and would yet be scarcely worth acceptance; and in higher offices, such as those of the civil and criminal judges, the Salaries must be augmented more than ten-fold. For, [437] greatly to the credit of their patriotism and moral character, the Maltese Gentry sought these Places as honourable distinctions, which endeared them to their Fellow-countrymen, and at the same time rendered the yoke of the Order somewhat less grievous and galling. With the exception of the Maltese Secretary, whose situation was one of incessant labour, and who at the same time performed the duties of Law Counsellor to the Government, the highest salaries scarcely exceeded £100. a year, and were barely sufficient to defray the encreased expences of the Functionaries for an additional equipage, or one of more imposing appearance. Besides, it was of importance that the Person placed at the head of that Government, should be looked up to by the Natives, and possess the means of distinguishing and rewarding those who had been most faithful and zealous in their attachment to Great Britain, and hostile to their former Tyrants. The number of the employments to be conferred would give considerable influence to his Majesty's civil Representative, while the trifling amount of the emolument attached to each, precluded all temptation of abusing it.

Sir Alexander Ball would likewise, it is probable, urge, that the commercial advantages of Malta, which were most intelligible to the English Public, and best fitted to render our retention of the Island popular, must necessarily be of very slow growth, though finally they would become great, and of an extent not to be calculated. For this reason, therefore, it was highly desirable, that the Possession should be and appear to be, at least inexpensive. After the British Government had made one advance for a stock of Corn sufficient to place the Island a year before-hand, the sum total drawn from Great Britain need not exceed 25, or at most £30,000. annually; excluding of course the expenditure connected with our own Military and Navy, and the repair of the Fortifications, which latter expence ought to be much less than at Gibraltar, from the multitude and low wages of the Labourers in Malta, and from the softness and admirable quality of the stone. Indeed much more might safely be promised on the assumption, that a wise and generous system of policy were adopted and persevered in. The monopoly of the Maltese corn Trade by the Government, formed an exception to a general rule, and by a strange, yet valid, anomaly in [438] the operations of political Economy, was not more necessary than advantageous to the Inhabitants. The chief reason is, that the produce of the Island itself barely suffices for one-fourth of it's Inhabitants, although fruits and vegetables form so large a part of their nourishment. Meantime the Harbours of Malta, and it's equi-distance from Europe, Asia, and Africa, gave it a vast and unnatural importance in the present relations of the great European Powers, and imposed on it's Government, whether native or dependent, the necessity of considering the whole Island as a single Garrison, the provisioning of which could not be trusted to the casualties of ordinary commerce. What is actually necessary is seldom injurious. Thus in Malta bread is better and cheaper on an average than in Italy or the Coast of Barbary: while a similar interference with the corn Trade in Sicily impoverishes the Inhabitants and keeps the Agriculture in a state of Barbarism. But the point in question is the expence to Great Britain. Whether the Monopoly be good or evil in itself, it remains true, that in this established usage, and in the gradual inclosure of the uncultivated district, such resources exist as without the least oppression might render the civil Government in Vallette independent of the Treasury at home, finally taking upon itself even the repair of the Fortifications, and thus realize one instance of an important possession that cost the Country nothing.

But now the time arrived, which threatened to frustrate the patriotism of the Maltese themselves and all the zealous efforts of their disinterested Friend. Soon after the War had for the first time become indisputably just and necessary, the People at large and a majority of independent Senators, incapable, as it might seem, of translating their fanatical anti-jacobinism into a well-grounded, yet equally impassioned, anti-Gallican-ism, grew impatient for Peace or rather for a *name*, under which the most terrific of all War would be incessantly waged against us. Our conduct was not much wiser than that of the weary Traveller, who having proceeded half way on his journey procured a short rest for himself by getting up be-hind a Chaise which was going the contrary road. In the strange Treaty of Amiens, in which we neither recognized our former relations with France or with the other European Powers, nor formed any new ones, the com-promise concerning [439] Malta formed the prominent feature: and it's nominal re-delivery to the Order of St. John was authorized in the minds of the People, by Lord Nelson's opinion of it's worthlessness to Great Britain in a political or naval view. It is a melancholy fact, and one that must often sadden a reflective and philanthropic mind, how little moral considerations weigh even with the noblest Nations, how vain are the strongest appeals to justice, humanity, and national honour, unless when the public mind is under the immediate influence of the cheerful or vehe-ment passions, indignation or avaricious hope. In the whole class of human infirmities there is none, that makes such loud appeals to *prudence*, and yet so frequently outrages it's plainest dictates, as the spirit of Fear. The worst cause conducted in Hope, is an overmatch for the noblest managed by Despondence: in both cases an unnatural conjunction that recals the old Fable of Love and Death, taking each the arrows of the others by mistake. When Islands that had courted British protection in reliance upon British honour, are with their Inhabitants and Proprietors abandoned to the resentment which we had tempted them to provoke, what wonder, if the opinion becomes general, that alike to England as to France, the fates and fortunes of other Nations are but the Counters, with which the bloody Game of War is played: and that notwithstanding the great and acknowledged difference between the two Governments during Possession, yet the protection of France is more desirable because it is more likely to endure? for what the French take, they keep. Often both in Sicily and Malta have I heard the case of Minorca referred to, where a considerable portion of the most respectable Gentry and Merchants (no provision having been made for their protection on the re-delivery of that Island to Spain) expiated in Dungeons the warmth and forwardness of their predilection for Great Britain.

It has been by some Persons imagined, that Lord Nelson was consider-ably influenced, in his public declaration concerning the value of Malta, by ministerial flattery, and his own sense of the great serviceableness of that opinion to the Persons in Office. This supposition is however wholly false and groundless. His Lordship's opinion was indeed greately shaken after-wards if not changed, but at that time he spoke in strictest correspondence with his existing [440] convictions. He said no more than he had often previously declared to his private Friends: it was the point on which, after some amicable controversy, his Lordship and Sir Alexander Ball had *"agreed to differ."* Though the opinion itself may have lost the greatest part of it's interest, and except for the Historian is, as it were, superannuated; yet the grounds and causes of it, as far as they arose out of Lord Nelson's particular character, and may perhaps tend to re-enliven our recollection of a Hero so deeply and justly beloved, will for ever possess an interest of their own. In an Essay too, which purports to be no more than a series of Sketches and Fragments, the Reader it is hoped, will readily excuse an occasional digression, and a more desultory style of narration than could be tolerated in a Work of regular Biography.

Lord Nelson was an Admiral, every inch of him. He looked at every thing, not merely in its' possible relations to the Naval Service in general, but in its' immediate Bearings on his own Squadron; to his officers, his men, to the particular Ships themselves, his affections were as strong and ardent as those of a Lover. Hence, though his temper was constitutionally irritable and uneven, yet never was a Commander so enthusiastically beloved by men of all ranks, from the Captain of the Fleet to the youngest Ship-boy. Hence too the unexampled Harmony which reigned in his Fleet, year after year, under circumstances that might well have undermined the patience of the best balanced Dispositions, much more of men with the impetuous character of British Sailors. Year after year, the same dull duties of a wearisome Blockade, of doubtful Policy—little if any opportunity of making Prizes; and the few Prizes, which accident might throw in the way, of little or no value—and when at last the occasion presented itself which would have compensated for all, then a disappointment as sudden and unexpected as it was unjust and cruel, and the cup dashed from their lips!—Add to these trials the sense of enterprizes checked by feebleness and timidity elsewhere, not omitting the tiresomeness of the Mediterranean Sea, Sky, and Climate; and the unjarring and chearful Spirit of affectionate Brotherhood, which linked together the Hearts of that whole Squadron, will appear not less wonderful to us than admirable and affecting. When the resolution was taken of commencing [441] hostilities against Spain, before any intelligence was sent to Lord Nelson, another Admiral, with two or three Ships of the line, was sent into the Mediterranean, and stationed before Cadiz, for the express purpose of intercepting the Spanish Prizes. The Admiral dispatched on this lucrative service gave no information to Lord Nelson of his arrival in the same Sea, and five weeks elapsed before his Lordship became acquainted with the circumstance. The Prizes thus taken were immense. A month or two sufficed to enrich the Commander and Officers of this small and highly-favoured Squadron: while to Nelson and his Fleet the sense of having done their duty, and the consciousness of the glorious services which they had performed, were considered, it must be presumed, as an abundant remuneration for all their toils and long suffering! It was indeed an unexampled circumstance, that a small Squadron should be sent to the Station which had been long occupied by a large Fleet, commanded by the Darling of the Navy, and the Glory of the British Empire, to the Station where this Fleet had for years been wearing away in the most barren, repulsive, and spirit-trying service, in which the Navy can be employed! and that this minor Squadron should be sent independent of, and without any communication with the Commander of the former Fleet, for the express and solitary purpose of stepping between it and the Spanish Prizes, and as soon as this short and pleasant service was performed, of bringing home the unshared Booty with all possible caution and dispatch. The *substantial* advantages of naval service were perhaps deemed of too *gross* a nature for Men already rewarded with the grateful affections of their own Countrymen, and the admiration of the whole World! They were to be awarded, therefore, on a principle of compensation to a Commander less rich in Fame, and whose Laurels, though not scanty, were not yet sufficiently luxuriant to hide the *golden* crown, which is the appropriate ornament of Victory in the bloodless war of commercial capture! Of all the wounds which were ever inflicted on Nelson's feelings, (and there were not a few) this was the deepest! this rankled most! "I had thought, (said the gallant Man, in a letter written on the first feelings of the affront) "I fancied—but nay, it must have been a dream, an idle dream—yet, I confess it, I *did* fancy, that I had done my Country service—and thus [442] they use me. It was not enough to have robbed me once before of my West India Harvest—now they have taken away the Spanish—and under what circumstances, and with what pointed aggravations! Yet, if I know my own thoughts, it is not for myself, or on my own account chiefly, that I feel the sting and the disappointment; no! it is for my brave Officers; for my noble-minded Friends and Comrades—such a gallant set of Fellows! such a band of Brothers! My heart swells at the thought of them!"——

This strong attachment of the heroic Admiral to his Fleet, faithfully repaid by an equal attachment on their part to their Admiral, had no little influence in attuning their hearts to each other; and when he died it seemed as if no Man was a Stranger to another: for all were made Acquaintances by the rights of a common anguish. In the Fleet itself, many a private quarrel was forgotten, no more to be remembered; many, who had been alienated, became once more good Friends; yea, many a one was reconciled to his very Enemy and loved, and (as it were) thanked him, for the bitterness of his grief, as if it had been an act of consolation to himself in an intercourse of private sympathy. The tidings arrived at Naples on the day that I returned to that City from Calabria: and never can I forget the sorrow and consternation that lay on every Countenance. Even to this day there are times when I seem to see, as in a vision, separate groupes and individual faces of the Picture. Numbers stopped and shook hands with me, because they had seen the tears on my cheek, and conjectured, that I was an Englishman; and several, as they held my hand, burst, themselves, into tears. And though it may awake a smile, yet it pleased and affected me, as a proof of the goodness of the human heart struggling to exercise its' kindness in spite of prejudices the most obstinate, and eager to carry on its' love and honour into the Life beyond Life, that it was whispered about Naples, that Lord Nelson had become a good Catholic before his Death. The absurdity of the Fiction is a sort of measurement of the fond and affectionate esteem which had ripened the pious wish of some kind

Individual through all the gradations of possibility and probability into a confident assertion believed and affirmed by hundreds. The feelings of Great Britain on this awful event, have been described well and worthily by a living Poet, who [443] has happily blended the passion and wild transitions of lyric song with the swell and solemnity of epic narration.

> ——Thou art fall'n! fall'n, in the lap
> Of Victory. To thy country thou cam'st back
> Thou, Conqueror, to triumphal Albion, cam'st
> A corse! I saw before thy hearse pass on
> The comrades of thy perils and renown.
> The frequent tear upon their dauntless breasts
> Fell. I beheld the pomp thick gather'd round
> The trophy'd car that bore thy grac'd remains
> Thro' arm'd ranks, and a nation gazing on.
> Bright glow'd the sun, and not a cloud distain'd
> Heav'ns arch of gold, but all was gloom beneath.
> A holy and unutterable pang
> Thrill'd on the soul. Awe and mute anguish fell
> On all.—Yet high the public bosom throbb'd
> With triumph. And if one, 'mid that vast pomp
> If but the voice of one had shouted forth
> The name of NELSON: Thou hadst past along,
> Thou in thy hearse to burial past, as oft
> Before the van of battle, proudly rode
> Thy prow, down Britain's line, shout after shout
> Rending the air with triumph, ere thy hand
> Had lanc'd the bolt of victory.
>   SOTHEBY (SAUL, p. 80.)

I introduced this digression with an apology, yet have extended it so much farther than I had designed, that I must once more request my Reader to excuse me. Both for what has preceded and what is to follow, he will, I trust, consider it as some small excuse, that though I should have taken a long circuit in arriving at the particular point in view, the objects, which have tempted me from the straight road, are either more interesting than the point itself from which I have turned aside; or such, as I should have introduced elsewhere in the course of this Sketch, and which are therefore to be blamed rather as a defect in my arrangement than as digressions wholly irrelevant and impertinent.

[444] It was to be expected (I have said) that Lord Nelson would appreciate the Isle of Malta from it's relations to the British Fleet on the Mediterranean Station. It was the fashion of the day to style Egypt the *Key* of India, and Malta the *Key* of Egypt. Nelson saw the hollowness of this metaphor: or if he only *doubted* it's applicability in the former instance he was sure that it was false in the latter. Egypt might or might not be the key of India; but Malta was certainly not the key of Egypt. It was not intended to keep constantly two distinct fleets in that Sea; and the largest naval force at Malta would not supersede the necessity of a Squadron off Toulon. Malta does not lie in the direct course from Toulon to Alexandria: and from the nature of the winds, (taking one time with another) the

comparative length of the Voyage to the latter port will be found far less than a view of the map would suggest, and in truth of little practical importance. If it were the object of the French Fleet to avoid Malta in it's passage to Egypt, the Port-admiral at Vallette would in all probability receive his first intelligence of it's course from Minorca or the Squadron off Toulon, instead of communicating it. In what regards the refitting and provisioning of the Fleet, either on ordinary or extraordinary occasions, Malta was as inconvenient as Minorca was advantageous, not only from it's distance, (which yet was sufficient to render it almost useless in cases of the most pressing necessity, as after a severe action or injuries of tempest) but likewise from the extreme difficulty, if not impracticability, of leaving the Harbour of Vallette with a N. W. wind, which often lasted for weeks together. In all these points his Lordship's Observations were perfectly just: and it must be conceded by all persons acquainted with the situation and circumstances of Malta, that it's importance, as a British Possession, if not exaggerated on the whole, was unduly magnified in several important particulars. Thus Lord Minto, in a Speech delivered at a County Meeting and afterwards published, affirms, that supposing what no one will consider as unlikely to take place, that the Court of Naples should be compelled to act under the influence of France, and that the Barbary Powers were unfriendly to us either in consequence of French Intrigues or from their own caprice and insolence, there would not be a single Port, Harbour, Bay, Creek, or Roadstead, [445] in the whole Mediterranean, from which our men of war could obtain a single Ox or an Hogshead of fresh Water: unless Great Britain retained possession of Malta. The noble Speaker seems not to have been aware, that under the circumstances supposed by him, Odessa too being closed against us by a Russian War, the Island of Malta itself would be no better than a vast almshouse of 75,000 persons, exclusive of the British Soldiery, all of whom must be regularly supplied with Corn and Salt Meat from Great Britain or Ireland. The population of Malta and Goza exceeds 100,000: while the Food of all kinds produced on the two Islands would barely suffice for one fourth of that number. The deficit is procured by the growth and spinning of Cotton, for which Corn could not be substituted from the nature of the Soil, or were it attempted, would produce but a small proportion of the quantity, which the Cotton raised on the same fields and spun* into thread, enables the Maltese to purchase, not to mention that the substitution of Grain for Cotton would leave half of the Inhabitants without employment. As to live stock, it is quite out of the question, if we except the Pigs and Goats,

---

* The Maltese Cotton is naturally of a deep Buff, or dusky Orange colour, and, by the Laws of the Island, must be spun before it can be exported. I have heard it asserted, by persons apparently well informed on the Subject, that the raw material would fetch as high a price as the thread, weight for weight: the thread from it's coarseness being applicable to few purposes. It is manufactured likewise for the use of the natives themselves into a coarse nankin, which never loses it's colour by washing, and is durable beyond any cloathing, I have ever known or heard of. The Cotton Seed is used as a food for the Cattle, that are not immediately wanted for the market: it is very nutritious, but changes the fat of the animal into a kind of suet, congealing quickly, and of an adhesive substance.

which perform the office of Scavengers in the Streets of Vallette and the towns on the other side of the Porto Grande. Against these arguments Sir A. Ball placed the following considerations. It had been long his Conviction, that the Mediterranean Squadron should be supplied by regular Store Ships, the sole business of which should be that of Carriers for the Fleet. This he recommended as by far the most economic plan, in the first instance; secondly, beyond any other it would secure a system and regularity in the arrival of Supplies; and lastly, it would conduce to the discipline of the Navy, and prevent both Ships and Officers from being out of the way on any sudden [446] emergence. If this system were introduced, the Objections to Malta, from its great distance, &c. would have little force. On the other hand, the Objections to Minorca he deemed irremoveable. The same disadvantages which attended the getting out of the harbour of Vallette, applied to Vessels getting into Port Mahon; but while fifteen hundred, or two thousand British Troops might be safely entrusted with the preservation of Malta, the Troops for the defence of Minorca must ever be in proportion to those which the enemy may be supposed likely to send against it. It is so little favoured by Nature or by Art, that the Possessors stood merely on the level with the Invaders. Cæteris paribus, if there 12,000 of the enemy landed, there must be an equal number to repel them; nor could the Garrison, or any part of it be spared for any sudden emergence without risk of losing the Island. Previously to the battle of Marengo, the most earnest representations were made to the Governor and Commander at Minorca, by the British Admiral, who offered to take on himself the whole responsibility of the measure, if he would permit the Troops at Minorca to join our Allies. The Governor felt himself compelled to refuse his assent. Doubtless, he acted wisely, for responsibility is not transferable. The fact is introduced in proof of the defenceless State of Minorca, and its constant liability to attack. If the Austrian Army had stood in the same relation to eight or nine thousand British Soldiers at Malta, a single regiment would have precluded all alarms, as to the Island itself, and the remainder have perhaps changed the destiny of Europe. What might not, almost I would say, what *must* not 8000 Britons have accomplished at the Battle of Marengo, nicely poised as the fortunes of the two Armies are now known to have been. Minorca too is alone useful or desirable during a war, and on the supposition of a fleet off Toulon. The advantages of Malta are permanent and national. As a second Gibraltar, it must tend to secure Gibraltar itself: for if by the loss of that one place we could be excluded from the Mediterranean, it is difficult to say what sacrifices of blood and treasure the Enemy would deem too high a price for it's conquest. Whatever Malta may or may not be respecting Egypt, it's high importance to the independence of Sicily cannot be doubted, or it's advantages, as a central station, for any [447] portion of our disposable force. Neither is the influence which it will enable us to exert on the Barbary Powers, to be wholly neglected. I shall only add, that during the plague at Gibraltar, Lord Nelson himself acknowledged that he began to see the possession of Malta in a different Light.

Sir Alexander Ball looked forward to future contingencies as likely to increase the value of Malta to Great Britain. He foresaw that the whole of Italy would become a French Province, and he knew, that the French Government had been long intriguing on the Coast of Barbary. The Dey of Algiers was believed to have accumulated a treasure of fifteen million sterling, and Buonaparte had actually duped him into a Treaty, by which the French were to be permitted to erect a fort on the very spot where the Ancient Hippo stood, the choice between which and the Hellespont as the site of New Rome, is said to have perplexed the judgement of Constantine. To this he added an additional point of connection with Russia, by means of Odessa, and on the supposition of a War in the Baltic, a still more interesting relation to Turkey, and the Morea, and the Greek Islands.— It has been repeatedly signified to the British Government, that from the Morea and the Countries adjacent, a considerable supply of Ship-timber and naval stores might be obtained, such as would at least greatly lessen the pressure of a Russian War. The agents of France were in full activity in the Morea and the Greek Islands, the possession of which, by that Government, would augment the naval resources of the French to a degree of which few are aware, who have not made the present state of commerce of the Greeks, an object of particular attention. In short, if the possession of Malta were advantageous to England solely as a convenient Watch tower, as a centre of Intelligence, it's importance would be undeniable.

Although these suggestions did not prevent the signing away of Malta at the Peace of Amiens, they doubtless were not without effect, when the Ambition of Buonaparte had given a full and final answer to the grand Question: Can we remain in Peace with France? I have likewise reason to believe, that Sir Alexander Ball, baffled by exposing an insidious proposal of the French Government, during the negociations that preceded the recommencement [448] of the War—that the fortifications of Malta should be entirely dismantled, and the Island left to it's Inhabitants. Without dwelling on the obvious inhumanity and flagitious injustice of exposing the Maltese to certain Pillage and Slavery, from their old and inveterate enemies, the Moors, he shewed that the plan would promote the interests of Buonaparte even more than his actual possession of the Island, which France had no possible interest in desiring, except as the means of keeping it out of the hands of Great Britain. This was indeed an interest, which Buonaparte regarded as vital, as connected closely and by many links both with the commercial and the military prospects of his Empire: and this of itself furnishes a stronger argument in presumption of it's ultimate importance to us, even though Malta should only *negatively* assist us by prevention of evils, than all the facts that have been adduced in presumption of the Contrary.

(*To be concluded in the next Number.*)

COLOPHONS OF *THE FRIEND*
(1809–10, 1812)

COLOPHONS OF *THE FRIEND*
(1809–10, 1812)

	1809–10	1812
No 1	*Penrith: printed and published by J. Brown.*	*Penrith: printed and published by J. Brown.*
No 2	*Penrith: printed and published by J. Brown.*	PENRITH: PRINTED AND PUBLISHED BY J. BROWN; AND SOLD BY MESSRS. LONGMAN AND CO. PATERNOSTER ROW; AND CLEMENT, 201, STRAND, LONDON.
No 3	PENRITH: PRINTED AND PUBLISHED BY J. BROWN.	PENRITH: PRINTED AND PUBLISHED BY J. BROWN; AND SOLD BY MESSRS. LONGMAN AND CO. PATERNOSTER ROW, AND CLEMENT, 201, STRAND, LONDON.
No 4	PENRITH: PRINTED AND PUBLISHED BY J. BROWN.	[Same as No 3]
No 5	PENRITH: PRINTED AND PUBLISHED BY J. BROWN; AND SOLD BY MESSRS. LONGMAN AND CO. PATERNOSTER ROW, LONDON.	[Same as Nos 3, 4]
No 6	[Same as No 5]	[Same as Nos 3–5]
No 7	[Same as Nos 5, 6]	KENDAL: PRINTED BY M. & R. BRANTHWAITE; PUBLISHED AND SOLD BY MR. BROWN, PENRITH; AND MESSRS. LONGMAN AND CO. PATERNOSTER ROW, LONDON.
No 8	PENRITH: PRINTED AND PUBLISHED BY J. BROWN; AND SOLD BY MESSRS. LONGMAN AND CO. PATERNOSTER ROW, LONDON.	PENRITH: PRINTED AND PUBLISHED BY J. BROWN, AND SOLD BY MESSRS. LONGMAN AND CO. PATERNOSTER ROW AND CLEMENT, 201, STRAND LONDON.

	1809–10	1812
No 9	PENRITH: PRINTED AND PUB-LISHED BY J. BROWN; AND SOLD BY MESSRS. LONGMAN AND CO. PATERNOSTER ROW; AND CLEMENT, 201, STRAND, LONDON.	[Same as No 8]
No 10	[Same as No 9]	[Same as Nos 8, 9]
No 11	[Same as Nos 9, 10]	*Penrith; Printed and published, by J. Brown.*
No 12	[Same as Nos 9–11]	[Same as Nos 8–10]
No 13	[Same as Nos 9–12]	PENRITH: PRINTED AND PUB-LISHED BY J. BROWN; AND SOLD BY MESSRS. LONGMAN AND CO. PATERNOSTER ROW; AND CLEMENT, 201, STRAND, LONDON.
No 14	[Same as Nos 9–13]	[Same as No 13]
No 15	[Same as Nos 9–14]	[Same as Nos 13, 14]
No 16	[Same as Nos 9–15]	[Same as Nos 13–15]
No 17	[Same as Nos 9–16]	[Same as Nos 13–16]
No 18	[Same as Nos 9–17]	[Same as Nos 13–17]
No 19	PENRITH: PRINTED AND PUB-LISHED BY J. BROWN; AND SOLD BY MESSRS. LONGMAN AND CO. PATERNOSTER ROW, AND CLEMENT, 201, STRAND, LONDON.	PENRITH: PRINTED AND PUB-LISHED BY J. BROWN; AND SOLD BY MESSRS. LONGMAN AND CO. PATERNOSTER ROW, AND CLEMENT, 201, STRAND, LONDON.
No 20	[Same as No 19]	[Same as No 19]
Supernu-merary	PENRITH: PRINTED AND PUB-LISHED BY J. BROWN.	PENRITH: PRINTED AND PUB-LISHED BY J. BROWN.
No 21	[Same as Supernumerary]	[Same as Supernumerary]
No 22	PENRITH: PRINTED AND PUB-LISHED BY J. BROWN; AND SOLD BY MESSRS. LONGMAN AND CO. PATERNOSTER ROW, AND CLEMENT, 201, STRAND, LONDON.	PENRITH: PRINTED AND PUB-LISHED BY J. BROWN; AND SOLD BY MESSRS. LONGMAN AND CO. PATERNOSTER ROW, AND CLEMENT, 201, STRAND, LONDON.
No 23	[Same as No 22]	[Same as No 22]

	1809–10	1812
No 24	[Same as Nos 22, 23]	[Same as Nos 22, 23]
No 25	[Same as Nos 22–4]	[Same as Nos 22–4]
No 26	[Same as Nos 22–5]	[Same as Nos 22–5]
No 27	[Same as Nos 22–6]	[Same as Nos 22–6]

APPENDIX C

1. THE MANUSCRIPT OF *THE FRIEND*
2. ANNOTATED COPIES

1. THE MANUSCRIPT OF
THE FRIEND

---

2. ANNOTATED COPIES

1. FORSTER MS 112

THE partial ms of *The Friend* (1809–10), bound with letters and memoranda, is now in the V & A: Forster MS 112, folioed 1–16 for letters and memoranda, then refolioed 1–117 for *The Friend*. The ms sheets of *The Friend* vary in size, although from f 12 they are mainly in folio suitable for posting. A number of them have the name of the printer, John Brown, or his name and address, on the address side. The following is a brief description of Forster MS 112 to indicate content, break in continuity, and the handwriting. Where the hand is Sara Hutchinson's, Coleridge almost invariably supplies some, if not all, of the corrections. About the handwriting, perhaps a word of caution is needed. Although the attribution of hands in the ms has been made carefully, sometimes the line between hands is difficult to draw, especially when the new writer seems to continue with the same quill and ink. The unconscious imitation of handwriting within the Coleridge-Wordsworth circle is well known to readers of their mss. The numbers at the beginning of each entry refer to the folios of the ms.

Letters and Memoranda

1–2ᵛ. A letter from R. Thorne to John Brown 27 Mar 1809 concerning pica type sent from London.

3–7ᵛ. Three letters from C to Brown concerning *The Friend*, 4 Apr, 4 Dec 1809, and n.d., pub *CL* III 186–7, 261–3, 190–1 (dated c 9 Apr 1809).

8. A letter from WW to Brown (n.d.), in MW's hand, marked "Y" at the top, containing two new opening sentences for No 20 and an inserted sentence for par 4 of the same number. See *Friend* (1809–10) 305, 306; above, II 260 lines 1–4 ("The remarks . . . illustration."), 261 lines 6–7 ("But . . . Letter."). See also below, f 87.

10. A letter from C to Brown (n.d.), pub *CL* III 220–1 (dated 11 Sept 1809).

11–11ᵛ. Copy for part of the motto for No 9 that had been eaten by rats (from "for better examination" to the end); see above, II 122. Also a note: "This is more than the mutilated passage; but it contains it—& the remainder will point out when to begin & end—". This is followed by a letter from C to Brown (n.d.), pub *CL* III 245–6 (dated c 14 Oct 1809). The ms for the entire motto is also on ff 58–58ᵛ; see below.

12–13ᵛ. A letter from C to J. J. Morgan postmarked Jan 1818, pub *CL* IV 796–9. See above, Introduction, I lxxxiv and n 1.

14. A leaf in C's hand correcting the prospectus as it was printed at the end of No 1; it contains the sentence beginning "In the words 'Dejection of Mind'..." and the final four paragraphs. See *Friend* (1809–10) 15–16; above, II 19, 20. A sentence explaining the reason for including the Prospectus—"Several Subscribers having requested it, the original Prospectus is added with the necessary Advertisement to this first Number"—does not appear in No 1.

15. A list of subscribers in SH's hand, together with a note to Brown by C: "The friend is no longer to be sent to Mʳ Norris, Bookseller, Taunton; but to Dʳ Blake, of Taunton (if his name be not already on the List of Subscribers—) but the two first Numbers, and the postage of two letters are to be charged to Messʳˢ Longman &c on the account of the said Mʳ Norris.—"

16. A list of subscribers "from the 1ˢᵗ No", in SH's hand, most of the names crossed out.

The Friend

1. Motto of No 1, in C's hand. See *Friend* (1809–10) 2; above, II 5. This is actually copy for the Prospectus, for overleaf there is a cancelled passage from it.

2. Copy for the specimen pages (see below, ff 116–117), also part of No 1, in C's hand. See *Friend* (1809–10) 4–5; above II 7 line 13 ("and from the..." to 8 line 15 ("... implied").

2ᵛ. A note from C to Brown (n.d.), pub *CL* III 209 (dated May 1809).

3–11ᵛ. Copy for No 1, with omissions and the paragraphs sometimes in an order different from that of the printed version, in C's hand. See *Friend* (1809–10) 5–13; above, II 8 lines 13 ("Of so mysterious...") to 15 line 20 ("... Power.").

12–13. Copy for the end of No 3 and the opening of No 4, with footnotes, in C's hand. Paper watermarked 1804. See *Friend* (1809–10) 45–52; above, II 47 line 43 ("But how...") to 54 line 1 ("... Welt.").

13ᵛ. A note from C to Brown (n.d.), pub *CL* III 217–18 (dated Late July 1809).

14–14ᵛ. Copy for No 4, continuing from f 13, in C's hand. Paper watermarked 1807. See *Friend* (1809–10) 52–4 and n; above, II 54 line 1 to 55 line 32 and n.

15–15ᵛ. A note from C to Brown (n.d.), pub *CL* III 218 and n (dated Late July 1809). The word "sea" appears at the top of f 15; see below, ff 16–17ᵛ.

16–17ᵛ. Copy for No 4, continuing from f 14ᵛ, in C's hand. See *Friend* (1809–10) 54–60; above, II 55 line 33 ("It argues...") to 59 line 41 ("... sunk into the"). The concluding word of the sentence, "sea", is written at the top of f 15, possibly indicating that ff 16–17 (a double sheet) were enfolded within ff 14–15 (also a double sheet).

18–19^v. Copy for three footnotes, the first for No 4, the second beginning in No 4 and ending in No 5, and the third in No 5, in SH's hand. See *Friend* (1809–10) 58n, 64–6n, 70n; above, II 58n, 62–6n, 68n.

19^v. A note from C to Brown (n.d.), pub *CL* III 218–19 (dated c 24 Aug 1809).

20–23. Copy for the end of No 4 and the first half of No 5, continuing from f 17^v, in SH's hand, except for ff 20–1, most of which is in C's. See *Friend* (1809–10) 60–72; above, II 59 line 41 ("We have reason . . .") to 70 (the quote from *Samson Agonistes*). At the bottom of ff 20^v, 21, in C's hand, is a footnote for No 4. See *Friend* (1809–10) 62n; above, II 60–1n.

24–27. Copy for the end of No 5 and the beginning of No 6, continuing from f 23, in SH's hand. See *Friend* (1809–10) 72–83; above, II 70 line 32 ("This is not . . .") to 82 line 26 (". . . Commentator.").

27. A note from C to Brown, not pub in *CL*, beginning "To Mr Brown You will be so good as to print the Latin Quotation as a Note, with the translation &c which I have sent you in my letter—and to let the *Text* run thus . . .", C continuing with the text as it appears above, II 79 line 10 ("With this Faith . . .") to 82 line 5. The Latin quotation is that from Giordano Bruno (f 26^v), which begins, above, II 79n.

27–27^v. Copy for No 6, one paragraph and the beginning of another, in C's hand, continuing where SH left off, the first few lines being written above the note to Brown. See *Friend* (1809–10) 83–4; above, II 82 line 27 ("It is of . . .") to 83 line 31 (". . . give form").

28–29^v. Copy for No 6, continuing from above, in SH's hand. See *Friend* (1809–10) 84–9; above, II 83 line 31 ("and body . . .") to 88 line 2 (". . . Poets.").

30. At top in C's hand: "Mr Stewart—3 New Street—Bishopgate St London to be discontinued." See below, App E, II 460.

30–30^v. Copy for No 6, the translation of the Bruno passage and the continuation of the footnote, in C's hand. See *Friend* (1809–10) 81–2n; above, II 80–82n.

31–31^v. A letter from C to Brown, dated "Saturday Night", with a note to Brown on the address side in SH's hand, pub *CL* III 219 and n (dated 27 Aug 1809).

32–33. Copy for No 6, half of the introduction to *The Three Graves*, in C's hand, on small leaves of the same size as those in Notebooks 17 and 18 ($4\frac{5}{8} \times 4\frac{1}{2}$ inches). See *Friend* (1809–10) 89–90; above, II 88 line 3 ("As I wish . . .") to line 34 (". . . O Edward!").

33^v–43. Copy for No 6, *The Three Graves*, in Sarah Stoddart's hand, with alterations by C, on small leaves as above. See *Friend* (1809–10) 90–6; above, II 89–96.

44. Copy for No 6, the remainder of the introduction to *The Three Graves*, in C's hand, on a large sheet. See *Friend* (1809–10) 90; above, II 88 line 34 ("indeed . . .") to 89 line 29 (". . . metre.").

45–49. Copy for No 7, in SH's hand. See *Friend* (1809–10) 97–108; above, II 97–105 line 21 (". . . *Contrat Social*,").

48ᵛ–49ᵛ. Footnotes for No 7, at foot of ff 48ᵛ, 49, and at top of 49ᵛ, in C's hand. See *Friend* (1809–10) 107n, 112n; above, ıı 104–5n, 108n.

49ᵛ. A note from C to Brown, not pub in *CL*, beginning: "To Mʳ Brown. Observe, that the Note at p. 12, marked ⊕, is to begin with the following words which are to come immediately before the Latin, Neque, &c . . .", and continuing with copy for the introduction to the Latin in the footnote in *Friend* (1809–10) 112n; above, ıı 108n. The Latin "Neque . . ." is the quotation from Pliny.

50–51ᵛ. Copy for the end of No 7, continuing from f 49, and the first two paragraphs of No 8, in SH's hand, except for a footnote and nine lines on f 50, which are in C's. See *Friend* (1809–10) 108–14; above, ıı 105 line 21 ("and the . . .") to 111 line 2 (". . . Spirits."). The copy includes the remainder of the footnote, above, ıı 108–9n.

52–56ᵛ. Copy for Essay v in No 8, in SH's hand. See *Friend* (1809–10) 114–28; above, ıı 111–21.

57. A letter from C to Brown (n.d.), pub *CL* ııı 223–4 (dated c Sept 1809).

58–63ᵛ. Copy for the entire No 9, in SH's hand, with additions and corrections in C's. See *Friend* (1809–10) 129–44; above, ıı 122–33.

63ᵛ–64. An insertion in No 9, in C's hand. See *Friend* (1809–10) 140–1; above, ıı 130 lines 27–43 ("Reason . . . last hour!").

64. A letter from C to Brown, dated "Friday Night", pub *CL* ııı 224–5 (dated 22 Sept 1809).

65–66. Copy for the letter to R. L. (second half) and the two Wordsworth sonnets in No 11; the first 27 lines of f 65 in SH's hand, the last 21 lines on f 65, all of 65ᵛ, and the first 5 lines of f 66 in C's hand, and the WW sonnets in MW's or SH's hand. See *Friend* (1809–10) 168–71; above, ıı 151 line 32 ("be supposed . . .") to 154.

66ᵛ. A letter from SH to Brown:

Monday Night Octʳ 23

To Mʳ Brown

Mʳ Coleridge will write by the next post—Mʳ C. supposes that the Essay "on the Errors of both parties, or extremes meet," will extend a few pages over one Sheet, and has therefore sent the accompanying Copy to fill up the 11ᵗʰ Number. If however you should have set the 11 Nº with the Essay on the Taxes (which ⟨he⟩ should regret chiefly because in that case two Nᵒˢ will run over) you will take this to fill up the 12 Nº—If the Essay on Taxes will not fill a sheet alone you must write immediately to say how much will be wanting— The Poetry must be printed in the same Type with the Text—and ⟨with⟩ a somewhat larger Space between the lines if the sheet will allow it—

SH's letter may have been sent not only with ff 65–66 to fill the issue, but also ff 67–68ᵛ, which completed No 11. Brown began No 12 with the essay on taxes, as requested.

67. Copy for the first of the "Specimens of Rabbinical Wisdom" in No 11, in SH's hand. See *Friend* (1809–10) 172–3; above, ıı 154–5.

67ᵛ–68ᵛ. Copy for the *Hymn Before Sun-rise* in No 11, in C's hand. See *Friend* (1809–10) 174–6; above, ıı 156–8.

69. Copy for the conclusion of the essay on taxes in No 13, in SH's hand. See *Friend* (1809–10) 191; above, ıı 169 lines 32–41 ("the state of . . . Nonsense!—").

70-70ᵛ. Copy for the introduction to the Wrangham poem, in C's hand, and the poem, in SH's hand, in No 18, followed by the advertisement to subscribers in No 16, in C's hand. See *Friend* (1809-10) 275, 256; above, II 235-6, 221.

71-73ᵛ. Copy for most of "Satyrane's Letters" III in No 18, in SH's hand. See *Friend* (1809-10) 276-85 and nn; above, II 236-44 line 30 (". . . Schiller's 'Robbers' ").

74-74ᵛ. WW's translation of the Chiabrera epitaphs in No 19, in MW's hand. See *Friend* (1809-10) 289-90; above, II 248-9.

75-75ᵛ. A letter from C to Brown 22 Dec, pub *CL* III 264, containing the motto from Chiabrera (and C's translation) to the essay "*Does* Fortune Favour Fools?" in No 19. See *Friend* (1809-10) 291 and n; above, II 249 and n. On the address side of the sheet, in SH's hand, is the two-sentence note to Brown printed as a postscript in *CL* III 264.

76-80ᵛ. Copy for the remainder of No 19, in SH's hand, with additions in C's. This includes the essay "*Does* Fortune Favour Fools?" (with cancelled passages), "Christmas Within Doors", "Christmas Out of Doors" (which ends with the WW poem), and the list of errata. In ms "Christmas Out of Doors" (with the poem) preceded the "Within Doors", and on f 79 C notes: "After the Essay print *first*—Christmas within Doors—from p. 9.—then what follows—and the Poem to conclude." The WW poem was originally entitled *Boys Scating*, which was altered in C's hand to *Growth of Genius . . . Early Youth*. In ms the list of errata is written sideways in the margin of the poem. Before "Christmas Within Doors" C notes: "This to follow immediately after the Essay—then 2.—and last of all the Poem." See *Friend* (1809-10) 291-304; above, II 249-59.

80ᵛ. A letter from C to Brown 24 Dec, pub *CL* III 266-7.

81-86ᵛ. Copy for WW's reply to Mathetes in No 20, in MW's hand, with changes in WW's. See *Friend* (1809-10) 306-18; above, II 261 line 7 ("Protection . . .") to 269 line 33 (". . . M.M."). For cancelled passages within these sheets see directly below.

82. A cancelled passage after "his mind", above, I 397 line 17, II 263 line 28:

Autumn for him has risen, she has mounted her Air; the Clouds have coloured round the radiant Goddess and he has seen the Hours dance hand in hand before himer strewing the path with roses; he has seen the bright Company, and for him they are no longer in the Sky. Granted that the jocund and brief time is past—this gladness, this freshness, and this unsullied purity, and if we will may speak of what ourselves have felt and remember [that the sacred light of Childhood . . .]

A note to Brown reads: "see letter marked X"—i.e. f 88, which see.

84. A cancelled passage before "Range against each other", above, I 402 line 9; II 267 line 5:

In fact, there are no conclusions, relating to points which in any stage of life could admit of a doubt, ⟨there is⟩ nothing, which that can be fairly called matter of speculation or opinion, upon which the mind can so confidently repose as those truths which are the direct opposite of errors once rapturously cherished, and which have been passed through and are rejected for ever.

There is a note to Brown to "see letter marked X"—i.e. to substitute f 88, which see.

85. A cancelled passage after "upon itself", above, I 404 line 28, II 268 line 43:

> The hound may be led forth by the Hunter; be cheared by his voice, animated by his presence; but he must follow perseveringly by his own scent: if, the moment he is at a loss or foiled, the Hunter is unready to step in, and, having seen the course which the game took, lays the Dog close at its heel the chase is deemed dishonorable, and the instinct of the Dog animal will be impaired or destroyed.

85ᵛ–86. A cancelled passage at the end of WW's reply to Mathetes, after "philosophical Poet", above, I 405 line 16, II 269 line 19:

> thinking of morality as implying in its essence voluntary obedience, he transfers, in the rapture of imagination, the law of morality to physical natures, and contemplatesing all modes of existence as subservient to one harmony he concludes his addresses to the Power of Duty in the following words—

> Through no disturbance of my soul,
> Or strong compunction in me wrought,
> I supplicate for thy controul,
> But in the quietness of thought.
> Me this uncharted freedom tires;
> I feel the weight of chance desires:
> My hopes no more must change their aim name,
> I look long for a repose which ever is the same.

> Yet not the less would I throughout
> Still act according to the voice
> Of my own inborn wish; nor doubt
> That my submissiveness was choice.
> Not seeking in the school of pride
> For "precepts over dignified,"
> Denial and restraint I prize
> No farther than they breatheeed a second Will more wise.

> Stern Lawgiver! yet thou dost wear
> The Godhead's most benignant grace;
> Nor know we any thing so fair
> As is the smile upon thy face:
> Flowers laugh before thee on their beds;
> And Fragrance in thy footing treads;
> Thou dost preserve the Stars from wrong;
> And the most ancient Heavens through Thee are fresh and strong.

Cf *Ode to Duty* lines 32–56: *WPW* IV 85–6. Before the above cancellation, on f 85ᵛ, there is a note to Brown: "here use the former old Letter X"—i.e. f 88, which see.

86ᵛ. A note from C to Brown: "I would have the verses printed as the Sonnets &c were in Nọ 11—if the Essay should not be enough for a

Number without it.—" However, WW cancelled three of the stanzas—(see above), and two Chiabrera epitaphs fill the issue (see below).

87. An insertion near the beginning of WW's reply to Mathetes in No 20, in MW's hand, with a note to Brown to continue with the letter marked "Y"—i.e. f 8 of the first foliation of Forster MS 112, or the sentence, "But . . . Letter." See *Friend* (1809–10) 305–6; above, II 260 line 27 ("has been visited . . .") to 261 line 5 (". . . mind."). A continuation of this insertion has been cancelled:

And assuredly little evil is to be apprehended from this quarter in a case like that of my Correspondent, who seems so well aware of the many causes within and without of himself, which are at work to check or turn him ~~from~~ out of that course which he feels was by Nature ~~marked out~~ appointed for him and along which ⟨he knows that⟩ it is his duty to advance—But I must refer to (*To be continued*) a future occasion the rest of the remarks which I wished arising out of my Correspondent's Letter to a future Occasion. MM

88. A note to Brown, headed "X", in MW's hand, to substitute the following passage for "a sentence which he will find towards the latter part of the second Sheet of the Essay marked No 18—which ⟨Essay⟩ begins with the words 'in answer to the letter of Mathetes'—The sentence alluded to begins 'In fact there are no conclusions relating to points which in any stage of life could admit of a doubt' [see above, f 84, a cancelled passage] for which print as follows 'We may safely affirm that, in relation to subjects which could in any stage of life admit of a doubt, to points which can fairly be called matter of speculation or opinion, there is nothing ~~upon~~ whereupon the Mind reposes with a confidence ~~as firm~~ as equal to that with which it rests ~~upon~~ on those conclusions, by which truths have been established the direct opposite of errours once ~~fondly~~ rapturously cherished, ~~and now~~ and which have been passed through ⟨and⟩ are rejected for ever. Range". But this passage, too, was not printed; see above, I 401 line 37 to 402 line 9, II 266 line 43 to 267 line 5, the passage as it was apparently finally corrected. After the substitution above, on f 88, there is a note in the same hand: "The above Essay was sent off in a great hurry & being written in a hand which Mr Brown is not used to it will require particular care to be taken in the printing—one word very ill written, of which the first ~~word~~ letter is almost defaced is '*blank* unsignalized Shield'. [See above, I 401 lines 15–16, II 266 line 23.] Should this Essay not fill up a whole No. add the following", i.e. the two Chiabrera epitaphs.

88–89. WW's translation of the Chiabrera epitaphs in No 19, in MW's hand, with corrections in WW's. See *Friend* (1809–10) 319–20; above, II 269–70. On f 88ᵛ, at the end of the first epitaph, in SH's hand: "if there be room add also the following to the same sheet but not to crowd the number; in which case keep it for a future occasion".

89ᵛ. Copy for the conclusion of WW's reply to Mathetes needed when the earlier verses from the *Ode to Duty* were cancelled, in MW's hand. It is prefaced with: "I must further trouble Mr Brown to search for a passage in the M.S. (which I think will be found towards the end of the first, or beginning of the second sheet) where he will find words to this effect "knowledge in which word is included Virtue" *for which print* "Knowledge efficacious for the production of Virtue"—N.B. the Sentence ends ~~with the~~ or contains the words complacency & repose. I mention this that Mr B. may not mistake the passage—". See above, I 399 lines 38–9, II 265 lines 20–1. The note then concludes: "The ⟨latter part of the⟩ *concluding* sentence of the Essay print thus", followed by the end of the essay. See *Friend* (1809–10) 318; above, II 269 lines 19–24 ("having thought . . . following words:"). Also on f 89ᵛ a note from SH to Brown on the address side of the sheet (a corner has been torn off): "The non arrival of the Friend this [. . . . .] conclude that you have not recᵈ the [. . . . .] it is a fortnight this day since Mʳ Cookson [for]warded them from Kendal—*Monday Dec.* 11ᵗʰ".

90–90ᵛ. Copy for the Irus fable in the supernumerary, in SH's hand, except for the last paragraph, which is in C's. See *Friend* (1809–10) 321–3; above, II 271–2.

91–92ᵛ. Copy for the address to subscribers in the supernumerary, in C's hand, except for the last 30 lines on f 92ᵛ, which are in SH's. See *Friend* (1809–10) 323–8; above, II 272–6 line 38 (". . . that Fact"). Cancelled at the beginning of the address on f 91 is the following: "As the twentieth Number of THE FRIEND, which must be considered its second starting-post, (I speak as a Tradesman—not as an Author, and of the *Publication* rather than of the Work) included in the past week, which each Number is supposed to represent, the departure of the old and the commencement of the New Year". (No 20 was 4 Jan 1810.)

93–93ᵛ. Copy for part of the address to subscribers in the supernumerary, in SH's hand. See *Friend* (1809–10) 331–6; above, II 278 line 35 ("As . . .") to 283 line 7 (". . . philosophical").

94–96ᵛ. Copy for the first half of No 21, in SH's hand. See *Friend* (1809–1810) 337–46; above, II 285–92 line 29 (". . . that the calum-").

97–97ᵛ. Copy for the opening of No 22, in SH's hand. See *Friend* (1809–1810) 353–6; above, II 298 (excluding the prefatory paragraph to subscribers) to 300 line 45 (". . . sight, what").

98–98ᵛ. Further copy for No 22, in C's hand. See *Friend* (1809–10) 359–362; above, II 303 line 13 ("the extension . . .") to 305 line 28 (". . . of the Future."), not including the footnote.

99–99ᵛ. Further copy for No 22, in C's hand. See *Friend* (1809–10) 363–7; above, II 306 line 5 ("and he . . .") to 308 line 38 (". . . existence?").

100–101ᵛ. Copy for the beginning of No 23, in SH's hand. See *Friend* (1809–10) 369–75; above, II 310–14 line 33 (". . . proceed").

102–102ᵛ. Further copy for No 23 (after a gap of several lines), in SH's hand. See *Friend* (1809–10) 375–7; above, II 314 line 42 ("such immense . . .") to 315 line 48 (". . . Love?").

102ᵛ. An insert for No 23, in C's hand. See *Friend* (1809–10) 373; above, II 313 lines 11–15 ("There can . . . *grafted on.*"). Also on f 102ᵛ a note from SH to Brown:

The remainder of the Essay will be sent tomorrow by the Kendal Post to be at Penrith on Friday Evᵍ at all events by Saturdays Coach.

Send to the Revᵈ J. Lambert Trin. Col. Cambridge all the Noˢ of the Friend from the first that you have and those wanting when reprinted and ~~signify~~

write with a pencil upon one of them ~~that~~ "the others will be sent corrected & and amended as soon as reprinted" Mr Coleridge will write to say how you go on with the No^s. to be reprinted and if convenient would be glad if you could come over some Saturday ⟨to spend a day or two here,⟩ and bring your Accounts.

103–103^v. Copy for No 23, continuing from f 102^v, in SH's hand. See *Friend* (1809–10) 377–82; above, ɪɪ 315 line 49 ("I return . . .") to 319 line 41 (". . . boundless void,").

104–104^v. Copy for the life of Ball in No 26, in SH's hand. See *Friend* (1809–10) 419–21 and n; above, ɪɪ 348 line 30 ("as it was above . . .") to 350 line 3 (". . . main hope").

105–105^v. Copy for the life of Ball in No 26, in SH's hand. See *Friend* (1809–10) 423–5; above, ɪɪ 351 line 27 ("the English think . . .") to 353 line 7 (". . . justified.").

106. Copy for "To Correspondents" in No 26, in SH's hand. The bottom of the leaf has been cut off. See *Friend* (1809–10) 430–1; above, ɪɪ 356–7 line 9 (". . . disguise").

106^v. Further copy for "To Correspondents" in No 26, in SH's hand. See *Friend* (1809–10) 431–2; above, ɪɪ 357 line 24 ("the motive . . .") to 358 line 4 (". . . disquisition. I").

107^v. A note from SH to Brown on the address side of the sheet dated 24 Feb [1810]:

Send 2 Copies of the 1st N^o next week with the Books & 1 of the 2nd *without fail*—they need not be stamped ones—

108–112. Copy for the life of Ball in No 27, in SH's hand, except for 28 lines on f 110^v, which are in C's. The first 9 lines of C's are cancelled, and an insert in SH's hand is attached. See *Friend* (1809–10) 433–43; above, ɪɪ 359–66 line 38 (". . . impertinent.").

112. At the end of the above copy, a note from C to Brown (n.d.), pub *CL* ɪɪɪ 285 (dated c 28 Feb 1810).

113–113^v. Continuing copy for the life of Ball in No 27, in C's hand. C began on f 113, continued on 114, and returned to 113^v. He apparently intended to end there, for the leaf finishes: "To be concluded in the next Number." See *Friend* (1809–10) 444–5, 446–7, 448; above, ɪɪ 366 line 39 ("It was . . .") to 368 line 2, 368 lines 36–48 ("Minorca . . . Light."), and 369 last line.

114. Copy for the life of Ball in No 27, in C's hand. See *Friend* (1809–10) 445–6, 445n; above, ɪɪ 368 lines 3–36 ("Against . . . been."), 367n.

115. Copy ending life of Ball in No 27, in C's hand. See *Friend* (1809–10) 447–8; above, ɪɪ 368 line 49 ("Sir Alexander . . .") to 369 line 41 (". . . the Contrary").

116–117. Corrected facing specimen pages (numbered 4, 5) with an insert in C's hand attached to f 116. Cf *Friend* (1809–10) 4–5; and see above, f 2 (second foliation).

2. ANNOTATED COPIES

The Friend (1809–10)

Only one copy is described, and two others are worth noting, though having no definite connection with C.

1. Unidentified copy. Hagen Sale, Parke-Bernet 24 Apr 1945. Parke-Bernet catalogue 5 Dec 1949 describes the copy as "With Coleridge's autograph and two epigrams".

2. BM C 126 k 8. Inscribed "J. D. Coleridge 6 Southwick Crescent 1862". Inscribed in pencil on the front flyleaf: "Given by Coleridge to Mr Slaughter"; but the "Coleridge" is not identified and no direct connection is established.

3. J. D. Campbell's copy. Sotheby Sale 13–14 Jun 1904, lot 87: "With 3 interesting autograph letters, numerous MS. memoranda, and printed extracts inserted". The description probably means that the ms memoranda were inserted and therefore not C's. A copy now in my possession contains printed extracts and may be this copy.

The Friend (1812)

1. Hugh J. Rose's copy—Copy R in the notes to the *CC* text.
Owned by John Thornton, Oxford.
Presentation inscription to "Hugh Rose Trin. coll. from the Author." Numerous additions and corrections in C's hand. For the circumstances of presentation to Rose in Sept 1816 see *CL* IV 669–72, 683–5.
Full description and transcript of the notes by Jonathan Wordsworth "Some Unpublished Coleridge Marginalia" *TLS* No 2885 (14 Jun 1957) 369. See below, Index, for references to notes quoted in *CC*.

2. Sir John Sinclair's copy.
Not located. Sotheby Misc Sale 2 Mar 1891. *C Bibl* (Haney 1903) 49. Samuel Sale, Sotheby 1 Jul 1907, 35 (bought by Dobell). Dobell Catalogue 1909. No further trace.
"Inserted . . . is the original . . . prospectus . . . containing several corrections in the autograph of Coleridge, and addressed in his handwriting to Sir John Sinclair, with postmark. 'It is not unknown to you, that I have employed almost the whole of my life in acquiring, or endeavouring to acquire, useful knowledge, by study, reflection, observation, and by cultivating the society of my superiors in intellect, both at home and in foreign countries.' " *Samuel Sale Catalogue.*
This appears to be not a marked copy, but a copy into which the marked Prospectus of the 1809–10 edition has been inserted. The quotation above is the beginning of the Prospectus, which is also printed at the end of No 1 in both 1809–10 and 1812 editions.

3. Southey's copy.
Owned by the Rev N. F. D. Coleridge.
Signed "Robert Southey" in his hand and later "Sara Coleridge 10 Chester Place Regent's Park" in her hand. It bears a label: "Bound by

J. Brown, Penrith". There are some pencilled notes in a hand that might be SC's, but none by C.

The Friend (1818)

1. Thomas Allsop's copy—Copy A in the notes to the *CC* text.
Harvard *EC8 C6795 810 fc (A) (formerly 19476.336.11*). Hodgson Sale, 28 Jan 1925. *C Bibl* (Haney 1934) 125.

Inscribed by C: "To my honored Friend T. Allsop in grateful and affectionate remembrance and in cheerful confident hope, these Volumes, the introduction to my philosophical labors. S. T. Coleridge 1 Jan.ʸ 1820. Highgate." For C's covering letter of presentation 20 Mar 1820, see Allsop I 24–7, where C writes of his "MS corrections, and additions", referring particularly to that on III 263, which Allsop gives I 28–31.

C has written corrections and additions to all three volumes. There are besides a number of objections and comments written in what appears to be Allsop's hand. A number of C's notes have been published by Cecil C. Seronsy "Marginalia by Coleridge in Three Copies of His Published Works" *Studies in Philology* LI (1954) 473–7 ("most of the textual revisions are not here transcribed"). See below, Index, for references to the changes and additions (retranscribed from the Harvard copy) given in the notes to the *CC* text.

2. DC's copy—Copy D in the notes to the *CC* text.
PML 49356–8 W 18C.

DC's bookplate, and many corrections and additions in C's hand in all three volumes. Vol III contains a cancelled leaf (pp 191–2). Extra leaves are bound at the beginning and end of each volume, containing notes in C's and other hands (not referring to *The Friend*), and some sheets of irregular size have been inserted in vols II and III, watermarked 1821 and 1824.

This is probably the "interleaved" copy mentioned by HNC in the Preface to *The Friend* (1837) as bequeathed to DC's wife, from which he took additions and corrections. (Cf notes from Copy D with those corrections made by HNC, some of which correspondences are given in the *CC* notes.) It may also be the copy sold to Currer for £11 at the W. H. Forman Sale, Sotheby 3–8 Jul 1899. *C Bibl* (Haney 1903) 50: "Coleridge's own copy, with numerous valuable additions and corrections on flyleaves and margins". See below, Index, for references to the changes and additions from Copy D given in the notes to the *CC* text.

3. Another DC copy.
Owned by the Rev A. D. Coleridge.

DC's bookplate, many notes in DC's and EHC's hands, and (on III 66–7) a letter from C to DC, pub *CL* IV 885–6.

4. Ralph Waldo Emerson's copy.
Harvard *AC85 Em345 Zy818c.

No notes by C. Emerson's autograph in all three volumes, a few passages marked and noted on the back boards, two notes about the pages in vol III that C considered so important, and (on I 56) a marginal note: "Borrowed from Lessing". See above, I 39 and n 1.

5. Joseph Hughes's copy—Copy H in the notes to the *CC* text.
Manchester College Library, Oxford.

Inscribed by C on front flyleaf of vol I: "The Reverend M.ʳ Hughes from the Author: in testimony of Esteem and Regard, and in the humble hope that the Bread cast on the fluctuating Waters of the Author's mind by M.ʳ Hughes in early manhood and years long gone by, will be here found again, neither innutritious nor unmultiplied. Nov.ʳ 1819 Highgate." The inscription and two notes in C's hand; other notes of C's authorship in another hand.

C had met Joseph Hughes at Cottle's house in Bristol, before Hughes left for London in 1796, where he became secretary of the British and Foreign Bible Society. See John Leifchild *Memoir of the Late Rev. Joseph Hughes* (1835), which also prints C's inscription p 465n. Copy H was described, with transcript of a note by C on III 263 (not in his hand in this copy), by F. H. Heinemann *N&Q* CLXXVIII (1940) 455–6. For a letter from C to Hughes on the presentation of several of his works in Nov 1819, see *CL* IV 965–6. *The Friend* was probably one of these works, for the inscription, like the letter, is dated Nov 1819. Also, although *CL* IV 965n does not positively identify as Joseph Hughes the "Revd Mr Hughes" to whom the letter is addressed, see a letter from C to Hughes 24 Nov 1819 in which he asks Hughes to draw his attention to "any passages in my 'Friend' . . . which shall have struck you . . . as *objectionable*. . . . My philosophy (as metaphysics) is built on the distinction between the Reason and the Understanding. He who, after fairly attending to my exposition of this point in the 'Friend' (vol. I p. 254–277,) and in the Appendix to the *first* Lay-Sermon, can still find no meaning in this distinction . . . for him the perusal of my *philosophical* writings, at least, will be a mere waste of time". This letter, dated 24 Nov 1819, which does not appear in *CL* IV, was printed in Leifchild pp 464–6. For the full text of the letter see below, App F, II 503–4.

6. Hyman Hurwitz's copy.
Harvard *EC8 C6795 810fc (B). *C Bibl* (Haney 1903) 51.

Inscribed by C: "To Hyman Hurwitz from S. T. Coleridge, with that regard and respect, which Men who reverence themselves pay to those whom they know worthy to be revered. Highgate, 27 April 1821."

The corrections in vols I and III and the addition in III 90 (from the errata) correspond to those in other corrected copies but are not in C's hand. There are many light pencil marks in the margins.

7. John Kenyon's copy.
Owned by W. H. P. Coleridge.

This is a ms transcript of the original, which is neither located nor described. A note in the book shows that it was given by John Kenyon (author of *A Rhymed Plea for Tolerance*) to a Mr Booth, and by Booth to Lord Coleridge. (C calls Kenyon "a particular friend of our friend, Mr Thomas Poole": to RS [31 Jan 1819]: *CL* IV 916). The transcription, in a hand similar to the transcripts in the Hurwitz copy, has been done with care; and since the initials S.T.C. and his signature have been attached to the notes, this copy was until about 1956 described as containing notes in C's hand. The notes conform, with minor variations, to those in Copy L. Inscribed in an unknown hand: "John Kenyon. London. 1820. from the Author—with his corrections and additions written by himself."

8. John Gibson Lockhart's copy—Copy L in the notes to the *CC* text. NYPL Berg 340073–75B (copy 1).

Inscribed by C on the half-title: "To the Author of 'Peter's Letters to his Kinsfolks', = Dʳ Morris, εἰ μὲν ἄν ⟨ουτος⟩ ἔνας, εἰ δὲ καὶ ἄν δύας ἤ [whether he be one or a pair], from the obliged Friend, S. T. Coleridge. Id quidem vera laus est, a laudate viro laudari [It is true praise to be praised by one who has himself been praised]. 13 Novʳ 1819. Highgate".

There are many corrections, additions, and notes. This copy, like Copies D and A, is one of the most heavily annotated. See below, Index, for references to the changes and additions given in the notes to the *CC* text. The note on Hobbes, on I 46 (see above, I 31 n 2), was printed in *C 17th C* 67.

For the letter C sent to the author of *Peter's Letters to His Kinsfolk* (1819), whose identity he did not then know, when sending him "all my works, of which I possess a copy", see *CL* IV 966–70.

9. Samuel Mence's copy—Copy M in the notes to the *CC* text. Bristol Central Library B 7051–3.

Inscribed on the half-title: "Revᵈ Samuel Mence in testimony of sincere respect from the Author." A typewritten letter of 17 Oct 1902 from Richard Mence, presenting the volumes to the Bristol Library, inserted, testifies that this copy "was given to my Father [who] also was the incumbent of Highgate, when Coleridge lived with Mr. and Mrs. Gillman. . . . I remember Coleridge well, as a little boy. My father performed the ceremony when he was buried, and helped to draw up the inscription on the tablet to his memory. . .".

There are numerous additions and corrections in an unidentified hand, probably copied from Copy D, to which they conform.

This copy was described by James Ross in *TLS* No 2401 (7 Feb 1948) 79.

10. Thomas Fanshaw Middleton's copy. Not located or described.

This copy is known only from the ms transcript recorded in *Blackwell Catalogue 570*, lot 751: "The notes in ink at end of Vol. III were transcribed from S.T.C.'s own MS. notes in a copy presented by him to Bp. Middleton, his old school friend." Middleton (1769–1822), C's friend at Christ's Hospital and at Jesus College, Cambridge, New Testament scholar, and Bishop of Calcutta (1814).

11. Hugh J. Rose's copy. Not located or described.

A letter from C to Rose 19 Nov 1818, sending corrections, seems to imply that C had sent him a copy. See *CL* IV 881–2.

12. Francis Wrangham's copy. Not located or described.

On 5 Jun 1817, more than a year before publication, C promised to reserve for Wrangham one of "the few Copies, which I can claim of . . . the Rifacciamento of the Friend . . . in 3 volumes". *CL* IV 737. (Wrangham had been a subscriber and contributor to the 1809–10 *Friend*.) On 28 Sept 1819 C sent "the first set" of his works: "They will have an accidental value in your eyes, from the numerous M.S.S. corrections which I have made in your set and which from the time required for transcribing will remain peculiar to that set . . .". *CL* IV 949.

13. Unidentified copy.
Owned 1952 by Raphael King, London.
In Feb 1952 Raphael King offered Kathleen Coburn vol III of C's annotated copy of *The Friend* from Richard Heber's collection. (Heber's library was dispersed in a series of sales in c 1833 by Sotheby; the catalogue does not show an annotated *Friend*.) At a Sotheby sale 17 Dec 1945 King bought for £26 a copy of *The Friend* (1818) described as "Inscribed presentation copy"; this would appear to be the copy offered for sale in 1952.

APPENDIX D
COLLATION TABLES

COLLATION TABLES

TABLE 1

Collation of pages of 1818 *Friend* with those of the editions of 1809–10, 1812, 1837 (HNC), and *CC*

Essay	1818	1809–10	1812	1837	*CC*
[Intro]	I			I	I
I	1–12	8–11, 6–8	9–11, 8, 6–8	1–9	7–13
II	13–20	327–9	327–9	10–15	14–17
III	21–33	165–9	165–9	16–25	18–24
IV	34–48	27–31	24–9	26–37	25–33
V	49–64	33–4, 26–7, 34–40	23–4, 33–9	38–50	34–43
VI	65–77	40–5	39–44	51–60	44–50
VII	78–82			III 330–3	51–3
	82–9	45–9	45–8	61–9	53–7
VIII	90–102	49–54	48–53	70–9	58–66
IX	103–7	54–6	53–5	80–3	67–9
X	108–21	56–60	55–9	84–94	70–6
XI	122–32	60–7	59–65	95–102	77–82
XII	133–48	64–6n	63–6n	103–15	83–90
XIII	149–65	67–9	66–8	116–28	91–9
XIV	166–78	69–75	68–74	129–39	100–6
XV	179–89	75–8, 80, 81–2	74–81	140–8	107–13
XVI	190–212	81n, 82–9	81–8	149–66	114–26
1 LP					
I	215–26	114–19	114–19	169–77	129–34
II	227–43	119–23, 125–8	119–26	178–91	135–43
III	244–50	123–5	126–8	192–6	144–7
IV	251–62			197–205	148–53
V	263–77	350–2	350–2	206–17	154–61
§I					
I	281–8	98–100	98–100	221–6	165–8
II	289–302	100–6	100–6	227–37	169–75
III	303–21	106–14	106–14	238–51	176–85
IV	322–56	129–44	129–44	252–78	186–202

Essay	1818	1809–10	1812	1837	CC
	II			II	I
v [I]	1–36	145–60	145–60	1–27	205–22
vi [II]	37–46	161–5	161–5	28–35	223–7
vii [III]	47–80	177–91	177–91	36–61	228–44
viii [IV]	81–91	225–30	225–30	62–9	245–50
ix [v]	92–114	230–40	230–40	70–87	251–62
x [vi]	115–42	355–67	355–67	88–109	263–75
xi [vii]	143–54	369–73	369–73	110–19	276–81
xii [viii]	155–67			120–9	282–8
xiii [ix]	168–84	385–91	385–91	130–42	289–97
xiv [x]	185–215	391–400, 430–2	391–400, 430–2	143–66	298–312
xv [xi]	216–40	373–84	373–84	167–85	313–25
xvi [xii]	241–64			186–204	326–38
2 LP					
I	267–300	193–208	193–208	207–32	341–55
II	301–14	337–9	337–9	233–44	356–62
III	315–28	321–3, 300–4	321–3, 300–4	245–55	363–9
IV	329–36	172–4, 367–8	172–4, 367–8	256–61	370–3
	III			III	I
Intro	1–64	257–72, 305–18	257–72, 305–18	1–50	377–405
§ II					
I	67–92			53–73	409–23
II	93–11			74–89	424–35
III	112–32			90–107	436–47
IV	133–51			108–22	448–57
V	152–63			123–31	458–63
vi [v]	163–75			132–42	464–71
vii [vi]	176–92			143–56	472–81
viii [vii]	193–203			157–65	482–7
ix [viii]	204–16			166–75	488–95
x [ix]	217–36			176–92	496–506
xi [ix]	237–65			193–216	507–24
3 LP					
I	269–77	291–5	291–5	219–25	527–31
II	278–88	295–300	295–300	226–34	532–8
III [II]	289–304	340–7	340–7	235–46	539–46
IV	305–11	347–9	347–9	247–52	547–50
V	312–42	417–30	417–30	253–76	551–64
VI	343–75	433–48	433–48	277–301	565–80

TABLE 2
Collation of pages of 1809–10 *Friend* with those of 1812, 1818, and *CC* Vols I and II (App A)

1809–10	1812	1818	CC	CC
1 (Jun 1809)			Vol I	Vol II
2	2	⟩1, 6–7n	7, 9n	5
2–3	2–3			5–7
	3 [add.]			7n
4–6	4–6			7–9
6–8	6–8	⟩9–14	11–14	9–10
	8 [add.]	⟩8–9	10–11	10n
8	8			10–11
8–11	8–11	⟩2–6, 7–8	7–9, 10	11–13
	11 [add.]	I 6–7	9–10	12n
11–13	11–14			13–15
13	14	⟩13	14	15
14–16	14–16			16–19
16	[deletion]			19–20
2 (8 Jun 1809)				
17–26	17–23			21–31
17	[deletion]			2n
18–20n	29–32			22–6n
	21 [add.]			28n
26–7	22–4	⟩49–52	35–6	31–2
27–31	24–9	⟩36–48	26–33	32–6
32	[deletion]			36–7
3 (10 Aug 1809)				
33	[deletion]			38
33–4	33	I 49	34–5	38
34–5	33–5	I 53–6	37–9	38–40
35–6	35–6			40
36–43	36–42	I 57–73	39–48	40–6
43–4	42–3			46
44–5	43–5	I 74–7	48–50	46–7
45–8	45–8	I 82–8	53–7	47–50
4 (7 Sept 1809)				
49–60	48–59	I 88–117	57–74	51–9
60–4	59–63	I 122–31	77–82	59–63
64n	63n	I 135–38, 144	84–6, 88	62–3n

1809-10	1812	1818	*CC*	*CC*
5 (14 Sept 1809)			Vol I	Vol II
65–7	64–5	I 131–2	82	64–6
65–6n	64–6n	I 138–44	86–8	64–6n
67–9	66–8	I 150–5	91–4	66–8
69–78	68–77	I 166–87	100–111	68–75
	74n [add.]	I 177–8n	106n	72n
	78n [add.]			79n
78–80	78–80n			75–8
80	77–8	I 187	112	78
6 (21 Sept 1809)				
81	78	I 187–8	112	79
81–2	81	I 188	112	79–81
	81n	I 190–1	114–15	81n
81–2n	88–9n	I 193–4, 194–7n	115–18	79–82n
82–4	81–3	I 195–202	117–20	82–3
84n	83	I 202	120–1	83n
84–6	83–5	I 202–7	121–3	84–5
86–7	85–6	I 207–9	123–4	85–6
87–9	86–8	I 209–12	124–6	86–7
89	[deletion]			87–8
89–96	89–96			88–96
7 (28 Sept 1809)				
97–112	97–112	I 281–317, 316–18n	165–82, 182–4n	97–109
8 (5 Oct 1809)				
113–14	113–14	I 318–21	183–5	110–11
114–23	114–23	I 215–36	129–40	111–17
123–5	126–7	I 245–8	144–6	117–19
124–5n	127–8	I 248–50	146–7	118n
125–8	123–6	I 236–43	140–3	119–21
9 (12 Oct 1809)				
129–44	129–44	I 322–56	186–202	122–33
10 (19 Oct 1809)				
145–60	145–60	II 1–36	205–22	134–45

1809–10	1812	1818	*CC*	*CC*
11 (26 Oct 1809)			Vol I	Vol II
161–5	161–5	II 37–46	223–7	146–9
165–8	165–8	I 22–7	19–21	149–51
168–9	168–9	I 27–30	21–3	151–2
169–71	169–71			152–4
172–4	172–4	II 329–34	370–3	154–6
174–6	174–6			156–8
12 (9 Nov 1809)				
177–91	177–91	II 47–80	228–44	159–69
192				170–1
	192			170n
13 (16 Nov 1809)				
193–208	193–208	II 267–300	341–55	172–82
208	208			183
14 (23 Nov 1809)				
209–24	209–24			184–96
15 (30 Nov 1809)				
225–8	225–8	II 81–9	245–9	197–9
228–9	228–9	89	249	199
229	229			199–200
229–40	229–40	89–114	249–62	199–208
16 (7 Dec 1809)				
241–56	241–56			209–21
17 (14 Dec 1809)				
257–72	257–72	III 2–35	377–92	222–32
18 (21 Dec 1809)				
273–88	273–88			233–47
19 (28 Dec 1809)				
289–91	289–91			248–9
291–9	291–9	III 269–87	527–38	249–55
299–300	299–300	III 287–8	538	255–6
300–4	300–4	II 320–8	365–9	256–9
20 (4 Jan 1810)				
305–18	305–18	III 35–64	392–405	260–69
319–20	319–20			269–70

1809–10	1812	1818	*CC*	*CC*
(11 Jan 1810)			Vol I	Vol II
321–3	321–3	II 315–19	363-5	271–2
323–27	323-27			273–6
327–9	327–9	I 14-20	14-17	276-7
330–6	330-6			277–84
21 (25 Jan 1810)				
337–9	337–9	II 301–7	356–9	285–7
339–40	339-40			287
340–9	340-9	III 289–311	539–50	287–94
349–50	349-50			294
350–2	350-2	I 271–7	158–61	294–7
22 (31 Jan 1810)				
353–5	353-5			298–9
355	355	II 115–16	263	299–300
355	355			300
355–67	355–67	II 116–42	263–75	300–8
367–8	367–8	II 334-6	373	308–9
368	368			309
23 (8 Feb 1810)				
369–73	369–73	II 144-54	276–81	310–13
373–84	373-84	II 217–40	313-25	313–20
384	384			320
24 (15 Feb 1810)				
385–400	385–400	II 169-208	289–308	321–33
25 (22 Feb 1810)				
401–16	401–16			334–46
26 (1 Mar 1810)				
417–30	417–30	III 312–42	551–64	347–56
430-2	430-2	II 210-5	310-12	356–8
27 (15 March 1810)				
433-43	433-43	III 343-65	565–76	359–66
443	443			366
444-8	444-8	III 365-74	576-80	366-9
448	448			369

TABLE 3

Collation of folios of Forster MS 112 with pages of the 1809–10 *Friend* and reprint in *CC*; an asterisk before the number indicates complete ms for the issue

MS	1809–10	CC
	1 (Jun 1809)	Vol II
f 1	2	5
f 2	4–5	7–8
f 3	5	8–9
ff 4–4ᵛ	5–6, 6–7	8, 9
f 5	6	9
f 6	7–8	10–11
f 7	8–9	11
ff 8–8ᵛ	9–10	11–12
f 9	10–11	12–13
ff 10–10ᵛ	11–12	13–14
ff 11–11ᵛ	12–13	14–15
	3 (10 Aug 1809)	
ff 12–12ᵛ	45–8	47–50
	*4 (7 Sept 1809)	
ff 12ᵛ–13	49–52	51–4
ff 14–14ᵛ	52–4 & n	54–5 & n
f 15	60 [one word]	59
ff 16–17ᵛ	54–60	55–9
ff 18–19ᵛ	58n, 64–6n, 70n	58n, 62–6n, 68n
ff 20–21	60–4, 62n	59–63, 60–61n
	*5 (14 Sept 1809)	
ff 21–23	65–72	64–70
[See above, ff 18–19ᵛ]		
ff 24–26ᵛ	72–80	70–8
	*6 (21 Sept 1809)	
ff 26ᵛ–29ᵛ	81–9, 81n, 84n	79–88, 79–80n, 83n
ff 30–30ᵛ	81–2n	80–2n
ff 32–33	89–90	88
ff 33ᵛ–43	90–6	89–96
f 44	90	88–9

MS	1809–10	CC
	*7 (28 Sept 1809)	Vol II
ff 45–48^v	97–107, 106n	97–104, 103n
ff 48^v–49^v	107n, 112n	104–5n, 108n
f 49	107–8	105
ff 50–51	108–12	105–8
ff 51–51^v	112n	108–9n
	*8 (5 Oct 1809)	
f 51^v	113–14	110–11
ff 52–56^v	114–28	111–21
	*9 (12 Oct 1809)	
ff 58–58^v	129	122
ff 59–63^v	130–44	123–33
ff 63^v–64	140–1	130
	11 (26 Oct 1809)	
ff 65–66	168–71	151–4
f 67	172–3	154–6
ff 67^v–68^v	174–6, 175n	156–8, 157n
	12 (9 Nov 1809)	
f 69	191	169
	16 (7 Dec 1809)	
f 70^v	256	221
	18 (21 Dec 1809)	
ff 70–70^v	275	235–6
[See also above, f 70^v]		
ff 71–73^v	276–85, 280, 281–2n	236–44, 240n, 241–2n
	*19 (28 Dec 1809)	
ff 74–74^v	289–90	248–9
f 75	291, 291n	249, 249n
ff 76–78^v	291–8, 297n	249–55, 254n
f 79–80^v	298–304	255–9
	20 (4 Jan 1810)	
ff 81–86^v	306–18	260–9
f 87	305–6	260–1
ff 88–89	319–20	269–70
f 89^v	318	269

MS	1809–10	*CC*
	(11 Jan 1810)	Vol II
ff 90–90^v	321–3	271–2
ff 91–92^v	323–8, 323n, 325n	272–6, 272n, 274n
ff 93–93^v	331–6	278–83
	21 (25 Jan 1810)	
ff 94–96^v	337–46	285–92
	22 (31 Jan 1810)	
ff 97–97^v	353–56, 354n	298–300, 299n
ff 98–98^v	359–62	303–5
ff 99–99^v	363–7	306–8
	23 (8 Feb 1810)	
ff 100–101^v	369–75	310–14
ff 102–102^v	375–7, 373	314–15, 313
ff 103–103^v	377–82	315–19
	26 (1 Mar 1810)	
ff 104–104^v	419–21, 419n	348–50, 348–9n
ff 105–105^v	423–5	351–3
f 106	430–1	356–7
f 106^v	431–2	357–8
	*27 (15 Mar 1810)	
ff 108–112	433–43	359–66
f 113	444–5	366–8
f 113^v	446–7	368
f 114	445–6, 445n	368, 367n
f 115	447–8	368–9

APPENDIX E
SUBSCRIBERS
TO THE PERIODICAL *FRIEND*

SUBSCRIBERS TO
THE PERIODICAL *FRIEND*

As friends sent Coleridge their own and other names as subscribers to *The Friend*, Sara Hutchinson copied them into a notebook (N 62, now in VCL).[1] There are 398 names in the notebook, accounting for 446 copies (De Quincey took five, the bookseller Ford eight, and so on). Many of the letters of subscription are in DCL; lists of subscribers in these letters reappear in exact order and time-sequence in Sara's notebook list. The first name in the notebook is the Bishop of Llandaff, who wrote to Coleridge 4 December 1808 to become a subscriber.[2] The last names in the notebook are those of Gibson, a printer at Malton, who subscribed 27 June 1809,[3] and De Quincey's mother and two of her friends, who subscribed before 16 August 1809.[4]

John Brown, the printer, who mailed the copies to subscribers, kept an account-book of names and numbers of copies. As new subscribers came in, Sara or Coleridge sent him the names, which he "inserted in the Catalogue".[5] To answer Stuart's question of how much paper was on hand, and how many copies were printed, Coleridge wrote to Brown c 14 September 1809, asking for a list of all booksellers as well.[6] Brown replied c 15 September: "The number of *copies* on the list is 632"; he also listed booksellers and the number of copies each took (eight booksellers accounted for eighty-five copies). "We print", he continued, "a dozen copies more than the number on the list".[7] Such was the state of things shortly after *Friend* No 5 had appeared.

Two years after *The Friend* ceased publication, Brown went into bankruptcy, and, Coleridge wrote, the "Account Book, which contained [subscribers'] names & by which alone I could know who had & who had not payed, suddenly disappeared under circumstances not mysterious only because they were of the most suspicious kind".[8] Some persons were saying that *The Friend* had ruined Brown, but Anthony Harrison, the Penrith

---

[1] SH to Mary Monkhouse 27 Mar [1809]: *SHL* 17. See also below, II 481, Stuart's letter to C 26 Jan 1809 advising him to keep "a Small Alphabetical memorandum book" in which to enter "every Customers name, when he begins, when & what he pays, when he leaves off &c".

[2] DCL Folder C.

[3] DCL Folder E.

[4] De Q to DW 16 Aug [1809]: *De Q to W* 245.

[5] C to Brown c 24 Aug 1809: *CL* III 218.

[6] C to Brown c 14 Sept 1809: *CL* III 223–4.

[7] DCL Folder E.

[8] C to Richard Sharp 24 Apr [1812]: *CL* III 388–9.

attorney, agreed with Sara Hutchinson that it could not possibly have done Brown harm and was "sure that B. rec^d as many subscriptions as paid him".[1] The names of all the subscribers, which presumably had been in the account-book, are not known. Still, from the notebook as well as from other sources a fairly complete list of subscribers can be pieced together. Forster MS 112 contains a "List of names on the inky Paper" Coleridge enclosed in a letter to Brown c 24 August 1809.[2] A few of these names are not in the notebook. Names of many subscribers appear in letters to Coleridge and Wordsworth now in DCL;[3] a number of these are also not in the notebook. Coleridge mentions several subscribers in his correspondence.[4] Sara Hutchinson copied twenty-six names of subscribers living in or near Bridgwater for a letter Coleridge sent to Poole 12 January 1810: "The names on the other side were written out in the hope of receiving a letter from you, and that you might collect the Sum"; this, with the money the Bristol subscribers owed, "would have more than repaid you the advance [for paper]".[5]

Since there is no complete list, it is useless to conjecture on the missing. A coolness developed between Humphry Davy and Coleridge over Coleridge's dismissal of Savage as printer of *The Friend*,[6] yet there is no certainty that he was not a subscriber. It seems unlikely that William Sotheby did not subscribe (his name is on no extant list), nor the Quaker Pim Nevins, a friend in Leeds.[7] Coleridge sent 30 Prospectuses to Southey's brother Henry and another bundle to William Taylor of Norwich,[8] yet neither person is on a subscriber list. The names of known subscribers are, however, sufficiently revealing. In identifying them, emphasis has been placed on connexions with the Coleridge circle—the friends of *The Friend*, a constant theme of the subscribers' letters and of the periodical itself. Clarkson and Montagu procured the greatest number of subscribers, so it is not surprising that many were Quakers and members of the bar. Friends and acquaintances from childhood days in Devonshire, from Christ's Hospital, and from Cambridge appear among the names. Friends from Bristol and *The Watchman* days also appear—all five of Jedediah Strutt's children, Cottle and Biggs, his early publishers, many Lloyds and their ladies, to mention a few. Interesting connexions among the subscribers can also be traced: for example, Mrs Palmer of Holme Park, Sir George Armytage of Kirklees, and W. Sturges Bourne of the Treasury. The first was a daughter of Oldfield Bowles, Sir George Beaumont's friend and

[1] SH to John Monkhouse 28 [–29] Mar [1812]: *SHL* 46.

[2] *CL* III 218.

[3] DCL Folders B, C, D, and E.

[4] *CL* III passim.

[5] *CL* III 272 (the list is not given). The letter is in BM Add MS 35343, the list on f 369.

[6] See C's letter to Stuart [28 Mar 1809]: *CL* III 185–6.

[7] See C's long letter to him on *The Friend* c 31 Dec 1808: *CL* III 157–9.

[8] C to RS c 4 Dec 1808: *CL* III, 130. William Taylor of Norwich was, however, definitely not a subscriber; he wrote to RS 28 Mar 1810 that his bookseller had not sent him *The Friend* as he had desired, which, he reported, "some one compared . . . in [his] hearing to a muddy waterfall,—sonorous but not transparent": J. W. Robberds *A Memoir of the Life and Writings of the Late William Taylor of Norwich* (2 vols 1843) II 288–9.

fellow-Etonian; the other two were married to her sisters. Seven members of the Friday Club of Edinburgh, a literary club modelled on Dr Johnson's at the Turk's Head—Alison, Elmesley, Jeffrey, Walter Scott, etc—were subscribers.[1] The subscriber list gives telling evidence of Coleridge's assertion that his readers did him a disservice "by giving out every where that [*The Friend*] was an *unreadable* work".[2] An adverse criticism bounced like a ball from one hand to another—from, for example, Robert Lloyd in Birmingham to Lamb in London, on to Rickman, and then to Poole in Nether Stowey. Clarkson spoke to nine subscribers in Bury,[3] and Joseph Strutt to fourteen in Derby,[4] both men eager for Coleridge to succeed and yet helping to undermine his position.

Emphasis on the relationships of the subscribers with each other and with Coleridge should not, however, obscure *who* they were. Coleridge was writing "for those, who by Rank, or Fortune, or official Situation, or Talents and Habits of Reflection, are to *influence* the Multitude".[5] Both Commons and Lords were well represented in the subscriber list, and the Church, from bishop to deacon. There were many men of the bar, several physicians, and a number of military men. There were newspaper proprietors, wealthy landowners and merchants, and men of letters and learning.

The list that follows is in alphabetical order. The names and addresses appear as they do in notebook and letters. Where no city or town is given, the address is usually London. It is a wonder that there were not more fugitives to puzzle a postmaster than Coleridge noted.[6] Names preceded by * are taken from N 62; cf *CN* III 3450 for the order in which they appeared. Abbreviations used below (but not elsewhere in this work) are:

AC   *Alumni Cantabrigienses* pt II ed J. A. Venn (6 vols Cambridge 1940–54).

AO   *Alumni Oxonienses . . . 1715–1886* ed Joseph Foster (4 vols 1887–8).

BCG   *Boyle's Court Guide* (1808–10).

BLG   John Burke and Sir John Bernard Burke *A Genealogical and Heraldic Dictionary of the Landed Gentry of Great Britain and Ireland* (3 vols 1846–9 [1843–9]).

DMD   *Deans & Co.'s Manchester and Salford Directory* (Manchester 1808–9).

E P-O   *The Post-Office Annual Directory . . . in . . . Edinburgh* (Edinburgh 1813).

[1] See the list of members in J. G. Lockhart *Memoirs of Sir Walter Scott* (5 vols 1900) II 113–14n.

[2] To Poole 12 Jan 1810: *CL* III 271.

[3] Clarkson to C 19 Jun 1809: DCL Folder B.

[4] John Edwards to C 28 Oct 1809: DCL Folder D.

[5] C to Davy 14 Dec [1808]: *CL* III 143.

[6] Brown wrote to C 18 Sept 1809 that the Leeds postmaster could not find a bookseller there named Pearson and that No 4 to "Charles Fairfax, Esq. Gilling Castle, Bristol" had been returned, marked "unknown": DCL Folder E. Gilling Castle is in Denton.

Farington	Joseph Farington *The Farington Diary* ed James Greig (8 vols 1922–8).
G	*Gore's Directory of Liverpool and its Environs* (Liverpool 1810).
GD	*The Glasgow Directory* (Glasgow 1813).
HAD	*Holden's Annual Directory . . . comprising . . . London and Separate Towns in England, Scotland, and Wales* (1814–16).
J	*Johnstone's London and Commercial Guide and Street Directory* (1817).
JCG	*Jollie's Cumberland Guide and Directory* (Carlisle 1811).
K	*Kent's Directory . . . for 1808* (1808).
L P-O	*The [London] Post-Office Annual Directory* (1808–10).
MBD	*Matthew's Complete Bristol Directory* (Bristol 1813).
MTA	*Register of Admissions to the . . . Middle Temple* ed H. A. C. Sturgess vol II 1782–1909 (1949).
T	*Holden's Triennial Directory for 1809, 1810, 1811* (1811).

SUBSCRIBERS

John Ackland Esq[re]   Fairford—Bridgewater

John Acland of Fairfield was a friend of Tom Poole. C had suggested to Poole sending Acland a Prospectus: 4 Dec 1808: *CL* III 131. Poole replied that Acland was "disposed I know in every respect to serve you": 17 Dec 1808: DCL Folder B. Acland's name appears in the list of subscribers living in or near Bridgwater that was sent to Poole 12 Jan 1810: BM Add MS 35343 f 369.

★ M[r] J. Acraman—Redcliffe Parade   Bristol

John Acraman, a deal merchant: *MBD*. C called him "the father of the Fine Arts" in Bristol: "On the Principles of Genial Criticism" I: *BL* (1907) II 222–3. He subscribed through W. Hood: Hood to C 24 Jun 1809: DCL Folder E. He also paid his subscription to Hood: Hood to C 3 Feb 1810: ibid. His name also appears in Forster MS 112 f 15.

★ John William Adam Esq[re]   at Longman & Rees'   Paternoster Row, London

Longman & Rees acted as a London agent for *The Friend*.

★ M[r] E. Addison   Porcher & C[o]   Devonshire Sq.

A brother (?) of Richard Addison (q.v.). Porcher, Redhead & Co were East India agents: *L P-O*. E. Addison is mentioned in a letter of SH to John Monkhouse 6 Feb [1827]: *SHL* 335. His name appears among those who subscribed through Tom Monkhouse (q.v.).

★ M[r] H. Addison   76 Lombard S[t]

Henry Addison, a brother of Richard; see DW to Richard Wordsworth 23 Mar 1810: *WL (M)* I 362. Probably subscribed through T. Monkhouse.

* M͏ͬ R. Addison   11 Staple Inn

Richard Addison, an attorney, Richard Wordsworth's partner. His sister Isabella married John Monkhouse (1806).

Alfred Club

Thomas Bernard wrote to C 25 Jun 1809: "My copies of the friend I have left on the Table of the new literary Club, the Alfred, which it is ordered for in future": DCL Folder D. The Alfred Club was at 23 Albemarle St, near the Royal Institution. At first jokingly called the 'Alf-read, it soon acquired a reputation for sobriety. Byron called it "a decent resource in a rainy day", and Lord Alvanley, when asked whether he was still a member, replied: "When the seventeenth bishop was proposed I gave in. I really could not enter the place without being put in mind of my catechism". John Timbs *Clubs and Club Life in London* (1872) 203.

* Rev͏ͩ Arch͏ͩ Alison   Buntsfield Links   Edinb͏ʰ

Archibald Alison (1757–1839), miscellaneous writer, was a friend of Jeffrey, through whom he may have subscribed. Wordsworth also knew him: see SH to MW 11 Sept [1820]: *SHL* 201. Like Walter Scott, a member of the Friday Club.

* W͏ᵐ Allen, Plough Court, Lombard S͏ͭ   London

William Allen (1770–1843), Quaker friend of Davy and Clarkson (C sent 200 Prospectuses to Clarkson care of Allen), scientist and philanthropist. C once procured a clyster from him: see C to Allen 19 May 1814: *CL* III 494. Allen subscribed through Basil Montagu: Montagu to C 22 Feb 1809: DCL Folder B.

* Earl of Altamont   10 Grafton Street   London

Howe Peter Browne (1788–1845), 4th Earl of Altamont, 2nd Marquess of Sligo (1809), governor-general of Jamaica (1833–6). He subscribed through the Rev George Caldwell: Caldwell to C (n.d.): DCL Folder B. As Lord Westport, he had been a boyhood companion of De Quincey.

* M͏ʳˢ Apreece—No 1 North Audley Street

Jane Kerr Apreece (1780–1855), said to have been the model of Mme de Staël's heroine Corinne, was then a wealthy widow. She subscribed through Clarkson: Clarkson to C 21 Apr 1809: DCL Folder B. When she married Humphry Davy in 1812, a friend of Clement Carlyon sent him the following epigram (Carlyon I 251):

> Though many a clever man has seen
> His talents underrated,
> Davy must own that his have been
> Richly Ap-pree-ce-ated.

* S͏ͬ Geo. Armytage B͏ͭ   Kirklees N͏ͬ Leeds

Sir George Armytage (1761–1836), 4th bt, married to Mary Bowles and therefore related to other subscribers; see above, II 408–9.

* M͏ͬ Sam¹ Ash—Kings Square—Bristol

A linen merchant: *MBD*.

* Fra. Duckenfield Astley Esqre

    Francis Dukenfield Astley of Manchester: *AO*. He subscribed through the bookseller William Ford: Ford to C 4 Jan 1809: DCL Folder E. He and his brother were friends of John Wilson; Wordsworth called them Wilson's "Merry Men": see DW to De Q 25 Jun [1809]: *WL* (*M*) I 330, and C. M. Maclean *Dorothy Wordsworth* (1932) 307.

* Mathew Atkinson Esqre   Temple Sowerby

    Matthew Atkinson (1769–1827), of a land-owning family of Temple Sowerby, Westmorland; he was related to the Mackereth family, Wordsworth's neighbours.

* John Awdry Esqre   Notton House   Chippenham   Wilts

    John Awdry (1766–1844), a magistrate for Wiltshire; his son John became chief justice of the supreme count of Bombay: *BLG*. He was distantly related to Southey's friend John May, and Southey had met him: *S Letters* (Warter) I 338.

G. D. B., Liverpool

    Writing from Liverpool 9 Jan 1810, he began a long letter to C: "Sir—As the sincere friend of your 'Friend' and with every wish that it may obtain the extensive circulation amongst all good men, which its superior excellence deserves, I trust you will excuse the liberty I take in addressing you"; he was surprised at complaints of obscurity against *The Friend*: DCL Folder D. See above, Introduction, I lxv n 4. None of the known Liverpool subscribers has the initials with which he signed his letter, "G. D. B."

* John Backhouse & Co   Darlington   2 Copies

    Probably Jonathan Backhouse of Darlington, who subscribed four times to Montagu's Society for the Diffusion of Knowledge upon the Punishment of Death: [Montagu] *An Account of the Origin and Object of the Society . . .* (1812) 16. Probably subscribed through Montagu.

* H. Ballard Esqr   11 Change Alley

    Of Rainier, Ballard & Co, bill brokers: *J*. Possibly a friend of Thomas Monkhouse, for his name appears in Mary Monkhouse's part of the list in N 62: see SH to M. Monkhouse 27 Mar [1809]: *SHL* 17. See also below, T. Monkhouse.

* —— Banister Esqr   Worcester Col.   Oxford

    John Banister (d 1870): *AO*. He subscribed through De Quincey: De Q to DW 21 Mar [1809]: *De Q to W* 115.

* David Barclay   Walthamstow   n^r London

    A descendant of the Quaker apologist, Robert Barclay, David Barclay was a London brewer; he was married to Rachael Lloyd, sister of Charles Lloyd Sr: *BLG*. Probably also a friend of Montagu, for his name appears among the subscribers to Montagu's Society: [Montagu] *Account* p 16 (see above, John Backhouse & Co).

* Robert Barclay Esqre   56 Lombard S.^t

    He was a banker: *K*. Probably of the Barclay family related to C's friends the Lloyds.

Charles Bardswell Esqre   Liverpool

He was an attorney: *G.* C wrote to Brown c 14 Oct 1809: "Send all the Numbers from the beginning as far as you have them to Charles Bardswell Esqre. Liverpool: & continue them": *CL* III 246 and Forster MS 112 f 11^v.

★ Miss Barker   Sr E^d Littleton's   Tedsely Park   Staffordshire

Mary Barker (later Mrs Slade), Southey's friend, whom he addressed in his letters as "My dear Senhora", for he had first met her in Lisbon. She lived for a time in Keswick, a next-door neighbour at Greta Lodge. Sir Edward Littleton's seat was Teddesley Park. From a letter from RS to Miss Barker 29 Jan 1810, it appears that she compared C's faults of style in *The Friend* to Edmund Burke's: see *S Letters* (Warter) II 188–90.

★ John Barnard Esqre   Knapton   n^r North Walsham ⟨ Norfolk⟩

He subscribed through Clarkson: Clarkson to C 11 Mar 1809: DCL Folder B.

★ T. Barnard Esqre   Wimpole S^t

Thomas Bernard (1750–1818), the philanthropist who helped found the Royal Institution. He subscribed in a letter to C 16 Dec 1808, also giving the name of the Bishop of Durham as subscriber: DCL Folder D. He wrote to C 11 Apr 1809 that he and Sir George Beaumont were to give a dinner-party with Sotheby, Davy "& some other of your friends, in Order to see what can be done" to further *The Friend:* ibid. He paid his subscription to G. Ward: Ward & Middleton account 10 Jan 1810: DCL Folder E. For his rôle in *The Friend* see above, Introduction, I xxxvii–xxxviii, xlix n 1; also I 238 n 3.

★ Mr B. Barry—High S^t—Bristol

Bartholomew Barry, bookseller and stationer who provided a reading-room for his customers. He subscribed through Longman & Co: Longman to C 4 May 1809: DCL Folder E.

★ Barwise Esqre   Temple   London

John Barwis, son of a Devizes physician, called to the bar 1804: *BCG* and *MTA.* Possibly a friend of Montagu; perhaps the Barwis mentioned by Mary Lamb in a letter to Sarah Stoddart 23 Oct 1806: *LL* II 24.

Bp. of Bath and Wells

Richard Beadon (1737–1824). His name appears in the list of subscriptions for collection sent to Poole 12 Jan 1810: BM Add MS 35343 f 369. C wrote to Poole 9 Oct 1809: "I have written to Brown concerning the Bishop of Bath & Wells—I will take care when all the Numbers have been reprinted, to have a copy sent to him, with my respectful &c—": *CL* III 236.

★ Lady Susan Bathurst   Cadogan Place N° 3

Lady Susan Bathurst (b 1768), daughter of the 2nd Earl Bathurst, Lord High Chancellor, and youngest sister of Henry, 3rd Earl Bathurst, who was foreign secretary briefly in 1809 and secretary for war 1812–27. She was a friend of Lady Beaumont.

★ Geo. Beauchamp Esq.ʳᵉ—Thetford—Norfolk

George Beauchamp married Charlotte Palmer, a sister-in-law of Mrs Palmer of Holme Park, who was also a subscriber: *BLG*. He subscribed through Clarkson: Clarkson to C 21 Apr 1809: DCL Folder B.

★ Lady Beaumont   Dunmow   Essex

Either Margaret (Willes), Lady Beaumont (1755–1829), wife of Sir George, or his mother, Rachel, Dowager Lady Beaumont (d 1814). The former wrote to C 20 Feb 1810 that she read *The Friend* with her sister (Mrs Fermor, also a subscriber), "light seem[ing] to break in upon us from the awakening power of sympathy"; she thought Clarkson must have been speaking ironically when he called *The Friend* a very dear work: DCL Folder B. She wrote to DW 13 Dec 1809: "The Friend must grow popular, I have heard so painful an account of the effect of the german Tale ["The Story of Maria Eleonora Schöning"] on my sister Fermor that I accuse myself of harshness in bearing it so well": Letters from Sir George Beaumont to WW, together with some from Lady Beaumont, DCL Folder I.

★ Sʳ G. Beaumont, Bᵗ, ~~Dunmow, Essex~~ Grosvenor Sq

C had known Sir George and Lady Beaumont since the summer of 1803. Beaumont (1753–1827), 7th bt, landscape painter and art patron, helped found the National Gallery.

★ Revᵈ Andrew Bell, Swanage, Dorset.

Bell (1753–1832), founder of the Madras system of education; C expounded it in his Royal Institution lectures of 1808. See above, I 102 and n 4. In a letter to C 6 Apr 1809 he asked to become a subscriber, having read an advertisement for *The Friend* in the *Courier*: DCL Folder C. He later paid £2 for his subscription directly to C: letter of 3 Feb 1810: ibid.

★ Daniel Bell Junʳ Esqʳ   6 Freemans Court   Cornhill

Bell was of a Quaker family related to the Barclays. His sister, Priscilla Wakefield, founded the first savings-bank and wrote many children's books. He subscribed through Clarkson: Clarkson to C 17 Feb 1809: DCL Folder B.

★ P. Bennet Esqʳ   Bury   Suffolk

Philip Bennet (1771–1853), a magistrate and high sheriff of Suffolk (1821): *BLG*. Probably a friend of Clarkson, who wrote of speaking to nine subscribers who lived in Bury: Clarkson to C 19 Jun 1809: DCL Folder B.

★ The Revᵈ Chaˢ Berry   Leicester

A Unitarian minister, Charles Berry (1783–1877) was also scholar mathematician, and schoolmaster.

★ Countess of Beverley   Portman Square

Isabella Susannah (Burrell) Percy (1750–1812), wife of the 1st Earl of Beverley. Her sister, the Marchioness of Exeter, and her daughter,

Viscountess St Asaph, were also subscribers. They were friends of the Beaumonts.

★ Mʳ J. L. Bickley, Portland Square   Bristol   from Nᵒ 3
He subscribed through Hood: Hood to C 24 Jun 1809: DCL Folder E. He also paid his subscription to Hood: Hood to C 3 Feb 1810: ibid. Bickley also appears in a list of subscribers in Forster MS 112 f 15.

★ Mʳ Biggs   1 Gough Square
Nathaniel Biggs, formerly of Biggs and Cottle, Bristol printers who had published C's *Poems* (1796, 1797) and printed *LB* (1800). Biggs had also printed *The Watchman*. Biggs, then printer and wholesale stationer in London, subscribed through G. Ward: Ward to C 21 Apr 1809: DCL Folder E.

★ John Bill Esqʳᵉ   Manchester
A surgeon: *DMD*. A member of the Manchester Literary and Philosophical Society, the *Memoirs* of which C read. Bill subscribed through Ford: Ford to C 4 Jan 1809: DCL Folder E.

★ Mʳ M. Birbeck Junʳ   Wanborough, near Guildford, Surrey
Probably a friend of Montagu: Morris Birkbeck, Junr., Wanborough, also appears in the list of subscribers to Montagu's Society: *Account* p 17 (see above, John Backhouse & Co). Birkbeck bought 16,000 acres of land in America, a parcel of which he sold to Keats's brother George. Known as "the Emperor of the Prairies", he wrote *Letters from Illinois* (1818) and other works; he was drowned 1825. See *The Letters of John Keats* ed Maurice Buxton Forman (Oxford 1947) I 235n and Edmund Blunden *Keats's Publisher* 57–8.

★ Mʳ Blair, Dudley   nʳ Birmingham
He subscribed through Knott & Lloyd: Knott & Lloyd to C 13 Jun 1809: DCL Folder E. Possibly Alexander Blair, John Wilson's friend, co-author of Mathetes' letter: see above, I 377 n 2. Blair, staying with Wilson at Elleray in the autumn of 1809, threatened to follow up *The Friend* each week with a satirical counterpart he would call *The Enemy*. Blair was professor of English literature at University College, London, 1830–6.

★ Dʳ Blake   Taunton
Probably Malachi Blake (d 1843), Taunton physician; the Blake Ward in the Taunton and Somerset Hospital is named after him. C wrote to Brown (n.d.) to send *The Friend* to Dr Blake "if his name be not already on the List of Subscribers": Forster MS 112 f 15. Blake probably subscribed through J. Norris (q.v.). Blake's name also appears in the list of subscriptions for collection sent to Poole 12 Jan 1810: BM Add MS 35343 f 369.

Marquis of Blandford   Grosvenor Square
George Spencer (1766–1840), later 5th Duke of Marlborough, styled Marquess of Blandford till 1817, was a noted book-collector. He subscribed through G. Ward: Ward to C 3 May 1809: DCL Folder E. His sister, Lady Elizabeth Spencer, was also a subscriber for a time.

★ Thos Bleaymire Esqre Penrith   ~~Templesowerby~~
   Thomas D. Bleaymire, an attorney: *HAD.*

★ Mr Blount, Surgeon—Birmingham
   John Blount: *T.* He subscribed through Knott & Lloyd: Knott &
   Lloyd to C 13 Jun 1809: DCL Folder E.

★ Very Revd Dean of Bocking
   Christopher Wordsworth (1774–1846), WW's youngest brother,
   married to Charles Lloyd's sister Priscilla; later master of Trinity
   College, Cambridge.

★ Boddington   Upper Brook S^t
   Samuel Boddington, a director of the Bank of England and business
   partner of Richard Sharp, through whom he subscribed: Sharp to
   C 12 Dec 1808: DCL Folder C.

★ Mrs Bolton   Storrs   Kendal
   Mrs Bolton, wealthy widow of a Liverpool merchant, lived at Storr's
   Hall, Windermere; she was a well-known hostess in the Lake country.
   William Green (see below, Mr Green) described the property as "the
   most splendid on the banks of Windermere": *A Description of Sixty
   Studies from Nature* (Kendal 1810) 17.

★ Stourges Bourne Esqre 14 Charles St Berkley Square
   William Sturges Bourne (1769–1845), then lord of the treasury (with
   his friend Canning he resigned from the cabinet during the year),
   wrote to C 25 Jan 1809: "Mr Sturges Bourne informs Mr Coleridge
   that Mr Canning and Mr William Rose as well as himself desire the
   Friend may be sent to them. 14 Charles Street Berkeley Square":
   DCL Folder C. Sturges Bourne was married to Anne Bowles, whose
   sister, Mrs Palmer, was also a subscriber.

★ Revd W. L. Bowlis   Brunhill   Calne   Wilts
   William Lisle Bowles (1762–1850), vicar of Bremhill, whose *Sonnets*,
   C once wrote, gave him more pleasure, and did his heart more good,
   than all the other books he read, except the Bible: C to Mrs Thelwall
   18 Dec 1796: *CL* I 287. C maintained a friendship with Bowles for
   over thirty years.

★ Mr Bowman   5 Bread St Cheapside
   Possibly a friend of Thomas Monkhouse, for his name appears among
   a group of his subscribers (see above, H. Ballard).

★ Mr John Bowman   14 Water Lane   Thames S^t
   A brandy merchant: *L P-O* and *K.* He subscribed through SH's
   cousin, Thomas Monkhouse; see SH to Mary Monkhouse 27 Mar
   [1809] on a contradiction in names of subscribers on two lists:
   "Tom's had one address 'Mr Bowman Water Lane *Thames St*' the
   Clarks '*Tower St*'. We have taken *Tom's* down into the Book; but
   if it is wrong tell us . . .": *SHL* 17. It was wrong: *L P-O* and *K* have
   "Tower St".

★ Mr Bowyer, Pall Mall, London
   Robert Bowyer (1758–1834), miniature-painter, who also produced a
   multi-volume illustrated Hume's *History of England.* Clarkson wrote

to C 1 Jan 1808 [1809] to have him send his "Poem on the Great Event of ye Abolition, for Bowyer's splendid Work, which will come out in March"; Clarkson thought that it might help procure subscribers, and had "prevailed upon Bowyer to stop the Press for three Weeks" to wait for C's poem: DCL Folder B. Bowyer's work was *Poems on the Abolition of the Slave Trade* (1809), containing poems by James Montgomery, James Grahame, and Elizabeth Benger and "embellished with engravings from pictures painted by R. Smirke" as well as portraits and biographical sketches of the anti-slavery leaders such as Clarkson. It had been planned to commemorate the abolition of the slave-trade in 1807, but was two years in the press.

* Mr G. Braithwaite, Stricklandgate, Kendal
George Braithwaite was married to Mary Lloyd, sister of Charles, Jr. A Quaker, from whom C once requested the loan of a library book: see C to Thelwall 26 Nov 1803: *CL* II 1020. *T* lists rope-makers and dry-salters of that name at Strickland Gate, Kendal.

* Isaac Braithwaite   Kendal
He was married to Anna Lloyd, sister of Charles, Jr. He was a publisher, with whom Wordsworth did business: see DW to R. Wordsworth 6 Apr 1809: *WL (M)* I 283.

Charles Brandling, Esq., M.P.   Newcastle
Charles J. Brandling (1769–1826), MP for Newcastle-on-Tyne (1798, 1802, 1806, 1807–12, 1820), withdrew from Parliament to devote his time to his mines and industries. He was involved with Humphry Davy in the controversy over the miners' safety-lamp. He was married to the daughter of another *Friend* subscriber, W. R. Fawkes, and subscribed through Wrangham: Montagu (quoting Wrangham) to C 23 May 1809: DCL Folder B. Brown wrote to C c 15 Sept 1809: "Yesterday I rec^d a letter from C. Brandling, Esq of Newcastle saying he never subscribed to the Friend, and desired them to be discontinued": DCL Folder E.

* Mr G. Brebner   Glasgow
George Brebner, keeper of Bridewell, Duke Street: *GD.*

* Richd Bright Esqre   Haw Green   N.^r Bristol
Richard Bright, merchant and banker; his son Richard, the pathologist, discovered "Bright's disease". He subscribed through Danvers: Danvers to C 3 Jan 1809: DCL Folder D. *MBD* lists his address as Hampne Green.

* Revd J. Brook   Jesus Coll: Cambridge
John Brooke (1773–1821), fellow and tutor of Jesus College: *AC.* He subscribed through George Caldwell: Caldwell to C (n.d.): DCL Folder C.

* Miss Brown, Meeting House Lane   Peckham
She subscribed through Clarkson: Clarkson to C 11 Mar 1809: DCL Folder B.

* The Revd T. Brown—Connington—St Ives—Huntingdonshire
Thomas Brown (1761–1829), rector of Conington; son of "Capabil-

ity" Brown, head-gardener of Hampton Court for George III: *AC*.
A friend of Clarkson, through whom he subscribed: Clarkson to
C 17 Feb 1809: DCL Folder B.

★ Richard Bruce Esq.ʳᵉ   Frenchay   N.ʳ Bristol
Robert Bruce, a merchant: *MBD*. He subscribed through Danvers:
Danvers to C 3 Jan 1809: DCL Folder D (Danvers lists him as
"Robert").

★ M.ʳ Thoˢ Buchannan   Dalmarnock   n.ʳ Glasgow
Thomas Buchanan, Dalmarnock dye-works: *GD*. Possibly one of
Thomas Monkhouse's subscribers (his name appears among a list
of such).

★ John Buck Esq.ʳ   18 South Street   Finsbury Sq.
Catherine (Mrs Thomas) Clarkson's brother; he subscribed through
Clarkson: Clarkson to C 17 Feb 1809: DCL Folder B.

★ M.ʳ Rob.ᵗ Buck   Bury   Suffolk
Another brother of Mrs Clarkson; he also subscribed through his
brother-in-law: Clarkson to C 11 Mar 1809: DCL Folder B.

★ M.ʳ Samuel Buck   Bury   Suffolk
Another brother of Mrs Clarkson: he subscribed through his brother-
in-law: Clarkson to C 11 Mar 1809: DCL Folder B.

★ W.ᵐ Buck Esq.ʳ   Bury   Suffolk
Mrs Clarkson's father; he probably subscribed through his son-in-law.

R. B. Buller Esq.ʳᵉ   Stowey   Bridgewater
Probably Richard Buller, married to Sarah Beadon, sister of another
subscriber, the Bishop of Bath and Wells (q.v.). His name appears
in the list of subscriptions for collection sent to Poole 12 Jan 1810:
BM Add MS 35343 f 369.

★ M.ʳ Dan.ˡ Burges—Small S.ᵗ   Bristol
Daniel Burges was an attorney: *MBD*.

Capt. Burney, 26 James Street, Pimlico
Fanny Burney's brother James (1750–1821), who had sailed with
Capt Cook on his second voyage, subscribed through Lamb: Lamb
to Brown 24 Aug 1809: DCL Folder C. Burney gave whist parties
for Lamb, Rickman, and other friends of Coleridge: *CRD* I 157.

★ M.ʳ Burroughs   Mall   Clifton
Benjamin Gustavus Burroughs, an apothecary: *MBD*. He sub-
scribed through De Quincey's mother: De Q to DW 16 Aug [1809]:
DE Q to W 245. His name also appears in a list of subscribers in
Forster MS 112 f 16.

★ James Burton Esq.ʳ   9 Bedford Place   Bloomsbury
Architect and builder (1761–1837), he built Russell Square in Bloomsbury, Waterloo Place, and many of Nash's terraces in Regent's Park;
father of the architect Decimus Burton. He subscribed through
Montagu: Montagu to C 22 Feb 1809: DCL Folder B. Montagu later
sent a copy of a letter he received 30 Sept from Burton asking that his
copies of *The Friend* be forwarded to Tunbridge (see also C to Brown
c 14 Oct 1809: *CL* III 246). Burton, in a letter to C 31 Jan 1810, dis-

continued his subscription, sending "a trifle" to make up for "disappointment or inconvenience": DCL Folder E.

★ Mr C. Butler   44 Ormond Street

Charles Butler, of the above address and Lincoln's Inn: *BCG*. Butler (1750–1832), the first Roman Catholic barrister since the Revolution of 1688, was co-editor of *Coke upon Littleton* and author of the continuation of *Lives of the Saints*. He subscribed through Montagu: his name appears in a list on a Prospectus that Montagu sent C (n.d.): DCL Folder B.

★ Mr Cadwell   9 Paternoster Row

Possibly Thomas Cadell the younger (1773–1836), of Cadell & Davies, booksellers.

★ Revd G. Caldwel   Jesus Coll: Cambridge

George Caldwell (c 1773–1848), an intimate of C's college days. He sent C a list of subscribers (n.d.) and offered to distribute Prospectuses to the booksellers, but asked C to send them to the Rev T. Cautley if they should be likely to arrive in his absence: DCL Folder C. C sent Cautley the Prospectuses.

★ Wm Calvert Esqre   Keswick

William Calvert, an intimate friend of Wordsworth. C, WW, and Calvert once intended to study chemistry together in a laboratory Calvert—"an idle, good-hearted, and ingenious man"—was to build at Windy Brow, near Greta Hall: C to Davy 3 Feb 1801: *CL* II 670–1. C asked RS c 4 Dec 1808 to speak to Calvert about getting subscribers in Carlisle: *CL* III 130. It was through Calvert that Southey met Shelley, then at Keswick: Shelley to Elizabeth Hitchener 26 Dec 1811: *The Letters of Percy Bysshe Shelley* ed Frederick L. Jones (Oxford 1964) I 212.

★ The Right Honble Geo. Canning   Downing Street

George Canning (1770–1827) was foreign secretary when he subscribed to *The Friend*, shortly before his duel with Castlereagh, minister of war. A year before, he had helped found the *Quarterly Review*. He subscribed through Sturges Bourne: Sturges Bourne to C 25 Jan 1809: DCL Folder C. See also C to Poole 3 Feb 1809: *CL* III 174.

★ A. Carlysle Esqr   Soho Square

Anthony Carlisle (1768–1840), surgeon, a friend of the Montagus, whom C consulted in 1810: see above, Introduction, I lxxiii and n 5. C and Davy had discussed the subject of "pain" with him: C to Davy 2 Dec 1800: *CL* II 648.

★ Mr Carr   Great Russel S^t

T. W. Carr, 105 Great Russell St: *BCG*. Thomas William Carr was a solicitor who subscribed through Montagu: his name appears in a list on a Prospectus that Montagu sent C (n.d.): DCL Folder B. Crabb Robinson calls him Solicitor to the Excise and an old acquaintance of WW: *CRB* I 86.

★ David Carrick Junr   Carlisle

A linen- and woollen-draper of that name is listed in *T*. Possibly a relation of the cotton-mill-owner whose son later painted Wordsworth. *JCG* lists a banker of that name at Carlisle.

* Mͬ John Carruthers   50 Cheapside
  The wholesale haberdasher of 32 King St, Cheapside? *L P-O*. Possibly a friend of Thomas Monkhouse, for his name appears among a group of his subscribers.

* Mͬ W. Carruthers   Mitre Court   Cheapside
  William Carruthers, a lace merchant: *L P-O* and *K*. Possibly a friend of Thomas Monkhouse.

* Mich! Castle Esqͬ   Old Market Sͭ   Bristol
  A friend from early *Watchman* days, Michael Castle subscribed through J. J. Morgan: Morgan to C 26 Dec 1808: DCL Folder C. He paid his subscription to Morgan's friend, Hood: Hood to C 3 Feb 1810: DCL Folder E. In 1813, Castle, then mayor of Bristol, gave C an elegant snuffbox: *CL* III 460, 587.

* Mͬ Thoͣ Castle   Milk Sͭ   Bristol
  He subscribed through Morgan: Morgan to C 26 Dec 1808: DCL Folder C. He paid his subscription to Hood: Hood to C 3 Feb 1810: DCL Folder E.

Rev. T. Cautley, Jesus College, Cambridge
  A possible subscriber, Thomas Cautley was a friend of George Caldwell. C sent him 100 Prospectuses at Caldwell's suggestion (Caldwell was away from Cambridge at the time): C to Stuart 23 Jan 1809: *CL* III 170. Also listed for 100 Prospectuses in BM Add MS 34046 f 82.

Sir George Cayley, Brompton, Yorkshire
  Sir George Cayley (1773–1857), 6th bt, scientist and pioneer in aviation, was related to Francis Wrangham by marriage (Wrangham's second wife was Dorothy Cayley). Cayley subscribed through Wrangham: Montagu (quoting from a letter of Wrangham) to C 23 May 1809: DCL Folder B.

* S. Chatfield Esqͬ   Coopers Row   Tower Hill
  Samuel Chatfield was a wine merchant: *J*.

* Messͬˢ Christopher & Jennet   Stockton
  Christopher & Jennett, booksellers and printers, subscribed through Longman & Co: Longman to C 10 Jun 1809: DCL Folder E.

John Chubb Esqͬᵉ   Bridgewater
  A wine merchant, friend of Poole, whom C once asked to procure a cottage for Thelwall: C to Chubb [20 Aug 1797]: *CL* I 341–3. His name appears in the list of subscriptions for collection sent to Poole 12 Jan 1810: BM Add MS 35343 f 369. Chubb was an indirect descendant of the deist writer Thomas Chubb.

* Dͬ E. D. Clarke, Sͭ Andrews Sͭ   Cambridge
  Edward Daniel Clarke (1769–1822), antiquary and mineralogist, professor of mineralogy at Cambridge (1808) and author of *Travels in Various Countries of Europe, Asia, and Africa* (6 vols 1810–23). A friend of Wrangham and R. P. Knight; he subscribed through George Caldwell: Caldwell to C (n.d.): DCL Folder C.

* John Clarkson Esqre Purfleet   near Grays   Essex
> Thomas Clarkson's brother, formerly a naval officer, governor of
> Sierra Leone in 1792: see E. L. Griggs *Thomas Clarkson* (1936) 66–8.
> Probably subscribed through his brother.

* T. Clarkson Esqr Bury   Suffolk
> Thomas Clarkson (1760–1846), Quaker who had fought to abolish
> the slave-trade. C reviewed Clarkson's *History of the . . . Abolition
> of the . . . Slave-Trade* (1808) for the *Ed Rev.* C asked Stuart 23 Jan
> 1809 to send Clarkson 200 Prospectuses: *CL* III 169–70. For the rôle
> of "the Moral Steam-Engine" (as C called him) in *The Friend*, see
> above, Introduction, I xxxviii, xl, xlv, lxviii.

William Innell Clement, 201 Strand
> Clement (d 1852), bookseller who acted as C's London agent: see
> above, Introduction I lii, lv. Clement sent C a list of subscribers
> 1 May 1809: DCL Folder E. He forwarded subscription payments to
> C 19 Jan 1810: ibid. From his account, he sold twenty-four copies
> each of Nos 1–4 and twelve each of Nos 9–20. Clement later pur-
> chased a share of the London *Observer* and, on the death of James
> Perry in 1821, the *Morning Chronicle*.

* Mr Clementson   72 Sun Street   Bishopgate S.^{t}
> No information found.

Wm Coleman Esqre Bridgewater
> His name appears in the list of subscriptions for collection sent to
> Poole 12 Jan 1810: BM Add MS 35343 f 369.

Revd Geo: Coleridge, Ottery   Devon
> C's brother George (1764–1828) wrote to him 16 Mar 1809: "As far
> as my influence will allow you shall find me an active Patron of the
> Friend", promising to "hunt about for Subscribers &c as will brother
> James": DCL Folder B. He sent C a list of subscribers 28 May 1809,
> including his own name: ibid. See also above, I lxiii, and below, II 496.

James Coleridge Esq, Ottery   Devon
> C's oldest surviving brother (1759–1836) subscribed through their
> brother George: G. Coleridge to C 28 May 1809: DCL Folder B.

John Coleridge, Corpus Christi, Oxford
> C's nephew, son of his brother James, John Taylor Coleridge (1790–
> 1876), later judge of the queen's bench. He wrote to C 20 Jun 1809
> asking that *The Friend* be sent to Devon during the long vacation
> and enclosing a list of C's ms poems in his possession, which he
> thought C had perhaps forgotten: DCL Folder B. John Taylor
> Coleridge had been at Eton with Shelley.

William Hart Coleridge, Christ Church, Oxford
> C's nephew (1789–1849), son of his brother Luke (d 1790), later bp of
> Barbados and the Leeward Islands. He wrote C an affectionate letter
> 24 Apr 1809: ". . . You may be assured, my dear Uncle, that you have
> one at Oxford who will be happy to assist"; he included the names of
> his cousin John and Edward James as well as his own as subscribers:
> DCL Folder B. He also wrote that Parker, the Oxford bookseller

(q.v.), suggested that C send him twenty copies and a Prospectus for Parker. George Coleridge also sent in W. H. Coleridge's name as subscriber: G. Coleridge to C 28 May 1809: ibid.

Mr Commins   Bookseller   Tavistock
He ordered through Longman & Co: Longman to C 4 May 1809: DCL Folder E.

★ Messʳˢ Constable & Co   Booksellers   Edinbʰ
C sent the company fifty Prospectuses: BM Add MS 34046 f 83. Constable received twelve copies of *The Friend*: Brown to C c 15 Sept 1809: DCL Folder E. Archibald Constable published the *Ed Rev.*

★ Mʳ Cooke   Leicester
Probably D. Cooke, an attorney there: *HAD*. He subscribed through Montagu: his name appears in a list on a Prospectus Montagu sent C (n.d.): DCL Folder B.

★ Mʳ Cookson   Kendal
Thomas Cookson and his wife were friends of SH from childhood, and later friends of the Wordsworths. C had his paper for *The Friend* sent to Cookson, whom he described as "Manufacturer": C to Stuart 2 May 1809: *CL* iii 207. *T* lists him as a linsey manufacturer.

★ The Revᵈ Dʳ Cookson   Binfield   Berks
William Cookson, Wordsworth's uncle. He paid his subscription to G. Ward: Ward & Middleton account 5 Mar 1810: DCL Folder E.

Mr Coombe   Bookseller   Leicester   2 Copies
Thomas Coombe, bookseller, subscribed through Longman & Co: Longman to C 4 May 1809: DCL Folder E. He received two copies: Brown to C c 14 Sept 1809: ibid.

★ John Corbyn   300 Holborn
Of Corbyn, Stacy, Messer & Swaine, chemists: *L P-O* and *K*. The Corbyns were Quakers, friends of the Fosters of Bromley (see Joseph Foster, below), the Hanburys (see Sampson Hanbury, below), and the Barclays: R. Hingston Fox *Dr. John Fothergill and His Friends* (1919) 264.

Earl of Cork   Hamilton Place   London
Edmund Boyle, 8th Earl of Cork and Orrery (1767–1856), subscribed through G. Ward: Ward to C 3 May 1809: DCL Folder E. See above, Introduction i lxxi.

George Cornish, Esqʳ, Salcombe Hill, Sidmouth, Devon
A friend of early days, Cornish had visited C, then Dragoon S. T. Comberbache, in Reading: see C to Cornish 12 Mar 1794: *CL* i 72–3. Cornish subscribed through C's brother George: G. Coleridge to C 28 May 1809: DCL Folder B.

★ Revᵈ J. Corrie, Shackbrook   Birmingham
John Corrie, father of the first Bishop of Madras; he subscribed through Knott & Lloyd: Knott & Lloyd to C 13 Jun 1809: DCL Folder E.

★ Joseph Corsbie Junʳ Esqʳ   3 Artillery Place
A merchant: *L P-O*. He subscribed through Clarkson: Clarkson to

C 17 Feb 1809: DCL Folder B. The Corsbies and Clarksons were later related by marriage: see DW to Mrs Clarkson 31 Jul [1812]: *WL (M)* II 516–17.

* Joseph Corsbie Esqr   Wm Bucks Esqr   Bury   Suffolk
Father of the above. He also subscribed through Clarkson: Clarkson to C 17 Feb 1809: DCL Folder B.

Joseph Cottle, Brunswick Square, Bristol
The bookseller (1770–1853) who published C's *Poems* (1796, 1797) and the *LB* (1798) and later wrote *Early Recollections* (1837) and *Reminiscences* (1847) of C. Cottle wrote to the Kendal postmaster 28 Feb 1810, asking him to pay C an enclosed pound note for the "20th N^o of the Friend, that excellent Paper": DCL Folder E.

John Coulson, Clifton Wood, Bristol
A lawyer, a friend of C's from *Watchman* days. The Coulson family of Massachusetts, loyalists during the Revolutionary War, settled in Bristol; they were close friends of the Poole family. C wrote to Coulson c 18 Apr 1809, asking his help in obtaining subscribers: *CL* III 198–9. Coulson replied 28 Apr 1809 with a list of subscribers, including his own name: DCL Folder D.

Mr Thomas Coulson—Bristol
A brother? John Coulson sent in his name as subscriber: Coulson to C 28 Apr 1809: DCL Folder D.

Mr Craig, Glasgow
He wrote to C 6 Feb 1810, asking forgiveness for "having neglected to pay for the Friend, so long": DCL Folder E. A friend of Robert Grahame (q.v.)?

* Geo. Cranstoun Esqre   George S.^t   Edinb.^h
George Cranstoun (d 1850), then an advocate, later Lord Corehouse and a judge; a friend of Walter Scott and a member of the Friday Club.

* R.^t Honb.^{le} Lady Craven   Lower Grosvenor S.^t
Louisa, Countess of Craven (c 1785–1860), had been an actress before her marriage (1807). C had known her father, John Brunton, and her sisters (and probably herself as well) in Cambridge in 1794; her sister Ann had been one of his early loves.

* Mrs Crawford, 29, Park S.^t   Grosvenor Sq.^{re}
Wife of Robert Craufurd (1764–1812), general? Southey sent the widow his inscription *For the Walls of Ciudad Rodrigo* (at the assault of which Craufurd lost his life): *S Letters* (Curry) II, 464, 466. She paid her subscription to G. Ward: Ward & Middleton account 5 Mar 1810: DCL Folder E.

* Dr Crompton   Eaton   Liverpool
C had known Peter Crompton since 1796, when he contemplated running a day-school at Derby on the doctor's advice, and had later consulted him professionally: "I must, I must, I must, see him—", C wrote Southey [13 Feb 1808], "and in he dashes—rattles away, & when I am near sinking under him, cries—Now—now—you are quite

well.—I never saw you look better. God bless him! he is a noble-hearted fellow . . . and I like his company too very much, only not in hours of Disease or Dejection": *CL* iii 69. Crompton, whose seat, Eton, was five miles from Liverpool, became a brewer. In his letter to C 3 Feb 1810, enclosing £2. 7 for his and his sister's subscriptions, Crompton wrote to continue them, "& if it be as good in future as it has been for the last 10 numbers, you I believe will be tired of writing before we shall be tired of taking the work": DCL Folder E.

★ Miss Crompton   Eaton   Liverpool
Dr Crompton's "excellent Sister": C to Morgan 18 Feb [1812]: *CL* iii 370.

★ Miss Crosthwaite   Keswick
Of M. and D. Crosthwaite, mercers, drapers, and grocers: *JCG*. A Keswick merchant with whom C traded: see C to Mrs C 5 and 16 Dec 1802: *CL* ii 891, 898. De Quincey sometimes sent letters and parcels to the Wordsworths care of Miss Crosthwaite, for speedier delivery: De Q to DW 11 Mar [1809]: *De Q to W* 105.

★ J. G. Crump Esqre   Liverpool
John Gregory Crump, an attorney, owned Allan Bank, which Wordsworth leased from him. C asked him for information about another Liverpool subscriber: C to Brown c 24 Aug 1809: *CL* iii 219.

★ H. Curwen Esqre   Youngfield   Dumfries
Henry Curwen (1783–1861), son and heir of J. C. Curwen (q.v.).

★ J. C. Curwen Esqre   Workington Hall
John Christian Curwen (1756–1828), MP for Carlisle, who franked all the numbers of *The Friend*—"an honest Country Member, always on the right side, & . . . a stirring & enthusiastic Agriculturist": C to Poole 11 Apr 1809: *CL* iii 191–2. Cf his letter to Stuart 15 Apr 1809: *CL* iii 194.

★ Chas Davers Esqr   Bristol
Charles Danvers (d 1814), a friend from early Bristol days, was to C "the spirit of Southey made perfect. He had his Sanctity without his Severity—his fortitude without his Frown": C to J. Wade [10 Jan 1796]: *CL* i 175. Danvers sent in his and other subscriptions in a letter to C 28 Dec 1808: DCL Folder D. He sent a later list of names 3 Jan 1809: ibid. He promised to pay his and John King's subscriptions to G. Ward, but cancelled his subscription after the twentieth number because he could not afford the expense now that his brother and the latter's family were starving in a garret and needed his help: letter to C 3 Jan 1810: ibid.

Dr. Martin Davy, Caius College, Cambridge
Martin Davy (1763–1839), master of Caius, was also a physician. He subscribed through George Caldwell: Caldwell to C (n.d.): DCL Folder C.

★ Mrs de Quincey   Westhay   n^r Wrington   2 Copies
Elizabeth Penson De Quincey, De Quincey's mother. The second copy was for her brother, Major Penson, in the East India service:

see De Q to DW 16 Aug [1809]: *De Q to W* 245. "My mother", De Quincey wrote to DW, "is the only person that I have seen who sincerely and *thoroughly* likes the Friend hereabouts: she has been used to read a great many old religious books—and is therefore not unwilling to give the necessary attention to the transitions—the train and bearing of the arguments &c": ibid. Mrs De Quincey had sent Prospectuses to the East Indies, distributed them amongst her friends throughout the kingdom, and put down two other names of subscribers: ibid.

* Thos de Quincey Esqre 5 copies

De Quincey (then of Worcester College) was a frequent visitor to the Lakes, where he hoped to set up a press: see above, Introduction, I xliv–xlv. He sent DW a list of seven subscribers 21 Mar [1809] and wrote of a letter listing four others from Liverpool that had gone astray; he had received copies of the Prospectus and hoped to procure other names: *De Q to W* 114–16. He reported to DW 7 Jul [1809] that he had read only No 2 of *The Friend*, which he had bought at Clement's; it was Clement's last copy, and when Capt Pasley came to buy one there were none, so he lent his No 2 to Pasley: ibid 242. After reading No 3 he wrote to DW 16 Aug [1809] of the complaints about the obscurity of *The Friend*: ibid 244; see above, Introduction lix. De Quincey seems to have cancelled four of his five copies; in a note to Brown with copy for No 9, C wrote: "I have sent back some odd Friends that had been sent to Mr De Quincey & shall send back the rest all but one of each when I can put my hands on them. You will continue to send *one* to him weekly": Forster MS 112 f 64.

* Mr R. Dickson Stockton

A friend of the Hutchinsons: see SH to J. Monkhouse 23 Aug [1800]: *SHL* 6.

Revd. James Donne, Oswestry

The Rev Dr Donne (1764–1844), headmaster of the Oswestry Grammar School, subscribed after reading an excerpt from *The Friend* in the *Courier*: Donne to C 10 Dec 1809: DCL Folder D. Cf C to Brown 22 Dec [1809]: *CL* III 264. Donne paid his subscription 29 Jan 1810, telling C that he "could wish for fewer 'words of learned length & thundering sound' ": DCL Folder D.

* John Douglas Glassford Street Glasgow

He subscribed through Robert Grahame: Grahame to WW 21 Apr 1809: DCL Folder D.

* Philip Ducarel Esqre—Walford House n^r Bridgewater

Son and heir of John Ducarel, descendant of an ancient French family: *BLG*. His name, spelled Ducarrel, appears on the list of subscriptions for collection sent to Poole 12 Jan 1810: BM Add MS 35343 f 369.

* David Dunlop Bleacher at Craigdton Glasgow

Of Dunlop, Hamilton & Co, linen merchants and bleachers: *GD*. He subscribed through Robert Grahame: Grahame to WW 21 Apr 1809: DCL Folder D. Grahame's letter also implies that Dunlop secured other subscribers; unidentified Glasgow subscribers were perhaps therefore his.

⋆ William Dunn   John Street   Machine Maker   Glasgow
He subscribed through Robert Grahame: Grahame to WW 21 Apr 1809: DCL Folder D.

⋆ The Bishop of Durham
Shute Barrington (1734–1826), philanthropist, friend of C, who interceded as arbitrator with Savage the printer: see above, Introduction, I xxxvii. See also above, I 238 and n 3. He subscribed in a letter to C 15 Dec 1808: DCL Folder C. Thomas Bernard also sent in the bp of Durham as a subscriber a day later: DCL Folder D. Durham paid his subscription to G. Ward: Ward & Middleton account 10 Jan 1810: DCL Folder E.

⋆ —— Dyne Esqʳᵉ   Bruton—Somerset
Edward Dyne, an attorney: *AO*. His name, spelled Dynes, was on the list of subscriptions for collection sent to Poole 12 Jan 1810: BM Add MS 35343 f 369.

Messʳˢ Eddowes, Shrewsbury
Booksellers who subscribed through Longman & Co: Longman to C 4 May 1809: DCL Folder E.

⋆ Mʳ Edmondson   Keswick
John Edmondson, the apothecary and physician who treated C and the Wordsworths; he had recommended C's taking the Scottish tour of 1803: C to RS 14 Aug 1803: *CL* II 974–5. C used as ink the gout medicine Edmondson once prescribed: C to Sir George and Lady Beaumont 1 Oct 1803: *CL* II 999.

⋆ Mʳ Blooms Edwards   Bloomsbury Square   Great Russel Sᵗ
Of Lyon and Edwards, solicitors: *J*. Possibly Thomas Edwards (c 1775–1845), legal writer. He subscribed through Montagu: his name appears in a list on a prospectus Montagu sent C (n.d.): DCL Folder B.

John Edwards, Irongate, Derby
Edwards (b c 1772), a friend of C and the poet Montgomery (q.v.), subscribed 25 Sept 1809, enclosing a pound for the first twenty numbers and sending a poem and a few other trifles of his composing: DCL Folder D. It was typical of C to offer to send him free copies, but Edwards wrote that he could afford to pay: 28 Oct 1809: ibid. Wordsworth quoted an Edwards poem in his "Essay on Epitaphs": see above, II 340–1. Edwards also appears in a list of subscribers in Forster MS 112 f 16.

⋆ Nathˡ Edwards Esqʳᵉ   Derby
Nathaniel Edwards was a solicitor: *T*. Possibly subscribed through Joseph Strutt (q.v.).

⋆ Revᵈ Mʳ Edwards   Bedminster   Bristol
John E. Edwards subscribed through Morgan: Morgan to C 26 Dec 1808: DCL Folder C. He paid his subscription to Hood: Hood to C 3 Feb 1810: DCL Folder E.

* Mr Elam   Leeds
T lists two firms of merchants on Woodhouse Lane, Leeds: Elam, Granger & Co and Elam & Glover.

Revd L. W. Eliott, Peper Harrow, near Godalming, Surrey
Lawrence William Eliot (1777–1862), rector of Peper Harow (1801–62): *AC*. He subscribed through Clement: Clement to C 1 May 1809: DCL Folder E.

* Revd Mr Elmesley   St Mary Cray   Kent
Peter Elmesley (1773–1825), Southey's friend, classical scholar, contributor to the *Ed Rev.* C called on him in Edinburgh in 1803: C to RS [13 Sept 1803]: *CL* II 988. Like Scott and Jeffrey, a member of the Friday Club.

* Dean of Ely   Jesus College   Cambridge
William Pearce (1744–1820), master of Jesus College, who had appointed C librarian in 1793. He subscribed through George Caldwell: Caldwell to C (n.d.): DCL Folder C.

* G. T. Estcourt Esqre M.P.   17 Curzon Street   London
Thomas Grimston Bucknall Estcourt (1775–1853), MP for Devizes (1805–26). Possibly an acquaintance of the Merewethers, who lived near Devizes (see *CL* IV 617), for the names follow in the notebook list.

* J. Estcourt Esqre   Estcourt   Tetbury   Gloucestersh.
J. Estcourt, of the family of the above, was MP for Cricklade (1807).

* R. E. Estcourt Esqre   Estcourt   Tetbury   Gloucestershire
The Rev Edmund William Estcourt (c 1782–1856), brother of T. G. B. Estcourt (above), rector of Long Newnton (1808): *AO*. He wrote to C from Estcourt 13 Jun 1809 to subscribe to the projected Essays and Poems advertised in *Friend* No 2: DCL Folder E.

* Mr Estlin   Bristol
As early as autumn 1795 C had John Prior Estlin (1747–1817), a Unitarian minister of Bristol, correct his *Religious Musings* because of his "implicit confidence in the soundness of [Estlin's] Taste in compositions of the higher cast": C to Cottle [Oct 1795]: *CL* I 162–3. C sent Estlin a Prospectus, with a warm letter written on its blank pages 3 Dec 1808: *CL* III 127–9. Danvers (q.v.), in a letter to C 28 Dec 1808, wrote: "Dr Estlin has I believe give you his own name [as subscriber]": DCL Folder D.

* Mrs Evans   Darley   N.^r Derby
Elizabeth Evans, Jedediah Strutt's daughter, once wanted C to educate her children: see C to John Fellows 28 Jul 1796: *CL* I 227–8. C wrote Thelwall 6 Feb 1797 that she was "without exception the greatest WOMAN, I have been fortunate enough to meet with in my brief pilgrimage thro' Life": *CL* I 306. Her brother-in-law and her three brothers were also subscribers.

J. Everard Esqre   Hill, n.^r Bridgewater   (2 copies)
John Everard (1769–1848), of Hill House, a barrister: *BLG*. His name appears in the list of subscriptions for collection sent to Poole 12 Jan 1810: BM Add MS 35343 f 369.

★ Marchoiness of Exeter   Whitehall

Elizabeth Anne (Burrell) Cecil (1757–1837), widow of the 10th Marquess of Exeter (d 1804), was the divorced wife of the 8th Duke of Hamilton and the sister of the Countess of Beverley, also a subscriber.

★ Rev.d Charles Fairfax Esq.re   Gilling Castle

Charles Gregory Pigott, who assumed the name of Fairfax 1793 (1768–1845), of Gilling Castle, Yorkshire; of the famous Fairfax family of Virginia. Brown wrote to C 18 Sept 1809 that Fairfax's copy of No 4 had been returned, marked "unknown"; "if unknown", Brown asked, "what has become of the former numbers, as he was on the list from the first?" DCL Folder E. In his letter Brown located Gilling Castle in Bristol.

Walter Ramsden Fawkes, Esq.re, Farnley Hall, Ottley, Yorkshire

Fawkes (1769–1825), MP for York, miscellaneous writer, and friend and patron of the painter Turner, subscribed through Wrangham. Wrangham noted in a letter to C 12 Jun 1809 that Fawkes's copy had come by mistake to him: DCL Folder B.

★ Richard Fell No 8, Princes Place, Kennington Road

A friend of Montagu? Richard Fell, Southwark, appears in the list of subscribers to Montagu's Society: *Account* p 18 (see above, John Backhouse & Co). Crabb Robinson had tea at Lamb's 24 Apr 1811, when C and "a Mr. Fell" were there: *CRB* I 31.

★ M.rs Fermor   Albion Place   Bath

Frances (Willes) Fermor, Lady Beaumont's sister. "I receive a deeper delight", C wrote to Lady Beaumont 21 Jan 1810, "from the knowledge that I have half a dozen readers, like your Sister, than I should have from as large a promiscuous sale, as Avarice could crave or Vanity dream of": *CL* III 277. Mrs Fermor took lodgings close to C in Ashley in 1814 "to have the comfort of [C's] religious openings & consolations": C to Morgan [1] Jun 1814: *CL* III 502.

★ Rev.d R. Finch   9 Lower Brook S.t   Grosvenor Sq.

Robert Finch (1783–1830) had been private sectetary to both Pitt and Fox. He was ordained 1807, lived the latter part of his life abroad, and bequeathed his library to the Ashmolean Museum. He subscribed through De Quincey: De Q to DW 21 Mar [1809]: *De Q to W* 115.

★ Tho.s Fitzgerald Esq.re   Old Buildings   Lincoln's Inn

Thomas Fitzgerald of 10 Lincoln's Inn: *BCG*. He was a special pleader: *J*. He subscribed through Anthony Spedding: Spedding to C (n.d.): DCL Folder E.

★ W.m Ford   Books.r   85 Market S.t Lane   Manchester   8 Copies

William Ford (1771–1832), bookseller and bibliographer, wrote to C 4 Jan 1809 that George Philips of the same town having sent him Prospectuses he had found eight subscribers: DCL Folder E. Brown listed Ford as receiving eight copies c 15 Sept 1809: Brown to C: ibid.

* D. Forester   Derby
   Richard French, who changed his name to Forrester (b 1771), a
   physician: *AC*. Possibly subscribed through Joseph Strutt (q.v.).

* Thos Forster Esq.re   Five Houses   Clapton   near London,
   or St Helens   Bishopsgate Street, London
   Thomas Furly Forster (1761–1825), botanist, fellow of the Linnaean
   Society, friend of Porson and Sir Joseph Banks. He paid his subscription to G. Ward: Ward & Middleton account 5 Mar 1810:
   DCL Folder E. Possibly subscribed through Montagu, for his name
   appears in the list of subscribers to Montagu's Society: *Account*
   p 18 (see above, John Backhouse & Co); he was a member of the
   business committee of the society.

* Joseph Foster, Bromley, near Bow, Middlesex
   Joseph Foster, of Bromley House, was married to Sarah Lloyd, a
   cousin of Charles Lloyd Jr: *BLG*.

* Saml Fox⟨ Esq.re⟩   Mulston Grange   N. Derby
   Samuel Fox was married to Martha Strutt, sister of Mrs Evans and
   G. B., Joseph, and William Strutt, all subscribers. Fox paid his
   subscription to G. Ward: Ward & Middleton account 3 Jan 1810:
   DCL Folder E.

Francis Freeling Esq.
   Freeling (1764–1836), secretary-general of the post-office, subscribed
   through Ridout: Ridout to C 24 Apr 1809: DCL Folder D. C and
   his friends thought of complaining to Freeling about the delivery
   of the post between London and Grasmere: C to Montagu [7 Jan
   1809]: *CL* III 162.

* D. French Esq.   Barrister   Temple
   Daniel French, admitted to Lincoln's Inn, 1802. Possibly the "half-
   crazy Catholic" who angered Lord Ellenborough by declaring, in
   defence of a client accused of publishing a blasphemy, that blasphemy
   had been justified by an Act of Parliament: *CRD* I 493 (24 Nov
   1823).

* Revd   Froude   Dartington   N. Totness   Devon.
   Robert Hurrell Froude (1771–1859), rector of Dartington and later
   archdeacon of Totnes, father of the historian James Anthony Froude.
   He subscribed through C's brother George: G. Coleridge to C 28 May
   1809: DCL Folder B. Mrs Froude's brother, Anthony Spedding
   (q.v.), was also a subscriber.

* Edward Fuller Esq.re   Carlton   N. Saxmundham   Suffolk
   Edward Fuller (b c 1782): *AO* and *AC*. He wrote to C 27 Sept 1809
   cancelling his subscription because he was leaving the country, and
   wished to know whom to pay: DCL Folder E.

Miss Gale, Sheffield
   One of three sisters, Anne, Elizabeth, and Sarah, who continued
   the bookselling and stationery business of their brother, Joseph
   Gales, proprietor of the *Sheffield Register*, when he fled to America
   in 1794 to avoid arrest on a charge of conspiracy. The poet James

Montgomery, then in the editorial department of the paper, bought up its assets to issue his *Iris*; he lived the rest of his life with the sisters, his especial friend being the youngest, Sarah. Miss Gales subscribed through him: Montgomery to C 16 Dec 1808: DCL Folder C.

⋆ Samuel Gralton Esqʳ   Birmingham
Samuel Galton, Quaker gunmaker and banker (1753–1832), was related to the Lloyds. He subscribed through Knott & Lloyd: Knott & Lloyd to C 13 Jun 1809: DCL Folder E.

⋆ Oliver Gammon Esqʳ   Jefferies Square   Sͭ Mary Axe
Oliver Gamon, an oil- and seed-broker: *L P-O* and *J*.

⋆ Mʳ Gasgarth—Matron Ground   nʳ Bowness
Isaac Gaskarth & Sons, cotton and linsey manufacturers: *HAD*.

⋆ Mʳ Jackson Gaskill   4 Minoriers
L P-O lists Jas. Gaskill & Jackson, woollen-drapers, at 4 Minories.

⋆ Mʳ J. George Junʳ   Brunswick Square, Bristol
James George subscribed through Hood: Hood to C 24 Jun 1809; DCL Folder E. He also paid Hood his subscription: Hood to C 3 Feb 1810: ibid. His name also appears in a list of subscribers in Forster MS 112 f 15.

⋆ Mʳ James German   Highfield   nʳ Wigan
No information found.

⋆ Mʳ Thoˢ German   Preston   Lancashire
No information found.

⋆ Miss Gibbons   Ashley Place   Bristol   from Nᵒ 3
She subscribed through W. Hood: Hood to C 24 June 1809: DCL Folder E. She also paid Hood her subscription: Hood to C 3 Feb 1810: ibid. Her name also appears in a list of subscribers in Forster MS 112 f 15.

⋆ Wᵐ Gibbons Esqʳᵉ   Ashley Place   Bristol
William Gibbons, ironmonger, was mayor of Bristol in 1800: John Latimer *Annals of Bristol in the Eighteenth Century* (n.p. 1893) 536. C mentioned his art collection in "On the Principles of Genial Criticism" i: *BL* (1907) ii 222–3. He subscribed through Morgan: Morgan to C 26 Dec 1808: DCL Folder C. He paid his subscription to Hood: Hood to C 3 Feb 1810: DCL Folder E.

⋆ Mʳ James Gibson, Printer—Malton
He subscribed through Wray: Wray to C 4 May 1809: DCL Folder D. He also wrote himself to C 27 Jun 1809 to order *The Friend* from the first number: DCL Folder E. He also appears in a list of subscribers in Forster MS 112 f 15.

⋆ Thoˢ Gibson Esqʳᵉ   Old Bank   NCastle Tyne
He subscribed through Anthony Spedding: Spedding to C (n.d.): DCL Folder E. The Gibsons and the Speddings were related.

⋆ T. Gill Esqʳᵉ—Thetford—Norfolk
He subscribed through Clarkson: Clarkson to C 21 Apr 1809: DCL Folder B.

* Glasgow Public Library—care of M.r Lumsden—Bookseller
   The library subscribed through Robert Grahame: Grahame to WW
   21 Apr 1809: DCL Folder D.
* J. Gleed Esq.r   Barrister   Temple
   John Gleed (b c 1771), who went to Trinity College, Cambridge?
   AC.
* Rev.d H. Glossop   Rickmansworth   Hertfordshire
   Probably Henry Glossop (1780-1869), who was ordained 1805; later
   rector of West Dean with East Grimstead, Wilts: *AC*.
* P. L. Godsall Esq.r   242 Oxford Road
   Probably Philip Lake Godsal (b c 1784): *AO*.
* I. Goldsmid Esq.r   Spital Square
   Isaac Lyon Goldsmid (1778-1859), financier, philanthropist, reformer,
   and book-collector; instrumental in passing the Jewish Disabilities
   Bill, he was the first Jewish baronet, created (1841). He was an
   acquaintance of Southey and a friend of Crabb Robinson.
* M.rs Maxwell Gordon   Albany S.t   Edinb.
   She paid her subscription (13 s.) to G. Ward: Ward & Middleton
   account 10 Jan 1810: DCL Folder E.
* Rob.t Grahame   Ingram Street   writer   Glasgow
   A friend of Wordsworth, Robert Grahame was a solicitor. WW
   wrote to him 26 Nov [1808] asking him to collect names of sub-
   scribers and informing him that his brother in Edinburgh (the poet
   James Grahame) had also been sent a packet of Prospectuses for
   similar reasons: *WL (M)* i 248-9. Grahame replied 21 Apr 1809
   (perhaps in answer to a later letter) with a list of nine subscribers from
   Glasgow: DCL Folder D.
* M.r Grant   Kendal
   No information found.
* M.r Jamesohn Grave, Keswick
   One John Grave was a woollen manufacturer (*HAD*), another, a
   baker (*JCG*).
John Green Esq.re   Dell Lodge, Black Heath, London
   His name appears in a list of subscribers in Forster MS 112 f 15.
   Farington describes a dinner at Green's, at Dell Lodge, 13 Jul 1808:
   Farington v 88; Greig ibid v 88n identifies Green as "Probably George
   Green, of the firm of Green, Wigram, and Green, well known as
   builders of East Indiamen".
* M.r Green   Ambleside
   William Green of Ambleside, the Lake artist (1760-1823). After
   completing the first standard survey of Manchester (1787-94) and
   studying painting in London, he settled in Ambleside (1800). An
   etcher and engraver as well as a water-colourist, Green held yearly
   exhibitions at Ambleside and Keswick. Wordsworth, who owned
   Green's *The Tourists' New Guide to the Lakes* (2 vols Kendal 1819),
   wrote his epitaph. (The *Wordsworth SC* 36 describes the *Guide* as
   "*very scarce*"; there is no copy in the BM.) Hartley Coleridge, a great

admirer of Green, wrote of him: "He taught his pencil, too, as he taught his children—to speak the truth": *Essays and Marginalia* (2 vols 1851) 253.

Mʳˢ Griffiths, Ottery, Devon
She subscribed through C's brother George: G. Coleridge to C 28 May 1809: DCL Folder B.

★ Mʳ Thoˢ Griffiths —Sᵗ James Barton—Bristol
Thomas Griffiths was an apothecary: *MBD*.

★ Mʳ John Gutch   Bristol
A schoolfellow of C's at Christ's Hospital, Gutch (1776–1861) owned and printed *Felix Farley's Bristol Journal* and once owned the Gutch Memorandum Book, C's notebook of *RX* fame. He subscribed through Danvers: Danvers to C 28 Dec 1808: DCL Folder D. He later printed the sheets of *BL*: see above, Introduction, I lxxix n 3, lxxxiv n 1.

★ W. Hall Esqʳᵉ   14 Birchin Lane
L P-O lists Hall & Co, merchants, at the address.

★ Mʳˢ Anthony Hamilton   Sʳ Walter Farquhar   Conduit Sᵗ
Charity (Farquhar) Hamilton, wife of a clergyman noted for his benevolence and his preaching, the daughter of Sir Walter Farquhar. She subscribed through Clarkson: Clarkson to C 21 Apr 1809: DCL Folder B. She discontinued after No 20: Clement to C 19 Jan 1810: DCL Folder E.

★ Mʳˢ Eliz Hamilton   Edinburgh
Elizabeth Hamilton (1758–1816), author of *Memoirs of Modern Philosophers* (1800) and other works, had lived in the Lake country in 1804.

★ Sampson Hanbury Esqʳᵉ
Hanbury (1769–1835), a London brewer, was a cousin of Charles Lloyd Jr: *BLG*. The Hanburys were friends of William Allen (one was Allen's business partner).

★ Joseph Hardcastle Esqʳᵉ   Old Swan, London Bridge, London
DW calls him Mrs Clarkson's uncle: letter of 28 Mar [1808]: *WL* (*M*) I 184. C knew him: see his letter to Stuart c 18 Apr 1808 and to Hardcastle 8 Jun 1812: *CL* III 91, 412. Joseph Hardcastle, Son & Co, of 9 Old Swan Stairs, were merchants: *L P-O*. Hardcastle was treasurer of the London Missionary Society; his "counting-house and offices" were "the birth-place or nursery of some of the noblest institutions that Britain or the world contains: John Leifchild *Memoir of the Late Rev. Joseph Hughes* (1835) 190–1.

★ Joseph Hardcastle Esqʳᵉ Junʳ   Old Swan, London Bridge, London
Son of the above (q.v.).

★ John Harden Esqʳᵉ   Brathay
John Harden, of Brathay Hall (1772–1847), painter, a friend of the Wordsworths; about the time of *The Friend* he left Westmorland for Edinburgh to edit the *Caledonian Mercury*, owned by his father-in-law: [Mary] Gordon *"Christopher North"* I 151.

*M.**rs** Harden   Dublin

Jane Webster of Dublin, who married William Harden 1767: *BLG*. Mother of the above.

* Tho.**s** Hardiman Esq.**re**   Manchester

He subscribed through Ford: Ford to C 4 Jan 1809: DCL Folder E.

* Miss B. Harding   M.**r** Bremridge's   Barnstaple—Devon

Probably care of Samuel Bumridge, a woollen manufacturer: *HAD*. Miss Harding also appears in a list of subscribers in Forster MS 112 f 15.

* Earl of Hardwicke   S.**t** James Square

Philip Yorke, 3rd Earl of Hardwicke (1757–1834), lord lieutenant of Ireland (1801–4). A friend of Thomas Bernard, he was a fellow of the Royal Society and a trustee of the British Museum.

* R. P. Harris Esq.**r**   147 Fenchurch Street

L P-O lists P. Harris & Son, corn- and seed-factors at that address. Harris subscribed through Clarkson: Clarkson to C 17 Feb 1809: DCL Folder B. Harris wrote to C 28 Jul 1809 that he had received the first two numbers, but no more; he assured C that he wished to subscribe and would reimburse him. "Though a perfect Stranger to you personally", he wrote, "I am not a stranger to your writings": DCL Folder E.

* M.**r** W.**m** Harris—Trinity S.**t**—Bristol

Wintour Harris, chamberlain of Bristol: *MBD*.

* M.**r** W.**m** Harris Jun.**r**—Small S.**t** Bristol

Wintour Harris Jr, an attorney: *MBD*.

* M.**r** Harrison   Surgeon   Kendal

Thomas Harrison, surgeon, acquaintance of the Wordsworths: see WW to C [early May 1809]: *WL* (*M*) I 304. He wrote a pamphlet on the Kendal riots of Feb 1818.

Richard Hart Esq   Exeter

Hart's sisters had married C's brothers Luke and George. When told that C and Mrs C had separated, Hart answered an inquiry about C with "I know nothing and wish to know nothing about such a Fellow": C to G. Coleridge 11 May 1808: *CL* III 103. Yet, a year later, he subscribed through G. Coleridge: letter to C 28 May 1809: DCL Folder B.

* Rev.**d** T. Harward   Worcester Col.   Oxford

Thomas Harward (c 1776–1856), fellow of Worcester: *AO*. He subscribed through De Quincey: De Q to DW 21 Mar [1809]: *De Q to W* 115.

* Rev.**d** H. Hasted   Bury   Suffolk

Henry Hasted (1771–1852), lecturer at St James's, Bury St Edmunds (1803–42); friend of William Hyde Wollaston. He paid his subscription to G. Ward: Ward & Middleton account 10 Jan 1810: DCL Folder E. One of Montagu's subscribers? His name appears in the list of subscribers to Montagu's Society: *Account* p 19 (see above, John Backhouse & Co).

★ Mʳ T. L. Hawkes, Birmingham
  Thomas Hawkes, an early friend of C's (see C to J. Wade [22 Aug] 1796: *CL* ɪ 230), who may have introduced him to the poet Charles Lloyd (see *CL* ɪ 235n).

★ B. R. Hayden Esqⁱ   Great Marlbro' Sᵗ
  Benjamin Robert Haydon (1786–1846), painter and critic, who put Wordsworth's portrait into his vast *Christ's Entry into Jerusalem*. Haydon wrote C 10 Nov 1809 that he could not "avoid expressing my thanks, to you dear Sir, for the elevated, heavenly feelings, your sublime, enthusiastic hymn, has raised in me—if you never write again, this will immortalize you": DCL Miscellaneous Coleridge Letters. (The *Hymn Before Sun-rise* had appeared in No 11.) Haydon subscribed through G. Ward: Ward to C 21 Apr 1809: DCL Folder E.

★ Mʳ Hazlewood   Fitzroy Square
  He subscribed through Montagu: his name appears in the list of subscribers on a Prospectus that Montagu sent C (n.d.): DCL Folder B.

★ G. Heald Esqʳᵉ   Barrister   Lincoln's Inn
  George Heald (c 1775–1834): *AC*. He subscribed through Montagu: Montagu to C 22 Feb 1809: DCL Folder B.

Alexander Henderson, 22 Prince Street, Edinburgh
  Henderson (1780–1863), physician, author of *A Sketch of the Revolutions of Medical Science* (1806) and other works. He wrote to C 21 Aug 1809 offering to contribute—especially an article on fashion: DCL Folder D. In a letter of 1 Nov 1809 he said he liked No 12: ibid. He paid his subscription 23 Jan 1810: ibid.

★ George Hibbert Esqʳᵉ M.P.   Mincing Lane
  Hibbert (1757–1837), merchant as well as MP, helped found the London Institution. A friend of Richard Sharp, through whom he subscribed: Sharp to C 12 Dec 1808: DCL Folder C. Hibbert was a well-known book-collector; the sale of his library took forty-two days.

★ Lᵈ Hichingbroke   Grafton Street   Bond Sᵗ
  George John Montagu (1773–1818), Viscount Hinchingbrooke, MP for Huntingdonshire (1794–1814), 6th Earl of Sandwich (1814). He subscribed through his relation, Basil Montagu: Montagu to C 22 Feb 1809: DCL Folder B.

★ Revᵈ Ed. Higginson   Manchester Hill   Stockport
  Edward Higginson (1781–1832), Unitarian minister and schoolmaster at Stockport and Derby. Possibly subscribed through Joseph Strutt (q.v.). Higginson paid his subscription to G. Ward: Ward & Middleton account 5 Mar 1810: DCL Folder E.

Thomas Hill Esqʳᵉ   Queenhithe   London
  Hill (1760–1840), "Prince of Dry Salters" (C to RS [24 Mar 1808]: *CL* ɪɪɪ 80), book-collector, and part owner of the *Monthly Mirror*, appears in a list of subscribers in Forster MS 112 f 15. In a "Commen-

tary on Coleridge's Three Graves" (the poem had appeared in No 6) running over three issues, the *Mirror* printed a savage attack on the poem (see *Monthly Mirror* VIII—Jul, Aug, Sept 1810—26–31, 98–105, 186–196), and in the Nov issue *The Friend* was described as "known to few, and understood by none, the author included" (VIII 322).

Mrs Hincks, 29 Somerset Street, Portman Square
> According to Clement's account of 19 Jan 1810, she had ordered No 4 and all subsequent: DCL Folder E. She also wrote to C 22 Jun 1809 to subscribe to the Poems and Essays advertised in No 2; " . . . at the same time", she wrote, "she cannot help expressing a wish, that the *Essays on Shakespeare, partly promised* to the public, in the Lectures delivered by Mr Coleridge last year, at the Royal Institution, may be *included* in the intended Publication": ibid.

★ Benjamin Hobhouse Esq M.P. 11 Manchester Buildings London
> An acquaintance of C's from early Bristol days, Hobhouse (1757–1831), then MP for Hindon, Wilts, subscribed through Danvers: Danvers to C 28 Dec 1808: DCL Folder D. His son, John Cam Hobhouse, later Lord Broughton, was Byron's friend.

★ Mr Hodgson 67 Lombard Street
> Of the banking-house of Brown, Cobb & Co, at that address? *L P-O.*

★ L. B. Holingshead Esqre Manchester
> Laurence Brock Hollinshead (1778–1838), descendant of the famous chronicler: *BLG.* He subscribed through Ford: Ford to C 4 Jan 1809: DCL Folder E.

★ Henry Holland Esqre—Albany—London
> Son of the architect famous for his alteration of Carlton House and construction of Drury Lane Theatre (destroyed by fire 1809), Henry Holland had been MP for Okehampton (1802–6). His address, Albany, was another of his father's buildings. He subscribed through Clarkson: Clarkson to C 21 Apr 1809: DCL Folder B. He paid his subscription to G. Ward: Ward & Middleton account 5 Mar 1810: DCL Folder E.

Jarvis Holland Esqr Teignmouth Devon
> He subscribed through John Coulson: Coulson to C 28 Apr 1809: DCL Folder D.

★ Richard Holland Esqre Madley n^r Hereford
> He subscribed through Clarkson: Clarkson to C 21 Apr 1809: DCL Folder B. He cancelled his subscription after No 16 because he was leaving the country, and asked how to pay: Holland to C 16 Dec 1809: DCL Folder E.

★ G. L. Hollingsworth Esqre Darlington
> Of Mowbray, Hollingworth and Co, bankers? *HAD.*

Timothy Holmes Esqr—Bury St. Edmunds
> He subscribed through J. Wilkinson: Wilkinson to C (n.d.): DCL Folder C. He paid his subscription to G. Ward: Ward & Middleton account 5 Mar 1810: DCL Folder E.

* Mʳ Hood   Brunswick Square   Bristol

William Hood, Morgan's wealthy friend (and later a benefactor to C), subscribed through Morgan: Morgan to C 26 Dec 1808: DCL Folder C. "My Zeal for promoting your Friend", Hood wrote to C 24 Jun 1809, "is inferior to that of no one, & I have to regret that my Friends are Friendless"; however, he parted with his own copies to satisfy curiosity and so sent in a list of subscribers: DCL Folder E. He also collected subscription payments, sending £10 to C 3 Feb 1810: ibid. As late as 10 Feb 1812 C was authorising Hood to collect these payments: *CL* III 366.

* S. Horrocks Esqʳ Junʳ Esqʳ   Bread Street

Samuel Horrocks, manufacturer, whose sister Jane married SH's cousin, Thomas Monkhouse. Probably subscribed through Monkhouse.

* Luke Howard, Plough Court, Lombard Sᵗ   London

Quaker chemist and meteorologist, Howard (1772–1864) was the business partner of William Allen, also a subscriber. He subscribed through Montagu: Montagu to C 22 Feb 1809: DCL Folder B. He paid his subscription to G. Ward: Ward & Middleton account 10 Jan 1810: DCL Folder E.

* J. Huddart Esqʳᵉ   Merton

Joseph Huddart (1741–1816), who patented a new method of cordage, or his son Joseph?

* H. Huddleston Junʳ Esqʳ   11 Gray's Inn Square

Henry Huddleston, counsellor: *BCG*. He subscribed through Montagu: Montagu to C 22 Feb 1809: DCL Folder B.

* Lady Anne Hudson   Yorkshire

Wife of Harrington Hudson of Bessingby Hall, Bridlington, and daughter of George, 1st Marquess Townshend. She subscribed through Wrangham: Montagu (quoting Wrangham) to C 23 May 1809: DCL Folder B. Her niece, Lady Harriet Townshend, was also a subscriber.

* John Hull   Uxbridge   Middlesex

A friend of Montagu? He subscribed to Montagu's Society: *Account* p 20 (see above, John Backhouse & Co).

* Samuel Hull   Uxbridge   Middlesex

A friend of Montagu? He also subscribed to Montagu's Society: *Account* p 20 (see above, John Backhouse & Co).

The Revᵈ J. J. Hume   West Kington   near Chippenham Wilts

James John Hume (c 1777–1816), vicar of West Kington: *AO*. He subscribed through John Coulson, who described him as "a great friend of [W. L.] Bowles": Coulson to C 28 Apr 1809: DCL Folder D.

* Mʳˢ Hustler, Ulverstone

The Hustlers, a Quaker family, later moved to Dale End, Grasmere. Sara Fox (née Hustler) became a friend of Hartley Coleridge.

* H. Hutchinson 〈Junr 〉Esqre Stockton
Henry Hutchinson (1769–1839), SH's brother, whose release from the Navy C secured after Hutchinson had been impressed: see *CL* III 74–8.

* Mr J. Hutchinson Stockton
John Hutchinson (1768–1833), SH's brother. For his part in advancing money for paper for *The Friend*, see above, I lxiii, lxvi.

* Mr Jackson Keswick
Probably William Jackson, owner of Greta Hall, C's "dear & highly respected Friend & Landlord", who died in Sept 1809: C to Brown [22 Sept 1809]: *CL* III 224.

* Mr Sam! Jackson Manchester
Samuel Jackson, a merchant: *HAD*. A member of the Manchester Literary and Philosophical Society. He subscribed through Ford: Ford to C 4 Jan 1809: DCL Folder E.

* Revd Ben. Jackson Alston-moor
Vicar of Alston, he also officiated at the chapel at Garrigill: *JCG*.

* Wm Jackson Esqr Circus, Exeter
Son of the musician William Jackson (1730–1803) of Exeter? William Jackson, Jr, was in the W. L. Bowles circle of friends: Garland Greever *A Wiltshire Parson and His Friends* (1926) 154, 155. The Jacksons were friends of Thomas Russell of Exeter (q.v.). See C to RS 30 Sept [1799], 15 Oct 1799: *CL* I 533, 539. His name also appears in a list of subscribers in Forster MS 112 f 15.

* Wm Jacob Esqr M.P. 1 Dartmouth St Westminster
William Jacob (c 1762–1851), MP for Rye (1808–12), subscribed through Ridout: Ridout to C 24 Apr 1809: DCL Folder D. Jacob was in Spain 1809–10 (during publication of *The Friend*); his letters home were published as *Travels in the South of Spain* (1811).

* Geo. Jacson Esqr Preston Lancashire
George Jacson (b 1783), later of Barton Lodge: *BLG*.

Mr. Edward James, Christ Church, Oxford
James (b c 1790) matriculated at Christ Church 1808: *AO*. He subscribed through C's nephew, William Hart Coleridge: W. H. Coleridge to C 24 Apr 1809: DCL Folder B. John Coleridge wrote C 20 Jun 1809 that James's address during the long vacation was College Green, Worcester: ibid.

* Hals Mr Halsey Janson Bull Head Passage Wood S.^t
Janson was married to Lucy Lloyd, a cousin of Charles Lloyd Jr: *BLG*. Janson & Coventry owned a flannel warehouse at the above address: *J*. Janson subscribed through Clarkson: Clarkson to C 17 Feb 1809: DCL Folder B. He paid his subscription to G. Ward: Ward & Middleton account 10 Jan 1810: DCL Folder E.

* Francis Jeffrey Esqr 62 Queens St Edinburgh
C sent Francis Jeffrey (1773–1850), editor of the *Ed Rev*, "a small parcel of Prospectuses" c 7 Nov 1808, entreating him "to disperse them as favourably" as he could: *CL* III 126–7.

Joseph Jeffrey Esqre, Bridgewater

> J. Jeffery, an attorney: *HAD*. His name appears in the list of sub-scriptions for collection sent to Poole 12 Jan 1810: BM Add MS 35343 f 369.

★ Mrs Johnson   8 Crescent   Weymouth

> A letter to C from Weymouth, dated 7 [? Jan/Feb] 1809, reads: "Anna Buxton informs S T Coleridge that Sarah Johnson one of the Mistresses of a Girls Boarding School here, wishes to be supplied weekly with a paper of the 'Friend' ": DCL Folder E.

★ Dr Johnstone, Edgbaston—Birmingham

> Edward Johnstone, a physician, of Edgbaston Hall: *BLG*. He sub-scribed through Knott & Lloyd: Knott & Lloyd to C 13 Jun 1809: DCL Folder E.

★ P. Johnstone Esqre 11 Somerset St Portman Square

> Peter Johnstone: *BCG*. He subscribed through Montagu: Montagu to C 22 Feb 1809: DCL Folder B.

Mr. Jolliffe, Grouville Barracks, Jersey

> Charles Jolliffe, an army officer who fell at Waterloo? *BLG*. He subscribed through Capt Wyatt: Wyatt to C 27 Apr 1809: DCL Folder E.

★ —— Jones Esqr Worcester Col.   Oxford

> Probably Theophilus Jones (b c 1788), at Worcester 1808: *AO*. He subscribed through De Quincey: De Q to DW 21 Mar [1809]: *De Q to W* 115.

The Revd Dr Jones—Redland—Bristol

> Thomas Jones, who ran a classical seminary for young gentlemen at Redland (d 1812). He subscribed through John Coulson: Coulson to C 28 Apr 1809: DCL Folder D. Probably the "Jones, Dublin" (he had been educated there) who paid G. Ward £2. 2 for his subscription (and probably that of Henry Lane, whose copies of *The Friend* were sent care of him): Ward & Middleton account 5 Mar 1810: DCL Folder E.

★ Wm Jones Esqre Manchester

> He subscribed through Ford: Ford to C 4 Jan 1809: DCL Folder E.

Thomas Kaye, Liverpool

> Kaye owned and published the *Liverpool Courier*. He wrote to C 14 Sept 1809 that he had not yet obtained any permanent subscriptions, offered to publish an extract from *The Friend* in his paper, and won-dered what to do with the numbers he had on hand: DCL Folder D. C asked him to return unsold copies to Brown: C to Brown [22 Sept 1809]: *CL* III 224. Kaye may have subscribed through De Quincey; see De Q to DW 11 Mar [1809], in which he speaks of a lost letter con-taining names of four subscribers from Liverpool "and some hints for it's [*The Friend*'s] management (which however, coming fm. the Editor of a News-paper, *might* have been very valuable)": *De Q to W* 105. See also ibid 114.

★ Michael Keane Esqre Derby

> Probably Michael Kean (d 1823), miniature-painter who owned the

Derby china factory. Possibly subscribed through Joseph Strutt (q.v.).

★ John Kelsall Esq.ʳ

Formerly a clerk to De Quincey's father, John Kelsall of Manchester, a rich merchant, acted as the De Quincey banker and adviser. See De Q to DW 11 Mar [1809]: *De Q to W* 106.

★ Miss Ann Kemp   28 Richmond Place   Clifton   Bristol

She subscribed through De Quincey's mother: De Q to DW 16 Aug [1809]: *De Q to W* 245. Her name also appears in a list of subscribers in Forster MS 112 f 16.

★ Mʳˢ Kerrich   Harleston   Norfolk

Elizabeth Walker, married to John Kerrich of Harleston? *BLG*. There were, however, several Kerrichs in Harleston: see *AC* and *AO*.

★ G. E. Kiddell—Cumberland Sᵗ.   Bristol

George Kiddell, a Bristol merchant. C called him "Kiddle the Immutable! So have I christened him—for he is the *very same* Being I knew 20 years ago—& a most worthy Being it is": to Mr & Mrs Morgan [17 Nov 1813]: *CL* III 457. Kiddell subscribed through Hood: Hood to C 24 Jun 1809: DCL Folder E. He also paid his subscription to Hood: Hood to C 3 Feb 1810: ibid. His name also appears in a list of subscribers in Forster MS 112 f 15.

★ Thoˢ Kindee Esqʳᵉ   Sᵗ Albans

Thomas Kinder, of St Albans, Herts, who went to Trinity College, Oxford: *AO*. The Kinders were friends of Mrs Barbauld; see *CRB* I 78.

★ John King Esqʳᵉ   Dowry Square   Bristol

King (1766–1846), Dr Beddoes's brother-in-law, the surgeon who treated both C and his son Derwent, subscribed through Danvers: Danvers to C 28 Dec 1808: DCL Folder D.

★ Thoˢ King Esqʳᵉ   Grasmere

Wordsworth's neighbour, who infuriated him by planting larches: De Q *Literary and Lake Reminiscences* ch 9: *De Q Works* II 429–30.

Sir Robert Kingsmill Barᵗ—Sidmanton House, near Newbury, Berks

Sir Robert Kingsmill, 2nd bt (1772–1823), was the nephew of Admiral Kingsmill: *BLG*. He subscribed through John Coulson: Coulson to C 28 Apr 1809: DCL Folder D.

★ R. Knight Esqʳᵉ   Henley in under Warwickshire

Henry Knight, an army officer: *BLG*. He subscribed through Montagu: Montagu to C 22 Feb 1809: DCL Folder B (where his initial is "H."). He paid his subscription to G. Ward: Ward & Middleton account 3 Jan 1810: DCL Folder E.

★ William Knight   Chelmsford   Essex

He subscribed through Clarkson: Clarkson to C 17 Feb 1809: DCL Folder B. Knight and his family were kind to Charles and Mary Lamb during one of her attacks of madness: see Lamb to Thomas and Catherine Clarkson Jun 1807: *LL* II 36.

* Wᵐ Knight Junʳ—Chelmsford—Essex

He also subscribed through Clarkson: Clarkson to C 17 Feb 1809:
DLC Folder B.

Knott & Lloyd, Birmingham

See below, Lloyd Bookseller.

* James Knox   Queen Street   Glasgow

He subscribed through Robert Grahame: Grahame to WW 21 Apr
1809: DCL Folder D.

* T. Koster Esqʳᵉ   Liverpool

John Theodore Koster, a gold merchant whom Southey had met in
Portugal: see RS to Miss Barker 26 Oct 1807: *S Letters* (Warter) ɪɪ
24. According to De Quincey, Koster was an eccentric who denied
that the battle of Talavera ever took place: De Q *Literary and Lake
Reminiscences* ch 3: *De Q Works* ɪɪ 233.

Charles Lamb, No. 4 Inner Temple Lane, London

Lamb (1775–1834), C's schoolfellow and lifelong friend, subscribed
with No 4 (he had bought the earlier numbers from Clement the bookseller). In a letter to Brown 24 Aug 1809 he complained: "They
[copies of *The Friend*] have been ordered at Clement's in the Strand, &
Mʳ Clement refuses to send them, because he says it is an irregular
publication": DCL Folder C. Brown wanted to know if C wished to
continue Clement as his London agent, C replying no: see C to Brown
[11 Sept 1809]: *CL* ɪɪɪ 220. See also above, Introduction, ɪ lv, lxiii.
Lamb also sent in the names of Rickman and Capt Burney as subscribers: DCL Folder C. In a letter to Robert Lloyd 1 Jan 1810 Lamb
wrote that he found *The Friend* "occasionally sublime", but Mathetes'
letter in No 17 "stupid . . . nothing better than a Prospectus, and
ought to have preceded the 1st Number": *LL* ɪɪ 88.

* Revᵈ Jaˢ Lambert   Trinity Col.   Cambridge

James Lambert (1741–1823), Greek scholar, subscribed through
Clarkson: Clarkson to C 11 Mar 1809: DCL Folder B. A note to
Brown with copy for No 23, in SH's hand, asked him to "Send to the
Revᵈ J. Lambert Trin. Col. Cambridge all the Noˢ of the Friend from
the first that you have and those wanting when reprinted and write
with a pencil upon one of them 'the others will be sent corrected &
and amended as soon as reprinted' ": Forster MS 112 f 102ᵛ.

* The Bishop of Landaff, Calgarth

Richard Watson (1737–1816), bp of Llandaff, a neighbour and an
acquaintance of many years, subscribed in a letter to C 4 Dec 1808:
DCL Folder C. In 1801 C thought him "that beastly Bishop, that
blustering Fool": letter to Poole 5 Jul 1801: *CL* ɪɪ 740. According to
De Quincey, *The Friend* was nicknamed *The Delphic Oracle* by the
bishop's daughter, "the kindest of the nicknames which the literary
taste of Windermere conferred upon it": De Q *Literary and Lake
Reminiscences* ch 7: *De Q Works* ɪɪ 372.

* Wᵐᵗ Landor Esqʳᵉ

Walter Savage Landor (1775–1864), recently returned from Spain,

sent C a letter 14 Dec 1808: "Sir   I beg permission to be a sub-
scriber to the publication you announce. Mr Southey sent me the
Prospectus. It followed me from Warwickshire to Clifton, and from
Clifton to Bath. Hence arises my delay in acknowledging the pleasure
I received from it and in offering the congratulations it gives me the
liberty to make": DCL Folder C. On the outside of the folded leaf
C wrote: "Send it back, as I should like to have a specimen of the
Handwriting of so remarkable a man, and of a Genius so brilliant
and original". Landor paid his subscription to G. Ward: Ward &
Middleton account 3 Jan 1810: DCL Folder E.

Henry Lane Esqr.— at Dr Jones   Redland   Bristol
Lane subscribed through John Coulson: Coulson to C 28 Apr 1809:
DCL Folder D. Dr Jones (q.v.) probably paid his subscription.

★ Revd Dr Lawson   Heversham—Milnthorpe
George Lawson (1765–1842), vicar of Heversham, Westmorland: *AC*.

James Lean Esqr   Bristol
Lean was a banker: *MBD*. He subscribed through John Coulson:
Coulson to C 28 Apr 1809: DCL Folder D.

John Ellis Lee Esq   Ottery   Devon
He subscribed through C's brother George: G. Coleridge to C
28 May 1809: DCL Folder B.

★ Heris Grace the Duehesske of Leeds
George William Frederick Osborne, 6th Duke of Leeds (1775–1838),
master of the horse to George iv. He subscribed through Wrangham:
Wrangham to C 12 Jun 1809: DCL Folder B.

Robt Leigh Esqre   Bardon, nr Taunton
Robert Leigh of Bardon (b 1774), a deputy lieutenant for Somerset:
BLG. His name appears in the list of subscriptions for collection
sent to Poole 12 Jan 1810: BM Add MS 35343 f 369.

Wm Leigh Esqre   Bardon, nr Taunton
William Leigh purchased the estate of Bardon from his brother
Robert (above): *BLG*. His name also appears in the list sent to
Poole 12 Jan 1810: BM Add MS 35343 f 369.

★ Abraham Levy Esqre   Templesowerby
No information found.

★ Dr Wm Lewis   Ross   Herefordshire
William Lewis was a friend of Thomas Prichard, who wrote to
C 28 Jun 1809 that he had given Lewis's name to Clarkson: DCL
Folder E. Clarkson had sent in his name to C 11 Mar 1809: DCL
Folder B. His name also appears in a list of subscribers in Forster
MS 112 f 16.

★ Wm Lewis Esqre   23 Berners St   Oxford St
Listed at that address in *BCG*.

★ Lloyd   Birmingham   25 Copies
Robert Lloyd's firm (see next entry).

★ —— Lloyd   Bookseller   Birmingham
Robert Lloyd (1778–1811), Charles's brother, a close friend of Lamb,

and partner in the firm of Knott & Lloyd, which had ordered twenty-five copies of No 1 and included its own name among a list of subscribers sent to C 13 Jun 1809: DCL Folder E. According to a letter of Brown to C c 15 Sept 1809, the firm was sent twelve copies: DCL Folder E. It requested eleven copies of No 3, but Brown had none on hand: ibid.

* Lloyd Esqre   Hawkshead field—Kendal

A member of the large family of Charles Lloyd Sr? Charles Jr was then living at Old Brathay. Possibly his younger brother Thomas (d 1811) or Plumstead (b 1780).

* Mr Chas.^s Lloyd, Banker—Birmingham

C had found the elder Charles Lloyd "a mild man, very liberal in his ideas, and in religion an *allegorizing Quaker*": C to Poole 24 Sept 1796: *CL* I 236. Lloyd subscribed through Knott & Lloyd: Knott & Lloyd to C 13 Jun 1809: DCL Folder E. "I believe thy publication", Lloyd suggested to C 7 Nov 1809, "would please much better if it were more adapted to the capacities of thy general readers many of whom are incapable of comprehending the depth of thy thoughts": DCL Folder C. He also suggested monthly publication, felt that the continuation of essays from one number to another broke "the thread of reasonings", and warned that the numbers were "injured by being folded up as newspapers". He liked Nos 10 and 11 better than the earlier ones.

* Charles Lloyd Esqre

Charles Lloyd Jr (1775–1839), the poet, whose education C had supervised. In late May or early June 1808 WW wrote to C that Lloyd was on the edge of madness: *WL (M)* I 218–19. Lloyd sent his brother Robert Prospectuses of *The Friend* and asked him to procure subscribers: E. V. Lucas *Charles Lamb and the Lloyds* (1898) 240–1. He later wrote to his brother (12 Jun 1809): "I certainly think the first number of The Friend abstruse and laboured in the style—it is evidently written with great difficulty. I cannot say that I am more pleased with the second. . . . If [C] is excited by a remark in company, he will pour forth, in an evening, without the least apparent effort, what would furnish matter for a hundred essays—but the moment that he is to write—not from the present impulse but from preordained deliberation—his powers fail him . . . his inspirations are all *oral*, and not *scriptural*": ibid 244. In appreciation of *Friend* No 23, Lloyd wrote C a long letter on the same subject, faith, 10 Feb 1810: DCL Folder C.

* Mr Robt Lloyd—Birmingham

Robert Lloyd, a banker of the firm of Taylor & Lloyd: *T.* (Taylor's and Lloyd's names follow on SH's list.) He subscribed through Knott & Lloyd: Knott & Lloyd to C 13 Jun 1809: DCL Folder E.

* Mr Saml Lloyd   Banker—Birmingham

Samuel Lloyd (b 1768) married a daughter of George Braithwaite of Kendal; he was a cousin of Charles Lloyd Jr: *BLG*. He subscribed through Knott & Lloyd: Knott & Lloyd to C 13 Jun 1809: DCL Folder E.

Samuel Edw.ᵈ Lloyd Esq.ʳ—Bristol
He subscribed through John Coulson: Coulson to C 28 Apr 1809: DCL Folder D.

★ Mʳ Ralph Lodge   Stockton
Lodge was a brewer: *HAD*.

★ Capel Lofft Esq.ʳᵉ   Troston, Nʳ Bury, Suffolk
Writer and reformer, Capell Lofft (1751–1824) subscribed through Clarkson: Clarkson to C 11 Mar 1809: DCL Folder B. He was a friend of the Wordsworths, and C quoted him in *The Friend*: see above, ɪ 198.

★ E. Lomax Esqʳ   New Square   Lincoln's Inn
Edmund Lomax (1778–1847), a barrister: *AC*. A friend of Montagu?

Longman & Cᵒ.   Paternoster Row
The bookseller and publisher subscribed in a letter to C 4 May 1809, sending a list of other subscribing booksellers: DCL Folder E. A later letter (10 Jun 1809) included the names of two more subscribers and ordered "a dozen more of Nᵒ 1 & 2 dozen of Nᵒ. 2. Clement has also sold all he had": ibid. See above, Introduction lii. According to Brown's letter to C c 15 Sept 1809, Longman received thirty-six copies of each issue: ibid.

★ Countess of Lonsdale   Charles Sᵗ.   Berkley Square
Augusta (Fane) Lowther (1761–1838), wife of the Earl of Lonsdale. (From the address, it was unlikely to have been the Dowager Countess of Lonsdale, widow of the "bad earl", who lived till 1824.)

★ The Earl of Lonsdale   Charles Sᵗ.   Berkley Sq.
William Lowther (1757–1844), Earl of Lonsdale (1st earl of the 2nd creation, 1807), Wordsworth's patron. He blamed C for excluding party politics from the plan of *The Friend*: C to Stuart 13 Jun 1809: *CL* ɪɪɪ 214.

★ J. Losh Esq.ʳ   Jesmond   NCastle
James Losh (1763–1833), attorney and man of letters, recorder of Newcastle. C had read a pamphlet the "good man" had translated (C to Thelwall 6 Feb 1797: *CL* ɪ 308), and in 1802 had dined with him in London (to Mrs C 19 Feb 1802: *CL* ɪɪ 786). James Losh paid his subscription to G. Ward: Ward & Middelton account 5 Mar 1810: DCL Folder E. A fighter for civil liberty, Losh, who had joined the Quakers, was active in the reform movement and was a spokesman of the Whig party in Newcastle: Richard Welford *Men of Mark 'Twixt Tyne and Tweed* (3 vols 1895) ɪɪ 82–8.

John Losh Esqʳ   Woodside—Carlisle
John Losh (1756–1814), brother of the above, a chemist who had founded the Walker Alkali Works, was the squire of Woodside and a friend of J. C. Curwen (q.v.): ibid ɪɪɪ 90–2. He subscribed through J. Wilkinson: Wilkinson to C (n.d.): DCL Folder C.

★ Lady Anne Lowther
Daughter (b 1788) of the Earl of Lonsdale (q.v.).

★ Lady Elizabeth Lowther
> Daughter (1784–1869) of the Earl of Lonsdale.

★ Lady Mary Lowther
> Daughter (1785–1822) of the Earl of Lonsdale.

★ Lord Lowther
> William Lowther (1787–1872), styled Viscount Lowther (1807–44), son of the Earl of Lonsdale, succeeding to the earldom 1844. He was MP for Cockermouth (1808–13). In Disraeli's *Coningsby* he appears as Lord Eskdale. Lowther subscribed through Wrangham: Montagu (quoting Wrangham) to C 23 May 1809: DCL Folder B.

★ Willm Lucas, Junr, Hitchin, Hertfordshire
> A friend of Montagu? William Lucas, Sr and Jr, subscribed to Montagu's Society: *Account* p 20 (see above, John Backhouse & Co).

★ Mr Luff   Patterdale
> Capt Charles Luff, a friend of C, Wordsworth, and the Clarksons. C sometimes broke his journey from Keswick or Penrith to Grasmere by spending the night at Luff's: *CL* ii 911, iii 211.

★ The Revd J. Mackenzie—Thetford—Norfolk
> James Stuart Mackenzie, PC of St Mary Magdalene, Thetford, Norfolk (d 1811): *AC*.

★ Mr Mackereth, Ambleside
> George Mackereth, Grasmere innkeeper and parish clerk (he signed the register when De Quincey was married, Feb 1817: *De Q to W* 278). He is mentioned in the Wordsworth letters: *WL* (*M*) i 44, 54.

★ Mr R^d Macpherson   76 Lombard S^t
> Of the banking-house of Willis, Wood, Percival & Co, of 76 Lombard St? *L P-O*. See below, R^d Percival.

★ Miss Mainwaring—Manchester
> Possibly related to Peter Mainwaring, physician, a member of the Manchester Literary and Philosophical Society. She subscribed through Ford: Ford to C 4 Jan 1809: DCL Folder E.

★ Dr Manson   Golden Square
> Dr Thomson of Golden Square subscribed through Montagu: his name is in a list of subscribers on a Prospectus Montagu sent C (n.d.): DCL Folder B. (In Montagu's rapid hand, the name could be misread "Manson".) Possibly William Thomson (1746–1817), miscellaneous writer; C quoted from two of his travel-books in *The Watchman*. Southey calls him "Dr" Thomson in a letter of 1819: *S Letters* (Curry) ii 198. *BCG*, however, lists a Rev Dr Thompson at No 8 Golden Square.

★ Mr Marshall   New Grange   Leeds
> John Marshall (b 1765), a deputy lieutenant of the West Riding of Yorkshire, whose wife Jane (Pollard) was a childhood friend of DW. The Marshalls were also friends of the Lloyds and the Rawsons. For DW to Mrs Marshall about *The Friend* see *WL* (*M*) i 356.

⋆ Rev.ᵈ H. Martin, Cucklington   n.ʳ Winnaston   ⟨Wimarton⟩
Somerset
   Henry Martin, of Jesus College, to whom C had dedicated *The Fall
   of Robespierre*: see *CL* I 106–7. From 1807 Martin was rector of
   Cucklington. He subscribed through Longman & Co: Longman to C
   10 Jun 1809: DCL Folder E.
⋆ Rev.ᵈ E. Master—Tarleton n.ʳ Ormskirk
   Possibly Edward Masters, later rector of Rufford, Lancs (1816):
   AO.
⋆ M.ʳ Maude, Sunnyside, ⟨Sunderland⟩ Durham
   Perhaps Jacob Maude (1757–1840) or his son Warren (1786–1841),
   who married a daughter of Thomas Wilkinson: *BLG*. Another branch
   of the Maude family lived in Kendal.
⋆ John May Esq.ʳᵉ   Hole   Downton   Wilts
   May (1775–1856), a wine merchant, of Hale, was a friend of both
   Southey and C's brother James; see C's letter to him 27 Sept 1815:
   CL IV 588–90. Southey sent May a Prospectus 4 Dec 1808, one of
   many that he was sending off, "which I do with no very good heart, tho
   certainly not without hope that Coleridge may essentially benefit
   himself and the public": *S Letters* (Curry) I 494–5.
Mr. Mayne, Litchfield
   Perhaps John Mayne of Litchfield (BA 1802): *AO*. He paid G. Ward
   17 s. for his subscription: Ward & Middleton account 10 Jan 1810:
   DCL Folder E.
Alex.ʳ M.ᶜLeay ⟨Esq.ʳ ⟩   N⁰ 12 Queens Square
   Alexander Macleay (1767–1848), of an old Scots family, was secretary
   of the transport board (1806–18) and colonial secretary for New
   South Wales (1825–37). A fellow of the Linnaean Society and the
   Royal Society, he was a noted entomologist. His name appears in a
   list of subscribers in Forster MS 112 f 15.
Kenneth M.ᶜLeay Esq.ʳ   Wick, Caithness   North Britain
   Kenneth Macleay, antiquary and physician practising in Glasgow;
   author of *Historical Memoirs of Rob Roy and the Clan Macgregor*
   (1818). His name appears in a list of subscribers in Forster MS 112 f 15.
⋆ M.ʳ Meggison   Harcourt Buildings   Temple
   Probably Holker Meggison, admitted to the Middle Temple 1806:
   MTA. He subscribed through Montagu: his name appears in a list
   of subscribers on a Prospectus that Montagu send C (n.d.): DCL
   Folder B. The Meggison who "very loudly and before [C] had left
   his rostrum began to abuse him" c 18 Nov 1811? See *CRB* I 51.
⋆ M.ʳ M. L. Merac Jun.ʳ   Aldermanbury
   M. L. Merac were merchants of Old Jewry: *HAD*.
⋆ H. A. Merewether Esq.ʳ   20 Southampton S.ᵗ   Bloomsbury
   Henry Alworth Merewether (1780–1864), barrister in 1809, later
   sergeant-at-law, author of *A New System of Police* (1816) and other
   works. An elder brother of Francis Merewether: see below, Merry-
   weather.

* Rev.ᵈ Francis Merryweather   Haverhill   Essex

   Francis Merewether, younger brother of the above (1784–1864), vicar of Haverhill (1808–15). A friend of Sir George Beaumont, he was rector of Coleorton (1815–64).

* J.ⁿ Miller Esq.ʳᵉ   Worcester Col.   Oxford

   John Miller (1787–1858), fellow of Worcester (1810–23), author of *A Christian Guide for Plain People* (1820) and other works. C sent him 100 Prospectuses: BM Add MS 34046 ff 55, 82. De Quincey wrote to DW 21 Mar [1809]: "I fear that Miller has not come up to college this term; and that the prospectuses may have been sent, and may now be lying unopened in his rooms: I shall therefore immediately write to his brother-in-law, requesting him to distribute them": *De Q to W* 115.

* J. K. Miller   Trinity Col.   Cambridge

   Joseph Kirkman Miller (c 1785–1855), fellow of Trinity (1808), later vicar of Walkeringham, Notts: *AC*. He subscribed through G. Ward: Ward to C 19 Nov 1809: DCL Folder E.

* M.ʳ Miller   3 New S.ᵗ   Bishopgate S.ᵗ

   An associate of Mr Stewart, another subscriber at that address?

* Tho.ˢ Miller Esq.ʳ   at Horrocks & Co   ~~St Mary Axe~~   Preston   Lancashire

   Possibly subscribed through Thomas Monkhouse (q.v.).

* Andrew Mitchell   Ingram Street   writer   Glasgow

   Mitchell (1774–1845), Robert Grahame's apprentice and later his partner; he was active in the anti-slavery movement: [M. D. Acworth] *Recollections of Andrew Mitchell* (Glasgow 1868). He subscribed through Grahame: Grahame to WW 21 Apr 1809: DCL Folder D. Brown wrote to C c 15 Sept 1809: "Mitchell returned 11 Copies of the Friend some time ago, as he has only one subscribed for": DCL Folder E. But this Mitchell would seem to be a bookseller rather than the above attorney.

* Miss Mitchinson   Carlisle

   JCG lists a baker and flour-dealer, M. Mitchinson, and a grocer and flax-dealer named John. Perhaps a member of either family.

* Rev.ᵈ J. Mitford   Kelsales   N.ʳ Saxmundham

   John Mitford (1781–1859), curate of Kelsale (1809), vicar of Benhall (1810), editor of the *Gentleman's Magazine* and of the works of Gray, Cowper, Goldsmith, and others; a friend of Bernard Barton and Lamb. According to Clement's account of 19 Jan 1810, "Mr Mitford, Harlestone" paid his subscription but did not send it post-paid: DCL Folder E.

* John Monkhouse, Hindwell

   SH's cousin, who took a farm in Wales with her brother Thomas; she went for a visit there in the spring of 1810, during the final weeks of *The Friend*. See C's letters to him: *CL* III 121–2, 178–9 298–9.

* M! Monkhouse 10 Charles S! Middlesex Hospital
George Monkhouse, chemist and druggist: *J.* Of the Monkhouses who were SH's cousins?

* M! T. Monkhouse 21 Budge Row
Thomas Monkhouse, SH's cousin. C asked Stuart 28 Dec 1808 to send Monkhouse 20 to 30 Prospectuses: *CL* III 151. Sometime in Feb 1809 he was sent 100: BM Add MS 34046 f 82. He began to collect names of subscribers, which his sister Mary then transcribed and sent to C or SH: see SH to T. Monkhouse 27 Mar [1809]: *SHL* 17. A few weeks later he "decided not to trouble himself any further about *The Friend* until he sees it—there are no want of subscribers": SH to Mary Monkhouse 19 Apr [1809]: *SHL* 20.

* Basil Montagu
Wordsworth's friend (1770–1851), the illegitimate son of the 4th Earl of Sandwich; called to the bar 1798. For his help with *The Friend*, see above, Introduction, I xl, lxviii, and for his part in the Coleridge-Wordsworth quarrel, above, I lxxiii. C sent him 100 Prospectuses at Lincoln's Inn: BM Add MS 34046 f 82. Montagu and Clarkson supplied the longest lists of subscribers.

* Mathew Montague Esq!e Portman Square
Matthew Robinson Montagu (c 1763–1831), MP for St Germans (1806–12), nephew of the bluestocking Elizabeth Montagu, whose correspondence he published (1809–13).

* J. Montgomery Sheffield
James Montgomery (1771–1854), the poet; when C was collecting subscriptions to *The Watchman*, Montgomery was in prison for a libel on a magistrate that appeared in his paper the *Iris*: see C to John Edwards 4 Feb [1796]: *CL* I 182–3. A friend of Mrs Basil Montagu, Montgomery was sent a packet of Prospectuses c 10 Dec 1808: *CL* III 138–9. He subscribed in a letter of 16 Dec 1808, writing that he had sent the Prospectuses round but would be "as much surprized as delighted" if C got two subscriptions from his efforts: "We have no taste for literature in Sheffield": DCL Folder C.

* —— Moore Esq! Worcester Col. Oxford
John Moore (1788–1851), scholar of Worcester (1806–14), fellow (1814–18). He subscribed through De Quincey: De Q to DW 21 Mar [1809]: *De Q to W* 115.

J. J. Morgan, N? 7, Portland Place Hammersmith near London
C had known John James Morgan since 1795. Morgan not only procured subscribers himself (he sent C a list 28 Dec 1808: DCL Folder C), but also had his friend Hood (q.v.) do the same. C lived with the Morgans after his quarrel with Wordsworth.

* M! Morrison Alston-moor
Probably John Morrison, bankers' agent: *HAD.*

J. C. Mottley, Bookseller, Portsmouth
Mottley was Stuart's Portsmouth correspondent; C stayed with this

"dashing Bookseller" while awaiting his ship to Malta: C to RS 28 Mar 1804: *CL* II 1111. C had several Prospectuses sent to him: C to Street [7] Dec 1808: *CL* III 138, and BM Add MS 34046 ff 55, 83.

⋆ M! Mounsey   21 Old Compton Street

Thomas Mounsey, a wine and brandy merchant: *J*. Perhaps related to the Mr Mounsey, a neighbour of the Wordsworths, whose house was of an offensively ugly colour: see DW to Lady Beaumont 7 Nov [1805]: *WL (E)* 538.

⋆ Miss Mune   Exeter   Whitehall

Probably a miscopying of "Mure". Her name follows that of the Marchioness of Exeter in SH's list. In the Glenbervie journals there is an item, dated 20 Nov 1796, of a dinner-party at the Duchess of Hamilton's; among those present was "a Miss Muir, who lives with the Duchess": *The Diaries of Sylvester Douglas* (*Lord Glenbervie*) ed Francis Bickley (2 vols 1928) I 98. The Duchess of Hamilton later became the Marchioness of Exeter.

⋆ John Muney Esq!   Geo. S!   Edinb!

An error of transcription for John Murray, advocate at 122 George St, Edinburgh? *E P-O.* John Archibald Murray (1779–1859), later Lord Murray and a judge, was one of the original joint editors of the *Ed Rev.* A member of the Friday Club.

⋆ M! C. A. Neep   76 Lombard S!

Of the banking-house of Willis, Wood, Percival & Co, of 76 Lombard St? *L P-O.*

Duchess Dowager of Newcastle, Charles Street, Berkeley Square, London

Anna Maria (Stanhope) Clinton (1760–1834), widow of Thomas Pelham Clinton, 3rd Duke of Newcastle, married to Lieut-Gen Sir Charles G. Crawfurd. She subscribed through Clarkson: Clarkson to C 25 Apr 1809: DCL Folder B.

⋆ Josiah Newman   Ross   Herefordshire

A Quaker friend of Thomas Prichard, Newman subscribed through Clarkson: Clarkson to C 11 Mar 1809: DCL Folder B. Prichard wrote to C 28 Jun 1809 that he had given Newman's name to Clarkson: DCL Folder E. Newman aroused C's ire by his "meanness in the mode of payment & discontinuance": "I have received this evening", C wrote Poole 28 Jan 1810, ". . . . N.B. Three days after the publication of the 21st No.—and 16 days after the publication of the Supernumerary—A Bill upon a post master—an order of discontinuance and information that any others, that may come, will not be paid for—: as if I had been gifted with prophecy—and this precious Epistle directed—To Thomas Colerdige, of Grazemar.—And yet this Mr Newman would think himself libelled, if he were called a dishonest man": *CL* III 280.

⋆ M! Newton   Ambleside

Robert Newton, innkeeper, an acquaintance of C and the Wordsworths: see *CN* I 512n, *WL (M)* I 373, 459.

Rev.ᵈ W. Newton, Old Clive, Taunton
> William Newton (b Stowey c 1784)? *AO*. His name is in the list of subscriptions for collection sent to Poole 12 Jan 1810: BM Add MS 35343 f 369.

J. Norris, Taunton
> Norris edited the *Taunton Courier*. He wrote to C 6 May 1809 ordering *The Friend* "regularly . . . until further Notice: if I should get any other Order, I will immediately forward it to you": DCL Folder E. C wrote to Brown c Sept 1809: "The friend is no longer to be sent to Mʳ Norris, Bookseller, Taunton", and asked Brown to bill Longman & Co for postage of two letters from Norris: Forster MS 112 f 15.

* Sᵣ Stafford Northcote, Bᵗ Pynes—Exeter
> The Northcotes had been C's neighbours at Ottery St Mary; Sir Stafford (1762–1851), 7th bt, had found him after a childhood runaway escapade and an all-night search. Northcote's name also appears in a list of subscribers in Forster MS 112 f 15.

Norton & Sons. Booksellers. Bristol
> The London bookseller George Robinson (q.v.) complained that Norton had not received No 1, although No 2 was out: Robinson to C 17 Aug 1809: DCL Folder E. James Norton & Sons were booksellers, stationers, and picture-dealers: *MBD*.

* Alex. Oswald of Shieldhall—Glasgow
> Alexander Oswald, a Glasgow merchant who owned the estate of Shieldhall; he lived to the age of ninety. He was the father-in-law of Andrew Mitchell, another *Friend* subscriber: [Acworth] *Recollections* pp 53–5. He subscribed through Robert Grahame: Grahame to WW 21 Apr 1809: DCL Folder D.

* Dᵣ Paley Halifax
> Robert Paley (1780–1859), a physician; he married a daughter of William Paley, author of *Principles of Moral and Political Philosophy*, a favourite target of C in *The Friend* and other works.

* Mᵣˢ Palmer Holme Park Nʳ Reading
> Jane (Bowles) Palmer (1771–1812), widow of Richard Palmer, an attorney; her eldest son Robert later became MP for Berks: *AC* and *BLG*. She was the daughter of Oldfield Bowles, Sir George Beaumont's old friend and fellow-Etonian. Beaumont sent WW a sample of the poetry she wrote, 12 Dec 1808: DCL Letters from Sir George Beaumont Folder 1. Two of her brothers-in-law were also *Friend* subscribers: Sir George Armytage (married to her sister Mary) and W. Sturges Bourne (married to her sister Anne).

Parker, Oxford
> Joseph Parker, bookseller and publisher, had been at Christ's Hospital with C. George Coleridge had suggested him to C as Oxford agent for *The Friend*: letter to C 16 Mar 1809: DCL Folder B. C's nephew W. H. Coleridge wrote to C 24 Apr 1809 that Parker wanted twenty copies and a Prospectus: ibid. According to a letter

from Brown to C c 15 Sept 1809; Parker received three copies: DCL Folder E.

C. W. Pasley

An army officer, a military engineer, and a military authority of his time, Charles William Pasley (1780–1861) was acquainted with C since the Malta days: see *CN* II 2449 and n. Pasley, who was wounded at the siege of Flushing Aug 1809, paid his subscription to G. Ward: Ward & Middleton account 10 Jan 1810: DCL Folder E. Later that year Pasley published his *Essay on the Military Policy and Institutions of the British Empire*, which soon ran through four editions. See above, De Quincey; also above, I 311 n 1, 544 and n 1.

Henry Patteson, Drinkston, Woolpit

Patteson (1757–1824), rector of Drinkstone, Suffolk (1805–24); his son John married C's niece, Frances Duke Coleridge (1824). Patteson wrote to C 13 Sept 1809 that he had not received Nos 2 and 3: "I must therefore request you to send me Noˢ 2 & 3, & to continue sending the Work as soon as published": DCL Folder E.

★ Miss Pearce, Sidbury, nᵣ Sidmouth, Devon

A relation of William Pearce, master of Jesus College? Her name also appears in a list of subscribers in Forster **MS** 112 f 15. She lived near another subscriber, George Cornish.

Pearson, booksellers, Leeds

Brown wrote to C 18 Sept 1809 that the Leeds postmaster could not find "any Person of the name of Pearson, a bookseller there. I have him on the list for 8 copies": DCL Folder E. C replied [22 Sept 1809]: "Be so good as to desire the Leeds Post Master to send back to you all the numbers sent to the imaginary Pearson": *CL* III 224.

★ Miss Penny   Ambleside   Kendal

Either Jane Penny, daughter of a Liverpool merchant, who married John Wilson May 1811, or a sister.

★ ~~Major Penson~~

Mrs. De Quincey's brother, Major Thomas Penson. His name was deleted because his copy was sent to his sister: see above, Mrs De Quincey.

★ T. W. Pepy's   Sᵗ Johns   Cambridge

Probably Henry Pepys (1783–1860), fellow of St Johns (1806–23), bp of Worcester (1841), a liberal in politics: *AC*.

★ Rᵈ Percival Junᵣ   76 Lombard Sᵗ

Of the banking-house of Willis, Wood, Percival & Co, of that address? *L P-O*.

★ J. Perry Esqᵣᵉ   Morning Chron.   Strand

James Perry (1756–1821), proprietor and editor of the *Morning Chronicle*, an old friend: see C to RS 17 Dec 1794: *CL* I 138. Perry had offered C a job writing for the paper in London, and it was in the *Chronicle*, C said, that his "*first* poetic efforts were brought before the public": C to Perry 25 Jan 1818: *CL* IV 815.

Mrs Peters   56 Park Street   Grosvenor Square
C. Morrison Peters, wife of a banker: *AC*. She subscribed through
Clarkson: Clarkson to C 21 Apr 1809: DCL Folder B.

Geo Philips Esq.
George Philips of Manchester was a friend of Wordsworth: see DW
to Jane Marshall 2 Jun [1806]: *WL (M)* I 27. Having received Prospectuses (probably from WW), he sent them to W. Ford, a Manchester bookseller, through whom he then subscribed: Ford to C 4 Jan
1809: DCL Folder E. Philips had been vice-president of the Manchester Literary and Philosophical Society.

* Richd Phillips, 32 East Street, Red Lion Square, London
Sir Richard Phillips (1767–1840), bookseller and proprietor of the
M Mag, who, after hearing C's conversation at a dinner-party, said
that he wished he had C in a garret without a coat to his back. See
C to RS 18 Feb [1800]: *CL* I 573. Phillips once threatened to sue C;
see C to Poole 19 Jan 1801: *CL* II 665 & n-6. Phillips subscribed
through Montagu: Montagu to C (n.d.): DCL Folder B.

* Honble Mrs Phipps   Harley S.^t
She lived at No 24: *BCG*. Maria (Thellusson) Phipps, wife of the Hon
Augustus Phipps (1762–1822), commissioner of excise stamps, taxes, and
inland revenue (1792–1822). The Phippses were friends of the Beau-
monts. "Mrs. Phipps sd. [1 Jun 1808] Coleridge is no favorite with
Mr. Phipps, & he sd. He . . . was oppressed by Him": Farington v 70.

* Henry Pilkington Esqre   Derby
Henry Pilkington, a barrister (b 1787): *BLG*. Pilkington paid his
subscription to G. Ward: Ward & Middleton account 3 Jan 1810:
DCL Folder E. The "Dominus Pilkington" C asked Brown to strike
from the list of subscribers? See C to Brown c 28 Feb 1810: *CL* III 285.
Perhaps Pilkington had subscribed through Joseph Strutt (q.v.).

* Thos Place Esqre   Spennithorne   n.^r Bedale
Probably Thomas Place, vicar of Kirklington, Yorks (1802–28):
AC.

Revd John Poole, Enmore
Tom Poole's cousin. Poole wrote to him 19 Apr 1809 asking him to
subscribe: *Poole* II 232–3. His name appears in the list of subscriptions
for collection sent to Poole 12 Jan 1810: BM Add MS 35343 f 369.

Thos Poole Esqre, Stowey, Bridgewater
Thomas Poole (1765–1837), tanner ("Lord Chancellor Hyde" to the
Taunton wits), C's intimate friend. For his part in *The Friend*, see
above, Introduction, I lxiii and n 4. Poole wrote to his cousin John
19 Apr 1809: "I have said to some of my friends: 'If you like Coleridge,
take in the work; if you do not like Coleridge, *take it in* and he will
make you like him'": *Poole* II 232. His name is included in the list of
subscriptions for collection that C sent him 12 Jan 1810: BM Add
MS 35343 f 369.

* Mr Porter   Castle Green   Bristol
Joseph Porter, a friend of Morgan, through whom he subscribed:

Morgan to C 26 Dec 1808: DCL Folder C. For his later relations with C see *CL* III 442–3, 444, 445, 451, 452, 507, 514.

★ James Potter   Chelmsford   Essex

A woollen-draper: *HAD.*

James Powles, Ross, Herefordshire

A friend of Prichard, who promised to pay his subscription: Prichard to C 28 Jun 1809: DCL Folder E. His name also appears in a list of subscribers in Forster MS 112 f 16.

Mr Pratt, Malton, Yorks.

A surgeon who subscribed through Wray: Wray to C 4 May 1809: DCL Folder D. He paid his subscription to G. Ward: Ward & Middleton account 3 Jan 1810: DCL Folder E.

Rev⁴ Jaˢ Preedy   Sᵗ Albans

James Preedy (c 1752–1836), ordained deacon 1775: *AC.* He subscribed through G. Ward: Ward to C 3 May 1809: DCL Folder E.

★ T. Prichard   Brook End   Ross   Herefordshire   (2 Copies)

Thomas Prichard, a Quaker friend of Clarkson. Clarkson sent in his name and the names of Prichard's friends Lewis and Newman, saying that the copies could be sent to Prichard: Clarkson to C 11 Mar 1809: DCL Folder B. Prichard wrote to C 28 Jun 1809 that he lacked one copy of No 2 and proposed to pay quarterly for a list of names subjoined: DCL Folder E. C informed Brown: "Thoˢ Prichard Esqʳ of Ross, Herefordshire, received 2 Copies of the 1ˢᵗ Number—of the 2ⁿᵈ but one—The deficient Copy must be sent to him—& 2 Copies of every future number—": Forster MS 112 f 16. Prichard's son James, a physician, who also knew C, was the first to recognise the disease "moral insanity".

Mr Jonathan Priestman, Malton, Yorks.

A Quaker who subscribed through Wray: Wray to C 4 May 1809: DCL Folder D. Priestman wrote to C 2 [? Jan/May] 1810, from Newcastle-on-Tyne, apologising for late payment, sending one guinea to cover the cost of the twenty numbers plus the supernumerary; "I am glad to find the work is continued", he wrote, "for if it had been given up at the end of the 20th No. it would not have been making a fair trial of the Author's powers . . .": DCL Folder E.

Mr Purday   Nᵒ 1 Paternoster Row

He subscribed through Longman & Co: Longman to C 4 May 1809: DCL Folder E.

Samuel Purkis, Esqʳᵉ   Brentford

Like his younger friend, Tom Poole, a tanner; C made his acquaintance in 1798. He acted as Poole's agent in purchasing paper for *The Friend*: see above, Introduction, I lxi–lxii, and C's letters to him [11 Oct 1809], 20 Oct [1809]: *CL* III 243–5, 251–3.

Jaˢ Pyke—Esqʳᵉ   Bridgewater

Of the banking-house of Pyke & Sons? *HAD.* His name appears twice (once for postage due) in the list of subscriptions for collection sent to Poole 12 Jan 1810: BM Add MS 35343 f 369.

W. H. Pyne Esq. N⁰ 38 Great Argyle Street, London
William Henry Pyne, also known as Ephraim Hardcastle (1769–1843), painter and writer, author of *The Costume of Great Britain* (1808) and editor of the *Somerset House Gazette and Literary Museum.* He subscribed through J. Wilkinson: Wilkinson to C (n.d.): DCL Folder C.

★ Fletcher Raincock Esq. Barrister at Law Liverpool
Fletcher Raincock (1769–1840), of Penrith, later deputy judge advocate-general: *BLG.* He was related by marriage to Anthony Harrison, the Penrith attorney who helped proof-read *The Friend*: see DW to Mrs Clarkson 5 Feb 1808: *WL (M)* I 174.

★ Rob. Rankin Esq.ʳᵉ Bristol
Robert Rankin was a merchant: *MBD.* He subscribed through Danvers: Danvers to C 3 Jan 1809: DCL Folder D.

★ M. F. Rawlinson Stable Inn
An associate of Addison and Wentworth, whose office was 11 Staple Inn? See above, M. R. Addison. In 1835 Crabb Robinson dined at the Hardens' with "a Mr. Rawlinson,—a barrister of no practice, but a gentleman residing here of considerable fortune, a very unpleasant man": *CRB* II 472.

★ Stansfield Rawson Esqʳᵉ Breek Halifax
Stansfeld Rawson, of the Breck, Halifax (1778–1856): Joseph Foster *Pedigrees of the County Families of Yorkshire* (1874). Related to the Wordsworths.

★ Wᵐ Rawson Esqʳᵉ Halifax
William Rawson was married to a cousin of Wordsworth's mother; she had brought up Dorothy.

Robert Renell, Exeter
A merchant of Deanery St: *HAD.* He wrote to C 7 Oct 1809 that he had subscribed through Woolmer, the Exeter bookseller (see below, Woolan), and asked that *The Friend* be sent direct to him or c/o John Cole & Co, 72 Basinghall St, London: DCL Folder E.

★ R. Reynolds Esq. Barrister Bedford Row
Henry Revell Reynolds (1775–1853), commissioner of bankrupts (1806–20). He subscribed through Montagu: Montagu to C 22 Feb 1809: DCL Folder B.

★ J. Rhodes Esqʳᵉ Halifax
Possibly a friend of Wordsworth's relations the Rawsons. Of Rhodes & Briggs, merchants? *HAD.*

Mr. Rickman, New Palace Yard, Westminster
John Rickman the census-taker (1771–1840). He subscribed through Lamb: Lamb to Brown 24 Aug 1809: DCL Folder C. For his opinion of *The Friend*, see above, Introduction, I lxvi. He told Poole that he would call on G. Ward in London to pay his subscription: *Poole* II 238.

J. G. Ridout, Paternoster Row

Ridout, a surgeon, Thomas Ward's uncle, was a manager of the Equitable Assurance Society with which C had insured his life for £1000. Ridout wrote to C 24 Apr 1809, enclosing a list of subscribers and promising to send future ones to Longman & Co; he hoped C would not immure himself in the country; "occasional retirement is pleasant, is necessary, but this is the sphere in which you should principally act": DCL Folder D.

George Robinson, Bookseller, 25 Paternoster Row

G. Robinson Jr (d 1811) wrote to C 17 Aug 1809 that too few copies had been sent for their customers; that Norton & Sons had not received No 1; that he had written to Longman & Co, which had referred him to Clement, who had no copies left: DCL Folder E.

Henry Crabb Robinson, 59 Hatton Garden

Crabb Robinson (1775–1867) the diarist, friend of C, WW, and the Clarksons, subscribed through Mrs Clarkson: "I sent your name as a subscriber a little while ago": Mrs Clarkson to HCR [15 May 1809]: *CRC* I 55. He paid G. Ward for two subscriptions: Ward & Middleton account 5 Mar 1810: DCL Folder E.

★ Mʳˢ Robison   17 Sᵗ Mary Axe

Probably a friend of Thomas Monkhouse: SH, in a letter to him, sent her regards to the Robisons: *SHL* 110. Also, Mrs Robison's name occurs in a sequence of subscribers suggesting the list Mary Monkhouse sent SH: see SH to M. Monkhouse 27 Mar [1809]: *SHL* 17.

★ Sʳ Samˡ Romilly   Russel Square

Sir Samuel Romilly (1757–1818), the law reformer, was a friend of the Bishop of Durham, Montagu, and other friends of C's.

★ Wᵐ Roscoe Esqʳ   Liverpool

William Roscoe (1753–1831), author of lives of Lorenzo the Magnificent (1796) and Leo X (1805), an early admirer of C: see C to J. Wade [22 Aug] 1796: *CL* I 230. Roscoe had been "much concerned" when C discontinued *The Watchman* and been "deeply affected" by C's concluding address in that paper: Henry Roscoe *The Life of William Roscoe* (1833) I 232. C described him as a "man of the most delightful manners", with a nice matronly wife and nine children: to Poole 24 Jul 1800: *CL* I 607. Historian, botanist, and banker, Roscoe helped found and was first president of the Liverpool Royal Institution (1817). An anti-slavery fighter and a leader in the struggle for Catholic emancipation, he had been briefly MP for Liverpool (1806).

★ Wᵐ Rose Esqʳᵉ M.P.

Rose subscribed through Sturges Bourne (q.v.). "Among my subscribers", C wrote to Poole 3 Feb 1809, "I have . . . Mr W. *Rose* of whose moral Odor your nose, I believe, has had competent experience": *CL* III 174. C had confused William Stewart Rose (1775–1843), poet and translator, friend of Sir Walter Scott, with his father, George Rose (1744–1818)—a confusion he made again seven years later: see C to John Murray 27 Apr 1816: *CL* IV 635, in which he admits to the confusion. William Rose became reading clerk of the House of Lords.

* Hercules Ross Esqre Peebles n.^{r} Arbroath—N Britain

Ross (d 1816), an intimate friend of Lord Nelson, was a wealthy landowner. He subscribed through Clarkson: Clarkson to C 21 Apr 1809: DCL Folder B.

* Mr Sergeant Rough Bedford Row

William Rough (1772–1838), lawyer and poet, had known C at Cambridge: see *Studies* 92–3. He became sergeant-at-law (1808), judge in Demarara (1816), and chief justice of the supreme court of Ceylon (1836). He subscribed through Montagu: his name appears on the list on a Prospectus Montagu sent C (n.d.): DCL Folder B. A friend of Crabb Robinson, Rough influenced his decision to become a barrister.

* Wm Rowland Esqre Derby

Possibly a relation of Samuel Rowland, mayor of Derby in 1809; he may have subscribed through Joseph Strutt (q.v.). Rowland discontinued after the twentieth number but did not pay: Ward & Middleton account 10 Jan 1810: DCL Folder E.

* J. Rowley Esqre St Neots—Huntingdonshire

Of a well-known family whose seat, the Priory, was at St Neots: *BLG*.

* J. R. Rowntree Esqre Stockton

A woollen-draper: *HAD*.

* Revd J. Rudd Cockermouth

John Rudd of Cockermouth (1771–1834): *AC*. He was a friend and schoolfellow of Wordsworth: *WL* (*L*) II 728. See SH to Mary Monkhouse [autumn 1810] on a sale of livestock: "Mr Rudd bought 3 highest priced Cows—one for 400 Gs another 410 Gs & the third 365 Gs ": *SHL* 24.

* J. Russell Esqr Worcester Col. ~~Cambridge~~ Oxford

Jesse Watts Russell (1786–1875), MP for Gatton (1820–6): *AO*. His father was "an eminent Soap maker . . . worth £500,000": Farington VI 231 (15 Jan 1811). He subscribed through De Quincey: De Q to DW 21 Mar [1809]: *De Q to W* 115. He paid his subscription to G. Ward: Ward & Middleton account 5 Mar 1810: DCL Folder E.

Mr Thomas Russell, c/o J. Green, Esqr., 18 Guildford Street, Exeter

The father of C's friend, Thomas Russell (see below), he subscribed through Longman & Co: Longman to C 20 Feb 1809: DCL Folder E. Russell was a banker who carried on "the great business of the waggons which carry goods to & from London": Farington VI 166 (2 Nov 1810).

Thomas Russell, Esqre, Junior, Russell Waggon Office, Exeter

C had met Russell, then studying art, in Rome in 1806, visited Florence with him, and returned to England on the same ship. C ordered twenty-five Prospectuses sent to him: C to Street [7] Dec 1808: *CL* III 138. Russell wrote to C 20 Feb 1809 that C had mistaken the name of his Exeter agent: it was Woolmer and not Woolan (see below); he also suggested that C send Prospectuses to Edward Upham (q.v.). Russell promised to write to C's agent to send his copies to his "cara sposa", whom he was marrying in April: DCL Folder C. He later wrote G. Ward (16 Dec 1809) that his friend Mr Austwick would pay for the first twenty numbers and asked if Ward could supply a copy of No 1, which he had lost: DCL Folder E.

* James Rust Esqre—Huntington

A banker: *HAD*. He had subscribed through Clarkson: Clarkson to C 21 Apr 1809: DCL Folder B.

Mrs Ryland, Savage Gardens, Tower Hill, London

The widow of Dr Johnson's friend, John Ryland (née Hawkesworth), a merchant who contributed to the *Gentleman's Magazine*. She paid £2 on her subscription to G. Ward: Ward & Middleton account 5 Mar 1810: DCL Folder E.

* Viscountess St Asaph   Berkley Square

Charlotte (Percy) Ashburnham (1776–1862), Viscountess St Asaph, second wife of George Ashburnham, Viscount St Asaph, and daughter of the Countess of Beverley, also a *Friend* subscriber. She was a friend of the Beaumonts; her daughter Jane was the poet Swinburne's mother.

* Wm Salmon Esqre   Devizes

William Salmon, a solicitor, was town clerk of Devizes: *T*.

* Mr Scambler   Ambleside

Richard Scambler (d 1820), the local apothecary and physician who attended the Wordsworth family and to whom C confided his addiction to opium, receiving the answer that it could not be abandoned at once without loss of life; relieved at having no secret to brood over, C claimed that he reduced his dose to one-sixth of what he had formerly taken, and his appetite, health, and mental activity were greater than he had known them for years: C to John Prior Estlin 3 Dec 1808: *CL* III 127–8. Scambler may thus be partly responsible for C's ability to carry through *The Friend*. For SH on Scambler's death, see her letter to Mrs Swaine 19 Sept [1820]: *SHL* 208–9.

Mr Henry Schimmelpenning—Bristol

Probably Schimmelpenninck, a well-known Bristol family of Dutch origin related to the Galtons. He subscribed through John Coulson: Coulson to C 28 Apr 1809: DCL Folder D.

Miss Schimmelpenning—Bristol

See directly above. She subscribed through John Coulson: Coulson to C 28 Apr 1809: DCL Folder D.

Messrs A & D Scott   Book^sr   Glasgow

Booksellers who subscribed through Longman & Co: Longman to C 4 May 1809: DCL Folder E.

* Mr Scott   72 Sun Street   Bishopgate S^t

John Scott (1783–1821), journalist, writer of travel books, and editor of the *London Magazine*? He was a friend of Haydon and Lamb.

Scott died of a wound from a duel provoked by his controversy with Lockhart and *Blackwood's*.

* Walter Scott Esqre Edinburgh

Sir Walter Scott (1771–1832), the novelist; see above, I 122n and n 2. He wrote to RS 20 May 1810: "What is become of Coleridge's *Friend*? I hope he had a letter from me, enclosing my trifling subscription": *The Letters of Sir Walter Scott* ed H. J. C. Grierson (12 vols 1932–7) II 343.

* W. B. Scott Esqre 15 Bucklers Bury

Of Scott and Milne, stock agents: *HAD*. He subscribed through Montagu: Montagu to C 22 Feb 1809: DCL Folder B.

Ed. Sealey Esqre Bridgewater

Edward Sealy, a banker: *HAD*. His name is in the list of subscriptions for collection sent to Poole 12 Jan 1810: BM Add MS 35343 f 369.

* Humphrey Senhouse Esqre Maryport

Senhouse (1781–1841), a naval captain, Southey's friend.

* J. Selmon Esqr Grays Inn Square

Thomas Sermon of 3 Gray's Inn Square, a solicitor: *BCG*. He paid his subscription to G. Ward: Ward & Middleton account 10 Jan 1810 (where his name is "T. Sermon"): DCL Folder E.

* Richd Sharp Esqre Mark Lane   2 copies

Richard Sharp (1759–1835), called "Conversation" Sharp; MP, critic, and wealthy merchant of Boddington & Sharp, 17 Mark Lane; friend of C, WW, and Montagu. He begged to be set down for two copies and also added the names of his friends Boddington and Hibbert: letter to C 12 Dec 1808: DCL Folder C. For his kindness to C in supplying paper, see above, Introduction, I lxiii–lxiv.

Mr Shepherd, Wine Street, Bristol

William Sheppard, bookseller and stationer: *MBD*. C ordered 200 Prospectuses sent to him: C to Street [7] Dec 1808: *CL* III 138; also BM Add MS 34046 f 82. "Great Complaints" were made of him, C wrote Brown c 24 Aug 1809: *CL* III 218; he had used C "most cruelly", C wrote Poole 9 Oct 1809: *CL* III 236. De Quincey told DW 21 Mar [1809] that his sister told him that Sheppard "had received a *great many* names": *De Q to W* 115. Later (16 Aug) De Q wrote DW that Sheppard knew and cared little about the work: ibid 245. According to Brown's letter to C c 15 Sept 1809, Sheppard received eight copies: DCL Folder E.

* Mr Sherer   34 Reg^{t} Grouville Barracks   Isle of Jersey

Moyle Sherer (1789–1869), who took part in the Peninsular War; author of *Sketches of India* (1821) and other works. He subscribed through Capt Wyatt: Wyatt to C 11 Apr 1809: DCL Folder D.

* Saml Shore Esqre Meersbrooke   Sheffield

Samuel Shore (1738–1828) of Sheffield and Mearsbrook, high sheriff of Derby: *BLG*. C had met Shore on his *Watchman* tour: see *CL* I 182–3.

★ Wm Shore Esqre   Tapton   Sheffield

William Shore (1752–1822), a banker, brother of Samuel (above); his son married the daughter of William Smith of Parndon, also a subscriber: *BLG*.

John Sillifant Esq, Coombe, Crediton, Devon

Sillifant (b 1765), a magistrate and deputy lieutenant for Devonshire: *BLG*. He subscribed through C's brother George: G. Coleridge to C 28 May 1809: DCL Folder B.

★ Revd T. Simpson   Worcester Col.   Oxford

Thomas Wood Simpson (c 1784–1868), fellow of Worcester (1812–18): *AO*. He subscribed through De Quincey: De Q to DW 21 Mar [1809]: *De Q to W* 115.

★ Emmot Skidmore, Rickmansworth, Hertfordshire

Emmott Skidmore, coal merchants: *HAD*.

★ Lieut. Col. Sleigh   Stockton

William Sleigh (1758–1825), lieut-col of the 83rd foot. His younger sister, Elizabeth, married John Hutchinson. To SH Sleigh was "the most noble-minded man breathing": to T. Monkhouse 17 Feb 1817: *SHL* 104–5. He was passed over as heir to George Sutton, another *Friend* subscriber.

Mr E. Smedley   Trin: Col: Cambridge

Edward Smedley (1788–1836), contributor to the *British Critic*, editor of the *Encyclopaedia Metropolitana* (1822), and author of *Religio Clerici* (1818). He subscribed through Clement: Clement to C 1 May 1809: DCL Folder E.

Smith & Sons, Glasgow

According to Brown's letter to C c 15 Sept 1809, these booksellers received four copies of each issue. John Smith, of Smith & Son, Glasgow booksellers, was a friend of John Wilson.

★ J. Smith   29 Haymarket

L P-O lists F. Smith, chemist and druggist, at that address. He subscribed through Montagu: his name appears on a list of subscribers on a Prospectus that Montagu sent to C (n.d.): DCL Folder B.

★ J. Smith Junr   29 Haymarket

See above. Probably also subscribed through Montagu.

★ John Smith, Mercer, Thirsk

No information found.

★ Mrs Smith   Coniston   Kendal

Juliet Smith, mother of Elizabeth Smith (1776–1806), Oriental scholar. Southey found Mrs Smith's haughtiness and harshness "exceedingly offensive": RS to J. N. White 30 Sept 1808: *S Letters* (Warter) II 90.

★ Thomas Smith, at the Bank, Uxbridge.

No information found.

★ Thos Woodruffe Smith Esqre   Stockwell Park   Surrey

Smith sent C a present and a letter of approbation of the principles on which *The Friend* was founded: see C's letter to Thomas W. Smith

22 Jun 1809 on *The Friend*, ending with an invitation to Grasmere and Keswick, where Smith would find "house-room & heart-room, and a heaven without to those who have peace within": *CL* III 215–17. Smith (d 1817) was a friend of Southey.

★ Wᵐ Smith Esqʳᵉ   M.P.   Parndon   nʳ Harlow   Essex
William Smith (1756–1835), MP for Norwich, a friend of the Clarksons. C spent several days at Smith's country-seat, Parndon: C to Mrs C 16 Sept 1806: *CL* II 1180–1. Smith attacked Southey in the Commons when *Wat Tyler* was published: see above, I 221 n 3.

★ Wᵐ Smith Esqʳᵉ   Sᵗ Albans
No information found.

★ Professor Smyth   Peter Coll: Cambridge
William Smyth (1765–1849), professor of modern history. He subscribed through George Caldwell: Caldwell to C (n.d.): DCL Folder C. Caldwell wrote C that Smyth was "too much engaged in preparing for his lectures in Modern History" to contribute to *The Friend*: ibid.

★ Mʳ J. Soulby   Bookseller   Ulverstone
John Soulby, printer and stationer, established a circulating library in 1797 "of new and well-chosen books in the superior departments of literature": William Green *Tourists' New Guide* I 22–3.

Soulby, Penrith
Anthony Soulby, printer and bookseller. C mentioned his name as agent to sell *The Friend* and as a possible printer of it: to Stuart 23 Jan 1809, to John Monkhouse 8 Feb 1809: *CL* III 169, 178.

Lieut. Southey   HM Ship Dreadnought, Plymouth Dock
Southey's younger brother Thomas (1777–1838), of whom C wrote to RS 15 Feb 1803 that he had "not for a very long time met with a young man who has made so unpleasant an impression on my mind": *CL* II 925–6. On the face of a letter from Clement to C 7 Oct 1809 was the direction: "Friend Nᵒ 1 & continue to Lieut. Southey HM Ship Dreadnought, Plymouth Dock": DCL Folder E. Lieut Southey paid his subscription to G. Ward: Ward & Middleton account 5 Mar 1810: DCL Folder E. The *Dreadnought*, a ninety-eight, was the ship of Admiral Sotheby, brother of the poet, C's friend.

★ R. Southey Esqʳᵉ   Keswick
Robert Southey (1774–1843) proof-read *The Friend*. For his part in it see above, Introduction, I xlvii, lviii–lix, lxii. In sending some Prospectuses to H. H. Southey 7 Dec 1808 he wrote: "Make what use of them you can in the way of distribution. They are upon too horny a paper for any other use . . .": *S Letters* (Warter) II 114.

★ Mʳˢ Spalding   Devizes   Wiltshire
Possibly the wife of a physician of that name: *T*.

★ Anthony Spedding Esqʳᵉ   46 Gower Sᵗ   Bedford Sqʳᵉ
Anthony Spedding (b 1775) sent C a letter (n.d.) with his own name and those of others wishing to subscribe from the first number: DCL Folder E. The Speddings were friends of the Wordsworths, and Anthony's sister Margaret was married to R. H. Froude, another

Friend subscriber. James Spedding, the editor of Bacon, was Anthony Spedding's nephew.

Mr Spence, Hull
William Spence (1783–1860), a merchant in Hull before he turned to the study of entomology. At the request of his friend Wray, he inserted an advertisement for *The Friend* in the *Rockingham and Hull Weekly Advertiser*: Wray to C 4 May 1809: DCL Folder D. C sent the Hull paper to Stuart: C to Stuart 2 May 1809: *CL* iii 206. Wray describes him as the author of the pamphlet *Britain Independent of Commerce* (it went through four editions 1807–8).

Lady Elizabeth Spencer   Wheatfield House   Tetsworth
Lady Elizabeth Spencer (b 1764), daughter of the 4th Duke of Marlborough, married her cousin, Lord John Spencer. She subscribed through G. Ward: Ward to C 3 May 1809: DCL Folder E. Her brother, the Marquess of Blandford, was also a subscriber. In DCL Folder E there is a slip reading: "W. Clement 201 Strand has had none of N⁰ 5—Lady E. Spencer's paper to be stopped". C wrote to Brown c 14 Oct 1809 to stop her subscription: *CL* iii 246.

Miss Stables, N⁰ 6 Harley Street
Ward & Middleton wrote to C 5 Mar 1810 that she requested C to forward her a set of the papers: DCL Folder E. *BCG* lists Mrs Hibbert at that address—a connexion of George Hibbert, also a subscriber? In 1812 Crabb Robinson dined at Carr's (see above, T. W. Carr), and among such guests as Davy, WW, and Joanna Baillie was Miss Stable, "a large, no longer young, nor perhaps a handsome, but a most elegant figure and fine interesting face: her looks delighted me more than the words of the rest of the party": *CRB* i 91.

* Mr Stewart   3 New St   Bishopgate St
An associate of Mr Miller, another subscriber at that address? At the top of copy for No 6 sent to Brown there is a note to discontinue his subscription: Forster MS 112 f 30.

* George Fredirick Stratton Esqre   Rangers Lodge, near Enstone, Oxfordshire
George Frederick Stratton (1779–c 1834) married a grand-niece of the bluestocking Mrs Delany, friend of Swift and Burney: *BLG*. Possibly subscribed through Montagu, for he also subscribed to Montagu's Society: *Account* p 22 (see above, John Backhouse & Co).

* G. Street Esqr   Courier Office   Strand   London
T. G. Street was co-proprietor and managing editor of the *Courier*. See above, Introduction, i xl and n 4, lvii, lx and n 3. Stuart ordered Street's copy from C: letter to C 30 Mar 1809: DCL Folder B.

* G. B. Strutt Esqre   Derby
George Benson Strutt (d 1841), Jedediah Strutt's second son: *BLG*. C had met Jedediah Strutt, inventor and cotton-spinner, and his sons while canvassing subscribers for *The Watchman*. G. B. Strutt paid his subscription to G. Ward: Ward & Middleton account 5 Mar 1810:

DCL Folder E. All five of Jedediah Strutt's children were subscribers.

★ Joseph Strutt Esqre   Derby

Joseph Strutt (1765–1844), the third son of Jedediah, was the first mayor of Derby: *BLG.* C had once described him as "every way amiable": to Thelwall 6 Feb 1797: *CL* I 306. The poet John Edwards wrote to C 28 Oct 1809 that he had written to Strutt to take *The Friend*, only to discover Strutt a friend of C and already a subscriber; Strutt also reported that he had got C fourteen subscribers, "but that some of them did not like it, on account of its dryness & abstruseness": DCL Folder D. J. Strutt paid his subscription to G. Ward: Ward & Middleton account 5 Mar 1810: DCL Folder E.

★ Wm Strutt Esqre   Derby

William Strutt (1756–1830), eldest son of Jedediah, was also an inventor who worked out systems of ventilation and heating. C once described him as "a man of stern aspect, but strong, very strong abilities": to Thelwall 6 Feb 1797: *CL* I 306. W. Strutt paid his subscription to G. Ward: Ward & Middleton account 5 Mar 1810: DCL Folder E.

★ D. Stuart Esqr   36 Brompton Row   Knightsbridge ⟨2 Copies⟩

Daniel Stuart (1766–1846). For his connexion with *The Friend* see above, Introduction passim, and below, App F, II 474–94. Stuart paid G. Ward £2 for his subscriptions: Ward & Middleton receipt of 18 Jan 1810: BM Add MS 34046 f 120.

★ Geo Sutton Esqre   Stockton

George Sutton (1735–1817), a magistrate of Durham: *BLG.* The, wealthy uncle of Mrs John Hutchinson (née Elizabeth Caroline Sleigh), he passed over Lieut-Col Sleigh (q.v.) to leave his fortune to the Hutchinsons' son, on the condition that the boy take the Sutton name.

★ Sr J. E. Swinburne   Capheaton   Newcastle

Sir John Edward Swinburne (1762–1860), 6th bt, grandfather of the poet Algernon, whom he greatly influenced. "It was said that the two maddest things in the North Country were his horse and himself": A. C. Swinburne to E. C. Stedman 20 Feb 1875: *The Swinburne Letters* ed Cecil Y. Lang III (Oxford 1960) 10–11.

★ Charles Sydebotham Esqre   Liverpool

G lists him as a merchant at 41 Stanhope St; he was therefore a neighbour of the Wordsworths' landlord, J. G. Crump, who lived at No 42. Their names also follow in SH's notebook list.

Richd Symes Esqre   Bridgewater

Richard Symes, an attorney, a friend of Poole; he once tore Paine's *Rights of Man* to pieces and stamped it underfoot (1792): *Poole* I 35–8.

★ Dr Symmons   Richmond   Surrey

Probably the Rev Dr Charles Symmons (1749–1826), at Cambridge to take a DD soon after the trial of William Frend; like C, he expressed sympathy for the French Revolution. He was the author of a *Life of Milton* and a translator of Virgil. He subscribed through

Montagu: his name appears in a list of subscribers on a Prospectus Montagu sent C (n.d.): DCL Folder B.

★ Miss Talbot   6 Southampton S.ᵗ, Bloomsbury

Possibly Frances Talbot (c 1781–1857), daughter of a Norfolk surgeon and apothecary, who married Lord Boringdon 23 Aug 1809. Faringjton, 10 Oct 1809, found Lady Boringdon in a "school with the mistress & scholars" and thought it "a good trait of her Disposition, which promised more happiness than [Lord Boringdon] could have enjoyed with His late divorced vicious wife": Farington v 285; cf ibid v 291. She subscribed through Clarkson: Clarkson to C 21 Apr 1809: DCL Folder B.

★ James Taylor Esq.ʳ   Banker—Birmingham

Of the banking-house of Taylor & Lloyd: *T.* He subscribed through Knott & Lloyd: Knott & Lloyd to C 13 Jun 1809: DCL Folder E.

★ Rich.ᵈ Taylor   38 Shoe Lane

Richard Taylor (1781–1858), printer, naturalist, and linguist, subscribed through Montagu: Montagu to C 22 Feb 1809: DCL Folder B. In an earlier letter from Montagu to C, 11 Feb 1809, Taylor filled the second half with information on type and printing, warning C not to be his own printer (it was the time C was contemplating a printing-press at Grasmere). "But if your friend M.ʳ De Quincy intends to have a press for other purposes (from which, however, he must not calculate on any profit) this will remove the objections", he wrote, ". . . I have a great respect for amateur Printers, and should be very proud to give M.ʳ De Quincy any instruction in my power that he may desire": ibid.

★ M.ʳ W.ᵐ Taylor   ⟨at⟩ M.ʳ Smith's   Preston   Lancashire

Possibly a friend of the Horrocks family.

★ Will.ᵐ Taylor Esq.ʳᵉ   S.ᵗ Helen's   Aukland

William Taylor, of St Helen's, Auckland, Durham, a friend of the Hutchinsons. C sent him a packet of Prospectuses, asking him to disperse them, c 10 Dec 1808: *CL* III 139–40. Taylor replied 29 Dec 1808, subscribing and offering to make arrangements with booksellers in Darlington, Durham, Sunderland, and Newcastle: DCL Folder D.

★ Andrew Templeton   Banker   Glasgow

He subscribed through Robert Grahame: Grahame to WW 21 Apr 1809: DCL Folder D.

Mr P. Thompson   Boston   Lincs.

Pishey Thompson (1784–1862), historian of Boston who moved (1819) to the United States. He subscribed through Clement: Clement to C 1 May 1809: DCL Folder E.

★ Tho.ˢ Thomson Esq.ʳᵉ   Castle S.ᵗ   Edinb.ʰ

Thomas Thomson (1768–1852), an advocate then, a friend of Sir Walter Scott and editor of the *Ed Rev* in Jeffrey's absence. Possibly subscribed through Jeffrey, to whom C had sent Prospectuses. A member of the Friday Club.

* Mrs Merely Tofts, Brandon, Norfolk
  She subscribed through Montagu: her name appears in a list on a Prospectus that Montagu sent C (n.d.): DCL Folder B.
* Miss Pearce Tofts—Brandon Norfolk
  Daughter or sister-in-law of the above?

Jon. Toogood Esqre   Bridgewater
  Jonathan Toogood (1783–1870), a surgeon, founder of the Bridgwater infirmary, author of *Hints to Mothers* (1845) and other works. His name is in the list of subscriptions for collection sent to Poole 12 Jan 1810: BM Add MS 35343 f 369.

Lady Harriet Townshend
  Lady Harriet Ann Townshend (b 1782) was the daughter of the 2nd Marquess Townshend. She subscribed through Wrangham: Montagu (quoting Wrangham) to C 23 May 1809: DCL Folder B.

Revd G. Trevelyan, Nettlecombe, Taunton
  George Trevelyan (1764–1827), rector of Nettlecombe, whose son, Sir Charles Edward, became governor of Madras. His name is in the list of subscriptions for collection sent to Poole 12 Jan 1810: BM Add MS 35343 f 369. According to the Ward & Middleton account of 5 Mar 1810, a "Revd Trevillion" paid his subscription but discontinued.

* Mr E. Upham, Bookseller, Exeter
  Edward Upham (1776–1834), bookseller and orientalist, mayor of Exeter (1809). An acquaintance of C's brother George, who proposed Upham as C's Exeter agent: G. Coleridge to C 10 Dec 1808: DCL Folder B. Thomas Russell (q.v.) wrote to C 20 Feb 1809 to send Prospectuses to Upham, "king of the 'Cormorants at the Tree of Knowledge' in this place": DCL Folder C. Upham's name also appears in a list of subscribers in Forster MS 112 f 15.

* T. Vipond Esqre—Thetford—Norfolk
  Probably Thomas Vipan, a Thetford brewer: *HAD*. He subscribed through Clarkson: Clarkson to C 21 Apr 1809: DCL Folder B.

* Mr Jacob Wakefield   Kendal
  Both a cotton manufacturer and a banker of that name in Kendal: *HAD*. Jacob Wakefield was one of the owners of the *Kendal Chronicle*: A. Aspinall *Politics and the Press* (1949) 354.

* Mr John Wakefield   Kendal
  Probably John Wakefield (1761–1829), Kendal banker: *BLG*.

* Mr G. B. Ward   24 Skinner Street
  George Ward, London bookseller and stationer, brother of Poole's partner, Thomas Ward. C considered him as a possible publisher of the projected "Comforts and Consolations": C to Poole 30 Jan 1804: *CL* II 1046. Ward did many services for *The Friend*: he procured subscribers (letters to C 21 Apr and 3 May 1809: DCL Folder E) and collected subscription payments (Ward & Middleton accounts of 3 and 10 Jan, 5 Mar: ibid). Although he wrote to C 29 Jan 1810 that he could not collect all the subscriptions, he continued to do so.

For Ward's rôle in *The Friend* see above, Introduction, I lxix–lxx; also II 221 and 274.

★ John Ward Esqre　　Bruton—Somerset
Probably a member of the Ward family (above and below). His name is also in the list of subscriptions for collection sent to Poole 12 Jan 1810: BM Add MS 35343 f 369.

★ Mr J. S. Ward—Bruton　　Somerset
The brother of Poole's partner, Thomas Ward. He was a silk manufacturer and merchant: *HAD*. He subscribed through G. Ward: Ward to C 21 Apr 1809: DCL Folder E. He also paid his subscription to Ward: Ward & Middleton account 5 Mar 1810: ibid. His name is also in the list of subscriptions for collection sent to Poole 12 Jan 1810: BM Add MS 35343 f 369.

Thos Ward Esqre　　Stowey　　Bridgewater
Poole's partner, Thomas Ward, whom C had known since Ward was an apprentice. His name appears in the list sent to Poole 12 Jan 1810: BM Add MS 35343 f 369.

★ Revd John Warren　　Ottery St Mary, Devon
Headmaster of the King's School, Ottery St Mary. He also appears in a list of subscribers in Forster MS 112 f 15.

★ Miss Weatherburn　　Sunderland
Possibly related to Ralph Wetherburn, ship-owner: *HAD*.

Josiah Wedgewood Esqre　　Etruria　　Staffordshire
Josiah Wedgwood, son of the potter; together with his brother Thomas he conferred a life annuity of £150 on C in 1798: see also above, Introduction, I lxxviii n 1. C lists him as a subscriber in a letter to Brown [11 Sept 1809]: *CL* III 221 and Forster MS 112 f 10. Wedgwood wrote to Poole 23 Apr 1810 that he did not think *The Friend* would "either raise Coleridge's reputation, or do much good, for very few, I presume, can understand it": *Poole* II 240. Two months later he wrote Poole: "I see the wreck of genius with tender concern, and without a hope": 26 Jun 1810: ibid.

Mr Wells—York-buildings, n^r Baker Street—London
BCG lists W. Wells at 33 York Buildings. Perhaps William Wells (1757–1817), physician at St Thomas's Hospital and contributor to *Phil Trans*. He subscribed through J. Wilkinson: Wilkinson to C (n.d.): DCL Folder C.

Jos. Welsh Esqre　　Bridgewater
His name is in the list of subscriptions for collection sent to Poole 12 Jan 1810: BM Add MS 35343 f 369.

Thomas Westfalling, Esqre, Reed Hall, nr. Ross
He subscribed through Prichard, who promised to pay his subscription: Prichard to C 28 Jun 1809: DCL Folder E. His name also appears in a list of subscribers in Forster MS 112 f 16.

★ Westminster Library　　Jermyn Street
Founded c 1790 as a public library "for the general use of every class

of readers" (prospectus, "Association for the General Advantage of the Republic of Letters": BM 1879.b.13 [19]), it included among its trustees Sir George Leonard Staunton, Henry Beaufoy, James Petit Andrews, David Scott, and Thomas Christie. In 1808 Lord Moira was president of the library: see *LL* II 51. In 1821 its stock, together with that of the London Library, was sold at auction; a copy of the sale-catalogue is in the BM. In Oct 1811 C had "been obliged to spend [his] mornings in Westminster Library": to Godwin *CL* III 335.

★ Mʳ J. Wheelwright 21 Budge Row

The business partner of SH's cousin, Thomas Monkhouse, through whom he probably subscribed. For SH's opinion of him, see her letter to T. Monkhouse 22 Mar [1818]: *SHL* 129–30.

★ Fred White Esqʳᵉ Wallington—Somerset

An acquaintance of Poole in Wellington? Frederic White is in the list of subscriptions for collection sent to Poole 12 Jan 1810: BM Add MS 35343 f 369.

★ Mʳˢ White Bury Suffolk

She subscribed through Clarkson: Clarkson to C 11 Mar 1809: DCL Folder B.

★ Wᵐ Whitehead Esqʳᵉ Worster Col. Oxford

William Baily (or Bayley) Whitehead (1787–1853), fellow of Worcester (1812–13); he helped found a labourer's friend society and promoted the temperance movement. Probably subscribed through De Quincey, then at Worcester.

★ Miles Whitelock Esqʳᵉ Old Change

Of Cowper, Whitelock & Co, "Scotch warehousemen", at No 51: *J.*

★ Mʳ Wilkinson, 18 Change Alley

Possibly James John Wilkinson (d 1848), special pleader and later judge, father of the famous Swedenborgian, James John Garth Wilkinson. He subscribed through Montagu: his name appears in a list of subscribers on a Prospectus that Montagu sent C (n.d.): DCL Folder B.

The Reverend Joseph Wilkinson, Thetford

A friend of Clarkson, Wilkinson sent him a list of subscribers he had obtained: letter to C (n.d. but written after receipt of No 1): DCL Folder C. Wilkinson read No 1 "with much pleasure & interest" and added a few more names of subscribers; he also sought C's and WW's assistance in making a collection of prints "more perfect and acceptable to the public than it otherwise would be": ibid. WW wrote the introduction to these prints, Wilkinson *Select Views in Cumberland, Westmoreland, and Lancashire* (1810). Wilkinson paid his subscription to G. Ward: Ward & Middleton account 5 Mar 1810: DCL Folder E.

★ Thoˢ Wilkinson Yanwath ⟨Penrith⟩

Thomas Wilkinson (1751–1836), a Quaker, friend of C and WW (he was the "friend" of the lines *To the Spade of a Friend*). C wrote him a long letter on *The Friend* and Quakerism 31 Dec 1808: *CL* III 155–7.

Prior to publication of *The Friend* C spent a week with Wilkinson, which made him, according to DW, "the Father of *The Friend*": see her letter to Mrs Clarkson 15 Jun [1809]: *WL* (*M*) I 325.

* Miss Willis   at Col Willis's   Kensington Palace
One of the daughters of Col Henry Norton Willis, FSA, comptroller of the household to the Princess Charlotte of Wales. "He has one Son & three daugrs. the eldest daugr. towards 30 years of age,—the second abt. 23 or 4 highly (Classically) educated": Farington IV 36 (28 Oct 1806). Willis was Col of the Kensington Corps of Volunteers.

* J. Wilson   Trinity Col.   Cambridge
John Wilson, exhibitioner at Trinity College, Oxford (1806–12), fellow (1816–50). He sent C a letter 12 Mar [1809] requesting that he be put on the list of subscribers; his address is "Trinity Col. Oxford", not Cambridge: DCL Folder E. One wonders if he received his copies.

* Mr John Wilson   3 New Court Temple
Possibly John Wilson, of a Stockton family, called to the bar 1811, or, more likely, John Wilson (1785–1851), barrister, author of *Reports . . . of the Court of Exchequer* (1805–17).

* Thos Wilson Esqr   Knights Land   N^r Barnet
Thomas Willson of that address subscribed through G. Ward: Ward to C 21 Apr 1809: DCL Folder E.

* Mrs Witham   Durham
Possibly Elizabeth (Meynell) Witham, widow of Dr Thomas Witham of Durham: *BLG*.

Sir Francis Wood, Bart., Henworth, Pontefract, Yorkshire
Sir Francis Lindley Wood (1771–1846), bt, father of the 1st Viscount Halifax. He subscribed through Wrangham: Wrangham to WW 12 Jun 1809: DCL Folder B.

* Jonathan Wood Esqr   Queen Street
L P-O lists J. Wood, importer of French cambrics, at 86 Queen St, Cheapside.

* W. Woodstock Esqr—Banker   Coventry
An error for Woodcock: it is clearly Woodcock in the letter of Knott & Lloyd to C 13 Jun 1809 where his name appears as subscriber: DCL Folder E. Little & Woodcock was a Coventry banking-house: *HAD*.

Woolan, Exeter
An Exeter bookseller whose name was actually Woolmer: see above, Thomas Russell Jr. Probably Edward Woolmer (1789 or 1790–1856), proprietor and editor of the *Exeter Gazette*. C sent him twenty-five Prospectuses: BM Add MS 34046 f 83. C included "Woolan" in a list of booksellers in a letter to Stuart 23 Jan 1809: *CL* III 169.

Charles Woollam   Esqr   St Albans
He subscribed through G. Ward: Ward to C 3 May 1809: DCL Folder E.

* F. Wrangham Esqre   Hunmanby   Bridlington   Yorkshire
The Rev Francis Wrangham (1769–1842), C's friend from Cambridge days. C sent him 100 Prospectuses (BM Add MS 34046 f 82), and

WW wrote him to circulate them: WW to Wrangham 3 Dec [1808]: *WL* (*M*) I 249–50. For Wrangham's translation of a French poem that appeared in *The Friend*, see above II 235–6; the ms is in DCL Folder B. Wrangham wrote to C 27 Nov 1809: ". . . I look for the post of Saturday with the impatient eagerness of one, who expects the arrival of a valuable *Friend*": ibid.

* Mr Wray   Malton   Yorkshire

Mr and Mrs Montagu, in a letter to C 23 May 1809, quoted Wrangham (obviously in answer to C's query): "Of Mr Wray of Malton, I never heard—it is generally speaking a profligate unliterary place—There is a very intelligent Mr Wray of Hull, who has two sons both ci-devant and lately of Trinity, and that is the only *Ray* of information I can give you upon the subject": DCL Folder B. William Wray was not one of the sons; he was an attorney. Perhaps he is the Wray mentioned by Mary Lamb in connexion with Sarah Stoddart's mother's pension: M. Lamb to S. Stoddart [? 18 Sept 1805]: *LL* I 398. He sent C a letter 4 May 1809 saying that he had put an advertisement for *The Friend* in the *York Herald* and had his friend Spence put one in the Rockingham paper: DCL Folder D. Later, he prepared extracts of *The Friend* for the York and Hull papers: to C 24 Nov 1809: ibid. He paid his subscription to G. Ward: Ward & Middleton account 3 Jan 1810: DCL Folder E.

* Capt Wyatt   34 Reg^t Grouville Barracks   Isle of Jersey

Capt John Wyatt (d 1814), of the 34th Foot or Cumberland Regiment, first wrote to C 11 Apr 1809 that he had heard of C at Cambridge, had read some of his works, and was confident that *The Friend* would "meet the approbation of every classical and ingenuous mind": DCL Folder D. He and his friend Mr Sherer wished to subscribe. A fortnight later he wrote to C 27 Apr 1809: "The Mess Committee of my Reg^t, I am happy to say, shew their Taste by having given an Order for your *Friend*"; Mr Jolliffe of the regiment also subscribed: DCL Folder E. C wrote to Brown c 14 Sept 1809: "I suspect, that Captn Wyatt, my Subscriber, was killed at Talavera—I would not therefore send any more with his Address—if he be alive, we shall soon hear from him—": *CL* III 223. Brown replied 18 Sept 1809 that Wyatt and two other officers had been sent on overseas service and had requested that copies be reserved, for they wished to remain subscribers: DCL Folder E. Capt Wyatt was at Jesus College, Cambridge 1795–9: *AC*.

APPENDIX F

LETTERS CONCERNING
THE FRIEND

LETTERS CONCERNING
THE FRIEND

I. An unpublished letter from John Broadhead to William Wordsworth. See above, Introduction, I xxxviii.

Leeds, 25th of 8th mo. 1808

Resp^d Friend

Having heard of thy intimacy with S. Coleridge and that he intended calling on thee on his way home and not knowing whether his friends might be
under some anxiety from not hearing from him &c I thought this information might be acceptable—

That Thos Clarkson drew my attention to him by Letter which has induced me frequently to seek his Company with which I have been highly
gratified; he has been detained at Leeds about 3 weeks by indisposition
and the sufferings he experiences through the weakness of his nervous
system has excited the sympathy of all who have become acquainted with
him in this place. Though yet very poorly he left this place yesterday in
company with a friend of Leeds going to Lancaster they intended only
going to Bradford last evening & to take the Kendall Coach from thence
this morning & my friend would leave that road near Settle—If S. Coleridge
was well enough to go on he would reach Kendall this evening if not he
would probably stop a night with the Birkbecks at Settle but should he not
reach you in a day or two after the receipt of this I fear he may again be
detained by indisposition and require the care of his friends—

The short acquaintance I have had with S. Coleridge has interested me
exceedingly in the restoration of his health & should he not be well enough
to write me on his arrival—do me the favour to announce it by letter which
would greatly relcive and oblige

thy unknown friend
John Broadhead—

Isaac Wilson of Kendall who is the bearer of this Letter thither may
probably know if S. C. be detained on the road and where—

[Wilson then added a postscript]

Isaac Wilson's respects to W. Wordsworth and in addition to the annexed, can inform him that he yesterday was in company with S. Coleridge
at Settle who had reached that place the preceding Evening he gave a
better acc't of his health than when he left Leeds & purposed continuing

his journey in a day or two he wished to see Maltham Cove and Gordal Scar—if the weather was favourable, which seemed to be the only objects to detain him, so that should he continue as well as he then was he will probably join [you in a] few days—
Kendal 8 month 27th 1808.[1]

II. A letter of subscription from Richard Watson, Bishop of Llandaff, to Coleridge: DCL Folder C. See above, I 19 and n 1.

Calgarth Park 4th Dec[r] 1808

Sir/

I have perused your Prospectus and beg to become a subscriber to the Friend, wishing that it may have an extensive circulation; supported by the sincerity of that wish, I take the great liberty of suggesting to you a measure, the adoption or rejection of which I leave entirely to your own judgment of its expediency or inutility. From my short acquaintance with you, I cannot vouch (which I should wish to do) for your political principles being diametrically opposite to those democratic principles which common fame (perhaps unjustly) imputed to you; and which, with the warmest attachment to the civil and religious liberty of mankind, have always appeared to me unwise principles; but as the prejudice against you has, on that account, been general, I submit to your consideration whether, in the outset of your undertaking, it would not be of use publickly to abandon those principles if you ever entertained them, or to reprobate as calumny the imputation of them if you did not.

I wish talents such as yours not to be obstructed by misrepresentation, or diverted from their progress in promoting virtue, and in advancing knowledge by prejudice and ignorance. When you differ from Locke, I shall probably think that you differ from truth, tho' truth may be with you, & error of opinion with me, but I assure you that prejudice shall not be with me, for I will read with patience whatever you write even against my favourite. Men at my time of life seldom change their opinions on Theoretical Subjects, and one reason of this adherence to præcognita et præconcessa may be, that from the decline of their faculties they shrink from the exertion of that mental energy which is requisite for the investigation of truths not previous[ly] ascertained to them, and instead of positive knowledge, which is rarely to be met with except in the abstract

[1] The cover was addressed by Isaac Wilson: "William Wordsworth Grasmere"; above, Mary Wordsworth wrote: "Mr Cookson's Kendal", and below: "If Mr. Wordsworth has left Elleray Mrs. W. will be exceedingly obliged to Mr. Wilson to forward this letter to him at Kendal this evening—It is of the utmost consequence—". Later the last six words were crossed out. This letter, found in EHC's copy of *L*, is now in the possession of Mr W. H. P. Coleridge.

sciences they rest contented with probability, with verisimilitude instead of truth. Will you allow me to observe that whatever may be your reason for substituting *futuri* in the place of *victuri*, the former I think should have been printed in a different letter.[1]

> I am, Sir, with much esteem your
> faithful Servt
>
> R Landaff

III. A letter to Coleridge from William Savage, printer to the Royal Institution, with his proposals for printing *The Friend*: DCL Folder E. See above, Introduction, I xxxix, xl–xli.

Dear Sir,

I received the copy of the Prospectus of "The Friend" and will immediately print 1000 of it according to your desire; but I do not think the number will be nearly sufficient, to give that publicity which is necessary for a new work: I would recommend at least 10000 in the first instance, and that it should be in octavo, uniform in size with the work, so as to bind up with it, and to circulate them in the Reviews, &c. to the amount of 2000 each month, for twelve succeeding months. This is only to a small extent compared with what is generally done when a new work is wanted to be established.

In the last conversation which I had with you on this subject, it was agreed, if my recollection be correct, that the Copyright of the work should be your property; that I should take the risk of the publication; that is defray the expenses of printing, paper, and advertising, and be repaid out of the first proceeds of the sale; and then the profits to be equally divided between us; I having always the printing and the publishing of the work; and the power of printing it in different sizes in any subsequent editions, if I should think proper, so as to match the usual editions of what are called the "British Classics" or "British Essayists", to which I look forward to its becoming a part: always understanding that the expenses attending these editions will be born by me; and that I shall be repaid, as in the first instance, out of the first receipts of the sale of such edition, and then the profit to be equally divided between us.

I really think that this provision is necessary, as it will tend to make the work have a more extensive, as well as a more permanent, sale, and of course make it a more productive concern, these are my only objects; and it is not with any view to the advantage of printing that I make them, but to meet the Public, after the first edition is disposed of, with sets that will be uniform with their Spectators, &c. as I feel confident of its being a work that will bear to be frequently reprinted.

[1] See above, II 17 and n 1.

The Accounts should be made up every 3, or 6, months, at your option. And I think there should be an understanding, that either party might be at liberty to recede, on giving the other 3 months' notice, or any other period that might be agreed on.

I do not see the practicability of sending the numbers by the post, as you propose. It would certainly be better to let it pass through the Booksellers hands; for when you depart from established rules in trade, you generally get into confusion. I should have, according to the plan of sending them by the post, to open, probably, 500 accounts with people who are perfect strangers to me; and the difficulty, and trouble, of obtaining payment of such subscriptions, particularly where the parties reside at a great distance, is incredible. It would be much easier and simpler to let every gentleman who takes the work receive it through the medium of his bookseller; by which means the accounts will be easily settled, more regularly paid, and the credit given will be much shorter.

If the statement which I have made be correct, you will have the goodness to inform me, when I will have a short agreement drawn up for our signatures; as it is, in my opinion, in transactions of this kind, much better not to leave any thing to future explanation, which may easily be provided for at the first; as it frequently prevents misunderstandings. You will also be so good as to give me your opinion of the size of the paper, whether demy, or royal; and of the type and page, which you would prefer; this you may easily do by referring to English modern books, and informing me which you choose. If you think of demy octavo, which is the most common size, I think it would be an advantage to the sale of the work to make the price of each number *Six pence*, instead of *One Shilling*. The price affects the sale of a book greatly, particularly a periodical publication, unless it be very finely printed, or embellished with plates; and $1\frac{1}{4}$ Sheet may be afforded very well for 6^d which would make it only the price of a weekly Newspaper, an expense that nobody thinks an object.

I remain, Dear Sir,
Yours very faithfully,
Willm Savage.

N° 28, Bedford Bury,
London,
7th December, 1808.

IV. Letters from Daniel Stuart to Coleridge: DCL Folder B. See above, Introduction, I passim.

No. 9. upper Brompton Row
Dear Coleridge
I received your Letter about a week ago, & on monday I obtained your Letter to Street.[1] On tuesday I called on Mr Savage, who not being

[1] For the letter to Stuart [c 6 Dec 1808] see *CL* III 133–4; for that to Street [7] Dec 1808, *CL* III 136–8.

at home, I wrote to him and received a written answer stating he had written to you on the 7th instant and was in dailey Expectation of your Reply. In writing to Mr Savage I made an extract from your Letter to Mr Street. Mr Savage's address is No. 28. Bedford Bury Covent Garden. It seems to me very necessary that you should settle with Mr Savage before you publish. From your conversations, if I recollect rightly he was the Projector of the work & though there was in reality nothing in that, yet he might say you had adopted his plan, leaving him out of it. Let him declare off or on with you.

In giving your Prospectus as an extract of a Letter to a Correspondent, it seems to me, you do not treat the Public with proper respect. The Public itself should be addressed, & to do this would probably require but the alteration of a few words.

The Prospectus should be printed in the shape and on the type precisely as the intended work, thus shewing the Public what it is to be in respect of Size, Paper & type.

You are not aware that no periodical Paper is suffered to be published unless it pays the Stamp duty; especially if a dailey or a weekly Paper. I can recollect an instance as far back as fifteen years of a weekly Paper being set up which neither gave news or advertisements, but was a political Paper like Cobbet; or rather I should say it professedly and carefully avoided giving any thing that could be called news for the purpose expressly of avoiding the stamp duty; but the stamp office interfered and compelled it to pay the Stamp duty. They would compel you also.

All cities & Towns & even villages I believe have communication with the Post. Certainly any Person that would buy your Paper can give you an address by which he will receive it post free.

Why make it a sheet *and a quarter*? A sheet will be quite enough, even for the shilling. Surely you do not take Cobbets price as your Rule, and add a quarter of a sheet because you charge two pence more? Besides Expence to you, the quarter sheet will occasion great trouble. The Paper must be folded and Stitched like a Pamphlet, whereas one sheet is but one piece & folded or not folded no part of it can be lost.

These points adjusted you should publish your prospectus & it should be circulated in the towns you mention. I know Persons in Plymouth & Shrewsbury who will circulate it. We will insert it in the Courier as it now stands, but it would be desireable that you should make a very short address for the purpose of its being advertised in several Papers, & you should have some place of reference in London; some Bookseller perhaps, to answer questions & receive orders, as the Publisher.

When once you begin I have no doubt of your obtaining a sufficient number of Subscribers. I will circulate your Prospectus & I shall be able to obtain a few Customers.

The Essays on Spain & Portugal from Mr Wordsworth have not arrived; but we shall be very glad indeed to receive them, & to pay for them too, if you think that will be agreeable. But at any rate let us have them. The subject is extremely important; the present situation of Spain abounds with new & important subjects for reflexion. I wrote the Letters of X.Y. & should write much more, but I am so indignant about Military affairs that scarce dare trust myself. Never did I hear any Measure so universally execrated as the Cintra Convention. Burrard & Dalrymple are drivelling old women; Wellesley is a bold dashing fellow without brains.[1] Your opinion had struck me strongly before I saw your Letter of Wellesleys saying none of the French from Portugal had yet entered Spain. From several such circumstances he might Easily be proved a weak Fellow. I agree with you that there is much sickness of heart in the Country, among the middle & better part of the People, but I do not see any symptoms of change, nor any Persons or way [to] effect a change. The Public would rejoice if a change were made but they are too much afraid of mischief to make any serious efforts to effect it.

I am very happy to hear that your health and spirits are so well restored, and that you are so comfortable in Grassmere. You may there write your work and publish in London with the greatest ease.

With compliments to M[r] Wordsworth & Family I remain dear Coleridge

Yours sincerely

D Stuart

Friday night 16 Dec[r] 1808.

(turn over).

Saturday morning.—Happening to come to the office I have found your Letter.[2] I shall go to Savage & do as you desire, & shall see Ward— Savage's proposals would have led you into a gulph of debt or obligation; they are most ruinous. You would have been like a young girl who gets into a House of ill fame, & whom the old Bawd always keeps in Debt, stripping her of every Shilling she gets for prostitution. I shall write again soon   Ds

Brompton Saturday Evening

17 Dec[r]

Dear Coleridge

Since I put my Letter to you into the Post I have seen M[r] Savage, and have told him he was not to print the 1000 Prospectuses which he tells me he had not printed. I further stated to him that you considered the probability of any connexion with him in the work as at an end, and that you intended to employ another Printer. He asked my name complained of having been prevented by you from continuing his work, but said he would continue it. I told him yours would be quite a distinct work not interfering with his, & we parted under the understanding of all connexion between you & him being at an end. His plan of circulating so

---

[1] Sir Arthur Wellesley (1769–1852), later the Duke of Wellington, had won a victory over the French in Portugal, but was halted from pursuing the French army by his senior in command, Sir Harry Burrard (1755–1813), who had just arrived. Sir Hew Whitefoord Dalrymple (1750–1830) took command the following day, and the Convention of Cintra followed. All three generals concurred in the convention, which called for the French to evacuate Portugal, and all three, recalled to England following the public reaction to it, were examined by a board of enquiry.

[2] For the letter [c 14 Dec 1808] see *CL* III 141–2.

many Prospectuses and printing so much, though he may very honestly have recommended it, such a plan being necessary for particular works; would however have incurred great expence, in all of which he would have had a large profit, & would have laid you under the necessity of working for a long time, to bring up the arrears, nay a very tolerable circulation would still have left the concern in debt; and if you had declined or been irregular in writing, Mr Savage would have had just cause to complain of your leading him into great expence, leaving him without the chance of repayment, & I think he might in that case have brought an action against you for damages. But as you have totally done with him there is no occasion to say more about him, or to comment at length on his Letter, which otherwise I would do at great length. I made use of a gross simile in the note to my last Letter, but it is tolerable just.

You must allow me to observe that you seem to have proceeded in this Business without due consideration, and, that, now pressed by the approaching new year you would begin rashly and prematurely. This you should by no means do. I think your publication will come under the description of a newspaper, in which case the Proprietor, Printer, and Publisher must personally appear & register themselves on oath at the Stamp office, giving Security for advertisements, & making oath where it is intended to print & publish &c. The Provisions of the act of Parliament are very numerous & must be observed. With regard to a Publisher I have no doubt of being able to find one easily at some Pamphlet shop in the Strand; I dare say I can find a good Printer too; but that they will Register at the Stamp office, standing the chance of prosecutions for Libels in a Newspaper, for that is the terrific light in which they will view the transaction, is what I cannot promise. Here you see is a great difficulty which with Savage could not have arisen. I will put the question to the Stamp office and send you the answer.[1]

Now supposing all these points settled, it will be necessary for you to consider what will be the expence and the profits. The Stamp duty will be 3½; (if a sheet *and a quarter* 7^d!) the Paper will be 1^d making 4½ for Stamp & Paper. We allow out of ^{d}6 to the Newsmen about 1⅛ quite as much as we get ourselves, we having all expences to pay out of *our* profit. I don't suppose you can allow your Newsmen and Publisher less than 3^d so that you will have 4½ for yourself out of which you must pay the expence of printing. This I think will be very much below 5£ (I will enquire)   A sale of 250 would probably pay all current expences & if you sold 500 you would probably have a profit of 300£ per ann:—if 1000, of about 800£

You see how many difficulties arise to me; so many that it would be idle to write more till I enquire. 1st whether the Stamp office will consider yours a Newspaper. 2^d what will be the expence of printing a sheet like Cobbet, & 3^d what does Cobbet allow his Newsmen & Publisher? Savage would have put to rest all this uneasiness; but it appears to me, that, working for him you would be working for nothing. Have you ever considered of a monthly publication? That would be no Newspaper.

<hr/>

[1] See above, Introduction, I xli and n 3.

I approve of your Plan of Principles and objects in the Publication & make no doubt of its success, though you must not expect it to start all once with a great circulation. When it has been published a little time it will be gradually more & more talked of & more and more [will] extend itself. I approve of the price at one shilling ⌐? but that⌐ would take a Sale of 1500 to pay expences! Savage is probably ⌐aware⌐ that it must be stamped.

*Saturday 24 Dec*ᵗ—I have waited a week to get an answer from the Stamp office but have failed though I called twice & wrote a formal application; and as the holidays have begun I have no chance of answer till the end of next week. But I can learn that you may sign the Bonds if necessary, in Cumberland. They say Politics are considered as news; but in the absence of politics & news, they do not think yours would be considered a Newspaper. This is said by the Secretary & a chief Clerk, but I have no answer from the Board. I believe they are at a loss what answer to give though I sent them a Prospectus.—The printing per sheet of 500 copies will cost, like Cobbet, about 5 gˢ—Cobbet allows his publisher one guinea per week, and the News vendors 2 per sheet. As the Paper & stamp must cost him about 4½, he therefore has 3½ profit on each sheet, of which he pays expences of printing publishing &c.—

I have just received Mʳ Wordsworths Packet & shall take it to Brompton to read.—

Yours sincerely
D Stuart.

Brompton—Monday
[10 January 1809]

Dear Coleridge

I wrote you so full a Letter on friday; of instructions about publishing as a Newspaper, that it is scarcely necessary to answer yours which I received on Saturday;[1] but that nothing may be left undecided I send you this to say

As a newspaper you cannot *print* even but on stamped Paper. The Law says we shall not print; and if an unstamped newspaper were found in our office, printed but for the purposes of the Business, never having been out of our office, it would subject us to the Penalty of 50£.—For our own Files even we print on Stamped Paper. Whether you might hereafter *re*print on unstamped Paper, is a question I cannot positively answer. The Law seems to allow of no such thing, & yet I think you might do it.

I disapprove of your having many Persons, say Booksellers for receiving subscriptions & selling the Work. They will lead to confusion & loss. The Post office will do all. It will be sufficient to have 1ˢᵗ Yourself at Grasmere; 2ᵈ One at Kendall; 3ᵈ in London; 4ᵗʰ in Edinburgh; 5ᵗʰ in Bristol; 6ᵗʰ in Exeter & 7ᵗʰ one in York a little metropolis, the head of an extensive great Country. I should disapprove of Exeter even but that you have a

---

[1] Probably C's letter of 28 Dec 1808: *CL* ɪɪɪ 150-2.

local influence there. On this ground you may add any other towns if you please, as Sheffield & Manchester; but in keeping down the number who are to receive Subscriptions & to have on *trust* the work to sell, you will ultimately find a great advantage. If a man at Norwich wants the Work let him write to you for it, & you must send it from Kendall directed to him. At the end of the quarter, half year, or year you may call on him for the price. This is precisely the way, these are the grounds on which the London Papers are served all over the Kingdom by the Newsmen. It should be your object to serve as many as possible, yourself from Kendall, as on each of those your agents serve they will require a profit of $2\frac{1}{2}$ at least, while you may do it from Kendall by giving your publisher $\frac{1}{4}$ on each. This mode indeed will require the employment of a small capital *permanently* but so would the other mode, for sometime at the beginning. If the Paper were published in London indeed, this difficulty of Capital would be removed, as the Newsmen would pay ready money for every sheet they took, they running the risk of being paid by the person they served. This, as you will see is a great convenience to the London News-papers, which thus have no trouble with customers & run no risk of money. To the Newsmen in consequence they allow a large profit, about a penny & a half a farthing per sheet.

But the Capital you would require would be so small that surely it could be no difficulty to your carrying on the Work. Say you began with 200 Subscribers & printed 250. The Stamps and Paper for 250 would cost about 4£—the printing say about 3: 10: 0—you would require about 7 G^s per week. If your number increased to 500, the expence of your Paper & Stamps would be doubled; but your printing would not be increased more than 4 or 5 shillings. I think your friends might prevail on their friends to pay you half a years Subscription in advance, & this might set you a going, or rather keep you a going after you had begun. For begin I would; & when once you had begun & were going on, there would be no difficulty about money.—Your Printer would surely trust you a few weeks, & you could have no difficulty in finding a few pounds for Stamps & Paper.

The Distributor of Stamps who will take your Bonds will supply you with Stamped Paper, on the Sale of which he has a profit. But you should order *good* Paper to be stamped & should see a sample of it, before it is sent for stamping. You may see a sample at Kendall, which the Distributor can send to London, ordering a certain quantity of that to be stamped & sent down to him. I suppose you cannot order less than 1250 which is what is called a quarter of a warrant, the smallest number stamped at the Stamp office. They will cost you about 19 or 20 £. The Stamp money is always ready money at the office in London; but the Distributor may trust you if he chooses.

Persons living in retired Places may either remit to you, or to your London or Kendall Agent, a 20 shilling note for so many weeks, or may pay in the Money to the nearest Post office, & get an order payable to you at Kendall, or payable to your Agent in London. You can say nothing in the Advertisement respecting the mode of payment. It is quite unusual to call for money before hand, & such a call would not be attended to; but your friends may privately procure Subscriptions in advance.

I am surprised you should attach so much importance to the Prospectuses. They should not be issued till the whole plan is settled; you should not ask persons to engage to take your Paper, till you have settled what it is they shall have & how they shall have it. There is nothing in your Prospectus that can persuade a single subscriber: it is your name & your name alone that will procure them. Whenever you start they will follow. There will be no want of Subscribers.

But I have directed 1000 Prospectuses to be printed and distributed as you have desired.

Sincerely yours
D Stuart

Brompton 26 Jany 1809

Dear Coleridge

I received your Letter a few days ago, in which I see you prefer the Newspaper to the Pamphlet,[1]—quite with my concurrence. I had no other reason for enlarging about the Pamphlet, than that it seemed to have been your own original Plan, which I had led you from, that it came nearer to the idea of *a Book* your ultimate object, that there would be less risk or loss in printing a number on speculation, and that the inconveniences of a Newspaper in giving Bonds &c would be avoided. The expence of the Stamp is in reality nothing to you. If you had printed as a Pamphlet you must have been at the expence of another half sheet, which would have been equivalent to the Expence of the Stamp. And the Newspaper has this great convenience, great indeed it is, that one man can put your whole publication into the Post office, & in a minute say,—there;—all your Customers are served, served regularly & infallibly.—

The Letter I wrote last thursday is an answer to yours which I received on monday; but to lose no time, in answer to your last; say the Newspaper.

1 You should go to Kendall agree with your Printer about the price of printing each sheet. For such as Cobbet I was asked 5 G^s a sheet for 1000. For such as Wordsworths Pamphlet 2 G^s for 500. There is but little difference in the number of Sheets; the difference is in the number of Types, the smaller Type having the greater Number. 500 of Cobbet would be at least 4½ G^s You should print on a size or two smaller than Wordsworth, say just one size larger than Cobbet. The Public will expect quantity of matter if not quantity of Paper for a shilling. I would print as you say in Octavo, the lines going right across the Page, not in 2 Columns like Cobbet. You should Print on very good Paper. It will be expected for the money. I suppose the printing of 500 in the way I mention, on the size I allude to will cost about 3 or 3½ G^s Having agreed with your Printer about terms of printing, you must then ask him if he objects to registering as Printer of a Newspaper in which Situation he is also responsible for advertisement Duties. On these two points you may overcome his objection's should he have any, by saying, that by the act of Parliament he must

---

1 For C's letter [18 Jan 1809] see *CL* III 166–8.

print his name to every Pamphlet or handbill he issues, & that in registering as a Newspaper Printer he will incur no more danger than in printing the same matter as a Pamphlet. As to advertisement Duties, you can tell him, you intend to insert no advertisements therefore the risk can be nothing; but as the act says, all Newspapers must give Bonds of security for Advertisement duties, such Security must be given. Some of the weekly Newspapers in London, profess to give no advertisements & really give none, yet they must give Bonds of security for Advertisement Duties, & though they insert no advert^{ts} yet they are charged with trifling sums as Duties. Any thing which benefits an individuals private interests is charged as an Advertisement. The announcing of a new play (in giving an acc^t of its first performance) for a *particular* night is charged as an Ad^t for instance though no charge would be made if no future night were named. Having settled with your Printer about the Price of printing and his signing the Bonds you should next propose to him to be publisher also. As such he must sign the Bonds, no additional risk being incurred he in them already as Printer. As Publisher you may then agree with him how much you should allow him. Here you may make a monstrous saving to yourself. If you publish through the London Newsmen, you must allow them two pence or $2\frac{1}{2}$ per sheet, they paying your agent ready money & running all risks of payment themselves; but yours being a limited, select work going chiefly among your friends, you have no occasion to suffer such a deduction. If you allow your Kendall Publisher, as such, one halfpenny per sheet for his trouble in folding, directing, taking to the Post office & finding Paper for an *open* cover, open at each end, you will allow him liberally. Thus your Stamp per sheet will cost $3\frac{1}{2}$. your Paper nearly 1^d your Publisher $\frac{1}{2}$—in all 5^d so that you will have 7^d each number for yourself. If you print but 250, they being sold & paid will yield a profit after paying for printing of about 4£   If your number rises high the profit will be very great. I would not advise you to print more than 100 beyond your first number of Subscribers, as large impressions on speculation have ruined many a work & individual. You can reprint at any time. You can tell your Publisher that you pay him so little as you will run all the risk of payment from the Subscribers, the consideration for which large profit is allowed. In fact your Publisher will rather be your Agent. He must keep a set of Books for you, a Ledger perhaps, alone, will do, in which should be entered every Subscribers account, when & what he pays &c—You should pay the Printers Bill weekly & the Publishers Bill weekly. And whatever money he receives on your account, he should pay you weekly. You should each keep a cash account against each other. I think you should also yourself keep a Ledger, the counterpart of his, in case he should use you ill. For if he had all Knowledge of your customers & you had not he might domineer. When I say Ledger, I perhaps frighten you. A Small Alphabetical memorandum book is all that is necessary in which should be entered every Customers name, when he begins, when & what he pays, when he leaves off &c—a few words, not to say lines would keep such an account for years. Your Ledger should be corrected by the Publishers weekly & his by yours. You will order & pay for the printing of a certain number weekly. Of this you must keep an account, & weekly you should count the numbers unsold, comparing them with the numbers for which the Publisher has accounted, settling the Cash &c—This will frighten you by the vastness of the Business; but it may all be done in as short a time as I have been writing.

2 Having settled with your Printer, and as such, Publisher also, Country Printers being usually Shopkeepers or Booksellers, you will next go to the Postmaster, (Post office) of the town (Kendall). Tell him what you intend to do, & that as he may be astonished at finding some hundreds of Newspapers popped into his Letter Box some night, you think it best to apprize him before hand. The Law says respecting Newspapers that only such shall go free of postage, as shall be sent pursuant to an order signed by a member of Parliament given in to the Post office of the district, which order shall specify the name & address of the Person to whom the Member wishes the Paper to be sent. And then the Paper must be folded in a cover open at each end, that it may be seen to be a Newspaper, pulled out & examined for the Stamp if necessary, and above the direction must be written the name of the Member, say: "J. C. Curwen Esq.ʳ M.P."— Though the Law says all this yet it is found impossible & unnecessary to attend to the Law. In fact the Newspapers pay such a monstrous revenue to Government that the Law is knowingly by Government, & necessarily & wisely, overlooked. Of the 20 or 30,000 Papers which go off every night through the general Post office, I dare say not twenty or 30 go off according to Law, & that if any M.P. were to send a formal order to the P.O. for sending or rather franking a Paper to a friend his order would be laughed at & thrown into the fire. It is however understood that he who thus franks a Newspaper has the permission of the M.P. whose name he uses. So far appearances are kept up. But most of the Papers are sent off in the names of Members of Parliament who know nothing of the Person who uses their name, & I should have no more hesitation in franking a Newspaper with the name of the Lord Chancellor or of one of the Royal Princes than with that of any M.P. whom I most intimately know. The only case I have heard of enforcing the Law strictly was against an Edinburgh Newspaper called the Scots Chronicle, about 14 years ago, at the time of the Scottish Convention with Muir, Palmer, Skirving, whose part this Paper took,[1] &c, and the enforcing of the Law of franking strictly against it, knocked it up. It is very difficult to obey the Law strictly. Its enforcement would half ruin the London evening Papers, would hurt the revenue & compel the Post office to double their number of Clerks. Suppose you send a great number to any particular town; say you send 200 to London. I would have you send each directed to the individual to whom it was destined & each would then be delivered as regularly as a Letter; but should you have occasion to send a large quantity to one hand, be not afraid of this. We send 2 quire every night to Liverpool franked in the Common way of a single Newspaper though making a Parcel as large as my thigh, & I should have no fear of sending safely & regularly to you at Grasmere a quantity of Papers which would require

1 Thomas Muir (1765-98), T. F. Palmer (see above, i 334 n 2), and William Skirving were separately tried for sedition and sentenced, 1794, to transportation to Botany Bay.

a cart to be carried, free of expence. Having explained to the Kendall Postmaster that he may not be taken by surprise and embarrass you, you will tell him that you have Mr Curwens permission for franking all your Papers. You may as well get a Letter from Mr Curwen to him to that effect, which should mention you, the name of your Paper, & the town in which it is to be published & the Printer & publishers name. Tell the Postmaster then to satisfy himself previous to your first publication, that he may not embarrass it; and that if he finds any difficulties, Mr Curwen or other friends by application to Mr Freeling at the Gen P.O. London may in time remove them.

3^d. Having settled with your Printer, Publisher, and the Post office you will next proceed to the Distributor of stamps for the District. Tell him your intention of publishing a Newspaper &c—Give him in writing: 1st your own name as Proprietor, & the name of the Person at Kendall as Printer & Publisher, stating that you reside at Grasmere & intend residing there; that your Printer & Publisher resides at —— in Kendall & intends residing there, and that it is your intention to print and publish the said Paper naming it, at the House of the said —— in Kendall.—2 you will give him on another slip in writing, with a view to a Bond for Security of Stamp Ad^t Duties; your own name as Proprietor, the name of your Printer & Publisher, who *must* be responsible, & the names of 2 friends as Securities. Wordsworth & Southey will be quite sufficient, or any two, or any one person perhaps. The Security will only be for 100£ or 200£. This Bond does not render the Parties liable for libels; only for Ad^t duties. The first Bond is with a view to Libels. Having given in these particulars, you will ask the Distributor when the Bonds will be ready, that you may fix your time of publication. You will then consult him about supplying you with stamped Paper to print on which he will be anxious to do as he gains a profit by it. About your Paper you should have previously consulted your Printer, & have obtained a sample, which you should give the Distributor, desiring him to let you have 1000 (perhaps he will recommend 1250, which you may take) by such a day & asking if you can rely on him. A thousand will cost about 14£. You must tell the Distributor you mean to sell at more than ^{d}6 per sheet as this makes a difference in the amount of stamp Duties, & the Paper must be differently stamped. Papers selling at or below ^{d}6 are allowed 12 per cent discount on the Duty.

4 And now having settled with your Printer & Publisher, having explained to the Post office & Distributor of Stamps, & having a reasonable Prospect of being enabled, *permitted*, to publish by a particular time; Now you should set about your *Prospectus*, which may be printing and circulating while the Stamp & Post offices are settling your other Business. To the Business part of your Prospectus only I speak. You should state in it the size, the sized Type, the quantity, the price, the day of publication, that it like other Newspapers will go to all of Britain free of postage. To Ireland, I think a penny must be paid with each, to the Colonies none. You should date your prospectus from Grasmere near Kendall, saying you yourself desire to receive all orders, subscriptions & communications (postage free) but that your Printer & publisher, M^r —— of Kendall is

authorized to receive them and so is M^r —— of London, M^r —— of Edinburgh &c—I would say nothing of beginning *when* you had a certain number of Subscribers, but *I would begin* printing only 250. unless you have more than 200 orders. When your friends & the Public see the work afloat then the Subscribers will come in. I would advertise the first number well, and all the numbers a little in the London Newspapers. A short advertisement, with your name, the name of the Paper, the Price & where it was to be had would be quite sufficient. It is your name alone which will bring customers in the first instance & your abilities which will retain them. There is no occasion for any long story to induce persons to subscribe. I have not the slightest doubt of the success of the work if you keep it up with spirit; but you must not expect to start with a large body of subscribers. They will follow you to a certainty. There is no necessity for your publishing on Saturday more than on any other day. There are so many trumpery weekly Papers in London, that publishing from the Lakes will be a recommendation; and as to circulation, the G.P.O. will do all that for you, so that it will be the same to your Subscribers whether you date at Grasmere & print at Kendall, or date at Grasmere & print in London

And now I wait your commands respecting the Prospectuses. Will you print them in Kendall or London? I have all your Letters & know where to send the different Parcels. If you send me a Copy finished agreeably to my instructions in this Letter I will get what number you desire printed in London, & sent or circulated from hence; but I have more reliance on a few Advertisements in the London Papers, when once you shall have published No. 1. than on all the Prospectuses. If the Public know *you* are publishing they will find out the way to read. It is not the custom with Newspapers to expect Subscribers to pay in advance, nor should you require it. Such as do pay in advance may assist you in going on. You may stipulate for payment every quarter. A very small capital will carry on the work for a quarter, & the profit will be so large in proportion to the sale that if you lose $\frac{1}{3}$ you will gain, on the whole. Subscribers should subscribe in writing, by Letter say, & enquiry should be made, where it can be made, in great towns, such as London into their character. A London agent will be essential, and a good one. A shop the best, (Booksellers) where some one will always be in the way to answer questions, & some numbers should be here for sale. Bristol Exeter & Edinburgh should also have Agents, none of them being agents for distribution which will be done by the Post office, but all of them for chance sale & getting subscribers, for answering questions, circulating Prospectuses &c. But Kendall & London would ultimately be the only two spots for agents. The Post office would obviate all necessity for them Elsewhere. I would have you date every number from Grasmere: it will be signed with your own name, (in print) must have your Kendall Printers & Publishers name & should name your London Agents also. I suppose you may start in the first week of March. I am Dr Coleridge

yours sincerely
D Stuart

Dr Coleridge

Mr Clarkson has ⌈. . . . .⌉ some days & has written some ⌈. . . . .⌉ at your not appointing Longman ⌈. . . . .⌉ that you could not with ⌈. . .⌉ appoint any others; he will do the whole for 5 per cent &c.[1] This has puzzled me much respecting the Prospectuses, as I cannot put a London Booksellers name to them, consequently cannot, advertise in the London Papers as I intended that the Prospectuses are to be had at such & such Booksellers. However I shall print a thousand & send them round as you have directed, without any London agents name.

I have seen Mr Clarkson this Day. He thinks if you make the Work a Newspaper that possibly, it would not then be convenient or necessary for Longman to be concerned. He thinks it should not be a Newspaper; but a ⌈? Pamphlet. In that⌉ case Longman would ⌈. . . . .⌉ off your hands, on the ⌈. . . . .⌉ with Savage of 5 per ⌈. . . . .⌉ there will be no risk. This would be a good plan.—You will recollect I inclined to this at first, but yielded to the Newspaper Plan which has its advantages.

Mr Clarkson agrees with me in not printing the Prospectuses on quite so large a Size. They will be out tomorrow.

I am Dr Coleridge
Yours &c

Tuesday 7 feb   D Stuart

Dear Coleridge[2]

The Prospectuses are out. yesterday I sent 100 to Mr Monkhouse by Mr Clarksons desire, & 100 to Mr Clarkson himself; also 100 to Basil Montague. Parcels go off this Day to Cautley, to Oxford, to Wrangham, to Bristol to Stowey. Tomorrow, or thereabouts I shall have finished my List, when I will send it you correct. In a day or two I shall put in an Advertisement; so that every thing shall be done by me to get Subscribers names. By the inclosed you will see I have had the Prospectuses set up on both sizes, this & yours. Mr Clarkson & myself decidedly approved of this size & so I have printed 1000 on it; but you may have others on the large size if you desire them. That I might not lose time by boggling about Longman as publisher, I have inserted his name without asking his permission. Mr Clarkson would write to you on that subject; & I shall say no more; except to observe that I still think the Pamphlet plan has its advantages, (*I do not say beyond* the Newspaper Plan). If Longman printed [&] published as a Pamphlet, taking only 5 per cent & his profits as a Bookseller, you would have no sort of trouble beyond producing your M.S. & you would require no money to go on with. For Longman would no doubt deem himself well secured by seeing a List of your Subscribers & knowing that they were to pay their money to him. As a Pamphlet too you might print a large number for future sale without risking much loss. I merely state these circumstances, hoping they will not bewilder you. Either plan has its advantages. For my own part I cannot decide.

[1] See above, Introduction, I xlv–xlvi. The top of the sheet is torn, making the beginning and end (overleaf) of the letter difficult to read.

[2] This letter is written on the blank pages of the Prospectus.

Your scheme of printing at Grasmere, I approve highly. The great difficulty will be in finding a steady good Printer. He should be a married man, & you should know his character & habits well. If one failed you could no doubt get another. Upon all this Business Mr Pennington can advise you better than me. I know that Country printers are bred to work *Press* & *Case* (Compositors) I do not suppose there can be any difficulty getting a Press & Types long before the 1st May. We had a new press lately & got it in a fortnight. You should print on the same types as this Prospectus & I have no doubt a sufficient quantity for your purpose might be found at any Founders. There is an excellent Type-Founder at Glasgow, the name of Nelson, who sends a great deal of type to London to the best Houses. The Morning Chronicle is printed on it. You may send to him for a specimen & to know if he has any ready. You can have a Press &c from Glasgow or Edinburgh also, these towns being but half the distance of London, the Articles being as good or better, & cheaper. Perhaps you must have a man from Edinburgh to fix up the Press, as common Carpenters know nothing of the matter, but on this Mr Pennington will advise you. Indeed on all points he must be your Adviser; [? for do not come] to me on all points of detail, such as the quantity of type, the Sorts, the Press, Cases, furniture, Store, chases, Ink &c &c There will be a great multitude of little things to get, but they are not expensive. As to the Plan itself, if *I* were in your Situation, I would adopt it with delight; of all things it would please me. It did not escape me; I long ago thought of it, but I would not recommend it. For you will excuse me in saying there is a great difference between you & me; and you and your friends should well consider how far it is wise thus to accumulate sources of anxiety & vexation on you who are so easily disheartened.

I recollect M^r De Quincey perfectly & envy him the pleasure he will feel in pursuing his proposed Plan. I know nothing of Lord Stanhopes Press. You should take care not to be misled by it—consult Mr Pennington. I see no difficulty in the way of your Plan, no objection to it, but the trouble in which it will involve you. I have made no Enquiries because I am sure the Types & Press may be had in time. The *Printer,*—he is the great object of consideration.—A man of your Country would be much better than a Londoner. On this Mr Pennington can advise you. There must be plenty in Newcastle & Liverpool; a greater plenty still in Edinburgh & Glasgow; & several no doubt at Kendall, Penrith, Lancaster, Whitehaven & Carlisle. You should not look south for a man. I should prefer a steady intelligent man from Edinburgh or Glasgow, to one from London; but the Printer is *of great importance.* He is every thing.— There are many advantages; & to me there would be many pleasures in printing at Grasmere. I should approve the Plan, whether as Newspaper or Pamphlet; excepting for *the trouble,* so take care of that.—

You expressed your opinion of the Duke of York's case on the second days examination.[1] I also was then of your opinion; but the Business is

[1] Frederick, Duke of York, commander-in-chief of the army, had been charged in the Commons with misusing military patronage. His mistress, Mary Ann Clarke, had demanded and received bribes from officers eager for promotion, and he was accused of sharing in the proceeds. Though

now most awfully altered. By yesterdays examination York convicted in his own hand writing. He must go to trial, & that will be as bad as conviction; for we can scarcely expect the House of Peers to convict the King's 2ᵈ, his favourite Son. This business must produce great changes: it may be the death of the King, or may derange the Ministry. There is no saying what it will do. It is unfortunate that it should happen at such a time; it must occupy the attention of Ministers to the exclusion of the affairs of Spain &c which they are determined to support; but it is most fortunate in itself, that such a millstone about our neck as the Duke of York should be got rid of.

I am Dʳ Coleridge

Yours &c

Tuesday 14 febʸ 1809   D Stuart

The Courier is the only Paper which has dared speak out agˢᵗ the Duke.—

Dear Coleridge

On Saturday 1250 of Stamped Paper left London by the waggon for Penrith, addressed to Mʳ John Brown Printer there, & I was assured it would reach Penrith in 8 days. On monday I wrote to you, to this Effect; & as I have heard from Mʳ de Quincey this day that you are remaining at Penrith till the first number is published I address this Letter to that place.

You may publish No. 1. on Saturday the 15ᵗʰ of april, & certainly no reference to the beginning of a month should delay you. Early next week I will advertise, the whole Prospectus shall be inserted in the Courier & I will endeavour to have the same done in the Morning Post. When once you begin there can be no doubt of your obtaining a sufficient number of Subscribers. I would not have you print many beyond the actual demand; not certainly more than 50. The Stamps and Paper of 50 if lost would cost as much as reprinting a sheet, which you might afterwards do either with or without Stamps, as the Expence will only be 1: 7: 0.—Send me 2 Copies to Brompton Row No. 36.—and send Street one at the Courier office.

Fourdrinier & Co the Stationer, in Sherborne Lane, Lombard Street does I find supply Stamped Paper. You had better write to him, sending him a Copy of your first number. We have no transactions with them. I have sent a note to Bernard to pay the 60£ to the Courier office;[1] but I have not yet heard from him.

Whoever folds up your Papers to go by Post must leave them open at both ends, as Newspapers are, that it may be visible what they are & you

---

acquitted, he resigned as commander-in-chief, only to be reappointed two years later. For C's opinion of Gwyllym Lloyd Wardle, the soldier and politician who pressed the charges, see a letter to Poole 3 Feb 1809 and another to Stuart 15 Apr: *CL* iii 174, 195. See also above, i 260 and n 2.

[1] Thomas Bernard, of the Royal Institution; see above, Introduction, i xlviii–xlix, xlix n 1.

must put a Member of Parliaments name on—In all this do precisely as Newspapers do.

I am Dr Coleridge yours sincerely

D Stuart

36 Brompton Row
30 March 1809

Brompton, Tuesday night
[19 April 1809]

Dear Coleridge

I yesterday put a Letter into the Post to you, & this day I received a Letter from you. Your observation about the want of a leading paragraph made me laugh.[1] I had not been in town that day & was really as much surprized as your friends; but I soon understood then guessed the reason to be the late arrival of the gazette, the anxiety to insert it all & the necessity of going to press, circumstances which squeezed out the leading paragraph. I have never even mentioned the circumstance to Street. Out of your Letter I have written a paragraph or two. I am sorry Mr Curwen who acted so ably & independently lately & who I think properly supports the Character of a Country Gentleman should be captivated by such a silly Sarcasm as Burdetts about Gentlemen agriculturists. Politics & Agriculture are perfectly compatible. Burdett himself does not work so hard in politics but that he might cultivate Farms. He comes forward but now & then; but he dislikes seeing independent men of weight in the Country joining his mob standard; therefore he had a fling at Coke, Curwen, Byng, Whitbread &c &c.—this infamous desertion of poor Paul,[2] without even a pretext shews this to be his spirit or rather perhaps the spirit of Horne Tooke.[3] Wardle as you will have seen has declined the Whig Club.[4]—I have no doubt that the Grenvilles & Howicks[5] are feeling their way to power through the Duke of York, who is in reality at this moment the King of this Country. Both Ministry and Opposition are equally corrupt

[1] For C's letter of 15 Apr 1809 see *CL* III 194-6; it was the *Courier* that lacked the leading paragraph.

[2] Thomas William Coke (1752-1842), Whig MP, later Earl of Leicester of Holkham; Sir John Byng (1772-1860), then a lieutenant-colonel, a veteran of the Walcheren expedition, later the Earl of Strafford; Samuel Whitbread (1758-1815), Whig MP whose motions for peace split his party in 1809. James Paull (1770-1808), also a Whig politician, formerly a friend of Burdett and Whitbread, fought a duel with Burdett in 1807 (they were both wounded), resulting in a pre-election attack by John Horne Tooke (1736-1812), who published *A Warning to the Electors of Westminster* (1807). Paull replied with *A Refutation of the Calumnies . . .* (1807) and, when he lost the election, which he attributed to Whitbread, published *A Letter . . . to Samuel Whitbread*. Ill of his duelling wounds and in debt from gambling, Paull committed suicide.

[3] See above note.

[4] See above, II 486-7 n 1.

[5] William Wyndham, Baron Grenville (1759-1834), Whig statesman, had been lord of the treasury (1806). Charles Grey, then Viscount Howick (1764-1845), later Earl Grey, was at this time trying to control the dissident Whig leaders such as Whitbread.

Parties, only the one is in the other out of Place. Indeed they are in character but one Party. The Burdett Revolutionists are another; the Saints as they are called a third, having more real weight both in & out of the House of Commons than any one section of the Court Party. I think them the most honest & valuable Party. There is a great tendency I think between certain parts of the Ministry & certain parts of the opposition to unite & form another "All the talents" Ministry. Alarm at the Public danger will be the pretence, & such a step will aggravate the danger. Indeed they are a selfish set on both sides, though there are some good men among them. Cannings speeches of late have not at all pleased me. They have been pert & personal; seeing only in the D.Y.s case the splendour of the King's son sinking out of sight the responsibility of a Public servant. About state policy & morality, I think you mean one & the same thing. The Copenhagen say was immoral but policy made it moral, for nothing can be politic which is not moral, consequently state policy and public morality are one & the same thing. Copenhagen is immoral at first view but go into the reasons & they make it moral—so with other things.

I shall insert your advertisements as you have directed. Clement will I suppose expect to serve the orders he gets & to have a profit out of them. I wrote to you to send him 1 or 2 dozen. They will be asked for & in London at least they should be to be had. I can get you a Bookseller both in Plymouth & Portsmouth, Mottley—but they will expect to serve their Customers & get a profit—However that can be arranged hereafter. I know not your plan about paying; but it is not the custom with such works to get payment till a Bill has been given. However I think you may ask payment at the end of 20 weeks & give notice of your intention so to do. There is a way of remitting money through the G. Post office, not by Bank notes, but by money orders which is perfectly secure. The money is paid into the Post office say at Bridgwater & an order given payable at Penrith. The expence of this is either sixpence or 1^{sh} in the pound which with postage would indeed deduct about 2^d per Paper. But in great towns particularly in London the Money may be collected by an Agent & the expence of remitting 20£ will be no more than in remitting 20^{sh} Then you may be able to let some of your Customers in retired situations go on a year without paying which will diminish the expence of Collection. I have got the receipt on Bernard. The money I shall lay out in Stamps & Paper as soon as you direct. The 60£ will buy nearly 4000.

I am Dr Coleridge,
Yours sincerely
D Stuart

I shall write to Mr Wordsworth tomorrow (turn)
of course you have got the Paper at Penrith. How do you like it?

Dear Coleridge

Not being satisfied with the Report of the Clerk & Porter I this day went into the City purposely to enquire after the Parcel of stamped Paper. It was taken in at a waggon Inn in friday Street, from thence sent to the Red Lion Inn Aldersgate Street, where on the 25 March it was put into the

Waggon & left London. The London waggoners are Deacon & Co. And this Red Lion waggon does not go by York but by Halifax & Kendall. Deacon & Co convey to Halifax to Clarkson & Co.—Clarkson & Co at Halifax convey to Kendall;—to Docker at Kendall—it is thought. And Docker at Kendall conveys to Penrith. On my return from Aldersgate Street [I] yesterday wrote from the Courier office: to Clarkson at Halifax—to Docker at Kendall & to your Printer Brown at Penrith acquainting them with the whole of the Circumstances & urging them to see the Goods forwarded.

The Paper is a large sized Octavo. In size & quality as nearly as possible I believe the same as Cobbet, who prints upon very costly Paper.

Being in the City I enquired at Baldwins about Wordsworths Pamphlet, & was much vexed to hear Mr Baldwins account of it. He says that in the whole course of his Business, he never knew so much chopping & changing, so much cancelling & correction, that he supposes he has got the whole but in forming that supposition he has several times already been deceived, & that he cannot say when it will be done, till it is done. He plainly told me that the multitude of alterations, corrections & cancels would greatly inflame the expence of printing. And I know him to be a very honest man.

Now this is the very thing I wished to guard against in the first instance. I, of myself changed the long notes, into an appendix as I know notes inflame the expence, & I ordered only 500 to be printed distinctly stating to Wordsworth that there would soon be an opportunity of making a second Edition in which he might set all to rights, which it would be impossible to do in the first one. About 3 or 4 weeks ago I informed M^r De Quincey to the same effect & even remonstrated against notes & many great alterations; urging the necessity of publishing immediately after the Easter Holidays & making him promise to write to Wordsworth. Now the whole of my prudence is upset. The Expence of printing will be great, the Edition small, the Season nearly expired.—

I do not know what understanding may exist between Mr de Quincey & Mr Wordsworth; probably my fears arise from mistake: but I wish Mr Wordsworth had trusted to himself to send the Pamphlet to Press. We got on much faster when it was in his own hands. I am quite satisfied of Mr de Quinceys amiable character & kind intentions;—but these are nothing on such an occasion.

I scarcely know whether it is right in me to write to Wordsworth, to interfere between him and Mr de Quincey, & therefore leave the matter [to] your discretion

I am Dr Coleridge
Yours &c &c

26 april 1809   D Stuart

I have got the Receipt, but not yet the money from Mr Bernard.

Dear Coleridge

On the 15th of this month there were sent 1250 more Stamps & Paper by the Kendall Waggon from the Bull & Mouth directed Mr Cookson, manufacturer,—& marked J. B. I hope they have arrived safely. The remainder of the 60£ in Greens hands, shall be laid out in Stamps & Paper, as soon as you direct. As I have heard nothing of the *Friend* I am afraid you are indisposed. For this last month I have been dissipating very much, dining or dancing out almost every day, neglecting business and almost forgetting politics. I am glad to tell you Wordsworth's Pamphlet is out, after many delays which have vexed me much. I have great confidence in its success in all ways,—in political influence—in popularity & in money—

I am Dr Coleridge

Yours &c

D Stuart

27 May 1809

36 Brompton Row

7 July 1809

Dear Coleridge

On wednesday last went off by the Kendall Waggon directed Mr Cookson Kendall, as the preceding Parcel, 1250 Stamps; and on friday went off another Parcel containing 1250 more, so that you have now enough for 8 numbers in all, & I will send sufficient for 2 more before it is wanted.

You should have some general Agent, a man of Business, in London, to receive your Subscriptions & buy Stamps. Longmans House appears to me the most proper for this Business & I make no doubt they will forward to you the necessary Stamps for carrying on your Paper agreeably to the plan laid down in my last Letter.

I am Dr Coleridge

Yours &c

D Stuart

at Stiles's Boarding House, Cheltenham

Septr 25th 1809

Dear Coleridge

I have been here two months. A few days ago I received your Letter with your 3. 4. & 5. Numbers which I have read with great satisfaction, particularly the 3^d The 5th seems to me liable to the objection of which you are aware, namely, abstruseness; but it may so seem to me without really having the fault. I am glad to find you are making such rapid progress with the Work & make no doubt of its doing you great honour as well as being very profitable; but still I doubt the wisdom of the plan of publication, more now than I did at first, when I expressed my opinion, in favour of a monthly publication without a stamp. Your work, even less than I expected requires immediate circulation. Can you suppose that all your Readers read it instantly on receiving it as they do a Newspaper? Most assuredly they do not. You send a piece of an Essay beginning & ending in the middle of a sentence, & yet you imagine the Public will be as eager to read the Scrap as if it contained the account of a riot in the

Theatre or a Duel with Mr Canning? Rapidity of circulation cannot constitute any part of the value of your work. The matter it contains constitutes its value, & that is not of a transient nature. By publishing once a month you will save a great expence to your Readers & will present them with the work in a better form, while you will greatly if not wholly remove all the difficulties in the way of your continuing the work from want of stamped Paper. The work may Either be printed at Penrith or in London. Its circulation will be perfectly certain & sufficiently expeditious. You feel for your friends in remote Corners. What corner is so remote that it cannot procure the monthly reviews?—none. On this subject you have an overweening anxiety, an anxiety about trifles. Depend on it all those desirous of your work will find it whatever the corner may be in which they live. What a picture of confusion does your Letter display![1] Confusion as to the commercial concerns & conduct of your work; & what hope can any man entertain of any thing but loss & disappointment if you continue your present System? I hope you will excuse me for speaking thus freely, but really it becomes an act of duty to speak my mind to you. The stamped Paper I sent amounted to 5,000 sheets in all, & cost somewhere about 90£. I calculated that it would print 8 numbers in all. You will therefore have enough for 3 more. In my last Letter I laid down at length a plan for your proceeding, the particulars of which I forget but I suppose you can recur to it. There must be some mistake about Clement.[2] He is a worthy man & was particularly desirous of being civil.

With the extracts from Pasleys Letters I have been much pleased.[3] They contain precisely the opinions I formed with the Expedition & continued to form during its progress. *All* our force *united*, should have gone into the heart of Germany at *once* or into the heart of Spain. I have to Street abused the Expedition from the beginning saying so selfish an object as a few ships & a Dock Yard were unworthy of us who pretend to be the Deliverers of Europe. With the whole of our military plans I have been quite disgusted & as to the Execution of them, it has been as good as we had any right to expect. With public affairs I have been out of humour & have not written a Line these six months. In what the disturbed state of the Ministry will settle I know not; but I fear as you have hinted the root of all the evil is the Kings Will, to which all factions of any weight in the State equally bow for the Sake of place & power.

I am Dr Coleridge,

yours sincerely

D Stuart

The Letter you mention to come through Brown has not arrived.[4]

[1] See C's letter to Stuart [11 Sept 1809]: *CL* III 221–2.

[2] See above, Introduction, I lv–lvi.

[3] C enclosed passages from three letters of C. W. Pasley to make his letter to Stuart "worth the Postage": *CL* III 222.

[4] C had sent his printer a letter to Stuart to be enclosed in Brown's account of the paper received and expended: to Stuart [11 Sept 1809]: *CL* III 222. However, he ordered it back again: "indeed all my latter letters to you have been written in far too tumultuous & uneasy a state of mind": to Stuart 30 Sept 1809: *CL* III 227.

Stiles's Boarding House
Cheltenham 5 Octr 1809

Dear Coleridge

Last night I received your Letter[1] & this day I have written to Green to send you 1250 Stamps for 2 numbers as I promised. This will enable you to publish 10 numbers. The Plan I proposed was that you should constitute Longman or some such Person your Agent in London for receiving Subscriptions, that he should provide the Stamps for the next 5 numbers & that in the 15th number you should request payment of your Subscribers for 20 numbers, a step which would soon reimburse your Agent & enable you of yourself to go on. I cannot suppose that Longman or any other would refuse this as you are ten numbers in advance which must be to him a sufficient security. You cannot go on in any case without a proper Agent in London; another might, but you cannot. I have been from the beginning of opinion & am now more confirmed in it, that your plan is a bad one. You should publish once a month without a Stamp. You see the difficulties arising from printing on Stamps & what good purpose does it answer? Why; that the numbers as soon as printed go instantly to the hands of the Customer! & of what value is this to the Customer? What necessity for expedition in a publication professedly not temporary, and in reality not at all temporary, a publication too which by continuing one number into another you deprive of all pretence to a temporary character or to circulation in haste, and which by your lapses in its production is still further proved not to be temporary. Excuse me for saying that this desire of instant circulation seems to me to arise from a feeling unworthy of you a desire of producing on the public and receiving on yourself an instant impression. The design of the work itself has [a] nobler & more permanent object & a great mind doing great things should be able to proceed, stimulated only by conscious rectitude and power, regardless of temporary notice. I once or twice had almost likened your anxiety about the Prospectuses before your plan was thoroughly settled, to a gig horse I had a few years ago. He was extremely restless & eager to proceed while waiting at the Door to set out on a journey but before he had gone a mile he became quite sluggish & required much driving. I hope you will excuse me for making thus free with you, but I think it the duty of a friend sometimes to give good advice at the hazard even of giving offence. Of the merit & of the Success of your work there can be no doubt: all that is wanted is a good steady settled System. When the Public know where, how & when the Stream flows they will certainly resort to it for nourishment & refreshment.

I am much obliged to you for the Extracts from Pasley's Letters. In all opinions I agree with him. On the present Ministerial squabbles I look down with contempt & indifference, & so do the Public. They excite no interest & scarcely any conversation in this place, so full of public persons from all quarters.

With compliments to M^r & Mrs Wordsworth and all other friends at Grasmere, I am Dr Coleridge   yours &c
                                                            D Stuart

[1] For C's letter of 30 Sept 1809 see *CL* III 227–9.

36 Brompton Row 10 Nov[r] 1809

Dear Coleridge

I have been in town a week, but so busy with pressing private concerns that I have had no time to write to any one, though I am sadly in arrear of Letters to India. Next week I intend to return to Cheltenham to *Smiths Hotel.*—

Clement informs me there was nothing wrong between you & him. He says he wrote mentioning that some Gentlemen were vexed at the irregular delivery of the Friend. This gave rise to some misunderstanding, but on writing to you personally all was rectified. At Longmans I saw Brown the managing man who informed me they had sent you no stamps, consequently I concluded you had not made them your agents to receive money and advance Stamps. Green is getting 1250 ready for you, which with 1250 unstamped Paper go off on tuesday by the Waggon. In the 15 number you should call on your Subscribers to pay for 20. Some will & some wont till the 20 are expired, many reluctantly even then, if then. I now see it would have been much better for you to have done as Newspapers do;—allow the Newsvendors 20 or 25 per cent profit, in consequence of which they pay ready money for all their Papers. Thus you could have been in no want of money to proceed; but I recollect you were quite unwilling to let so much profit go out of your own hands and I approved of your feeling under the opinion that you could command the means of accomplishing the present plan. I doubt now whether you will not find it necessary to print your work in London & let it issue like Cobbet and other Newspapers. You may still live & write at Grasmere with perfect convenience.

I am puzzled by your order to advertise No. 7. when in the same Letter you acknowledge no. 10. is out. No. 12. is a most brilliant one. I shall make a long extract from it in the Courier and another in the Morning Post, and I shall send a short advertisement to each; to which I will add the Ad[t] of No 7. I have spoken to Street about the extract respecting Charlemagne. He says he could not find the part you mean. On such occasions the best way is to prepare the extract for the press yourself and send it up in a Letter. In the whirlwind of business in which an Editor is involved he forgets or postpones such things as are not pressed on him by the day.

With politics & Parties I am quite out of humour & have not & shall not interfere with them for some time. Your sentiments on the Duel are quite mine—Irish Gentlemen Bullies.[1]

I am D[r] Coleridge
yours
Nov[r] 13   D Stuart

---

[1] Castlereagh and Canning, both former cabinet ministers, had fought a duel 21 Sept 1809: see C to Stuart 27 Sept [1809]: *CL* iii 227.

V. Two letters from Southey concerning *The Friend.*

Coleridge had asked Southey 20 Oct 1809 to "look over the eight numbers" of *The Friend* "and to write a letter . . . in a lively style, chiefly urging, in a humorous manner, my Don Quixotism in expecting that the public will ever pretend to understand my lucubrations, or feel any interest in subjects of such sad and unkempt antiquity, and contrasting my style with the cementless periods of the modern Anglo-Gallican style, which not only are understood *beforehand*, but, being free from all connections of logic, all the hooks and eyes of intellectual memory, never oppress the mind by any after recollections, but, like civil visitors, stay a few moments, and leave the room quite free and open for the next comers. Something of this kind, I mean, that I may be able to answer it so as, in the answer, to state my own convictions at full on the nature of obscurity, &c . . .": *S Life* (CS) III 260 and *CL* III 254. See above I 19 and n 1. Southey's first reply is printed here from a ms in the possession of the Rev N. F. D. Coleridge. The second, a formal attempt to fulfil Coleridge's request, together with an informal covering letter, was published in *S Life* (CS) III 261–5.

My dear Coleridge
  The Porter kept your letter, manuring it in his Pocket till Tuesday, & it then found its way to me at such an hour that as soon as I could get pen in hand to answer it news came that the carriers were going.—I will endeavour to do what you desire so as to send it on Saturday.
  The Friend is faulty in nothing but its mode of publication, which certes is the most unsuitable that could possibly be chosen for matter of close reasoning & high philosophy. The mischief however is only temporary,— the objections applying only to these Essays while they are appearing in weekly sheets, & ceasing as soon as they are in a collected form. It would be better to intersperse numbers of amusement,—indeed to give three four or five in succession, so as to put the great children who read it in good humour; give them sugar plumbs so that they may be ready with open mouth to swallow a tonic bolus every now & then before they are aware of what is coming. At present they expect physic & make up their mouths accordingly, & what is worse their stomachs too. Any dislocation of the logical order of the Essays is an inferior consideration, that can be remedied in reprinting them. At present the one thing needful is to amuse the readers for a while & give them something that they can *talk about.*— Heaven help us—it is for this end only that the precious "Public" condescend to read.
  You told me you had proved those mad scenes in Jeronymo to be Shakesperes.[1] I have no doubt they are so. But make this the subject of

[1] Probably the "mad scenes" from Thomas Kyd's *Spanish Tragedy: or, Hieronimo is mad again* preserved by Lamb in *Specimens of English Dramatic Poets* (1808) 6–12. Lamb suggests that they may have been written by Webster. Cf *TT* 5 Apr 1833: "The parts pointed out in Hieronimo as Ben Jonson's bear no traces of his style; but they are very like Shakespeare's; and it is very remarkable that every one of them re-appears in full form and development, and tempered with mature judgment, in some one or other of Shakspeare's great pieces." *The First Part of Jeronimo* (1605), generally

an early number—there will be something for the talkers, & for the mud-larks & gold-finders of literature, & for the Magazine-men to discuss,—besides its own value.

Will you have an Essay upon the Spanish Ballads—showing how much worse they are than the English, & introducing three or four specimens of the different kinds which happen to be lying by me? I do not propose them as any thing striking, tho it may turn out better than the subject promises, —but merely because I know not what else to offer.

G. Coleridge's conduct exemplifies the precious consequences of substituting faith for good works, & talking about religion till you cease to feel it.[1] In general men degrade their intellects by corrupting their hearts: he has gone thro the opposite process which is rather the worst of the two. —What do you mean about Stuart,—*that* was the most unpleasant part of your letter,—the rest related to light vexations & evils all removable.[2]

I have undertaken the whole historical part of Ballantyne's New Register, at unseasonable notice & ill prepared for the task,—but he was in distress, having been disappointed in the sample he received from the person originally engaged—(whom I suspect to have been Wm Rose, old Georges son)—& he made me an offer which it became me to accept.[3] I am working at this, & greatly pressed for time. The first Chapter is printed,—it will displease the Foxites as much as your Letters did,[4] & it will offend all parties in turn, being tolerably strong & stinging.—Will you give me as briefly as you please the history of that Maltese Regiment which behaved so ill at Scylla last year?[5] I will tell any truths about Sicily that you may think fit to be told.

---

supposed not to be by Kyd, and *The Spanish Tragedy* are reprinted in Dodsley's *Old Plays*—in vol III of the 1780 edition. For the evidence that C read Dodsley's collection see *CN* II 2964n.

[1] See C's letter to George Coleridge [18 Oct 1809]: *CL* III 249–51; it was a reply to his brother's refusal to help him financially with *The Friend*.

[2] C's letter of 20 Oct 1809 to RS (*CL* III 253–4, reprinted from *S Life*—CS; see above) has been truncated and contains no references to C's brother or to Stuart. Stuart's letter that caused this reaction is probably that of 5 Oct 1809, printed above (II 493), containing the phrase "your plan is a bad one". See also above, Introduction, I lvi–lvii.

[3] An offer of £400 a year; for a full account, see *S Life* (CS) III 270–2 and J. Simmons *Southey* (1945) 130–1.

[4] C's "Letters to Mr. Fox" published in the *M Post* 4, 9 Nov 1802: *EOT* II

552–85. For reactions to them see *CL* II 912 (C to RS [8] Jan 1803), 954 (C to RS [29 Jun 1803]) and *CN* II 2064 (4)n.

[5] Probably a slip on Southey's part for Capri. There was an assault on Scylla, which had been captured by the French in 1806, after the British took Ischia and Procida in June–July 1809, but the Maltese regiment was not involved. For the unfortunate loss of Capri on 4 Oct 1808 the Maltese regiment under Major Hammill was much blamed. It fled before an attack on both flanks, "returning only a feeble fire"; Hammill was killed, and "the greater part of his men huddled themselves together into their barracks and were surrounded and taken". The Maltese loss was 25 killed and wounded and 680 prisoners, against the Corsican troops' loss of 15 killed and wounded and 20 missing. For a full account see J. W. Fortescue *A History of the British Army* (1910) VI 138–47.

I have asked Sir G Beaumont to use his influence with Lord Mulgrave on behalf of my brother Tom. This was done with no little reluctance & gizzard-grumbling on my part,—but knowing how intimate Sir G. is in that quarter, I thought it was not justifiable to let my own dislike to asking favours stand in the way here. What may come of it God knows. Sir G. wrote me an answer sufficiently kind recommending me rather to apply to Ld Lonsdale.—That however was out of the question. He has county & borough applications of that nature out of number

Your 8ᵗʰ Nᵒ was very interesting. I did not venture being no German to alter the name of *Munster*, tho I believed it should be *Muncer*,—& I was in hopes you would have said more of him, he being one of my Worthies of the World.[1] At present the little mention you have made of him leaves him under his usual load of obloquy. Would the lives of Loyola & Wesley be fit for the Friend? The one you know I have by me, & the materials at hand for amplifying or amending it,—there is none that I know of in our language except slight second-hand notices,—nor is there any account of Wesley except those which have been written by his disciples.[2]—Tell me any thing that I can do, & I will purloin time to do it.

Poor Mʳˢ Fricker is released at last,—a great blessing for herself & poor Martha—[3]

God bless you

RS.

—

Thursday 26ᵗʰ [4]
Mrs C expected to hear that the Applethwait[5] was received, which was sent in a letter by young Benson.

For C's comments on the Maltese regiment and the Corsican rangers see *CL* III 265, a letter to RS c 24 Dec 1809; though this seems rather late as a reply to RS's request here, there may have been other letters, now lost, between the two men.

[1] See above, I 131 and n 3.

[2] C heavily annotated RS' *Life of Wesley* when it appeared in 1820; the notes were first published in the 1846 ed. The "Life" of Loyola, if written, has never been published.

[3] C's mother-in-law, who had been "almost bed-ridden" for some time, had been nursed by her daughter Martha. C had for many years kept up, almost without fail, a small annuity for her. Among many references see esp *CL* III 60–1, 238, letters to J. J. Morgan [10 Feb 1808] and to G. Coleridge 9 Oct 1809.

[4] That is, 26 Oct 1809, the only near and likely "Thursday 26ᵗʰ" (and, in-

cidentally, the publication date of No 11, which contained the "Letter to R. L."). Southey's letter of 26 Oct and C's dated "Early November 1809" (*CL* III 259–61) may have crossed in the post, for Southey's news of Mrs Fricker's death seems to have been known to C, according to the next-to-last paragraph in his letter (*CL* III 261), concerning letters Mrs Lloyd and he had written Mrs C (presumably of consolation). Although Southey proofread most numbers of *The Friend*, Nos 10 and 11, which are pertinent here, were exceptions (see above, Introduction, I lviii), so he would not have seen the "Letter to R. L." before it appeared in print. The sequence of letters between C and RS was probably this: 20 Oct, C requests a letter from RS criticising *The Friend*; 20–3 Oct, C, not waiting for RS' reply, writes an answer to an imagined letter of criticism, published in No 11 as "Letter to R. L.";

TO THE FRIEND

Sir,

I know not whether your subscribers have expected too much from you, but it appears to me that you expect too much from your subscribers; and that, however accurately you may understand the diseases of the age, you have certainly mistaken its temper. In the first place, Sir, your essays are too long. "Brevity," says a contemporary journalist, "is the humour of the times; a tragedy must not exceed fifteen hundred lines, a fashionable preacher must not trespass above fifteen minutes upon his congregation. We have short waistcoats and short campaigns; everything must be short —except lawsuits, speeches in Parliament, and tax-tables." It is expressly stated, in the prospectus of a collection of extracts, called the Beauties of Sentiment, that the extracts shall always be complete sense, and *not very long*. Secondly, Sir, though your essays appear in so tempting a shape to a lounger, the very fiends themselves were not more deceived by the *lignum vitae* apples, when

> They, fondly thinking to allay
> Their appetite with gust, instead of fruit
> Chew'd bitter ashes,

than the reader is who takes up one of your papers from breakfast table, parlour-window, sofa, or ottoman, thinking to amuse himself with a few minutes' light reading. We are informed, upon the authority of no less a man than Sir Richard Phillips, how "it has long been a subject of just complaint among the lovers of English literature, that our language has been deficient in lounging or parlour-window books;" and to remove the opprobium from the language, Sir Richard advertises a list, mostly ending in *ana*, under the general title of "Lounging Books or Light Reading." I am afraid, Mr. Friend, that your predecessors would never have have obtained their popularity unless their essays had been of the description Ὅμοιον ὁμοίῳ φίλον [like is pleasing to like],—and this is a light age.

You have yourself observed that few converts were made by Burke; but the cause which you have assigned does not sufficiently explain why a man of such powerful talents and so authoritative a reputation should have produced so little an effect upon the minds of the people. Was it not because he neither was nor could be generally understood? Because, instead of endeavouring to make difficult things easy of comprehension, he made things which were easy in themselves, difficult to be comprehended by the manner in which he presented them, evolving their causes and involving their consequences, till the reader whose mind was not habituated to metaphysical discussions, neither knew in what his arguments began nor in what they ended? You have told me that the straightest line must be the shortest; but do not you yourself sometimes nose out your way,

---

26 Oct, RS answers C's letter of 20 Oct (above letter); 28 Oct, having promised to send the critical letter "on Saturday" —i.e. two days later—RS writes the letter C had requested (see letter below, from *S Life*—CS—III 261-5, undated); late Oct or early Nov, C writes letter in *CL* III 259-61.

⁵ The ms of *At Applethwaite*, WW's sonnet on the property Beaumont had given him? See *WL (E)* 383. Or the address of a subscriber from that village?

hound-like, in pursuit of truth, turning and winding, and doubling and running when the same object might be reached in a tenth part of the time by darting straightforward like a greyhound to the mark? Burke failed of effect upon the people for this reason,—there was the difficulty of mathematics without the precision in his writings. You looked through the process without arriving at the proof. It was the fashion to read him because of his rank as a political partizan; otherwise he would not have been read. Even in the House of Commons he was admired more than he was listened to; not a sentence came from him which was not pregnant with seeds of thought, if it had fallen upon good ground; yet his speeches convinced nobody, while the mellifluous orations of Mr. Pitt persuaded his majorities of whatever he wished to persuade them; because they were easily understood, what mattered it to him that they were as easily forgotten?

The reader, Sir, must think before he can understand you; is it not a little unreasonable to require from him an effort which you have yourself described as so very painful a one? and is not this effort not merely difficult but in many cases impossible? All brains, Sir, were not made for thinking: modern philosophy has taught us that they are galvanic machines, and thinking is only an accident belonging to them. Intellect is not essential to the functions of life; in the ordinary course of society it is very commonly dispensed with; and we have lived, Mr. Friend, to witness experiments for carrying on government without it. This is surely a proof that it is a rare commodity; and yet you expect it in all your subscribers!

Give us your moral medicines in a more "elegant preparation." The Reverend J. Gentle administers his physic in the form of tea; Dr. Solomon prefers the medium of a cordial; Mr. Ching exhibits his in gingerbread nuts; Dr. Barton in wine; but you, Mr. Friend, come with a tonic bolus, bitter in the mouth, difficult to swallow, and hard of digestion.

My dear Coleridge,
All this, were it not for the Sir and the Mr. Friend, is like a real letter from me to you: I fell into the strain without intending it, and would not send it were it not to show you that I have attempted to do something. From jest I got into earnest, and, trying to pass from earnest to jest failed. It was against the grain, and would not do. I had re-read the eight last numbers, and the truth is, they left me no heart for jesting or for irony. In time they will do their work; it is the form of publication only that is unlucky, and that cannot now be remedied. But this evil is merely temporary. Give two or three amusing numbers, and you will hear of admiration from every side. Insert a few more poems,—any that you have, except Christabel, for that is of too much value. There is scarcely anything you could do which would excite so much notice as if you were *now* to write the character of Bonaparte, announced in former times for "tomorrow," and to-morrow and to-morrow; and I think it would do good by counteracting that base spirit of condescension towards him, which I am afraid is gaining ground; and by showing the people what grounds they have for hope.
God bless you!   R. S.

VI. The "inspiriting Letter" to Coleridge from "the Friend's friend, & a Cantab.": DCL Folder D. See above, II 247.

[Tenbury] *Dec.* 4.th 1809.

Dear Sir,

The vivid & varied delight, the comfort, the strength, & the profound hope that I have drawn from the "Friend" shall no longer be dissipated or silenced by the engagements & necessities of ordinary life; but shall find a time to speak, tho' it be in the voice of a distant stranger. Having declared myself such, if I disclaim all presumption, I leave my letter without an object. I shall therefore plead guilty to as much of this as you chuse to impute to me, when I say (in the tantalizing rush of thoughts & feelings which crowd upon me, as definitely & integrally as I can) that my object is encouragement to you. You will perhaps not be very apt to conceive what this means, when it comes from a nameless individual to the conductor of a great public work. Let me therefore explain myself a little more fully. It constitutes the greater part of those grateful feelings which the Friend has inspired in me, that I perceive in it a decided & energetic opposition to the proud & weak wisdom of modern philosophy—that darkness of a false & insufficient light; & an acknowledgement of that pure & essential light, which shone once, & is for ever from whence the rays of the other borrowed supply a set of men, the produce & the disgrace of extended knowledge, with twilight to talk of passions which they do not feel, & wisdom "which they do not understand." Whether this opposition be systematic or no, I know not: nor is it of much consequence while it is uniform in that tendency.

But it is not only for the principles which are its basis that I admire the Friend—but for the manner & spirit in which they are conveyed. I have long regretted to see the right side maintained by indifferent calculation, over-care, personal invective, uncandid insincerity, & lately in particular by unequal imitation of excellences that fairly belong to their opponents. It is not by following, at an irrecoverable distance, a race that is lost on these terms, that any hope can be entertained of permanently withstanding error, or establishing truth. Those who are thus opposed will look with contempt (their predominant & ever-ready feeling) on unworthy motives & real inferiority; & only strengthen themselves the more in the castle of their pride, when they see it attacked by weaker arms & ungenerous warfare. The defence of what is dearest & highest must be entrusted to other hands, & wrought by other means: & I consider you, Sir, as the captain & the hope of this great cause:—in you, (as far as I have seen yet) rests the only chance, at least in this our time, of stemming the force of (I believe) a moral current, & blind vortex in the minds of men: and I most earnestly exhort & entreat you, if I rightly comprehend your plan & feelings, rejecting all party passions, & as if unconscious of contention, to press forward steadfastly to the mark of permanent utility & the salvation of right principles, ever keeping & looking to as a rule & light, the spirit of Truth, & Love, & Good Taste: that whether men shall struggle thro' this torrent, or be immerged & not rise again till He who directs it shall ordain, you at any rate may have set up a beacon & a monument, to tell that their have been those who saw the danger, & would have averted the error.—I should not have been easy if I had not thus given vent to feelings which have been for some time forming & acquiring strength. But I cannot conclude without thanking you for the very exquisite pleasure I have received from parts of the Friend that are of lighter mood & less grave office; in which I have often found my own dark thoughts & lesser principles adopted, illustrated, & confirmed.

With every hope & wish for the success of the Friend, & entreaty for your perseverance in the plan you have adopted, I am, dear Sir, your very obedient servant,

Neither Holly, Larch, Hicory, nor Sycamore,[1] & yet
the Friend's friend, & a Cantab.

VII. A letter to Coleridge from his "very kind Malton Correspondent", William Wray, an attorney: DCL Folder D. See above, II 247.

Dear Sir.

A brief Opportunity presents itself and I avail myself of it to thank you for 13 Nos of "The Friend" which I do in all sincerity for never has a work in appearance so completely calculated to meet my moral and intellectual Wants come under my Eye. Some may complain of its Obscurity and so could I but I must in that case first forget that the cause is in myself[;] others may tax it with want of agreeable Variety but such a Charge is very unreasonable for by means of your frequent Digressions notes &c you have it seems to me admirably contrived to make it as pleasantly miscellaneous as it is at the same Time gravely and instructively systematic: and my most fervent Wish is that you may enjoy Health and Spirits and *much more* than enough of public patronage to enable you to prosecute it to the conclusion you meditate. The Allocation you have recently announced in accommodation to the Wants of so many of your Readers must be acquiesced in by such others as are in quest of better Things for the Reasons you assign and I think one may fairly confide in your Discretion not to indulge those lighter gentry with any disproportionate Share of your Attentions. That such a work must eventually succeed with all serious and meditative Minds I think cannot well be doubted but of this Class comparatively few I am afraid have hitherto become acquainted with its Merits: it has you know been little advertized and it would have many prejudices to encounter. The Extracts however from Time to Time given in the Courier—must have been of great Service to the Circulation— such Notice is by far the most efficacious mode of advertizing: The York & Hull Papers have copied an Article or two from the Courier but the

[1] See above, II 186.

Editors of these Papers seem to know nothing of the original Work[.] I have therefore made a few interesting Extracts which in a Day or two I mean to forward for Insertion in these papers taking Care to "give Honor to whom Honor is due". This Liberty I trust you will excuse. I must endeavour some Return for the great gratification you afford me and from which you never detract but when you fail in your weekly visit. Apologizing (an Operation at which I am but clumsy) for intruding on your Leisure with a Letter so little to the purpose as the present I hasten to proscribe myself—in Terms of which you have so kindly set me the Example

Dear Sir

Your Friend & obliged Servt

Will: Wray

Malton 24th Novr 1809

I cannot but thank Mr Wordsworth (an old poetical Acquaintance) for his excellent Occasional contributions to the Friend & express my surprize that Robert Southey (he would forgive my plain Language) who has helped to mar my political Taste if Messieurs the Edinburgh Reviewers may be credited has not yet graced your pages. If Mr Wordsworth be not in the Habit of seeing such Things it may be worth while to point out a singularly eloquent Critique on his late Pamphlet in the last No but one or 2 of the Eclectic Review.

VIII. A letter to Coleridge from "A Veteran": DCL Folder D. See above, Introduction, I lxx–lxxi n 8.

Sir

I am sorry to see your apprehensions come in confirmation of my own that there would be a considerable falling off among your Subscribers at the first decent opportunity—which is afforded by the twentieth Number. Indeed I could not in consistency with the opinion I have long been compelled to entertain of the present generation of my countrymen form any strong hopes of the popularity of a work which requires in the outset the laborious thought of a zealous and vigorous student and which only promises to bring us back at last to where we were an hundred and fifty years ago. It is a great evil, and, as far as I can see, an unmixed one, that those who wish to labour for the benefit of mankind should often depend for the power of doing so upon the immediate acceptance of their labours by the said mankind: and that we should be obliged to bring together the two ideas of Truth and Money.—But since it is so, and that they who have no love to any good work do chiefly signify the same by keeping their purse strings undrawn,—it behoves them who care for the Truth to seek in the same quarter for a language of approbation to oppose to the *expressive silence* of those worldlings:—I have therefore to beg that the enclosed may be admitted as the expression of my wish for the success of your work.

I am Sir
(in more than one meaning of the word)
A Veteran

London. January 21. 1810.

IX. A letter from Coleridge to the Rev Joseph Hughes 24 Nov 1819. See above, I 161 n 1, II 390.

24th November, 1819.

DEAR SIR,—Having no one in the circle of my common acquaintance who is at once competent and interested in religion *theologically*, I had additional pleasure in the opportunity of conversing with you. In part, from constitutional temperament not duly disciplined; but in part likewise from the very circumstance above mentioned, my thoughts, all born and shaped inwardly in consequence, and in solitary meditation, communicate their own continuity, and (to use a phrase of Jeremy Taylor's) *agglomeration* to my conversation. Whenever the so rare occasion presents itself of conversing concerning these subjects, I am most conscious that I hurry forwards, *run over*, and tread upon my own arguments, and leave at last on my auditor an impression of dazzle and crowd, where so much has been said that little or nothing can be distinctly remembered. When indeed I am on my guard:—as for instance, when I am ostensibly, and, as it were, officially engaged in *teaching*, and my companion is with me as my acknowledged pupil,—then I err, if at all, in the opposite extreme; by anxiety in arrangement, and in the effort to secure for my pupil a firm footing at each step, and to obtain proofs from himself that he has full possession of the ground before I advance. And even in conversation, I can affirm most sincerely that any interruption, or admonition that I have lost the bit and curb, and am reducing the conversation to a mono-drama, or dialogue (in which one of the two *dramatis personæ* is forced to act the mute) of tongue *versus* ear, is received by me not only thankfully, but with unfeigned pleasure. I wish from my very heart that every one of my acquaintance, not to say my friends, made a point of doing this. "*Lente! ferruminandus est!*"

Of no mean importance therefore, as a *service*, would it be, and a solid gratification, if you should have at any time half an hour's leisure that you could employ in drawing my attention to any passages in my "Friend," or "Lay Sermons," which shall have struck you during the perusal of them as *objectionable*, whether as unscriptural in the doctrine or rash and uncandid in the application or language.

My philosophy (as metaphysics) is built on the distinction between the Reason and the Understanding. He who, after fairly attending to my exposition of this point in the "Friend," (vol. I. p. 254—277,)[1] and in the Appendix to the *first* Lay-Sermon, can still find no meaning in this distinction,—if it still appear to him the same as if I had attempted to contradistinguish a black from a *negro,*—for him the perusal of my *philosophical* writings, at least, will be a mere waste of time. I can only suggest to him, in prevention of any contemptuous feelings and judgments on his part, that from the first philosopher, Pythagoras, even to the present age, there has not been a single century in which this distinction has not been made and impressed by some one or more philosopher or divine of acknowledged eminence; that in the works of others it is clearly *implied,* though not *expressed;* and that, in some, sundry errors and obscurities are attributable to the confusion of terms, from the absence of a previous distinction. But, should the reader admit that the distinction conveys a *meaning,* he admits in fact that it is a *truth;* and I should dare hope, that for him the Essays on Method in the third volume would be intelligible throughout, and serve as the first elements, or alphabet, of my whole system—should it be the will of the Most High that I should live and have power to publish it. As among the secondary and merely confirmative arguments, I would challenge any learned Unitarian to give such an interpretation of the θρόνημα σάρκος, σύνεσις τῶν συνετῶν, ἐκ κόσμου,[2] &c. as would not impeach the philosophic apostle of the puerile and tautological truism that folly is folly, and wicked opinions displeasing to God.

I am most solicitous on this point, from the deep conviction, grounded in constant experience, that it is to the mistaken identification of reason and the understanding that the undervaluing of,—nay, the suspicious aversion to,—all intellectual ἄσκησις among so many truly pious Christians is owing; and on the other hand, the over-rating of the intellects of sundry impious men and writers, who in fact are eminent (if eminent at all) in those faculties which differ from animals in degree only, except as far as that the reason irradiates these even in despite of their possessors, who, in this life of probation, and while even the shadow of the image of God is yet vouchsafed to them, *cannot* be as base as they themselves try to become; but who (comparatively) are idiots in all that is properly and peculiarly *human.*

I fear, that if my thoughts are intelligible, my writing will scarcely be legible,—but be so kind as to divide the fault between the pen and your obliged friend.

S. T. C.

---

[1] Above, I 149-61.
[2] Cf Rom 8.7, 1 Cor 1.19, 1 Cor 5.10; tr "carnal mind", "understanding of the prudent", "out of the world".

APPENDIX G
THE FABLE OF
THE MADNING RAIN

THE FABLE OF
THE MADNING RAIN

Coleridge read the fable during his freshman term in Cambridge "in a modern Latin Poet: and if I mistake not, in one of the philosophical Poems of B. Stay": see above, II 11, I 7–10. Benedetto Stay *Philosophiae recentioris* bk V lines 2435–2503 (Rome 1755–60) II 195–7:

A c male quam mixtus furibundis, quamque locatus
Difficili statione foret pacatus, inermis,
Et sapiens inter stulta, irrequietaque corda,
Clarius ut noscas, age, percipe, fabula quondam
Quod facile in terris vulgata, & credita profert;
Nimirum prisco sapientes tempore, sudo
Sub Divo vixisse homines, cum lactea forsan
Flumina manabant rivis, & roscida mella
Sudabant silvae, cum nullo agitante tumultu
Aurea per laetos florebant saecula campos.
Sidera namque ferunt tum quendam, aviumq[ue] volatus
Perdoctum vidisse, brevi fore, ut horridus imber
Decidat, atque nova quem forte asperserit unda,
Excusso cogat velut insanire cerebro.
Horruit, & Mundo vulgavit triste periclum,
Nequidquam, nam nullus erat tum cognitus Augur;
Cavit at ipse sibi, atque illo adventante subivit
Antra die, caecosque aditus, terramque profundam.
Ecce tonante ruit Caelo pluvia unda profuso,
Irriguique natant campi, montesque superne
Evolvunt rapido torrentes gurgite lymphas.
Jam mortale genus, latis errabat ut arvis
Securum, subito madefactum est rore, novoque
Correptum pariter morbo; jam protinus omnes
Bacchantes latis homines excurrere campis,
Quassare & capita, & truculentas mittere voces.
At Sapiens terra latitans, ut nubila sensit
Disjecta, & Caeli specimen rediisse serenam,
Prossilit in superos, & luci redditur almae.

507

Spectaclum infelix! furiis immanibus omnes
Vidit agi; quae tum monstra ac portenta notavit!
Hunc vexare timorem, illum ambitione domari,
Illum & avaritia, & viso impallescere ab auro,
Multos ira, odiis, caecaque libidine multos
Correptos; spes ante oculos, & gaudia vana,
Et dolor, & lacrymae, & tristes nova nomina curae,
Omnia turbarum plena undique, & omnia victa
A ratione repulsa, in eo confusa tumultu.
Dum stupet, & sana se solum mente potiri
Laetatur; laetum sinere illi haud esse; repente
Ad monstrum veluti vis undique circumfusa
Irruit irridens hominum, atque huc pellit, & illuc,
Et vice mutata malesanum hunc incita clamat,
Jamque in dura parat detrudere vincula captum.
Ille malum miserans tantum nunc increpitabat,
Nunc frustra revocabat ad amissam rationem,
Et bona praeteritae repetebat perdita vitae;
Acrius urgebant illi, circumque premebant.
Quid faceret? vitam intutum sibi ducere durum,
Irrisamque fuit, cunctorum & ferre furores;
Scilicet haud illos proprium cognoscere morbum,
Stultitiamque suam caecos perferre libenter.
Illic forte lacus pluvia collectus ab unda
Nuper erat; mediam sese projecit in undam,
Involvitque luto turpi; stultissimus unde
Prodiit, atque hilaris nimium ratione relicta,
Stultorumque a concilio plaudente receptus.
Proin Sapiens inter mortalia saecla relictus
Nullus erat, prolem semper genuere Parentes
Insani non dissimilem, atque antiqua Nepotes
Semper in humano renovant deliria corde.
Quidnam etenim nostris medium est in rebus, & aequum?
Quae studia inter nos versamus, non ubi multum
Nostra habeat partem vesania consiliorum?
Omnibus in rebus virtutem audire, sequique
Semper quis suevit solam, solaque moveri?
Protinus invadit quaedam vis fervida pectus,
Qua rapimur, magnoque obstantia quaeque fragore
Dejicimus, non vitamus, non tarte movemus.

TRANSLATED BY A. G. CARRINGTON

C OME, hear what is told in a story which long ago was easily spread
and believed throughout the earth. You will then know more clearly
how the wise man, mingling with the mad and placed in a troublous
position—unarmed, and sage amid foolish and restless hearts—was evilly
overcome.

Doubtless wise men lived in former time, under a cloudless heaven, when, perhaps, the rivers flowed in streams of milk, and the forests oozed with honey instead of gum; when with no disturbance to mar it, the Golden Age flourished throughout the happy plains.

Wise men there must have been, for it is said that a certain man, steeped in lore about the stars and the flight of birds, perceived that in a short time a dreadful shower would fall. Whomsoever this strange flood should sprinkle, it would force him to act like a madman with stricken brain.

The wise man shuddered, and broadcast to the world its pitiful state of danger, but in vain; for no prophet had honour in those days. He himself took precautions, however, and when that day came, went into a cave, a hidden retreat deep in the earth. Suddenly the drenching shower of rain fell from the thundering heaven. The sodden fields swam, and the mountains rolled down torrential waters in swift streams. The human race as it wandered free from care in the wide fields was now quickly sprinkled, and was at the same time attacked by a strange disease.

At once all human beings ran forth on the wide plains like Bacchantes, tossing their heads and uttering challenging cries. But when the wise man lurking in the earth perceived that the clouds were scattered and that the sky had regained its calm appearance, he came forth swiftly from beneath the ground and was restored to the bountiful light.

What an unhappy sight met his gaze! He saw all men acting under the influence of hideous frenzy. What fearful and incredible things did he observe! Fear troubled one man; another was overcome by ambition, a third by avarice, growing pale at the sight of gold. Many were attacked by anger, hatred and blind lust. Hope fluttered before their eyes, and empty joys, and grief and tears, and cruel pains with new names.

All things everywhere were full of troubles. All things were conquered, and driven away from reason, being thrown into disorder amid that riot. While he watched in amazement and rejoiced that he alone had control over his senses, those men did not allow him to remain joyful. A great crowd of people pouring around rushed at him as against a monster and chased him to and fro, mocking him. With an exchange of rôles, they shouted excitedly that he was the madman. Already they were preparing to catch him and throw him into cruel chains. He, feeling pity for their great malady, now rebuked them, now tried in vain to recall them to the reason they had let go, repeating the lost blessings of their past existence. They jostled him all the more violently, pressing around him.

What was he to do? It was unsafe for him to lead a hard and despised life and to bear with the frenzy of all. It was plain that they did not know their own ailment, but gladly endured their own folly.

There happened to be at that spot a pond collected from the recent shower. He plunged into the midst of the water, and wallowed in the foul mire. He came out steeped in folly, only too happy to be rid of reason, and was welcomed by the cheering assembly of fools.

From that time no wise man has remained amid the centuries of human life, and the mad parents produced offspring not unlike themselves, and their descendants ever renew the ancient follies in the human heart.

For what is there, that is moderate and just in our times? In what pursuits do we engage without letting our insanity play a great part in our decisions? Who has been accustomed to listen to Virtue in everything, to follow her, and be influenced by her alone?

A kind of violence instantly entered our hearts, and by that we are swept along. All things that stand in our way we hurl asunder with a great crash. We do not avoid them, nor move them aside with skill.

INDEX

INDEX

procured by terror I 17 (II 277)
required for perception of linked
truths I 159–60 (II 296)
thought and I c, 14n, 16–17 (II 277),
25, 56 (II 49), 150, II 40
Atticus I 444n–5
Attius, Lucius *see* Accius, Lucius
attornies
Old Bailey I 345 (II 175)
attraction
and repulsion I 231 (II 161)
Atwood, George (1746–1807) I 496–7
*A Dissertation on the Construction and
Properties of Arches* I 496n
Supplement to a Tract I 496n
audience/auditor(s)/auditory
a.'s thoughts and feelings I 130 (II 111)
every man's opinion has right to pass
into common I 277 (II 310)
of literature I 278 (II 311)
of truth I 48–9 (II 46), 50 (II 47)
Augustine, St (Aurelius Augustinus)
(354–430)
and St Jerome on administrative pre-
varication I 38n
Epistolae
on censure q & tr I 276, 276n
on faith q & tr I 281 (II 313), 281n
on truth q & tr I 35 (II 38), 35n
Contra academicos I 11n
Augustus (Gaius Julius Caesar Octa-
vianus), Roman emperor (63 B.C.–
A.D. 14) I 82n
Augustus Frederick, Duke of Sussex
(1773–1843) I 294n
Aukland *see* St Helens, Auckland
Aulus Caecina *see* Caecina, Aulus
Aulus Gellius *see* Gellius, Aulus
Aurelius Antoninus, Marcus, Roman
emperor (121–180) I 12 (II 9)
Meditations I 12 (II 9), q & tr 377,
377n; tr Jeremy Collier I 12n; ed
Thomas Gataker I 377n
Auster II 248
Austerlitz I xxix
Australia I 203n
Austria I xxvii, xxxi, 265 (II 301), 270
(II 305), 311n, 578 (II 368), 578n
Austrius I 365 (II 272)
Austwick, Mr (fl 1809) II 456
author(s)/authorship I 227 (II 149)
aim to unsettle belief I 31 (II 35)
anonymous I 125 (II 86), 183* (II 108*)
biographers' aims and duties I 356–
360 (II 285–7)

contemporary a./writer(s) I 22 (II
152), 26, 388 (II 229), II 29, 218
demanding thought I 14–15 (II 276),
16–17 (II 277)
dullness of I 10
duty of I 15 (II 276), 29 (II 33, 33n)
elder writers I 20, 52, 537 (II 255), II
26
falsehoods of omission or error I 30–1
(II 34–5)
first paragraph gives most trouble to
II 5
foundations of a.'s edifice I 14, 21
(II 151)
French gentleman comparing French
and English writers I 262 (II 208)
intelligibility of I 26
living writer is sub judice II 282
modern lyrical writers II 244
obscurity *see* obscurity
of our more celebrated periodical
essays II 27–8
pen improves by exercise I 20 (II 150)
proofs of a.'s intentions I 81 (II 62)
readers and I c 53–4 (II 47–8), 55 (II
48), 356, II 278
seriousness of I 42 (II 42*)
of startling paradoxes I 50 (II 47)
success II 283–4
to think with I 25
utter thoughts to myraids I 53 (II 62)
who aim to instil self-knowledge I
114–15 (II 81n)
who pass judgements in blank assertions II 278
writer undeservedly forgotten I 53
writer will sometimes mislead through
excellence I 356
writers of prurient love-odes and
novels II 29
authority
dissent from I 27–8 (II 32–3)
great a. may be poor proof q I 488
habitual yielding to I 385 (II 227)
lust of I 193 (II 127)
authorizers
reverend a. of delusions I 54 (II 48)
autumn
for him has risen II 383
whirled about by gusts of I 349 (II 178)
Avars I 86 (II 64*)
aversions
gust-eddying stream of I 444
aviary
state of libel a vast I 82 (II 63)

COLERIDGE, SAMUEL TAYLOR (1772–1834)

I BIOGRAPHICAL AND GENERAL: (1) Personal references (2) Conversations
(3) Described by himself (4) Described by others (5) Habits and tastes (6) Health
(7) Observations from experience (8) Revision of views (9) Word-coinages
II POETICAL WORKS   III PROSE WORKS   IV CONTRIBUTIONS TO
NEWSPAPERS AND PERIODICALS   V ESSAYS   VI LECTURES   VII MSS
VIII PROJECTED WORKS   IX COLLECTIONS AND SELECTIONS (ed since 1834)
X LETTERS   XI MARGINALIA   XII NOTEBOOKS

first departure from native land II 187
French conversation interpreted for him by WW II 239n
French works, his reading I 181 (II 107), 181n, 475n
Friend central in his development I xxxv, civ
in Germany to finish his education II 22*; *see also* Germany
and Godwin I 110n
goes to French comedy II 216, 216n
at Göttingen I 25n, 36 (II 31), 154*–5, 154n
guessed author of Waverley novels I 122n
and Sara Hutchinson *see* Hutchinson, Sara
Jesus College, Cambridge I 134* (II 114*)
lecture on education (1813) I 103n, II 29n; *see also below*, VI LECTURES
library, at Keswick I 144–5 (II 117); Sir Gilfrid Lawson's I 411n; Westminster II 465
life-mask taken by Spurzheim I 415n
lines "composed during sleep" II 15n
Malta period I 247n, 562, 562n; *see also* Malta
marginalia I cii; *see also below*, XI MARGINALIA
never saw Gerrald I 334n
newspaper leader-writer *see below*, IV CONTRIBUTIONS TO NEWSPAPERS
notebooks I c, cii; *see also below*, XII NOTEBOOKS
Ottery St Mary neighbours subscribers II 449
pantisocracy I 224 (II 146), 224n, 238n
plan for a school at Derby II 423
plan to study chemistry at Keswick II 419
poems first in *Morning Chronicle* II 450
and printer Brown and his bankruptcy I lxxvi, 235n–6
private secretary to Sir A. Ball I 533 (II 252), 533n; *see also* Ball, Sir Alexander; *see below*, (2) *Conversations*
and publishers and booksellers I xlvi n, lv–lvi, lxxiv, lxxvi, lxxvi n, lxxviii, lxxix–lxxxv & nn, xciii n; *see also* Boosey & Sons; Clement, W. I.; Curtis, Thomas; Fenner, Rest; Gale & Curtis; Gutch, J. M.; Longman, T. N.; Murray, John

read WW's *Immortality Ode* to Humboldt in Rome I 510*
read WW's *Peter Bell* to Lady Ball in Malta I 543 (II 290), 543*, 543n
Sir William Scott personally unknown to him I 291* (II 322*)
secured Henry Hutchinson's release after impressment II 437
snuffbox a gift from mayor of Bristol II 420
songs set to music by Clagget I 465n
spoke Latin to Klopstock II 239
visited Leckie at Syracuse I 251n
Wordsworth quarrel I lxxiii, lxxiii n, lxxvi–lxxvii, lxxvii n, II 447
see also Chronological Table I xxv–xxxiv

(2) *Conversations*
conversations abroad used in *Friend* I 249 (II 200)
in German II 209
in Germany with Amptmann and Pastor in Ratzeburg II 236
in Germany with landlord of public-house I 259–60 (II 206)
in Germany with an old countryman I 259 (II 205–6)
in Germany with a professor I 260–1 (II 206–7)
in Helmstadt with an old schoolfellow of Klopstock II 240*
in Naples, on individuality of English I 557 (II 351)
in Naples, on Nelson I 575 (II 365)
in SW England, on taxation I 234 (II 163), 237 (II 165)
with American commander I 297 (II 326), 297n
with amiable Frenchman II 211
converting an atheist I 284n
with Ball I 533 (II 252–3), 533n, 537n, 539–45 (II 288–91), 542n, 549 (II 294), 551 (II 347), 553* (II 348*–9), 562 (II 354–5), 566* (II 360*), II 255, 299
with Dane and fellow-passengers aboard the Hamburg pacquet II 188–193
with R. Dennison I 217–18 (II 142), 218n
with C. D. Ebeling II 214–15
with Emerson I 261n, 411n
with friend from America I 238–9 (II 166), 238n
with gallant officer I 544 (II 290–1), 544n

Eytzinger/Aitsingerius, Michael von (d 1598)
De leone Belgico I 219n

fable *see* allegory
fact(s)
accumulating one sort of I 531 (II 252)
acquired by reflection II 7n
aid men by knowledge of II 27
conclusions from f. in flux I xci, II 6–7, 7n
correspondence of given words to given I 49 (II 47)
development of I 475
essential to intelligibility of my principles I 21 (II 151)
experience and I 119, 158–9 (II 295), II 28, 36
fundamental I 16 (II 277)
giving illustration to principles I 311 (II 358)
how mean a thing I 358 (II 286)
interval between knowledge of f. and discovery of law I 479
is a postulate II 279
matters of f. equally judicable q I 282
not received from senses I xci, II 7n
not to shew this or that f., as to kindle torch I xciii, 16 (II 276)
one f. worth a thousand I 481
publication of actual I 92–3 (II 67)
of science I 492
substantial matter-of- I 482
supernatural I 37n
symbol of new I 47 (II 45)
things of experience I 158 (II 295)
truth and I 158 (II 295), 358 (II 286), 466, II 6–7
faction(s)
artifices of I 242 (II 168)
struggles of contrariant I 329
faculties/faculty
comparing two f. with each other I 154
confusion of I 177* (II 104*)
discursive I 129 (II 111), 156
intellectual I 101 (II 68), 102 (II 69), 172n
moral I 102 (II 69)
scientific I 158
Fairclough, Henry Rushton (1862–1938) I 111n
Fairfax, Charles Gregory Pigott (1768–1845) II 409n, 428
Fairfield (Somerset) II 410

Fairford *see* Fairfield
Fairy-Queen
court of I 401 (II 266)
faith I cii, 98, 103 (II 70), 285n
article of my own II 9
barren I 283n
chaff of light I 63 (II 53*)
disputes concerning I 316 (II 315)
effective f. presupposes conviction I 104 (II 70)
enthusiastic I 227 (II 149)
intolerant person not master of grounds of I 279 (II 312)
man's principles on which he grounds I 97
men of sense having rejected I 502
men often talk against I 317 (II 315)
moral system uniting intention and motive I 325 (II 320)
my system of I 10 (II 12)
mysteries of I 433
not to find reasons for q & tr I 281 (II 213), 281n
old f. modern heresy II 17
personal realization of reason I 432
philosophy and I 519
reason and will united in I 432, 501
to reject all f. not possible II 279
slipped the cable of his I 133 (II 113)
sole principle of justification I 315 (II 314)
such a principle is called I 325 (II 320)
that never remains alone I 283n
there must be I 316 (II 315)
they regard more than charity q I 283
those who substituted one f. for another II 279
those who substitute obedience for I 316 (II 315)
to build a holy life upon a holy q I 284
through f. we understand q I 500
total act of soul I 315 (II 314)
we are justified by I 316 (II 315)
we live by I 97, 100 (II 68), 523n
without f. we perish I 97n
Falinus *see* Phalinus
fall II 279
mulct of our I 96
fallibility
deep conviction of our I 96
falsehood(s) I 80 (II 61*), 92 (II 67)
accommodating truth to I cii, 38 (II 39)
of adversary's reasonings I 337
are half-truths I 189 (II 124)

WORDSWORTH, WILLIAM (1770–1850)

I PERSONAL REFERENCES II POETICAL WORKS III PROSE WORKS
IV LETTERS

Yale University Library *see* New Haven

Yanwath (Cumberland) II 465

Yarmouth II 187, 194, 237

yawn/yawning
deaf while I 25, 25n
inapt medicine for I 13 (II 9–10), 13n

Yellow Dwarf, The I 326n

Yonge, Sir George, 5th Bt (1731–1812) I 148n

York I 393, II 467, 478, 490, 501
wars of Lancaster and II 260

York, Duke of *see* Frederick Augustus, Duke of York and Albany

York Buildings *see* London

York Herald I liii n, II 467

Yorke, Philip, 3rd Earl of Hardwicke (1757–1834) II 433

Yorkshire I 60n, 239 (II 166), 295 (II 325)

young/youth/youthful I 378–405 (II 222–32, 260–9) passim
adventurer in life I 379 (II 223)
benevolence I 187 (II 123)
bodily sensations in II 7
deceived in question of abstract politics I 222 (II 145)
enthusiasm kindled by French Revolution I 220 (II 144), 222 (II 145), 224–5 (II 147)
hardihood II 8
has many helps and aptitudes I 394 (II 261)
hireling hunters of I 438

leaving school I 401 (II 266)
less shocked by doctrine of necessity I 338n
minds of y. preached away I 443
and nature I 378 (II 222), 379 (II 223), 384 (II 226), 396–7 (II 263)
and reason I 195 (II 129), 397–9 (II 263–4)
virtues sacred attribute of I 404 (II 268)

Young, Arthur (1741–1820)
The Example of France a Warning to Britain I 327, 327n
Travels, During the Years 1787, 1788, and 1789 . . . in France q I 261* (II 207*), 261n

Zammit, Sir Giuseppe (1752–1823) I 569, 569n

Zaragoza *see* Saragossa

zeal/zealotry I 422

Zeno of Citium (c 335–c 263 B.C.) I 463*

Zeno of Elea (c 490–c 430 B.C.) I 437–8, 437n, 463, 523n

zoology I 155, 473–5, 474n–5

Zoroaster (fl c 6th cent B.C.)
Oracles q I 2, tr 2n, 433n, q 511, tr 511n, q 516*, tr 516n

Zouch, Thomas (1737–1815)
Memoirs of the Life and Writings of Sir Philip Sidney I 182n

Zwingli/Zuinglius, Ulrich/Huldreich (1484–1531) I 62 (II 53), 62n

**NORMANDALE COMMUNITY
COLLEGE**

9700 FRANCE AVENUE S.

BLOOMINGTON, MN 55431